THE MODERN MEXICAN ESSAY

THE MODERN MEXICAN ESSAY

edited by

JOSÉ LUIS MARTÍNEZ

translated by

H. W. HILBORN

UNIVERSITY OF TORONTO PRESS

Printed in Canada
Reprinted in 2018
ISBN 978-1-4875-7866-4 (paper)

Translator's Preface

ALTHOUGH THE MORE SUPERFICIAL FEATURES of the Latin-American countries are becoming better known to North Americans as a result of improved travel facilities, their cultural and economic problems still remain largely unappreciated. The Rockefeller Foundation, aware of this fact, has seen fit to encourage work of the kind here undertaken by supporting the translation of some of the more significant Latin-American scholarly and literary works into English. The translator would like to express his gratitude to the Foundation, to the Association of American University Presses, which administers the Foundation's grant for this purpose, and to the University of Toronto Press for assistance from its Publications Fund.

The original collection, entitled *El ensayo mexicano moderno,* was edited by José Luis Martínez and appeared in two volumes.[1] In selecting the essays to be included in this translation, I have had in mind primarily the presentation of a Mexican national outlook, in the hope that more people may be led to interest themselves in the psychological and spiritual aspects (as well as the economic and practical considerations) of the country that lies immediately to the south of the Rio Grande. It would be difficult to discover any problem confronting the modern Mexican, or almost any member of the Latin-American community of nations, that does not receive attention in this anthology of essays. The essays in this collection are not exercises in journalistic polemics. They are, almost without exception, of high literary quality, and they should make a profound impression on the English-speaking reader, except perhaps where the translator's efforts may have fallen short of the mark.

One important influence on the selection of this anthology of essays for translation was the recognition of the fact that Canada and Mexico have certain features in common. In 1953 Malcolm Ross published a

[1]*El ensayo mexicano moderno, Letras mexicanas* 39 and 40, Fondo de Cultura Económica, Mexico, 1958.

collection of essays by Canadian writers under the general title *Our Sense of Identity.*[2] The essays in that collection revealed clearly that Canada was developing a national consciousness, a consciousness of being unique, neither completely British nor completely American (that is, of the United States) in culture and outlook. Mexico, like Canada, received an Old World culture with the occupation of her soil by Europeans. Like Canada, too, she has sought emancipation from European rule, but by the revolutionary method of the United States rather than by Canada's slower evolutionary process. While Mexico resembles the United States in the method employed for the achievement of her independence, she is like Canada in her relationship to other powers and in her desire to develop a still unrealized national consciousness. Mexico and Canada often feel overshadowed, and perhaps even smothered, by the presence of the United States colossus on their frontiers. Both Canada and Mexico are confronted with the problem of economic dependence upon the United States and are striving to achieve greater independence in this sphere. Both want to be a nation, but they are unsure of their national status and stature. A national literature is essential for a nation that desires to be complete, but neither Canada nor Mexico feels absolutely certain of possessing such a literature, except as an appendage to an older literature.

The two volumes of Mexican essays translated herein are of much broader scope than the Canadian essays in *Our Sense of Identity.* A number of the essays in *El ensayo mexicano moderno* lie somewhat outside the specific area of an expression of national consciousness, and in order to reduce the great bulk of material by about one-quarter, certain essays have been excluded. This has been done with regret, because those omitted are generally by no means inferior in quality to those included (in a number of cases, *au contraire*), but their omission seemed to provide the remainder of the collection with a greater unity of theme than is evident in the original volumes. The essays that have been excluded fall under the following headings:

(1) Essays not intrinsically Mexican in theme, such as those by Antonio Caso, Carlos Díaz Dufóo (Jr.), Julio Torri, Francisco Monterde, Antonio Castro Leal, Alfonso Junco, Salvador Novo, Gabriel Méndez Plancarte, Rodolfo Usigli, Edmundo O'Gorman, Antonio Acevedo Escobedo, and Fernando Benítez;

(2) Essays relating to colonial times or to the early post-colonial period, such as those by Jesús T. Acevedo, Enrique Fernández Le-

[2]Ryerson Press, Toronto.

lectual modernity, marked by a decided break with the Romanticism which had lingered in Spanish America long after its decline in Europe. At first, however, this modernity was not a mark of real independence, although the influence in Spain of Rubén Darío of Nicaragua had suggested that cultural communications between Spanish America and Europe were already established as a two-way street. A development accompanying this realization was the recognition that Mexican literary culture must seek inspiration in its own linguistic heritage, and that French influences alone could not replace the ties with Spain that had been broken by the independence movement. These essays reveal Mexican cultural nationalism as a plant of slow growth, one grounded in a full consciousness of its roots. The important question of the extent to which these roots are European and the extent to which they are Indian is a constant source of debate. Ethnically, the Indian obviously predominates, but culturally the need for European inspiration, with Spanish as the only serviceable national language, is made manifest by the essayists.

The earlier essays in this anthology deal with Mexico's cultural past and the literary figures that contributed most significantly to it. Only a few of the essays belong to the period preceding the Mexican Revolution of 1910, which overthrew the dictatorship of Porfirio Díaz and initiated experiments in land redistribution and in political democracy, a process which is still going on. Although several essays reflect the struggles that followed this upheaval, a comparatively large number of them deal with purely literary and philosophical themes, from which one is tempted to draw the conclusion that their authors were insensitive to or detached from the political ferment of those days. Such a conclusion would be unjust, however, since the Mexican intellectual has not felt it necessary to confine his vision to the consideration of immediate realities in order to show his awareness of practical problems. Throughout the anthology, the authors' sense of responsibility for the Mexican as a man, and their consciousness of the need to foster his full development as such—with education and culture indispensable ingredients in this process—stand out clearly.

The depressing realities of social conditions in Mexico are not ignored in these essays. Iturriaga's analysis of the Mexican character, in his essay of 1951, is a sombre portrait, but the final note, typically, is one of faith in the Mexican's latent spiritual power and vigorous national personality. The contrast of opulence and misery is not regarded as permanent, and without exception the writers presented desma, Genaro Estrada (one of the three in the original collection), Héctor Pérez Martínez, and Silvio Zavala;

(3) Familiar essays on trivial themes (though written with charm and artistic skill), such as one essay by José Vasconcelos, two by Genaro Estrada, one by Alfredo Maillefert, one by Mauricio Magdaleno, and one by Andrés Henestrosa;

(4) Themes obscure for the English-speaking reader, such as essays by Genaro Fernández MacGrégor and by Eduardo Villaseñor.

As indicated, the reduction in bulk was made chiefly for the purpose of achieving greater concentration on a general unifying theme. Like the essays included, those omitted reveal much about the national culture and the psychology of the Mexican, but they do not give direct expression to a common national concern: *Mexicanism.* For this reason I have performed the rather presumptuous pruning operation which I hope will give a clearer view of the fruit without leaving too many traces of the pruning-hook.

The editor of the original collection, José Luis Martínez, is an eminent Mexican scholar and critic. In 1949, when just past the age of thirty, he published a two-volume book on twentieth-century Mexican literature,[3] and in 1955 he published two volumes dealing with Mexico's literary emancipation.[4] The anthology presented here in translation (with omissions as indicated) was published in 1958, and was doubtless an outgrowth of Martínez' monograph of 1955. The encouragement of a Mexican national spirit is patently the primary incentive throughout, but Martínez is also concerned with avoiding the taint of isolationism. While these essays broaden our understanding of what is distinctive in Mexicanism, they concentrate on presenting the Mexican consciousness of belonging to the whole of Western culture, and their appeal is therefore of a universal nature.

Martínez prefaces his anthology with a detailed study of the essay as an art form. The essayists are then presented to us in a roughly chronological order, and so a sense of the growing national consciousness is developed as one reads through them. The first of the essays date from the last decade of the nineteenth century, the point at which Martínez perceives the first flowering of Mexico's literary and intel-

[3]*Mexican Literature. Twentieth Century* (*Literatura mexicana. Siglo XX*), Antigua Librería Robredo, Mexico.

[4]*The Literary Emancipation of Mexico* (*La emancipación literaria de México*), Antigua Librería Robredo, Mexico; *The National Expression* (*La expresión nacional*), Imprenta Universitaria, Mexico.

to us through Martínez have something vital to say about their nation—a nation that they envision as one of great potentialities, seeking greatness in the conquest of poverty, disease, and ignorance, and in the moral, intellectual, and artistic progress of its people.

HARRY W. HILBORN

Note: Numbered footnotes are those of the translator. Footnotes appearing in the original edition are indicated by symbols.

Contents

TRANSLATOR'S PREFACE, by Harry W. Hilborn v

INTRODUCTION, by José Luis Martínez 3

Justo Sierra (1848–1912)
Prologue to the Poems of Manuel Gutiérrez Nájera 19
The Festival of Sodzil 33
Discourse at the Inauguration of the National University 37

José López Portillo y Rojas (1850–1923)
Prologue to The Plot of Land 55

Manuel Gutiérrez Nájera (1859–1895)
Aesthetics of Prose 61

Francisco A. de Icaza (1863–1925)
Mexican Letters 66

Luis G. Urbina (1868–1934)
Origin and Character of Mexican Literature 75

Amado Nervo (1870–1919)
Let's Speak of Writers and Literature 83

Rafael López (1875–1943)
Provincial Mayors 91

José Vasconcelos (1881–)
Sadness 96
Books I Read Sitting and Books I Read Standing 97
Glad Pessimism 100
The Embittered 105

Carlos González Peña (1885–1955)
Provincial Slumber 111

Martín Luis Guzmán (1887–)
My Friend Credulity 116
The Unpopularity of the Senses 118

Ramón López Velarde (1888–1921)
Masterpiece 122
In the Ancestral Home 123
The New Homeland 124
Ashes and Poplars 126
The Punitive Flower 127
Meditation on the Public Walk 128
Joseph of Arimathea 129
Filth 130
The Rout of Language 131
Mother Earth 136

Alfonso Reyes (1889–)
Palinode on Dust 141
Aristarchus or the Anatomy of Criticism 144
Parrasio or Moral Painting 155
Born in '89 168
Notes on the American Mind 169

Manuel Toussaint (1890–1955)
The House of Sugar-paste in Puebla 179
American Art 182

Jesús Silva Herzog (1892–)
Meditations on Mexico 187

Ermilo Abreu Gómez (1894–)
Literary Reflections 217

Julio Jiménez Rueda (1896–)
Mexico in Search of Her Expression 223

Alfonso Caso (1896–)
Is the Mexican Indian a Mexican? 230

Samuel Ramos (1897–1959)
Psycho-analysis of the Mexican 239
Creole Culture 250

Daniel Cosío Villegas (1900–)
American Problems 263

Jaime Torres Bodet (1902–)
Reflections on the Novel 281
Duty and Honour of the Writer 290

Xavier Villaurrutia (1903–1950)
Painting Unmarked 301
The Face and the Portrait 307
The Poetry of Ramón López Velarde 310

Jorge Cuesta (1903–1942)
Modern Art 327
Salvador Díaz Mirón 335
French Culture in Mexico 339
Mexican Classicism 343

Augustín Yáñez (1904–)
Meditations on the Indigenous Soul 356

Justino Fernández (1904–)
Orozco, Genius of America 369

César Garizurieta (1904–)
Catharsis of the Mexican 376

Andrés Iduarte (1907–)
Cortez and Cuauhtémoc: Hispanicism, Indigenism 395

Antonio Gómez Robledo (1908–)
Philosophy and Language 406

Leopoldo Zea (1912–)
Concerning an American Philosophy 424

Octavio Paz (1914–)
Introduction to the History of Mexican Poetry 438
The Disembodied Word 455

José E. Iturriaga (1914–)
The Character of the Mexican 472

Arturo Arnáiz y Freg (1915–)
Panorama of Mexico 492

Emilio Uranga (1921–)
The Mexican and Humanism 504

Pablo González Casanova (1922–)
Propaganda or the New Rhetoric 510

THE MODERN MEXICAN ESSAY

Introduction

Origins and Definition of the Essay

"THE WORD IS LATE, but the thing is ancient,"* said Bacon with respect to the term "essay." So ancient that essayistic touches may be recognized in oriental books and in books of the Old Testament, as well as in various Greek and Latin texts.† Nevertheless, the self-contained essay, with its own name and no longer intermingled with religious or philosophical meditations, does not appear in its plenitude and with all its shadings and possibilities until the *Essays* of Montaigne, the first version of which is dated 1580.

Among the many passages in which Montaigne reflects upon the nature of his own writings, one seems to me singularly illustrative since it defines not only the peculiar spirit which inspires the essay, but also the greater part of its characteristics.

> Judgement is a necessary instrument in the examination of every kind of subject, and for that reason I exercise it at all times in these *Essays.* If I am dealing with something I do not understand, all the greater is my reason for making use of it, sounding the ford from a great distance; then, if I find it too deep for my size, I stop at the shore. The conviction that I can go no further is evidence of the value of judgement, and evidence of the most cogent character. At times I take a fancy to build upon a trite and trivial theme, seeking something upon which to support and construct it;

*Bacon, *Essays*, Dedication to Prince Henry, 1612.

†For example, in *Proverbs*, *Wisdom*, and *Ecclesiastes* in the Old Testament; in the maxims of Confucius and the teachings of Lao-Tse; in various Greek texts and especially in the *Memorabilia* of Xenophon, the *Parallel Lives* of Plutarch, the *Dialogues* of Plato, Aristotle's *Poetics*, and Theophrastes' *Characters*; also in passages of Horace's *Poetic Art*, Quintilian's *Oratorical Institutions*, the letters of Pliny the Younger, Cicero's *Offices* and Marcus Aurelius's *Soliloquies*—perhaps, along with Seneca's *Moral Treatises*, the two books of antiquity which most merit being considered as essays—the *Confessions* of Saint Augustine, and Boethius' *Consolation of Philosophy*.

at other times, my reflections turn to a noble and thoroughly discussed subject in which nothing new can be found, since the road has already been travelled over so much that nothing can be done but follow the course others have taken. In the first type the judgement is unshackled, chooses the way that best suits its inclination, and among a thousand paths decides that this one or that one is the most attractive. I select at random the first theme. For me all are equally good and I never propose to exhaust any of them, because I contemplate none in its entirety; this is not the claim of those who promise to treat every aspect of a thing. Of a hundred parts and facets of any given thing, I select just one, sometimes to fondle it, sometimes to dally with it, and sometimes to penetrate to the marrow. I reflect about things, not with comprehensiveness but with all the profundity of which I am capable, and usually I like to examine them from the most uncommon angle. I would venture to deal with some subject with thoroughness if I knew myself less well and lacked consciousness of my limitations. Casting forth one phrase here, another there, like parts separated from the whole, wayward, without design or plan, it must not be expected of me that I produce a finished piece of work or that I make a concentrated effort. I take a new turn when it pleases me and yield to doubt and uncertainty, and to my habitual pose which is that of one who does not know.*

The features peculiar to the essay which Montaigne explicitly proclaims in this passage may be summarized as a voluntary lack of profundity in the treatment of a theme, a capricious and rambling approach to it, and a preference for the unusual point of view. We may here recall that Bacon in his *Essays*, published shortly after those of Montaigne (in 1597), defines the new genre as *dispersed meditations*. But in addition to these explicit features, in both Montaigne's and Bacon's essays, there are other features implicit which definitely establish the characteristics of the new genre. The new features are: discursive exposition, in prose;† the length, which varies greatly, and may range from a few lines to several hundred pages, but with the apparent presupposition that it can be read at a single sitting; finally, its typifying of the individualistic mentality which the Renaissance creates, and which is marked by, as Burckhardt has described it, "a multiple knowledge of individual things in all their shadings and

*Montaigne, *Essays*, Book I, Chap. 1, "On Democritus and Heraclitus." I follow the translation of Constantino Román y Salamero (Garnier, Paris, 1912), revising it with reference to the original text.

†Nevertheless, the English poets Dryden and Pope wrote authentic essays in verse on preceptive and philosophical themes. *The Metamorphosis of Plants* (*Die Metamorphose der Pflanzen*), by Goethe, is also an essay in verse.

gradations,"* in the form of descriptions of mental states, biographies, and external portrayals of human beings and animated scenes from life.

The most concise and exact expression that is current with regard to the essay is "literature of ideas."† In fact, the essay is a hybrid genre in that it contains elements of two different categories. On the one hand it is didactic and logical in the exposition of thoughts or ideas, but on the other hand, on account of its effusive flexibility, its ideological and formal liberty, in short, on account of its subjective quality, it generally has literary relief as well. According to the patterns and denominations established by Alfonso Reyes in *Boundaries,*‡ the essay is an ancillary mode of expression, that is, it carries on an interchange of services between literature and other disciplines expressed in written thought. By virtue of its form or its verbal artistry, it may have an aesthetic dimension in the quality of its style, but at the same time it requires a logical dimension, rather than a literary one, in the exposition of its themes. By its indicated subject matter it may relate to themes definitely in the domain of literature, such as those pertaining to fiction, but in the majority of cases it concerns itself with subjects belonging to other disciplines: history, science, etc. First of all, therefore, it is a peculiar form of the suggestive communication of ideas, in which the ideas abandon all pretensions to impersonality and impartiality in order boldly to take on the advantages and limitations of their personal basis and bias. In the purest and most characteristic essays any theme or subject is converted into an intimate and individual problem; it is shot through with human resonances, is frequently enlivened by a humorous touch or a certain intellectual coquetry and, abandoning whenever possible the fallacy of objectivity and of didactic seriousness, as well as exhaustiveness in exposition, it enters wholeheartedly into an "historicism" and presents itself as a witness, as a personal and provisional judgement. Nevertheless, even the most rambling and capricious mental game requires, to a greater or smaller

*Jacob Burckhardt, *The Culture of the Renaissance in Italy* (*La cultura del Renacimiento en Italia*), translated by Ramón de la Serna, Editorial Losada, Buenos Aires, 1942, pp. 250 ff.

†Xavier Villaurrutia called the essay "a form midway between journalism and philosophic system": *Texts and Pretexts* (*Textos y pretextos*), La casa de España en México, 1940, p. 104.

‡Alfonso Reyes, *Boundaries, Introductory Discourse on Literary Theory* (*El deslinde, Prolegómenos a la teoría literaria*), El Colegio de México, Mexico, 1944, pp. 30 ff.

degree, some expository precision; and precisely in the varying proportions of these two elements—originality in mode and form of thought on the one hand, and logical systematization on the other—lie the bases of the different types of essay. Opposed to the subjective, free, and capricious form of essay which comes into being with Montaigne, then emigrates to England to be reincarnated in the journalistic essays of Addison and Steele, and later flourishes with Lamb, Hazlitt, and Stevenson and returns to France with Gide and Alain, there soon arises another form, expository, organic, and impersonal, the origin of which may be attributed to Bacon. To this form, which reaches its apogee in the eighteenth and nineteenth centuries, belong the elaborate and extensive disquisitions in eighteenth-century style—like the *Essay on the Customs and the Spirit of Nations . . .* (*Essai sur les moeurs et l'esprit des nations et sur les principaux faits de l'histoire depuis Charlemagne jusqu'à Louis XIII*), 1756, by Voltaire or the *Political Essay on the Kingdom of New Spain* (*Essai politique sur le royaume de la Nouvelle Espagne*), 1811, by Humboldt—and in the age of Romanticism, the massive critical, philosophical, or historical essays of Macaulay, Emerson, Thiers, Saint-Victor, Brunetière, and Menéndez Pelayo.

Related Forms and Categories of the Essay

Such flexibility and amplitude in the definition of this "literature of ideas" has given rise, in the course of history, to ramifications into several forms closely related to the essay, which do not express either diversified functions of the mind or determined forms of written thought, but in general are simple stratifications of non-narrative prose which follow laws vaguely conventional, and in varying degrees approach or diverge from literature or the didactic treatise. The *article*, for example,* remains from its birth bound to journalism; it is usually shorter than the essay, its theme more immediate or "up to the minute" in its appeal, and its level of style "journalistic." The *critical study* "is a work of cold examination, indispensable erudition, and strict method," even though critical essays may also exist. In the *monograph* the intention is plainly didactic, treating a precise theme with exhaustiveness as the aim; but—as Medardo Vitier observes—"the subject itself leads to an essay if the author's attitude is contemplative, in spite of the scientific materials he may be interested in

*In this classification I follow, in part, Medardo Vitier's *On the American Essay* (*Del ensayo americano*), Tierra Firme, Fondo de Cultura Económica, Mexico, 1945, pp. 47 ff.

utilizing." *Criticism*, whether literary, artistic, historical, philosophical, or scientific, is, in general, a function of the mind which approaches the products of culture with different purposes, aims, and degrees of precision. Furthermore, it may make its selection from among the immense gamut of forms which range from the incidental impressionistic opinion to the monograph, but criticism encroaches upon the territory of the essay when, whatever its nature may be, it has in addition to those qualities of flexibility and formal and ideological liberty the subjective note and the interpretive character which mark the essay. The *treatise*, finally, stands at the opposite pole to the brief article or the essayistic excursion; it is the complete, organized, and precise study which aims to supply all that is presently known about a given theme, a genre which the specialization of our time has almost caused to disappear.

By intermingling or confusion, or through divergence from these related forms, there lives in modern thought this fluid substance which is the essay. Disregarding the question of whether or not it is found in its improbable purity, the essay nevertheless appears most frequently in the following categories:*

1. *Essay as a type of literary creation*. This is the most noble and illustrious form of the essay, being simultaneously invention, theory, and poem. In the literature of modern Mexico it is represented by Alfonso Reyes' *Palinode on Dust* (*Palinodia del polvo*), Ramón López Velarde's *The New Homeland* (*Novedad de la patria*), or Xavier Villaurrutia's *Painting Unmarked* (*Pintura sin mancha*).

2. *Brief, poetic essay*. This is similar to the type just mentioned but shorter and less connected; like lyrical philosophical notes or the recording of simple curious observation. Memorable examples are the short essays of Julio Torri,[1] the essay-epigrams of Carlos Díaz Dufóo Jr.,[1] and Ramón López Velarde's *Masterpiece* (*Obra maestra*).

3. *Essay born of fancy, wit, or casual meditation*, of an evident English type. It requires a whimsical freshness and wit, or that subtle art of deep and sincere reflection without loss of fluidity and apparent

*I follow the scheme of essayistic types which I initially applied to the essays of Alfonso Reyes in my study "The Work of Alfonso Reyes" ("La obra de Alfonso Reyes") published in *Cuadernos Americanos*, Mexico, January-February 1952. Angel del Río and M. J. Benardete, in the introduction to *The Contemporary View of Spain, Anthology of Essays, 1895–1931* (*El concepto contemporáneo de España: Antología de ensayos, 1895–1931*) [Editorial Losada, Buenos Aires, 1946, pp. 31–32], propose a division of essays into three types: the pure, the poetic descriptive, and the critico-erudite.

[1]Excluded from this translation.

lightness, as in Alfonso Reyes' *Born in '89* (*Matrícula 89*), José Vasconcelos' *Sadness* (*Tristeza*), and Salvador Novo's *The Advantages of Not Being in Fashion* (*De las ventajas de no estar a la moda*).[2]

4. *Essay-discourse or oration* (*instructional*).This is the transmission of cultural or civilizing messages. Formally it ranges from the oratorical style of the public address to the academic dissertation, but it is bound to the essay properly so called by its consideration and interpretation of material or spiritual realities. Some examples are Justo Sierra's fine *Discourse at the Inauguration of the National University* (*Discurso en la inauguración de la Universidad Nacional*), Antonio Caso's *The Four Modern Poets* (*Los cuatro poetas modernos*),[2] Jesús Silvia Herzog's *Meditations on Mexico* (*Meditaciones sobre México*), the homily of Alfonso Caso in defence of the Mexican Indian, and Jaime Torres Bodet's *Duty and Honour of the Writer* (*Deber y honra del escritor*).

5. *Interpretative essay.* This is the form that may be considered the most normal and common form of the essay: a brief exposition of a subject with an original interpretation. Among many possible examples, here are a few: José Vasconcelos' *Glad Pessimism* (*Pesimismo alegre*), Alfonso Reyes' *Parrasio or Moral Painting* (*Parrasio o de la pintura moral*), Manuel Toussaint's *American Art* (*Arte americano*), Daniel Cosío Villegas' *American Problems* (*Los problemas de América*), Agustín Yáñez' *Meditations on the Indigenous Soul* (*Meditaciones sobre el alma indígena*), and Andrés Iduarte's *Cortez and Cuauhtémoc: Hispanicism, Indigenism* (*Cortés y Cuauhtémoc; hispanismo, indigenismo*).

6. *Theoretical essay.* This differs by just a shade from the interpretative essay, since while the ideas expressed in the interpretative essay flow more freely and generally deal with personalities or historical or cultural events, those expressed in the theoretical essay, more closely knit, hold solely to the field of concepts. Some examples are Samuel Ramos' *Psycho-analysis of the Mexican* (*Psicoanálisis del mexicano*), Jorge Cuesta's *Mexican Classicism* (*El clasicismo mexicano*), Antonio Gómez Robledo's *Philosophy and Language* (*Filosofía y lenguaje*), and Octavio Paz's *The Disembodied Word* (*El verbo desencarnado*).

7. *Essay on literary criticism.* It has already been noted above that when literary criticism, of whatever kind it may be, has in addition the characteristics of the essay, it encroaches upon this territory, as is attested by two masterly studies, that of Justo Sierra on *Gutiérrez Nájera* and that of Xavier Villaurrutia on *Ramón López Velarde.*

[2]Excluded from this translation.

8. *Expository essay.* This is an exposition of the monographic type and with synthetic vision which at the same time contains an original interpretation, as occurs in Silvio Zavala's *Thomas More's "Utopia" in New Spain* (*La "Utopía" de Tomás Moro en la Nueva España*),[3] in Gabriel Méndez Plancarte's *Mexican Humanists of the Eighteenth Century* (*Humanistas mexicanos del siglo XVIII*),[3] in José Iturriaga's *The Character of the Mexican* (*El carácter del mexicano*), and in Arturo Arnáiz y Freg's *Panorama of Mexico* (*Panorama de México*).

9. *Chronical-essay or memoirs.* In this the essay is allied with historical or autobiographical reminiscences. An example of the first is the work of Artemio de Valle Arizpe on *Don Victoriano Salado Alvarez and Conversation in Mexico* (*Don Victoriano Salado Alvarez y la conversación en México*),[3] and of the second a large number of admirable passages in the memoirs of José Vasconcelos.

10. *Brief journalistic essay.* This is, finally, the light, passing record of the impulses, topics considered, opinions, and facts of the moment, noted as they flit by, but with a keenness or emotion which lifts them above simple journalism, as is exemplified by José Vasconcelos' *The Embittered* (*El amargado*), Rafael López' *Provincial Mayors* (*Los alcaldes de la provincia*), or Mauricio Magdaleno's *Second Class Train* (*Tren de segunda*).[3]

Antecedents of the Mexican Essay

There are passages in which reflections of an essayistic character are set forth in almost all our early historians and chroniclers, and in the humanists of the sixteenth and eighteenth centuries studied by Méndez Plancarte,* especially in the works of Bartolomé de las Casas, Francisco Xavier Clavigero, Andrés Cavo, and Pedro José Márquez.

At the beginning of the nineteenth century, when the political independence of Mexico made possible the free expression of ideas, one form of expression which was found to be most suited to the providing of an outlet for that personal, desultory, and restless outpouring of thoughts concerning so many situations about which there was disagreement, and concerning the remedies and solutions suggested,

**Mexican Humanism of the Sixteenth Century* (*Humanismo mexicano del siglo XVI*). Introduction, selection, and editing by Gabriel Méndez Plancarte, Ediciones de la Universidad Nacional Autónoma, Mexico, 1946, Biblioteca del Estudiante Universitario, 63; *Humanists of the Eighteenth Century* (*Humanistas del siglo XVIII*). Introduction and selection by Gabriel Méndez Plancarte, Ediciones de la Universidad Nacional Autónoma, Mexico, 1941, Biblioteca del Estudiante Universitario, 24.

[3]Excluded from this translation.

was a type of writing very similar to the essay, even though the name[4] had not yet appeared as applied to those texts.

Suggestions of the essay or actual essays constituted, indeed, the major part of the non-novelistic writings which Fernández de Lizardi published assiduously in his personal journals; genuine essays composed the most important part of the studies which José María Luis Mora collected in his *Casual Works* (*Obras sueltas*), and the digressions of the first part of *Mexico and its Revolutions* (*México y sus revoluciones*), which describe in so penetrating a manner the population of the Republic and the Mexican character; there are numerous essayistic passages in the work which Lorenzo de Zavala called, after Humboldt, *Historical Essay on Mexican Revolutions* (*Ensayo histórico de las revoluciones de México*), and also essayistic, in their richest productions, were Fray Servando Teresa de Mier, José María Gutiérrez de Estrada, Mariano Otero, and Lucas Alamán. Common to all of them, moreover, is a cultural tone characterized by a keen historical consciousness and by an eagerness to analyse and evaluate the social scene at that dramatic point where it touched their own lives, these being characteristics which, except for reaction or deviation at certain periods, will persist as distinctive traits of the Mexican essay.

During later years of the past century, the essay, though formless, understood principally as an expression of historical consciousness and an evaluation of existent society, will appear in some of the writings of Luis Gonzaga Cuevas, Francisco Zarco, Ignacio Ramírez, Ignacio L. Vallarta, Vicente Riva Palacio, Ignacio M. Altamirano, Francisco Bulnes, and Carlos Pereyra; it will confine itself to themes relating to cultural history in passages of the works of José Fernando Ramírez, Bernardo Couto, Manuel Orozco y Berra, Joaquín García Icazbalceta, Victoriano Agüeros, Francisco Pimentel, José María Vigil, and Luis González Obregón, and only in the last years of the century will the sensibility awakened by Modernism, with its more closely knit and elegant prose, its more pointed and original form of expression, bring our writers to attainment in its plenitude of the indefinable literary form called the essay.

A Persistent Theme: Mexico

A representative repertory of French or English essays would offer us reflections on aesthetic, philosophical, political, or moral questions, or mere feats of intelligence and wit, and only in exceptional cases would

[4]The Spanish text has *hombre* (man), an apparent misprint for *nombre* (name).

these essays confine themselves to national problems, doubtless because the authors find their countries already formed and with an established culture, and therefore they are free to turn to general or personal topics which best suit their own personalities. In Mexico, on the other hand, our authors are inclined persistently and tenaciously to explore a single field of inquiry, the national entity and national problems, whatever their personal perspective and discipline–philosophical or historical, scientific or literary–and whatever their ideology. The constant theme of most modern essays will be Mexico, Mexico in its totality or some of the topics relating to the formation of the country: its history, its culture, its economic and social problems, its literary and artistic creations, its past and its present.

This peculiarity of our essays, moreover, is not an exclusively Mexican trait, but one that applies to all Spanish-American thought, to countries in process of formation, with hopes predominating over the influences of the past, and less rich in achievement and conquests than in plans and enterprise. "All the essay writing on the continent," observes Alberto Zum Felde, "appears, in a greater or lesser degree, in a close relationship with its sociological background."* Since the time of Sarmiento, Bello, and Altamirano, right up to the present, the Spanish-American essay has been deepening its three principal channels†: the culture of our countries, problems of race and politics and economics, and the sense of history, channels which unite in the wider channel of national problems.

In exceptional cases there will appear themes of pure theory or of untrammelled imagination or of intellectual, poetic, or humorous divagation. And in scarcely any case, as Unamuno pointed out, can one discover moral, religious, or metaphysical themes, except in works of clerical writers which generally lie outside the field of the essay. But reflections of an independent character on moral themes, so frequent in French thought, as also those on metaphysical themes, which the English prefer, appear to have no place in the minds of our essayists.

Within its own limits, the modern Mexican essay is largely the history of Mexican thought, and by virtue of that very fact, a cultural history and an inventory of our problems. What I mean is that in our essays the intelligence and the sensibilities are rarely displayed for the sake of gratuitous solace or a purely intellectual or aesthetic

*Alberto Zum Felde, *Critical Index of Spanish-American Literature. The Essayists* (*Indice crítico de la literatura hispanoamericana. Los ensayistas*), Editorial Guaranía, Mexico, 1954, p. 9.

†Vitier, *On the American Essay*, p. 7.

gratification, but rather they are used in the service of fundamental examinations, either of a cultural character—literary or artistic expression, philosophic thought, the character of the Mexican, or the great historic and spiritual conflicts—or else of a social or economic character.

Stages of Thought as Expressed in the Modern Mexican Essay

The history of ideas in Mexico, as has already been indicated, can be identified only partially with the history of the essay, because ideas adopt varying forms of expression which cannot always be considered essays. Economic thought, for example, is hardly ever expressed with the originality and flexibility required by the essay; certain philosophical schools, like Neo-Kantism or Thomism, have never expressed themselves in this form, and the same is true of scientific themes. At certain moments the history of the essay is closely linked to the history of literature, but on occasion the essayistic form follows its own path, allying itself with the history of sociological or philosophical thought.

Furthermore, the Mexican writer who writes essays seldom does that alone. Usually his chief work is in the field of poetry, drama, the novel, or criticism, or else he cultivates another intellectual discipline, such as history, economics, anthropology, or philosophy, which occasionally finds its outlet in the form of essays.

In spite of the instability of these bounds inside which the essay moves, we may tentatively propose the following guide to the principal stages of the modern Mexican essay.

In the last days of the régime of Porfirio Díaz, writers express the aesthetic theories and the sensibility of Modernism or else they oppose this movement by clinging to the nationalistic doctrine which enjoyed favour during the nineteenth century. Justo Sierra founds the National University in 1910 and proposes for it a spiritual basis.

From that time on and parallel with the social revolution of 1910, the Athenaeum group, with Antonio Caso, José Vasconcelos, and Alfonso Reyes at the head, effects a cultural revolution in which the objectives are the return to philosophic spiritualism, to disciplined intellectual activity, and an alert universal curiosity. The group looks principally to Bergson and Boutroux as its leaders.

The impact of the Revolution, about the year 1915 and continuing till towards the end of the twenties, provokes a return to the recognition of national origins, a rediscovery of Mexico as it were, if not even a nostalgic flight to the past. López Velarde reveals the novelty of a more intimate nationhood, and the colonialists discover the charm of past ages in our country. One generation, that of 1915 (Alfonso Caso,

Antonio Castro Leal, etc.), rising above the confusion, feels the necessity of making fruitful, through thought and action, that terrible upheaval from which the Mexican nation was suffering.

A new sensitivity arises, with the so-called "Vanguardism," in the decade 1928–38. When the violence has passed, the group of writers called *Contemporaries* (*Contemporáneos*) devotes itself to the pure, disinterested practice of literary endeavour and to the mastery of the new art, in the theatre as well as in literature and painting.

In the same period writers of different generations and intellectual disciplines embark upon the tremendous task—uninterrupted up to our own day—of investigating and analysing the real essence of Mexico, in the field of cultural history as well as through social and economic studies and evaluations. There is initiated then the investigation of the Mexican—especially in the book *The Profile of Man and Culture in Mexico* (*El perfil del hombre y la cultura en México*), by Samuel Ramos—and, in general, knowledge of Mexico is worked into the fields cultivated by the disciplines of philosophy and the social sciences.

After 1940 there follow in succession such philosophical currents as historicism and existentialism, which for a moment dominate Mexican thought. One generation, with numerous allies, devotes itself to the task of meditating upon Mexico and all that is Mexican; then isolated groups engage in vain discussion of nationalism or universalism in literary expression. Other writers follow their own course: Christian humanism, aesthetic meditation or literary analysis, social philosophy or historical reflection.

These summarized stages of essayistic thought permit us to note a few significant facts. In the first place, in the field of ideas to which the essay belongs there is a relationship to political and social events which is much closer than the one manifested in the pure cultivation of letters or the sciences. Even in its forms least related to historical circumstance the essay is always concerned with reflection and testimony; this reflection most frequently takes for its theme immediate historical and cultural events, and in fact acts as an expression of a keen consciousness of reality.

Furthermore, precisely in this period and in this domain, there takes place in Mexico the transformation of the cultured man—one who has knowledge and interest in a vast field of human learning—into the specialist. The writers of the first truly modern generation, the members of the Athenaeum, still aspire to embrace the complete field of one or several disciplines: Antonio Caso, the vast territory covered by philosophy; Alfonso Reyes, all the notes of poetic expression, literary theory, and humanism; José Vasconcelos, philosophy, literature, and politics. On the other hand, the writers of the schools to follow keep moving progressively towards cultural specializations: Manuel Toussaint, colonial art; Alfonso Caso, anthropology; Jesús Silva Herzog, economics; Daniel Cosío Villegas, economics, and from 1950 a radical turn towards history; Samuel Ramos, Mexican philosophy and aesthetics; Francisco Monterde, Mexican literature, and the whole generation of *Contemporaries*, the exclusive cultivation of the literary.

There are no grounds for supposing that this reduction of cultural boundaries implies at the same time a reduction in intellectual quality; neither can it be affirmed that what has been lost in scope has been gained in depth. It is simply a matter of a change in perspective which is typical of the modern era, and writers and thinkers continue to have their own personal merits, independently of the extent of their territory.

Is There an Essayistic Style?

The anonymous writer of the prologue to the *Anthology of Contemporary French Essayists* drew attention to the fact that "essayists rarely belong to a definite school; at most they form part of a movement in ideas."* Now, a literary movement is recognized especially by new characteristics in style; but since in the essay the function of style is less important than the ideological element, only by exception do its characteristics permit us to discern clearly a genuine literary school. What form of verse and rhythm of phrase are to the creative writer, mode of expression and expository power are to the essayist. For that reason, from the formal point of view, the history of the essay fails to present precise outlines.†

When its authors are fundamentally literary writers, like Alfonso Reyes, Julio Torri, Rámon López Velarde, or Xavier Villarrutia, the essay may exemplify in an adequate manner the style of a period and especially a personal style. But when it comes to professionals in different fields of learning who express themselves through the medium of the essay, it seems to take on a style with no pretensions of a literary character except clarity and the effective exposition of the theme. Following the scheme of historical stages previously presented, it may be stated that there are certain common notes in the essays of the Modernist period, and that the same is true of the writers of the

**Anthologie des essayistes français contemporains*, Editions KRA, Paris, 1929, p. 8.

†*Ibid.*, p. 11.

generation of 1910 and the "Vanguard" group of 1928. But in the other stages, the features which enable us to group the thinkers and writers are rather coincidences of an ideological character, related cultural concerns, or a similarity in the approach to certain problems. Leopoldo Zea, José E. Iturriaga, and Emilio Uranga are alike in that they investigate the nature and character of the Mexican, but they are not connected by any stylistic peculiarity. And even in Artemio de Valle Arizpe, Manuel Toussaint, and Genaro Estrada, writers with literary intent and approximately contemporaneous, and who all write on colonial themes, the styles have nothing in common because the first is a novelist and essayist with a fondness for archaisms, the second an historian and a critic of colonial art, and the last an historian with an ironic attitude towards the archaizing mania. In other words, they treat the same theme from different perspectives and different mental outlooks.

For all these reasons it is erroneous to speak of a style common to each and every one of the stages of modern essayistic thought in Mexico. Perhaps the only valid notes are some of those which distinguish the Mexican character: sobriety, delicacy, a profound nationalistic instinct, measured gravity, a longing for universal understanding. And even in this summary definition one quickly perceives deficiencies, for where can one place the humour and irony of Julio Torri or Salvador Novo?

These crossways traced by the essay induced me to give as extensive an introduction as necessary of the individual authors who figure in this anthology, instead of avoiding this elusive, properly historico-literary treatment of the modern Mexican essay.

At all events, in the essays collected in this anthology are found some of the most brilliant pages in the literature and thought of modern Mexico. Although every artistic creation is not, strictly speaking, amenable to comparison, there may be established a resemblance, a parallel in aesthetic quality, in the literary essays of Antonio Caso, José Vasconcelos, Alfonso Reyes, Julio Torri, Rámon López Velarde, Xavier Villaurrutia, and Octavio Paz, to precise moments in the painting, poetry, and novel of the period. As for ideological or theoretical essays, like the one by Justo Sierra on the inauguration of the University, or those by Manuel Toussaint, Jesús Silva Herzog, Alfonso Caso, Jaime Torres Bodet, Daniel Cosío Villegas, Agustín Yáñez, Edmundo O'Gorman,[5] and Leopoldo Zea, it can only be said that their intellectual calibre is important to Mexican thought in such

[5]Excluded from this translation.

measure as their meditations have revealed, with more intense expressive power or greater originality, problems, and facts fundamental to our culture.

The Present Anthology

In the modern Mexican essays here collected there may be noted a panorama in which different aesthetic or intellectual disciplines are represented—history, philosophy, sociology, anthropology, literary and art criticism, and literature—that is to say, we shall recognize a characteristic feature of the modern age, specialization. Nevertheless, it would not be possible at the same time to point out an incongruous variety of ideas or criteria. In some way the present anthology of modern Mexican essays offers an ideological continuity—which could broadly be called liberalism—and a constant intellectual dignity. Does this imply that the thought here represented is the only Mexican mode of thought? No. Of course there are other thinkers who do not agree, for example, with the extolling of colonial life, with the indigene thesis of Alfonso Caso, or with the historical images of Jesús Silva Herzog and Arturo Arnáiz y Freg. I have selected the former group and not their opponents, both for reasons of personal sympathy with their way of thinking and, principally, because of their intellectual quality and because their texts do satisfy the requirements of the essay. This is an anthology of essays formed necessarily upon the basis of both an aesthetic and an intellectual criterion.

As for the themes of the essays selected, I have tried to present a repertory as broad as possible. In fact, with a few exceptions, it covers the most important cultural fields: metaphysical, religious, and moral themes, as already noted, and scientific themes, because—in spite of the existence of important scientists—our Bertrand Russell has not yet arisen in Mexico. In the field of science, it must be noted that there do not yet exist in Mexico sexologist essays—in the manner of Sigmund Freud, Havelock Ellis, or even Alfred Kinsey—which could continue in this area of human conduct the investigation into the character of the Mexican.* Political themes—on which we do have important essays

*Nevertheless, the theme has been given some initial investigation by Salvador Reyes Nevares, *Love and Friendship in the Mexican* (*El amor y la amistad en el mexicano*) [Porrúa and Obregón, Mexico, 1952, Collection "Mexico and things Mexican" ("México y lo Mexicano") 6], and by Dr. Alfonso Millán, "Looking towards an interpretation of love in the Mexican. Essay" ("Proyecciones hacia una interpretación del amor en el mexicano. Ensayo") [*Panoramas* 6, Mexico, 1957].

—are excluded from the present anthology because they will be the theme of another anthology planned by the Foundation for Economic Culture.

I cannot claim that all the pieces in the present collection are, strictly speaking, essays. Within the variety of forms and shadings which the genre allows, I have endeavoured to have my selections conform to the essential conditions established by mere force of custom, and also to have them marked by a literary quality or, failing this, to have them represent important stages in the history of ideas. In any case, the selection has taken into account above all else the real quality of the personalities representing the modern spirit. Nevertheless, many important expressions of modern thought and erudition are unfortunately omitted from this repertory because, in spite of their quality, they could not really be considered essays. Such, for example, are the excellent studies of Angel María Garibay on Náhuatl literature, which are strictly speaking critical studies or treatises.

As for chronological limits, I have adopted as my starting point Justo Sierra, and with him Modernism. My reasons are that if, according to the thesis which has been supported by Daniel Cosío Villegas,* the modern age in Mexico actually begins in 1867 with the restoration of the Republic, then literary and intellectual modernity will have a rich development until the last years of the century, and will find concrete expression in the *Blue Review* (*Revista Azul*) of 1894–96, in which the new generation of writers who made a definite break with Romanticism makes its appearance. For this reason Justo Sierra, guide and master of this period, opens the present anthology, which is closed by the youngest and most recent essayists in whom signs of maturity are already evident.

José Luis Martínez

*Daniel Cosío Villegas, "Call to the Public" ("Llamada general"), *Modern History of Mexico. The Republic Restored. Political life* (*Historia moderna de México. La República restaurada. Vida política*), Editorial Hermes, Mexico, 1955, p. 13.

Justo Sierra

(b. Campeche, Camp., Mexico, 1848; d. Madrid, Spain, 1912)

Son of the writer, historian, and jurist of Yucatán, Justo Sierra O'Reilly, Justo Sierra Méndez studied in Mérida and Mexico City, obtaining his law degree in 1871. His literary career began in 1868, under the eye of the master Altamirano, and a short time later he embarked upon his political career, which combined with his literary activities in a single cultural aspiration. Deputy, judge of the Supreme Court, teacher of history in the National Preparatory School, Minister of Education, and Minister Plenipotentiary to Spain, he was constantly a stimulator and organizer, through multiple channels, of the national cultural life. Among these channels were the *National Review of Letters and Sciences* (*Revista Nacional de Letras y Ciencias*, 1889–90), the Mexican Academy, of which he was director, his own historical works and those undertaken under his direction, his long effort in the field of education, which culminated in the organization he gave to the public educational system and in the founding of the National University (1910).

The centenary of his birth, in 1948, was commemorated with special solemnity by the National University of Mexico, which recognizes him as its founder. Agustín Yáñez directed the publication of his *Complete Works* (*Obras completas*); his mortal remains were transferred with great ceremony to the Rotunda of Illustrious Men in the Civil Pantheon, and the universities of the continent bestowed on him the title "Master of America."

Justo Sierra's essays, chronicles, and articles on literary criticism were written between 1869 and 1911, that is from a year after his introduction to a life of letters to one year prior to his death. Without interruptions, except those imposed upon him by his duties as a government official or by certain fortuitous events, Sierra published this part of his work in magazines and newspapers of those years, or as prologues to works of various kinds. Although mainly journalistic, his prose almost always overcame that superficiality and suggestion of improvisation which this kind of writing induces, and if many of his articles have, in the course of time, lost the interest which once gave them life, there still remains alive in them the enthusiasm they inspired in the mind of their author, and the verbal and imaginative richness which he was able to put into them. No other writer of the nineteenth century had to the same extent as Sierra that great gift of style which was capable of enriching both the great and the small with far-ranging suggestions, as if he were presenting it to the reader's eye illuminated by both heart and mind, lustrous and transfigured. When he turned his mind to his most revered literary masters—Victor Hugo, Altamirano, Gutiérrez Nájera—or when he defended his own convictions and literary predilections, or from the threshold of old age recalled the joyous life and songs of his youth on the beaches of Campeche, he wrote admirable pages which will be remembered with the best in our literary prose of his time.

ESSAYS: *Criticism and Literary Articles* (*Crítica y artículos literarios*), *Complete Works* (*Obras completas*), 1948, Vol. III.

PROLOGUE TO THE POEMS OF MANUEL GUTIÉRREZ NÁJERA

THE OBLIGATION was accepted over the grave of the poet. I feel myself incapable of fulfilling it; my powers, unequal in themselves to a task of such magnitude, are as though sapped away by the almost material proximity of our friend,* because the catastrophe, unfortunately not unexpected, but still sudden, has disturbed the morale of those of us who loved him with the love which he inspired; for we feel him near us, still warm with youth and affection; his sobbing, afflicted soul is wandering about in the very air we breathe. As the golden dewdrops of his verses saturate our poetic atmosphere, to the point of modifying and shading every line of our spiritual horizon, so the echoes called forth by his low and most gentle lamentations pass from heart to heart, and from this day they enter into us as part of our most intimate selves, and are reflected in all aspects of pain and human suffering, when we possess the serenity necessary to contemplate them. That quality of suggestiveness is the mark of the poetic work of Manuel Gutiérrez Nájera,[1] and it would be necessary to remove oneself a good distance from it to be able to judge it. It cannot be done today, because we are under the spell of his song. That magic influence will last long, and probably those who knew him and loved him will never be able to be judges of this marvellous outpourer of sentiment and music in the last hours of our dying century.

One day, seven or eight years ago, we were engaged upon a literary

*Manuel Gutiérrez Nájera died in Mexico City, February 3, 1895.

[1]See page 60 for a biography of Nájera.

publication; Manuel and I talked about his verses, and I think about my own too. "No," I said to him, "I will not write a prologue, but I would like to compose a psychological sketch of you; I shall go wide of the mark, but there all that I think and feel about you will be recorded, both what we so greatly admire you for, and what we love you most for."

The agreement which was entered into in this way, amid verses and laughter, in a casual moment of our lives, now suddenly rises up from a grave, solemn and stern. So then it must be faced, it must be honoured. . . . Shall I be equal to it?

I have just read his verses one by one. I shall read them again, I shall always be reading them. I shall make a selection of them and compose my anthology. With voluptuous devotion I shall savour the exquisite drops of his soul poured into those vessels of ethereal crystal, and so I shall live in long, perennial communion with him.

I have a feeling that to analyse this emotion will be for me an almost impossible task. My friend's verses retain the form of his dead body, which they still cover like a shroud; from a distance they appear as carved in pure, virginal, shining marble, but at close range, they live and suffer so! Under their immaculate whiteness, in an imperceptible network of throbbing veins, is there not flowing and living the pale, rhythmic blood of pain and tears? How can I proceed in this way to a study which would be almost a vivisection? Let us leave him wrapped up in the thin, vaporous tunic of his gay verses; let us clothe him in the gold-lined fabric of his sad verses, and covered with the mantle of glory, which is the poet's royal purple; let us watch over him, respect his slumbers, and let his mortal remains

> by fancy be guarded
> in crimson of sunset,

as d'Annunzio says.

I shall content myself with witnessing the spectacle, superb in its variety and romantic features, of the journey of this soul, pure and soft like the breath of a child, like the *animula vagula blandula* of the imperial poet, through silent inner storms, more terrible than those which dash to pieces the albatrosses against the rocks and break the wings of the eagles.

His life is a tragic idyll of which we know only the music: the verses of the poet. The result is a poem with notes gay, humorous, satirical, and yet in spite of this, perhaps because of it, ineffably sad. It must be followed step by step, and the metamorphosis of this select spirit studied. As in all poets who have had a very gentle, very loving, and very pious mother, Manuel's soul in its first notes is but a prolongation of the maternal soul; his first verses are songs of the nest, but of a nest hanging from the high coloured window of the church. His mother's mystic sighs pass through the strings of his harp (*The Cross* [*La cruz*], *Mary* [*María*], *God* [*Dios*], *The Faith of My Childhood* [*La fe de mi infancia*]).*

These fervent verses of a believer—nay, of one deeply devout, verses most sincere though rather conventional, and in which, in an occasional exalted and expressive strophe, one notes the eager desire to conform to the venerated models of sacred poetry with suggestions of the erotic and romantic, which was the delight of the generation of the second third of this century—these raptures of Catholic adoration hardly give us any indication of the future poetic personality of Gutiérrez Nájera, the most delicately sensuous and elegant of our lyric poets. But already he aroused enthusiasm, already he inspired faith and new aspirations. And this he did not only in the young; don Anselmo de la Portilla—the eminent Hispano-Mexican writer, one who, I shall venture to state, identified himself so completely, with the ingenuous fervour of his Spanish heart, with the hopes and aspirations of our native literature—introduced Nájera to the world of Mexican letters as a very precocious poet with inspiration and a future.

In Manuel's household this must have been a source of very great gratification and pride. How many kisses and blessings must have been showered upon that head, still with golden hair, of the fifteen-year-old boy! For while his mother was a soul at all times vibrant with religious emotion and tenderness (and mothers of this kind always produce poets), his father had a passion for literature and a love of good verses. Manuel's father also composed verses, giving spare moments to the writing of dramas which, at the end of his life, he submitted to the test of the impeccable good taste of his son. Manuel heard them with emotion, and possibly with exquisite and respectful tact, used his influence to prevent them from passing from their reading among intimate friends to the public stage.

If ever there was a poet both born and made, it was certainly Gutiérrez Nájera; he had the germ in his blood and he breathed in the atmosphere which fostered his early development. Catholic society in Mexico which, after the death of Carpio and Pesado, saw no sign on

*These poems appeared with dates 1876–78; we are sure that many others of the same kind were written by Manuel before those published here; but these, if not distinguished by an absolute spontaneity of inspiration, do reveal to us the writer of verse already nearly master of his art.

the horizon of any successor to those great writers of psalms—for Arango and Segura were elegant versifiers as a result of a select and superior literary culture, rather than by temperament or native genius—that Catholic society which was passing through an acute crisis of decomposition and compensation as a consequence of the definitive triumph of liberalism, saw in Gutiérrez Nájera its child sublime, as Chateaubriand said of Hugo, and hoped to see him wave aloft, to the accompaniment of matchless hymns, the *vexilla regis* of religion and art.

Two things must have been disquieting to this group: the eroticism and the looking towards France which the brilliant young verse-writer showed in his compositions—not yet an established preference, but still a tendency in that direction. But is there anything more sensuous than the prose of Chateaubriand, which by its music alone produces a material sensation of delight, and by its spirit turns the genius of Christianity into the very source of art in the most human, that is the most pagan, sense of the term; and was not he the latest of the Church Fathers, in the opinion of many orthodox poets? Gutiérrez Nájera, in his still inarticulate and indistinct eroticism, frequently in imitation, which was a natural note and gave tone to his compositions, was not rising in revolt against the Christian tradition. But this eroticism must, strictly speaking, take on classical dress and be more or less Latinizing or Hellenizing if it is not to be sinful; that is, in dealing with the deepest of human feelings, from which springs forth in an inexhaustible torrent the very sap of eternal poetry, it must, we say, try to appear in the eyes of the reader as a nicely contrived game, a shadowy imitation of the ancients; it must, in short, disguise itself and take on itself the classical stamp. The disquieting thing was that in Gutiérrez Nájera's strophes there resounded at times notes of a very penetrating and pleasant passion, exceptionally real and voluptuous, and in them there was neither classical pose nor mythological decoration.

And then the French element! In a study of our national literature in the first three quarters of this century, too cursory and incomplete for lack of sufficient information, but nevertheless the most accurate and of the greatest scope among all those that have been written on this theme, Mr. Menéndez y Pelayo[2] reproaches the youngest Mexican writers for their devotion, which he hyperbolically calls a superstition, to the latest in French literature.* The reproach may be just, but every

*Prologue to the first volume of the *Anthology of Spanish-American Poets* (*Antología de poetas hispano-americanos*).

[2]Famous Spanish literary critic and scholar of the late nineteenth and early twentieth century.

one of us deserves it at times. The French spirit in literature, on account of its amazing power to cast abroad the genius of that people; on account of the "assimilability," if I may be permitted the word, of its creations and transformations; on account of its very lightness; on account of the character of its aesthetic taste; well, indeed, for the identical reason which causes French fashions to be the most suitable for all human types, and the French cuisine the best adapted to all stomachs—the French soul, which has been the vesture of Latin humanity for two centuries, a vesture donned by Mr. Menéndez, in the same way as his body wears French frock-coats, though he appears not to realize it, that literature, we repeat, has been the nutritive juice of Spanish letters in recent times. The strange thing is that the illustrious writer has not explained the phenomenon to himself and has not understood that it was inevitable.

No people, engendered by another in the plenitude of its culture, and to which has been transmitted the necessary heritage of language, customs, and religion, has been able to create for itself, on the same level as its political personality, an intellectual or a literary personality; this has been, if it has occurred at all, the slow work of time and circumstance. To say to us, ironically, to us American sons of Spain, that our national literature is still non-existent, is not even the mark of a good critic. Does the illustrious academician think that our national literature reveals no evolution towards a certain characteristic form, one which bears the distinctive stamp of the Mexican group among all those of Spanish speech? Yes, there *has* been an evolution, and to achieve it assimilation has been necessary: first, indiscriminate imitation, almost unconscious; then, selective imitation, the reproduction of a model—this is what is called the assimilation of a literary or artistic element, and this we have done. And whom could we imitate? The Spanish pseudo-Classicism of the beginning of the century? This was an imitation of the French. The Spanish Romanticism of the second third of the century? This too was an imitation of the French. And yet we did imitate them: Quintana and Gallego, the Duke of Rivas and García Gutiérrez, Espronceda and Zorrilla[3] were our fathers' masters.

But later the imitation was more direct. Since we learn French at the same time as we learn Spanish; since in French we were able to inform ourselves, spasmodically, about exotic literatures, as we all did; since in French, in short, we made contact with the march of human civilization, and not in Spanish, to the French we went most directly. And that is what may be found in the present state of our intellectual

[3]These are all Romantic or pre-Romantic Spanish poets of the early nineteenth century.

evolution. Gutiérrez Nájera was one of the first to seek those waters, too impatient to wait for the thin trickle of the Spanish stream. But in that there was a danger, even an evil. The Spanish language, the vehicle we use now and always to express our ideas, became profoundly altered, not for the expression of the needs of our spirit, but for the factitious requirements of our rhetoric. The service rendered by the admirable poet we here commemorate was precisely to set the example, as an impetus, to accentuate the movement which led us to an intimate knowledge of the queen of Latin literatures in our era, and at the same time to defend the language of Spain as the only vessel out of which to drink the new wine. French thoughts in Spanish verses, such was his literary motto, we might say—an adaptation of the motto of André Chénier. And as years passed by he did achieve something; his purposes did not misfire. The Spanish language, not burnished or prim, yet pure and rich, took out naturalization papers in our literature principally in his poetry. The poets in the last boats, to take a phrase from Daudet, were proud to express themselves in the best Spanish at their command, through imitation of him, imitating not merely his verse, but his prose, which unfortunately is inimitable, and in which he expressed with marvellous colour and charm, in language generally pure and healthy, all the sentiments, all the longings, and even the caprices and petty desires of the modern individual.

It is but just to concede that in this task Gutiérrez Nájera found collaborators of the highest order: Pérez Galdós and Alarcón[4]—read and re-read today even as in former days, especially the former—renewed the language and style of our novelists and the appetite of readers; Valera,[5] thanks to his marvellous ability to overcome all linguistic difficulties with ease, provided his rich flavour in cosy intimacy for all people of good taste and for all those who doubted that the ethereal French *esprit* could become acclimatized in Spanish, a language by nature emphatic and precise. (The fact is that only Valera in Spain, and Gutiérrez Nájera here, have achieved it, though in different ways.) Menéndez y Pelayo himself, the prodigy of the learned and the delight of the cultured public—who overlook his sectarian bias out of consideration for his almost childlike good faith, and his efforts, unusual among neo-Catholic polemicists, to be impartial and just, and especially in view of the continuous and astonishing development of his powers—even he contributed towards bringing into fashion among

[4]Spanish novelists of the latter half of the nineteenth century.

[5]Another Spanish novelist of the same period, characterized by greater polish and refinement in his style than Pérez Galdós or Alarcón.

us a taste for Spanish of good sound stalk, so different from the affected, solemn, and straitened Spanish of the Classicists of the early part of the century, and also from the extravagant Gallicized Spanish of the Romanticists who followed them.

With these outstanding writers, and before and beyond them, our almost unreserved admiration (and I know not why I make mention of this reservation) was shared by Castelar in prose, and by Bécquer, Campoamor, Echegaray, and Núñez de Arce[6] in verse. The first of these, the only one who in the literary history of our century can be compared to Victor Hugo, not on account of his style or work, but on account of the infinite opulence of his elocution and his gift for thinking exclusively in images, was able to make an impression on our minds, fascinate them and hypnotize them (and as a matter of fact Castelar has had Latin America hanging on his magic words for more than a quarter of a century), but he had no influence upon our language, since his eloquence defied all imitation, which always sounded ridiculous and flat. The others were poets, and poets, with their restricted vocabulary and rhetorical devices, influence the general direction of the poetic spirit of a society, and are reflected in the style of other poets who are their contemporaries, but they do not refine the language; that is the work of prose-writers. But that reign of the poets was preparatory to the favourable change which for some time has been gaining momentum in our literature, which previously had flaunted inaccuracies and disdained grammar.

We called it a reign, and that is what it was, and in some measure still is. Bécquer held us for a long time under the spell of the semi-Germanic magic of his almost formless strophes, but strophes measured by the rhythm of an indefinably melancholy inner music, which appeared more adequate for the dolorous idealism of the modern lyric. Echegaray, another great lyric poet, with his tragic conflicts of conscience in his paradoxical and superb dramas of violent conflict, was also admired and applauded, as though his verses quickened the pulsations of the heart and brought illness out of emotion and tears. Núñez de Arce was and is the most highly esteemed; the pure sincerity of this great representative of Spanish Parnassianism shines through to the depths of the crystal-clear stream of his poetic eloquence, flowing through the white marble channels of a verse unfailingly sonorous and pure. All souls acclaimed him, all hands were extended to him, all crowns were offered to him. He still has among us hidden temples in

[6]Further references to leading writers of Spain in the latter half of the nineteenth century.

which his art is worshipped and in which the author of *Raimundo Lulio* and of *Fishing* (*La pesca*) occupies a place alongside the authors of two or three of the greatest books given to humanity, and he is the breviary in aesthetics for the most elegant women, in the best sense of the term, and for the most high-minded. Nevertheless, Campoamor is perhaps more delicate, of more profound psychology, and more transcendental; granting that he is less serious, with his smile and his irony he still achieves greater penetration, and brings forth more novel examples of passion and pain from the depths of the human soul. Yes, these inspired men were kings, shining suns. Most of our poets would have been their satellites if the attraction of French literature and other alien literatures with which we became acquainted through it had not marked an orbit of which the curve cannot yet be determined.

It may be said that the first ten or twelve years of the literary career of Gutiérrez Nájera (1876–1888)* were a continuous journey through all these influences, coming near to all of them, reflecting all of them, swimming in the waters of the new authors, enchanted, admiring, submerged, and at times showing on the surface of the waves, like Heredia's shark,[7] his shining fin of emerald and gold.

In that decade he revealed himself as an outstanding writer of prose, with no point of comparison in present-day Spanish letters, by the continual but most gentle glow, like that of glow worms, of his phrases, and by his very complex and fine style, saturated with poetry and with an indescribable faculty for an intimate, familiar, and caressing flow of words, which seemed to border upon a mannered style, but which adroitly eluded the reef by a movement filled with grace and good taste.

In his prose, a perpetual expression of his lyrical, love-filled heart, set like a fairy-made embroidery upon the course of worldly events which his work as a chronicler obliged him to relate, our Manuel formed his style, created his literary personality, and reached the full consciousness of his power and his art. Then he became popular, in learned circles and in the society of the *salons*, under the pseudonym of "Duke Job." This so well suited his modesty and his literary nobility, and harmonized so well with the mood prevailing in each of these

*The first articles of Gutiérrez Nájera appeared, from November 15, 1876, in the literary edition of *The Federalist* (*El Federalista*), under the general title of *Confidences* (*Confidencias*).

[7]The reference is to *Le récif de corail* (*The Coral Rock*), by the Cuban-French poet Heredia (1842–1905).

social groups, moods by him united with inimitable ease, that this young writer was really a prince of the realm of fancy, a magician who painted, on fans of lace and silk, delightful figures and landscapes, surrounded by an infinite dreamland.

But let us set aside the writer of prose: shall we be given the privilege of studying him some day? Without such a study, as perhaps we have already said, the standing figure of "the Duke" cannot be set up on the pedestal. Let us briefly follow the poet. His verses, less frequent than at first, more artistic, the work of one who knows and penetrates the most recondite secrets of technique, arise from his journalistic prose, and in the quiet pools of the rushing current, like the overflowing waters of the Nile, open up their splendid flowers like living stars joined by crystal links. His verses were indeed like flowers; and his poetic work, on the whole, is the most beautiful, the most sweet-smelling flower, the autumn flower of Mexican Romanticism. Within the elements of its vital fluid, in the juice with which it is coloured, one may find selected constituents taken from all the poetic productions which had recently come to light on both sides of the ocean, and in the poetry of the entire generation which follows Nájera this flower finds its corolla shorn of its leaves as though it had been immersed in a glass of strong wine.

We said the flower of Romanticism, and rightly did we say it. First of all, the truth is that all our poetic literature since 1830 is Romantic. It is the form of realistic works that has influenced us, not the bias or the spirit, or at least such influence is very slight; we have been and shall still be for a long time Romantic, in spite of the transformations undergone by the schools of our overseas masters. We have never succeeded in composing purely objective poetry; in all our verses we pour forth all our feeling, all our personality; we have produced nothing but subjective poetry. Latterly, heroic attempts have been made, we might say, considering our temperament, to depart from the old channel and impersonalize our emotion—in short, to produce a little indifferent realism in verse (I have in mind the *Cruel Poems* [*Poemas crueles*]). It is doubtful if the result has been anything but splendid samples of psycho-pathological poetry. The brilliant descriptive poetry of Pagaza, Othón, Delgado, Valenzuela, and a group of refined young artists, turns out to be barely semi-objective, on account of its religious, erotic, or moral purpose. Let us glance at the magnificent miscellany of Gutiérrez Nájera: *Tristissima nox*. There one has a sample of objective poetry; there one finds surprising insights into nature, and yet, how much of his suffering feminine soul is dispersed throughout those shadows, how much lyricism sprinkles with gold the wings of that great dark butterfly!

Individualistic poetry in which not lyricism—for, according to my professor of French literature, lyricism is not a genre but a state of mind that may be common to different poetic genres—but rather that which most characterizes the individual, that which most differentiates his personality from others, in short, sensibility rather than intelligence, predominates, is what we call Romanticism. This poetry of sensibility or, in poetic terms, of sentimentalism, is that of Gutiérrez Nájera. His sentimental lyricism, even when he frolics and laughs, is essentially elegiac; take a hundred of the compositions here published, and with most of them one can make up a bouquet of elegies, white, perfumed, and sad, like the last flowers of a dying garden. Such an anthology might be entitled "Love and Tears," and this title alone would recall the apogee of Romanticism.

But Manuel's elegy, a genuine flute song (this was the primitive Helenic elegy), on account of its dolorous and subtle sweetness, and not because in musical rhymes it reveals a soul, ceases to be of its time and to mark the interminable transition from Romanticism to pure Realism, which today the mysticism of the new schools brightens with the spectral colours into which the light of the sun beyond the grave decomposes. It is a song of love or pain, or usually both at once; it is soft to the point of languor, sensuous to the point of delectation, like those of his master Musset; but sometimes he goes further, and from the vertex of his sadness, our poet contemplates that fragment of the world and of universal life which it is given us to know, like a segment of shadow and despair that cuts off and measures the two lines of spirit and matter which form the angle of our existence, and then Manuel is a pessimist, and his poetry expresses with such precision the torment of many, yes indeed, of very many, that he becomes almost impersonal and ceases to be Romantic in order to be eternal.

Let us laugh at pessimism with the Dumas and with the Nordaus; let us laugh, life is good; the proof of it is that we seize upon it furiously; yes, indeed, we do. But this we do either because it is an instinct, that is, through the influence of the least intellectual part of ourselves, or out of duty, on account of the lives of others. "The pessimism of the young is a pose, it is not a genuine feeling!", say the glorious spiritual disciples of Pangloss. So then, the loss of one's course in mid-ocean (because science serves, though indeed admirably, only for coastal navigation along the shores of the known), the invincible sense of the immensity of the unknown, the eclipse of that most ancient polar star that was called religion, the derangement of that compass that was called the free conscience, afford no reason for supreme anguish; they are incapable of rising above all our sensibilities and casting gloom over our lyre, in the same way as they engulf the soul in densest darkness! And this you say is not worthy of being mourned and bewailed in immortal sobs and cries! Ah! If all this is a pose, it is the pose in which civilization has placed us, the pose of Laocoon amid the coils of Apollo's serpents.

The sublime Mexican composer of elegies had a golden thread attached to his foot, and no sooner would he flutter out into the night of pessimism (*Tobe* [*Tobe*], *The Monologue of the Doubter* [*El monólogo del incrédulo*], *Dead Waves* [*Ondas muertas*], *Orphan Souls* [*Almas huérfanas*]) than he would return to his Romantic nest, lined with the feathers of his fantasy, softened by the warmth of every love, and from there he would continue to strike up ineffable melodies, tearful and divine. Divine indeed (*Pax animae, Non omnis moriar, To Cecilia* [*A Cecilia*], etc.), divine without hyperbole, because from the volcanic upheaval produced in his heart by pain and disillusionment (*My Mourners* [*Mis enlutadas*], *Punished* [*Castigadas*], *Butterflies* [*Mariposas*], *The Serenade* [*La serenata*], *Afterwards* [*Después*]), from the petrified lava decorated with thorny cacti flowering in vases of blood, there arose very high peaks, very serene and snow-clad—those peaks upon which the ancients placed the gods, whence the moderns see the sky more unfathomable and blacker, but also the stars more refulgent.

A poet tormented by the desire for happiness and by the thirst for truth is a tragedy which sings along its way through the human masquerade. Such was Manuel, such was that soul made ill by the ideal, a soul which, as someone has said about Joubert, was hemmed in and inhibited by any kind of body encountered by chance. He came to believe in happiness when he was at the end of his life, in the warmth of the hearth, and there is in his verses something like an echo of the immortal plea of Faust to Time, to the fleeting moment: "Oh, stop, thou art so beautiful!" But the eagerness to understand everything (the dream of Goethe) would again disturb him, drive him on, and in advance he would feel himself beaten, and the Muse would whisper in his ear the words of Shelley (whom Manuel worshipped): "Sleep, sleep on! Forget thy pain; my hand is on thy brow, my spirit on thy brain, my pity on thy heart, poor friend. . . . Sleep, and with the slumber of the dead and the unborn, forget thy life and love; forget that thou must wake forever. . . . Forget lost health, and the divine feelings which died in youth's brief morn; and forget me, for I can never be thine." Oh no! The Muse, the archetype of beauty and goodness which we struggle to reach in life, is like those women who give themselves, but do not surrender themselves. It is the delightful life of our pink and blue aurora which, in the end, in the fullness of life, turns pure, absolute darkness—

darkness, shoreless shadow, that,
that which sees not, ends not,
darkness in which the sight is smothered,
that's what I seek for my soul.

The darkness sought by the poet is the eternal darkness, that of the tomb. Let us stop at its threshold; it is very high. From the other shadow, alas, not so distant (the life of the "Duke" was so short, as life normally is!), from the mystic shadow of the penumbra, of the temple, emerges the heavenly body, and we can trace its curve of light: Bécquer, Campoamor, then all the French poets of the modern, the new, and the very new generation, from those of the Romantic caravel to those of the latest craft, from Hugo, Lamartine, and Musset to Richepin, Rollinat, and Verlaine, including on the way Gautier, Baudelaire, and Coppée—all have marked, like constellations, the course of the orbit of the great planet. Of these constellations, those which have shone most brilliantly in Gutiérrez Nájera's firmament have been Campoamor and Musset, just as in his prose are reflected the style of Gautier and Paul de Saint Victor and the limpid, crystalline moulds of don Juan Valera which, from time to time, have a delightful archaic touch, like the song of the king of Thule, in Gounod's *Faust*.

In the last six to eight years, already complete master of himself, not in the style of his masters, but yet in one that his masters would not have repudiated and which was unique in our literature, the poet, "Duke Job," succeeded in achieving in his writings the goal of his dreams: an amalgamation of French spirit and Spanish form. In the midst of his progress towards the ideal, by dint of the mastery already acquired over his genius and his expression, came the cruel and sudden end.

As the course of a comet is calculated and marked by the elements of its curve, so we might forecast what Gutiérrez Nájera was to be; one senses what he had still to say, the notes of his unsung song. And I believe that he would have been the great religious poet of the dawn of Latin America's century. I say religious and mean Christian, not, of course, a Christian after the manner of the Pesados or the Carpios, nor in the likeness of our Pindaric Prieto who is more Deist than Christian and who worships in Christ the people made divine, but a serene and delicately sensitive Christian, profoundly moved to pity upon contact with poverty and suffering in society, and with doubt and despair in individuals—a sectless Christianity—such would have been the basis of his last poems. And he would have won many souls, not by the tragic sublimity of his *De profundis* or his *Dies irae*, but by the tender, balsamic unction of his *Ave Maris Stella* and his *Te Deums*. It is true that the elegant and exquisite quality of his verses would not have given him influence over the masses and that he would never have been popular. But he would have played, as upon the strings of the lyre, upon the fibres of the tortured hearts of the intellectual aristocracy, and it is these who have need of a faith and an ideal, and not the people, who possess them in a form that is simple, absurd, and divine.

But this was not to be; everything came to an end in the full light of day and at the height of his endeavours. The work of Gutiérrez Nájera goes on, but in the writings of others who came after him, in which the light he shed is at the same time reflected and refracted. For it may be said that he was the great awakener of poetic vocations, and it may be added that the crowd of singers (I speak of the genuine singers) who today fill the air with their notes, here and perhaps in all Spanish America, first awoke inside his nest and soared in their first flight thanks to the magic power of the voice of Manuel.

And what lay deep down within this elect soul, what was his inborn faculty, that faculty which serves as a key to his elegance, his tenderness, his erotic and melancholy inspiration? It was one that is very difficult to explain, impossible to define and make tangible, but one which we all understand when it is named: it was grace, a sort of smile of the soul, which to any kind of utterance lends an indescribable delicate, winged rhythm, which in impalpable waves like those of light, penetrating through all the fine ramifications of style, lends them a certain peculiar magic which produces in the mind an impression like that of a difficulty overcome without effort, which turns into delight and enchantment. This gift of grace in our poet shines through all the themes of his admirable compositions in verse and prose. Whether mournful, serious, humorous, classical, satirical, or tender, all his work is made, through the effect of grace, diaphanous, ethereal, and imponderable. His laughter, his tears, his patriotic notes, his art criticism, his gay or sad tales, even his political articles, yea everything, from the account of a salon to a study on Hamlet, from the verses with champagne sparkle written to the dear "Duchess," to the infinitely gentle murmurs of *Non omnis moriar*, everything reveals that peculiar irradiation from the varied facets of the poet's personality; it is as though Roentgen's X-rays, penetrating a wall, caused the photographic plate to burst into flower.

The distinction, brilliance, and elegance of his style are but manifestations of the native grace of the man, which is the quality that best prepares for the development of taste, that other indefinable faculty made up of balance, proportion, and harmony. The good taste of the "Duke" was outstanding: his *Brief Odes* (*Odas breves*), true amphoras of the potter, show this clearly. All of us who knew Manuel know that he could go on indefinitely producing those samples of immaculate art, those jewels, some of them worthy of figuring in the anthology, which were child's play to him.

And this sovereign faculty, which gives to the artistic work of Gutiérrez Nájera all its variety and movement, also forms its unity. The heightened imagination like that of an Athenian, the delicacy of feeling, the tenderness of heart—all these are doubtless the psychological and moral conditions which permit the use, in a fecund manner, of this gift of the gods. These were the distinctive marks of the character of Manuel.

Either I or someone else will later take it upon himself to trace the psychological biography of our friend. The complete magnetization of his soul, which exerted upon all those who came into contact with him the irresistible attraction of the goodness and purity of his sentiments, redeemed intact from a youth subjected in its flower to every kind of sensation and exposed to contact with every kind of filth, will pose a problem. Another problem will be to explain why there was no loss of mental and aesthetic virility in an intellect wrung to the point of martyrdom in continuous toil over a period of from ten to twelve years. In this toil a man who was admirably endowed for dreaming and singing was converted into the galley-slave of journalism, feeding into the press, in series indefinitely renewed, now studies of the more serious literature, now poetic studies in enamel, gem, and gold—in which he drew upon his artistic skill without exhausting or even lowering the springs of his aesthetic instinct, which remained unpolluted and virgin despite the tireless writer's reckless prodigality of power and light—now serious articles of political controversy, and also daily trifles impregnated with Attic irony and gay humour. How could this be? Herein lies the secret of a life and a death.

Poor Manuel! Never was it granted to him to live with himself, to realize the *secum esse secumque vivere* of Cicero—never! And for this reason he felt, at times, an overwhelming lassitude which was instantly fought off with strong, treacherous stimulants. And this man, who had lived a hundred lives by dint of the intensity of his cerebrations and his feelings, found his heart and faith unimpaired for setting up a home, for crowning with immortal flowers the brow of his beloved, and for succeeding, by the power of his affection, in transfusing his angelic soul into the soul of his little Cecilia, a seraphim to whom our unhappy Martí[8] consecrated his last most admirable song.

We shall shed light upon these painful problems. In this way, or by some other path, we shall go back towards our friend; we shall ever keep going back. To bid him farewell here, I shall beg from Shakespeare, the poet who knew and felt all, the words of Horatio before the body of Hamlet (our "Duke" too was a prince of art): "Good night, sweet prince, and flights of angels sing thee to thy rest!"

Prologue to: Manuel Gutiérrez Nájera, *Works. Poems* (*Obras. Poesía*), Establecimiento Tipográfico de la Officina Impresora del Timbre, Mexico, 1896, pp. iii–xvii.

THE FESTIVAL OF SODZIL

FOLLOWING THE EXAMPLE of my fellow-speakers, I shall be very brief. All we men of letters say this when we set out to force our defenceless victims to endure the torture of listening to a lucubration which was produced in sixty hours of work and condensed into one hour of reading time. What more can we do? Or what less? Nothing more nor less. So get ready to suffer a little; you have enjoyed the sweet honey with which the poets have regaled you; you have savoured the exquisite joys which this little select paradise offers to the eyes and to the soul, thanks to the charming Castilian maids of Sodzil, and it is only fair that a little boredom and suffering should set in relief the fine quality of the sweet pleasures that are here offered you.

When I learned that four of us Yucatán poets were to read their work here, I naturally thought of writing in prose. Where could I find time, in spite of the great mass of time petrified in the marvellous

[8]Cuban poet and patriot (1853–95).

ruins of Yucatán, to forge that work of the devil that is called "poetry"? The time that exists there, alas, is past time, and I needed present time.

And then I said to myself: "What shall I write about? What shall I read even in prose?" My first answer, the natural answer to any old hand in literature, was this: write about politics. It is the first thing a writer thinks of—his formula is: lots of politics and little administration. So let us do some political literature. Let us say to the President: "Mr. President, you have finally given to Yucatán a cordial embrace; you have felt beating next to your own heart the heart of a people, a great heart too; you have made it eternally yours. Yucatán will not forget you, and when you have begun the period of monuments and statues, when you start your life of marble and bronze, a piece of bronze and a piece of marble will commemorate, in an imperishable form, the gratitude of the people of Yucatán. That does not die, I well know it does not die. And you have come here, fearless in the face of great danger of which you have preferred not even to speak, in order to finish, in a splendid fusion of your trust and our enthusiasm, the work of the indestructible union of Yucatán and the nation. The son of those who in bitter times believed the little unit of power to be a necessity swears to you that merely by your coming here, merely by your extending your hand to us, you have sealed the final reconquest of Yucatán for the larger unit. Nothing, no material, economic, or political interest, compelled this union. It had to be a union of souls, and for that reason imperishable; it is now completed, and you have accomplished it. And as a witness of this work of the spirit, you have brought with you the lady who has been a peerless collaborator in your social benefactions. To your power of will in conjunction with the crying needs of the Mexican people you owe your political prestige, but this element of brightness and smiles necessary for any kind of social prestige you owe to her. This Yucatán feels, and sends off after her a great song of love and of benediction, soft, melancholy, and profound, like the farewell verses of Peón Contreras[9] transposed into sobs by the guitar of Chan-Cil.[10] The presence of Carmelita has made of your salute to Yucatán not only an embrace, but a kiss. In legendary days there came to these parts an empress, an unhappy lady.[11] Many remember here. Today there has come one of those sovereigns whom republics and democracies bless, one whose crown

[9]Yucatán poet and dramatist (1843–1908).

[10]A popular guitarrist of the district.

[11]The reference is to the Empress Carlota, welcomed in Yucatán on her arrival in 1864. The Mexican Empire fell in 1867.

is formed out of her modesty, her goodness, the spotless virtue of her life, and the divine gift for making herself beloved. None will forget her.

But my political theme is not proper for the Sodzil Festival. Politics among flowers reminds me of a verse of Horace, which at this moment escapes me (perhaps because I did not know it), but which in essence says that at times the asp springs forth from the flower-bud. If I had the temerity to stress my congratulations to the master of this house, or nest, or tuft of flowers, on the renewal of his powers to continue his splendid service to the State which owes so much to him, the opposition would come out and confront me, led by the most charming, influential, and irresistible of leaders, by Teresita Molina, the bright, lovely girl who, with the instinctive, egotistic gentleness of filial affection, would wish to compete against the public weal for the attentions of her father, needed by his home, and the well-spring of its life.

Well then, ladies and gentlemen (how many tight places I am getting myself into!), we will choose one, two, or three historical themes. Yucatán is the most historical place in America; that is to say, it tried to be the most historical. Unfortunately, before the earnest questioning of our curiosity, the great books of stone, full of speech, thought, beliefs, and history, remain mute. In them lies what was felt and said, not by the builders, who were mere poor, subjugated tribes, but by those who conceived their building, the great nobles, the priests, the kings, the despots, those who presented to us those sublime relics impregnated with mystery and art. Blessed may they be! What hopeless desperation it is to keep turning over an enigma without finding a way to dispel it! The temple, the tomb, the relief in stone, all turn out to be one great exasperating work of irony. Once I managed to crawl up to the carved head in the funeral crypt, at the foot of the Temple of the Diviner in Uxmal. There is nothing more beautiful in all that has been left us from ancient times in the Orient, in Greece, or in India. In the veiled smile of that mouth filled with sensuous sweetness and with the desire to live and to give life, in the Egyptian eyes which see without pupils, which for that reason see more and see farther, in the voluptuous palpitation of the fine nose with its golden ring, there is such a readiness to speak, to reveal, to tell, to confide the feelings of a soul compressed by the stone hand of ritual, like a bird crushed in the claws of a Chacmol,[12] that one standing in its presence silently awaits a word, a sob, a kiss.

Let us leave this theme; no kisses, no sobs, no words. But shall we

[12]A reclining figure with flexed knees, found in prehistoric remains.

actually be leaving it? Really, can we say that Yucatán has ended its history, back there in the unknown past? No, colonial Yucatán still lives in many of the towns of the peninsula, especially the Yucatán of yesterday—the Yucatán of caste warfare, the rebellion of those who had formerly fallen under the control of the Itzá and Toltec priests, accustomed probably to drowning alien civilizations in blood, lives on too, that rebellion which tried to burn up the peninsula and leave in its cities no stone upon another, to kill or enslave their white inhabitants, and which almost succeeded in its purpose. And what do the Yucatán poets do with this epic? Why does there not burst forth from their lips the epic song, the song of the reconquest, the song of desperate anguish, native instinct, and valour? They do not sing it, but the story is told by the ruins of yesterday which are not yet restored by the new breath, the new force which has made a magic wand out of the bristling thorn of the maguey. The story is told by the houses eviscerated by the sharp claw of the invasion, the stripped altars, the church towers bereft of their tongues of iron, the charred traces of the torch, the blood marks left by the machete. Yes, many of the flowers of Yucatán are still the flowers of the cemeteries. Fortunately, as a promise that here nothing will or can die, the sempervivum, emblem of the immortal, grows everywhere over the streets and highways in amazing profusion.

No, this is a gloomy theme; let us look for another. A friend said to me in Lerma: "Are you in prayer before the sea?" I *was* in prayer before the sea. (Here a piece of description would be appropriate: the sun was like a golden egg slipping out from some unknown womb of blue; on the sea the tiny clouds—in that sunset none was large—were like swans of the bay, slowly furrowing the blue sky.) All was memory, all was pain, all was a cruel, deep ecstasy; it was the resurrection of my forgotten soul, of my soul fluttering on the edge of youth, of the fountain which we all believe to be eternal. "And why do you not compose another 'beach song'?"—asked suddenly, at the height of my rapture, the clear, innocent voice of a girl from Campeche. "Oh, no!"—I answered, startled—"it would be a sob, a lamentation of agony; the pearls I found in the waves would turn to tears. The 'beach song' is Youth. Farewell, youth! We old men keep entertaining ourselves with this farewell each day, but the farewell receives no answer. Youth is already a long way off."

And why do I have these sorrows, these sad feelings of nostalgia? What more do we old men desire, than to have channelled our youth into the youth of others, than to have given it away, to have seen it bud in other souls formed from ours? As for me, what great longing of mine have I not seen almost gratified? What have I asked of life that it has not given me? A hearth alive, giving warmth to other hearths, and, as the singer of Junín said, a smile from our homeland, what more can I ask? I have had a heart that could love: my helpmate and I have together lit a lamp which will burn over our joint graves. How about our homeland? Well, I have been a humble priest of its cult. What more can a poet wish?

I want to compose the "beach song," I want to compose the "beach song" of old age. Why not? When the soul hovers on the brink of death, one has strange revelations, loves unexpressed, ineffable intuitions; the sweet little girl does not come from the nearby hill, but descends from the soul to be met at the beach. Yes, let us redo the "beach song," that of old age.

Of this I sing: the sea, barely green, close to black, woven with gold, with the moon lightly touching the sky with the pearl of its pale gleam. The voice which will sing this song will be my own soul, my whole life. The inspiration, as the rhetoricians say, is already upon me: the wave rises from the heart to the lips. Here is the beach song; the sea song is on. . . . Here it is. . . . Listen.

February, 1906

An address at the festival on the Sodzil Estate in honour of the President of the Republic, General Porfirio Díaz, during his visit to Yucatán in 1906. It was published in the local newspaper and taken from there by the publishers of *El Reproductor Campechano*, who reproduced it in No. 4–5, of July–October 1947. It is very interesting to contrast the attitude of Justo Sierra at this festival in honour of Porfirio with the account of the same festival given by Fernando Benítez in his book *Ki: the Drama of a People and of a Plant* (*Ki: el drama de un pueblo y de una planta*), F.C.E., Mexico, 1956, pp. 96–117.

DISCOURSE AT THE INAUGURATION OF THE NATIONAL UNIVERSITY

TWO CONSPICUOUS WORSHIPPERS of force made law are the authors of *The German Empire* and of *The Strenuous Life.*[13] The first of these conceived of force as an instrument of domination, as the major weapon of what Nietzsche calls the will to power. The second sees force as an agent of civilization, that is, of justice. These two writers are chiefly responsible for having instilled into the minds of all people capable

[13]W. H. Dawson and Theodore Roosevelt, respectively.

of looking towards the future a deep longing, with tenacious purpose, to transform all their activities: their mental activities, in the way that light is transformed; their emotional nature, as heat is transformed; and their physical nature, as motion is transformed—all into one single form of energy, into a kind of moral electricity which is precisely what integrates the man, what makes him into a value, what causes him to enter as a conscious molecule into the different evolutions which determine the direction of human evolution in the torrent of eternal becoming. . . .

This resolve to be strong, by which the ancient world achieved magnificent results in select groups, and which is now coming into the field of great achievements realized by entire nations, shows that the heart of any problem, whether social or political, taking these words in their broadest sense, necessarily involves a pedagogical problem, a problem of education.

For, with regard to individuals, and let this be very clear, to be strong is to integrate their whole development—physical, intellectual, ethical, and aesthetic—in the formation of a character. Obviously the essential element in a character is the will. To force it to evolve with intensity, by means of physical, intellectual, and moral cultivation, from childhood to manhood, is the main purpose of the primary school, or "the school" by antonomasia. The character is formed when there has been impressed upon the will that mysterious magnetism analogous to that which attracts the compass in the direction of the pole, the magnetism of the good. To cultivate wills to attain selfish ends would mean the bankruptcy of pedagogy. It is necessary to magnetize characters with love; it is necessary to saturate the man with the spirit of sacrifice to make him have a sense of the tremendous value of the corporate life, to make him into a moral being, in all the serene beauty of that expression. To sail ever along the course of this ideal, to keep reaching towards it day by day, minute by minute—such is the divine mission of the teacher.

The University, you will tell me, cannot be an educator in the complete sense of the word; the University is a simple producer of learning. It is an "intellectualizer"—it serves only to develop intellectuals. I could then add, it would be most unfortunate if the group of Mexicans who have already been initiated into human culture, scaling the huge pyramid with the ambition of getting a clearer view of the stars, and of being viewed in turn by an entire people, as our Toltec ancestors did, would end by forming a shrine around which would be formed a caste of the learned, a caste more and more removed from its earthly function, more and more removed from the soil which sustains it, more and more indifferent to the pulsations of the turbid, heterogeneous, barely possessed of consciousness, social masses, whence it derives its nurture and upon whose highest peak its greatness of mind may be lighted like a lamp, shining out into the solitude of space.

Again I say it: this would be a misfortune; already the leading psycho-sociologists have told us so. No, in our times it would be inconceivable that any group, created by a society aspiring to take a more and more active part in human enterprise, should feel itself freed from the bond that would unite it vitally with its mother's body in order to belong to an imaginary land of souls unbound to a native soil. No, the University will not be something destined never to turn the eye away from the telescope or the microscope, even though around it a nation is falling apart. The taking of Constantinople will not catch them discussing the nature of the light of Tabor.

I think of it in this way: a group of students of all ages adding up to just one age, the age of full intellectual capacity, forming a real personality by virtue of unity of purpose and consciousness of mission, which, taking advantage of any source of culture, wherever it may show itself, provided the lymph is pure and diaphanous, would take upon itself the task of acquiring means whereby they might nationalize science and Mexicanize learning. Turn the telescope to our sky, a compendium of prodigious formations of stars where amid the blackness, formed of the mysterious and the infinite, gleam at one and the same time the septentrion eternally inscribing the Arctic furrow about the virginal pole star, and the sidereal diamonds which fix in the firmament the Southern Cross. Turn the microscope on the germs which swarm about invisible in the retort of the organic world, germs that in the cycle of their incessant transformations make of all existence a medium in which to perform their evolutions, that ensconce themselves in our fauna, in our flora, in the atmosphere in which we are immersed, in the stream of water that flows over the ground, in the flow of blood coursing through our veins, and that conspire, with as sure an effect as if they were conscious beings, to decompose all life and to extract from death new forms of life.

Life would probably be exhausted on our planet before science would complete its observation of all the phenomena that enter into our making and the making of life. Our subsoil, which in so many ways justifies the description of "new" that has been given to our continent, is one of them. Another is the peculiar conformation of our territory, formed by a gigantic horseshoe of mountain ranges which, having risen from the ocean inside the torrid zone, transforms it into the temperate zone and carries it right on to the frigid zone, and raises it up to seek the snowy diadem of its volcanoes in an atmosphere completely polar, and there, in those altitudes, the inner arc of the horseshoe ending in a series of plateaux which die away towards the north, it presents us with an ethnic fact which is perhaps unique on the earth. Here we have large groups of human beings organizing themselves and persistently continuing to exist and evolve to the point of constituting large societies, a nation resolved to live, at an altitude where, in other analogous regions on the earth, either human societies have not succeeded in growing, or they have not succeeded in establishing a fixed abode, or they vegetate without any capacity to form nations conscious of themselves and with an urge to progress.

And a most interesting point is that on account of such conditions not only do social, and consequently economic, demographic, and historical phenomena, here have forms *sui generis*, but the other phenomena, those which are most plainly produced within the limitations of the inescapable uniformity of natural law, have them also. Physical, chemical, and biological phenomena here show peculiar features so intimately related to meteorological and barological conditions that they constitute, within the vast domain of knowledge, a province not indeed autonomous, because all nature falls within the sovereign domain of science, but yet distinct and characteristic.

And if from nature we pass on to man, who, of course, is an atom, but an atom that not only reflects the universe, but ponders it, what a multitude of strange things we encounter! Did one single race dwell here? Do the morphological differences in the languages spoken, even though of like structure, indicate different origins related to a diversity, not indeed psychological, but nevertheless in the bodily form and appearance of the inhabitants of these regions? If this continent of ours is not a centre of creation, where is the primitive stock of these groups? Is there, by any chance, a latent unity in this human family which runs along the meridians from one pole to the other? These men who built stupendous monuments in the midst of cities, apparently conceived by a single gigantic brain and brought into being by several generations of conquered tribes or of slaves of religious passion, serving a desire for domination and pride, but convinced they were serving a god, also erected in their cosmogonies and theogonies spiritual monuments greater than those merely material. These monuments, with motley peaks like those of their temples, touched eternal problems, problems in whose presence man is but man, in all climes and all races, that is, he is but an interrogation cast into the night. Who were these men, whence did they come, where are their living relics in the depths of this indigenous sea over which from prehistoric times has passed the levelling weight of superstition and servitude? But still this sea reveals to us, from time to time, its formidable latent energy in individuals charged with the spiritual electricity of character and intelligence.

Then there is the history of the contact of these strange aboriginal cultures, as they appear to us, with the most energetic representatives of Christian culture, and the extinction of that culture which had developed here in so many different forms. This is the effect resulting from a contact begun four hundred years ago and not yet consummated, with the persistence of the indigenous soul coupled with the Spanish soul, but not identified or fused, even in the new race, in the genuinely Mexican family, born, as has been said, of the first kiss of Hernán Cortés (Cortez) and Malintzin.[14] And then there is the necessity of finding in a common education the means to that final unification of the nation. If all these things are studied in relation to whither they are leading us, and in relation to the series of phenomena which determine our social condition, what a profusion of themes for our intellectual workers to study, and what a rich treasure for human knowledge, will be extractable from these still hidden veins of revelations embracing the whole field of learning of which man is at once subject and object!

By carrying out this vast work of culture and by drawing upon all the energies of the Republic, wherever these are fitted for intellectual effort, our University will merit the name of "national" which the legislator has given it. It must demonstrate that our personality has indestructible roots in our nature and in our history, and that, even while we share certain elements with other American peoples, our manner of life is such that it constitutes an entity quite distinct from all others, and that the words of Tacitus, *tantum sui simile gentem*, may properly be applied to the Mexican people.

In order that this work may be not only Mexican, but human, not only must we not waste a single day of the century in which it is to be achieved, but the University dare not forget, lest it risk using up the oil of its lamp without renewing it, that it will be necessary to live in intimate communion with the march of general culture, that its methods, investigations, and conclusions cannot acquire definitive value until they have been tested upon the touchstone of scientific

[14]Called by the Spaniards doña Marina.

investigation carried out in our age, principally through the universities. Science advances projecting its light before it, and its light is method, which is like an immaculate theory of truths in pursuit of the truth. We must and we will take our place in this divine procession of torches.

The educational work of the University will therefore stem from its scientific activity, bringing to it select groups of intellectually-minded Mexicans and intensely cultivating in them the pure love of truth, tenacity in their daily work in pursuit of it, the conviction that the interests of learning and those of the state must be added together in the heart of every Mexican student. This will create types of character destined to crown and seal the great work of popular education which school and family (the latter being the great school of example) set upon a splendid foundation when they work in harmony. Emerson, quoted by the eminent president of Columbia University, says: "Culture consists in suggesting to man, in the name of certain higher principles, the idea that there is in him a series of affinities which serve to temper the violence of master notes which sound discordant in their scale, affinities which are a help to us against ourselves. Culture reestablishes the balance, puts man in his place among his equals and his superiors, reanimates in him the exquisite feeling of sympathy and warns him in time of the danger of solitude and of antipathetic impulses."[15] And this suggestion of which the great American moralist speaks, this suggestion of higher principles, of right ideas being transmutable into altruistic sentiments, is the work of all the men who have a voice in history, who acquire a decisive vote in the moral problems which vex a society. It is the work of those men who, unconsciously, from their tomb or from their writing desk, their workshop, their camp, or their altar, are true social educators. Victor Hugo, Juárez, Abraham Lincoln, Léon Gambetta, Garibaldi, Kossuth, Gladstone, Leo XIII, Emilio Castelar, Sarmiento, Bjoernson, Karl Marx, to speak only of those alive but yesterday, have greater influence and power of suggestion for our present-day democracies in formation than all the moral treatises in existence.

This diffusive and penetrating education by example and uttered word, which throughout a certain period of time saturates the atmosphere of the national life with ideas made power, the University must concentrate, systematize, and send out into action; it must strive to present fruitful incarnations of those higher principles of which

[15]Quoted by Nicholas Murray Butler, President of Columbia University from 1901 to 1945. This is a free rendering from Emerson's essay *Culture*, Complete Works, Centenary Edition, Houghton Mifflin, Boston, 1903, Vol. VI, pp. 136–37.

Emerson speaks. It must carry out the tremendous task of receiving within the school doors, where the teacher has succeeded in inculcating moral and physical habits which incline our natures towards the good, the child who is going to make of his instincts the constant auxiliaries of his reason when he passes into the decisive stage of adolescence, and who is going to acquire mental habits which lead him towards the truth, and aesthetic habits which make him worthy of appropriating the exclamation of Agrippa d'Aubigné:

> Oh! Celestial beauty,
> Fair daughter of heaven, torch of eternity!

When the youth becomes a man, the University must either send him out to struggle for a living at a higher social level, or lift him to the lofty heights of scientific investigation. Nevertheless, this must be without ever forgetting that all contemplation must be preliminary to action, that it is not permissible to the university person to think only for his own interest, and that even if inside the doors of the laboratory spirit and matter may be forgotten, as Claude Bernard[16] said, we shall not be able, morally, ever to forget either humanity or the nation.

The University, then, will have sufficient power to co-ordinate the main lines of the national character, and before the nascent national consciousness of the Mexican people it will ever hold high, so that it may project its rays into every place of darkness, the beacon of the ideal, an ideal of health, truth, goodness, and beauty. This is the torch of life of which the Latin poet speaks, the torch which generations in their course pass on one to another.

Have we a history? No. The Mexican University born today has no genealogical tree; it has roots, of course, roots in a compelling inclination to organize itself, which in all its manifestations reveals the national mentality, and therefore no sooner does the shoot spring from the soil than it becomes covered, at the first kiss of the sun of the homeland, with sprouts and buds, harbingers of leaves, flowers, and fruit. Already it is strong, and we sense that the fruit will come. *It will work by itself.* If it has no ancestry, our University does have forerunners. The governors and faculty of the Royal and Pontifical University of Mexico are not for us our forebears, they are the past. And yet, we remember that University with a certain involuntary sense of filiation, involuntary, but not devoid of emotion or interest. It was born in the Colony, in the society engendered by the Conquest, when

[16]Professor at the Collège de France, who died in 1878.

it possessed no branches of learning except those which the conquerors themselves offered or tolerated. It was the brain-child of the First Viceroy, the magnanimous don Antonio de Mendoza, and an expression of the saintly Father Las Casas' steadfast love for the new country, and it could not come into existence until the votes of the Mexico City Council were heard, ardently supported by another great viceroy who won from his contemporaries the title of Father of the Country.[17] A short distance from this site was erected a large white house, decorated with large gratings of Basque manufacture, on the banks of one of those endless canals which traversed the magnificent city in all directions, and passing by the Marquis' establishment (today the National Palace), ran to seek an outlet through the irrigation ditches which, as in Aztec times, crossed Cortez' capital. The indigenes who rowed in their long flat canoes, swollen with vegetables and flowers, heard in astonishment the confusion of voices and the murmurings of the enormous cage in which the great dignitaries of the Church governed chairs patronized by crowds of students, in which they explained abstruse problems in theology, canon law, jurisprudence, and rhetoric, problems already solved, without any possible revision in case of error, by the authority of the Church.

There was nothing left for the University to do in the matter of the acquisition of knowledge, little in the matter of religious propaganda, of which the religious orders took charge with brilliant success, but there was everything to do in the matter of providing instruction, by slow selections from among the colonial group. It was a verbalizing school; "wordism," to cite Leibnitz, prevailed in it. It was the word and always the Latin word, of course, which was the magic shuttle which functioned incessantly in the endless weaving of dialectal concepts. On the doors of the University—we might have said of universities—there should have been inscribed the exclamation of Hamlet: "Words, words, words." But the Mexican University, surrounded by the Chinese wall erected by the Council of the Indies between the American colonies and the outside world, was almost completely insulated from the formidable seething of intellectual currents known as the Renaissance, and knew nothing of the great religious and social schism known as the Reformation. So it continued to live under the same conditions as had prevailed in the universities of the fifteenth century, a century before. What could it do? For it time did not pass, it was intellectually walled up. But as it wished to speak, it did speak

17Don Luis de Velasco, Second Viceroy of Mexico from 1550 until his death in 1564.

through the mouths of its students and teachers, veritable prodigies of memory and of knowledge of dialectical technique.

So passes its first century, already housed in a large, noble building which we have seen ourselves obliged to tear down in order to save it from falling into ruins while it was occupied by our National School of Music. It was demolished with the intention of rebuilding it, in the not too distant future, with its characteristic type of architecture and its artistic decorations in stone and wood which we are carefully preserving. The University of Salamanca, which today is sponsoring our University at its birth, gave it the model for its form of government, which soon was half stifled through the operation of parasitical adherences. Then into its cloisters was projected the noble, battling shadow of Bishop Palafox, who reduced everything to regulations, quite intricate, but at the same time quite clear, and these were the definitive guide of that house of studies in which the intellectual New Spain centred its pride until there appeared on the horizon the terrible rivals, those who were to monopolize all Catholic education *ad majorem Dei gloriam*.

We are rightly proud of our wonderful inventions, of our discoveries of unimaginable importance. We are looking into the universe towards all its dark spots. We are pursuing the mystery of all things right into the most remote areas of the night of what is. We ask of science the last word pertaining to the real, and it answers us and will always answer us with the penultimate word, leaving between it and the ultimate truth of which we seek a glimpse the great immensity of the relative. In this domain, what a swarming multitude of new facts, of unsuspected phenomena, of surprises in nature solicited with eager zeal by the mind armed with an instrument superior to the compass for the discovery of new worlds: armed with *method*! The present period of human revelation matches that of divine revelation, from which, after the triumph of militant Christianity, in the form of Catholicism, arose the pious centuries of the monastic orders, the theocratic popes, the Crusades, and scholastic theology. That period, the mediaeval period, issued from the cross of the temple, from God, and travelled entire centuries through human thought, to be lost in a formidable theological labyrinth in search of the metaphysical union linking the rules of human conduct and the divine idea. It sought man with the scholastic lantern, when the splendid dawn of the Renaissance extinguished the lantern and revealed man. From this man made up of passions, but controlled by reason, not by faith, forming a harmonious unity as pagan philosophy had conceived it, the new science came forth. You know the episodes of this amazing journey, that of circumnavigating truth over shoreless seas, of which Littré speaks in a devastating vision. Science, the new revelation, dares to sail upon those seas, bound for mountains rising higher and higher, crowned with a mysterious glow. When one of the great men in science, the eminent English physicist Thomson, described them, he said a short time ago in an assembly of scholars: "Great are the works of the Lord!" Can it be that the science of man is a world travelling in search of God?

We have, then, all the discoveries, already countless, which science has achieved in this journey. We have the applications and the behaviour of electric energy, which before the eyes of the philosopher is being converted into a sort of soul of the universe, compared to which matter and the ether appear simple concepts of our minds. We have the discoveries that have shown the way to retain in a copper wire a world of sounds which disappear by a simple metallic contact. We have those which have brought within the field of the photographic telescope myriads of stars hidden in the darkness which a few years ago a poet would have called eternal, and we have those which have brought to the eye of the microscope the inconceivable multitudes of organic nebulae which compose the infinitely small, and decompose into individuals better endowed to propagate death than Attila, Tamburlaine, or Ahuizotl.[18] Then there are those discoveries which have found in Roentgen rays, in the properties of radium, and in the radio-activity of bodies an eager endeavour to add to the visible world another unsuspected world, a world which we might call supernatural if nature were really known to us. There is all that sort of stirring of the cosmos effected from the inner recesses of the laboratory, by which in each day of work and observation there is awakened a new form of a latent force. From there arise, with the problem of their continuity unsolved, the analysable phenomena, describable through the processes of science, which acts as an inflexible measure applied by our minds to the endless fabric of things that are. But yet all this cannot be compared in importance for humanity, in influence upon the destiny of the human being, to the invention of printing or the discovery of America in the fifteenth century, just as these latter discoveries pale into insignificance beside the voluntary production of fire, without which man would have succumbed at the dawn of the quaternary period.

[18]Aztec emperor of Mexico, who reigned from 1486 to 1502.

Printing engendered the book, which put the mind into contact with itself, and the discovery of America completed humanity, which felt itself deficient, and replaced theological faith by scientific faith. Out of both these discoveries was born the modern age. Out of both these discoveries was born the University of Mexico which, with that of Lima, constitutes the first attempt by Spanish monarchs to give wings to the American soul, which was just beginning painfully to form itself.

The place of studies was not a harbour for ships which dared to plough through the new seas of the human intellect in the time of the Renaissance. No, that we have already said. The basis of learning was scholastic. In the meshes of this school the doctrines of the great Catholic thinkers who, with St. Thomas Aquinas and Vives, had disappeared from the scene, had turned to flowers of rags. Until the appearance of Cardinal Newman the void remained, not indeed with regard to intelligence and mystic sentiment, which were always abundant, but with regard to genuine philosophic creation. Ever making deductions from dogmas above or beyond reason, or from the commentaries of the Church Fathers, and most expert in the use of dialectal or rhetorical formulae, the university teachers, here as in old Spain, carried on the work of Penelope and taught how to reason indefinitely, following the syllogistic chain, without ever hitting upon a new idea or a sure fact. It was an oral spider's web made out of the very substance of the word, and the *quod erat probandum* proved nothing but what was already proved in the original proposition. And this technique was applied to canonical, juridical, medical, and philosophical studies, since theology spoke as ruling mistress, and the other sciences as slaves.

There could well be produced, as there were produced, university men who were reasoning prodigies of memory and syllogistic logic, among both professors and students in our University. This body was transmuted into a case of vegetable life and later into a sample of mineral life. It was the flagstone of a tomb. The epitaph was written by Father Agustín Rivera, in the *History of Philosophy in New Spain* (*Historia de la filosofía en la Nueva España*).

In vain did Bishop Palafox, full of hatred for the Jesuits, try to galvanize that corpse in the seventeeth century. Soon it fell again into impotence, debility, and decomposition. Jesuitical education is radically defective in that it bases all character training upon blind and mute obedience, and because it makes knowledge of the classics the principal element of its teaching, but without being able to penetrate into the true classical spirit which was that of the Renaissance, which it declares anathema. In Mexico this education was in the hands of men of signal virtue, so well versed in the learning of their age, so human, so self-denying as missionaries, so pliable as courtiers, so tolerant–in the social sense of the word–so penetrating as psychologists and so zealous in their efforts to uplift the Mexican soul, that the University entered into a rapid decline of the moon in the presence of that moral and mental sun which was rising before it. It declined irremediably, even as a school for the training of priests. Soon the conciliar seminaries, born of the Tridentine prescriptions and adapted to them, made of the University a very practical and effective instrument. The degrees gradually became a despised honour, a means of providing resources for the old university doctors. Not even the expulsion of the Jesuits, decreed by Charles III, which left the University a free field, was of any service to it. Not even then could it attract a Creole clientele, since the Creoles were completely on the side of the expelled fathers and revived their teachings. There was nothing to be done about the University. Its agony was very slow, but irremediable. It knew no way, and perhaps, indeed, it would in any case have been impossible, to open a gateway for the new spirit and refreshen its air and reoxygenize its old body, which was gradually turning to stone. The University knew no way to do it. It was the seminaries that prepared the way for the spirit of philosophical emancipation, obliging their students to become familiar with it through the refutations that were made of it, or through some books clandestinely brought into the classrooms. And it was the seminaries, not the University, that secretly cultivated the great souls of the insurgents of 1810, souls in which, for the first time, the native land came to be.

When the worthy leaders who in 1813 brought to the government the conscious aspirations of the Reform Movement pushed open the doors of the old University building, there was hardly anyone or anything there. There were some large old objects, some of them venerable, others moth-eaten. . . . They threw into the waste-paper basket the rag relics, the doctoral tassels, the age-old registers, in which it was shown that the Royal and Pontifical University had not had a single idea of its own, or accomplished a single important purpose in the intellectual life of Mexico. It had done nothing but argue and re-argue through dazzling exercises in mental gymnastics, in the presence of archbishops and viceroys, for three hundred years. And so the University born today can have nothing in common with the other. Both have stemmed from the desire of the representatives of the State to lay upon men of great learning the task of utilizing the national resources for scientific education and investigation, because they constitute the body best prepared to fulfil these functions; for the State knows of no functions more important, and does not believe that the State itself is the most capable of fulfilling them. The founders of the former University said: "The truth is known, teach it." We say to the university people of today: "The truth is in process of being known, seek it." The first would say: "You are a select group charged with the task of inculcating a religious and political ideal, summed up in these words: God and the King." We say: "You are a group in perpetual process of selection, from within the body of the people of the nation, and you have entrusted to you the realization of a political and social ideal which is summed up thus: democracy and liberty."

To succeed more quickly—not in attaining its ends, because the history of human thought proves that they are never attained, though they are in the process of being attained each day, but rather in mastering the means to attain them—the legislator has seen fit to limit the direct activity of the new institution in order to intensify its operation. Nevertheless, we have not for this reason set it up completely apart from any concern for primary education, the most fundamental, and the most necessarily national type of education; but this concern could not go beyond the limit of giving precise information taken from the most authoritative source. Its concern had to stop there, because our laws establish an agreement between the people and the government, which reserves for the latter everything relating to primary education. This is indisputable, and we Mexicans regard it as indisputable. It belongs to the political order. The government holds that, being deeply persuaded of our ineluctable duty to make the Mexican people into a nation, a democracy, we are obliged to use, directly and constantly, the most important means of achieving this purpose, namely, the primary school. All other means are subsidiary; there is not one of all the means that lead to peace and progress which is not educative, because not one of them fails to increase the coefficient of cohesion in peoples and to foster love for work and facilitate the progress of the school. But the school, which suggests habit making, which tries to convert external into internal discipline, which unifies the language, establishing a national language over the dust of all the languages of indigenous stock, thus creating the fundamental element in the soul of the nation—this school, which systematically moulds the child into the citizen, instilling in him devotion to the native land and the cult of civic duty, forms an integral part of the State, constitutes one of its prime obligations, and must be considered as a public service. Indeed, it is the State itself foreshadowed in its future function.

This is the first reason for our system, and this is why the normal schools have been kept outside the sphere of the University, in spite of the fact that we are quite aware of the present tendency to replace normal school training by university pedagogical training. I do not know what the results would be elsewhere, but here we condemn such a system as disastrous in the present stage of the development of our schools.

The University is responsible for national education in its higher, more intellectual areas; it is the high point where the fountain gushes, clear as the crystal of the Horatian spring, coming down to water the plants which have germinated in the national soil and rising up into the soul of the people however high it is held. Meanwhile, our pedagogical plan in present circumstances, with close dependence on the State, will include all that forms part of concrete and utilitarian disciplines, those disciplines relating to new necessities upon which the present-day life of the State is in part dependent, such as commercial and industrial studies, these being a field for future universities. Included also will be everything in the economic order that it is necessary zealously to protect (because the poor climate in which it is evolving requires the temporary creation of artificial means to encourage it) that evolution which we hold to be indispensable to the national culture, namely, that of aesthetic studies.

So, then, the new University will make its selection out of those whom the primary school sends to the secondary; but already at this stage it will appropriate them, refine them in tough crucibles, out of which it will finally extract the gold which, in the form of medals engraved with the national coat of arms, it will put into circulation. This secondary education is organized, here as in almost the whole Republic, in a double series of programmes which follow each other, one being a preparation for the other in both logical and chronological order, and in both the scientific and literary branches. This system is preferred to that of coincident studies, because our experience and the Mexican type of mentality seem to credit it with greater didactical value. It is, of course, somewhat at variance with present-day scientific interdependence, but its accordance with the history of learning and with the psychological laws founded upon passing from the less to the more complex is undeniable.

Upon this scientific series which informs the plan of our secondary education, "the series of abstract sciences" as named by Auguste Comte, is erected that of the higher professional studies paid for by the State and supported by it with all the generosity of which it is capable—not because it believes it to be its mission to provide gratuitous courses for individuals who have been able to attain to that third or fourth stage of selection, but because it regards it as necessary for the good of everyone that there should be good lawyers, good doctors, good engineers, and good architects. It believes that social peace, social health, and social wealth and decorum, which satisfy needs of prime importance, require it. These studies are the base of the School of Advanced Studies. There selection attains its ultimate. There division into many fields of learning is to be found. There an ever-widening distribution of individual work-groups will be brought into being. There we shall bring together, so far as we are able, the princes of science and of the humanities, because it is our wish that those who receive the maximum degree of preparation in our system of national education will be able to listen to the voices of highest prestige in the world of learning, the voices that come from the highest eminences and that travel the farthest. We wish to bring them not only the voices which stir up ephemeral emotions, but those that initiate, inspire, reveal, and create. One day such voices will be heard in our School. They will inculcate love of learning, a divine love, because of its serenity and purity, which brings forth ideas just as human love brings forth human beings.

Our ambition is that in this School, the highest point in the university edifice, established to reveal in knowledge the broadest and most open horizons as well as those that can be contemplated only from the loftiest eminences on our planet, people will be taught to investigate and to think by investigating and thinking, and that the substance of investigation and thought will not crystallize into ideas contained inside minds, but that those ideas will become dynamisms continually translatable into teaching and into action, for only in this way can ideas be called forces. We should never like to see ideas reserved for ivory towers or a contemplative life, or for raptures seeking the artist who will utilize them; that sort of thing may exist elsewhere, and perhaps it is well that it should, but not here, in our School.

An imploring figure has for some time been wandering about the *templa serena* of our official educational system, namely, Philosophy. Nothing is more worthy of our respect and nothing is more beautiful. Far back in the centuries when the mystic doors of the Oriental sanctuaries were opened, it served as a guide to human thought, which sometimes is blind. This figure stood with thought on the pedestal of the Parthenon, which it would have preferred never to leave. It almost lost contact with thought in the confusion of the barbarous ages. Rejoining it and guiding it anew, it stopped at the doors of the University of Paris, the *alma mater* of thinking humanity in the Middle Ages. This imploring figure, Philosophy, is a tragic figure which leads to Oedipus, to him who sees through the eyes of his daughter the only thing worth seeing in this world, the thing that does not end, the thing that is eternal.

How we have been called cruel, and perhaps stupid, for keeping closed the gates leading to the ideal Antigone! The truth is that in the plan for positive education the scientific programme constitutes a fundamental philosophy. The higher studies which begin with mathematics and end with psychology, moral philosophy, logic, or sociology constitute a philosophic education; they are an explanation of the universe. Nevertheless, even though we could not give to philosophy its marble throne in our programmes as an autonomous subject of study, having traditions to respect but none to continue or follow, and even though we could show the constitution of the universe so far as science had projected its reflectors, we could not go further and give a place in our catalogue of subjects to the splendid hypotheses which attempt to explain not merely the how but the why of the universe. And this does not mean that we have adopted the philosophic creed of Positivism. You need only compare the programme adopted by us with the series of abstract sciences proposed by the great thinker who founded that creed to assure yourselves of this. No, in our schools a laic spirit prevails. Here, on account of circumstances peculiar to our history and institutions, the State could not, without betraying its trust, impose any creed. It leaves to all absolute liberty to profess whatever creed is convincing to them, whether one of reason or one of faith. The metaphysical lucubrations which are the expression of an irresistible urge of the spirit, and which constitute a sort of religion in the sphere of the intellect, cannot be the concern of science. They are superimposed syntheses which soar over it and frequently lose contact with it. They are always the work of the intelligence, sometimes the genius, of the individual mind. There is nothing to equal this form of mental exercise for elevation of the soul, or for contentment of mind, even when, as commonly happens, there follow tragic disillusionments.

There is, however, the work of co-ordination, the attempt to sum up knowledge, which does have its entire basis in science, and one section of the School of Advanced Studies includes this under the heading of Philosophy. There we shall open courses in the history of philosophy, beginning with that of modern doctrines and the new systems, or the renovated systems, from the appearance of Positivism up to our own day, the day of Bergson and William James. And we shall leave free, completely free, the field of negative or affirmative metaphysics, both monism and pluralism, so that we may be made to think and feel while we pursue the pure vision of those eternal ideas which endlessly appear and reappear in the current of intellectual life: a God distinct from the universe, a God immanent in the universe, a universe without God.

What should we have achieved if on realizing this dream we had merely added a Mexican star to a constellation which did not shine in our skies? No, the new man, whom devotion to science forms in the young neophite who has in his veins the sap of his land and the blood of his people, cannot forget to whom he owes himself and to whom he belongs. The *sursum corda* which issues from his lips at the foot of the altar must be directed to those who have loved, and have suffered, with him. Let him hold up before them a promise of liberty and redemption, the immaculate host of truth. In the temple that is erected today we do not desire the worship of an Athene without eyes for humanity or without heart for the people within her contours of white marble. It is our wish that the best Mexicans will come here in endless columns to worship Athene *Promakos*, the science that defends the homeland.

1910

Discourses, Complete works (*Discursos, Obras completas*), 1948, Vol. V, pp. 447–60. Excerpt.

José López Portillo y Rojas

(b. Guadalajara, Jalisco, 1850; d. Mexico, D.F., 1923)

Like so many other Mexican writers, the Jaliscan José López Portillo alternated duties as a public official with juridical and literary activities. He was a deputy in the Union Congress and in the Jalisco legislature, a deputy circuit judge and deputy judge of the Supreme Court, a senator, a professor of political economy and of penology and mining law, a delegate to the Second Panamerican Conference, an under-secretary of education, a Secretary for External Affairs, and a governor of the State of Jalisco. Furthermore, in Guadalajara he founded *The Literary Republic* (*La República Literaria*), 1886–1890, an excellent journal, and belonged to the literary organizations of Mexico City and to the Mexican Linguistic Academy, of which he was a president.

López Portillo wrote travel stories, verses, novels, and short stories, a few essays, studies in economics, sociology, and miscellaneous subjects, and one book on politics, *Rise and Fall of Porfírio Díaz* (*Elevación y caída de Porfírio Díaz*), 1921. He owes his prestige to his works of fiction, and especially to *The Plot of Land* (*La parcela*), 1898, a novel with a rural setting, written with restraint and a firm literary quality (within the limits of literature on social customs), and inspired by Spanish Realism.

Occasionally López Portillo wrote some well-thought-out essays, like the one which he used as a prologue to *The Plot of Land*. The importance of this essay lies in the fact that it is an exceptionally lucid doctrinal exposition concerning a problem or a policy in Mexican letters, a live issue in his day as it still is today: the problem of nationalism.

ESSAYS: *Egypt and Palestine. Travel notes* (*Egipto y Palestina. Apuntes de viaje*), 1874; *The Novel* (*La novela*), 1906; *Eulogy of Manuel José Othón* (*Elogio de Manuelo José Othón*), 1907; *Rosario de la Acuña: A Chapter in the History of Mexican Poetry* (*Rosario de la Acuña, un capítulo de historia de la poesía mexicana*), 1920; Other essays scattered throughout the *Reports of the Mexican Academy* (*Memorias de la Academia Mexicana*), the *Modern Review* (*Revista Moderna*), *The Literary Republic* (*La República Literaria*), in different newspapers, and as prologues.

PROLOGUE TO *THE PLOT OF LAND*

OUR RURAL INHABITANTS are the nerve of Mexico, the most direct and most genuine product of the different factors which are unifying our people. In their physical aspect, they represent the fusion of different indigenous and European races, but they lack a definite resemblance in character to either of these groups, and show a manner of life, tendencies, and habits that are original. With the colonial tradition broken, they do not try, and it does not even occur to them, to imitate foreign customs, of which they know nothing. At the same time, severed from the aboriginal stock, they have nothing in common with the inertia, the stubbornness, or the vengeful animosity so characteristic of that stock. These people are the new plant which has sprouted in the warmth of our sun and under the influence of our climate, the alluvium of the many races that have been depositing their fertilizing clay upon our territory.

Our cities may be more or less vague copies of European and American capitals, with their crust of ideas, customs, sciences, and arts imported from outside. Our fields, on the other hand, are the young nation, which is being formed in the wake of our political upheavals, like the forming of fine, healthy flesh over a wound at one time large and painful. Upon this very solid, substantial base of beliefs and toughness is to be erected the edifice of our future greatness, crowned by the civilization of the age.

At the present time, there is among these people a great passion which dominates and controls them, one which both spurs them on to work and incites them to take part in the struggle: love of the soil, of Mother Earth. The peasant has always worshipped it; but this love today has among us something that is special, something epic and primitive, one might almost say fierce. The disputes which it very frequently causes deeply stir the rustic folk, and furnish arguments full of interest to anyone who observes this phenomenon closely or describes it faithfully.

From the portrayal of such scenes may arise revelations of major importance, and among others, that of our essential, intrinsic national character. True examinations of the social conscience always give good results. Incidentally, in the midst of the work, the observer hits upon deep-seated vices that enter into the framework of the narrative. Presented in this form to the eyes of the public, these vices may move and stir people, arousing in their minds the desire to see them eradicated. Just as Mrs. Beecher Stowe produced in the United States a salutary reaction against slavery, with her novel *Uncle Tom's Cabin*, so also did Charles Dickens exert a powerful influence in England towards the abolition of imprisonment for debt with *Pickwick Papers*, for the reform of the primary schools with *Nicholas Nickleby*, and the protection of homeless children with *Oliver Twist*.

It is true that art must live as art and without didactic purposes, but it is true also that in the exact portrayal of life social blemishes appear as if they were crystallized, caught in their ugliest deformity. And how often that portrayal alone brings about hatred for the evil and its abolition!

The late Liceo Hidalgo (God rest his soul) years ago devoted some of his meetings to a discussion of the question as to whether Mexico should or should not have a special literature. If my memory serves me right, don Francisco Pimentel y Heras and don Ignacio M. Altamirano were the leaders in the opposing arguments, and over this question they became involved in most learned discussions, the latter of these debaters voting for a distinctly national literature and the former for a continuation of Spanish literature. The debate remained unsettled, and since that time nobody, so far as we know, has started it up again.

We shall not be the ones to blow on those ashes to stir up some latent spark, since we are among those who consider a compromise between such extremes to be possible. Our literature, in the matter of form, must remain orthodox, that is, very faithful to the dogmas and canons of the rich Spanish language. Nevertheless, this does not eliminate its autonomous faculty of enriching itself with indigenous words, or words created by our own invention and as a result of the powerful influences of character, nature, climate, and temperament which are peculiar to us alone. But even in these neologies, we must endeavour not to depart from the genius of the mother tongue, and not to break its splendid classical moulds. It would be madness to reject such an illustrious ancestry and open an abyss between ourselves and the Golden Age of Spanish literature. In the Iberian Peninsula, where the tradition of the sixteenth and seventeenth centuries is kept alive, and where there are so many eminent authors who cultivate the language with the profundity of sages and the finesse of artists, are to be found today, without any doubt, the standard and model of good speech. We Latin Americans must not lose sight of the masterpieces which come to us from over there, but we must approach them as closely as possible in purity of expression and beauty of phrase. Who can deny don José M. de Pereda his place as leading writer in the Hispanic world, a kind of revived Cervantes, capable of transporting the mind of the reader to the times when, to general astonishment, *Don Quijote* appeared? Who can deny don Juan Valera his charming Atticism, his most felicitous inventive faculty and the elegant, impeccable correctness of his periods? Who can deny Pérez Galdós and Pardo Bazán[1] their marvellous skill in manipulating the language?

Our origin, therefore, and the glory of Spanish letters, and our desire for progress, must keep us ever faithful both to the genius and sanctions of our language and to the course followed by the great writers of our old mother country.

But so far as its essential substance is concerned, our literature should be national in every possible way, that is, in accord with the character of our race, with the nature that surrounds us, and with ideals and tendencies which originate from both these factors. God save us from trying, for this reason, to shut ourselves up within the narrow limits of our horizons, and thus turn our literature into petty jingoism. We well know that the majority of subjects which fall within the realm of art, such as love and pain—eternal bases for poetry—are cosmopolitan, and not the patrimony of a special people or a special race. All we wish to say is that we must fix our attention, more than is our wont, on our own affairs, and make felt more forcibly in our creations the influence of our own temperament.

We Mexicans, up to the present, have been excellent imitators, but very poor inventors. We quickly pick up the fashions which reach us from outside, not only in costumes and customs, but even in ideas and systems, and we vie with one another in imitating quickly and precisely the new things from abroad. In order not to depart from the solely literary field, we shall not illustrate this observation with examples taken from legislation, politics, or social usage. So far as letters are concerned, nobody can fail to see that ours, with honourable exceptions, are nothing but a sad imitation of literature from overseas, chiefly French. Proof of this is our absurd Decadentism, which has no reason for existing among us because, being a new people, we have not yet reached the extremes of degeneracy or of refinement which this novelty presupposes. Decadentism can be understood in old nations of mature civilization, where the springs of sensibility, worn out with use

[1]Except for Cervantes, who is of the sixteenth and seventeenth centuries, the writers mentioned in this paragraph are all important Spanish novelists of the nineteenth century.

and abuse, require subtle and refined handling in order to function. But this is not true of an incipient society, where culture is only partial and has in its favour the freshness and strength of youth. Decadentism is less a literary school than a special psychic state, and cannot be faked.

Held under the spell of European books, our poets and novelists compose poems and novels of pure caprice, on subjects foreign to the real nature of our life and feelings in the present day, thus producing false creations, which here neither correspond to anything real, nor copy, except in a deformed and monstrous fashion, the exotic and refined. To convert Mexico City into a diminutive Paris, and attribute to it by artifice the excellences, meannesses, vices, and virtues of the French capital, is the most transparent aim of not a few of our best writers, for they strive to be elegant and voluptuous like Musset, solemn and paradoxical like Victor Hugo, obscene like Zola, and fanatical phrase-filers like Flaubert and the Goncourts. Every writer has a model like those mentioned, and tries to imitate him precisely, come of it what may. This is how, in our Republic, worlds are dreamed up which do not exist, with refinements, passions, languors, and despairs which do not suit us. Thus works are produced which in their negligence have neither the appeal of truth, nor the charm of a senile but perfected art.

Beautiful form must, obviously, be imitated by the writer who aspires to perfection, but not states of mind—as Bourget says—, not the private psychic states of individuals or the general spiritual climate of society. Every people is subject to peculiar influences which determine its character, and at each stage of civilization there is a corresponding development of definite vital fibres.

It would be absurd to demand of every writer that he be a genius and strike off over unfamiliar roads; but it is not absurd to ask him to be sincere and to make of his works a faithful mirror of real passions and fancies. There is no reason to scorn the surroundings in which we live (which are very beautiful, God be thanked) and to take pleasure only in distant views and scenes. Even though we may not have about us, unless by way of exotic exception, refined strollers on the boulevards, nobles fallen into penury, ridiculously conceited high-born ladies, degenerate nannies, magnificent palaces, and Daumont-style carriages, we do possess in their place a thousand other things worthy of observation and which can serve as an inspiration to us for the singing of loves, sorrows, and joys, in tones vibrant with life and truth.

Beauty is manifold and shines anywhere, even in the primitive state, even in the most dismal, sterile landscapes.

The only thing we need in order to exploit the rich possibilities surrounding us is to collect ourselves within ourselves, and to diffuse ourselves less in extraneous matters. Our national life is still as unexploited by art as our natural resources are by industry. Among us all is virgin–forests and customs, the material earth, and the moral climate which surrounds us. Our splendid coastlines, lofty ranges, vast plains, rich forests, and brilliant cloud effects still await the emotion-filled brush to paint them, and the eloquent pen to describe them. The same can be said of our colourful population, made up of sad-looking indigenes, proud Europeans, and shrewd mestizos. The vices, passions, inclinations, and virtues peculiar to them require inspired artists to portray them, who know how to utilize for their creations this interesting period of transition through which we are passing. Day by day, old habits die one by one; new customs take root and everything before our eyes becomes crisis: clash of interests and conflicting aspirations—the chaos that precedes order and beauty. So it goes continually, when in history's laboratory there boil and fuse together disparate elements destined to become amalgamated in a great people.

1898

Prologue to *The Plot of Land* (*La parcela*), 1st edition, Mexico, 1898. Library of Mexican Authors, Vol. II, 3rd edition, by Antonio Castro Leal, Editorial Porrúa, Mexico, 1945, pp. 1–8. Collection of Mexican Writers, Vol. II.

Manuel Gutiérrez Nájera

(b. Mexico, D.F., 1859; d. Mexico, D.F., 1895)

The man who was to be one of the most productive and significant of Mexican writers never attended school. His mother taught him his primer, and a few masters instructed him in Latin and mathematics. At the age of thirteen he began to write articles and poetry for *Iberia* (*La Iberia*) and *The Federalist* (*El Federalista*), and later for almost all the newspapers and magazines of the last third of the nineteenth century. He contributed to them daily—with a grace and polish that were new in Spanish letters—political and literary articles, news articles, travelogues, short stories, and poems which he signed with various pseudonyms, one of which, "Duke Job," was to become permanent.

Among so many tasks as galley-slave of the pen, which he performed with unfailing cheerfulness, Gutiérrez Nájera undertook an enterprise which I imagine brought him special pleasure and which was to be decisive in the introduction of Spanish-American Modernism, the *Blue Review* (*Revista Azul*), 1894–96, which he managed in collaboration with Carlos Díaz Dufóo. When the *Review* was not yet a year old, its founder died, without ever having abandoned the pen, exhausted by his tremendous literary efforts.

Amid the rich forest of the writings of Gutiérrez Nájera—explored, but only partially collected—his poems, short stories, and news articles have been most successful. His essays and literary studies, on the other hand, are rarely mentioned and have never been reprinted. Nevertheless, there is in them a vivid and an understanding view of Peninsular,[1] American, and European literature, with most lucid meditations and theories concerning the impulse towards new creation, which in his poetry was the gateway to modernity.

ESSAYS: *Works of Manuel Gutiérrez Nájera. Prose* (*Obras de M. G. N. Prosa*), Vol. II, 1903; *Loose Leaves. Various Articles* (*Hojas sueltas. Articulos diversos*) 1912.

[1]Term used with reference to the Iberian peninsula, i.e. Spain (with little thought of Portugal as part of that peninsula).

AESTHETICS OF PROSE

*Open letter to Mr. Ángel Franco**

FIRST OF ALL, Mr. Ángel Franco, please pardon the tardiness of my reply and do not, please, attribute it to discourtesy on my part, for I am not resigned to being in the bad books of one who, even though I do not know him, is already my friend: I was prevented by unavoidable duties and concerns from writing this letter at the proper time. You say, addressing your words to me, what I am copying out below to save myself the trouble of explaining the problem, though I state in advance that the words of praise you shower upon me I attribute only to excessive benevolence:

"You, who are so intelligent and so learned, must be kind-hearted. The greatness of your mind must not humiliate those who come to you respectfully in order to learn. Let the illuminating counsel come down from the heights. In this day when mean or false glory is subjected to the comic spectacle of encountering your wrath, incited to the inspiration of satire, please teach us, poet, what the noble attitude of a man of merit ought to be.

What has your fame to fear, that unforgettable, most beautiful, luminous and chaste vestal virgin? Do you not know that empresses oft descend to enter humble cottages? Do you not know that they return to their palaces with the imperial purple unspotted?

In the midst of this seething mass of mad presumptions and desperate struggles, your example will be most useful.

Permit me to question you, and may your goodness of heart and my admiration and respect for you serve to induce you to teach me something by answering me.

I was reading with delight your most beautiful address read in honour of Altamirano, when a friend of mine who was listening to me interrupted me with the question:

'Is it verse or prose?'

It is that most delicate music of Gutiérrez Nájera, I replied.

But when he asked me another question, I stopped reading and gave the paper to my friend. He, like a lucky diver, brought out this treasure of pearls."

Here you string off a lot of my lines which bear no resemblance to pearls, but *almost all* of which contain rhyme; and then you add:

*Answer to a letter written to Gutiérrez Nájera by José Ferrel, using the pseudonym indicated above. The title is the present editor's.

"Now, poet, I ask you respectfully: Is 'prose in verse,' like prosaic verse, a literary defect in Spanish?

Your answer will be a useful lesson to me, and you, who are so kind, so intelligent, and so learned, will not refuse me. Men like you, sir, are the men who ought to teach. Their glory imposes upon them this noble obligation."

Mr. Ángel Franco, you must surely be very young, and that is why you think me very learned and consider me capable of teaching you, and even succumb to the unpardonable and reprehensible weakness of admiring me. I do not wish to be admired. I want to be liked, and I am very proud because I believe I am achieving it, for you yourself, editor of the *Democrat* (*Demócrata*), a daily whose "obstructionist" mania I oppose and intend to oppose out of conviction, as a striking illustration of this publish in it the unmerited words of praise which I have copied out. I speak, then, to the friend, the stranger who likes me, not to the pupil, because I say to you, not with the modesty which in plain Spanish is called hypocrisy, but from the heart: I completely lack the indispensable qualities with which the educator must be endowed, from the learning acquired at the proper time and methodically organized, to the severity necessary to anyone who has to impart that learning. And as for the matter in question, my ignorance is even greater, since I know nothing at all about rhetoric. I have forgotten, if indeed I ever knew, all I was taught by some literary lawmakers, and by dint of reading French books, for which I have an inborn affection—and I advise you not to carry such a habit to excess and to a frenzied obsession—I have strayed far from the straight path in Spanish.

Having made the foregoing reservations, I now go on to answer your question "amicably."

Is prose in verse a defect? I do not think so, if the subject in its essence is poetic, but prosaic verse certainly is.

When I rapidly wrote—as unfortunately I write everything—the brief address to which you refer, my state of mind was as follows: I did not wish to remember the man, the master Altamirano in flesh and blood, because in remembering that friend I loved so dearly I should not have been capable of writing a single line. I did not feel competent to judge the literary work of such a great Mentor, and that task, in my opinion, was one for Justo Sierra, that man of high thoughts and deep feelings; neither did I have the leisure or peace of mind necessary for making up verses under the discipline of rhyme. I recalled, heaven knows how, the date it was, which corresponded to that on which the ancients celebrated their Feast of the Manes. There came rushing into my mind, as in a torrent, the memory of my talks the previous year with the

Horatian Singer of the Bees, of his fervent devotion to the Greek and Latin poets, and of his tender feeling for Italy. Then, dematerializing him, seeing him just in his spirit, I wrote something which, though prose, unwittingly expressed itself in verse. I did not do it purposely, it was not an artifice; it just came out that way. I heard, like a distant echo, concealed in a dense wood, the *Neniae*, the Orphic singing intoned by the Romans at the Feast of the Manes, similar to that struck up by the Greeks on the same day of the month of Anthesterion to the one who awoke the silent, white shade of Eurydice. Was that singing verse? Was it prose? The ignorance of us all with respect to the pronunciation of the Greek and Latin languages renders it impossible to solve this problem, but in any case it was a hymn cadenced and free, subject to no special rules. I imagine it to be like our blank verse, but much freer than blank verse, and so in that way, though in very bad form, there came out of me spontaneously, following no deliberate plan . . . what you wrongly praise. Verses just dropped into it, because it happened that way . . . and those verses are bad ones, as mine are, but it is not a bad thing to insert verses into prose.

How, then, could you expect anyone not to enjoy seeing a pretty girl with a camellia on her bodice, or a rose in her hair? Prose of good stock is dressed in Andalusian style, as in *The Three-Cornered Hat* (*El sombrero de tres picos*).[2] It is dressed as a nun; it wears the Greek cothurnus or moves about like a frolicsome maid of Paris; sometimes it declaims; at other times it counts; on appropriate occasions it also forms verses; *Spiritus flat ubi vult.*

What concerns us is to pass on to others our own sensation. Anyone who achieves this is truly a writer. Zorrilla,[3] in my opinion, was a great musician, and if he is in heaven, as I hope, he must have gone to the sphere or circle in which Saint Cecilia plays. The point is that he succeeded in making us hear incomparable melodies, and for that we are grateful to him. Others "feel a colour" and reflect it in the souls that are in sympathy with them. Leconte de Lisle feels a line and carves it on the brains of those who know how to read him.

But, you will tell me, these are poets, and I am talking of prose-writers. Well, my answer is that in matters of art there are not poets or prose-writers, only artists and non-artists. Prose has its hidden rhythm. In Quevedo[4] it sounds like laughter; in Fray Luis de Granada,[5]

[2]Written by Alarcón, a Spanish novelist of the nineteenth century.

[3]A Spanish dramatist and poet of the Romantic school in the nineteenth century, famous for his *Don Juan Tenorio*.

[4]Spanish poet and satirist of the seventeenth century.

[5]Spanish mystic of the sixteenth century.

like a sacred hymn; but both of these, without any deliberate purpose on the part of the ascetic or the satirist, have a certain special, perceptible cadence. The Bible is written in what is close to, and very close to, verse. The *Contemptus Mundi*, commonly called Kempis,[6] is a *Miserere*, a *De Profundis*, a sacred hymn. The prose of Castelar, which is the most conspicuous contemporary example of genuinely Spanish prose, is actually nothing but a string of enlarged royal octaves. In that of Renan, verses abound, and in the prophetic prose of Carlyle they are still more abundant.

Mr. Ángel Franco, what I say to you in a friendly way is that you should adjust your prose to the subject you are treating. If the subject is dry and arid, let the prose be so too. If it is designed to instruct, let it be clear. But if enthusiasm comes, ushered in by the rolling of drums; if ideals catch fire; if the sun warms up the bayonets—in such cases let the fulminating iambus surge forth from that prose, and let the martial verse penetrate through its tight ranks, as the call of the bugle comes in to shake up unawakened energies.

Then the "r" rolls, the period sounds out, the bold phrase flashes fire, the pen digs scratches into the paper on which we write, the words roar as they scurry along; and when the goal is reached, on the peak, the banner is hoisted, proud, resplendent, full of life, warmth, and sunshine. It matters little that verse should enter into prose; it is an ally . . . it is the regimental music.

When sadness creeps in slowly, verse arises, for the same reason that at nightfall the stars come out, shining tremulous as tears. Let us not leave this verse outside; it is alone, naked, and begs hospitality. It was going to be an elegy, but its parents would not permit it! It is a good thing for prose to have verses on certain occasions, because it is a good thing to weep, and verse is often a tear which falls on the paper.

Above all, Mr. Ángel Franco, it is a good thing to possess the gift, and I am sorry that I cannot say to you that you have it, because I know nothing about you and because you have been kind enough to praise me. I do believe I have perceived a friendly feeling, and it is that feeling which I sincerely return. Ask for lessons from those who know more, and be my friend.

ca. 1893

Works. Prose (*Obras. Prosa*), printed by the Oficina Impresora del Timbre, Mexico, 1903, Vol. II, pp. 307–11.

[6]After the famous author of the *Imitation of Christ*, Thomas à Kempis (1380–1471).

Francisco A. de Icaza

(b. Mexico, D.F., 1863; d. Madrid, Spain, 1925)

At the age of twenty-three, Francisco A. de Icaza went to Madrid, accompanying General Vicente Riva Palacio, Minister Plenipotentiary designate, and from then until his death, except for his sojourn in Germany and his brief returns to Mexico, he remained in Madrid, on diplomatic missions or on assignments in historical investigation. He was therefore a writer who had intimate relationships with Spanish letters and the intellectual circles of Madrid, a member of the Academies of Language, History, and Fine Arts, and vice-president of the Athenaeum of Madrid. A poet of contained emotion and sober bearing, his principal work is that of critic, and the greater part of his excellent studies, on Cervantes, Lope de Vega, the *Dance of Death* (*Danza de la muerte*), and the Sevillian writers of the sixteenth century who came to Mexico, were to be on Spanish themes. In them he corrected errors, cleared up questions of authorship, and gave new life to men and books of remote periods with both learning and artistic sensibility. His first book of this character, *Study of Critics* (*Examen de críticos*), is a well informed exposition of the different schools and doctrines of criticism, all culminating in an implacable exposure of certain plagiarisms of the then famous writer Emilia Pardo Bazán.

The fact that, in addition to knowing the past of Mexican letters and its Spanish roots, he liked and understood Mexican poetry subsequent to Modernism, is demonstrated by the lecture which he gave in the Athenaeum of Madrid in 1914, under the title of *American Letters* (*Letras americanas*), as an introduction to a reading of the five poets there discussed: Gutiérrez Nájera, Díaz Mirón, Othón, Urbina, and González Martínez. The importance of this essay by Icaza lies precisely in the fact that in him, for the first time, the group of "greater gods" in modern Mexican poetry becomes isolated and detached. In the same year, 1914, was to appear the first edition of *The Hundred Best Mexican Poems* (*Las cien mejores poesías mexicanas*), by Castro Leal, Vázquez del Mercado, and Toussaint, in which the selection is strengthened by adding Amado Nervo to the "greater gods," as they were to be called by Henriquez Ureña in his Prologue (1915) to *Gardens of France* (*Jardines de Francia*), by González Martínez.

In his last days, Francisco A. de Icaza, as the fruit of his study in

Germany, published some volumes of a projected *Critical Anthology of Foreign Poets* (*Antología crítica de poetas extranjeros*), with introductions and studies from his own pen. In them appeared texts from Liliencron, Dehmel, Hebbel, Nietzsche, and Turgenev. His last book, the *Autobiographical Dictionary of Conquerors and Settlers of New Spain* (*Diccionario autobiográfico de conquistadores y pobladores de Nueva España*), 1923, was to be the cause of heated discussion regarding authorship.

CRITICISM AND ESSAYS: *Study of Critics* (*Examen de críticos*), Madrid, 1894; *The "Exemplary Novels" of Cervantes* (*Las "Novelas ejemplares" de Cervantes*), Madrid, 1901; *The German University* (*La Universidad Alemana*), Madrid, 1915; *Concerning How and Why "The False Aunt" Is Not By Cervantes* (*De cómo y por qué "La tía fingida" no es de Cervantes*), Madrid, 1916; *Frauds and Errors in Cervantes* (*Supercherías y errores cervantinos*), Madrid, 1917; *The Quijote Through Three Centuries* (*El Quijote durante tres siglos*), Madrid, 1918; *Real Events Which Seem Imaginary in Gutierre de Cetina, Juan de la Cueva, and Mateo Alemán* (*Sucesos reales que parecen imaginados de Gutierre de Cetina, Juan de la Cueva y Mateo Alemán*), Madrid, 1919; *Lope de Vega, His Loves and Hates* (*Lope de Vega, sus amores y sus odios*), Madrid, 1919; *Of Poets and Poetry* (*De los poetas y de la poesía*), Madrid, 1919; *Autobiographical Dictionary of Conquerors and Settlers in New Spain* (*Diccionario autobiográfico de conquistadores y pobladores de Nueva España*), Madrid, 1923.

MEXICAN LETTERS

Intimate Anthology

PERHAPS YOU THINK with me that contemporary art must be studied in the private galleries. There scarcely exists a museum of modern art worthy of the name; everywhere the work of genius is lost among the mass of mediocre and bad pictures, and there is nothing that so resembles such museums as the anthologies of living poets, different in every way from the classical anthologies and the museums of ancient art.

A bust, a torso, a fragment of any kind of Greek or Roman sculpture, or an anonymous strophe preserved in the memory of the people and contained in the Greek or Latin collections, is worth more in our eyes than all the heterogeneous mass of official modern art. The selection of the relics of the past was made freely; those of which the only merit is their age were left out in the garden of the museum; those which have a relative and historical value were arranged in chronological order in vestibules and corridors; the place of honour in the halls was reserved for the Torso del Belvedere and the Venus de Milo.

Anyone who loves poetry—and by loving it I do not mean lavishing one's affections upon it, but knowing how to discern the superior—ceases to feel that he is carrying in his memory an anthology very similar to a classical museum. There are books of which one remembers only one page, poems of which one retains one strophe, and strophes of which one preserves only the rhythmic beat of one verse: the poetic vein of many generations of artists brought to our souls, in passing, those gold-bearing sands, just as the current leaves them behind in the channels of certain rivers.

From a private collection, from my personal anthology, I tear the leaves which I am about to offer you.

Something on the Mexican Lyric Poetry of the Present Day and Its Immediate Precursors

He was right who said that the best of the Spanish-American muse was the first and the last, and so far as Mexico is concerned, in his plaudits he passed from Alarcón and Sor Juana right on to Manuel Acuña.[1] I would open this critical account of the modern poets of my country with a page from Acuña if introducing or recalling to you the precursors of our current lyric renaissance were not a matter for independent treatment. At the moment I prefer to speak of those whose work is still completely contemporary, though some have prematurely disappeared from our midst. In short, this time the last shall be first: the chronological last, be it understood, among those already crowned with success.

Manuel Gutiérrez Nájera

With brotherly concern, kindly hands collected the entire work of a poet whose death while he was at the height of his creative powers brought a sad loss to our lyric muse. They reconstructed the formation of the artist, from his first efforts as a lover of verses and his imitations as an adolescent versifier right to his success in the domination of form, which was the external manifestation of his personality; and this latter expression of his literary personality was not discovered by Gutiérrez Nájera—for this is the name of our poet—either in his Romantic songs in the style of de Musset, or in his ingenious *pastiches*

[1]That is, from the seventeenth to the nineteenth century. Alarcón (to be distinguished from the nineteenth-century novelist) was a famous dramatist, Sor Juana Inés de la Cruz a famous poetess, and Manuel Acuña (1849–73) a medical student who, on committing suicide, left behind him some excellent poems that were later published by his friends.

of exotic inspiration, but in a kind of diaphanous symbolism, with human roots and a human transcendency, and in the simplicity of his classical verses, steeped in the sensuous sadness of the Latin elegiac poets.

Gutiérrez Nájera, before Samain, Moréas, and Régnier, followed the course of the experience of these writers, at first roaming over the most intricate paths of the new lyric, but as time went on preferring the plain road. In their way, these will be as Classical in the future as those whom in the beginning they appeared to abominate. And this is because the poetry of the *Jardin de l'infante*[2] and of *Les Syrthes*[3] was not vainly artificial, nor was that of *Aux flancs du vase*[2] and *Stances*[3] necessarily impassive. Neither are the symbols of *My Ladies in Mourning* (*Mis enlutadas*) puzzling plays on words, nor is the Classicism of the *Brief Odes* (*Odas breves*) forged in the cold. In both Gutiérrez Nájera is profoundly human; sometimes the work of another gave him the mould for his vessel, but the essence was his own. It is an essence exquisitely erotic, with voluptuosities frankly pagan or with morbid sentimentalities of a seer or of a man unwell. He could have been and he wished to be the poet of joy, but plagued by daily mental toil that was both painful and unrelenting, he was forced to quicken his brain with stimulants which burned him up as they kindled his fire. Clairvoyant in everything, he sensed the approach of death and pleaded with it in tender words—you will hear them presently—to such an extent that death, the implacable, deceived him by mercifully retreating only to return anew.

Life is ungrateful; it loves those who hate it. It does not wish to leave the sad even when they try to wrest themselves from its arms by force. It flees from its ardent lovers . . . and abandoned the poet at the height of his powers and fame.

Salvador Díaz Mirón

The lyric poetry of Gutiérrez Nájera requires a selection; the posthumous book in which it was collected is a volume of rough drafts with a few pages put into final form. It is all very well not to scorn anything, but the definitive pages could so appropriately and so easily be gathered together in a special edition.

On the other hand it is now not only difficult, but impossible, to select the best of the first writings of a poet perhaps more famous with the Latin American public than Gutiérrez Nájera (I am referring to

[2]By Samain.
[3]By Moréas.

Salvador Díaz Mirón), since the unevenness found in that first manner of his is inherent in his artistic methods.

Gutiérrez Nájera said:

> I do not write my verses, nor do I create them;
> They live within me; they come from without;
> One, flighty, was formed by desire;
> Another, full of light, by the springtime.

Díaz Mirón wrote in a somewhat affected manner, but with commendable sincerity: "At times I find myself accompanied for entire weeks by an aeriform archetype which refuses to be subjected to the sonorous atoms of the sung word, and which day and night holds my attention, until it becomes condensed and crystallizes."

This explains their chief differences. The rough drafts of the lyric poems of Gutiérrez Nájera are of small worth, but those of Díaz Mirón are not. The two poets achieved beauty in different ways. While Gutiérrez Nájera, in his plenitude, fused flawless bronze or carved smooth marble, Díaz Mirón was making mosaics, Byzantine jewels, and windows of coloured glass. The general tracing is perfect; but at close range one sees the workmanship, the junctures of the stones, the soldering and the leaden framework of the panes, even though in them the light may be broken or condensed into coloured figures.

For this reason Díaz Mirón, who later severely disciplined his technique—you will soon come to know something of his new and purified manner—makes an unjust and too drastic repudiation of those first splendid verses, though at heart I suspect that he will retain for them a father's love. It is a significant accomplishment that entire poems are condensed into one rhythmic phrase, that they show his earlier personality and brought after them a host of imitators, for even in Spain there were those who traced facsimiles of his strophes.

In the verses *To Gloria* (*A Gloria*) we have all of the first Díaz Mirón: his Romantic spirit in the style of Byron, his brilliant Hugoesque images, and his invertebrate poetic form in which each part subsists for its own sake in such a way that the composition can either be prolonged indefinitely or shortened by cutting out strophes.

That technique of Díaz Mirón's, which on the whole mars this part of his work, favours isolated phrases and allows him to compose marvellous independent verses to such an extent that it is almost impossible to quote separately any that are more beautiful and in which the feeling of the author appears more complete.

The literary figure of Díaz Mirón is also portrayed completely in his verses *To Hugo* (*A Hugo*). Díaz Mirón regards Hugo as something that is his own. He considers him his master and sings to him in verses which in their contexture flow with a continuity that is unusual in his works.

He does not admire the pious poet of the *Contemplations* (*Contemplaciones*), but the wrathful poet of *The Punishments* (*Les châtiments*). He does not perceive the tenderness with which the patriarch of French Romanticism subdues even the hostile. He does not foresee that he himself will later exclaim in a sentence which is a poem:

> . . . . There is a reason why
> the lyre has curves and nerves like a woman.

If everything is different in the condition governing the poetic expression of the two poets, everything in the essence of their inspiration is likewise in contrast.

> The voluptuous muse
> that inspires my erotic songs,
> cowed and tremulous, rejects
> the Pindaric lyre,

says Gutiérrez Nájera; Díaz Mirón, on the contrary, loves struggle, and finds nothing more worthy of his inspiration. If the one speaks of his pleasure and his pain, the other wants to sing

> Not his pain, but the pain of humanity.

And yet, by one of the frequent paradoxes of life, Nájera's most beautiful verses are intended for others and on behalf of others, while the best verses of Díaz Mirón are those in which he sings to himself.

Manuel José Othón

Manuel José Othón—lost to our world of letters at the height of his fame like Gutiérrez Nájera—won the applause of the moderns and the sympathy of the upholders of classical tradition. This is a strange fact, but explicable in this instance. Othón came to find what might be called a way of his own, within the rigid orthodoxy of the language. This accounts for his relations with the Hispano-American purists, perhaps more exacting with regard to the purity of the language than the Spanish purists themselves. But since for him being "a man for whom the outer world exists" was a reality and not a literary commonplace, he copied nature as he saw it, without recourse to conventional models, and the revolutionaries in matters of art, those who rebelled against routine, declared him an innovator. He practised art in silence, in the fields and in the mountains. A man extraordinary in all respects, on one of his hunting expeditions, in which he simultaneously indulged his leisure as a rural judge and directly collected sensations for his *Rustic Poems* (*Poemas rústicos*), he discovered a mine, not of ideas as was usual with him, but of silver. He was thereafter able to go down to the cities more frequently, and there to spend prodigally, with the health he had acquired in the forests and the mountains, the metal extracted from the rocks, never abandoning what in a certain unpublished autobiography he called his "mountain life" without bringing the jewel carved in his retreat and the song learned from some wild bird, imitated on a primitive flute or arranged with learned Beethovenian polyphony. Othón is a poet of conscious impressions, whose temperament no one could know by reading only one isolated composition. He is completely unlike Bello[4] or his forerunners. He does not portray from memory and in his study, but in the open air and from nature. A landscape artist with broad and varied palette, he can copy anything, but he has more feeling for the steep rocks and the old twisted trees than for the landscapes obscured by crepuscular half-tints. He describes marvellously, yet his true merit does not consist in describing, but in understanding nature and making it loved and felt.

Luis G. Urbina

Justo Sierra, in his prologue to Urbina's first book of poems, said that Urbina's inspiration, caressing to the ear, was suited to transmitting intimate and gentle emotions; today, that inspiration of adolescence has become strengthened and broadened, without losing any of its initial qualities. His rhythmic phrase has none of the martial bugle-sound of the verses of Díaz Mirón, or the lofty symphonic solemnity which Othón puts into his pastorals, but carries within itself all the musical suggestiveness of the poetry of Gutiérrez Nájera. In faint or supplicating melodies, sweet or dolorously melancholy, Urbina unfolds, in a series of confidential half-tones, the initial theme of his song. His poetry, predominantly melodic, links the idea to the music and knows how to discover in it the expression of the ineffable. Gently it calls forth emotions and sensations; one would say that his inspiration controls even his own sufferings: "Music tames wild beasts." This does not mean that he is not at times also pictorial, and he tends towards this in his last book, where the verse becomes colour in order to hold on to fleeting realities: the more immaterial elements of the landscape, shape

[4]Venezuela-born Chilean scholar and poet (1781–1865).

of clouds, colour of lakes and skies, sunsets with the whole gamut of crepuscular golds.

When barely more than a child, Urbina appeared as a poet who already knew all the secrets of his art. The first compositions can figure alongside the last without anyone seeing in them the vacillations and gropings of the beginner. Hardly can a shrewd examination detect in the earlier ones any foreboding of pain or pleasure, or in the later ones reveal any painful experience, since Urbina, like all those who became men early, preserves in maturity a good deal of childlike tenderness.

Enrique González Martínez

The artistic perfecting of González Martínez is on the contrary discernible, and from the first to the last of his books it moves on a steeply ascending scale. The flexible, vibrant strophe, which by exception appears in *Preludes* (*Preludios*) in the ranks of rigid hendecasyllabics and alexandrines, becomes more and more frequent in *Lyrics* (*Lirismos*), the final compositions of which already have the fluidity and intimate resonance of *Hidden Paths* (*Senderos ocultos*).

González Martínez formed his own verse by way of a perfect Castilian interpretation of the most incompatible foreign poets. With great rhythmic and mental dexterity he passes from the neat and ordered sentimentalism of Lamartine to the pathological hallucinations and spasms of Poe; he reflects Verlaine's *clair de lune* and the gloomy thought set in the polished verse of Baudelaire, the objective plasticity of Heredia's hendecasyllabic, the primitive charm, in form and thought, of Francis Jammes, the vivid classicism of Samain. He thus succeeds in achieving that technique which today characterizes his completely original poetry, since he infused blood and life into the poetry of others without making demands upon any. Master of the mechanism of expression, his verse is so united to the feeling that prompts it that it appears to be produced without any need of external means.

There is a pantheism which, in making the world divine, worships the world and oneself within it. This was in a certain measure the pantheism of the demigod Goethe. There is another type which makes nature divine, and loves it devoutly even in the lowly. This is the pantheism which González Martínez carries through *Hidden Paths*, when "he seeks in all things a soul and a sense." . . .

If Urbina sings of the temporary nature of joy with a kind of resigned pessimism, González Martínez, a melancholy optimist, senses the temporary nature of pain, which in normal life is just as impermanent as pleasure, and of both he sings, when they have passed, with a vague melancholy tenderness, since for the poet pain is no frightening guest, but a wayfarer who rests in one's home, and who tomorrow at daybreak, shaking the dust from his sandal, will start off again.

I began my prologue speech by comparing my intimate anthology to a museum of old art. You are now on the threshold, and I withdraw, for I am not going to be like those keepers who plague visitors to art galleries with comments upon the beauties they contain, which all like to appreciate unaided.

Review of Books (*Revista de libros*), Madrid, January, 1914.

Luis G. Urbina

(b. Mexico, D.F., 1868; d. Madrid, Spain, 1934)

Of humble family, Luis Urbina received little formal education. At a very early age he began to publish poems and articles, and years later he became a writer of editorials, a news commentator, and a reviewer of the theatre for *The Impartial* (*El Imparcial*) and *The Illustrated World* (*El Mundo Ilustrado*). He was private secretary to Justo Sierra (then Minister of Education), a professor of Spanish literature, and director of the National Library. In the Revolutionary period (1915) he went to Havana and proceeded from there to Madrid and then to Buenos Aires, as a journalist and lecturer. He returned to Madrid as secretary to the Legation and later as representative of the "Del Paso and Troncoso" Commission. In 1921 he was in Mexico, but he returned to Madrid, where he lived until his death.

He has been called the last Romantic, and he is also one of the most representative of our lyric poets. A poet of autumn and melancholy, of twilights and intimate voices, he described the landscapes of the world and of his soul with an art more and more profound and a gift of tears increasingly steeped in learning. As a news commentator and a writer of tales, like Gutiérrez Nájera, Urbina followed in the footsteps of his predecessor with a facile, spirited prose which preserves the outstanding characteristics and the temper of the first quarter of our century.

In his maturity Urbina undertook critical studies, one on literature in the period of the struggle for independence (prologue to the *Anthology of the Centennial* [*Antología del Centenario*]), and another on the literary life of Mexico. The former, which is one of the best panoramic views in our literary historiography, is more carefully composed and more complete, but does not by virtue of that fact obscure the lectures which make up the latter, a kind of sentimental history of our letters, full of shrewd insights and excellent prints.

STUDIES: *Mexican Literature during the War of Independence* (*La literatura mexicana durante la guerra de Independencia*), Madrid, 1917; *Literary Life in Mexico* (*La vida literaria de México*), Madrid, 1917.

ORIGIN AND CHARACTER OF MEXICAN LITERATURE

THE HISTORY OF MEXICAN LITERATURE, like that of many other countries of America, has not yet been deeply and definitively studied from the point of view, very interesting to us, of its being an expression of our national life.

Therefore, when on special occasions in my career as a professor in my country, I found it necessary to reflect upon this question of our literature, for the purpose of orienting and organizing my views, I made the following reflections, according to which I have patterned my investigations in this matter.

Of course, I was assailed by that worn-out idea, incessantly repeated: Mexican literature, and in general all Spanish-American literatures, are nothing but a reflection of Peninsular literature, a family of that ancient and most noble matron from whose bosom these weak literatures of the new continent, incapable of nourishing themselves independently, draw their nutriment. Late in their development, imprecise in their features, such literatures imitate, through their inability to create, the externals of the evolution of letters in Spain, and they are something like the projection of a shadow from a body, or like the echo which reproduces a voice.

Undoubtedly, in this old concept there is an incontrovertible truth: in Spanish America we are tied forever, in our march towards civilization, by the unbreakable bond of language. All our thoughts about imaginative beauty, all our lucubrations in speculative philosophy, all we experience in sensation or sentiment—in short, all we have to communicate or to bring forth through the natural effort of our minds—we shall express in the mother tongue, in the language which definitively gives us our character in the literary world and unites us to the other peoples who, in the tree of the living word, form one of the branches of the Romance languages, perhaps the most vigorous, the most full of vitality, though not as expressive, flexible, and ample as Italian, nor as patiently and learnedly wrought as French. And because we are in this position, because we are perpetually bound to one of the Romance languages, we have a right to believe and feel that we are a diffusion, more or less remote, but with virginal auguries, of the Latin soul.

The Spanish language is the only form which has given us and will ever give us a literary personality in the world of ideas.

This is how, by virtue of the persistent use of the word, the turn of phrase, the idiom, the analogical formation, the syntactical bond, the pet phrase and the apothegm, we approach, in never ending relationships, the spirit of our progenitors, while at the same time we draw near to the spirit of our brothers of America. And in this way we not only speak the same language, but we normally coincide in ideas and sentiments and present an example of collective mentalities, in the cultural groups of our countries, which on being compared, show a resemblance which approaches identity.

The psychological paradox that thought is an inner language is evidently founded upon a true observation. To speak the same language habitually from childhood implies a series of mental operations which oblige us, so to speak, to focus our thoughts in a special and peculiar manner. To speak in Spanish is, in a way, to think and feel in the Spanish fashion. A psychic mystery permeates and crystallizes, in an indivisible unity, form and essence, voice and thought, matter and energy.

Accordingly, it is an absolute certainty that in the succession of vital phenomena, in the biological, ethnical, and social transformation of the nations conquered by the Spanish genius, the language is one of the most powerful distinguishing elements, one of the most profound marks which the domination left in its trail. And that language, learned and disseminated with necessary persistence by missionaries and soldiers, the learned and the ignorant, the good and the wicked, for three hundred years—that language which, trying to invade all the districts having autochthonous languages, seeks in my country the realization of the great ideal of drawing heterogeneous expressions through a single and vast philological channel—that language takes control of us and makes us do homage to a monumental literature: the Spanish.

It is true, I said to myself: Mexican literature derives its merit from imitation, as a reflection of Spanish letters. And I began to recall the principal points of our literary existence, from the first attempts by those friars—some of whom were select examples of human goodness—like the seraphic Gante, Motolinía, Sahagún, Durán, passing over the Latinizing poets and the erotics and the writers of sacred verse of the sixteenth century who came from the Peninsula to that part of America that today is called Mexico and brought in their ears and hearts echoes of the eclogues of Garcilaso, the odes of Herrera, and the unctuous *liras* of Fray Luis,[1] until I came to the glorious appearance in Madrid

[1]Spanish poets of the sixteenth century.

of don Juan Ruiz de Alarcón, and the amazing prodigy Sor Juana Inés de la Cruz,[2] the divine flower, flower of the heart, *Yoloxóchitl*, the exquisite perfume of which, enveloped in *culto*[3] subtleties, still transcends paradisical verses. And I recalled likewise the luxurious rooting which spread to this land, along with the prolific seed, of the extravagance of the seventeenth century; I recalled the Colonial epic and lyric, and saw how we followed the contours and sinuosities of the rhetorical figures, of the literary patterns, on the tracing paper of imitation. And I ratified my conclusion: our literature is transplanted, it is genuinely and purely Spanish. In our country, whether we like it or not, it bears fruit less juicy and fragrant and with a less delicate flavour than the fruit which customarily comes to us from our verbal homeland.

Nevertheless, with the idea of transplantation I associated, necessarily, that of modification, that of circumstantial alteration, transformation, a variation of the primordial type, in short, that of the incessant work of nature which decomposes organisms into different families according to the influences of the medium in which they develop, without making them lose the fundamental characteristics of the species.

And then I extended my field of observation and directed my gaze to different horizons. It is known that the mingling of two races, the aboriginal and the conquering, which has constituted the Mexican type, the *mestizo* (let us call him by the name that is suggestive), has produced physiological alterations that scholars are studying today in the seclusion of their studies. Anthropological measurements, anatomical calculations and comparisons, minute investigations, show that the corporeal structure of the Mexican differs both from the Spanish type and from the primitive American type. Physiologically we are neither one nor the other; we are something different, we are ourselves, we are an ethnic type that is differentiated and nevertheless has a share in both parent races. And both struggle to coexist and survive in our persons.

"Well then," I asked myself, "why should what happens in the physiological world not also happen in the psychological world?" Most certainly it does. That same mingling, that same struggle, that same coexistence, take place in matters of the spirit and have finally pro-

[2]Sor Juana Inés de la Cruz and Ruiz de Alarcón are the earliest Mexican writers to achieve international fame.

[3]A very ornate and artificial style, of which the Spanish poet Luis de Góngora (1561–1627) is the chief exponent.

duced, or will produce, a psychic type well defined and differentiated, one parallel to the new physiological type of the Mexican.

Then I looked around me. And carefully I made a quick analysis of the national atmosphere. Drawing my thoughts from literature, I directed them towards other ideas correlative to the one which was the object of my investigations; I thought of architecture and music. And I thought of these because even though they are individual expressions, they interpret personal feelings less than they do feelings that are collective or social. Nothing better portrays a people, if you consider it carefully, than its buildings and its songs. Music, says a modern aesthete, is an architecture of sounds; architecture, a music of lines. They are intended for multitudes, and often they are anonymous, and frequently the result of obscure collaborations. In them resides, as in none of the other fine arts, the soul of a people.

And calling to mind our old colonial houses, our old churches, our old fountains, I saw that they bore a special stamp, a characteristic look, distinctive traits, elements all their own, which lend variety to the whole and give it a tonality which, to put it bluntly, is no longer Spanish, but Mexican. The materials of construction, the glazed tile, and the *tezontle* (building stone), in combination or isolated, contribute to the peculiar character of the buildings. And immediately the detail, the capricious alterations in the styles, the carving along which runs some fret belonging to the times before Cortez; Churriguerra's abundant flowers and leaves in stone, retouched here and there by a more eager desire for excessive ornamentation; an occasional decorative motif that vaguely recalls the reliefs of the *teocalli* (great structures of the Aztecs)—all this contributes to the peculiar character of the architecture of the devout and dazzling times during which the national spirit was being formed, that spirit which, spreading and multiplying itself, is to bring a uniformity to my country, which would be in danger of perishing if in the end this great purpose were not fulfilled.

And what about music? When in my country we hear a languid, sensuous, tearful song, a dance which sweetens voluptuosity with a sickly tenderness, a simple and impassioned melody, one which prolongs in moaning tones its trivial and piercing laments, we immediately say: that is Mexican music. The strumming of the Andalusian guitar does not accompany pleasant songs of oriental idleness, or sighs of gypsy love in our country; there it is transformed into the ardent dance of the coast country, into the sad erotic song of the *Bajío* (sand bank), into the fresh and gay *mañanitas* (songs of dawn), into the playful and roguish *jarabe* (love song), in the manner of the gallantry of the ranch. This is another revelation which distinguishes us, and which releases us from our hereditary ties with Spain. The musical folklore is complete. Truly there sings within it the sensibility of the people.

"And if architecture and music reveal a clear differentiation," I asked myself again, "why does poetry not abandon the maternal bosom? Why does it continue in its original servitude as an imitator of the Peninsular muse? Why should that which takes place in the plastic and the eurhythmic not also take place in the lyric, and in literature in general?"

Indeed, if one examines our literary phenomena with curiosity, one sees that the same differentiation has actually taken place, confined, naturally, within the form imposed by the language.—The wine does not alter the contours of the glass.

And as though led to me by the hand, there come to my mind the phonetic alterations which we have made in the language. Do we fail to pronounce as we were taught, or were we badly taught to pronounce? When the pertinent investigations are made, we find that the first answer is the right one; we do not pronounce as we were taught. That is to say, the autochthonous groups which received the first instruction in the language, when they did not succeed in pronouncing it well, extended and propagated the phonetic alterations. This fact is extremely interesting. All the American peoples resisted the Castilian pronunciation of the *c*, the *ll*, and the *z*.[4] And they rejected such pronunciations to such an extent that after a number of centuries not even pedagogy, bent on restoring them, has been able to achieve it.

In this connection the new-fangled linguistic theories tell us that it is not true that the modifications in pronunciation are due to caprice or to any individual defect, but that the unconsciousness of the phenomena is sufficient proof that a mysterious force, of which the speakers have no knowledge, directs these developments. The phonetic changes taking place in the same period, independently and unconsciously, among millions of individuals, are according to these theories not a mere matter of chance; the cause of such phenomena is of a physiological nature (the Germans call it the displacement of the muscular senses), and consists in the continual adaptation of the vocal articulations to the organic faculties.

But we have not only changed the pronunciation of the language,

[4]The sound of *th* in English *thin* is referred to for the *c* and *z*. In Spanish America it becomes like *s* in English *sit*. The *ll* is pronounced somewhat like *lli* in English *million* in Spain, but in Spanish America it becomes like *y* in English *yes*.

we have also changed the way of intoning it. The elocution, emphatic and harsh in the mouths of Spaniards, is soft, sweetish, and contracted, so to speak, in ours. The Castilian tongue, altered phonetically in the different regions of Spain, suffers fresh alterations, of like kind, among us—Mexican alterations.

The customs and practices of ordinary life have moved us likewise to modify the vocabulary, introducing into it, usually Castilianized, names of utensils, places, articles, fruits, furniture, and thus enriching the lexicon with words that are added to the common language, and to which the Dictionary of the Academy is gradually opening up its tightly closed columns.

The phonetics altered, the vocabulary enriched, and the poetry a slave? That can not be, and in fact, it is not true.

The sixteenth century, with its movement of Iberian culture back and forth, with its flux and reflux of ambition and piety, sends to New Spain poets who arrive with their cargo of dreams and their baggage of illusions, like Gutierre de Cetina, the contriver of that unforgettable jewel, the madrigal to a pair of bright eyes; like Eugenio de Salazar, the author of the epistle to don Hernando de Herrera; or like Bernardo de Balbuena, concerning whose poetry, in which the atmosphere exercises its influence, Quintana says that it resembles "the immense country that received him, at once fertile and uncultivated, and in which thorns are found confused with flowers and treasures with dearth." In the seventeenth and eighteenth centuries this influence gradually gets under way, and in the beginning of the nineteenth Fray Manuel de Navarrete, neo-Classicist, bursts forth into Anacreontic verses already sweetened by the fruit of our gardens. And there comes to us the doleful and sceptical Romanticism of Espronceda, and the musical and legendary Romanticism of Zorrilla, also the subtle verse and easy rhyme of Campoamor, the tearful Germanic strain of Bécquer, and the theatrical sonority of Núñez de Arce; and at each step, at each novel incident, we keep on showing a differentiation which we possess more and more, not boldly divergent from the original, but yet ever more profound and confident. This derives from the fact that the control of our literary individuality is becoming stronger, that we are seeking and finding our characteristic expression, that for four hundred years we have been elaborating the forms adaptable to our collective and personal spirit, and finally, that in the language which we appropriated, as was necessary and natural, we follow at the same time the physiological and psychological alterations in our nature.

And the temperament, which is the result of these alterations, impresses itself upon the speech and the plasma in its fashion, in accordance with its needs. The Spanish soul has left a great deal within us, but beneath this heritage there palpitates, with a dominating force, the indigenous sediment. To the gaiety of Sancho, and the delirium of Quijote, are united within our hearts the sadness of the Indian, the untamed force of time elapsed, the inherited distrust of the subjugated, the unorganized gentleness of the aboriginal native. And if we are Mexican in our way of living, we are Mexican also in our speech, our dreams, and our songs.

So these are the elements, the materials, with which we compose our work of art. And it must be noted that if there is anything that is our principal distinguishing mark in our departure from the literature of the motherland, it is that indigenous element which we, unwittingly and involuntarily, have put into our verse, our prose, our voice, our home, and our music—namely, melancholy.

Looking upon the fields of the central tableland, of a grey gilded and dotted with the green prickly clusters of the agave, and upon the compressed disks of apparent volcanic rock formed by the cactus shrubs, and looking over our broad plains inflamed by the setting sun, and up at our mountains with their pale violet fading away on the horizon, we feel that in our breasts there stir obscure nostalgias and vague feelings of uneasiness, and then we feel ourselves impregnated with the hieratic melancholy of our ancestors the Colhuas. A sentimental resurrection takes possession of our character as Neo-Spaniards. And for that reason we are continually inclined to turn our emotions towards melancholy. A touch of melancholy is cast or imposed on everything, and not only in the lyric notes, but even in our epic outbursts, even in our pleasant wit or our momentary humour, we usually put a grain of this melancholy. We perfume merriment and suffering with a drop of copal from the Toltec perfumery.

The Literary Life of Mexico (*La vida literaria de México*), Madrid, 1917, pp. 13–16. 2nd ed. of Antonio Castro Leal (Mexico, 1946) in the Collection of Mexican Writers (Colección de Escritores Mexicanos), Vol. XXVII.

Amado Nervo

(b. Tepic, Nayarit, 1870; d. Montevideo, Uruguay, 1919)

At the age of nine Amado Nervo went to Jacona, and later to the Seminary at Zamora, Michoacán, where he received his secondary school education. He began a law course, but being obliged to look after his family, he turned to journalism in Mazatlán and in 1894 came to Mexico City, where he quickly became famous. Here he wrote, in accordance with the taste of the period, news articles, stories, and poems in the newspapers and magazines of the day. He was one of the promoters of the *Modern Review* (*Revista Moderna*) and of the Modernist movement. In 1900 *The World* (*El Mundo*) sent him as a correspondent to Paris, where he met Verlaine, Moréas, Wilde, and the Spanish-Americans who were residing there or happened to be there, among them Rubén Darío. Back in Mexico, he resumed his former duties as a journalist and became a teacher of Spanish in the National Preparatory School. In 1905, as Assistant Secretary, he went to our Legation in Madrid, where he resided until 1914. As Minister Plenipotentiary he visited Argentina and Uruguay, his last journey.

In the abundant lyrical works of Amado Nervo the sentimental tendencies of our poetry were intensified. Religious by upbringing and tradition, erotic and sensitive by temperament when he began his work, he later sought a simplicity and a reserve which, expressed with an unctuous spirituality and a contagious lyricism, won for him a host of proselytes. Keen-witted, sensitive, colloquial, pensive, given to reverie, Nervo's work had and still has the virtue of expressing the meaning of adolescence.

Of his articles and essays Francisco Gonzaléz Guerrero says that "the ideas and the style become more and more refined as they are transformed into short essays, but they preserve many of the characteristics of his prose of the earlier years, composed to communicate with a large number of readers, such as sprightliness, transparency, fluency, brevity, and the emotion that reflects everyday reality."

ESSAYS AND ARTICLES: *Exodus and the Flowers on the Way* (*El éxodo y las flores del camino*), 1902; *Jane of Asbaje* (*Juana de Asbaje*), Madrid, 1910; *They* (*Ellos*), Paris, 1912; *My Philosophies* (*Mis filosofías*), Paris, 1912; *The Modern Woman and Her Role in the Present-day Evolution of the World* (*La mujer moderna y su papel en la evolución actual del mundo*), Buenos Aires, 1919; *Essays* (*Ensayos*), Madrid, 1920; *Will o' the Wisps and Sweet Pepper* (*Fuegos fatuos y Pimientos dulces*), 1951; *Complete Works* (*Obras completas*), Madrid, 1951, 1956 (2 vols.).

LET'S SPEAK OF WRITERS AND LITERATURE

I RECALL that on a certain occasion a man with whom I had kept up a lively correspondence concerning an infinite number of philosophical and literary topics, and for whose distinguished and powerful intellect I had the most profound esteem, invited me to dinner. We knew each other only through our writings; over the rough pathways of this life we had never once met. But our souls were acquainted.

This was sufficient. I admired him too much to wish to be in his company.

I thought of all the disillusionments that lurk behind an admiration, that lie in wait for us right next to the most beautiful element in our enthusiasm, that remind us with cruel frequency that "behind the cross is the devil," that man is a thing of brightness clad in a garb of wretchedness . . . and I did not accept my friend's invitation.

Later I was offered the opportunity to enjoy the company of a great poet, who at that time often went to a house where I called frequently, and I saw to it that we never came there at the same time.

"I admired him too much to wish to be in his company."

Not long afterwards, a woman who claimed to be young and beautiful began to write me delightful letters which culminated in an appointment. I answered the letters but did not keep the appointment.

I was afraid of breaking my toy.

What instinctive modesty guided me then, what an exalted and beautiful modesty, and why did it not go with me to Paris! Why was my mind more influenced by the vain curiosity that prompted me to approach some of those I had long worshipped in my heart than moved by the fear of tarnishing this worship permanently!

At all events, the punishment was cruel, because from this excursion to the country of letters I returned with far fewer objects of affection and many more of scorn, lamenting the impairment of that candid capacity to admire which gives peace to our souls and, as it were, enlarges them.

Some swollen with vanity, in Buddhistic contemplation of their navels, their ears open to any murmur of adulation, officiating in a priesthood in which they do not believe; others, beneath their feigned respect for the masters, eager for a following which they would like to be as extensive as that accorded to those masters, trafficking in ideals, confusing art with *métier* and literature with beauty, and turning themselves into professional specialists in the latter, stooping to any means for the acquisition of a profitable notoriety. The alien poet adulating the Parisian and beseeching him for a mention in a periodical, for his support with a word, or a flattering statement, or at least begging to have it recorded that he was present in his company so that later he would be able to say to the credulous folk of his little homeland, with more appearance of veracity: "Régnier said to me. . . . Moréas pointed out to me. . . . One day when I was with Rémy de Gourmont. . . . ," in this way openly confessing his own worthlessness and his urgent need of a consecration (that wretched business of a consecration) which in that vast Parisian sea can be won by no other means, the *cher maître* displaying himself replete with arrogance, wherever he can, and saying to everyone by attitude and expression: "Here I am; look at me and worship me." The beginner cultivates originality in dress, in *art nouveau* rings, in studied imitable habits, while he either finds or does not find it along the pathway of talent. At each step he tries to *épater le bourgeois*, allowing the little virility he has left to be shattered against forced aesthetic phrases and exotic effeminacies. . . . And all, all of them, hate one another, envy one another, prick one another with epigrams, cast forth sarcasms, seek an audience, and set themselves up as leaders of ridiculous coteries, piteous *poseurs*, false and cheaply gaudy. . . . All of them are incapable of feeling and loving the ideal, of which literature is the mortal enemy. Some deceive the masses with fictitious causes; some pose as martyrs, others as politicians; but all of them are incapacitated for faith, enthusiasm, or love. . . .

Sad indeed was that journey to the literary country, sad but brief! I came back from it stripped of illusions and full of disgust; but I came back in time, forever cured of my vanity, and finding quite ridiculous and pitiable the vanity of my Mexican fellow-writers who within the narrow limits of this beloved geographical accident called Mexico, fight, theorize, instruct, found parties, and carry on their faces a cheerful self-satisfaction with their regional renown and the expression of an Atlas supporting the world. Yes, I came back from that journey cured forever. . . . Later, how pleasant my solitude was! I was alone and lost in the enormous, radiant Paris. I was alone in the arms of that monster that would never spell my name. I was nothing, capable of nothing, if my being and my capacity depend upon such wretched "consecrations." But . . . I again found my self, I again felt the pure integrity of my artistic personality.

I was never to see my name on the yellow mask of one of those books that are piled up in show windows; my efforts and my life would pass by unknown to those folk. The "consecrating" Paris would never consecrate me, nor would I do anything to have myself consecrated. . . . But how happy I was, happy with the admirations I still had left and I clutched them to my heart for fear they would get away; happy with my verses and my readings, happy in my museums, happy in the harmony around me, in the unique city; happy roaming pensively along Avenue Henry Martin, through the park at the hour when it is deserted, or watching the sun sink like a golden buckler behind the glorious rectangle of the *Arc de Triomphe*!

I was happy with my own people: with Darío, with Díaz Rodríguez . . . whose silhouettes, along with others, will be seen by anyone who reads upon the white screen of the following pages:

Darío[1]

The man so named, a precious gem, is tall, sturdy, unexpressive—small, dark, and keen eyes—a broad nose, with nostrils sensuously open—slightly curled beard and hair—"hands of a marquis." He has a grave and awkward bearing, and is slow and somewhat stammering in his speech, but he is always elegant and refined.

He is proud—"I have pride and you have vanity," he said on one occasion to Gómez Carrillo.[2]

He is a sybarite and a gourmet of good stock. During the nine months we lived together he used to treat us—alas, the times were not always easy!—to rich golden pheasants ("The golden pheasant told his secrets"), modernistic galantines, ultra-subtle truffles, etc. In the evening there would be a "Prince of Wales" cocktail in the Continental Tavern, the one beloved by Huysmans.

For him life, full of unhappy incidents, has not diminished his inner goodness. He is kind-hearted. He is a child—a child selfish or affectionate, capricious or serene—jealous of his affections, susceptible as a violet, and on account of that very susceptibility he is capable of understanding and feeling all the shadings of a word, a gesture, or an attitude: a big nervous child.

[1]The Nicaragua-born father of Spanish "Modernism" in literature.
[2]Spanish novelist and journalist, born in Guatemala.

I owe to him this most beautiful and remarkable sonnet, written in five minutes one night in Paris, one of those nights when a premature blue summer dawn—in Paris the dawns are blue, are they not, Manuel Mercado?—lends a pensive tinge to the mad gold of the champagne. I copy it without vanity and more than anything else for fear that it will be lost:

Amado is the word uttered in love,
Nervo[3] is the vibration of the nerves of evil.
Blessed and pure be the song of the poet,
who thoughtlessly cast his crystal phrase.

Friar of sighs, celestial anchorite
who holdest in whiteness the sugar and salt,
show me the pure lily thou followest in thy course;
let me hear the echo of thy astral soul.

Generous and subtle as a butterfly,
find in me the honey of my gifts
and enjoy in me the sweet fragrance of the rose.
Seek not in my gestures the spirit 'neath my face;
I desire what grows tranquil, seek what rests
and hold like a jewel the pearl of Peace.

On a certain occasion when, apropos of my *Sister Water* (*Hermana Agua*) we were discussing things gentle and crystalline, the great poet said to me: "As for me, I should like to be a great piece of topaz, really big, and have the light of the Sun strike me on all sides, pass through me on all sides, and shine on all my facets. I want to be nothing else but a piece of topaz. . . ."

De Groux

No, I did not believe in ghosts until I met De Groux—Henry De Groux—tormented Dantesque Belgian painter.

From what witches' Sabbath did he come, from what night of Walpurgis, from what page of Edgar Poe, of Hoffmann, of Villiers de L'Isle Adam or of Jules Bois came forth this gentleman of darkness?

Rachitic and wasted, pale, with a face bearing a rare likeness to that of Louis XI, framed in straight greyish manelike hair, with a frock-coat of the time of Lamartine and a pair of everlasting checked trousers—thus did he pass through the nightmare of life.

One day he came to our house to see Darío. Darío was ill and I received him. We spoke, naturally, of Dante, Baudelaire, and Poe.

[3]A play on the name of the writer: *Amado*, loved; *Nervo*, nerve.

That was his beloved trinity. After that he kept coming for a long time. I, apropos of one of his endless misfortunes, wrote to him somewhat as follows:

> My dear De Groux: Léon Blois says in the *Ungrateful Beggar* (*Mendigo ingrato*) that you carry misfortune with you wherever you go. If you go into a house, a thunderbolt falls, somebody in the family dies, or the ceilings tumble. Since I have nothing to lose, I fear nothing. Come and see me. We'll share the bread and salt.

That was *foudroyant* for our artist; he answered me with a thousand protestations of affection, and from that time he almost lived with us in our cottage in the Faubourg Montmartre.

At night I used to be awakened by the feline sound of footsteps. It would be De Groux, wrapped in his red *manteau*, with a hood (which had been forgotten and left behind in the house by a lady friend of Gómez Carrillo). Not being able to sleep, De Groux would be intending to wake me and read me "his memoirs," which done, he would flee again into the darkness, his *bienheureuses ténèbres*, as he called it in his cabalistic diary.

How many unforgettable hours, "between approaching night and departing afternoon," I spent in his studio contemplating the enormous and marvellous canvases of his *Divine Comedy* (*Divina comedia*), his tragic portraits of which the mournful eyes followed me everywhere, his marvellous fragment of the *Christ Mocked* (*Cristo de los Ultrajes*), his Napoleon in Russia, beset by a snow less livid than his face, his Zola insulted by the crowd. . . .

And one day that illogical personage disappeared, impelled by some sort of tragedy, and hid himself in some bit of shadow. . . . I never saw him again.

Díaz Rodríguez

How many hours of quiet vagaries, of calm speculation, of pleasant idling, during which one placidly spins impressions, ideas, furtive sensations, do I owe to that exquisite, noble Manuel Díaz Rodríguez, the indisputable master of style, the indisputable master and authority with respect to the language in America, the diaphanous and profound author of *Confidences of Psyche* (*Confidencias de Psiquis*), *Tales of Colour* (*Cuentos de color*), *Broken Idols* (*Ídolos rotos*), and travel notes filled with elegance and life!

It has always seemed to me so improbable that a writer under the age of forty should succeed in making himself master of that intricately organized instrument which is our language, in stamping with his own unmistakable style beautiful medallions, in impressing his lion's claw or his soft dove-like fingers upon living pages, that I believed Díaz Rodríguez to have reached at least the aforementioned age. To my surprise I found that he was still very young, that what others acquire and master after exhausting that "long patience" which is called Art, he had conquered like an Alexander, in the flower of his years. Elegant, refined, with soft and expressive eyes, slender, with complexion slightly swarthy, slow in speech, radiating from his entire person an expression of kindliness and friendliness, it is difficult to know him without esteeming and loving him. Nothing in his actions contradicts this first impression. Nature, which commonly writes a warning on repulsive faces, likewise frequently deceives us with certain pleasant physiognomies or certain harmonious figures: the cat, the most beautiful and elegant of the domestic animals, is cruel, ungrateful, and hypocritical; the elephant, primitive, crude, ugly, and rough, is noble, faithful, and chaste. . . . This is nothing new; I think I read it in my first reader—pardon me!

With Díaz Rodríguez Nature has been logical. There is no contradiction between what his countenance reveals and the inestimable worth of his spirit. He is good and noble "through and through," if I may be permitted the expression.[4]

He became my brother, and he is that across the broad lands which separate our cordial hands, but not our spirits, which are swift as light and migratory as the air.

Moréas

Papadiamantópulos (Jean Moréas) was sipping some concoction or other in a café on the boulevard when Gómez Carrillo went and said to him: "Over at Calisaya (Calisaya is an American bar on the Boulevard des Italiens), there is a poet who has come from Mexico just to meet you."

Moréas rose immediately, and with that elastic gait and blustering look which characterize him, went to Calisaya accompanied by Gómez Carrillo.

There, in a dark and inconspicuous corner, with Darío and an actress from the Grand Guignol, Lola Noyr, a friend of Carrillo, was the poet who had come to Paris, from Mexico, "just" to meet the Greek.

That poet was "yours truly." . . .

[4]Expressed in Spanish by the word *medularmente*, "medullarly."

"Where is the poet who has come from America to meet me?"—asked Moréas in a stentorian voice.

Carrillo pointed me out, and I got up respectfully, with my hat in my left hand and my right hand extended towards his.

Papadiamantópulos clasped it with a frank and effusive handshake, and with the conversation already under way I was able to observe him at my ease.

His appearance was extremely attractive: his complexion a light brown, his face aquiline and lighted by large expressive eyes, to which a military air was imparted by his thick, twisted, and stiff moustache. His whole appearance suggested a Turkish soldier or a Persian sultan.

A monocle with a black rim, attached to a broad silk ribbon, and a certain style of dress bordering upon the elegant, although a little bit affected; also, on each hand a little rat-coloured glove which lent emphasis to that figure at once manly and refined.

That day Papa . . . etc. and I never separated. Nor that night, since Moréas invited Carrillo, Darío, and me to dinner, and afterwards we walked through the horrible streets of Montmartre till a very late hour of the night. I went arm in arm with Moréas, who showered me with affection (Of course! A poet who had crossed the ocean to see him!). And puffed up with pride, I was saying to myself:

"Arm in arm with Jean Moréas! You're walking arm in arm with Jean Moréas! Who would have told you you would ever do that, man! Who would have told you, when you were playing chicken and coyote in the beautiful streets of your town, that some day, or rather some night, you would be going through Paris, France, arm in arm with Jean Moréas, the author of the *Passionate Pilgrim* (*Pèlerin Passionné*). . . ."

"So you came from Mexico only to see me. . . ." (What a man this Gómez Carrillo!)

"Why yes . . . I came just for that." It's true that I said to myself: "Incidentally I'll see the Exhibition, I'll get to know the capital of the world, I'll travel around a bit; but just incidentally. . . ."

"Fine, fine!"

And we spoke of his work, the *Pilgrim*, of course, and naturally of that *Pilgrim* that moved Anatole France to say: "Jean Moréas is one of the seven stars of the new Pléiade. I consider him the Ronsard of Symbolism."

We spoke of *Eriphyle*, of *Aenone with the Pellucid Face* (*Enone au clair visage*), of which I recited a part translated by me, and of the *Stanzas* (*Estancias*), permeated with a serene pantheism in the style of Rousseau, which at the time were beginning to appear, indeed, in the form of an autograph manuscript.

Moréas was in excellent humour, and as we walked along, he recited to me something very beautiful, that ballad:

> Whack, whack, whack—he nails with rapid strokes,
> Whack, whack—the carpenter for the dead.
> "Good carpenter, good carpenter,
> In fir or walnut wood,
> Make a coffin big and heavy,
> In which to lay my love. . . ."

Before we parted he promised of his own accord to bring his *Passionate Pilgrim* to Calisaya for me the following day, with the accompanying dedicatory inscription. What a delight! . . . And I kept saying to myself: "Who would ever have told you, when you were playing chicken and coyote in the beautiful streets of your town, that some day, or rather some night, you would be going through Paris, France, etc., etc.

What happened the next day? I do not know. Perhaps I was ill, perhaps my very bad memory played a trick on me; in any case I did not go to Calisaya. According to what Darío told me later, Moréas came looking for me; he was carrying his book under his arm, his book with its dedication! He did not find me, and in anger he tore up the page he had autographed, completely. . . .

And that was all.

Papadiamantópulos and the poet who had gone from Mexico to Paris, just to see him, never became friends again. When they met, the first pretended not to remember the second (who had crossed the ocean!), and the second finally resigned himself. . . . All had been lost, save honour!

Exodus and the Flowers on the Way (*El éxodo y las flores del camino*), printed by the Oficina Impresora de Estampillas, Mexico, 1902, pp. 123–31.

Rafael López

(b. Guanajuato, Guanajuato, 1875; d. Mexico, D.F., 1943)

Rafael López studied in the State College of Guanajuato, and began his literary career there and also in León. At the beginning of the century he came to Mexico City, worked in the Department of Education, and began to write for *The Impartial* (*El Imparcial*), *The Illustrated World* (*El Mundo Ilustrado*) and *The Modern Review* (*La Revista Moderna*). Then he joined the Youth Club (Ateneo de la Juventud) and became a teacher of literature at the Normal School, where he had as students Francisco González Guerrero, Rodrigo Torres Hernández, and Gregorio López y Fuentes, already poets. Later he was for many years director of the National Archives and of the Institute for Aesthetic Research of the University of Mexico.

"Master of colour and rhythm," Alfonso de Reyes called him on the appearance of his first book of poems, *With Open Eyes* (*Con los ojos abiertos*). He was at that time a thoroughly Modernistic poet, but with a note all his own, that of civic and historical touches, that is to say, he preferred the Parnassian side of that literary school. And even though he purified the sculptural and sonorous bias in his last book of poems, he was always the poet of the single vibrating line.

Week after week, in the good old days of *Review of Reviews* (*Revista de Revistas*), Rafael López wrote news essays that continued the school of the later Romanticism, although with a style and a sensibility already new, less lyric and rambling than those of Gutiérraz Nájera, and on the other hand more sober and close-knit, with a sentimentalism tinged with irony. He collected the best of these news-essays in *Prose of the Day* (*Prosas transeúntes*), his literary club book.

ESSAYS: *Prose of the day* (*Prosas transeúntes*), 1925.

PROVINCIAL MAYORS

THE TUNE SUNG BY MAYORS from outside the capital along the avenues, in the centre of the squares, and in the auditoriums of the theatres of the metropolis is interesting, picturesque, and rather melancholy. Something of the quiet boredom of the provinces is given off from those good-natured figures with their broad-brimmed hats, and about whose necks the autumnal cold begins to bring forth premature and extraordinary scarves, scarves of eloquent colouring, in which the palette of Saturnino Herrán appears to be laughing.

For the most part they are agriculturists, industrialists, or merchants; perhaps occasionally a born politician, on account of being descended from a political boss. It is well known that in our country the political bosses were always the feudal lords of the municipalities. They come in their Sunday best (in those clothes that sleep all week in old chests, to come out with the Sunday sun and the call to mass), bound for the parish church to receive the blessing which the priest pronounces over the bowed heads of the parish proprietors. It is to be hoped that the sessions of the Conference of the Municipalities end soon and that the representatives return to their respective regions with their beliefs intact. The winds that blow in this city are completely hostile to the maintenance of religious morality and the practice of the faith. And there is danger in the fact that the mayors fill in the pauses in their sessions with an eleven o'clock cocktail, with the *pelota* games, and the songs of La Conesa, in addition to other less venial lapses. More than one mayor will have to return to his town council with knapsack full of bitter nostalgias.

Meanwhile, there they go submerged in the magnificent metropolis, up to their necks in the city traffic, with great difficulty saving their municipal integrity from the avalanche of electric cars and of trucks which threaten them from north, south, east, and west.

The establishment of the free municipality has coincided with such an abundance of vehicular traffic that the streets are already too narrow to carry it. Only a short time ago we knew nothing of traffic lights; in the matter of signals we knew nothing but the sacred ceremony of the manual sign. The measured trot of the blacks and the sorrels, drawing Victorian landaus, had no need of the new police service. Even the gouty were allowed to cross the street without any great difficulty. A vehicle that would run over anyone was more incredible than the bed with mother-of-pearl arabesques which fanciful antiquarians point out as the authentic property of the harsh conqueror don Nuño de Guzmán. Today we are gasoline-propelled and rush towards the future in missiles swift as arrows and wrapped in gusts of wind like Ariel. So much the worse for those who fall under the wheels or are smashed up in a collision. The world is getting more interesting every day and it would be too bad if our contemplation of its dramatic film were interrupted.

Let us calculate the situation of the mayors in this democratic Babylon. They must be overwhelmed, longing for the quiet mask of the parish clock which marks off the provincial and countryside hours in lethargic minutes, hungry for surprises and excitement that abound in the life of the city. They must feel eager to return to the tranquillity of their estates, to the peace of their horizons, to the unbounded comfort of their ample mansions.

To those complicated bilingual "menus" which they bravely digest at the restaurant tables, failing to recognize under their foreign appellations the garden products of their motherland, they will prefer the thick nourishing broth and the savoury stew of the ancestral pot, the pure foamy milk in which "La Pinta"[1] collaborates for the benefit of the family. Rather than ride in those diabolical vehicles of chimerical speed, they would like to caress, wearing their tight native head-dress, the back of the dappled pony, the unforgettable "Palomo," with the quiet solemn stride. And rather than the brightness of the avenues, dazzling with the lights of street lamps and show windows, they would prefer to watch from the domestic courtyard "The Seven Kids" and "The Three Marys," which shine in the skies as the adornments of the night.

They have been seen at the performance of *The Mayor of Zalamea* (*El alcalde de Zalamea*),[2] moved by the misfortunes of Elizabeth and enthusiastic over the energy, good sense, and the admirable moral grandeur of Pedro Crespo. Although it is a work that is the flower of the Spanish theatre and of the most brilliant century of its literature, I suspect that, like these small-town magistrates, there are here a large number of literary men who do not know it. Here is the theme in two lines. One of Philip II's captains abducts the daughter of a peasant in whose house he is a guest. The peasant is the mayor of Zalamea, and after exhausting good arguments to induce the captain to repair the honour of the wronged maiden, orders him hanged because the abductor refused to honour his claim. The masterpiece of Calderón, so dramatic, with a plot so firmly constructed about a core of simplicity, with characters so human in the Spanish atmosphere which surrounds them, must have enthralled our mayors by its undeniable good qualities. The beautiful civic and domestic virtues of Pedro Crespo are so fundamental that they flourish in his mayor's

[1]The family cow (Brindle), with a suggestion of mixed colours.

[2]A famous play by Calderón de la Barca (1600–1681), Spanish dramatist.

rod with a remarkable and lasting aroma, like roses on the mystic rod of this municipal Saint Joseph.

It is quite credible that a knowledge of *The Mayor of Zalamea* might have a beneficent influence upon these fellow-mayors, rather rustic like the mayor in the play, and for that reason capable of great moral improvement. With something of the integrity, honesty, and clear intelligence which give lustre to the name of Pedro Crespo, the provincial magistrates will be able to lend prestige and dignity to the municipal institution, which has been studied in such a precise and learned manner in the writings of Fustel de Coulanges. Good ideas thrive better in provincial minds than in the too sophisticated minds of the capital. Feeling for one's country is found in peaceful men who practise agriculture and industry far from the refinements of the large cities.

There is no need to be greatly upset if the provincial mayors find difficulty in speaking on the platform and are guilty of a few mayor-like utterances that go with their position. One cannot expect them to discourse on fine arts with the assurance of a member of a literary club, or to orate on social problems with the eloquence of Dr. De Alba. Neither should they be regarded with scorn because they are less dexterous in pulling on their gloves than our practised dandies.

Men of good will are what we need in order to remedy as far as possible our infinite social ills, even though they leave something to be desired with respect to their intellectual and physical refinement.

It is a well known fact that as soon as one begins to understand the marvels of the Ninth Symphony, one becomes too easy-going to serve the interests of the nation.

Prose of the day (*Prosas transeúntes*), Aztlán Editores, Mexico, 1925, pp. 15–19.

José Vasconcelos

(b. Oaxaca, Oax., 1881)

The life of José Vasconcelos is one of the most intense, impassioned, and contradictory to be found among modern Mexicans. After living a few years in his native city he went to Piedras Negras and, after visiting other places in the Republic, studied at the Campeche Institute. In Mexico City he entered the Preparatory School and later took the course in law. In 1907 he graduated, writing a thesis on *Dynamic Theory of Law* (*Teoría dinámica del Derecho*), which he afterwards published in the *Positive Review* (*Revista Positiva*). About 1910 he belonged to the Youth Club (Ateneo de la Juventud), with the tone of which he finally showed himself in disagreement, but at the rise of the Revolutionary movement he preferred to be one of its soldiers rather than one of its victims. He fought with the followers of Madero and later shared in the adventures of the new leaders, following a very personal course: Madero, Villa, Eulalio Gutiérrez, Obregón. During the brief presidency of Eulalio Gutiérrez he was Secretary of Education, and at the triumph of the Revolution Obregón appointed him President of the University and later, once again, Secretary of Education (1921–24). This was the zenith of his intellectual and political career. He organized popular education, established libraries, published the classics, promoted mural painting, encouraged a generation of poets, contributed towards the formation of a Spanish-American consciousness, and discovered Gabriela Mistral.[1] After this brief moment of brilliance, our contemporary Renaissance, political disillusionments began to corrode this great figure. An implacable enemy of the Calles régime, he first failed as a candidate for the governorship of Oaxaca, went into profitable exile in Europe and the United States, and then undertook the great adventure of his life, with his candidature for the presidency of the Republic in 1929. After his failure and persecution there came another exile in Europe and South America, which did not end until 1940. On his return to Mexico he was a totally different man from the one who had once won the title "Master of Youth."

He has received honours for the extraordinary merit of his intellectual work. He is Director of the Library of Mexico City, a member of the Linguistic Academy and of the National College.

[1]Famous Chilean poetess, winner of the Nobel Prize for Literature in 1945.

Whether literary, historical, or philosophical, Vasconcelos' books unmistakably reveal the man, and are imbued, as it were, with the warm reflex of impassioned breathing. His most constant tone is that of the summing up of an allegation, whether he is dealing with persons or with philosophical propositions. He has a notorious incapacity for the objective exposition of doctrines not his own, but on the other hand he possesses a clear capacity for understanding and expressing reality, both objective reality and that of the spirit, through his own vibrant crystal. He never pays much attention to methods, fine points of style, and academic techniques, always being absorbed in the spirit and the particular emotion with which he views events. According to what he tells us in his writings, he prefers in his prose the oratorical style, which in him is the product of the intensity and richness of his thought, and not a sought after or superimposed effect. He believes, and rightly so, that "a good style identifies itself with the act of thinking," that it is "substance and not foliage," and this he practised throughout his long, varied, uneven, and admirable career as a writer.

ESSAYS AND AUTOBIOGRAPHY: *Gabino Barreda and Contemporary Ideas* (*Gabino Barreda y las ideas contemporáneas*), 1910; *Mexican Intellectuality* (*La intelectualidad mexicana*), 1916; *Pythagoras, a Theory of Rhythm* (*Pitágoras, una teoría del ritmo*), Havana, 1916; *Aesthetic Monism* (*El monismo estético*), 1918; *Literary Vagaries* (*Divagaciones literarias*), 1919; *Hindu Studies* (*Estudios indostánicos*), Madrid, 1920; *The Cosmic Race* (*La raza cósmica*), Barcelona, 1925; *About India* (*Indología*), Barcelona, 1927; *Glad Pessimism* (*Pesimismo alegre*), Madrid, 1931; *Magic Sonata* (*Sonata mágica*), Madrid, 1933; *Bolivarism and Monroeism* (*Bolivarismo y monroísmo*), Santiago de Chile, 1935; *From Robinson to Odysseus* (*De Robinsón a Odiseo*), Madrid, 1935; *What is Communism?* (*¿Qué es el comunismo?*), 1936; *What is Revolution?* (*¿Qué es la revolucion?*), 1937; *Ulysses a Creole* (*Ulises criollo*), 1936; *The Storm* (*La tormenta*), 1936; *The Disaster* (*El desastre*), 1938; *The Proconsulship* (*El proconsulado*), 1939; *At the Sunset of My Life* (*En el ocaso de mi vida*), 1957.

SADNESS

THEY DO TALK of our sadness too. When tyranny gives way, there is nothing gayer than a Mexican Sunday, with processions and music and sunshine, unless it is a Sunday in Madrid. If one is homesick for Spain, that too can be understood. For where could the festivity one sees every morning in the Retiro[2] be surpassed? Or the music of women's conversations in the Castellana?[3] Or the luxury of the trains in the sunshine? Or the proximity of the bright canvases of Goya? Or the

[2]A park in Madrid.

[3]A boulevard in Madrid.

orgeat drunk at tables along the sidewalk converted into a hall? Or the excitement of the coming bullfight? Or the melodious sound of the Latin soul? One may well miss all this, but those who speak of loneliness and homesickness think rather of rain-soaked panoramas and of an atmosphere in which the soul itself must don the straitjacket of a foreign language, for what woe is ours if we come to master it, because it is at the cost of a hurt which deforms the sensibilities!

A lot is said about our sadness in America, but is there any desolation comparable to that of a Sunday in London? And is there anything more painful than the Sunday crowds in the Boulevards from the Boulevard des Italiens downwards? Pale faces, short sleeves and trousers to save cloth, a slow walk with nowhere to go. There is no panorama and there is no gaiety. And they are less poor than the poor of Madrid. And also less poor than the common folk of Mexico, but they have lost, or they have never had, that creation of the sunshine: carefree, boisterous laughter.

What does the Argentinian know of sadness who has never spent a Sunday in the Bowery? And where is there loneliness like that of the lone immigrants who droop their heads on the benches of Battery Place?

Bolivarism and Monroeism (*Bolivarismo y monroísmo*), 2nd edition, Santiago de Chile, 1935, p. 155.

BOOKS I READ SITTING AND BOOKS I READ STANDING

TO DISTINGUISH BOOKS, I have followed the practice for some time of using a classification which corresponds to the emotions they arouse in me. I divide them into books I read sitting and books I read standing. The former may be pleasant, instructive, beautiful, splendid, or simply stupid and boring, but all are incapable of arousing us from our normal posture. On the other hand there are some books which, the moment we begin reading, make us get up, as though they derive from the earth a force that pushes against our heels and obliges us to make an effort to rise. In these we do not just read: we declaim, we assume a lofty pose, and undergo a genuine transfiguration. Examples of this kind are: Greek tragedy, Plato, Hindu philosophy, the Gospels, Dante, Spinoza, Kant, Schopenhauer, the music of Beethoven, and others, if more modest, not less exceptional in their qualities.

To the quiet type of book, which one reads without being stirred up, belong all the rest, of infinite number, in which we find instruction, delight, charm, but not the palpitation of our consciousness which lifts us up as if we were witnessing a revelation of a new aspect of creation, a new aspect which incites us to move in order to be able to contemplate it in its entirety.

Moreover, writing books is a poor consolation for being unadaptable to life. Thinking is the most intense and fruitful function of life, but descending from thought to the hazardous task of writing it down weakens pride and reveals a spiritual inadequacy, indicating a fear that the idea will not live if it is not put in writing. This is an author's vanity and a little fraternal solicitude on the part of a traveller who, for the benefit of future travellers, marks along the arid way the points where there has been found the ideal water, indispensable for the continuance of the journey. A book, like a journey, is begun in anxiety and finished in melancholy.

If it were possible to be profound and optimistic, books would never be written. Men filled with energy, free and fecund, would not devote themselves to imitating with dead letters the ineffable worth, the perennial self-renewing of a life which absorbs and fulfils its impulses and all its longings. A noble book is always the fruit of disillusionment and a sign of protest. The poet does not barter his visions for his verses, and the hero prefers to live his passions and heroisms rather than sing them, however capable he might be of doing so in full and sumptuous pages. The people who write are those who cannot do things or are not satisfied with what they do. Every book says, expressly or between the lines: nothing is as it ought to be.

Woe to the man who takes up his pen and begins to write, while outside there is every potential which attracts human endeavour, when all the unfinished work calls forth emotion to consummate it in a pure and perfect reality!

But woe also to the man who, devoted to the world outside, neither reflects, nor becomes revolted, nor has ambitions ever more exalted! This man lives complacently only for the external and does not give up and die only because he is not yet born or reborn. For to be born is not merely to come into the world, in which life and death persist together and succeed each other; to be born is to proclaim oneself a non-conformist; to be born is to tear oneself away from the sombre mass of the species, to rebel against every human convention, to wish to strike out and rise up under the stimulus of the books that are read standing, books radically unsubmissive.

I do not know to what we are born when, like Buddha or Jesus, we renounce the world, but there is certainly no doubt about the nobility of a renunciation which anticipates the fatal dictum of death and defies death. Yes, unquestionably it is necessary, after knowing life, to be able to say to it: "That's enough!" Without that renunciation and without that demanding of something better, it appears that life has no value for us. It appears that new incarnations will be necessary in order that we may again attempt to surpass in our hearts all that is human, in order to rise to the state of the demigod, the angel, or the blessed.

Good books reprove life, without for that reason giving in to discouragement and doubt. To understand this, it is sufficient to read them, and to observe how strong, healthy temperaments judge them; because the sick man desires health, as the weak man reveres strength and as the mediocre man seeks happiness, and all three are optimistic. But the man who is healthy and glad of heart, the valiant and the bold, become demanding and clamour for what is not found here. Before the sybarite who offers me pleasure and the prophet who points out to me the vale of tears, I may waver, but I understand and respect the one who says to me: "It is necessary," and I laugh with scorn when I come upon the one who exclaims: "How beautiful!" or "How splendid!"

This is because truth is expressed only in a prophetic tone, and is perceived only in the tremulous atmosphere of catastrophe. So it speaks in the word of Aeschylus, so it is woven gloriously into the dialogue of Plato, so it bursts forth in the opulent modern symphony.

Euripides too, one of the free and great who have passed by, had such a clear understanding of the human that, moved by compassion, he began to write his visions, taking care to repeat at every moment the wise and sincere counsel, to which we are so deaf: "Be distrustful, be not puffed up in your joy. Call not yourself happy till the hour of your death; before then you know not what fate has in store for you. Why do you wish glory, beauty, and power. . . . Look at the house of Priam; listen to the lamentations of Hecuba. The faithful Andromache shares the bed of the victor! The little son of Hector has just perished, and of all the illustrious race there remains only the procession of Trojan slaves, imploring in vain as they march towards exile. Why have children!"

But as the truth inspires terror and many are alarmed by the corollaries which any thoroughly sincere spirit might deduce from these immortal gospels, the representatives of those who refuse to die, and who still, furthermore, indulge the instinct to engender offspring—

the representatives of such beings, the intelligent men, with Aristotle at the head, invent for us attenuated interpretations, as they do in telling us that tragedy gives relief because the portrayal of pain causes joy, and that in this way the principle of life triumphs over its negations. They seem to fear that some day men will understand, and therefore they write books which restore our calm and good sense, books which deceive us: books which we read sitting because they attach us to life!

Literary Vagaries (*Divagaciones literarias*), 2nd ed., Mexico, 1922, pp. 9–13.

GLAD PESSIMISM

THE PROGRESS OF CIVILIZATION is the tragedy of personality confronting the monsters that would devour it. Above all temporal interest, above environment, above the State, above the country of our birth and as the only mainspring of action, stands the heroic eagerness to maintain triumphant the highest value of personality.

In man there will always endure the will to overcome obstacles. How could immortal Prometheus, who dared to rebel even against the gods, fail to keep himself on guard against his own creations, the social systems, the politico-economic doctrines, the fashions, the opinions, and the times?

Periodically man liberates himself, even though afterwards his exercise of liberty is of short duration. He liberated himself from barbarism, from superstition; at times he liberates himself from ignorance. And just as other periods have achieved their triumphs consistently in favour of the total and transcendental human personality, so we today must be alert to liberate ourselves from the modern monsters: the State, political fanaticism and reaction, whether Bolshevist or Fascist.

A new man is going to emerge after the period of economic stress which we are presently enduring; he will once more be a perfect expression of the eternal man who survives his own orderings and external manifestations.

The total man is the only eternal aspiration. The other men, the partial men, are exhausted in their task and are confused with their age. They fulfil their mission as instruments, as simple raw material in the progress of history. After every great crisis, the total man is reborn from the ashes of the age that has been obliterated. He is ever victorious over the temporal forms of the economic or political society which has begotten him!

Not that the total man must withdraw himself from the work of his time—on the contrary, he will have to embrace it passionately, but he will not devote himself to it completely unless he wishes to cease being total, falling thus within the limitations of the sectarian, with the obstinacy of one who works with no vision of a beyond.

I work and I dream; this formula the perfect man cannot relinquish, with the understanding that on the side of the dreams one must place one's whole mind. The hands are made for work, and if intelligence has any part to play in it, it must always do so like the part which controls the mechanism, and only in order to make the impulse continue on its course and achieve its purpose. The great sin of capitalism has been to utilize the best of the mind in the lust for gain. The most unselfish workers become criminals if they make the single task of production their entire aim. And the other pole of capitalism, Communism, falls into the same evil when it converts its systems into nothing but machinery of production.

The economic man has base aspects and generous aspects; but it is necessary that the eternal man should prevail over the economic man. The economic man of the period of scarcity and material suffering will have to be replaced by the complete man of tomorrow. Again he will be the total man of the good times, enriched by economic experience, but not its slave.

Divided into pessimists and optimists, the partial men, men who are slaves of their present, follow routes that are apparently opposed to each other, but strictly speaking they are identical. Some have been optimists because they see the possibility of earthly happiness; others are pessimists because they see happiness on earth as impossible. But both will be left without a task to perform—deprived of the corpse required for the function of the mourners. The pessimists of the earth will no longer have anything to mourn. . . . The world will solve its economic problem. It is solving it by the double method of science and economic doctrine, by production multiplied by the machine and work organized without profit to the capitalist; without private capitalism it is already easy to foresee the world of a morrow soon to come.

Paradise will be made on earth. The last of Satan's temptations, or perhaps his real triumph—what less can one expect of the planet than that it should feed its beasts? And if the very beasts in the jungle have their morality, which gives them all a chance to live, why should men not conquer the beast, capitalistic competition, to bring in the morality of common sense, sharing according to need and merit?

One would have to dismiss intelligence from our service if in five thousand years of culture it had not yet perceived the clearest and most just solution to the problem.

But it is not sufficient that the economic man should triumph, nor is it sufficient that the triumph should go to the mere man of intelligence. We have already said that the eternal man is the total man or the one who aspires to totality. And this alone is worthy of the effort of the millenniums of culture.

And then, in the hour of the approaching *Eureka*, when earthly justice and good fortune are intoxicating men, it will be necessary to shake up their vitals again with the implacable fist of Prometheus. The work of the spirit will begin again with vigour the day of the fraternal banquet of the peoples. The different races, fed, contented, and healthy, will lift their heads to heaven. Stronger than ever will then be the new call to non-conformity . . . on the most dangerous day in all creation!

And there is nothing new in saying that it will be then that the work of the spirit will begin in earnest. First the miracle of the loaves was performed, food and drink were given, and later came the Sermon on the Mount!

The miracle of the loaves will take on the flesh of reality: it will become a daily occurrence. The daily bread comes to all, given out by the Father, by the way of work, intelligence, and justice. Work as a blessing will replace work as a curse.

But in the very reality of terrestrial happiness lies implicit the danger of a worse, more terrible curse. He who has not eaten dreams of food and is eager to seek and enjoy it. But the problem starts all over again after one has eaten. And for that reason it is necessary that all should eat, so that all may experience disturbance of the conscience, which no longer has to run wild like the beasts, incited by appetite.

Alone with our conscience. . . .

The well-fed body will appear repugnant in a way that the hungry body has never been. And every conscience will feel the desolation of satiety; a desolation greater than that of suffering.

And then we shall need a new doctrine. It will be called the post-economic doctrine by those who use circumscribed glasses which allow them to see only their own times. It will continue to be called the eternal doctrine by others, by those who do not use glasses when they look....

And once all these problems which today affiict us are solved, the problems of the cook, the supplier, and the producer . . . , other ancient problems will again occupy the foreground. . . .

What do we do with the life left over after eating and loving? . . . What do we do with our good life, this good life of the mere economic man, as soon as that good life begins to produce yawning and nausea?

Then the multitudes will turn towards the eternal man. . . . The peoples will not ask their questions of the economist or the technician: one does not ask the cart-wheel what is the cause of motion or the motor-propeller the reason for its revolutions.

The peoples will again ask their questions, as always, of the poet.

And the just man will not be the one who shares well; no sharing is necessary when economics is a function and not a monopoly. . . . The just will be the one who lives according to the highest values. . . . The definer of the highest values.

And so the men of God will again reign over the men of the earth.

And again will sound forth the old imprecation: "Of what use to you is your good life? Swine of the planet, before you another Antichrist, the Antichrist Mohammed, already preached a paradise of earthly stamp. . . . He wished to carry to heaven the infection of the earth, and on the earth he allowed violence to remain as law. . . . Take heed that you make not satiety your law. . . . The paradise of Mohammed has come down to earth, and has been realized upon the earth. . . . But souls go in and swine come out in harems, in the paradises of the corporeal senses. . . ."

"Of what use to you is your good life?" the new prophets will repeat in the day of abundance, as of old did Solomon and Ecclesiastes. With the difference that now all will be in the same happy state as Solomon and they will not be blinded by the mirage of a pleasure not possessed. Like new Buddhas they will be led to flee from life by the happy state attained and within our reach. . . .

And who can say which is more terrible: the desolation of the good life or the desolation of suffering?

A Solomonic humanity, wise and powerful, will curse its very affluence and will complain of its plenty. . . . And the new prophets will say: "Cursed be plenty. . . ."

And then will come the decisive culmination. The powerful will abdicate; the happy will repudiate their happiness. . . .

And each destiny will be able to incarnate the tragedy of the Mount of Temptation. . . . To each, the eternal Satan will be able to say: "Behold nature at your service. . . . Press a button and the forces of the world will work for you . . . , and there are a thousand hearts eager for abundance and pleasure; intoxicate yourself with life. . . ." And again those who feel within them the gift of the higher life will say: "No, not that! . . ."

And this is the way I understand today what years ago I called, upon a mere glimpse of it: glad pessimism. . . . A fundamental pessimism which says no to happiness. . . . Strictly speaking that is the only valid pessimism; the pessimism which succeeds in bringing happiness within its grasp and renounces it because it knows that this is not its place. . . .

Inexorable pessimism of the elect. . . . It is something more likely to become general and popular by the way of satisfaction of wants than by the hard way of suffering.

And also it will be easier to free transcendentalism from its falsifications.

Renunciation of happiness and the forthcoming of a vital heroism, in place of the misguided heroism of the Nietzscheans. The morality of the life triumphant which exceeds itself and liberates itself, in place of the fetid contemporary morality of the disqualified. . . . Strength interpreted by Nietzsche, who could scarcely conceive of what health is. . . . Love judged by the perverts or by the inadequate. . . . Any humble beast can teach them a lesson. The Nietzscheanism of the sickly has a remedy: the sanatorium. . . . The lost can forget themselves or convert their aspirations into health . . . All this is therapeutics, not heroism. Heroism is the requirement of excellence. Heroism is the achievement of the normal, and still more beyond it. . . .

With life mastered and with the mind reaching out beyond intelligence and beyond humanity, then begins the terrible journey. . . . Cold, terror, hope, light? No signal responds to the strange immersion in profundity. Less than any, the erotic symbol which a certain period of mysticism had so abused. . . . This is a true, a pure mysticism. Just as men have spoken of the pure idea—which makes no sense—let us speak of pure emotion, which is indeed a tangible reality. Pure, deep emotion. Stirred just barely by a vague passing impulse. . . . A post-Dionysiac escape, beyond passion. . . . A mystic way. . . . Consummation in the absolute.

Glad Pessimism (*Pesimismo alegre*), Madrid, 1931, pp. 232–41.

THE EMBITTERED

"DO YOU KNOW what is being said of you in Mexico?" asks a travelling companion of mine, and I answer:

"I'm not much interested in knowing, but all right, tell me."

"Well, they say you are an embittered man."

"Well!" I exclaim, "they used to call me a spiteful man!" They have now become convinced that I am not seeking position and money at any cost and they have to abandon that adjective, because the spiteful man is one who cannot get what he wants, even though he is ready to pay for it by sacrificing his honour. The question of being embittered perhaps requires more careful examination. Before analysing it and as a beginning, I ask you to recall the faces of those people who think I'm embittered: yellow skin, lips swollen with alcohol and blotches, the expression of a jail-bird. And just look at my face. You yourself have just admired its healthy colour, the skin fresh in spite of age, the clear eyes. Let us take a look at things from this corner. I challenge you to see who is the first to read the names of the buses coming up the avenue, and in spite of the fact that I have read my way through a lot of libraries without glasses. After this test, it seems to me pointless to show you my tongue, free from any coating, and full of sound to condemn the iniquity which is weighing upon our people. I do not require much reflection to tell you the effect upon me of the pity of those who call me embittered. The effect is just like that on a person finding himself suddenly in a fraternity of pickpockets, in a den of the underworld, among perverts and gangsters, who hears himself pitied because he does not share their perversions. But let us dig down a little deeper into this. Who is there who does not experience bitterness? Even though it does not arise from the causes which torment the poor unfortunates who live on the piracy of politics!

As soon as I search into my heart I am tormented by the bitterness of my poor human condition, of the consciousness that cannot embrace totality and for that reason does not reach the plenitude of understanding; a soul which longs to unite itself with everything and love all that exists and barely finds fire for only an occasional concrete passion; a destiny which wearies of being alert and has to lose almost half its time sleeping, when the soul wishes to be ever in the light like an archangel. But what do the poor helots who think me embittered know of all this? What they imagine is that I suffer because I do not figure in the lists of those who share the plunder from the public treasury. I do not believe they consider me a failure in the matter of fame, because with a single hour of my years of glory any one of them would have sufficient honour and renown for a whole lifetime. And in any case I cannot imagine what it is that any honest, or even sensible, person could envy these who pity me: the abject position in which they live, or the money they do not know how to use, because when they leave the tequila it is only to turn to whisky, and the palaces which they appropriate for themselves they leave untouched by art; or the entire life of vices, which gains for them no other adornment than the low morality of their more or less collectivized mistresses?

Let us investigate, nevertheless, whether from the external and mundane point of view there is any reason why I might feel embittered, at over fifty years of age, and enjoying good health and a robust will. As a preliminary we shall note that everyone feels disappointed or successful only in relation to what his colleagues and contemporaries achieve. And though I am not one of those who take their own works very seriously when brought before those who call me embittered, it is natural that I should make comparisons and ask: "Has any one of you accomplished a more important piece of work than what I achieved in the Department of Education, which in spite of its having been destroyed by the enemies of Mexico is still the most distinguished on the continent since the termination of the efforts of the Catholic missionaries?" If there is bitterness from the destruction of that work which the country has been unable to defend, perhaps even unable to understand, in any case the remorse and the hurt are not mine. The harm suffered falls upon the country. And in like manner it is the nation that suffers on account of the opportunity it lost because it could not defend it, the opportunity of having me carry out in the Presidency a work similar to what I achieved as Minister of Education, but of more scope and substance. The hurt which I suffer is infinitesimal compared with the harm that will be suffered by the children of the present generation, now that this generation itself has nothing to lose, because it has become irredeemable and hardened.

Moreover, it is doubtful that I should lament, for my own sake, that I did not become President. My work in the government would have been exceptionally good compared to the misgovernment of so many inept and wicked men, but still not good enough, on account of the poor material that I should have had at my disposal. In any case I should have been overcome by vanity, by virtue of the fact that the defeats inflicted by the world encourage and stimulate the effort of the soul. A forced detachment from the affairs of state has enabled me to accomplish a mental output which, even though it is, like any human work, quite limited, is still superior to the most perfect political action. In general, all that we little men of this anaemic New World have been able to accomplish up to the present is of little worth, but within that relative setting, I would not exchange my *Aesthetics* (*Estética*) for the best of the battles of Bolívar . . . ! Don't laugh, remember there is nothing wrong in a boast which serves as a battering ram against injustice!

I am, then, a man who has attained wordly success. Nevertheless, there are men who have been successful in works of the mind and, while knowing notoriety and fame, still bear within them the bitterness of some one of those terrible, unconfessable, or inconsolable sorrows. I do not find in my life anything like this up to the present, and may God spare me from it in the future. The greatest misfortune that can befall us is one that has its cause in those we love: an invalid father, a paralyzed son, a wayward daughter, an unfaithful wife; none of this do I have to lament. On the contrary, God has blessed me in my children. If there is in life a greater source of happiness, I do not know of it. . . .

In spite of this, I have certainly suffered. Like anyone who has loved to excess, I have known the anguish of desire, false happiness, and the pain of disillusionment. Again and again the soul errs, doubtless because we demand the absolute of the poor creatures that we are, whom zeal exhausts and time changes. And in us breaks that passion we believed to be eternal, sometimes through natural attrition and tedium, at other times through error or fate. And out of each passion we come as from an infectious fever whose microbe corrodes the soul. We believe we are filling our solitude, and again we find ourselves empty. One there was whom I remember frequently because she was inside me, as the sphere fits inside its circles. But her will weakened at the moment when the course appeared to us as it was, long and rough. Fearful, perhaps, of bungling, and with her noble nature not allowing her any disloyalty, she preferred to pass on to the refuge of death. Her loss left me rent, but not embittered. The Lord, no doubt, received her in his mercy. Man is not judge of man. Mystery envelops us all and fate for some is benign, for others terrible. Who would dare to condemn, save what is base and disloyal?

When one has descended into abysses so deep, one knows of certain hours, desolate and mute, when the heart of one's being is tortured and consumed and imagines that it will never again recover. But also when it rises from the abyss purified, thereafter facing any contingency, the soul will feel invulnerable. And this is not because the heart has become insensible; like the unprotected child it will be proof against the feigned caress, the insincere admiration, and the hunger for love which nothing satisfies while one is cut off from the Absolute, which is our life.

And he who travels through different lands will leave in each one a bit of his heart. And behind a veil of tears are seen again friendly faces of loyal men and virtuous women. Can anyone who carries in his heart such a treasure of affections have time for resentment and bitterness? What rises within him, and abundantly, is indignant passion against injustice and hypocrisy, against those who are the cause of the ills of our fellowmen and our country. For I have hated, but never anyone who was more helpless or of humbler station than myself.

I have already mentioned my country, and some think that being far away from it is a reason for bitterness, and to that I reply that all depends upon the reason for one's absence. He who changes his country because of his privilege of being persecuted by the police always finds within his soul brighter skies than those made by climate and geography. And there is no better country than the one each of us wins for himself in his soul. And this reminds me of the pleasant thought of an Argentinian friend who, seeing me with my little granddaughter by my side, said to me: "You carry your country along with you." And this indeed was true, and for that reason that exile did not bring me grey hairs. And today when periodically I am away from her, I still have left the consolation of thinking that she, some day, if she is not infected by the filthy atmosphere about her, will be proud and feel strengthened in her trials by the remembrance that her grandfather preferred to deny himself the pleasure of her company rather than to smile at imbeciles and rogues; or rather than tolerate their smiling at me—I know not which is worse. Oh, how disgusting are these little people who do not attain the category of personal enemies of mine, but who still are a sore in the dishonoured body of our country!

The life of him who writes these lines is a life of suffering; but as I keep kicking my burden ahead of me, perhaps of greater weight than my own afflictions is the suffering of the people for whose morrow I struggle unceasingly and hopelessly. Fortunately, alongside the minor task, which is the service of my country, there is the urgent need of the soul which demands that I produce thousands of printed pages. Anyone who thus devotes himself to protean but coherent activities has no time for the kind of bitterness which springs from envy of others; neither is there time for complaint that fate, having given us what is more important, has denied us the less important. The energy I have left still feigns vigour, but it is barely sufficient for what I must strive to accomplish. In the distance sound the celestial trumpets and the merry toll of bells. The highways of the earth are obstructed, but there are portents in the wind. The minor tone of bitterness is extinguished and expands into the solemn chords of destinies. . . . Over and above all this, Mercy triumphs, which is the word of Christ, the Universality of the Holy Spirit, and the Grace of the Father. Amen.

What is the Revolution? (*¿ Qué es la Revolución?*), Mexico, 1937, pp. 81–88.

Carlos González Peña

(b. Lagos de Moreno, Jalisco, 1885; d. Mexico, D.F., 1955)

Although associated for a time with the cultural enterprises of the Athenaeum of 1910, González Peña came to the group with a sensibility already formed, which was to remain with him throughout his entire work. His work as a novelist remained attached to the realistic and naturalistic tradition of the end of the nineteenth century, and as a news-writer and composer of articles he might be considered a somewhat untimely heir to the genre in which Gutiérrez Nájera and Urbina excelled. He perhaps lacked the loftiness and the light charm which animated the prose of those masters of Modernism, but he possessed a superior polish and correctness, as of one who was a master of grammatical studies. He knew the secret of evocation and the art of animating, in a plain, expressive style, the themes of his sketches and articles, which appeared every Thursday for many years in *The Universal* (*El Universal*). In his *History of Mexican Literature* (*Historia de la literatura mexicana*), González Peña gave body to the partial contributions already in existence, and in spite of his lacunae and misunderstandings, he produced the most connected and complete manual we possess on the development of our letters.

A journalist from his youth, he continued as such until his last day in *The Illustrated World* (*El Mundo Ilustrado*), *Art and Letters* (*Arte y Letras*), *Review of Reviews* (*Revista de Revistas*), and finally *The Universal*, in which, besides his weekly articles, he wrote editorials. He was furthermore a teacher of language and literature and a member of the Linguistic Academy throughout his active career. In 1947 he received the Manuel Ávila Camacho Prize for Literature.

ARTICLES AND ESSAYS: *The Courtyard Under the Moon* (*El patio bajo la luna*), 1945; *Flowers of Passion and Melancholy* (*Flores de pasión y de melancolía*), 1945; *Musical Enchantment* (*El hechizo musical*), 1946; *My People* (*Gente mía*), 1946; *The Illuminated Niche* (*El nicho iluminado*), 1947; *Watching Life Pass* (*Mirando pasar la vida*), 1947; *Brightness in the Distance* (*Claridad en la lejanía*), 1947; *The Soul and the Mask* (*El alma y la máscara*), 1948; *Beyond the Sea* (*Más allá del mar*), 1949; *People and Landscapes of Jalisco* (*Gentes y paisajes de Jalisco*), 1949 (Prologue by Alfonso de Alba).

STUDIES: *Manual of Spanish Grammar* (*Manual de gramática castellana*), 1921 (several editions); *History of Mexican Literature* (*Historia de la literatura mexicana*), 1928 (several editions); *A Course in Literature. The Garden of Letters* (*Curso de literatura. El jardín de las letras*), 1944.

TRAVELS: *The Tumultuous Life. Six Weeks in the United States* (*La vida tumultuosa. Seis semanas en los Estados Unidos*), 1920; *Paris and London. Travel Tableaux* (*París y Londres. Cuadros de viaje*), 1950.

PROVINCIAL SLUMBER

TO LEAVE MEXICO CITY to seek rest and calm in some city of the provinces, to leave one's daily tasks occasionally, at least for a week each year, is advisable not only for hygienic, but also for poetic reasons.

As we go to the small towns to tone up our systems, renewing expended strength and creating fresh energy, so do we go there also to gratify the eyes and the spirit with the contemplation of beautiful landscapes, the temporary return to humble ways, and the company of beloved and not-forgotten people: those whose whole bodies smile, on our provincial horizon, illuminated by the kindly light of remembrance.

So then, the rest is certainly complete, unsurpassably so. We get off the train at the solitary station. We go into the city along the sleepy streets. We enter the old house—oh, that unforgettable house, with its bright courtyards, its quiet reddish courtyards, and its spacious rooms where our ancestors lived and died! And in an instant, we are right in the room where we have retired to sleep, in the room filled with the sweetness of slight shadows barely attenuated by the flickering glow of the candle, and there we suddenly feel that a deep peace and a great stillness surround us.

That peace and that stillness will continue as the days go by. They will be ever with us. They will be with us in the streets where every stone is a memory, in the sunny little squares, in the bright-hued gardens along the river bank, in the dusty roadways: in all those points and contours of the city, with their many ruins, where we clearly realize that the commotion, the turmoil, and the pleasant or unpleasant incidents of an active, persevering, and fruitful life of other times have disappeared, replaced by a tranquillity which bears many marks of abandonment and death.

And the joy of the return, and the tranquillizing atmosphere sought and obtained, are touched from that moment with slight tinges of melancholy.

We think the city is sad, and we are absorbed in its sadness.

But let us reconsider: Is this sadness only something pertaining to this city, to our picturesque, colourful, traditional city; or rather, have we been perceiving it, conjecturing it, sensing it all along the way, in each and every one of the cities and towns through which we have passed?

Sometimes we have been moved to think of something we would call provincial slumber.

Let us reflect. It is not a simple phrase. In this concept is expressed poetically the poignant reality of a sore spot in our national character. Like people who are ill, the provincial cities yield themselves to slumber because one can be certain that an intimate, persistent, and prolonged weakness is afflicting them.

Leaning with our elbow against the coach window, when the long train arrives at the stations and stops, we have seen the same, identical scene. Poverty unconcealed, frequently wretchedness that makes an open display of itself; boys semi-nude, loathsome women, the blind man with his doleful chant, the scraping of guitars and plaintive sounds; flashes of colour: the blanket being unfolded, bright embroidered gewgaws that make one conscious of fine, industrious fingers, the milky gleam of opals in copper-coloured hands, sweets and fruits, aromas and outlines in cool little baskets. . . . And the cries, and the hands held out, and the coins bouncing. . . . Then a sound of bells. A slow, heavy puff. And the train starts off again.

We are struck by the thought that those little crafts are the chief concern of life, the very fount of life for the humble people of the region.

As we pass fleetingly through cities and towns, in the persistent grey of the abundant adobe, we come to discover ruins, and more and more ruins. Streets that become lost as they terminate among groves of trees, or glimmering in the sunshine. Lone houses. Walls that wearily bend over, ready to fall.

Perhaps if we got off the train, we should discover that in those places which were formerly flourishing centres of population, with industries of their own, with their own ways of living, with their activities ever renewed and never interrupted, life now is hard. It is no longer possible to earn one's bread, except by farming. And this industry is so run-down, so limited, so small, that entire caravans of labourers emigrate, either to the northern frontier, or to other districts where they find themselves confronted with the same problem: the elusive daily wage.

And if this happens with people in the country, the truly urban population, which previously found work, and lived and even prospered from birth to death under the protection of the native town, has had no alternative to leaving the town, becoming scattered abroad, and vanishing.

Cities and towns are sleeping in lethal slumber.

It seems to be a verifiable fact that in our country, except for the capital of the Republic and the capitals of one or two of the States, the towns large and small, far from progressing, far from prospering and seeing their own resources multiply, have perceptibly declined for very nearly half a century. Perhaps this assertion has the defect of erring, as generalizations always do. Possibly statistics will come out to demonstrate by *a* plus *b* that such a decline is imaginary and pure fancy. But our travellers' eyes—poetic travellers' eyes, if you like—will not be able to help noticing the solitude and poverty of cities and towns, and their evident ruin and abandonment.

Those who recognize the truth of the above-mentioned phenomenon explain it by the transformation which has been effected in the national life by railways and heavy industry.

It would be interesting to investigate, nevertheless, how countries with many railways and formidably great industries—the United States, for example—at the same time as they have seen the rise of those monstrous industrial plants (which we, of course, refuse to recognize) have witnessed a normal, harmonious co-ordinated development of their obscure towns, in such a way that the large city does not absorb the small place. And not only interesting, but of general advantage, would be an investigation into whether, in any case, such a transformation—an industrial transformation of foreign stamp and only half-effected like ours—on bringing about the depopulation, the abandonment, and the impoverishment of the vast majority of the cities for the benefit of just a few, has not beclouded what must be a common ideal, the easy life, and has not furthermore created a tremendous unbalance.

Blasphemies, horrible blasphemies, all these observations will appear in pointing out unconfessed ills in Mexican life, to the formulators of the great, high-sounding economic theories of modern industrialism, today elevated to the rank of dogmas. They have put on us an embroidered coat, covered with braid and fringes, and though we feel uncomfortable in it, we are forbidden not only to say that it does not become our figure, but even to declare *sotto voce* that it is uncomfortable.

In the mornings, through the window, the light comes in. The bluish, clear, bright light of Jalisco, which is just as though there entered—according to the classic saying of our grandmother—"the grace of God." Some musical bells converse. Their peal expands, melodious and mysterious: voices of unspeakable tenderness in winged colloquies. . . . At the same time firm, slow footsteps are heard in the street. Let's take a look. The old women, wrapped up in their black shawls, are going to mass; two maidservants, muffled in their mufflers, meet and stop for a quiet chat; a sweet-potato vendor appears, and at a distance of ten paces raises his hand to the tray he is carrying on his head, and utters his brief piercing cry: "Spuds!"

At midday a great silence falls upon the city. The sun, the good and wonderful sun, pours down its rays in torrents. Creaking, bouncing along the pavement, goes a wagon loaded with alfalfa; the bright green tatters undulate as they cast their shadows over the powerful wheels; a dog that was sleeping, with legs apart, in the warmth of the stones of the sidewalk, jumps up and barks.

And after the twilight, a soft, slow twilight, with all the charm of a water-colour, comes the night. In the belfries sounds forth the call to prayers. We hear it as we cross a solitary little square. We then enter the steep street. There are footsteps in the distance. A window closes. A rap of the knocker, the old rusty knocker, at a rustic vestibule.

In the soothing softness of the courtyard to which we come, I wish to meditate. The atmosphere is filled with aromas; there is the pale brightness of the lamp which diffuses a pleasant half-light through the corridor; a persistent, lulling, mysterious chirp of the crickets. . . . I am glad to rest and to dream here.

There is a voice in my heart which says: "My city, my beloved city, how I should like to revive you!"

And I feel, with the quiet and the peacefulness, the deep sadness of the provincial slumber.

1926

The Courtyard under the Moon (*El patio bajo la luna*), Editorial Stylo, Mexico, 1945, pp. 15–21.

Martín Luis Guzmán

(b. Chihuahua, Chih., 1887)

Although he originally figured in the generation of the Youth Club (Athenaeum) and collaborated with some of its members in cultural enterprises, Martín Luis Guzmán has few ideological affinities with this group. His experiences in the Revolution not only provide him, as in the case of José Vasconcelos, with the theme of a significant part of his work, but they even mould the character of his thought. A prose-writer with an effective style, he has written essays, novels, and biographies about one predominating preoccupation, that of Mexican politics.

Martín Luis Guzmán established his literary prestige with two masterly novels, *The Eagle and the Serpent* (*El águila y la serpiente*), 1928, and *The Shadow of the Chief* (*La sombra del caudillo*), 1930, which narrate detached episodes of the Mexican Revolution. But his literary beginnings were as an essayist. His first book, *The Mexican Quarrel* (*La querella de México*), written while the Revolution was in progress (1915), is a pessimistic analysis of the moral calibre of Mexican men. His next work, *On the Banks of the Hudson* (*A orillas del Hudson*), 1920, groups together a series of dissimilar works—poems in prose, essays, criticism, and politics—written in New York. In these pages, more than in the rest of the work of Guzmán, can be seen the trace of the Athenaeum, not only in the dedications to José Vasconcelos and Alfonso Reyes, but even in the literary tone and the cultural atmosphere which they exhibit. But though the pleasant fancies in the volume do not lack distinction, his most interesting pages are undoubtedly those on politics. As his later work confirms, it will be in this field that Guzmán's thought moves with most assurance and authority, although the media—essays, biography, novel, journalism—are varied.

Martín Luis Guzmán studied in Veracruz and in the capital, where he entered the Faculty of Law. He was a teacher of language and literature, Director of the National Library, and a Congressman in the National Congress. He resided for some time in the United States, and from 1924 to 1936 lived in Spain, where he directed leading journals. Upon his return to Mexico he devoted himself fundamentally to journalism, through the periodical *Time* (*Tiempo*), which he has been directing since 1942, and to the defence and propagation of Mexican liberal thought. He is a member of the Mexican Linguistic Academy, at the first congress of which (Mexico City, 1951) he led an unsuccessful insurgent movement.

ESSAYS: *The Mexican Quarrel* (*La querella de México*), Madrid, 1915; *On the Banks of the Hudson* (*A orillas del Hudson*), 1920; *Democratic Adventures* (*Aventuras democráticas*), Madrid, 1931; *Notes on a Personality* (*Apuntes sobre una personalidad*), 1954.

MY FRIEND CREDULITY

THE BIOGRAPHERS OF HENRY JAMES tell us that the sound of a Remington typewriter was an inexhaustible source of inspiration for that consummate artist of English prose. The word has spread (it has spread with the readiness of any good recipe for obtaining impossible things—the same thing occurred with spiritualism and, still not so long ago, with Metchnikoff's[1] sour milk), and at the present moment the machines of the aforementioned manufacturer are in great demand on the market. Not wishing to be outdone by anyone, I resolved of course to rid myself of my faithful Underwood, in exchange for which, plus a small additional sum of money, I have acquired a brand-new sonorous Remington. What a melodious sound it makes!

The coming of the new machine has brought about a complete revolution in my home: it has transformed methods, altered customs, and modified characters. Since both my wife and my children thought, after the first audition, that no machine is superior to a Remington for evoking hidden harmonies, we have set aside the pianola and the phonograph, no longer remember Beethoven or Caruso, and take pleasure in listening, morning and evening, only to the great masters of the typewriter. Who would ever have thought that it is possible to execute—with one or both hands, in red and blue colour—anything from a canto of the Iliad to a proclamation by Marinetti![2] Divine music! Much, of course, depends upon the interpretation.

When the baby gets cross, when he is mad with rage because I do not give him his bit of soup, or something else of that kind, and when he makes the walls of the house tremble by knocking against them his soft little head, I run to my machine, hastily uncover it and play from memory some very classical piece (*The Sacred Fount*, for

[1]Russian doctor and biologist who died in Paris in 1916.

[2]French poet, born in Egypt, of the late nineteenth and the early twentieth century.

example, which is my favourite). As I have always thought that children are just wild beasts, I calmly await the outcome. Before I enter upon the second paragraph, my son becomes quiet and approaches hesitantly, wavering between laughter and tears.

On me personally, the influence of the machine has been no less profound. At night, particularly since I have learned to interpret Apollinaire and Max Jacob, I have the habit of seating myself in front of my typewriter and starting to improvise in the dark. This is a pleasure so exquisite and so full of surprises, and so easy to indulge in, moreover, that I shall never be able sufficiently to thank the two French masters just mentioned—the Schoenberg and the Stravinsky, so to speak, of the new art—and a few image-forming poets and not a few dramatists of the latest fashion, like Paul Claudel, for having initiated me into their secrets. When, after an hour or two of intense improvisation, I light the lamp and read on the long sheet of paper the alphabetical traces of the mechanical symphony, my eyes confirm the beautiful cadences which a few moments before were intoxicating my ears. Then I also confirm the interest my neighbours take in my nocturnal concerts, and I see why the most enthusiastic of them, and the boldest, open the windows opposite mine, in spite of the severe winter cold, and shout applause at me which I can hardly hear in the midst of my musical rapture. The tapping on my Remington stirs some of them as much as the best arias of Galli-Curci, and plunges others into that inner contemplation that is inspired only by the violin, the organ, and the orchestra.

Part of my improvisations, the ones most comprehensible to the crowd, I send to the magazines or to the great dailies. Some have caused surprise and others genuine stupefaction. The periodicals for young people always receive them with open applause; those of the old men, the academic journals, pretend not to understand them, and scorn them. It is the eternal dislike for all that we can no longer learn to do. But the young follow me with such zeal that a real school is beginning to be formed. At this very moment the people are stirred up and in complete disagreement about the distinctive essence of the new manner and the name that should be given to it. Is it a cubism or a vorticism of literature? Would it be euphonious to call it Remingtonism? Mechanicism, no doubt, is the name it ought to be given, were it not for the deplorable associations that such a word may arouse.

On the Banks of the Hudson (*A orillas del Hudson*), Librería Editorial de Andrés Botas e Hijo, Mexico, 1920, pp. 139–41.

THE UNPOPULARITY OF THE SENSES

IF SOME WELL-ENDOWED MORTAL EYES had intervened in the creation of the world, we should be living within one of Tintoretto's pictures and the problem would be solved. (In passing: Fra Angelico would be the Christian paradise and Sorolla[3] the true hell.) Unfortunately it was not done that way. The world was made in the absence of all the human senses—begging the pardon of the One who heard the eternal harmony of the spheres—and to us is reserved the task of giving order to the chaos of images or discovering the spontaneous groups of beautiful images. To that contemplative work is given the name of art.

Art must be, first of all, a pleasing of the senses—let us say it, plainly and boldly. To them the intelligence owes its having learned to enjoy beautiful spectacles. There is in the elemental, but noble, sensation something like the purity of a liquid running through the fingers, the beginning of an undeniable beauty. Or, as a contemporary "aestheticist" would say, through the elemental sensation an attentive mind—capable of heeding a single sensation—also harmonizes itself in that unique way which causes us to wander through regions situated beyond what is being contemplated. It is the vision of essences, we would say in Platonic metaphor—but only in metaphor, on account of an inexplicable longing on the part of limited beings that dream of the portals to the infinite: sincerely, only in the senses lies the birth or death of beauty. Through many lives we could live on them, for the little things, for the common things, or for the great things.

For the little things? On an uneven surface, in a street dirty and dark and full of deafening noise, a woman's feet advance agilely, delicately, and well-shod; swiftly among the black holes move the tiny bright forms of the feet; they pick their way without vacillations, they are not soiled, and they leave no mark; they trace a pure movement, with an original rhythm, fine and rapid, which attracts the eyes and deceives them, a movement which suddenly begins to play with our vision.

For the common things? There is in Plato, lost among the books of the *Republic*, that passage delightful for its sobriety, for its delicacy, and for its naturalness. "On reaching this place, Polemarch began to whisper to Ademantos, who was beside him, on the further side: *he stretched out his arm, caught Ademantos by his clothes, near the shoulder, and pulling him towards himself, as he also bent over, said in his ear. . . .*"

[3]One of the most famous of the modern Spanish painters.

For the great things? If the sea were colourless it would lack importance, unless it had the intimate calmness of glass. Without colour the sky also would not exist, nor would our eyes see the beautiful playings of light at the placid twilight hour, when over the Valley[4] live only the immense vault and the cathedral tower.

But who has ever thought justly about the senses? Now less than ever. We live in years of confusion and disorder, in which men are again finding everything mysterious. There is spreading over the world a modern wave of religiosity—though a new and strange religiosity—and intuition, another form of faith, reigns alone. They speak to us of a completely new way of understanding God, discernible even in the biological definitions of Metchnikoff; humanity is turning towards a profound sense of things. The revolutionaries in painting, from Cézanne to vorticism, disintegrate the real image in order to intellectualize it and thus produce an individual, synthetic, and untransmittable impression; they are moving towards a "profound realism." Modern musicians pass through sound like live coals, seeking a direct path to our souls. In the new poetry, the image-formers, confident in this modern trend, content themselves with the raw fact, shorn of emotive relations, certain that they will soon awaken our feeling.

And meanwhile the procession which men do not see continues. Isadora Duncan, one of Rubens' three Graces, has abandoned her canvas to dance among us; naturally, it is a Grace less worldly, more serious, more cognizant of the truths of life. And the beautiful little Isadoras—beautiful and adorable—seem to come out of an abode of many centuries in order to convert before us the drawings on a Greek vase into a divine animated substance: one sees them, and one experiences the ineffable caress of their eyes. The little Isadoras are tiny and delicate; along with their instructress they recall to us, by their proportions, the Laocoon group. They play around her, and then they are minor motifs surrounding the major motif of a *scherzo*; if they are not playing, they are walking; if they are not walking, they are running, and then they put forward their shining limbs and leave trailing behind them their dishevelled hair; their running pace is perfect, without jerks, without quick lunges, a continuous advance in which a conflict between repose and movement is resolved.

For this reason the spectators do not see the procession, they interpret it.

On the Banks of the Hudson (*A orillas del Hudson*), Librería Editorial de Andrés Botas e Hijo, Mexico, 1920, pp. 29–31.

---

[4]Valley of Mexico, in which Mexico City is situated.

Ramón López Velarde

(b. Jerez, Zacatecas, 1888; d. Mexico, D.F., 1921)

The stages of the life of Ramón López Velarde are similar to those of many other young men from the provinces who come to Mexico City to test the powers of their minds. In the year of the appearance of *Blue* (*Azul*), by Rubén Darío, López Velarde is born in a small provincial town. From age twelve to fourteen he is sent to study at the Seminary of Zacatecas, from which he goes on to the one at Aguascalientes. About 1906 he begins his preparatory studies in the latter city, and two years later he enrols as a student of jurisprudence in the University of San Luis Potosí. In 1910 he meets Francisco I. Madero, who is just beginning to show his revolutionary passion. López Velarde joins his cause and perhaps collaborates in the formulation of the San Luis Plan,[1] but he does not go on with the revolutionary adventure; instead, he continues with his course, which he completes in 1912, when he receives his diploma in law. His first post is as a judge in El Venado, San Luis Potosí; but, dissatisfied with his lot or impelled by the revolutionary turmoil, he makes his first trip to Mexico City. Here he at first experiences the obscure destiny of the ambitious who come to the capital without credentials. He works for several newspapers, occupies some modest bureaucratic and teaching posts, forms quick and effusive friendships in the little world of the journalistic bohemia, and begins with all his zest, but also with all his timidity and religious scruples, a love-life within reach of his possibilities. He also begins to publish his verses. In 1916 his first book appears, with a title and a warmth which reveal the man who has not yet forgotten either his province or his strong love for its purity: *Devout Blood* (*La sangre devota*). But a year later, in the Valley of Mexico, occurs the death of the woman who had inspired his first verses, Josefa de los Ríos, "Fuensanta," of whom nothing is known except that she was in some way related to him by marriage and was some years older than he.

This first love does not pass beyond verses, and with it Ramón López Velarde loses the bond which held him most firmly to the world of his

[1]Plan for the Mexican Revolution of 1910, formulated by Madero and his collaborators.

adolescence. In his second book, *Anxiety* (*Zozobra*), 1917, can be seen the imprint made on his mind by his experiences in the city: "flowers of sin" he calls them. He is already thirty-one years of age, is still unmarried, and being a lover of all women, he has none as a steady companion. Two years later he dies, in the early morning of June 19, 1921, choked by pneumonia and pleurisy, killed by two of those malignant powers of the city which he had so much feared: the prophecy of a gypsy woman who had predicted his death by asphyxia, and a walk by night, after theatre and supper, in which he tried to defy the cold of the Valley unarmed, because he wished to continue to talk about Montaigne.

Two years after his death his friends made up a volume of some of his essays, *The Minute-hand* (*El minutero*), and in 1932 some of the poems which had remained unpublished or scattered about were gathered together in *The Sound of the Heart* (*El son del corazón*).

To help us understand his complex poetic work and to drive home to us his message, Ramón López Velarde finally came to write his admirable essays and his only poem of patriotic inspiration, *The Gentle Homeland* (*La suave patria*). But though this poem has become, as it were, the central point of his work, his writings in prose, on the contrary, are barely remembered or valued, in spite of their rare quality and their documentary importance. It may be stated, nevertheless, that if no more of López Velarde existed than *The Minute-hand* and his other essays collected later, they would suffice to win for him a prominent place among our writers. Although these pages were written for a newspaper, there is nothing in them of mere passing interest; on the contrary, much in them will endure. There is in them perfect equilibrium between emotion and thought, and between humour and keenness of wit—qualities which ennoble almost all his themes. Some of his essays show a lack of effectiveness in their composition, and others appear to be nothing but either commentary or notes preparatory to the writing of some of his poems; but in not a few we learn more about the inner life and thought of López Velarde than we do from the poems themselves. As examples of this we have *Novelty of the Homeland* (*Novedad de la patria*), so penetrating in its doctrine, or those intense erotic or transcendental confessions of the essays entitled *Masterpiece* (*Obra maestra*), *The Punitive Flower* (*La flor punitiva*), *Joseph of Arimathea and Eve* (*José de Arimatea y Eva*), worthy of the most strictly selected anthology.

ESSAYS: *The Minute-hand* (*El minutero*), 1923 (Preceded by poems by José Juan Tablada and Rafael López); *The Gift of February and Other Prose* (*El don de febrero y otras prosas*), 1952 (Prologue by Elena Molina Ortega); *Political Prose* (*Prosa política*), 1953 (Prologue by Elena Molina Ortega).

MASTERPIECE

THE TIGER IS, say, a metre in length. Its cage will cover a space of somewhat more than a square metre. The beast never rests. Like a Jew wandering over himself, he describes the sign of infinity with such mechanical inevitability that his tail, by beating against the bars, bleeds in just one spot.

The bachelor is the tiger that writes eights on the floor of solitude. He neither recedes nor advances.

To advance, he needs to be a father. And fatherhood is terrifying because its responsibilities are endless.

With a son, I should lose my peace forever. It is not that I want to push aside this question with pride or foolish pretensions. Who will amend the pattern for fecundity? On taking up my pencil I have been made to tremble at the risk of sacrilege, in spite of the fact that my conclusions are drawn precisely from whatever there may be in me of clemency, justice, devotion to the ideal, and even of cowardice.

I hope that mine is no false humility, just as it is no false fear that moves me to give to life one single attribute: namely, that of being formidable.

In deference to the good which struggles with evil, I should like to drop to my knees in order to go on tracing these bold lines. Within my concept of things, to bring into being new hearts is conceivable only through a continuous and unclouded faith or through a great love.

We are kings, because with forestalling scissors of noble sincerity we can save from the terrestrial nightmare millions of men who hang upon a kiss. The law of daily life appears to be the law of mendicancy and asphyxia, but the free will to deny life is almost divine.

Perhaps while I am enjoying this great power, the woman destined to give me the son of greater worth than I am is thinking of me. To the unwed maidens it is given by the Most High to repeat, without irreverence, the words of the Unique Lady: "Behold the handmaid." . . . And my will finally capitulates at the blink of an eyelash.

But my negative son has existed for some time. He exists in the transcendant glory of not having either his shoulders or his brow vexed with the burdens of horror, sanctity, beauty, and disgust. Although he is inferior to the vertebrates, in that he lacks the dignity of suffering, he lives within my suffering as an absolute angel, a neighbour to the human species. Made up of rectitude, solicitude, intransigence, eagerness for joy, and self-abnegation, the son that I have not had is my true masterpiece.

IN THE ANCESTRAL HOME

AGAINST MY WILL I set out on my dreaded return journey to my old home. After seven years I again passed through the leagues and leagues of caper bushes, until I reached the bridge leading to my village, the bridge without arches, the dramatic endless bridge at the sight of which the carriages halt if the swollen angry river bars their entrance. A brief and painful struggle in the crossing, the bridge being so useless as to be barely good enough for the swallows, these friendly helpers that will make an effort to accompany me, flying at the level of the walk.

In the big old house, I am given the room on the right. Ghosts, ghosts, ghosts. At ten o'clock at night, I manage to escape. In a turquoise sky, the lightning flash flagellates feathery masses of cloud. The city of Jerez impresses me as a pleasant mixture of fossil and miniature. I wander through it with my mind reeling and I am nothing but a homeless animal passing through an imaginary town. Amid the terror of the Civil War the foxes came up to the front terraces and gardens. I cease my inquisitive prowlings, because I have aroused the suspicions of a lover. After I am already in my bed, as though stuck into a sarcophagus, the clock of the Sanctuary strikes twelve. The thunder rolls and everything becomes nugatory.

The reveille with which the birds waken me persuades me that they have inherited poetic mastery, keeping themselves free from the commonplace ideas and vulgar jingle of the poetic coteries.

The journey is an electoral one. This accounts for the inevitable presence of the comic side. I am called a decadent and apathetic. I pay my tribute to the sublunar farce and take my compensation in the jewel of the Scorpion, which has been gleaming over me in the blue nakedness like the persistent animality of the skies.

I have made one discovery: I no longer know how to eat. From one invitation to another, coddled by the legendary urbanity of this place, I have come to realize my decline. Neither the genuine lace tablecloths, nor the legitimist bread lavished over the table, vying in its sweet odours with the rosebushes, nor even the ice-cold milk, in glasses which even the fingers of Artaxerxes could not grasp, have been able to whet my appetite. The young ladies cast their sly smiles over their tucked up skirts, and the children too celebrate at my expense. I ate just the same as they did. Now, in the honest village abundance, the unpleasant after-effects on my senses call for, as a responsory for the sumptuous yesterday, the great, deafening, mad groan which only the mother of the Arabs[2] could utter.

THE NEW HOMELAND

THE MATERIAL CALM of the country, in thirty years of peace, supported the idea of a country pompous, fabulously rich, honourable in the present and epic in the past. The years of suffering have been necessary in order to conceive of a native land less external, more modest, and probably more worthy.

The present moment in the world, considering everything along with the tameness of the struggle, seems to be a subjective moment. What wonder, then, that there is a lack of epic, outgoing poets?

Likewise, our concept of our homeland is today an introspective one. Rectifications made through experience, reducing to just measure the fame of our victories over Spaniards, Americans, and Frenchman, and the grandeur of our republicanism, have revealed to us a homeland which is not historical or political, but intimately our own.

We have discovered it through sensations and reflections that are daily and incessant, like the continuous prayer invented by San Silvino.

We see it as something made for the life of each one of us. It is something individual, sensuous, resigned, full of gesture, immune to wrongs inflicted upon it, even if it is covered with salt. We almost confuse it with the land we dwell upon.

It is not that we despoil it of its moral and traditional dress. We love it typical, like the ladies now turned to dust—if their dust exists—who used to foretell the weather for the year.

A great artist or a great thinker might give us the formula for this new homeland. The lack of a name for it has not prevented us from cultivating it in verses, pictures, and music. The vogue of the colonial, even in the buildings of the great merchants, indicates the return to nationality.

We had abandoned it unconsciously, in peripheric excursions which hardly followed any direction but the pecuniary. We return to nationality through love . . . and poverty.

[2]Hagar, mother of Ishmael. See Genesis 16 and 21.

As prodigal sons of a country that we cannot even define, we are beginning to examine it. Castilian and Moorish, crossed with Aztec, when once we scrape off its body the labour union coating, it shows—let us say it with one of those wisecracks of the days of fury—the coffee and milk of its skin.

"Mere literature"—someone will exclaim, one of those who do not understand the real function of words, or who have no sense of the arterial system of vocabulary. But we do indeed possess a country of a culminating nature and of a spirit intermediate, tripartite, and including all flavours.

The country is renewed in the face of the havoc suffered and the millions of inhabitants whose only concern is for an animal existence. Through what fibres will this divination of mine operate?

In the singing contests, the judges chat, indifferent to vulgar throats, until one pupil captivates them. It is the mysterious moment of feminine domination through her voice. In this way has sounded, since the Centenary, the voice of nationality.

Many are inattentive—people without love, bored, eager to pull away the tablecloth, put the chairs on the table, and leave.

But not a few lovers are here too, faithful through thick and thin, mad pursuers of their sweetheart seven nights a week, ready to applaud the very contradictions which are scattered over her territory and summed up in the vast contradiction of the capital.

In this theme, as in all, only through the impulses of the heart do we come near the truth. How can one interpret, dispassionately, our genuine, gentle urbanity, which serves as a background for violence, and over this the present-day germinations, precarious as those of seeds planted on the rooftops?

A future is being stirred up within the diocesan placidity of our habits. At times, we think that what is finest in the world is about to die, that the hungry mob will destroy the traditional treasures, the achievements of thought, the finished expressions of emotion.

Will the new homeland still retain prudence? Its coach doors still cover the landaus in which rode those ladies, mistresses of the Virgins' bedchamber, and the families that hear of Lenine have their homes lighted by the candles of Baron de la Castaña.[3] . . .

The alchemy of the Mexican character does not acknowledge any apparatus capable of measuring precisely its components of wit and solemnity, heroism and apathy, negligence and tidiness, virtues and vices, which tremble inert before the foreign menace, as in the Holy

[3]An undistinguished member of the Colonial aristocracy.

Places of childhood we trembled before the passage of the dog of evil.

Absorbing the atmosphere of her enigma, the new homeland continuously calls to us with her hoarse, pectoral voice. Neglect and anger, the two enemies of love, can do or attempt nothing against the prodigal beckoner; she asks only for enthusiasm.

She admits to her table the sincere, those with just a single degree of sincerity. In the manner in which she fills our glasses, she does not vary so much that she appears to have lost caste, nor does she vary so little as to weary us. With her we are always in preliminary ceremonies, at any hour, official or astronomical. Let us not be so rude as to put the chairs on the table.

ASHES AND POPLARS

THIS MORNING, as my brain awoke, the blue fleet of phantoms which sail between wakefulness and slumber had as a background the ashes and poplars of my country. Poplars in which there quivers a nervous silver and ashes in which there lies an abundant vigour! Are the parade ground, the Brilanti Garden, and the public walk so far away from me that they seem to me an oasis on a planet where I lived eight hundred years ago?

When I wrote verses and groaned in childish fashion under that foliage, I still did not suspect that I was to write the confession which more or less runs as follows: "My life is a dull battle between the pessimistic view of things and the charms of Eve. It is a silent and unrelenting battle between units of the feminine army and conclusions favouring sterility. On the one hand, the bone-dry thesis; on the other, the intoxicating hair, worthy of our getting hanged in it at those moments when the intensity of life coincides with the intensity of death—breasts expanding and contracting, contracting and expanding like the inexorable waves on a methodical beach; mouths of fragile appearance and cruel design; knees that tighten together with strategic premeditation; feet that cross each other and torture as a sailor eager to disembark would be tortured by the dark-coloured or pink-coloured end of a forbidden continent."

No, I never expected to come to say anything like that. My sadness, though violent, was as simple as the consciences of the virgins who take communion at dawn and afterwards pray for two hours, and after two hours' prayer return home and drink water, obeying a laudable scruple. My first sonnet did not foresee the ardent wooing of material benefits, nor did my first tear see outlined in the distance the comforting silhouette of Epicurus. What would the poplars and ashes think if they discovered, in the face of their habitual visitor in those times, the traces of pleasure?

Today my sadness is not violent, but it is deep. It is not a storm of which the perils can be eluded, but an inviolable and permanent relic of the shipwreck.

There can be few emotions more voluptuous than loftiness of soul, nourished by its own bitterness and rejecting any external alleviation. I bear within me the old pride of that house of aristocrats of my town—corner of Parroquia and Espejo streets—that has been kept uninhabited and locked up from time immemorial, and which still preserves its interior arrangement as at the moment of the death of its mistress. Not even a chair, nor a candelabrum, nor the image of a saint, has been touched. The bed in which the old lady died is still unmade. I am like that house. But I have opened one of my windows to let in the piercing rays of the sun. And the sensuous warmth burns through my helplessness and the warm smile of the heavenly body sets afire the mortuary sheets and the faithful rays carry warmth to the inner recesses of my decayed being.

O ashes and poplars that heard my plea in hesitant verses! Ashes and poplars: no longer have I a plea! I am calm as I was those quiet autumn afternoons when I was taken by the hand to contemplate the way in which your piled up leaves burned as the gardener set them on fire. I remember with detailed exactness the dense smoke and the crackling of the writhing dead leaves, at once confessor and martyr. But to my serenity have been added two elements unknown to me when I was studying my primer: pain and the flesh. I am breathing, my dear ashes and poplars, not your fragrance, but the absurd atmosphere of a room from which a corpse has just been removed and which displays the still unspent candles and the wave of sunshine that comes like the warmth of a woman's breath.

I hear the echo of my footsteps with the resonance of those of a night prowler walking through a cemetery. . . .

THE PUNITIVE FLOWER

To Mario Torroella

REPEATEDLY INFECTED in the garden of delights, there came neither despair, nor vengeance, nor even the beginnings of loathing. Instead, there came the solemn complaisance of those bearing the mark of the goddess. And in the ritualistic resignations, only the blood, red like the flashing of a banner, eagerly sought definitive escape.

Whether she be a transient woman of Puebla,[4] or one of Turin, it is all the same. Masculine passion, without falling into silliness or baseness, cannot demand legality of the purveyors of experience, at times in the fashion of bedlam. Let us be grateful, on the contrary, for the fact that by seasoning our persons they free them from insipidity and inculcate in them a vital sense of the bitterness of every root.

The leaders of the multitude, whether they be called politicians, sages, or artists, would produce more illustrious work if there were shared among them a prudent number of infections.

If to pay is the role of man, let us pay for our supreme moments of happiness, abominating that healthiness which organizes the islands of the Aegean Sea into an insurance company.

An orang-outang in spring shares his pleasures with the libidinous oldsters and the young initiates. The frenzy of lust drops its molten lead on our manhood; it is useless and cowardly to try to save ourselves from the crapulous affliction. In the end, an unquarantined old age will sigh for the operating table.

MEDITATION ON THE PUBLIC WALK

PRÓSPERO GARDUÑO is a manifest incompatibility—an evident incompatibility between his name and his philosophy. Próspero is a pessimist. Próspero Garduño has not married because he is afraid to lead a young heroine, dressed in white, to the Tower of Fecundity. Próspero has got up today with his head filled with idleness, love, and fine weather, as a wit of the Renaissance would say.

Our man goes out from his house, located on the Plaza de Armas. It cuts off one corner of the sidewalks about the Square. He takes the walk leading to the prison and the courthouse. He passes through the "Paradise" (bar and billiard room). Soon he turns the corner at the approach to the Sanctuary, a corner at which he comes upon a branch with three oranges still green. And following the long street, "Las Flores," if you wish to call it so, he reaches the public walk.

Once there, the idleness, love, and fine weather mentioned above move him to meditation. And he meditates thus: "There are hours when nature is like an immersion in delights, with well-concealed treachery

[4]Mexican city east of the capital.

behind it. This sun which envelops me in feminine warmth will tomorrow refuse to warm my blood. The wine which so often has magnified in my eyes the panorama of my birthplace will deny me its generosity. On these rustic benches, under these poplars, couples will sit in joy and health, and I shall be ill. They will bury me in a cemetery in which the village craftsmen have been erecting stones chipped by a novice's chisel. My eyes, which took delight in the walls over which climbs the tea rose, will decay rapidly. My feet, which crush these poplar leaves with pleasure and even with levity, as though they were treading upon a lover's carpet, will be food for worms. And also my breast, and my hands that gave alms and supported the lyre, and leaned upon the trees as a human companion and glided along hills gentler than those frequented by Solomon. To what purpose is anxiety? To what purpose labour? I shall be buried, and all the women in my town will feel somewhat widowed. I shall be missed by the children who sat down in the "little garden" on the same bench with me, opposite the Hinojosa Theatre. And that will be all. A sterile life is better than a life of corruption extending beyond ourselves. As Thales said, let no trace be left of us. Why feed the cemetery? I shall live this hour of melody, calm, and light, for myself and for my descendants. So I shall live it with an incisive intensity, with the intensity of one who wishes to live in himself alone the life of his race."

It struck twelve o'clock. Próspero Garduño, intoxicated with his sterile conclusions, started back towards his house; but in the street of "The Flowers" he hesitated before a wall on which overflowed abundantly the verdure and roses of a garden. And in the approach to the Sanctuary, the branch with the three oranges, still green, showed its fruitful rebuttal. And fruitful too was the rebuttal of gibberish of little girls coming out of school. And in the square was the fruitful rebuttal of some young mothers who, taking away their offspring in little carriages, defended themselves from the June sun with bright-coloured parasols, over which played the dark reflection of the branches. And Próspero Garduño felt that his thought was pitiful beside those young mothers carrying parasols.

JOSEPH OF ARIMATHEA

IN THE SACRED AND DIABOLICAL SIMULTANEITY of the universe, there are occasions when the flesh becomes hypnotized, between sterile sheets.

The phenomenon occurs in any of the twenty-four hours; the silence and solitude permeate us, those vessels of communication in which nature places itself at the level of the soul.

An unnamed mistress, a mistress of uncertain baptism, lies naked, against the nakedness of the man. But a slow collapse of the powers of each impresses upon them a balsamic life of mummies. At the head of the bed nods a falcon. In the rocking chair, on the intertangled clothing of the couple, the cat is shaking itself, with the human alarm of one about to plunge into the somnolent antechambers of death. Nothing is stirred up, nothing even makes a move. Her breath, which is almost not hers, alternates with ours, which is almost not ours. Inside the bedroom, a climate of ether pearl, an evaporation of something in blossom or of something in flight. Suddenly, when the vital stimulus asserts itself, we leap away ten leagues, so as not to hurt the privileged virgin with such a narcotic judgement, the mistress anointed by Joseph of Arimathea.

FILTH

SOMEONE WAS SPEAKING TO ME about how the pitiful calamity of filth is becoming accentuated, reflecting that only the animal world is filthy. In the presence of the cleanliness of the mineral and the vegetable domains, filth imposes itself as the most lamentable of all forms of evil.

If the universal plan of salvation is linear, there is at the same time no line which falls into the aberration of the human line, either in conduct or physiognomy. Does there exist any being more heroic than a woman at the moment she is fighting against the powers of light? And conversely, is there any zoological species that grows old as tragically as the female of the human species? The expression, turned into a grimace, offends me, not merely in my poetical roots, but in my very moral dignity.

I know that at this point all those will smile who have censured me for not having any other theme but the feminine. But that is because I can understand or feel nothing except through woman. Through her, with deference to the rhyme of Gustavus Adolphus, I have believed in God; only through her have I known the icy dagger of atheism. Hence it comes that I approach even abstract questions with an erotic temperament.

To earth descend the sun, the firmament, yea even light. . . . So I am tortured by evil when it plunges the heart into enigmas as sordid as that of the buried virgin, for what she refused to the lover most distinguished in countenance, will, and thought, she yields to the lowest beast, which not a suspicion of light ever reaches.

The worm gnaws virginities and experiences. Some of the ingenuous blaspheme; others torture themselves with the hair shirt. The Manichean proclaims the immortality of the soul. The orthodox theologian puts into syllogisms the omnipotence of the infinite goodness of the Uncreated. Rather than imagine an unlimited power, I prefer to see, back of the mariner's compass, the great face of Jesus, afflicted because in the work of the Father was mingled a great love. And such a fiction may not be canonical; but it springs from the effort of a filthy demon.

The Minute-hand (*El minutero*), Imprenta de México, Mexico, 1923; pp. 19–21; 33–5; 39–43; 51–4; 83–4; 99–101; 165–6; 169–70.

THE ROUT OF LANGUAGE

I WISH TO SPEAK TO YOU this morning about the rout of language. That is, about the return of language to the primitive age in which it was the instrument of man and not his despot. I think, at times, that the barbarian artists who created the wheel and the axe with the words to designate them were less crude in their minds than the citizen of today, who is but a dead phonograph needle. I should like to arouse horror at the industrialism of language; but I protest that my intention is far from one of propaganda, and to that I shall even prefer that opinions differ from mine. The identity of ideas, in uniform like common soldiers, makes me just as uncomfortable as would the sight of an identical face in all women.

There can be few things more vain than talking for talking's sake. And few things are so much to the taste of Mexicans as just that. We are charmed by language as a final end, and we all broadcast our utterances in hollow tirades, from the young typist to the pretentious poet. In the truly literary circles, the abuse of words has been fostered, on occasion, by bad Peninsular prose, and on occasion too by the inhumane tendency of the Parnassians. Outside the literary circles, the factors which contribute towards supporting wordiness are less technical, but no less effective. Of course, vulgarity of mind moves people to declaim. Anyone who lacks an inner life naturally pretends to have one by nauseating people with his theatrical discourses. So, in order to feign a medical personality, the quacks hold forth, extravagantly reciting the curative powers of the serpent which they exhibit coiled around an arm. Here it is pertinent to mention also the advantage there is, in a society which neither reads nor thinks, in repeating loudly, obstinately, and profusely the accepted opinion. The buying of ready-made clothing is always an easy thing in a democracy. Looking at the question squarely, the charlatan is useful when he hammers away at what others have thought—just as the tailor is useful when he sells ready-made clothing. And I do not see why one should tolerate the tailor and at the same time detest the journalist who, for ten *centavos*, serves us every morning with ready-made poetry, ready-made politics, sensational reporting, and an editorial of spurious lineage.

Language has been converted from slave to cruel mistress. It no longer comes along docilely when called. Nowadays language is man's tyrant and tries at all times to ride him, spur him, and infect him with a comic loquacity. The victims of language can be counted by the thousands. I shall mention just one, one in whom Spain showed the greatest hope. Doubtless you have all noticed the verbal degeneration of Villaespesa, who publishes a book every second month.

Language, which in the infancy of the world so meekly lent itself to express the mind and heart of the sons of Adam, seems to have imitated the custom of those young ladies who, submissive and gentle while fiancées, once the papers are signed turn into an epidemic or into martial law. Everyone knows of more than one husband who has been beaten. And if language is the wife of the man of letters, I assure you that almost all our literary men are beaten by their wives.

What about the bachelor men of letters? They are even worse off, because they are scratched, prematurely, by their sweethearts.

Inversion, in the literary art, of rational processes and of vital processes, has filled the measure of the absurd. No longer does the mind dictate to language; now it is language that dictates to the mind. And wretched dictation it is that a slave gives to her master! Now they say "I have this phrase that sounds well"; but the question is: what shall I think or feel in order to express it by inserting this phrase that sounds well? The academic man has his wine cellar packed full of phrases; the Modernist has overstocked with phrases. But we ask: what will the academic man and the Modernist think or feel to put their phrases into use? This is the field in which language has won the victory and in which its rout would be advantageous.

These false artists, who claim to extract from language the sap of life, bear a resemblance, I know not whether lamentable or ridiculous, to the decrepit sages who, with the extinction of their sexual powers, strive eagerly to create a succession by spontaneous generation. Poor Fausts, over whose shoulders no power, diabolical or celestial, will cast the cloak of virile festivities! Poor Fausts, who in century after century of fruitless vigil will not succeed in lifting into folios or test-tubes the magic founts, the founts which the flaming sword of youth calls forth from the rock!

Both the poet who follows tradition and the one who goes along with the caravan of today possess recipes worthy of envy in any kitchen. The Modernist possesses, for example, this recipe: Heroic ducks. After cooking, cut into quarters, daub with Marquina[5] sauce, cover with a coating of verses from Darío's *Triumphal March* (*Marcha triunfal*), let soak, and when out of the fire decorate with condor beaks from Chocano.[6] The traditionalist will not know how to prepare heroic ducks, but he is master of the following recipe for classical stew. Cut a loin of pork into thin pieces. Put into a frying pan from Camacho's wedding.[7] Mix with it parsley from don José María de Pereda and vinegar from don Juan Valera. Set over the slow fire of a notary public's document, taking care that it does not burn. Serve decorated with archaisms from *El Cid*.[8]

Our writers concoct paragraphs and strophes like bad stew. In this way the practice of writing has turned into a huckster's trade and a swindler's snare.

Language has been divorced from spirit, which it hardly touches at a single point. It has been believed that luxuriousness of expression, and in general rhetorical ornament, must be sought far away from the flutter of the wings of Psyche. I am inclined to think, on the contrary, that to achieve the most exquisite elegance of expression there is nothing better than cutting the silk material of language upon the living form of the deity that animates us. If an artificial preciosity or a cold puristic correctness prompts us to cut purple cloth and brocade on patterns of grammar or rhetoric for the purpose of clothing the soul, we run the risk of having the concordant and elusive deity break the brocade and purple cloth, because we did not previously fit them to its butterfly form. Before putting pen to paper one must consult every fleeting shade of the butterfly's wing. I think that the soul

[5]Spanish poet of the Modernist school, led by Darío.

[6]Modern Peruvian poet.

[7]A wedding described in *Don Quijote*.

[8]The national epic of Spain.

of the coarsest man stores up, in its wings, swift-passing multiple shades of colour. Anyone capable of looking at these shades, one by one, and capable also of transmitting them, through a faithful and total adaptation of the language to the shade, will achieve the authentic splendour of language and will master it. For that reason the power of meditative writers becomes formidable, from Prince Góngora to Darío and Lugones—because they, in their quarter-hour of mental prayer, have penetrated down to areas of consciousness unsuspected by those who, on the level of the fallow land, entertain themselves with futile prattle. Doctor González Martínez has already said it, in the felicitous way in which he says everything: the soul is stirred by its exclusive joys, by its own instinct, and by its particular pain. The transmission of this individuality is not achieved by proclamations from the teeth out, nor by manifestos with source no deeper than the skin.

On more than one occasion I have tried to convince myself that the best attitude of the man of letters is that of a conversationalist. Conversational literature is based upon sincerity. Those who converse rid themselves of every sterile purpose. At the banquet table cordiality holds sway; the wines and viands, in their effect upon sociability, consolidate mutual intimacy; the guests try to reveal their hearts to one another precisely and naturally; but when the toasts come on, the guests put themselves under restraint and a tense expectancy comes over the gathering. That is because the time has come for the serious speech. Life has stopped being lived and is about to be reduced to rhetoric.

Dramatists and novelists resort to the same deceitful measures. The dramatist, following a superimposed strategy, will calculate, like any orator at a civic commemoration, just where the audience must applaud. It does not matter that the device oversteps the bounds of the crude. A husband will leave the house; the seducer will have slipped in, like the most apt pupil of the seducers of Seville; the unfaithful spouse will receive the descendant of don Juan de Mañara. Suddenly, the husband will surprise them. Then there will be a roar with a variant of that speech in the *New Drama* (*Drama nuevo*):[9] "The faithless spouse trembles, and ungrateful too!" The adulteress will rush upon the husband and cover his eyes. The seducer, taking advantage of the situation, will hide in a closet. The husband, throwing his Alice to the floor, will shoot off his revolver right and left. One of the shots will

[9]Written by Tamayo y Baus, a Spanish dramatist of the nineteenth century.

pierce the closet and kill the seducer. The audience will applaud the punishment of the culprit.

The startling effect is likewise sought in the novel. It really seems that all the pen-wielders take as their models those penniless suitors who, to get at the strong-box of a rich woman, virgin, or widow, exploit the fashion-plate and rush thither luxuriously attired. Today, as always, with a braggart's stance, he lands upon the noisy isle of fame and enters the harbour of a profitable marriage. The candidates for the laurel wreath and the bridal chamber go shares in the enterprise.

The solitary soul in the deep intimacy of its lofty castle knows how to distinguish the sincere page from the mercenary suitor. If this day I felt inclined to converse with my soul, I would address it in these terms: "I love you for your marvellous faculty of silence, because in silence you shower upon me your emotion, and involve yourself in mine, reclining upon the minutes, as upon deaf-mute slaves. Solitary and proud, you hang upon my neck only when we are a couple lost in the emptiness of solitude and the chaos of silence. Our gazes meet in a theosophical effluvium and copy one another like two parallel mirrors. My terrestrial lips have not spoken to you, but already you know the order in which I would kiss your mouth, your neck, and your eyelids. Oh soul, inseparable sibyl, I know not where you end and I begin: we are two turns of the same resplendent knot, the same knot of love! Because you are volcanic, I cling to you; because you are silent, I fear you. It seems to me that in your hatred of words you will finally mutilate me by tearing out my tongue by the roots and casting it from the ogival arch to the dogs of your fief. In your mouth, with its thirst for pleasure, the vowel does not link to the consonant when the pleasure is burning at a white heat; you break into an inarticulate cry. Since our embrace is a throb of eternity, a stirring of darkness over a dark passageway, let silence for us be absolute. Let the peace of the crypts where the statues lie come upon us. Let the smile of light, as in the crypts, filter in over us. And may our kiss, like the marble kiss of prostrate statues, be insatiable and unremitting.

Possibly the gravest consequence of artificial and prodigal language is the forsaking of the soul. With the rash outpouring of words, the soul is grieved, like a little girl who wants to tell us her feelings and cannot do so, because she is prevented by the uproar of a riot. The soul knows how to keep silence like a girl in love hurt by her lover's lack of attention and by his stupid forgetfulness for the sake of indulging in superficial eloquence. For my part, I confess that, in order to hear the laconic message of my own soul, I concentrate with that intensity with which in the depth of the night we feel the tireless throbbing of our temples and listen to the methodical passage of our blood over the pillow. The soul finds its delight in establishing its intimacy with us; but to do so it demands the solitude and the silence of the bedroom. My great desire is to reject any word or syllable which does not issue from the burning of my bones. And when I am eager to cast out the faintest suggestion of things foreign to my true nature, it is because within my palpitating soul there is an urge towards a religious and voluptuous dance of an Asiatic rite. And the dancer will not throw her nakedness or frenzy over my lips as long as she hears me mumble an idle syllable.

Lecture delivered at the University of the People (Universidad Popular), Sunday, March 26, 1916

Modern Life (*Vida Moderna*), Mexico, April 12, 1916. Reproduced in R. L. V., *The Gift of February and Other Articles* (*El don de Febrero y otras prosas*). Prologue and compilation by Elena Molina Ortega, Imprenta Universitaria, Mexico, 1952, pp. 232–39.

MOTHER EARTH

OUR FOREFATHERS DIED without fear concerning the fate that awaited their bodies in the dark slime of the grave. Religion taught our ancestors through the example of Jesus, Who was once in the tomb, and through the century-old custom of giving bodies an ecclesiastical burial. O you penitent men who suffered mortification heroically; O brave libertines who fearlessly sought carnal adventure; O nuns taught to see heaven each day in the perspective of ecstasy; O grandmothers who, in spite of all, with your many years and your innumerable children, with a few candles about you, seemed, by the blissfulness of your faces, to be sweethearts who had died still virgins; and even you unbelievers of yesteryear, is it not true that you were calm at the thought of sleeping your last sleep in the earth which men have called mother from the moment of the birth of Mythology?

Even the language of past years prevented the rise of doubt: dust returned to dust. There was nothing to fear.

But we, readers of hair-raising little gazettes, witnesses of vegetative phenomena in corpses, familiar with innumerable impressive contemporary statistics about crematory ovens, do not even have, as compensation for the daily worries of modern life, the firm belief in the peace of the tomb. A sophistical philosophy enervates us, and we fear, with the most terrifying of fears, an incorporation among the coffin boards of our twentieth-century bones, if the coffin still endures, slothful for virtue and powerless for evil. Pregnant women remind us in our pessimism of the daily procreation of beings destined to life, death, and the asphyxia with which the earth, in unknown ways, torments the flesh, the bones, and the dust of the dead.

Amid such anxieties, which like imaginary creations arise from common, familiar places in the wretched knowledge of humanity, to whom do we go in quest of salvation? To whom shall I turn my eyes to be cured of my horror of the grave, a horror which for me is a paternal heritage? I turn to you, whom I have loved. To you, woman of the autumn who arrives at the evening of life without having listened to disquieting theories. I turn to you, Lady of the Twilight, in complete faith—to you in whose adoration are consumed in an irresistible romantic fire sixty months of my youth; to you, a harvest which brought joy to farmer lads who today are scarcely a memory in your mind, now that you are a woman defeated by time; to you, fruit of past grape harvests for my adolescent mouth; to you, who in times when we knew each other had a heart like a beach where shattered boats augured that the shipwreck of your passion was inevitable; to you, who in your bedimmed pupils have the light of a shrinking room which makes clear the courses of my cunning fantasies. When I became enamoured of your charm (which you know, in spite of my perpetually sealed lips), I did not yet know the budding novelist to whom love is the great melancholy of the sex. You are certain that my head has become ennobled with thoughts that are yours; that my back would have endured obstinate downpours of rain to have colloquies with you at the rusty grating of oblivion; that the best day for my heart would be the one in which your ear would come listening to the diseased vitals, and certain are you too that my knee will never fail in the genuflexion it owes you. So then, free my knees, my heart, my back, and my head from a cruel and foreshadowed animation in the bosom of the earth. Heal me of this childish fear, for to do this you have the grace, in its two great senses: in the grave sense of theology and in the pleasant sense as shown in the beauty of woman, the power of song, the harmony of line, and the effectiveness of verse. Make me love Mother Earth.

Modern Life (*Vida Moderna*), Mexico, July 13, 1916. Reproduced in R. L. V., *The Gift of February and Other Articles* (*El don de febrero y otras prosas*). Prologue and compilation by Elena Molina Ortega, Imprenta Universitaria, Mexico, 1952, pp. 244–46.

Alfonso Reyes

(b. Monterrey, N. L., 1889)

In the very first literary productions of Alfonso Reyes, in those famous works of his youth, *Aesthetic Questions* (*Cuestiones estéticas*), 1911, one can detect the rudiments of his monumental work of later years. Classical culture, investigations into literary theory, the literature of Spain, France, England, and Mexico, the work of Goethe, inclinations which he will hold fast and develop in his later books, have in that book of his youth a propitious birth. As was then indicated, he was to be primarily an essayist, even though some consider him first of all a poet, on account of his beautiful lyrical works, and though he has also successfully cultivated narrative prose and drama. With a curiosity awake to all movements, always interested in expressions of the human spirit wherever they might arise, a master and disseminator of fundamental cultural traditions, Reyes, the man universal and encyclopaedic, manifests in Mexico the most perfect example of the man of letters.

With his essays alone one could make up an anthology which would illustrate most of the types and forms that are customary in the genre. And if we wished instead to make an inventory of his themes, we should see the multiple directions which those pages follow: pure divagations, literary criticism, humanistic themes, literary theory, meditations on America, and miscellaneous topics. Different forms and themes have alternated and combined in his work, following a distribution which suggests that of a well-ordered life—meditations on our American and Mexican destiny and poetic activities; reflections upon the phenomenon of literature and fantasies in which every form of curiosity finds its place; classical antiquity brought down to our present-day preoccupations and the calling of our attention to the excellence of modern thought, and even the wit and playfulness which keeps his face attractive amid the dryness of investigations, or the moral and philosophic lesson expressed so amusingly as to appear sheer frivolity.

The keynote of his style is not passion or the dramatic, nor is it imaginative exuberance or serene harmony of proportion, or keen brilliance or the warm tremor of feeling. These styles he handles with equal success and he goes from one to another with perfect mastery; he enriches himself with all types of experience and knows how to expose ideas with that subtle art of the musician in Proust's novel whose sonata seemed to reveal a "beautiful object" which already existed. He uses learning of the total kind, not only of the sciences and the arts but of all human experience, and it is remarkable how he can illuminate the most baffling cultural problems with a popular tale or an example bringing in personages from the animal kingdom. At times the richness of the elements, the multiplicity of incitations and allusions, and the virtuosity of the mental twist remind us of a certain baroque tendency, so frequent in our aesthetic productions. But Alfonso Reyes resolves this into a brilliant abundance of each of its beauties while remaining faithful to the classical architecture which regulates and supports his thought. He expresses himself with the easy elegance of a god ordering the universe. He possesses an infused grace which accompanies him in his undertakings, and we might wonder, like Sor Juana, whether he might owe it to the savoury condiments of soil.

The ever-abundant productivity which Alfonso Reyes has maintained from the beginning has created for Mexican culture work of the greatest splendour and one of its strongest claims to glory. While other Mexicans represent what is irreducible in our national entity, its obscure and violent originality, the work and personality of Reyes, one might say, start off from the precise point where that individuality begins to be intelligible to the rest of the world. In his long years of glorious fecundity, he has preferred the double task of preserving among us the operation of fundamental cultural traditions and attention to the witnesses of the spirit, while at the same time he has made communicable to the world what is best in us.

On account of the brilliant and lavish beauty of his style, his firm control over all the shadings in literary expression, and the clarity and originality of his studies and essays, especially in the field of literary theory, Alfonso Reyes is a writer who brings honour to Mexican culture.

Reyes began his studies in Monterrey, and in 1905 he moved to Mexico City to continue them in the National Preparatory School. In the same year he published his first verses in *The Spectator* (*El Espectador*), of Monterrey. While he was taking his law course, which he was to finish in 1913, he took part in the cultural activities of the Youth Club (Ateneo de la Juventud). Political events and the tragic death of his father, General Bernardo Reyes, brought about his departure for Europe about the middle of 1913. In France and Spain, where he remained from 1914 to 1927, he served in diplomatic posts and worked as a philologist in the Centre of Historical Studies in Madrid. From 1927 to 1939 he represented Mexico in Buenos Aires and in Rio de Janeiro. Early in 1939 he returned permanently to Mexico, where he organized and presided over the House of Spain (*Casa de España*), which soon became the College of Mexico (*Colegio de México*). At various periods in his life he has taught literature. Universities and other academic institutions of Europe and America have conferred upon him the greatest academic honours and have solicited for him the Nobel Prize. Since 1957 he has been President of the Mexican Academy, and he is an original member of the National College (Colegio Nacional). In 1955, having completed fifty years of his literary career, he had showered upon him the highest honours and acclaim, and the Institute of Economic Culture (Fondo de Cultura Económica) began the publication of his complete works.

CRITICISM, ESSAYS, AND MEMOIRS: *The "Rustic Poems" of Manuel José Othón* (*Los "Poemas rusticos" de Manuel José Othón*), 1910; *Aesthetic Questions* (*Cuestiones estéticas*), Paris, 1910–11; *Landscape in Mexican Poetry of the Nineteenth Century* (*El paisaje en la poesía mexicana del siglo XIX*), 1911; *The Suicide* (*El suicida*), Madrid, 1917, 1954; *Vision of Anáhuac* (*Visión de Anáhuac*), San José de Costa Rica, 1917–Madrid, 1923, 1953, 1956; *Cartoons of Madrid* (*Cartones de Madrid*), 1917; *Real and Imaginary Portraits* (*Retratos reales e imaginarios*), 1920; *Sympathies and Differences* (*Simpatías y diferencias*), Madrid, 1921–26, 1945 (2nd edition with Prologue by Antonio Castro Leal); *The Hunter* (*El cazador*), Madrid, 1921, 1954; *The Evolution of Mexico* (*L'évolution du Méxique*), Paris, 1923; *Calendar* (*Calendario*), Madrid, 1924; *Simple Observations about Mexico* (*Simples rémarques sur le Méxique*), Paris, 1926; *Gongorine Questions* (*Cuestiones gongorinas*), Madrid, 1927; *Discourse by Virgil* (*Discurso por Virgilio*), 1931–Buenos Aires, 1937; *By Return Mail* (*A vuelta de correo*), Rio de Janeiro, 1932; *On American Day* (*En el día americano*), Rio de Janeiro, 1932; *Political Wisdom* (*Atenea política*), Rio de Janeiro, 1932–Santiago de Chile, 1933; *Train of Waves* (*Tren de ondas*), Rio de Janeiro, 1932; *A Vote for the University of the North* (*Voto por la Universidad del Norte*), Rio de Janeiro, 1933; *The Fall* (*La caída*), Rio de Janeiro, 1933; *The Passing of Amado Nervo* (*Tránsito de Amado Nervo*), Santiago de Chile, 1937; *The Political Opinion of Goethe* (*Idea política de Goethe*), 1937; *The Vespers of Spain* (*Las vísperas de España*), Buenos Aires, 1937: Contains the *Cartoons of Madrid, In the Window of Toledo* (*En el ventillado de Toledo*), *Hours of Burgos* (*Horas de Burgos*), *The Dart* (*La saeta*), *Christmas Flight* (*Fuga de navidad*), and others not previously published; *Monterrey*, Correo Literario of Rio de Janeiro and Buenos Aires, 14 numbers, of which the penultimate has two editions, one for Rio de Janeiro and the other for Buenos Aires, 1930 to 1937; *Homily in Support of Culture* (*Homilía por la cultura*), 1938; *Those Days* (*Aquellos días*), Santiago de Chile, 1938; *Mallarmé Among Us* (*Mallarmé entre nostros*), Buenos Aires, 1938, 1955; *Chapters of Spanish Literature*. First Series (*Capítulos de literatura española. Primera serie*), 1939; *Criticism in the Athenian Age* (*La crítica en la Edad Ateniense*), 1941; *Immediate Past* (*Pasado inmediato*), 1941; *The Seven on Deva* (*Los siete sobre Deva*), 1942; The Old Rhetoric (La antigua retórica), 1942; *Land of Mystery* (*Última Tule*), 1942; The Literary Experience (La experiencia literaria), Buenos Aires, 1942, 1952; *The Boundary: Prolegomena to Literary Theory* (*El deslinde: prolegómenos a la teoría literaria*), 1944; *Trials and Orientations* (*Tentativas y orientaciones*), 1944; *Two or Three Worlds* (*Dos o tres mundos*), 1944; North and South (*Norte y Sur*), 1945; *Three Points in Literary Exegesis* (*Tres puntos de exegética literaria*), 1944; *Chapters of Spanish Literature. Second Series* (*Capítulos de literatura espanola. Segunda serie*), 1945; *Calendar and Train of Waves* (*Calendario y Tren de ondas*), 1945; *Panorama of Brazil* (*Panorama de Brasil*), 1945; *Juan Ruiz de Alarcón* (in English), in *Tribute to Albert Schweitzer*, Cambridge, Mass., 1945; *Discourses in the Mexican Linguistic Academy* (*Discursos en la Academia Mexicana de la Lengua*), 1945 (Contains discourses by Jaime Torres Bodet and A. R.); *Native Letters* (*las letras patrias*), in *Mexico and Culture* (*México y la cultura*), 1946; *It Was in May, in May* (*Por mayo era, por mayo*), 1946; *Work and Days* (*Los trabajos y los días*), 1946; *Tribute by the National College to The Teacher Antonio Caso* (*Homenaje de El Colegio Nacional al Maestro Antonio Caso*), 1946; *By Pencil* (*A lápiz*), 1947; *Literary Hoaxes* (*Burlas literarias*), 1919–22, 1947; *Pleasant Company* (*Grata compañía*), 1948; *Among Books* (*Entre libros*), 1948; *On an Author Censured in the "Quijote": Antonio de Torquemada* (*De un autor censurado en el "Quijote": Antonio de Torquemada*), 1948; *Panorama of the Greek Religion* (*Panorama de la religión griega*), 1948; *Letters of New Spain* (*Letras de la Nueva España*), 1948; *Syrtes* (*Sirtes*), 1949; *Viva Voce* (*De viva voz*), 1949; *Conference of Shades. Hellenic Studies* (*Junta de sombras. Estudios helénicos*), 1949; *My Idea of History* (*Mi idea de la historia*), Monterrey, 1949; *Madrid Conversations* (*Tertulia de Madrid*), Buenos Aires, 1950; *Four Great Minds* (*Cuatro ingenios*), Buenos Aires, 1950; *The Economic Horizon in the Early Days of Greece* (*El horizonte económico en los alberes de Grecia*), 1950; *Outlines of Literary History* (*Trazos de historia literaria*), Buenos Aires, 1950; *Relating to the Study of the Greek Religion* (*El torno al estudio de la religión griega*), 1951; *Anchorages* (*Ancorajes*), 1951; *Medallions* (*Medallones*), Buenos Aires, 1951; *The X on the Brow* (*La X en la frente*), 1952; *Marginalia. First Series, 1946–1951*, 1952; *Memories of Kitchen and Wine-cellar* (*Memorias de cocina y bodega*), 1953; *Powder Tree* (*Árbol de pólvora*), 1953; *Kinsfolk* (*Parentalia*), 1954; *Marginalia. Second Series, 1909–1954*; *Goethe's Trajectory* (*Trayectoria de Goethe*), 1954; *Complete Works* (*Obras completas*), I, 1955–II, III, and IV, 1956–V and VI, 1957; *True Hoaxes. First Hundred* (*Las burlas veras, Primer ciento*), 1957; *Hellenic Studies* (*Estudios helénicos*), 1957; *Complete Works* (*Obras Completas*), VII, VIII, 1958.

PALINODE ON DUST

IS THIS THE MOST TRANSPARENT REGION of the air? What have you done, then, with my high metaphysical valley? Why is it blurred, why is it turned yellow? The little whirls of earth run over it like will-o'-the-wisps. Upon it fall the coats of sepia, which rob the landscape of its depth and precipitate the far and the near into a single spectral plane, giving to its features and colours the unreality of a grotesque decalcomania, of an artificial old print, of a leaf prematurely withered.

With loathing we bite the sands. And the dust gets caught in our throats and with its hands cuts off our breath. It tries to asphyxiate us and strangle us. Subterranean howls come stealthily in the dust, which beneath its blanket kills the king. Invisible volleys come, a cunning attack against which there is no defence; a slow microbian dynamite; atoms in rebellion and inimical to any organized form; the superfluous energy of creation resentful in the knowledge that it is useless; persistent vengeance of dust, the oldest thing in the world. It is the final state of matter, which was born amid the blessings of the waters and—through the viscosity of life—is reduced first to mineral statuary, to break up finally into this diminutive disintegration of all that exists. It is a dwindling of things, on the way to being nothing, an annihilation without glory; a collapse of inertias, "entropy"; vengeance upon vengeance of the dust, the lowest thing in the world.

O driers-up of lakes, destroyers of forests! Cutters of lungs and breakers of magic mirrors! And when the mountains of andesite come down, in the slow landslide of the amphitheatre which guards and protects us, you will see how, sucked into the black revolving funnel, a waterspout of filth, our very valley disappears. The desert tires of the insults of the cities; tires of the human footstep, which urbanizes wherever it passes, crushing the dust upon the ground; tires of waiting for centuries and centuries. Behold: against the delightful flowers of stone, against the dwellings and the streets, against the gardens and the towers, it hurls the nefarious horsemen of Attila, the swift and savage troop of grey and yellow hooves. Vengeance upon vengeance of the dust. O planet condemned to be desert, the Mussulman wave of dust-clouds is preparing to sweep away all traces of you!

And once we are ants—the perfect state—we shall run along the avenues of cones made of chips and chaff, proud of having accumulated the sad residues and fuzz; incapable of unity, orphan addends of addition; incapable of being an individual, incapable of art and spirit—which were produced only in the most insolent societies, Greece and Renaissance Italy—perhaps repeating with the Romantic, whose voice is now scarcely heeded, that glory is a weary thing woven from dust and sunshine.

What a miserable future! Dust and torpor! Be not deceived, you people who build on soft subsoil, where the houses sink, the walls crack, and the façades tumble down. Your monuments fall one by one. Your bard, turned to dust, will no longer be able to sound his trumpet. Your churches, ships caught in undertow, with plummet broken, display their crosses a-tilt. O valley, you are a sea of frugal fluctuation! Its measure is unseen by the generations. O figure of Biblical punishments, you are sinking and being swept away! "A hundred cities stoned this valley," says your poet.*

*Carlos Pellicer, *Rhetoric of the Landscape* (*Retórica del paisaje*).

Come and buy: everything is carefully wrapped up in dust. The geological catastrophe is being awaited as we play: the origin of art, which is a way of making sport with death. Naples and Mexico: filth and song, Caruso used to say. Lands of volcanic disintegration, daughters of fire, mothers of ash. The pipe of lava is the compendium. An earthy Odysseus, furrowed with scars, smokes in it his dissolving philosophy. Stevenson one day confessed to himself, in horror, that all matter produces a contamination of dust, that everything is bound up with filth. What, O Ruskin, could be the true "ethics of the dust"? In dust we are born, and in it we die. Dust is the alpha and the omega. And what if it were the true god?

Perhaps dust is time itself, the supporter of consciousness. Perhaps the material corpuscle is confused with the moment of time. Hence the theories of Zeno, who ends by denying motion, an illusion of the moving thing mounted on a trajectory, swift-footed Achilles panting along behind a tortoise. Hence the exasperation of Faust, through whose fingers slips the single beat of happiness: "Stop. You *were* so beautiful!" Dust of moments which the mind weaves into an illusion of continuity, like that spun by the cinema. By the law of minimum effort—the conservation of energy, of Fermat—the person perceives in units, creating for himself that "biological arithmetic" of which Charles Henry speaks, that notion of cardinal numbers on which rests even the theology of Saint Thomas. The trace of successive static points deposits, in the receptacle of the soul, the illusion of the Bergsonian flow. The irreducible monads of Leibniz are bound together like interlinked atoms. Natural philosophy debates the conflict between the continuous and the discontinuous, between the physics of waves, considering the ether as horse, and corpuscular or radiant physics, which considers only the atom as rider. Does dust ride on the wave, or is it the wave? Infinitesimal calculation measures the stream of time, and the calculation of quantities fixes its immovable points. What of synthesis? Continuity, says Einstein, in a structure of space, a "field" as construed by Faraday. The unit is a focus of energy, a phenomenon, an atom, perhaps a grain of dust. Heraclitus, master of flux, allows himself to be measured in spans by Democritus, the capturer of sands. The river, Góngora would say, is resolved into a rosary of beads.

Why do we not imagine Democritus, at that morning hour when the Muses speak as the poets claimed, bending over his studies, his head resting on his hand, momentarily absorbed, in one of those lapses of attention which inspiration utilizes to pierce the consciousness with particles of surrounding reality, grapeshot of the world's dust, a cosmic wound which perchance nourishes thoughts? A ray of sunshine, still with the gentleness of the dawn, passes through the room like a banner of light, like the ghostly sail of a ship. A vibrating net which captures, in its course, the invisible life of space, shows to the eyes of the astonished philosopher that whole swarm of little dust particles which fill the air. A dance of luminous points moves back and forth, like a school of fish in confusion seeking in vain to escape the net-haul of light. The philosopher plunges his hand into the sunlight, shakes it about lightly, and organizes whirls of dust. Intuition springs into action: there arises in his mind the figure of the material atom, which would not exist without dust. The atom is the ultimate terminus of divisibility in matter—at least in intention, since it allows for divisors more and more intimate. Without the atom, matter would be destructible and not divisible. Every whole is a summation, a harmony of units. Therefore unit and atom and dust all come to be the same thing.

In its provisional schemes, science has not yet conceded the appropriate dignity to the dusty state, along with the gaseous, liquid, and solid. Undoubtedly it has characteristic properties, such as its suitability for dispersed or colloidal systems—where possibly life arises—and also (perhaps on account of its exposure of surface) its catalytic character, that mysterious influence of matter which is indeed so similar to the watchful care of an ordering mind. Can it be that dust aspires, further, to be spirit? And what if it were the true god?

Mexico, 1940

Anchorages (*Ancorajes*), Tezontle, Mexico, 1951, pp. 29–33.

ARISTARCHUS[1] OR THE ANATOMY OF CRITICISM*

1. *The paradox of criticism.* Criticism, that wet blanket, always received, like the rent collector, with the door just half open! The poor muse, when it comes upon this bastard sister, twists her fingers, touches wood, and runs as fast as she can to get disinfected. Whence came this paradoxical creature, this spoiler of the pure joy of life,

*Lecture read in the Palace of Fine Arts, under the auspices of the Symphony Orchestra of Mexico, August 26, 1941.

[1]Said to be first philosopher to hold that the earth revolves around the sun (3rd cent. B.C.).

this usurious toll which the arts pay for the capital they use? Does the principle of scarcity rule here too, as in the economic world, and set a price upon the commodity? It has often been said that to the Philistine the poet is a bird of bad omen, since he forces him to question himself. Well, what the poet is to the Philistine the critic comes to be for the poet in his turn; whence it follows that criticism is a second-grade nuisance and a final peril in the pathway of unpleasant encounters! It is an incident of the journey, and always moves against the current and enters streets in the wrong direction. It goes backwards and elbows its way through. It will examine everything, question and probe everything, destroy everything with its analytical investigation. If there is a picnic, it comes to forecast rain. "But, have you really thought this through?" it says in a low voice to the enthusiast. And it even slips into the most intimate chamber of delights to sow doubt. To the wooer, it points out the gold tooth and the little wrinkle in the neck, causing the sudden coldness. To the lover, it points out that suspicious emblem on the handkerchief which cost Desdemona her life. Ah, Athens was Athens, neither more nor less; and even so, it ended by killing Socrates! And do you know why? Here is the reason: simply because Socrates invented criticism. To invite an amiable group to reflect upon the nature of criticism may perhaps show a lack of urbanity and tact, like inviting them to take a walk through trees that bear prickly pears. It is too late for me now to beg forgiveness. I did not intend to make anyone uncomfortable. I will just explain myself.

2. *The paradox of man.* Are we sure of man? Is a man one man or several men? He is at least two: one who is going, and another who is coming. Almost always, he is two who accompany each other. While one lives, the other watches him live. What a strange contradictory creation! Man is both man and mirror. And that is because man does not walk alone. The poet Antonio Espina intuited this phantom companion, and called it "the one ahead":

> He always goes ahead. His hands behind his back.
> Irresolute. Dressed in black.
> I advance. And so does he.
> I stop. And he stops too.

And Antonio Machado,[2] long before, wrote: "I converse with the man who always goes with me."

[2]Espina and Machado are Spanish poets of the present century.

So, in this constant transcending of things, where everything is and also is not like the river of Heraclitus, we cannot even have confidence in ourselves, in the man one is, in our unique point of reference, which most probably is also—as in modern physics—a point in motion, or better still, a multiple and changing entity. We are action and contemplation, actor and spectator; anode and cathode, and spark from exchanging poles; a conflict and a conciliation between antagonistic principles; left and right; obverse and reverse, and the traffic that goes over them; we are poetry and criticism, action and judgement, Andrenius and Critilus. The middle term of Aristotle, virtue between extreme vices, is not to be regarded as a static milestone, but as a dynamic zone crossed by furious movements. And this comes to be our soul: the region of attractions and repulsions, the region of the thunderbolt. Nature operates through a schism in its complexes. It evolves by dialectics and by dividing its processes into two parts. All living is being, and at the same time an impulse of that being. The pendulous essence of man carries him from action to reflection and confronts him with himself at every moment. There is no need to go further. We can now define criticism. Criticism is this setting face to face or confronting, this calling to account, this conversing with the other one, the one who goes with me.

Criticism is conditioned being. Poetry is conditioning being. They are simultaneous, but theoretically poetry precedes criticism. All creation has infused within it a poetic art, in the same way as every creator bears creation within him. In Saint Thomas, the great master, the possibility is admitted that the universe may not have had an historical beginning, but that it coexists with God, from all eternity. Nevertheless, to approach the mystery, we accept as a theoretic aid a Day of Creation. Let us follow the symbol: our Day of Creation is confused with our Day of Judgement. Judgement and creation, precept and poem, thunder together in the womb of the poetic cloud. But the hour of division arrives in which one writes poetry and the other judges. Before reaching this final stage, the explicit dialogue, there are two previous stages of implicit dialogue. Let us go over a little anthropology, as much as is indispensable if we are not to be frightened off.

3. *Schism between poet and tribe.* If man is but an apparent unit, he is not even the first appearance in the critical series. The cell does not begin with him, but with the human group. Just as the child slowly develops consciousness of its own body through the confused mass of sensations which envelop it, so the poet, enveloped in the nebula of

the tribe, little by little gains a sense of his own autonomy and of his artistic proprietorship of the poem he produces. Poetry was born as a service which was institutional, religious, magic, agricultural, or political. The poem is primarily a rite, a formula, a decree, a contract, an historical review; deeds all collective, all verbs whose subject is not the individual, but the tribe. The poet is a mere instrument. If he does not yet belong completely to himself as an individual, much less does he belong to himself as a poet, inasmuch as his act is an elemental service to the tribe. He is the hero of the primitive tragedy, who appears and expresses himself only under the shadow of the combined energies of the entire chorus. The social circle requires, on account of the geometry of the spirit, that it be supported upon a point equidistant from its centre, and that it should revolve around it, and the centre comes to be the poet, perhaps a priest or chief. As centre, he is not the master of his posture: he is a necessity of the circle. He feels his words as others' words, as inspired, dictated by the collective will which moves him. What self-criticism can we expect in his elemental creations? Barely a vapour of consciousness, which he does not confess even to himself! But one day the schism occurs. The poet feels himself alone before his poem, and begins to consider it as something of his own. We shall not try to give historical descriptions of what never had any history, but merely conceptual explanations. This schism, in concept, may be understood as the effect of three concomitant causes: first, the slow development of individual feeling in all the members of the tribe; second, the suspicion, on the part of the poet, that he might have done better, as he perceives a possible failure of his formulas; third, the aesthetic concern which now appears, and leads him to desire revision, a striving towards perfection, and the best combinations of his verbal artifices. Moses reclimbs Sinai to forge his tables. He no longer consults the people. Alone, he receives them from God.

4. *Schism between the poet and the self-critic.* The first stage of implicit dialogue is thus bound to be second stage, before explicit dialogue comes in. The poet already marvels at his own gift, takes pride in it, while he imposes upon it correctives and norms; enthusiasm and doubt are intermingled. The candour of that first astonishment, the tremor of that first doubt, can be illustrated by an excellent example.

5. *Valmiki and the birds.* The old and almost legendary author of the *Ramayana* was walking through the country one day. I do not know what the country is like in India. I imagine it, like its extravagant

divinities, as a mass of trees with multiple arms which press one another. And under the vaults of green, hidden like terrible secrets, are the pagodas of ants. There is a heavy electric charge in the atmosphere, conducive to ecstasy or to panic. The viewer is overwhelmed by the spectacle, and nature easily engrafts it with the mineral, vegetable, and animal virtues which exist in man, regaining their patrimony. Valmiki has lost consciousness of himself, as he admires a pair of birds whose voices have taken on a singular sweetness because of the mating season. The pair woo in their manner—so superior to ours—with songs, flights, dances, and shaking of their plumage. But the destructive principle lies in wait for the joyous moment of life, and among the undergrowth, in some vague manner, shine the eyes of Vichnú. Victim of an unjust death, the male suddenly falls, struck dead at the height of his hopes. From the heart of Valmiki there pours forth a torrent of words, an unanticipated protest, a poetic complaint. And thus is born "kavya" poetry, a new literary genre. But the sound of his own voice awakens Valmiki. And he exclaims: "Is this myself, is it possible that I am the one who has uttered those divine words?" The poet has engaged in dialogue with his genius, he has opened himself up, doubted, and astounded himself with his own power.

6. *First document of doubt.* We now pass on to explicit dialogue. This is no longer self-criticism, but criticism. It is no longer the poet alone before his muse. There appears before him a stranger, a censor, a counsellor of doubt. The separation has become incorporated in two tragic persons: beside the hero, the protagonist, walks as a shadow the deuteragonist, the disturber. The oldest literary text recorded by human history is a set of teachings composed for the instruction of the untutored, by Ptahotep, an Egyptian ruler who lived forty centuries before Christ. The first thing that is counselled in that document is, to say it once for all, methodical doubt, distrust of handed-down beliefs, the need to revise them carefully on one's own. One foresees the coming of Aristarchus. One senses a foreshadowing of Descartes. Criticism, as a separate personage, now undertakes, before creation, his long intermittent dialogue.

7. *The coup d'état.* The deuteragonist gains confidence in himself and acquires firmness in his opinions. He is blinded with pride. He tries to usurp the role of hero, and makes a *coup d'état.* Criticism is not satisfied with following in the footsteps of the poem. Now it insists on

preceding it; it is now changed to Preceptive. It is a case of substitution of powers, of quarters, also a subject of mythology. It is an abuse of confidence on the part of Zeus, an interloping gallant of the north, who surreptitiously introduces himself into the murderous reign of Hera, begins by sharing her bed—to "divide the bed"—and finally becomes head of Olympus. It is the Arabian tale of the beggar, made vizir by the capricious sovereign, who one fine morning rises from counsellor to master. From division to usurpation there is a true abuse of confidence. But if a part of criticism starts off here along a mistaken course, another part of criticism, uncontaminated, preserves the use of its proper function. Let us examine it closely, avoiding henceforth all abuses or crooked paths.

8. *The critical scale and its steps.* First of all, criticism is not necessarily censure in the usual sense. Criticism also praises and applauds. Still more, it explains praise and enriches enjoyment. Let us set aside, then, the controversy over what there is in criticism that is positive and negative. The essence of entities is their constructive function. Let us allow provisionally that when criticism is negative, it is because creativity is not sustained, and does not exist. Otherwise we should be dealing not with criticism but with false criticism. Let us consider granted the excellence of the poem which is being approached by criticism. Only in this way shall we be submitting criticism to its crucial test.

How does criticism approach a poem? There are three steps in this scale: the impression, the exegesis, and the judgement. Along the scale, there are differentiations between the intellectual operation, the mere knowing, and the axiological or evaluating operation, which we may here call the operation of love; reason and the "reason of love" act differently.

9. *Impression and impressionism.* The impression, it is understood, is the indispensable condition, the capacity to be affected by the literary work. Without this there is no criticism, or exegesis, or judgement possible; neither knowledge nor love. Well now, the manifestation of this general and human impression could be denied to none. It is a natural right, if I am permitted such old-fashioned language. When this type of informal manifestation, without any specific obligations, ventures to speak aloud or to make use of the written word, it is commonly called impressionism. The philologists, the masters of exegesis, regard impressionism with a disdainful smile. Even the uncommitted men of

letters have allowed themselves a few absurdities in speaking of impressionistic criticism. The philologists are wrong in their disdain for several reasons:

(1) Because the aim of literary creation is not to provoke exegesis, but to illuminate the hearts of men, of all men in what they possess merely as human beings, and not in what they possess as specialists in this or that discipline. And impressionistic criticism is nothing more than the reflection of this illumination of the heart; it is nothing more than the human response, authentic and genuine, to the poem.

(2) Because the critic, at any point on the scale, if he does not bear within himself an impressionist, lacks the contact required in order to establish that mysterious communication with poetry, and remains, so to speak, outside the precincts. Impressionism is the common denominator of all criticism.

(3) Because impressionism, understood as the aggregate of the reactions of a period, or a society, or even of a single representative individual, is the indispensable index for the philologist—the one which tells him what the voice of the people has said; the one which indicates the direction for exegesis; the one which attracts the attention of the scholar or the literary historian to the presence and worth of the poem, encouraging them with a little pat on the shoulder. And this is true even in cases where the specialist opposes public opinion for the sake of correcting it. All this is an invaluable service. Culture, in general, is not made up of extravagances and secret singularities, unless these are absorbed into the sensibility of the human group which appeared to be waiting for them: a case of aesthetic revolution. And this information regarding the state of culture is the work of impressionism.

The literary men are wrong in the nonsense they talk in opposition to impressionistic criticism. To clarify this, let us reduce their nonsense to a scheme, a thankless task if there ever was one:

(1) Nonsense about the amateur. The amateur, as the name signifies, is a lover. The Frenchman calls him *amateur*, and the Portuguese *amador*. The amateur is, in societies, the one who is most sensitive to art, the person for whom art—and in our case, the poem—is not something juxtaposed, but a practical reality, a part of life, of one's habitual breathing. The Greek sophists considered it a mark of human dignity to accept seriously the illusions of art. The impressionist takes art seriously, without any professional obligation. This is indeed a thing of great dignity, in the pedigree of those who hardly eat or sleep!

(2) Nonsense about the supposed sterility of criticism. Does criti-

cism appear only when provoked by the poem of another? And what shall we then say about those who do not experience any provocation from the poem? Turning back to our previous argument: one who reacts to the illusion of art does so because he has risen above the level of vulgarity, because he has succeeded in incorporating art with the other realities of his life. Is this subordination to the work of others? Let us be clear: it is attention to the most excellent manifestations of humanity, which is something very different. It is sufficient to consider how often the impression goes far beyond its expression, and how many more times it matches it. The most generous attitude in this nonsensical view is represented by two positions. The first, that of Oscar Wilde: that criticism is a creation *within* another creation. The second, that of T. S. Eliot: that impressionistic criticism operates through outside fertilization and is almost a creation, without being able to achieve the complete expulsion of the creature. Whichever way you take it, from both positions the conclusion is that here the creature is a parasite. Biology has a more comprehensive word: not parasite, but "tenant." Of this criticism, which does not yet reach the lofty heights of the mind, we may say that it is a "tenant." But it is a tenant of life, just as poetry itself is, since the poetic object has here risen to the category of an object of life. Between criticism and life there is no metaphorical intermediary called poetry. Poetry is to criticism one more expression of life, the most effectual. Poetry and criticism are two orders of creation, and that is all. Why, even the modest grammatical commentary on the poem is a kind of creation! Much more so the expression of the emotions aroused by the product of art! It may even be that impressionistic criticism is not really such, in the strict sense of the word, and that in its own right it contains a high poetic value. This occurs with the commentary of Walter Pater on the portrait of Mona Lisa. And try to tell me that the emotion of a certain simple man, into whose hands fell a translation of Homer, is not worth many critical treatises, and many poems:

"I am reading," he said, "an extraordinary book. It is called the *Iliad*. I do not know what it is; but since my reading I see men with the stature of giants."

10. *Exegesis*. Half way between impressionism and judgement, there lies a zone difficult of access, which means that already it is a domain of specialists. It is that part of criticism which may be considered, at first glance, a mere exacerbation of didacticism. It is the domain of the philologist. This criticism, which for the present I prefer to call exe-

getic, allows the application of specific methods, and many call it the science of literature. Though it cannot disregard love, it stresses the aspect of knowledge. It informs, interprets, and also evaluates. It may also come to the point of judging, and in all cases the foundation is laid for it. If it does not always reach this point, it is because it stops and frequently entertains itself with the mere erudition of its themes, and also because these very themes, at times, besides having a definitive human value, have an inner value serving its own erudite purposes, a reference value only, to the end of establishing knowledge. In it the educative function is predominant; that is to say, the preservation of treasures we call culture. It is the only criticism that can be taught and learned, and therefore, in greater or lesser purity, it forms part of the academic programme. Its methods may be reduced to three that are fundamental, and only through the integration of methods does it acquire the right to aspire to the name of a science: (1) historical method; (2) psychological method; (3) stylistic method. Its content may be described by saying that it studies the production of the work in its mental and historical background; the psychological and cultural formation of the author; the peculiarities of his language and style; the influences of every kind—biographical facts or facts concerning his thought—which are discovered in the work itself; its significance at the time when it appears; the effects which in turn it has upon other works and upon the public of the time; its later success; its pure aesthetic value. It is inevitable, if it is to be complete, that it should be somewhat contaminated by sociological considerations which, although they go beyond the proper bounds, lie on the frontier. Yet it must not accept as determinative methods, but as simple aids, those which are taken from other disciplines. It is never simply a form of knowledge, but it fertilizes and renews aesthetic pleasure; in this, with its task of preservation, it offers its highest service.

11. *Judgement.* Thus do I call the last step in the scale, that criticism of last appeal which definitively places the work upon the balance-sheet of human acquisitions. Being neither without love, on which it is naturally founded, nor without the techniques of exegesis—although it does not operate in conformity with them, since it walks and even flies unaided, for it has already left behind the perambulator of method—it is the crown of criticism. It acquires ethical transcendence and acts as a guide to the mind. There is no teaching, and no learning. The heroic romantic name is appropriate to it: it is a work of genius. Not all

achieve it. It is neither all impressionism, nor is it all method. One who possesses a nature sensitive to literature, and who also has conquered the steep mount of method, has not for that reason fulfilled everything. Even if all the soldiers of the Little Corporal carry a baton in their knapsacks, to few is it given to be a marshal. The satyrs who draw near to the fire, in Aeschylus' fragment of the *Prometheus Pyropherus*, succeed only in scorching their beards. Grace is grace. All the raw emotive power and all the university degrees in the world are unable to arouse feeling to one not born to it, for the beauty of this simple verse: "The soft lament of two shepherds" (El dulce lamentar de dos pastores). The great interpretive faculty of Longinus, Dante, Coleridge, Sainte-Beuve, De Sanctis, Arnold, Pater, Brandes, Baudelaire, Menéndez y Pelayo, or Croce is not acquired through any commercial exchange, nor is it bought or sold at any price.

I should like now to tell of the delights which criticism provides. I shall illustrate, in conclusion, with three examples.

12. *The three lightning-flashes: speech, the swallow, and the falcon.*

SPEECH: Let us confront the man having a humanistic discipline with this sentence read by chance: "Poverty is abolished." There, where the ignoramus would appreciate only a certain inevitable humorous effect, the humanist has understood immediately that this is from a document of the French Revolution, a period when people thought they could remedy social inequalities by acts of faith and guarantee the rights of the individual by declarations and decrees. The political and spiritual picture appears to his eyes as in a painting. Before him pass, in the midst of a ragged mob, the orators with their Greco-Latin rhetoric, the tempestuous scenes, ideas in the form of daggers—all in one throb of the human epic, in a lightning-flash.

THE SWALLOW: Let us confront him now with that passage from Rousseau in which the latter tells that on opening his window—as a harbinger of the season—a swallow flew away. Where the ignoramus has seen only a trivial fact, though a pleasant one, to the humanist everything has appeared immediately as a turn in human sensibility; the time when frank feelings claim the attention of the philosopher, the time when the "thinkers" (a word of the period) question the foundations of society, which Providence has already let slip from His bosom. And all this, as in an allegorical print, where the hero meditates theatrically in the heart of the countryside—the countryside which he calls "nature"—while a swallow passes over the sky. The humanist knows that this is the first swallow in modern literature, the swallow already announcing the summer of Romanticism.* New avenues are opened to the eye, as in a lightning-flash.

THE FALCON: Let us now look at this two-line extract:

> In the master hand let the tempered bird
> nobly furbish his plumage.

And there, where the ignoramus has thought he saw a joke of the worst kind, the humanist has immediately recognized the style of the great aesthetic revolutions in which the Spanish Renaissance terminated. It is a perspective of brilliant images and linguistic voluptuousness, and that taste for entertaining the fancy with noble allusions. There comes to him the memory of books on hunting and falconry, rich in words and visual evocations, like those old treatises of the goldsmith on hunting with hawks which enraptured Heredia the Parnassian, the falcon—noble bird—tempered, as today we say "trained," as one tempers or tunes a bandore, his head freed from the hood, wearing the bell that sends messages about his flight. The falcon furbishes his plumage in the periods of rest, and rests in the gloved hand, the hand twice master because it possesses him and trains him. Perhaps the falconer goes on horseback, that Andalusian horse which "soaps the bridle with foam": a blemish which calls to mind verses of Góngora and Lope. And so continues the procession of figures and fine attitudes, as in a tapestry of the period, embroidered with heavy cords; and all, too, in a lightning-flash.

And here, in the twinkling of an eye, we have multiplied our limited existence three times, transporting ourselves on the two wings—emotion and knowledge—to the region where we receive adequate pleasure. A happy calling, then, is that which does not deny, but rather renews and multiplies for its initiates the resources and occasions of delight.

But it cannot be demanded of all that they possess the fine perceptions of the artist, this maker of mutations in the sensibilities of peoples. To initiate as many persons as possible becomes, for that very reason, an important social duty. Hegel once spoke of the "man condemned by God to be a philosopher." If, among the young people who have followed this examination, some have felt the stirring of a vocation, if

*Alfonso Reyes, Monologue by the author: "The First Swallow" ("La priméra golondrina") in *The Suicide, Complete Works* (*El suicida, Obras Completas*), Fondo de Cultura Económica, 1956, Vol. III, pp. 292–93.

some have heard the "You will be Marcellus" concealed in my words, this talk will not have been in vain.

The Literary Experience: Co-ordinates (*La experiencia literaria: coordenadas*), Editorial Losada, Buenos Aires, 1942, pp. 97–109.

PARRASIO OR MORAL PAINTING

WHAT CAN MORAL PAINTING BE except a portrait? Socrates enlightens us in this respect. Son of the stone-cutter Sophroniscus, he understood art and from childhood frequented his father's workshop. Son of a midwife, he learned from her to bring the soul to life. We friends of humane letters revere in Phenareta the patron of revealed vocations.

Socrates carried on his sport—the Mayeutic[3]—subjecting all to interrogation, asking them to give an account of themselves as he confessed them. Athens, irritated by the Peloponnesian Wars and the rebellion against the Thirty Tyrants, could not forgive him; hence the hemlock. He questioned the learned, and found them ignorant. He questioned the poets. He got little from them; he did not find them sufficiently lucid. He also questioned the artists, and kept forming his aesthetics amid impressionistic touches in the conversation. It is impossible to conceal the fact that his idea of beauty is infected—a deviation of long lineage—by that virus which an authoritative master characterizes as the iniquitous concept of utility. When his moral insistence begins to weary us, let us abstain from quick judgements; let us respect it, remembering that it is sincere and profound. He preferred to die rather than betray it.

Nietzsche states that this ethical preoccupation of Antiquity, from Socrates on, and this yielding oneself to reason to the point of utter absurdity, are actually symptoms of illness, collapse, and loss of the vital sense. If the heart starts to tamper with itself, it is because it is turning into an obstacle, because it is ill.

Will this explain why the poet Plato, when he perceives that the resistance is already weak, guards against the ravings of inspiration in the civil fortress of his *Republic*? Will this explain the tireless campaign of Aristophanes, in the name of ancient virtue, and of the rough men of Marathon, against the passionate deliquescences of Euripides?

Because Plato does not tolerate poets in his State, or just barely

[3]Method of discovering truth which takes one's own ignorance as a starting-point.

tolerates them as guests under suspicion, he gives them liberty on bail. And then he forces them into the role of pompous fools who have to be held in check by the rein to prevent the noxious outbursts of their fancy, regulating them according to crippling canons in the style of the Egyptians. And as for Aristophanes, scholars strive hard to justify in him a fault which he did not have. Aristophanes suffered from a hatred born of love for Euripides. He could not live without him. Even after his death, he evokes him and resuscitates him on the stage. He confesses that Euripides is an evil, but he admires him in spite of himself, which is evidence to support his clairvoyance. He knows him by heart and he is constantly recalling him to mind. Suddenly, between one satire and another, he catches himself almost praising him. This is a strange fascination which lasts twenty years, a stubborn poison. It is by no means a vulgar grudge, nor is it necessary for our admiration to defend him. It is a tempest in a cranium. It is the whole Athenian crisis vacillating between two destinies. The crisis, clothed in the phantom of the tragedian, passes through the soul of the comedian.

It was a time of moral conflicts, of dark, angry horizons. Socrates acted as a barometer. Pericles, from his high station, had committed his people to an imperialistic course which was the terror of the gentle, long-suffering islands, more like vassals than allies. Behind the laugh of Aristophanes—who takes a valiant stand against a provincial patriotism—there are roars of rage against the injustices of that lucky demagogue, that rascal Cleon. In Aristophanes one hears for the first time the strange word "Pan-Hellenism." (Or did it occur previously in the *Gorgias*?) A word thrown to posterity imploring, after such domestic bungling, a favourable outcome. In Thucydides, the contrast between the proud Athens and the sacrificed Melos forms an historical frown.

Socrates walks through the streets, barefoot and hatless, preaching about conscience as related to good. Not yet does light shine into this deep, dark valley. Good seems to him to be a thing of the intelligence, and both of these, a thing of beauty. At least, this seems to be true as far as it is possible to see through to Socrates in the intricate writings of Plato.

A formulation is not easy, because we know Socrates only by hearsay. The mean fellow never wrote a single line. This is an extreme case of the moralist. What does he care about writing? What does he care about being read? True moral influence must be by word of mouth, in the warmth of contact. In principle, for the moralist, the most important thing is the human presence. That absent man, the reader, at once suggests a highly intellectual relationship. The direct dialogue, in Socrates; the parable, in Christ—these are, for the moralist, the supreme instruments. Buddha writes, of course, and does not merely meditate and preach. From him, though without his signature, comes a novelistic treasure. In his hands the ear of corn sprouts. The grains, carried away through the stopping-points of the Near East—Persia, Arabia—reach, among other men, the Spaniards Pedro Alfonso and Don Juan Manuel, and spread through the European Middle Ages; they still germinate, in the Renaissance, with the writers of the *novella* and with the Elizabethan theatre; they are still revived, in our day, in being carried by the current of fables which touch everyone. But in Buddha—a great man of letters and, in this respect, a man of our profession—the intellectual order predominates over the other orders, as in Aristotle or in Saint Thomas Aquinas, although in very different ways. The theoretical Christ, the incorporation of an eternal principle, speaks for all humanity. Buddha speaks and dictates for spirit, accidentally split up into transitory individuals. Aristotle and Saint Thomas, concerned with essences, write for all spirits. Socrates speaks for his contemporaries, and is not interested in us, or at least he does not have us in mind even though he knows that his teachings will be imperishable, so far as demarcation is permissible.

Fortunately, along with the testimony of Plato, we possess that of Xenophon. This excellent narrator without genius has much less to say on his own account. It may be supposed that he gives us a more sober image of Socrates; or, to use the language of our subject, a minimum, uncoloured portrait. With this, and with an occasional opportune piece of information—though indeed from a distance—from the pupil of the pupil, Aristotle, it is not rash to infer an image of Socrates and recompose his outlines, dispersed in the "workings-over" to which his own creatures subjected him.

Unfortunately, while Plato transfigures Socrates in the fire of his genius—a moral portrait contaminated by a self-portrait, through the magic interpenetration of the two persons in the pictorial dialogue, artist and model—Xenophon on certain occasions simply deceives us. For does he not have Socrates discoursing on the strategy in Asia Minor, a theme familiar to the mercenary of the *Anabasis*, but not to the philosopher of the cicadas? Another time he has him discourse upon agriculture, when we well know that Socrates was the most urban of Greeks. According to Plato, "the trees had nothing to teach him." Let us interpret: the trees never answered his questions, they were not subjects of the Mayeutic. Morality means reciprocity and sympathy.

For the Socratics and their predecessors, the countryside was physics. Elements combine, but they do not love one another. Man uses them, he does not love them; they are not persons.

What mattered to Socrates was man, or his conduct. Whether truth or fiction, a story that makes very good sense tells us that some Hindus, who happened to be in Athens, went to Socrates and asked him what his profession was. "My work is to investigate man," he replied; and the Hindus laughed in his face. "How do you expect to understand man, without understanding the gods first?" they answered. It is not difficult to imagine, in a hypothetical portrait, the disillusioned smile with which Socrates allowed them to speak, in silence though without turning away his eyes from them.

Socrates was brave, patient, and, in the common sense, a sceptic. A head staunchly independent, that could not be turned even by wine. After the *Banquet*, while all the others roll under the table, we see him, gay as a lark, go out into the cool of the morning, lamenting that he has been left with no one to talk to. He was magnificently ugly, Silenus inhabited by Athenea, like the coffers or "silenas" that were sold at the market. His face portrayed evil passions. To one who told him so, he answered: "You, stranger, have found me out. But the point is that I control myself."

He was the least conceited of men, virtuous without affectation. He was not disturbed by the devotion of Alcibiades, a boy so tender in years that he pronounced "crow" as "clow," a rash boy whose life he had saved in a fight, and who will be absolved of many offences—including the scandalous mutilation of the Hermes—in consideration of his love and admiration for his Socrates.

Socrates, then, Xenophon writes, one day came up to the home of the sculptor Crito:

"How do you manage to infuse so much life into all those runners, wrestlers, boxers, and athletes?" he asked him.

Crito made a gesture of modesty, thinking he was being praised and not, as is said in law, being "put under questioning." "I see," said Socrates, "it is because you imitate living forms." Then the vague response:

"Yes, indeed. . . ."

"So you can also imitate, in the physical expressions of the gesture, the look, what is going on behind them?"

"I think so."

"I conclude that the secret of sculpture, in order that it may have real vitality, is in imitating, through the medium of form, the manifestations of the spirit."

We know little of Crito. We do not know whether, upon this discovery of Socrates concerning the hieroglyphic value of form, Crito, like many artists interested only in solving difficult technical questions, said to himself, like the elm of a certain unwritten fable: "So I, the elm, produce pears?"

Another day, Socrates went to the home of the painter Parrasio.

"I understand," he began, "that the art of painting consists of representing, through the medium of colours, the things the eye captures. But I see also that when you painters portray a beautiful figure, since nature is incapable of producing a perfect man, from one you borrow this, from another that, and so on, selecting the parts which you find most beautiful in each."

Parrasio (the silent man avoids trouble) answers with something that might be translated as: "M-m. . . ." Now you will see, Parrasio, what sort of man you are up against:

"But tell me," continued Socrates, "can you also imitate a gracious and gentle soul? Or does the brush fail to catch the soul?"

Parrasio, shaking his head, replies: "M-m! But, Socrates, the soul is not visible, it has no form, colour, or proportions; it has no tangible quality, or weight! . . ."

And though Xenophon does not say so, I think that Parrasio, to support his explanations, began here to put on airs and to make, with his thumb in the air, that well-known nasty little gesture.

"All right, all right, Parrasio. But tell me, does not the gracious and gentle expression of a soul show in the eyes and face?"

"That's different," agrees Parrasio.

"And can you not reproduce that expression imprinted on the face and eyes?"

"Why of course."

"Then you can also portray the workings of the spirit."

"Very true, very true."

Let us stop to consider what has happened. Socrates is seeking in the arts a moral expression. In the course of the talk, he speaks of odious and attractive characters, of temperaments amiable and disagreeable. All of that can be material for painting.

The lesson is short; its consequences, long.

The naturalist Pliny, a writer as intelligent and readable as the naturalist Buffon, tells us that Timantes, in his *Sacrifice of Iphigenia*, after painting the faces of all the characters tortured by grief, still succeeded in accentuating the portrayal of anguish in Menelaus, the uncle of the victim. Ah, but what about Agamemnon, the father, condemned to witness the sacrifice of his daughter so that those vessels

—according to the pronouncement of the diviners—can continue on their course towards Troy! Here Timantes, no longer able to heighten the tone in the portrayal of the pathetic, seized upon a good expedient: Agamemnon covers his face with his cloak! If this picture was painted after Socrates' onslaught in Parrasio's studio—which doubtless was much discussed at all the social gatherings in Athens—the reticence of Timantes may be considered a token of respect for the doctrine of moral expression.

As for Parrasio, it seems that the reaction was more serious. Parrasio had specialized in masculine figures, as Zeuxis had done in the feminine. We recall his Theseus, his Ajax, and his Odysseus quarreling over the arms of Achilles. And although Quintilian later will call him "an austere drawer," the Greeks—who had a better understanding of these weaknesses and had intimate acquaintance with Parrasio—observed in him his licentious sensuality and even gave him a suggestive nickname. I suspect that Crito was probably an artist more interested in technique than in ethical and aesthetic doctrines. Of Parrasio we can say this with less uncertainty, until the day of Socrates' memorable intrusion. Of him it is known that he took delight in seeking illusory effects. Zeuxis came to surprise him with his still-lifes: some fruits painted so naturally that the birds tried to peck at them. "Draw that curtain," Parrasio said to him, "so that we can see better." And Zeuxis, tricked, discovered at once that he was stretching out his hand towards one of Parrasio's pictures which represented a curtain. Zeuxis had deceived the birds. That is something. But Parrasio had deceived even the master Zeuxis!

Socrates, who chose his targets well, perhaps wished to entice Parrasio away from these games of a lower order; perhaps he wanted to make him concentrate upon nobler objectives, like that allegory of the Athenian people, in which the painter succeeded in giving to each face a different character. And the cautery was not without result. But Parrasio took the lesson as an artist, not as a moralist. He became more and more interested in the expression of pain, not in the pain itself. If we can believe Seneca, Parrasio years later bought one of the Olinthians that Philip caused to be sold as slaves, and—quietly—ordered him to be tortured in order to study quite coldly, with the absolute candour of an artistic demiurge, the grimaces and contortions of martyrdom. (As a matter of fact, this anecdote, like the one about Michelangelo,[4] presents chronological difficulties.)

In any case, Socrates' lesson, in that age, acted as a vaccine. Today,

[4]Various anecdotes have been told about Michelangelo, in his painting of the *Last Judgement*, with regard to his placing of known people in Hell.

though it may be on account of the accumulation of experiences, we are already immunized. We look for "that thing" in painting, or we look for a lot of other things. But in portrait painting, one cannot avoid consideration of the moral expression. This does not mean that the artist must hold to the processes of realistic imitation. At every step the mind comes up against the perversion that use effects in words. The "imitation," of which the ancients spoke so much and which they understood as "representation of nature," with a quite tolerable degree of latitude, finally turned into—taking the word literally—a sterilizing precept. To rectify the narrow point of view that has come to be called Realism, it is not necessary to become submerged in great aesthetic depths. Any sincere nature recognizes the moral truth in that portrait of Mallarmé which Whistler drew on a little piece of cigarette paper with just a few pencil strokes. Nothing more real, and nothing less realistic. There we have communicated to us the lively magic of a full presence. There we have the poet in full soul; but not in full body, because for the moral truth of the portrait there were many superfluous redundancies in the body. So if Crito, according to Socrates, constructed an archetype of the human figure through a selection of parts chosen from a number of individuals, the modern poet succeeds in representing the character of an individual—his moral truth—by the selection and use of only the expressive parts which the same individual carries in his corporeal cover.

The most extreme example of this procedure we are given in the caricature. It is a common experience to find greater truth in a caricature than in a corresponding portrait. Wherein lies the mystery of the caricature? The caricature is an etymology of the person. It is an investigation into the tendencies, the direction of a character. The tendencies have been exaggerated, in order to trace them better, as the anatomist puts an injection into a vein to mark more plainly its course among the network. The electrical focus becomes reduced to one incandescent fibre, to the skeleton of light. Aristotle, discussing a very different subject, has defined this principle thus: "Things," he says, "things *are* their tendencies."

Let us exaggerate the phrase in our turn, so as to bring out its sense more fully: "Things are *already* their tendencies." This is a rule of ontological thinking, a guide to critical thinking, since, when the tendency is once clearly established, it is always easy to mark the point where it stopped after it had manifested itself in every humble phenomenon. So the untutored man, who knew nothing of the reputation and past history of Socrates, was making a spoken caricature of

Socrates when he saw in his face the face of an evil person. Sincere unto death, Socrates confessed that his only merit was to recognize his bad tendencies and to prevent them from dominating him. Socrates thus marked the point of voluntary abortion in the development of the tendency. This act is morality, the art of operating on nature according to an idea of good freely chosen. We see here in what way the portrait leads us to moral doctrine.

But let us go one step further. If morality is psychic control or care of conduct, it is governed by a development in events, in time. The moral portrait supposes a time implication. How can one reduce to comprehensible terms the operation of painting in time? The idea of time is a terrible thing. The Argentinian philosopher Francisco Romero has written: "Time has lived philosophically incognito until a few decades ago." In fact, there are two reasons for its past misfortune: first, its difficult, fleeting nature; second, its bad company, its cohabitation with space. Well, let us come to the distinction. On the one hand there is real time, the sense of an inner unfolding, of a movement and flux that moves and fluxes nothing but a savour of flux and movement, a music without melody or notes which is what bears most resemblance to the soul, the *durée réelle* of Bergson, which–by the authority of the Marquis de Santillana–we might call in our language the real "has endured." On the other hand, there is physical time, that of science, the time measured by the clock, time that lies over space, time as the occurrence of a movement, of a movement which in its turn lies upon space to give us this stethogram which is called the trajectory. If the clock is considered as an absolute, as a static reference, we have the physics of Newton. If the clock is a relative reference, since in reality only by convention can there be fixed points, if the supposed static point in its turn suffers a temporal corrosion from the moment it is moved, we have the physics of Einstein. But, having made these abstract distinctions, let us go back and apply them in the artistic phenomenon, which operates in intuitive concretions. The aesthetic emotion of painting and the material substance of painting ineffably link the representations of time.

How is this? Has it not always been said that painting is an art of space, as opposed to the arts of time, like literature and music? Has it not been said that the only artistic synthesis is to be found in the dance, where there are both figure and succession? This digression would not take us too far. It is necessary to reinterpret the motifs of Lessing's *Laocoon* in the light of new experiences, now that we have a form of painting previously unsuspected, which has a pictorial space which moves, and then moves in physical time: the cinema. We must ask ourselves if the principles which appeared to be absolute are not merely descriptive lines of the artistic object, in a single moment of its history. Let us leave it there; let us not lose our way in dissolving photography. Let us go again to the stable art, painting.

With its space fixed, painting can refer to time only by symbolic implications, by ideograms. The landscape of the nineteenth century, for example, frequently shows us the storm cloud. We already know that the cloud is a changing thing, and more so if agitated by the storm. Now it assumes figures of a wolf, a leopard, and a bull, as in Aristophanes; now, as in *Hamlet*, a camel, a weasel, a whale. Well, the landscape, in this possible flux, cuts off a moment. And the possible flux remains suspended in the soul, as an evocation. The pictorial value is in the cutting, in the coagulation which is offered. But the psychological implications of the change whirl about it. The ideogram of time is here a mere allusion.

But at other times, and particularly in the portrait, the reference to time, more than a sense of a halt in the march, assumes a sense of a completion, a final summation, of a general effect of changes. It is better to deal with this in parables.

I now recall that Valle-Inclán[5] explained the calm of some of Velasquez' portraits by an effect of the change of light through the long hours of the day, in those huge rooms of the Royal Palace where he painted. Continual change, he came to say, leads to statism, to Molinistic quietism.[6] The accident disappears, and the essence remains. Velasquez does not paint what passes, but what endures. He does not see the gumboil that came out on the gentleman just that day. He does not see morning or afternoon, but total light. He does not paint the hour, but time. This is debatable, but worth debating. What parallel, indeed, is there between the theory of Socrates and that of Valle-Inclán? It is self-evident: Valle-Inclán sought in pictures a mystic sense, just as Socrates sought a moral. Molinism, a mystic doctrine, leads to an annulment of the change in time. But we cannot get away from time.

This leads me to another recollection: without being Socrates, I have the habit of talking with artists. As happened with Socrates, it is possible that I too, at times, seek in pictures the painting, and as well . . . (here an undecided coefficient). I generally refrain from saying to artists everything that comes to my mind, in order not to bother them.

[5]Spanish poetic novelist, of the late nineteenth and the early twentieth century.
[6]Doctrine of the sixteenth-century Spanish theologian, Molina.

Crito and Parrasio did not worry about theories: being creators, men all of one piece, souls undivided, Crito and Parrasio hardly answered Socrates. It is better not to distract them. It is better for them to keep on working. I was always more interested in the actual carvings of Mateo Hernández than in his aesthetic lucubrations. "Dumb Peter,"[7] said the Cid, explained himself better with the sword than with the tongue. Mateo explained himself better with his chisels. When he set them aside, he would start to rant, as he said, about the art of the "Egyptians."

Well then, many years ago a certain painter, whose name does not matter, said to me: "The important thing is not to paint the face the gentleman sees in the mirror when he shaves, but that face with which posterity will actually associate him."

Posterity, in this anonymous theory, is here another intrusion of time, and now in the form of a settlement, the settlement favouring an abstraction from accidents, the theory of Valle-Inclán, or on the other hand a final judgement, through a statement concerning the complete movement of a life, the Socratic theory. Here there is a bit of everything at once: psychology, aesthetics, ethics. When a man sees before him a peril to his life, as if the consciousness wished to enrich itself by compensation on learning that the end is near, he throws himself headlong upon his entire treasure, upon the past, and condenses it in the giddy memory of a single moment. When a man sees before him his portrait, one would say that in the artistic mind—according to the theory I am examining—a similar condensation has to take place quickly, with an eye upon posterity. In a certain fashion, the portrait is a peril to life.

The anonymous theory contains something more: the authenticity of the portrait separated now from its model; the authenticity of the portrait as a subjective representation of what the man might have been. And what guarantee do we have, we of posterity, of the authenticity of a portrait of a time passed, still tinged with the vague melancholy of things disappeared? Here we turn the idea upside down and find its true bottom. The aesthetic value—that is our only guarantee; the aesthetic value which presents us with a psychological unity and something which now resembles a paradigm; a harmony which imposes itself as necessary, and through which the portrait evolves from the individual to the abstraction, whatever the point of departure: mortal man or imperishable myth. Who would cast doubt upon the

[7]A literal translation of "Pero Mudo," nickname given by the Cid to Pedro Bermúdez.

authenticity of the *Gentleman with his Hand on his Breast*? A necessity superior to the contingencies confirms it. That is the way he was, we have no doubt about it; thus does the imagination conceive a man in his human category. If he was not like that, he made a mistake about himself. The artistic expression overrides the real thing which provokes it. The portrait detaches itself from its model, as the building detaches itself from its scaffolding, and begins to live on its own account. The gentleman, who wished to live on in his portrait, has been deceived. The portrait absorbed the gentleman, and killed him. The portrait is a vampire of the man. And if it is myth, look at *Eve Expelled*, by Masaccio. Adam, like the Agamemnon of Tirmantes, sobs by her side, covering his face, a picture of manly grief that prefers to "weep like the hidden fountain," in the words of the poet. Eve, meanwhile, as a portent of oppression and shame, since the female always gives herself, gives us her grief-stricken face, her eyes swollen with tears, and is as consistent as the fall of the eternal woman. We no longer care anything about the poor mortal creature who one day served as a model, as fodder for the minotaur of painting. This is the truth of art. Consequently, this is the moral of art.

Men are ruined by the casual and bad education which life keeps thrusting upon them. But children may understand this, since they never conceal their moral necessities. I knew a child, the son of a soldier, brought up in the atmosphere of the barracks. He had recovered from measles, and he was taken to the church to give thanks to God. They put him in front of a frightful crucifix. The child was terrified. "Go on," they said to him, "Give thanks to God." The child replied: "But is that God? That must be his assistant!"

If this does not indicate, in a negative way, the recognition of a moral truth in the arts, then I do not know what it does indicate.

Concerning this idea of human synthesis and harmony of inner necessities expressed by the portrait, it is mandatory, even though it may have been done a thousand times, to go back to the smile of *La Gioconda*. Allow me to quote from an old passage: "That fathomless smile, always marked by a sinister touch, always pursued in multiple juvenile attempts based on the sketches of Verrochio, which one day allowed itself to be captured, lulled by the charm of the flutes of the buffoons, like a live dove falling little by little under the hypnotism of the serpent."*

Walter Pater has sung of Mona Lisa, more alive in the posterity of canvas than in the fleshy dress of a past day, in these terms: "All the

The Collector (El coleccionador), in *Calendario*, Madrid, 1924, p. 168.

thought and experience in the world was brought together and stamped here, so far as it is possible to refine and give expression to external forms: the animalism of Greece, the gluttony of Rome, the fantasy of the Middle Ages composed of spiritual longing and meditative love, the return to paganism and the sins of the Borgias. She is older than the rocks that surround her. Like the vampire, she has already died many times and has wrested from the tomb its secret. She has plunged into deep seas, from which she brings that subdued light in which she seems to be immersed. She had trafficked in rare fabrics with merchants from the East. She, like Leda, was mother of Helen of Troy and, like Saint Ann, was mother of Mary. And all this, in her eyes, means no more than the sound of those lyres and flutes which entertain her smile. And all of that lives no more except in the delicate insistence that all this was able to model her mutable features, and give the colour to her eyelids and hands."

The idea of restful light, of which Valle-Inclán spoke in his manner, and the inevitable appearance of Leonardo, arouse in me still another recollection. One afternoon I was going through the Uffizi Gallery. Just when the light was beginning to soften, I found myself before the *Adoration of the Magi*, an unfinished work, like so many of the things done by that tireless investigator. Perhaps there is in this picture less fervour than in any of the "Adorations" I know. On the other hand, it possesses, among them all, a unique quality, a suggestion of noise and enthusiasm. The multitude throngs about the Virgin and Child with the movement of an onslaught, like a wave of curiosity. Up above are the bundles of presents. At the back, the Magi's horses are rearing up. And as evening was falling, the picture, which moreover is a very bright one, seemed to me to take on greater vigour. On returning to the Florentine inn, I thought I could solve the enigma through a certain passage I found by chance among the notes in Leonardo's notebooks, a passage in which he informs us that faces show their character best under a clouded sky: "I prefer for your portrait," he says, "the twilight hour, when there is vagueness and mist, because that is the time of perfect light."

And finally, to speak of what we are less ignorant, we shall consider the portrait not as an artistic object, but as a word. A student of grammar may be permitted to say here that, before the verb "portray"—a verb on a second level and derived from the noun "portrait"—we found in the old books the verb "retract," in the sense of reducing and concentrating something; of bringing out "retractions" (almost "extractions"), of extracting quintessences; or to say it in another way, to "break the bone and suck the substance-giving marrow," as Rabelais' dog does, a philosophical animal among all the animals.

So, in the *Portrait of the Andalusian Beauty*—a book of crude erudition, a book which bears on its cover the unhappy date of the sack of Rome by the Constable of Bourbon, and which appeared in Venice in the year 1528—the author says, referring to what he portrays in his work: "I tried to *retract* many things by *retracting* just one, and I *retracted* what I saw ought to be *retracted*." And further on, the author himself confronts his characters and rashly plunges into his own novel. His characters invite him to spend a while making merry in their company. But he, recovering his prudence, says: "I won't go, because afterwards they say I do nothing but watch and take note of what happens, to write later, and *that I take samples*." The author, Francisco Delgado, is a great maker of portraits. Of his book, Menéndez y Pelayo said: "A tremendous sample of photographic realism." As the instructing sergeant said: "Here we teach everything. It is not the way it is in the infantry." There one sees everything, and things of every sort. There one hears everything, even the intimate pantings of the bedchamber. The taking of samples, the retracting, the portraying in such lively fashion, caused Delgado many unpleasant experiences. For that reason he prefers not to go to the party. And it is because the retracting is a witchcraft that robs the models of their substance, takes control of their will, and subjects it to the portrayer. We have already said that the portrait is a peril to life, man's portrait his vampire. There is a reason for the portrait-maker's finding a stolid resistance in the unsophisticated, in the primitive. When he approaches, the superstitious bird nesting in his bosom trembles. The savage flees from the Kodak, because the one who takes away his image takes away from him his free will, his double, his astral body. Dorian Gray discharges into his portrait, into his double, the progressive decadence of his character, his growing cruelty, his acrimony, his vice, his aging, as Dr. Jekyll stores them in Mr. Hyde. Dorian Gray keeps himself intact: only in the portrait does one notice the scars of the years and sins. But Dorian Gray has come to be a lie. It is he—the model—who is deceived. The truth passes into his portrait, until one day Dorian Gray is drawn towards death, magnetically, by his portrait, by his portrait now tired of the real lie.

In precisely the same way it happened with that other snob of Thespias, the discoverer of the portrait: the handsome and disturbing

Narcissus, the first to see the reflection of his image and who, yielding to the mysterious magnet, allowed himself to fall into the waters.

Mexico, September, 1940

Conference of Shades (*Junta de sombras*), El Colegio Nacional, Mexico, 1949, pp. 179–96.

BORN IN '89

THINGS AND PERSONS OF THE SAME AGE, but contemporaries neither in knowledge nor form of government—I know some of these.

The poncho blanket I sometimes spread on my bed came to my house when I was born, and has been one of my things since then. It accompanies my fortunes and travels. Worn as it is, it lasts and lasts. It is just as bald as I am—and of the same mood. It serves me to combat the cold when I travel by automobile. It serves me as a rustic bed or as an improvised tablecloth in the country. I see it as part of my epidermis, my constant mate. I neither love it nor hate it: I no longer feel it. It is preparing itself to die with me, and so is solicitously accelerating its ruin, because we men burn up more quickly than our blankets. In it I have concealed evil designs and sins. On its account was it said: "Under my cloak, I kill the king." It is my cloak of which I make, when I wish, a coverall. It is my cloak that covers all. It is all that the proverbs say of it. And it is even called "Poncho," as I am called myself, that pet-name common back home.

Jean Giraudoux claims that he and the Eiffel Tower are contemporaries. When they were born, the "sentimentalists" of that time did not understand them or appreciate them properly. They seemed too geometrical, too ideological, too precise. Little by little they became filled with the music of the spheres, there was a stellar vibration in all the bones of the construction, and they invented wireless telegraphy, the antenna, the Citroën sign. I am correcting Jean Giraudoux, for in this statement they are robbing me of seven years at one stroke. Paul Morand, Waldo Frank, and I were actually born with the Tower.* And I can actually state that there was a time—although now I may be believed by no one—when the Eiffel Tower and I were of the same stature.

*I have since discovered that Charles Chaplin too was born in 1889.

Today I cannot match either it or them, but the figure ties us together, and we are sown in the same geological stratum of time.

> It is possible that for those who use their time well, learning and experience grow with life; but . . . .
>
> Montaigne, *Essays*, I, lvii.

1926

Calendar and Train of Waves (*Calendario y tren de ondas*), Edición Tezontle, Mexico, 1945, pp. 123–25.

NOTES ON THE AMERICAN MIND

1. MY OBSERVATIONS are confined to what is called Latin America. The need to abridge forces me to be inaccurate and unclear, and to exaggerate to the point of caricature. All I propose to do is to provoke or set moving a conversation, without trying to exhaust the groundwork of the problems I raise, much less to offer solutions. I have the feeling that, while using America as a pretext, I am doing nothing more than touching a few universal themes in passing.

2. To speak of American civilization* would be, in the present instance, inopportune: it would lead us into archaeological regions which lie outside our theme. To speak of American culture would be somewhat equivocal: it would suggest to us only one branch of the European tree which has been transplanted to American soil. On the other hand, we can speak of the American mind, and the American view of life and action in life. This will permit us to define, though only provisionally, the American colouring.

*The seventh meeting of the International Institute for Intellectual Co-operation was held in Buenos Aires, from the 11th to the 16th of September, 1936, on the theme: "Present relations between the cultures of Europe and Latin America." In it the following took part: G. Duhamel, P. Henríquez Ureña, J. B. Terán, L. Piérard, F. de Figueiredo, J. Maritain, B. Sanín Cano, A. Arguedas, E. Ludwig, [H. A.] Keyserling (by letter), F. Romero, R. H. Mottram, C. Ibarguren, W. Entwistle, A. Peixoto, J. Estelrich, A. Reyes, C. Reyles, E. Díez-Canedo, G. Ungaretti, J. Romains, and S. Zweig. Duhamel opened the discussion in the name of Europe, and the notes published here represent the introduction of the subject in the name of America, which was entrusted to us. The impossibility of exhausting such a vast and enticing theme in such short sessions occasioned our being called later to meet with Pedro Henríquez Ureña and Francisco Romero to continue the discussion on our own account. In several meetings, from October 23 to November 19 in 1936, we took some notes from which perhaps some day a work in collaboration will be produced.

3. Our drama has a stage, a chorus, and a character. By a stage I do not now mean a space, but rather a time, a time in almost the musical sense of the word: a beat, a rhythm. Having arrived late at the banquet of European civilization, America goes leaping over steps along the way, hurrying and racing from one form to another, without having given the preceding form time to mature completely. At times, the leap is bold and the new form looks like food taken away from the fire before it is fully cooked. Tradition has had less weight, and this explains the boldness. But we do not yet know whether the European rhythm—which we try to overtake with long strides, not being able to match it at its measured pace—is the only historical tempo possible; and no one has yet demonstrated that a certain acceleration of the process is contrary to nature. This is the secret of our history, our politics, our life, dominated by a call to improvise. The chorus: American populations are formed, principally, from the old autochthonous elements, the Iberian throngs of conquerors, missionaries, and colonists, and the later contributions of European immigrants in general. There are conflicts of blood, problems of cross-breeding, efforts at adaptation and absorption. In different regions, there is a predominance of the Indian or Iberian hue, the grey of the half-caste, the white of the general European immigrant, and even the huge marks of the African brought in past centuries to our soil by the old colonial administrators. The gamut allows every kind of tone. The laborious womb of America is little by little intermingling this heterogeneous substance, and day by day there is now coming into existence a characteristic American humanity, an American spirit. The actor or character in this case is the intelligence.

4. The American intelligence is operating upon a series of conflicts. Fifty years after the Spanish conquest, that is, in one generation, we already find in Mexico an American manner: under the influences of the new atmosphere, the new economic set-up, with the coming together of the sensibility of the Indian and the property instinct which arises out of having occupied the land, there appears among the Mexican Spaniards themselves a sense of a New World aristocracy, which already clashes with the aggressive ambitions of Spanish newcomers. On this point there are abundant literary testimonies: both in the satirical and popular poetry of the period, and in the subtle observations of the peninsular sages, like Juan de Cárdenas.[8] Literary criticism has centred this phenomenon, as in a luminous focus, in the figure of the Mexican dramatist don Juan Ruiz de Alarcón, who,

[8]Seventeenth-century Spanish theologian.

through Corneille—who passed it on to Molière—had the good fortune to bring influence to bear upon the modern French theatre of customs. And what I say of Mexico, because it is more familiar and better known to me, might be said to a greater or lesser degree of the rest of our America. In this incipient prickling, there was already throbbing the long yearning for the independence of the American states.

A second conflict: as soon as independence is won, the inevitable dispute between Americanists and Hispanists appears, between those who lay stress on the new reality, and those who lay it upon old tradition. Sarmiento[9] is above all an Americanist. Bello[10] is above all a Hispanist. In Mexico one recalls a certain polemic between the Indian Ignacio Ramírez and the Spaniard Emilio Castelar which revolves around the same themes. This polemic was often turned into a conflict between liberals and conservatives. The emancipation was so recent that neither father nor son had learned how to live with it in an attitude of mutual tolerance.

Third conflict: one pole is in Europe and the other in the United States. We receive inspiration from them both. Our constitutional utopias combine the political philosophy of France with the presidential federalism of the United States. The sirens of Europe and those of North America both sing to us at once. In a general way, the mind of our America (without for that reason denying affinities with the most select individuals of the other America) seems to find in Europe a vision of what is most universally and most basically human, and in closest conformity to its own way of feeling. Apart from historical suspicions, fortunately less and less justified and which must not be touched upon here, we dislike any tendency towards ethnic segregations. To keep to the Anglo-Saxon world, we like the naturalness with which a Chesterton or a Bernard Shaw contemplates the peoples of all climes, conceding to them equal human authenticity. Gide does the same thing in the Congo. We do not like to consider any human type as a mere curiosity or an amusing exotic specimen, because this is not the basis for true moral sympathy. The very first mentors of our America, the missionaries, lambs with hearts of lions, people of fierce independence, lovingly embrace the Indians, promising them the same heaven that was promised to them. The very first conquerors founded equality in their impulses towards cross-breeding: so, in the West Indies, we have Miguel Díaz and his Cacica, whom

[9]Argentinian reformer and educationist of the nineteenth century.
[10]Venezuela-born Chilean poet and scholar of the nineteenth centurv.

we find in the pages of Juan de Castellanos;[11] we also have that soldier, a certain Guerrero—who without this story about him would be unknown to us—refusing to follow the Spaniards with Cortez because he was getting along fine among Indians and, as in the old Spanish ballad, "had a beautiful wife and children most lovely." Likewise, in Brazil, we have the famous João Ramalho and el Caramurú, who fascinated the Indian women of San Vicente de Bahía. The conqueror Cortez himself enters into the secrets of his conquest when he rests upon the bosom of Doña Marina; perhaps there he learns to fall in love with his prize in a way that other captains with colder hearts could not (like Caesar of the Gauls), and begins to harbour in his mind certain ambitions for autonomy which, behind closed doors and within the family, he was to communicate to his children, later tortured for conspiracy against the Spanish motherland. Imperial Iberia, much more than she administered our affairs, simply kept bleeding herself over America. Here, in our countries, we continue to think of life in that way—as open and generous bleeding.

5. Such are the stage, the chorus, and the character. I have mentioned the principal alternatives in conduct. I spoke of a certain call to improvise, and I must now explain myself. The American mind is necessarily less specialized than the European. Our social structure requires it so. The writer here has closer links with society, and generally practises several professions. He rarely succeeds in being merely a writer, and is almost always a writer "plus" one or more other things. Such a situation offers advantages and disadvantages. The disadvantages: a call to action—the mind discovers that the order of action is the order of transaction, and this brings suffering. Frustrated by continual necessary duties, intellectual production is sporadic, and the mind is distracted. The advantages arise from the actual state of the contemporary world. In crisis, in the turmoil which keeps us all astir nowadays and requires the effort of all, and especially mental effort (unless we resign ourselves to allowing only ignorance and desperation to contrive to frame the new human patterns), the American mind is more accustomed to the air of the street; among us there are not, there cannot be, ivory towers. This new alternative of advantages and disadvantages also allows a synthesis, an equilibrium which resolves itself into a peculiar way of viewing intellectual work as a public service and a civilizing duty. Naturally this does not rule out, fortunately, possibilities of a withdrawal, of the luxury of pure literary

[11]Spanish poet and chronicler of the sixteenth century, who resided for many years in America.

leisure, a fount to which we must return to bathe with a salutary frequency. But in Europe, the withdrawal could be normal. The European writer is born, as it were, on the top level of the Eiffel Tower. With an effort of a few metres, he is right up on the mental heights. The American writer is born, as it were, in the region of central fire. After a colossal effort, in which often he is aided by a stimulated vitality which almost resembles genius, he just barely succeeds in getting up to the surface of the earth. Oh, my European colleagues, under many a mediocre American is frequently concealed a storehouse of qualities which certainly merits your sympathy and study. Evaluate him, if you please, from the standpoint of that profession superior to all the others, mentioned by Guyau[12] and by José Enrique Rodó:[13] the general profession of being a man. Under this light, there is no danger that learning would become detached from its main body, bottled up in its isolated conquests a millimetre long by another millimetre wide, a danger the consequences of which Jules Romains described to us so lucidly in his inaugural address to the Pen Club. In this peculiar American situation there is no danger either of a cutting-off of links with Europe. Quite on the contrary, I have a feeling that the American mind is called to fulfil the most noble complementary function: that of establishing syntheses, even though necessarily provisional; that of applying the results promptly, verifying the value of the theory in the living flesh of action. Along these lines, if the economy of Europe has need of us already, the very mind of Europe will in the end have need of us.

6. For this beautiful harmony which I foresee, the American mind offers a peculiar faculty, because our mentality, even though so strongly rooted in our own countries, as I have stated, is naturally internationalistic. This is explained not only by the fact that our America offers conditions for making it the melting-pot for that future "cosmic race" of which Vasconcelos has dreamed, but also by the fact that we have had to go looking for our cultural machinery in the great European centres, thus accustoming ourselves to handling foreign ideas as if they were our own. While the European has not had to go to America to construct his world-system, the American studies, knows, and lives Europe from the primary school. From this arises a most interesting consequence which I point out without vanity or rancour: in the

[12]Nineteenth-century French poet and philosopher.

[13]Uruguayan writer whose masterpiece, *Ariel* (1900), is a call to Spanish-American youth to appreciate and respond to their Hispanic cultural heritage, and to resist influences from English-speaking America.

balance of errors in detail or partial misunderstandings found in European books that deal with America, and those found in American books that deal with Europe, the count is in our favour. Among American writers it is actually a professional secret that European literature makes frequent errors in quotations in our language, the spelling of our names, our geography, etc. Our innate internationalism, happily supported by the historic brotherhood which unites so many republics, implants in the American mind an undeniable pacifistic inclination. It passes through armed conflicts, winning each time by dexterous manipulation, and makes itself felt in the international order even in groups most contaminated by a certain fashionable bellicosity. It will facilitate the delicate grafting of the pacifistic idealism which inspires the greatest minds of North America. Our America must live as if it were always prepared to realize the dream which its discovery inspired among the thinkers of Europe: the dream of utopia, the happy republic, which lent singular warmth to the pages of Montaigne, when he came to contemplate the surprises and marvels of the new world.*

7. In the new American literatures there is quite perceptible an insistence upon autochthonism which merits all our respect, especially when one does not cling to the easy note of local colour, but tries to extend the sounding right down to the heart of psychological realities.

*I thought these explanations would suffice to clarify the sense I gave to the concept of the synthesis of culture, a synthesis for which our America seems singularly fitted. In the volumes published in 1937 by the International Institute for Intellectual Co-operation, in Spanish and in French in Buenos Aires and Paris, respectively, in which appears the review of the talks to which these notes on America served as an introduction, it may be seen that Francisco Romero agreed with me in appreciating a certain synthesizing ability in the American mentality, a coincidence which was not the result of a previous interchange of ideas, and this makes it the more weighty. But, on speaking of "synthesis," neither he nor I was correctly interpreted by our European colleagues, who thought we referred to an elemental summary or compendium of European achievements. According to this superficial interpretation, the synthesis would be a terminal point. But no: synthesis here is a new point of departure, a structure made of previous scattered elements which, like any structure, is transcendent and contains new things within itself. H_2O is not only a combination of hydrogen and oxygen, but it is also water. The quantity 3 is not only the sum of 1 plus 2, but it is also something which neither 1 nor 2 is. This capacity to look at the incoherent panorama of the world and at the same time to establish objective structures, which signify a step further, finds in the American mind a fertile and prepared soil. As compared to the American setting, the European setting appears to be shut up behind a Chinese wall, and irremediably so, like a cultural provincial. So long as they do not perceive this and do not modestly accept it, the Europeans will not have understood the Americans. It is not a matter of vulgar judgements regarding what may be superior or inferior in itself, but of different points of view with respect to reality.

This pubescent ardour corrects that hereditary sadness, that bad conscience with which our elders contemplated the world, feeling themselves children of the great original sin, of diminution in stature on account of being American. I permit myself here to utilize some pages I wrote six years ago.*

The generation immediately preceding us still believed itself born within the prison of several concentric misfortunes. The most pessimistic felt this way: in the first place, the first great misfortune, which of course consisted of being human, according to the saying of the ancient Silenus picked up by Calderón:

> Because the greatest crime of man
> is to have been born.

Within this circle came the second, which consisted of having come very late to an old world. Still unsilenced were the echoes of that Romanticism which the Cuban Juan Clemente Zenea epitomized in two lines:

> My verses are those of ancient Rome
> And my brothers died with Greece.

In the world of our letters, a sentimental anachronism dominated the average person. The third circle, besides the misfortunes of being human and being modern, was the very specific circle of being American, that is to say, born and rooted in a soil which was not the present focus of civilization, but a branch-office of the world. To use a saying of our Victoria Ocampo, our ancestors felt themselves "proprietors of a soul without a passport." Once one was American, another handicap in life's career was to be Latin, or, in short, of a Latin cultural heritage. It was the period of "Wherein lies the superiority of the Anglo-Saxon?" It was the period of submission to the present state of things, without hope of a definitive change or faith in redemption. One heard only the harangues of Rodó, noble and ingenuous. Once belonging to the Latin sphere, another misfortune within it was to belong to the Hispanic sphere. The old lion had been in decline for some time. Spain seemed to have gone back home from its earlier greatness, and was now sceptical and weak. The sun had set over her dominions. And, to cap it all, the Spanish American was on bad terms with Spain, which was true until a short time ago, until before the present sorrow of Spain,[14]

*Monterrey, *Correo Literario* (*Literary Mail*) of A. Reyes, Rio de Janeiro, October 1930. No. 3, pp. 1–3, and *Sur*, Buenos Aires, 1931, No. 1, pp. 149–58: *A Bit of America* (*Un paso de América*).

[14]The Spanish Civil War, 1936–39.

which pains us all. Within the Hispanic world, we were still reduced to being a dialect, a derivation, something secondary, a branch-office once more: Spanish-American, a name bound together by a hyphen as with a chain. Within the Spanish-American, those near me still lamented having been born in the region where the Indian strain was strong: the Indian, then, was a burden, and not yet a proud duty and a strong hope. Within this region, those still nearer to me had reasons for distress at having been born in the fearful neighbourhood of an aggressive and plethoric nation, a feeling now transformed into the inappreciable sense of pride in representing the forefront of a race. Of all these phantoms which the wind has been blowing away or the light of day reforming into different shapes to the point of converting them, at least, into acceptable realities, something still remains in the corners of America, and it must be chased out, opening the windows to full width and calling superstition by its name, which is the way to put it to flight. But, basically, all that is now corrected.

8. Having established the foregoing premises and after this examination in court, I venture to assume the style of a juridical summing-up. For some time there has existed between Spain and us the sense of a levelling process and of equality. And now I say before the tribunal of international thinkers which is listening to me: acknowledge that we have the right to the universal citizenship which we now have won. We have attained our majority. Very soon you will get accustomed to having us with you.

Buenos Aires, September, 1936

Land of Mystery (*Última Tule*), Imprenta Universitaria, Mexico, 1942, pp. 131–45.

Manuel Toussaint

(b. Mexico, D.F., 1890; d. New York, 1955)

Manuel Toussaint y Ritter studied at the Normal School and at the National Preparatory School, then in the School of Fine Arts and the School of Higher Studies (later called the Faculty of Philosophy and Letters), and at a very young age began his work as a teacher, which was to be his principal activity. He was the founder of a memorable chair, that of the History of the Art of New Spain, in the Faculty of Philosophy and Letters, and from that chair he taught several generations to love our colonial art.

In 1917 the review *Pegasus* (*Pegaso*), managed by González Martínez, Rebolledo, and López Velarde in the shadow of the colonialist fashion of that time, published the first studies by Toussaint. Later don Manuel was artistic editor of the literary review *Modern Mexico* (*México Moderno*), 1920–23, and in the subsequent years he published texts by Sor Juana, Altamirano, Riva Palacio, and Cuenca, preceded by interesting studies. His fundamental work, nevertheless, was not to be literary criticism, but art criticism centred upon a single period, the colonial, of which for many years he was to be the investigator and master *par excellence*.

Toussaint travelled in Spain in 1921, as he relates in a pleasant book, *Fascinating Travels. Corners of Spain* (*Viajes alucinados. Rincones de España*), 1924. Later he travelled again, to Europe and America, on academic missions. He was founder and director of the Institute of Aesthetic Research from 1934 to his death. In 1928 and 1929 he directed the National School of Fine Arts, and from 1945 to 1954 he was head of the Committee on Colonial Monuments in the Republic, a branch of the National Institute of Anthropology and History. He was member of the National College, the Linguistic Academy, and many other cultural organizations, and received an honorary doctorate from the University of Mexico.

The copious studies and monographs by Toussaint on various aspects of colonial art and culture—architecture, painting, sculpture—have the double excellence of being prepared by a rigorous and analytic investigator and written by an artist who understood and loved the objects of his study. In his lectures Toussaint had the virtue of evoking with lively and impassioned eloquence the spirit of our colonial world, and that liveliness persists in many beautiful pages in which he reclaimed, ordered, and ennobled the art and life of New Spain.

ESSAYS: *Fascinating Travels. Corners of Spain* (*Viajes alucinados. Rincones de España*), 1924–Oaxaca, 1926.

LITERARY CRITICISM: Agustín F. Cuenca, *Select Poems* (*Poemas selectos*), Selection and Prologue by M.T., 1920; Sor Juana Inés de la Cruz, *Selected Works* (*Obras escogidas*), Edition and Prologue by M.T., 1928; Vicente Riva Palacio, *Tales of the General* (*Cuentos del general*), Edition and Prologue by M.T., 1929; Ignacio Manuel Altamirano, *Selected Speeches* (*Discursos escogidos*), Selection and Prologue by M.T., 1932.

MONOGRAPHS AND STUDIES: *The Cathedral of Mexico* (*La catedral de México*), 1917, 1924, 1948; *Saturnino Hernán and his Work* (*Saturnino Hernán y su obra*), 1920; *The Religious Architecture of New Spain During the Sixteenth Century* (*La arquitectura religiosa de Nueva España durante el siglo XVI*), 1927; *Sacramental Praise in Metaphor on the Streets of Mexico* (*Loa sacramental en metáfora de las calles de México*), 1927; *Tasco*, 1931; *The Lithograph in Mexico During the Nineteenth Century* (*La litografía en México durante el siglo XIX*), 1934; *Gothic Survivals in the Mexican Architecture of the Sixteenth Century* (*Supervivencias góticas en la arquitectura mexicana del siglo XVI*), 1935; *Illustrated Guide to Tasco* (*Guía ilustrada de Tasco*), 1935; *Painting in Mexico During the Sixteenth Century* (*La pintura en México durante el siglo XVI*), 1936; *The Story of Michoacán* (*La relación de Michoacán*), 1937; *Mexican Art* (*Arte mexicano*), Buenos Aires, 1937; *Impressions of Bolivia* (*Impresiones de Bolivia*), La Paz, 1937; *Maps of the City of Mexico During the Sixteenth and Seventeenth Centuries* (*Planos de la ciudad de México durante los siglos XVI y XVII*), 1938 (In collaboration with Justino Fernández and Federico Gómez de Orozco); *Portrait and Landscape in the Work of Cecil Crawford O'Gorman* (*Retrato y paisaje en la obra de Cecil Crawford O'Gorman*), 1938; *Lawsuit and Accusations against Simón Pereyns* (*Proceso y denuncias contra Simón Pereyns*), 1938; *Colonial Strolls* (*Paseos coloniales*), 1939; *Twenty Centuries of Mexican Art* (*Veinte siglos de arte Mexicano*), 1940 (In collaboration with Alfonson Caso, Miguel Covarrubias, and Roberto Montenegro); *Colonial Imagery* (*Imaginería colonial*), 1941 (In collaboration with M. Rodríguez Lozano); *The Art of New Spain* (*El arte de la Nueva España*), 1946; *Mexican Popular Art* (*Arte popular de México*), 1946; *Colonial Art in Mexico* (*Arte colonial en México*), 1948; *Mural Paintings in the Mexican Convents of the Sixteenth Century* (*Pinturas murales en los conventos mexicanos del siglo XVI*), 1949; *The Cathedral and the Churches of Puebla* (*La catedral y las iglesias de Puebla*), 1954.

HISTORY: *Don José de la Borda Restored to Spain* (*Don José de la Borda restituido a España*), 1933; *The Christian Doctrine of Brother Peter of Ghent* (*La doctrina cristiana de Fray Pedro de Gante*), 1933; *The Work of an Illustrious Cuban in Mexico. Doctor don Francisco Xavier Conde y Oquendo* (*La obra de un ilustre cubano en México. El doctor don Francisco Xavier Conde y Oquendo*), Havana, 1939; *The Conquest of Pánuco* (*La conquista de Pánuco*), 1948.

THE HOUSE OF SUGAR-PASTE IN PUEBLA

IN SPITE OF THE YEARS and neglect, the prestige of Puebla's colonial inheritance survives in its whole atmosphere. Ignorance persists in destroying the treasures of the past to set up at will all our modern architecture, artificial stone, cement, and stucco. When the traveller looks at old buildings, he adds to their peculiar beauty this other funereal charm which arises from the spiritual fragility of mortal beings as opposed to the persistence of stone; they are condemned in advance; their owner will kill them himself, ignorant of what he is losing. And, as if they acquired consciousness of their death, a twinge of uneasiness comes over them.

Puebla presents suggestive enchantments to anyone seeking traces of the art of other times. It is the Creole city of New Spain; it lacks the indigenous tradition, and clings tenaciously, almost furiously, to its old Spanish and Christian tradition. The special circumstances of its location have no little influence in lending to it its peculiar character. It is level, quiet, without great heights in the vicinity. It extends outward just as other cities—Guanajuato, Zacatecas, Tasco—are built in depth. The streets, uniform, picturesque in the motley groupings of the houses, end suddenly; there are no suburbs. The parish church of Santo Ángel de Analco hardly lifts up its aged crest in a wilderness of dust: it is a distant district, almost a town, and the same is true of Santiago. Of the modern colonies which have increased the size of the city recently, I prefer not to speak.

But the most distinctive thing is its climate. It is a dry atmosphere, of incomparable clearness. There are no transitions between light and shadow: you see a wall sunlit, dazzling, and in it, black and unfathomable, the opening of a door. This climate excites and oppresses. It is favourable to joy and melancholy, to laziness and voluptuosity, like those characteristic *ll*'s[1] which, on the lips of women, combine caress and nonchalance, at once inciting and indifferent.

The houses are admirably adapted to this climate. Everywhere you come upon ample entrances overflowing with shadow. Find refuge for your weariness in one of them; there is a delightful coolness in it. Behind the arch extends the courtyard, which is like an invasion of dazzling brightness. In the centre, there is the kindly green of a tree—an orange tree, a fig tree, a laurel—an oasis in that little desert. The stairway is not placed symmetrically as it is in the houses of certain

[1]Sound of *y* in "yes" for that of *lli* in "million."

periods in Mexico, but at the most convenient spot in the courtyard, pleasantly welcoming with a massive breastwork of rough masonry, the same as in the corridors; both rest upon brackets of stone set in the wall and joined together by cut-down arches. The whiteness of the courtyard seems to drive out life, but behind those dark blackish marks which form doors and windows, if you cross the irregular tiling, you will find life that is laughing, gay, and capricious—a lilting and piquant conversation.

But I can also show you a house with more sumptuous ornament. Look at that large edifice on the corner at Raboso Street. Is your attention attracted by that decoration on the walls, by that combination of glazed tile and brick? It is typical of Puebla; half of its houses have it. And note the wisdom it contains: the wall does not reverberate with the solar light, it absorbs the heat and the radiation, it protects our eyes and protects the inhabitant of the house, it plays the same role as the Mexican building stone—but alas! like the latter it has also been barbarously covered with whitewash in a large number of the houses.

The composition of the façade is admirable. Those horizontal lines divide it harmoniously and prevent the house from appearing too high or too low. And at the corner, the angle of the aforementioned lines breaks, giving to the building an incomparable grace. The fills and spaces are combined with great art. What modern architect can distribute twenty-six spaces over a façade without spoiling the equilibrium and without making the house appear an enormous dovecot?

But the principal merit of this mansion lies in its ornamentation. It is an ornamentation soberly concentrated, which is nil in the lower part and slowly ascends, lightening each story, until it reaches the voluptuous cornice, that undulating line which seems to be rocking itself in the clouds.

If you will go up with me to one of the top-floor balconies, you will be charmed by the gracefulness of the ornamentation, which on account of its fragility gives the house its name. Along the pilasters, like a fantastic and proteiform marine monster, creeps the reliefwork. It is low and simple at first; it is a simple garland which becomes gradually transformed as though yielding to a deep voluptuous desire. After passing the lintel of the door, one loses almost every trace of an architectural arrangement; there is only an accumulation of decorations, of volutes, conches, and stonework which seem to support, miraculously, the vastness of the canopies which cover the broad balconies. The consistency of the decorations, all made of a medley and refined by height, gives to the whole the most delicate effect; it certainly does resemble *sugar-paste*: a confection made only of sugar, fragile and translucent like a piece of porcelain.

Do not think that the façade has no defects. For example, look at the broad tiles which form the floors of the balconies, the *sardinel*[2] masonry; they are solidly set in the wall and do not present the slightest danger, but the most elementary law of architecture required that it should have something after the fashion of a bracket, at least one of those artificially wrought pieces of iron, so abundant in Puebla. I imagine that the architect, influenced by the plasticity afforded by his materials, and by the desire to fill his work with luxury in order to make it worthy of the prosperous colony, and also encouraged here by the pleasantness of the climate, forgot all rule and measure as he worked out the caprices of his fancy. You will find cornices in some houses in Puebla that have lost their architectural value and become something abominable: sumptuous and lineless, delicate and absurd, a monstrosity.

In the interior of the House of Sugar-paste there is still much to admire. After passing the vault over the entrance we come upon the ample courtyard. The stairway is most remarkable; it is crowned by a cupola which in the interior presents a magnificent appearance. The corridor, very wide, quite dark, has on one side a door superbly decorated; perhaps it is the chapel door, since it presents the same appearance as such doors in Mexico City. The corridors opposite are narrower. Like almost all corridors in Puebla, they rest on a series of low arches, supported on brackets of elegant outline; the shadow accumulates gently under the concave surface, lending vigour to the structure.

In style, through the use of the pilaster overcharged with ornament, this monument falls within the Churrigueresque[3] category, which is as abundant in the domestic buildings of Puebla as it is rare in other regions, such as in Mexico City. It is a magnificent example whose eighteenth-century grace contrasts with the severe and elegant baroque of the seventeenth century, which also exists abundantly in this beatific city.

Something can be said of the history of this house, even though the data be incomplete. According to Dr. Leicht, in his Germanic and therefore methodical book *The Streets of Puebla*, the house is mentioned by its present name as early as 1790; it had just been built by

[2]A style of Moorish origin, characterized by cut brick set in a design.
[3]A very ornate Spanish architectural style of the late seventeenth century.

the master iron-worker Juan Ignacio Morales, grandfather of the Pueblan painter don Francisco Morales, "Moralitos," who lived in it during the time that it was owned by his father and his sisters. In 1896 the philanthropist don Alejandro Ruiz Olavarrieta handed it over to the Public Charities of the State, and in 1926 the Regional Museum was installed in the building.

It is said that the architect of the monument was the famous don Antonio de Santa María Incháurregui, Master of Architecture and accredited Surveyor, Member of the Academy of San Carlos de México (this appears in the *Guides* of Ontiveros from at least as early as 1806), who died in 1827 at the age of seventy-five.

The Sugar-Paste Museum, as it is now called, is visited by all the tourists who come to Puebla. Its rooms are crowded with furniture, pictures, and archaeological and ethnographic objects. One's attention is attracted, on the ground floor, by the little stairways of the classical *outbuildings of cup and plate*, which were frequently used in Puebla.

Some departments of the Museum are well set up; others, unfortunately, on account of the excessive number of items, have the appearance of little bazaars in which the pieces of real merit are lost in a clutter which wearies our brain instead of delighting us.

Let us go again to the balcony, to the largest and most sumptuous. Is it not true that its ampleness and its spaciousness are symbolic? It is made as if it was intended to see life gliding by at its feet, preserving the imprisoned immortality in the colourless moss of its stones.

Colonial Strolls (*Paseos coloniales*), Imprenta Universitaria, Mexico, 1939, pp. 171–75.

AMERICAN ART

IS THERE AN AMERICAN ART? The question seems a senseless one and the answer obvious, but if we reflect a moment on the problem and insist upon precision in our concepts, we shall see that neither is it easy to come to a common agreement concerning it, nor does the solution appear so clear.

Of course, we must consider the artistic phenomenon in its entirety and not in local groups in space or time, and besides, if we are seeking an evaluation, as we believe we have a right to do, we shall not be satisfied with judging ourselves inside our own house, but we shall wish to compare our art with that of all humanity. So, paradoxically,

America has an art only when its artists go beyond its territorial frontiers. Moreover, what degree of importance are we going to concede to external influence? Was our colonial art, as some hold, only a colony of the Spanish art of the golden ages, in which Indian art served only as ballast? Or is this art valid only, as others say, when the indigenous spirit superimposes itself with most vigour on the European outline? Can we understand our present painting in Mexico without knowing modern French painting, from Renoir to Picasso? Does this mean that Mexican painting is a branch of French painting?

We see, then, that the subject is very complex and requires hard and careful study. At the moment we can only give our views in a general way.

Some deny the importance of nationalism in art and believe that the artistic movement of humanity through time is a single unit. For a mystical contemplation of a work of art, that may be true, but anyone who is concerned with the history and criticism of the phenomenon we call art must necessarily accept the fact that those activities, in essence, consist of the differentiation and co-ordination of this phenomenon in its two most important factors: man, or the creator, and the work, or its realization. And that differentiation and co-ordination must be made by stages: (1) the country, (2) the period, (3) the group, and (4) the individual. If this is not done, the figure is floating in a vacuum for lack of supports to connect it with reality. The man passes and the work remains; or rather, the man survives in his work, but the country and the period are necessary if we are to understand him or even be affected by him.

The countries of America have always been great producers of art. Before the discovery of the continent by the Europeans, art was at the service of divinity. It was, like divinity, recondite, and expressed itself in symbols. It was decorative and prolix. It knew how to enhance the terror which the gods had to inspire in order that they might be feared and worshipped. It brought together, in paintings which reveal a great imagination, its ritualistic secrets and its discoveries of times and seasons based on astronomy. As a concession from the major arts, its fondness for decoration passed to utensils, pottery, ritual jewels, woven and embroidered blankets, mosaics of feathers which seem to contain the entire spirit of the aboriginal races in the minute intricacies of the work, the harmony of the colours, and the force of expression.

Mexican indigenous art was not appreciated as such during the rule of the viceroys. Its works were considered valuable only as historical documents—Sahagún, Motolinia, Mendieta, Torquemada, Clavijero,

Boturini. In the nineteenth century, now in cultured Europe, it was followed in the same manner—Kingsborough, Dupais, Charnay, Loubat—and only in most recent times has its great importance as art been recognized. Although there does not yet exist a perfect demarcation between art and archaeology—a study of the anthropological phenomenon and not only the artistic—it must be recognized that the most valuable contribution of America to human art is precisely this.

The importance of colonial art, as it is called, has not been accepted until recent years. It was brought to our attention towards the end of the nineteenth century—Couto, Revilla, Baxter, for Mexico—and was taken as a branch, of more or less value, of Spanish art. Concerning it were pronounced, moreover, the two opinions fanatically opposed to each other, and for that reason absurd, that we have anticipated. Does not the good man who, for the glory of Spain, denies the slightest participation of the Indian in colonial art, actually denigrate that art? By his attitude he accepts, contrary to historical fact, a destructive fury in the conqueror which kills the spirit of the vanquished to the point of complete extinction. And he who seeks only for indigenous elements, more or less with the cramped outlook of the collector, places himself outside of a great historical achievement because, alongside the great pre-Hispanic creations, of what value are these others, already submerged by a different artistic mode?

If we place ourselves on a higher plane, and it is time we did, we can say that colonial art in America is not merely one or several divisions of Spanish art. On the new continent some of the great Spanish styles, like the Gothic and the plateresque, had an honourable end; the magnificent series of Spanish cathedrals terminated with dignity, and here culminated the baroque, already as an expression of our own spirit, but with elements received from the mother country—a glorious production of new countries, born under the protection of the old land. But at first the differential touch is given by indigenous technique and motifs applied to monuments of the European type, and later, in the baroque, by the new spirit, Creole and mestizo, which arose out of the mingling of the two peoples.

One of the proofs of the vigour of colonial art is given by our pitiful independent nineteenth century, in which, except for a few men of great talent—Velasco, Rebull—there is nothing worthy of mention, unless we count the popular art, which is a continuation of the popular art of the preceding century.

Now we come to contemporary art, developed more vigorously in Mexico than in other countries. Its air of modernity comes to it from

Europe, but it has succeeded in bringing together all experiences, the pre-Hispanic, the popular, the social movement, and even the experience of the great Italian painters of frescos in the Renaissance, without which Mexican mural painting would be inexplicable. This art, now recognized throughout the whole world, opens enormous perspectives to its cultivators in the New World.

From all that I have said it is seen that there are certainties which justify an affirmative answer to the question brought to your attention, however necessary it may be to extend these meditations and to advance more exhaustive arguments than those which can go into a simple periodical article.

Romance, Mexico, Apr. 15, 1940, Year I, No. 6, pp. 1–2.

Jesús Silva Herzog

(b. San Luis Potosí, S.L.P., 1892)

After studying in the Seminary of his native city, in a New York business school, and in the Faculty of Advanced Studies in the National University, Jesús Silva Herzog began teaching in the field of economics about 1919, and this occupation has been one of his most basic and most fruitful activities. In fact, he has taught for many years, and still continues to teach, different courses in economics in the Normal School, the Summer School, the Faculty of Philosophy and Letters, the Faculty of Law, the School of Economics, and the National College, of which he is a member. He founded and directed important journals like the *Mexican Review of Economics* (*Revista Mexicana de Economía*), *Oil in Mexico* (*El Petróleo en México*), and *The Economic Quarterly* (*El Trimestre Económico*); he also founded the Mexican Institute for Economic Research (Instituto Mexicano de Investigaciones Económicas), and occupied different public offices like those of Director of Economic Statistics, Head of the Department of Economic Records in the Department of Finance, Head of the Bureau of Economic Studies of the National Railways, Deputy Minister of Education, General Manager of Mexican Petroleums, Director of the School of Economics, Director of Financial Studies in the Department of Finance, and Deputy Minister of that department. He also belongs to the Mexican Linguistic Academy and to other cultural bodies. The majority of his books are devoted to the study of economic and social problems in Mexico; the rest of them are texts in which he expounds classical thought on that topic.

Since 1942 the greatest enterprise of Jesús Silva Herzog has been the direction of the journal *American Memoranda* (*Cuadernos Americanos*), a periodical of consistently high quality throughout its already long life, and an organ for the expression of the free thought of the continent.

The essays of Silva Herzog, written with restraint and with a strong love for Mexico, are deliberately kept free of rhetorical pretensions, but the clarity of the exposition, the firm grasp of the problems, and the honest passion which inspires them are their best ornamentation.

ESSAYS AND STUDIES: *Notes on the Economic Evolution of Mexico* (*Apuntes sobre la evolución económica de México*), 1927; *Sonora, Sinaloa,* and *Nayarit*, 1929

(In collaboration with several authors); *Economic Aspects of the Soviet Union* (*Aspectos económicos de la Unión Soviética*), 1930; *The Wages and Enterprtse of the Mexican National Railways* (*Los salarios y la empresa de los Ferrocarriles Nacionales de México*), 1930; *An Inquiry into the Cost of Living in Mexico* (*Una encuesta del costo de la vida en México*), 1931; *The Economy of Mexico* (*México económico*), 1928–1930 (In collaboration with several authors); *The Agrarian Problem in Mexico and Some Other Nations* (*El problema agrario en México y algunas otras naciones*), 1934; *Socialistic Thought* (*El pensamiento socialista*), 1936; *History and Anthology of Economic Thought. Antiquity and the Middle Ages* (*Historia y antología del pensamiento económico. Antigüedad y Edad Media*), 1938; *History and Anthology of Economic Thought. From the Sixteenth Century to David Ricardo* (*Historia y antología del pensamiento económico. Desde el siglo XVI hasta David Ricardo*), 1939; *Mexican Petroleum. History of a Problem* (*Petróleo mexicano, Historia de un problema*), 1941; *The Mexican Revolution in Crisis* (*La Revolución Mexicana en crisis*), 1943; *Essay on the Mexican Revolution* (*Un ensayo sobre la Revolución Mexicana*), 1946; *Economic Thought in Mexico* (*El pensamiento económico en México*), 1947; *Meditations on Mexico, Essays and Notes* (*Meditaciones sobra México, Ensayos y notas*), 1948; *Three Centuries of Economic Thought* (*Tres siglos de pensamiento económico*), 1950; *Nine Mexican Studies* (*Nueve estudios mexicanos*), 1953; *Homily for Future Economists* (*Homilia para futuros economistas*), 1956.

MEDITATIONS ON MEXICO

Geographical Survey

MEXICO IS A COUNTRY WITH AN AREA of two million square kilometres, situated between the United States and Central America, and between the Pacific and the Atlantic Oceans. It is said that its shape—a geographic irony—resembles the horn of plenty.

There are hot, temperate, and cold climates; healthful and unhealthful areas; deserts and forests; plains and mountains. There are primitive tribes, small colonial towns, and modern cities. For this reason, when we speak of some concrete problem—economic, social, or political—informed people always use the plural.

Many rivers are only seasonal, appearing in the rainy season. Then the currents swell and become fierce and threatening. Very few rivers are navigable, and still fewer throughout their whole course, so few that they can be counted on the fingers of one hand. How wonderful to have an Amazon, a Mississippi, or a Nile, a moving highway like those in history which have helped peoples to advance!

There are few places in which mountains are absent from the landscape. They are in almost every region, high and beautiful; covered with vegetation or looking as though an enormous razor had passed over their wrinkled surface. They are there, black by night; blue, grey, purple, or reddish by day, according to the distance or the hour. They are there, interposing themselves between man and man, hampering the interchange of the merchandise that brings wealth, and of the ideas next door. It is a young land, with a fruitful and prepotent matrix. Barely five years ago, it gave birth to a volcano.[1]

The coastlines are extensive in the east, the west, and the south; but there are no natural harbours, and constant dredging is necessary. Costly installations are necessary in order to utilize the sea, and to defend us against the sea; it is necessary to struggle against a hostile nature, continually and unrelentingly. Fishing is a profitable industry that is practised very little. The Mexican is not a sailor or fisherman. Always looking toward his mountains, he has forgotten the sea.

The rains are irregular, abundant in a few regions, but scant in most. Agriculture is casual, fortuitous, with the threat of early or late frost—it is poor, and the peasants wretched.

But man has the capacity to transform his dwelling-place. In Mexico it seems that he is already transforming it by irrigation projects, the utilization of electric power on a large scale, and by the conquest of the tropical regions. The destiny of the Mexican depends upon his efforts and his vision of the future.

The population is somewhat more than twenty-two million[2] and our soil can accommodate many millions more. A few are very rich; some are in moderate circumstances; the majority are extremely poor and distressingly ignorant.

Mexico is a beautiful country, one of the most beautiful on earth; but it is still under construction, and the important thing is to complete the work, the sooner the better.

In Olden Times

History is the drama of man, and the latter is, according to Croce, a compendium of universal history. It is a drama in which are mingled good and evil, suffering and joy, despair and the eternal eagerness to excel; and each human being is in himself a synthesis of his own generation and of past generations.

History never stops; it is a torrential river which flows towards an unknown sea; it is constant change and endlessly successive incidents. For that reason there are no vertical interruptions in history. It is made

[1]The reference is to Parícutin, a volcano that suddenly rose up in 1943.

[2]In 1964, the population of Mexico had passed the thirty-eight-million mark.

up of the errors and successes of the past, the anguish of the present, and the fervent, uneasy, or calm yearning for a better future.

And so, with a passionate desire for improvement, with misery and pain, triumphs and defeats, the Mexican people have been laboriously writing their history. But they are on their feet, scrutinizing the horizon to see if they can catch the first glow of an unforetold dawn; they are on their feet, like their thousand-year-old trees and their myth-bearing volcanoes.

It is said that the warring tribes that violated the mountains and valleys, the primaeval forests and the lakes, of the territory that now is Mexico, came down from the North little by little, so slowly that they took decades to establish themselves in the Centre and South. There were Toltecs, Mayas, Chichimecas, and Aztecs. There were many other groupings of humanity with different names that archaeologists and students of the prehistoric—poets of the remote past—have doubtless classified with astonishing accuracy, distinct peoples with certain peculiar characteristics in different regions. They contended with one another, and there were victors and vanquished—man ever the devourer of man.

History is confused with legend, and legend with history. There are mysterious personages that civilize and emigrate to be converted into stars; kings who tyrannize, kill, and die; kindly gods that send the growth-producing rain, or gods revengeful and with thirst for blood. And at the bottom of the picture are the shadows of the multitude working and struggling, suffering in silence, who are born and live to sink into their graves unremembered; the afflicted shadows of millions of anonymous beings who are those that, in large part, make history.

But these ancient peoples left their traces where they passed: Mitla, Teotihuacán, Monte Albán, Uxmal, Chichén-Itzá, and many other splendid monuments that show the degree of civilization and the creative capacity of their builders; monuments which astonish the traveller who studies them and arouse in the Mexican's heart a pride in his race. There they are, so that our man of America may take comfort and maintain confidence in his destiny.

The Epic of the Conquest

The Aztecs reached the Valley of Mexico in 1325; they arrived exhausted, destitute, and weakened by the privations and hardships of their long trek. There at last they discovered, on a nopal and devouring a serpent, the eagle which their augurers had indicated as the terminal point of their travels. Most certainly they felt fascinated by the charm of the exuberant vegetation, the tranquil lakes, the diaphanous skies, and the gigantic volcanoes, embellished by the snow which adorns their summits.

Slowly they constructed their city and later their empire: their city by toil, their empire by war. First they subdued their neighbours and formed military alliances with them; then they subjugated peoples and tribes that inhabited distant regions. Always, at all times and in all parts of the world, lust for power or glory on the part of the few who command, utilizing the ignorance and strength of the many who obey, has been the origin of great empires.

The characteristics of the Aztec empire were harsh subjection of the vanquished, with heavy tribute or slavery and human sacrifices, this with some moral principles of a kind that could have been taken from the Gospels. They taught respect for the aged, and consolation to the poor and afflicted by kindness in deed and word.

At the top was the emperor with the nobles, priests, and warriors; below were the unhappy, idolatrous, undernourished, and exploited masses. It was a contradictory society like all those that have been organized in the course of the centuries. What people, what nation, can throw the first stone? Man is an admirable but imperfect animal. His logic is admirable but all he achieves is imperfect. The only thing which saves him is his dissatisfaction with his imperfection.

Montezuma was reigning when Cortez arrived at Veracruz. The Spaniards numbered little more than five hundred, whereas, according to our information, the natives who peopled the territory now Mexican numbered as many as two million four hundred thousand. But never, in the hour of trial, have despots been able to count upon the help of those whom they tyrannize over and humiliate.

The empire, as we have already said, had been constructed by force of arms and was supported by the fear of the subject peoples, an unstable support because invariably it is brought down by the first flash, real or illusory, of liberty.

The indisputable genius of Cortez, stimulated by ambition for wealth, power, and glory, perceived, or rather sensed, that the public edifice of Montezuma was set on shifting soil, and then, with his men, he plunged into the epic of conquest.

The Spaniards were not alone in their struggle with the Aztecs; by their side fought hundreds and thousands of natives. The Spaniard was iron; the Aztec was bronze. There was a tremendous clash of two civilizations. The military technique of the Europeans overcame the brave hearts of the natives, but not at once and not without difficulties. Cortez knew the bitterness of defeat and wept with rage and despair one memorable night. The chroniclers call it "the sad night."[3]

The siege of Tenochtitlán[4] is one of the most heroic episodes in history. It has the grandeur of an epic and is still awaiting the poet with the creative imagination to exalt it and synthesize it in an immortal poem.

Heroism and daring in the besiegers; valour and heroism in the besieged—it was tit for tat, each adversary worthy of the other.

Basically, it was nothing but ambition for power and thirst for gold that animated the Spaniard; the native was motivated by his right to defend the soil of his ancestors. On this occasion, as on many others, right was vanquished.

The fighting went on day after day for weeks with the most extraordinary stubbornness. The natives kept retreating little by little over the bodies of their men and in the anguish of inevitable defeat. Hunger and pestilence consummated the disaster.

Cuauhtémoc, heir to the throne of Montezuma, fought as the best chieftains famed in history have fought; he fought with vigour and tenacity for his people, vainly and desperately. The fatal hour had come for a sturdy and warlike race; and the unsubdued hero, a splendid specimen of his race, understood with deep despair, so deep that it must have crushed his heart, that he was facing the end of his Empire in a blood-red sunset, without promise of a new dawn. He surrendered with dignity. "Kill me with that dagger, for I was unable to save my people," he said to the conqueror.

Time passed. Once more evil was victorious. The hero was assassinated, and became a statue.

But from the brutal clash in the cruel contest arose in the distance the beginnings of a new nation.

New Spain

Colonization lasted for three centuries. A long or a short time, depending upon the point of view; long in comparison with the lifetime of a man, considerably less long in the evolution of a people, and only a moment in the history of the planet, in the history of this little ball of

[3]July 1, 1520, when the Spaniards were forced to withdraw from the Aztec capital, with heavy losses.

[4]The Aztec capital, now Mexico City.

mud on which we dwell, which has been lost for thousands of years in the vastness of space.

The life of the native was very hard in the first few decades following the conquest. He was inhumanly treated, unjustly punished, and brutally exploited. He was obliged to work fourteen hours a day in the mines and in the fields of which the conquerors took possession; by threat of the sword he was forced to be converted to the mediaeval Catholicism of the Spaniard of that time, and to build with his hands, his sweat, and his blood the humble or magnificent temples of the new gods. As Alfonso Caso puts it, he was threatened with hell in the next life if he ventured to get out of the hell of this life.

Thousands of natives perished in the mines, exhausted by hard toil and insufficient nourishment, without knowing they were contributing to the building of the mercantile society. The gold and silver of America, the slave trade, and piracy form the diabolical triangle which accelerated the progress of capitalism.

There were those who doubted that the native was a rational being. There were disputes. Finally Pope Paul III, in a bull, declared that the Indian belonged to the human family.

Then came the Franciscans: trickles of light in the dark night of the vanquished. Later the Dominicans and the Augustinians arrived. Many of them were men of great virtue and filled with love for the humble; many were civilizing agents, true missionaries of the Jesus of the Gospels. They opposed the soldier and the estate-superintendent in defence of the weak, and instilled hope, the last refuge of all unfortunates, in the hearts of the vanquished. A beautiful example is that of Father Las Casas, who defended justice with passionate ardour and unfailing constancy. A still more beautiful example is that of the great Vasco de Quiroga, the first to show a burning desire to create in the New World a new world, inspired by the marvellous country which had been sketched by the wise and kindly genius of Thomas More.[5]

These are examples, nothing but beautiful examples. The civilizing task could not become generalized, in spite of the fact that a great deal was done. The political mistakes and the economic blunders at home, the conquests and the colonization, sapped the vitality of Spain and exhausted her creative power. She prolonged the Middle Ages, and without taking cognizance of the present turned her back on the future.

The Laws of the Indies, of which so much has been written, were also a beautiful example of nobility and good intentions; but unfortunately for thousands of human beings they were hardly ever observed,

[5]The reference is to More's *Utopia.*

because they were neutralized by distance and by the economic condition of the colonist. You see, laws cannot create reality; it is the other way round. This is obvious and quite clear. Nevertheless, man is obstinate in error, astonishingly and hopelessly obstinate. Experience teaches him only by the way of blood, his own blood and his own suffering. And at times, and this we are seeing now, not even by bloodshed.

In the course of time customs became somewhat softened. The ill treatment of the poor ceased to be the general system.

Twelve thousand churches were built so that the wretched people might pray to God for resignation and dream of heaven, enveloped in the smoke of incense and ill-smelling rags. Costly palaces were erected for the rich and highways were built to provide an outlet for the minerals and a means of entrance for the merchandise brought by fleets from Cadiz or Seville.

The land was seized by the Spaniard, the Creole, and most of all by the clergy.

The drama continued to develop on a paradoxical stage, amid a peace of slaves, and on a quiet pond.

It is true that very soon we had a Mint, a University, and a Press, and obviously all this honours Spain and honours us. Later other institutions of higher learning were established, other mints, and other printing establishments; but most of the coined silver and gold was taken to Spain and from there to the world at large. The Mexican silver *peso* was for centuries international currency. Copper coins were made too, so that the Indians could carry on their little transactions. The University was a centre of culture for the Spaniards and Creoles, but rarely for the mestizo. From the printing shops came a number of books, some good and some bad; food for the mind for a few, because the great majority of the population had not been taught to read. One may err on the side of optimism in stating that, at the beginning of the nineteenth century, the number of illiterates in New Spain was no less than ninety per cent.

Of course there were some illustrious individuals in science, literature, and the plastic arts: Ruiz de Alarcón and Sor Juana de la Cruz, world figures; Sigüenza y Góngora, a man of letters and a scholar; Clavijero, historian and philosopher; José Antonio Alzate, most eminent; Miguel Cabrera, a painter with some talent; and a few others, but not many, who stood out prominently inside the country and beyond the frontiers.

At the end of the eighteenth century the quiet pool began to lose its calm. There were lightning flashes on the horizon, and the wind of non-conformity was blowing. Some cultured Creoles who knew about the Independence of the United States and the French Revolution, who knew Rousseau, Voltaire, and the Encyclopaedists, felt the aspiration to build a country slowly rise, at first only with the vagueness of a dream; later, little by little, the dream became a fervid, irresistible longing. Meanwhile, the silent Indian was gnawing his crust of bread and awaiting the dawn.

Independence and Anarchy

Rebellions are organized by soldiers to take away power from one person and give it to another. Its source is the resentment or the ambition of some high military officer. Naturally, they always use high-sounding words—justice, liberty, the fatherland—which are used to conceal the worst instincts and the most perverse purposes.

Revolutions are brought about by peoples to subvert the established social order, with the purpose of improving living conditions, and with the conviction that this way, that of revolution, is the only way; these are bold measures, measures of the desperate and the suicidal.

The rebel is, in the majority of cases, ambitious and morally inferior; the revolutionary is fundamentally good, and may be an apostle or a hero. In Mexico we have had, in the course of our history, many rebels but very few revolutionaries; numerous uprisings in barracks, rebellions, and riots, but only three revolutions. The first was launched by a white-haired priest, high-minded and valiant, in a little town in the centre of the country on September 16, 1810, hours before the light of dawn broke in the east.

Hidalgo, the leader, spoke of independence and liberty. And those magic words awoke the masses out of their perennial lethargy. He was followed immediately by a ragged, enthusiastic, and vociferous multitude; he was followed by the poor man who had nothing to lose and something to gain in the hurly-burly of pillage; he was followed by a few literary men and soldiers, whose hearts had been kindled by the magnificent dream of making a free country out of the subjugated land in which they were born.

Hidalgo had his hour of glory. He won victory after victory and felt certain of quick and definitive success. In Guadalajara the abolition of slavery was decreed. This act alone is sufficient claim to our homage.

Later came defeat, the flight towards the north, loss of favour, and abandonment. The bishops excommunicated him for the crime of striving for the liberty of a people; and the hero, Father of the Country, was shot in the town of Chihuahua on July 30, 1811. The blood of heroes, martyrs in a noble cause, is the seed which impregnates and exalts the ideal for which they perished and arouses in the best people the desire to be like them.

The struggle for independence continued in the mountains of the South. Other leaders took up the heritage of the first, giving an example of patriotic love and stubborn self-abnegation. The priest Morelos, greatest of them all, a great statesman and a great general, saw clearly that the country's problem was not merely political, but also economic; that what had to be done was to give land to the peasants so that they could feed themselves and their wives and children. He also, like Hidalgo, was excommunicated by the clergy and later shot. Morelos is one of the greatest and most illustrious men of America.

Independence was achieved in 1821 through negotiations between the belligerents; it was solely a political independence from Spanish rule, neither more nor less—or, if you like, neither less nor more. The only ones to gain were the Creoles,[6] that is to say, the upper class, precisely the class that had fought against the insurgents. The Indian and the mestizo, the lower and the middle classes, continued as before to drag on in their poor, painful existence.

Later came a long and cruel struggle: the struggle to form a new nationality. There were rebellions and barracks uprisings, one part of the army against another, and this sort of game kept repeating itself over and over, bleeding the Republic. There were federalism and centralism—mistakes, failures, penury, shame, and anarchy. The tragic outcome was war with the United States and the loss of more than half the territory.

At that time the difference in power between Mexico and the neighbouring country was not great. The war was lost because of the government's lack of resources—they were in the hands of the clergy. When the latter were urgently asked for money, with the invaders not very far from the capital, they instigated a rebellion to keep their treasures intact and to save themselves from saving the country. To the causes of the defeat must be added the lack of patriotism or the incompetence of the generals. Only the cadets of Chapultepec and the common soldier knew how to do their duty, by giving the only thing they had—their lives as cannon fodder.

[6]Although the term "Creoles" commonly means persons of negro-white extraction, the reference here is to descendants of Spaniards born and raised in the New World.

The misfortune of Mexico in those dark years consisted in its fruitfulness in the production of uniformed pseudo-heroes and robed pseudo-saints. There were honest, serene, and patriotic voices. Their opinions and warnings found no echo and were lost in a tangled jungle of envy, ignorance, folly, and lust for gold and power.

Reform and Intervention

About the middle of the nineteenth century the clergy possessed great tracts of territory and numerous urban estates. The Church of that marvellous martyr of Judaea who preached virtue, love, and poverty was by far the most powerful economic organization in the country. That enormous wealth was inalienable, without any possibility of movement, stagnant, and therefore it impeded the development of the Republic.

Eminent men with clear political vision held, as early as just a few years after the winning of independence, that it was necessary to disentail this material property if the nation was to prosper; but not until 1855 was the first step taken, with the promulgation of the law ordering the clergy to sell their lands.

The clergy resisted and provoked another civil war, one of the most bloody and bitter recorded in the history of Mexico. The liberal government of Benito Juárez, that pure-blooded Indian with will of iron, whom Pérez Martínez has rightly called "the immovable," decreed in 1859, forced to it by the defiance of the Church, the nationalization of such property.

The Catholic writer Roque Barcía writes that the clergy form part of the organization of society and have a part in the political system, that they are a class, a category. He adds that when the organization of a country is altered, the organization of the clergy is necessarily altered too. But that class, that political institution, that social body, has been an obstacle to every creative impulse in the evolution of the Mexican people. The clergy have always been the enemy of the common people; they have always stood out against every effort to better the lives of those millions of human beings for whom it seems were made all of the world's sufferings and none of its joys. What a sad antinomy between doctrine and deeds, and between principles and actualities!

The liberals won the war, and Juárez established himself in power for a certain period. Then the losers sent a commission to Europe in search of an emperor to govern them. They found one in one of the old Houses of the old Continent. Napoleon III offered to send an army in support of the future mandatary, and he kept his word.

So the French army, defender of peoples, came to Mexico to fight against the people. On one occasion it was defeated by the Mexicans under the command of a good general, Ignacio Zaragoza. This happened on May 5, 1862. After this the foreigner won victory by his tactics, his numbers, and by the help of natives under the command of conservative generals, also natives. The French soldiers became masters of the soil on which they trod, but of nothing more, because the guerrillas of the liberals continually harassed them in the fields, hamlets, and small towns, while the patriots, almost always of the lower class, harassed them in the cities.

Maximilian and Charlotte were received with joy by the upper class and by the archbishops, bishops, and canons. There were solemn celebrations, secular and religious, in their honour, and a Court was improvised in Mexico City after the model of those of Europe. For three years that operetta with the tragic ending continued. The French, who had occupied a considerable number of geographical points in the country, but without succeeding in destroying the government of Juárez which had taken refuge on the northern frontier, found it necessary to abandon the country for well-known reasons of a character both national and international. Maximilian refused to abdicate, dreaming of the consolidation of his empire with the support of the native conservatives. He lost the contest. On June 19, 1867, he was shot in the town of Querétaro.

The blue blood of the blond archduke fertilized the seed of the liberty of a people.

The history of Mexico is reduced—Pedro Henríquez Ureña is reported to have said—to the struggle between two classes: honest pauperism and thievish respectability. The liberals belonged to pauperism; the imperialists, to the other class. The liberals won, and their government was established in the capital of the Republic. The conservatives were finished; they had suffered a mortal blow.

In Mexico, as elsewhere, the conservatives sometimes achieve temporary triumphs; but in the long run they lose out because they wish to preserve in perpetuity all that exists, because they want to see nothing changed, because they want to hold back time—and this is the greatest of absurdities. On the contrary, the progressives (let us give them that name because it is a fashionable one now) may suffer reverses in the struggle, but in spite of this they triumph in the end, and this is because they work in conformity with the laws of life and the course of history. To live, and we must not forget it, is to experience the occurrence of events; and there can be no occurrence of events without change, because change is their essence.

But let us return to our subject. After the defeat of the imperialists the liberals govern: Juárez and Lerdo de Tejada; the liberals and liberty rule. In those years the first railway is inaugurated, the educational reforms of Gabino Barreda are introduced, and progress is made in all departments. In those years Mexico opens her doors and offers asylum to the persecuted, to all the noble visionaries, among them, to José Martí,[7] the apostle of continental stature, who finds among us stimulation and cordial friendship.

The Peace of Slaves

General Porfirio Díaz seized power through a rebellion and held it for thirty years. Very quickly he established peace, a great benefit so long desired by all social classes. He was an energetic ruler, with a strong and sometimes cruel hand. Nevertheless, he did not make of cruelty a system of government, and on occasion he gave the impression of being a benevolent dictator.

It fell to his lot to rule in the latter part of the past century and the first part of our present century, when people had a blind faith in progress and in the miracles of "creative capitalism." Railways were built, the important cities were beautified, monuments were erected to the heroes of Independence and of the Reform movement, external credit was re-established, banking institutions were encouraged and budgets were balanced; but at the same time it must be remembered that, in accordance with government policy, the gold and silver mines, the oil deposits, the development of electric power, the few great secondary industries, and the many great business establishments were handed over to foreign corporations. In a word, the economy of the nation was denationalized, with the exception of agriculture, which remained in the hands of absentee proprietors, for the most part of Mexican origin.

The land was controlled by a small group. There were large estates with vast areas under cultivation, and with their own supply stores to reduce the small wage of the labourer. Debts passed from parents to children, and exploitation was without restraint or mercy. The landowner had his own mint, his own prison, and his own system of justice.

[7]Cuban poet and patriot who died in 1895, three years before the independence he fought for was achieved.

The workers could not organize in defence of their interests. Strikes were illegal. On one occasion the workers in a textile mill were showered with grapeshot because they had gone out into the street to ask for an increase in pay. For this the newspapers published editorials in praise of General Díaz. One of them was entitled: "That's the way to govern."

Assurance was given that this was progress, that the country was going ahead with gigantic strides, and the General Díaz myth was formed, presenting him as a statesman of genius, recognized by foreign powers, as was said.

The rich dressed according to Paris fashions. Not a few spoke French and were highly cultured; the rich had as good a life as can be had on this earth. In striking contrast, the great mass of the population lived in poverty, or even in destitution. They lived in the greatest ignorance, and by two myths: Don Porfirio Díaz and the Virgin of Guadalupe.

An author has written that peoples live by mythologies, because they seek in fables all the fancies that are indispensable to their lives. Nevertheless, in Mexico there was a moment when the fable indispensable to the existence of a people was not sufficient for their existence, because the artisans in the towns, the workers in the factories, and the labourers on the estates could no longer stifle their hunger for bread, for justice, and for liberty.

The above outline explains the Mexican Revolution. It was inevitable, because when the masses have not sunk into the depths of imbecility, their collective instinct of self-preservation is more powerful than the power of tyrants and of the greatest empires.

Years of Struggle

In September, 1910, the nation was wrapped up in the mantle of Porfirian peace. Those who had been lucky in life's game of chance were trustfully enjoying that peace, preparing to take an active part in the festivities celebrating the Centenary of Independence. All was going well. For them the future bore a rosy hue.

The "mad" Madero, as he was called by the followers of Porfirio, who had dared to oppose General Díaz in the last elections, was safely locked up in the San Luis Potosí prison. It was not then known that this madman, like other madmen in history, would a few years later rise to the highest and most splendid of human classifications, that of martyr and apostle of liberty.

But we must examine the reverse of the coin. What were the conditions among the poorer classes?

In the towns some were resigned and others concealed their discontent. They were not happy. Happiness does not nest in fireless hearths and has no liking for bare feet or empty stomachs. Happiness does not allow itself to be deceived by "the beatitudes." The poor man, workman or artisan, enjoyed only brief moments of gaiety, through alcohol that brutalizes and degrades the dignity of man. As for the farmlands, the situation was similar. It was only here that discontent was commonly expressed in acts of violence, an inevitable result of needs more pressing, and of crueler oppression on the part of the masters and the local authorities. Both, workers in the cities and workers in the fields, felt a deep uneasiness, and a flow of nebulous longing through their whole being for something new to happen, for something unexpected to come and change the hard conditions under which they lived. Such a pathological and social state, of course, is favourable to revolutionary movements. The important thing is that the leader should understand the vague aspirations of the masses, that he should assimilate them in his own flesh and spirit, and that he should be capable of giving them back those aspirations, clarified and magnified, in the form of a simple programme for immediate action. The masses will follow him, passionately, ardently, and ready for anything.

The centennial festivities were magnificent: the inauguration of splendid buildings, solemn ambassadors of countries with which Mexico had diplomatic relations; resounding military parades, bullfights, and dances at the palace. General Porfirio Díaz, the hero of peace and covered with glory, painfully rigid on account of the weight of his eighty years, with his divisional uniform, presidential sash, and medals so numerous that his breast lacked space for them, was in those festivities the central figure upon whom all eyes were tremulously fixed.

Meanwhile Madero, in the city where he was imprisoned, was preparing his plan for revolution.

On November 20 of that same year the struggle began. The sound of machine-gun fire deadened the final echoes of the fanfare, and the horizon became covered with dense, sombre clouds. It has been generally agreed to call that struggle the Mexican Revolution.

In the majority of cases revolutions are not carried out by professional soldiers; their interest is confined to rebellions. In Mexico the Independence revolution was led by Hidalgo, a priest; the Reform revolution by Benito Juárez, a lawyer; that of 1910 by Madero, a landowner in the northern part of the country, and upon his death, by Carranza, a provincial politician. In Mexico civilians have been, with exceptions that prove the rule, the ones who have launched the forward movements in history.

A further observation is that in the great struggles in the evolution of the Mexican people, between professional and temporary soldiers, it has always been the latter, in the end, who have defeated the former. It is probable that this will not occur again, here or anywhere, owing to the progress in military techniques and to the diabolical advances in the construction of murderous machines.

Of the professional soldiers in my country can be said, at least until a little while ago, what Antonio Machado says Mairena wrote concerning the Germans: "They are the great masters of war. About war they know everything—everything, except how to win it."

In 1910 non-professional generals assumed command, and there were uprisings in several districts in the country. About six months later, in my opinion to the surprise of most of the population, because both the friends and the enemies of the government were sure of its stability, Madero had triumphed. Naturally he did not win by the strength of his little army of ranchers, even though it is true that it had won resounding victories, but rather by the power of public opinion which, in a few months, inclined decidedly in his favour. Hungry peoples follow or support the first man who offers them something, whether it be a piece of bread to appease hunger, or pyrotechnical displays to help them forget it.

General Díaz presented his resignation and sadly sailed for Europe. He was leaving the land where for so many years he had been the first in command and in honours. The most difficult thing in life is the last act: to die with dignity, and soon enough. If General Díaz had died in 1907, for example, in spite of his mistakes he would have had, for he had good points too, monuments in every city of the Republic.

Madero became President, but he could not govern in peace. He thought that Mexico's problems were primarily political, and this was a gross error, because Mexico's problems were and still are primarily economic. His two most outstanding aides rose in arms against him: Orozco and Emiliano Zapata. The latter took up arms again with the cry "Land and liberty." The former based his campaign upon a broader programme, of greater scope and for those days very radical. Zapata and Orozco went much further than Madero in the matter of economic and social changes. It is usual that those who initiate a revolution in accordance with a system of ideas, with certain principles and plans, see themselves carried along, by the force of people and events, beyond their plans, their principles, and their system of ideas. Then there are only two solutions left to them: to swim with the current to reach the shore, or to stop and resign themselves to failure.

It is a serious matter to start a social conflagration, but it is still more serious to try to extinguish it when once started and in full flame. It must be allowed to continue its work of destruction and purification.

Orozco was finally defeated, and Zapata continued the struggle for a little more than five years under the protection of his southern mountains.

A disloyal soldier, Victoriano Huerta, forced Madero to resign the presidency of the Republic, and some days later he had him assassinated. He, Huerta, had himself named President. In Mexico City the nice people drank champagne; throughout the country, in spite of the mistakes of the leader, the people, that is the best people, always noble-hearted, wept with indignation and prepared for revenge.

The usurping President tried to turn back history; he tried to rule as they had ruled in 1840, but we were in the year 1913.

The Revolution could not be halted. Other leaders rose up: Carranza, Villa, Obregón, and many others. The soldier-assassin was beaten and had to flee abroad, where he died overcome by the weight of his crimes. After the victory there was still a struggle between factions. Carranza won out and was elected to fill the chair of the Chief Executive. The Revolution had triumphed.

The struggle lasted seven years. Much accumulated wealth was destroyed, and thousands of lives were lost. It really seems as though peoples achieve a little well-being only at a very high cost. For some the cost is less, but that is because in these cases the price is paid by other peoples. I am thinking (why not say it?) of the large empires.

The Mexican Revolution had precursors: Wistano Luis Orozco, Andrés Molina Enríquez, Filomena Mata, Paulino Martínez, Juan Sarabia, Antonio I. Villarreal, Librado Flores, Rosalío Bustamante, and Ricardo and Enrique Flores Magón. In different trenches they fought against the government of Porfirio Díaz; they sowed ideas which later germinated to produce a glorious bloom. These ideas contributed to the formation of revolutionary thought, whatever the proud men who claim the ideological paternity of our social movement may say about it.

It is well to remember here that there has been much discussion regarding whether the Revolution had or did not have, previous to military action, an economic and social doctrine, and a programme based on clear and well-defined ideas. In my opinion the San Luis Plan and the Guadalupe Plan, the former being that of the apostle Madero and the latter that of the leader Carranza, were merely political documents, except for an allusion in the San Luis Plan to the agrarian problem. Both plans were by-passed by reality as time went on, which is in no way surprising, because this has happened in analogous sociological phenomena. In the case of the Mexican Revolution it is certain that the radical ideas of the precursors slowly infiltrated among those who were fighting for it. This is clearly seen on examining the plan of Orozco. Besides, it must be remembered that the armed struggle lasted seven years. It would be absurd to suppose that ideas had remained static rather than in constant ferment, as was actually the case. One proof, among others, is the fact of the formation of the Ayala Plan, the Zapata Plan, and the law of January 6, 1915, signed by Carranza.

Moreover, attention must be drawn to the fact that the defenders of the régimes of Porfirio and of Huerta were the rich and the clergy, who were active adversaries. The inevitable result was that the revolutionaries were against the clergy and the rich, and that their social radicalism became accentuated. Upon its triumph the Revolution punished its adversaries. They, pretending to forget their past deeds, begged for justice from the very people against whom they had fought with the greatest ruthlessness.

Revolutionary thought was condensed into the constitutional principles of 1917, in which were maintained intact the ideals of liberty for which the men of the Reform Movement had fought and died sixty years before.

Those principles were the following:

(1) Nationalization of the wealth of the subsoil, to be subject to a system of concessions for its exploitation.

(2) Obligation to distribute land to the peasants.

(3) Guaranteed minimum wage to the workman, a weekly rest, and a share in the profits of the enterprise.

(4) Establishment of the eight-hour maximum work day, and a six-hour maximum for night work.

(5) Prohibition of the employment of minors.

(6) Protection of mother and child by means of prenatal and post-natal care.

(7) Regulative measures with respect to religious cults.

The essence of the reform was to improve the standard of living of the majority of the population, as a substantive basis for national progress.

Concerning these just and profoundly humane principles there has been no lack of ignorant detractors, especially journalists in the United States, who have spoken of Mexican Communism. Our Revolution had nothing in common with the Russian revolution, even superficially; also, ours preceded theirs. How then could we have imitated them? In Mexico's revolutionary literature, from the end of the past century to 1917, European socialistic terminology is not used; and the reason is that our social movement was born of our own soil, of the bleeding heart of the people, and became a drama at once painful and creative.

The Last Thirty Years

Since 1917 the generals of the Revolution have governed, sometimes well and sometimes ill, frequently quite badly, especially in the provinces. This political and sociological phenomenon of the governmental monopoly of generals is very far from being unusual in the history of Mexico and in that of other Latin-American countries. With brief interruptions, this situation has prevailed throughout one hundred and twenty-five years of national independence. In Mexico it appears that things are beginning to change. We are proud now to have a civilian president.[8]

Military men are the least capable in governmental functions. They know the art of war, and what is needed for governing is the reverse, that is to say, the art of peace. Military men are generally authoritarian and inclined to despotism; they are not to be blamed for it, since their psychological bent is the result of the training they have received; but the people are not to be blamed for it either.

Every soldier is normally a potential tyrant. Some conceive of the social order only in the manner of Charles Fourier: as based on "the power exercised by a minority of armed slaves over a majority of unarmed slaves." How I hope we have permanently left behind us the stage of military leadership!

In the last thirty years we have had ten governments. The last began in December 1946. All of them have followed in a general way the course marked by revolutionary principles, some in accordance with the will of the Chief Executive, others against his will; but not to do what was done would have been political suicide. The achievements are tremendously significant and have unquestionable positive

[8]Miguel Alemán, elected in 1946.

aspects even though, like any human endeavour, they are not free from error or blemish.

Millions of hectares of land have been divided among the peasants: agricultural instruction and credit for the cultivation of the fields have been furnished; irrigation systems and motor highways have been constructed; industry and credit have been developed in their various branches; and we have been given laws protecting labour along with popular and technical education.

The expropriation of the properties of the oil companies merits a separate chapter. The oil now belongs not to the foreigner, but to Mexicans.

Moreover, it is obvious that the scientific and technical progress achieved in the world in recent decades has contributed towards the transformation of the country.

Furthermore, stress must be laid upon the fact that the revolutionary governments have guaranteed liberty of thought, especially since 1935. To have made of Mexico in the last twelve years a country in which disagreement with official policy is not punished, and a refuge for those persecuted by any form of tyranny, is a source of deep and genuine satisfaction to the Mexican.

The shortcomings have been: improvisation and superficiality instead of serious technical study; the subordination of technique to politics, in all departments; lack of political education of the working class, which has contended only for the attainment of immediate goals; scorn for university education and culture in its higher categories; and, finally, lack of administrative honesty. It is noteworthy that some of these shortcomings have not been and are not now peculiar to Mexico; they are marks of the times through which contemporary society is passing.

The man of our times lives in anxiety, in a crisis of abysmal depth. Constantly and everywhere his face is being splashed with the waves of filth which wickedness and disillusionment increase and multiply. He does not know whither to direct his steps because he is always looking downwards, seeking the old paths which have been wiped out by grapeshot. He persists in refusing to recognize that salvation does not lie in the past, or in the present, but in the future; his salvation lies in always looking forward and upward to discover new horizons and the secret of some star.

And Mexico could not escape that crisis. Nobody has escaped and nobody will escape. It has already been said: a moral crisis and an ideological crisis. Honesty and clear thinking are needed. Man never has known what he is, whence he comes, or whither he is going. Now, in spite of his learning, he knows less than ever, even when he reduces his inquiry to life in his terrestrial abode.

In the revolutionary governments may be listed names of functionaries of exemplary probity. Of many this cannot be said; these have been the profiteers of the Revolution. There are some who, having acquired wealth in the government, or in business with the government in shady deals and trickery, are now honest men, socially respectable and even philanthropists. It is probable that they have thought and still hold to the belief that "the rich have an obligation to be honest, but not the poor"; it is possible that public gratitude will immortalize them for their good works and that their names will be read in the streets of the cities, on the front of some school or hospital.

The principles of the Constitution of 1917 have in some cases been exceeded, especially in labour legislation and in the matter of agrarian reform. The explanation is usually to be found in the political necessities of the moment and at times in urgent economic requirements. Owing to the fact that governments since 1917, and especially since December, 1920, have gone further to the left than the Constitution, they have quite properly been called, and we do not know who gave them the name first, revolutionary governments.

Well then, if we wished to represent graphically the progressionist trajectory of the revolutionary governments since 1917 in the economic and social domains, the line would be broken and oscillating, but with a marked tendency upwards, reaching the highest point at the end of the year 1938. Since then, if we extended the curve, its decline would be easily noted. The reason is that there is not just one social force, but a number of social forces opposing one another. Movements forward, however vigorous the initial impulse may be, cannot continue in that direction indefinitely, because they are checked by antagonistic forces. These negative forces, conservative or reactionary, never for long, if at all, force progressive movements back to the point of departure, which is what they desire and what they strive for; but they do always succeed, or almost always, and for a long time too, in pushing them backwards to the point of securing a relative and transitory adjustment between the contending interests.

However important they may be, men are nothing but the product or the toy of historical laws.

The first four years under Cárdenas, from 1935 to 1938, mark the zenith of the Mexican Revolution. It was able to go just that far; for in the two remaining years of his government the pressure of opposing forces, more and more aggressive and organized, made itself felt. Cárdenas, without perhaps fully realizing it, had to yield a small fringe of the ground gained, and this has continued in subsequent governments.

The old national *bourgeoisie* suffered a severe blow with the success of the Revolution, but it slowly recovered. It made money quickly, and slowly gained influence. In a few years it regained what it had lost. And that is not all. A new *bourgeoisie* joined it to form a new social class. The new elements kept breaking away from the ranks of the Revolution: public officials or former public officials grown rich, traffickers in government influence, or businessmen who profited from public works contracts or the sale of deteriorated merchandise. A few made their fortunes by methods approved by the morality of our time. So, at this point all the rich, united by their community of interest, constituted the neutralizing force of the Revolution. Moreover, all this has been fostered by the direction of the international policies of the great powers, especially those nearest to us.

The Mexican Revolution hastened the progress of Mexico. In my opinion the work achieved shows a favourable balance. The armed conflict lasted seven years and now the revolutionary governments, more or less faithful to the principles of the Revolution, have been functioning for thirty years. But we must bear in mind that we are dealing with an historical fact, and every historical fact is necessarily transitory. Consequently it may be said that we now find ourselves in a new stage in the evolution of the Mexican people, as José E. Iturriaga pointed out in a recent lecture.

A short while ago I wrote that the Mexican Revolution had its origin in the hunger of the people: hunger for bread, land, justice, and liberty. I wrote that as long as that popular hunger was not satisfied, the Revolution was in process of development, that it had not ended and would not end. Now I think that revolutions are not immortal. None ever has been, nor ever will be, immortal. They carry out their work of both destruction and creation and leave their deep traces in the very core of society. Later, new cultural constellations, and new developments among the social groupings, are formed in their perpetual eagerness for the comfortable life. On occasions there is retrogression or delay, but afterwards the march forward is always resumed.

The Mexican Revolution only partially satisfied some of the pressing needs of the masses, and perhaps it can be said that it fulfilled its mission in history in accelerating, at least in some regions of the country, the transformation of a predominantly semi-feudal economy into a capitalistic or pre-capitalistic economy. Now, in July, 1947, one can see in governmental action and in large sectors of society the indecision which accompanies any moment of transition. To achieve greater conquests it will still be necessary to strive again and again.

A Brief Pause

I recall that a Venezuelan writer wrote that there are men with only one window in the mind. I would say that it is not a window but a skylight, and that through it they view only one piece of the universe. It seems to me that such a biological species is the one to which specialists, United States style, belong; that this is a mutilation of the man and the citizen; that it is a monstrous creation of market and merchant. The human ideal is the opposite. One must have in one's mind wide windows open to all winds, to the four cardinal points both without and within. Our concern is to understand and to embrace in their totality both the world about us and the one we carry within ourselves.

The essential problem is the human element. The strongest aspiration of man is for happiness. All his actions tend towards that end, from the most mechanical and simple to the most complex and mysterious. For that reason he always tries to avoid pain and seek what provides him with satisfaction, pleasure, delight, or joy. At times his greatest suffering comes of feeling none, and repeated pleasure turns to satiety; but in spite of this, and whatever may be said about it, the truth is that the aim of the individual or society is the attainment of the greatest material and cultural benefits for the greatest number of people, here on our muddy little planet.

The discovery of paths leading to this goal, the age-old dream of suffering man, will require those broad windows in the mind. Utopia, which in the future may cease to be Utopia,[9] means the building of a new society composed of individuals different from those of yesterday and today in inner personality. Don Quixote and Sancho form the most beautiful and perhaps the most attractive human duality. If their psychological ingredients could be mixed together and a new man created with them, that man would be the superman—not that of Nietzsche, but that of all those possessed of a longing to excel.

Man needs first of all to satisfy his primal biological needs; nutrition and reproduction. Next, he needs housing, clothing, self-embellish-

[9]Utopia really means "nowhere." The play on words is obvious if this is borne in mind.

ment, and the rest of his material requirements. He must also understand the phenomena of nature, and create works of art or enjoy viewing them; and most of all, he must know himself, or in other words, know his own history. Only one who completely satisfies his animal or biological needs—I am thinking of the ordinary human being—can broaden the horizons of his mind and find in himself and in the outer world frequent sources of happiness.

All men, by virtue of their having been born, have the right to enjoy those material and cultural benefits. Governing means working to enable all to attain those benefits. And let no one tell us that governing means increasing the population or building roads, or other absurdities of the sort. Governing means striving indefatigably and fervently for the happiness of the people governed. Some examples of the contrary include Hitler, who did not govern Germany; he worked to destroy it. Also they include those great statesmen who now speak loudly of war in their public utterances, basically in defence of financial interests, and who are leading their peoples, or trying to lead them, into ruin; they are preparing themselves for misgovernment.

Some Problems

The existence of many complex economic, social, and political problems is not peculiar to Mexico. This has been so and will be so in all parts of the world at all times, as long as man inhabits the earth. This is because life means constant change, as we have said repeatedly, and for that reason it is a permanent problem. What is essentially Utopian in More, Bacon, and Campanella, the three most famous Utopians of the Renaissance, is not the construction of the worlds they imagined, but imagining them static in their organization and in their organic social life.

In a country like the United States the economic problems are not those of production but of distribution. Never in peace-time has it utilized all its productive capacity, which is always limited by market demand. In a country like Mexico the situation is different. We export a large number of agricultural products, but we do not produce wheat and corn in sufficient quantity to satisfy the needs of the population. Our agriculture is just beginning to be modernized by the use of fertilizers and machinery. We are on the right road; but the complete, or almost complete, transformation will take a quarter of a century at least. In the matter of secondary industry, in spite of the progress made in the last five years, our situation is very far from being ideal. We are just in the initial stage and consequently we are in large part importers of finished articles.

The industrialization of the country must be resolutely continued. It is the only way to increase domestic capital and raise the standard of living of large bodies of workers. I used the word "resolutely" because it is known that there are some elements in the plutocracy of the United States which do not view favourably the economic progress of Latin America. They would like to condemn us to a poverty without frontiers, to a dependence with no possible escape.

Obviously we must spare no effort to have industrialization carried out with a predominance of national capital.

Mining is one of the most important industries; but it is a foreign industry and leaves in Mexico nothing but wages, taxes, freight charges, and money for the purchase of some raw materials. The profits are at times reinvested in the business, and at others they are sent out to the benefit of the "sleeping partners" who live in London, Chicago, or New York. It is a bitter fate to have to send out to foreigners the wealth with which we have been endowed by nature, and at the same time to have to be grateful to them.

But if the problems of the production of wealth are serious and difficult, those of its distribution are still more so. In spite of the constructive efforts of the revolutionary governments, in spite of their unquestionable concern for the improvement of the living conditions of the masses, and in spite of the little success they have achieved, there are hundreds of thousands of families living in ignorance and poverty. The explanation is simple: it has not been possible to solve in a quarter of a century problems that had been accumulating for four centuries.

Nevertheless, it is urgent to try to solve those problems in order to put an end to the hunger for bread and justice, and to build a true nationality. We do not need leaders, but apostles, with wings on their thoughts and with hearts aflame with love of their people.

Problems of health are frightful. Most of the towns lack drainage and drinking water, which raises the mortality rate to an impressive figure, especially in children under the age of two years. The lowlands of the tropics contain enormous potential wealth. The problem lies in the indispensable drainage, and that costs hundreds of millions of *pesos*. Work of this character will necessarily have to be carried out over a period of many years.

I do not believe that outside of the Soviet Union there has been any country in which a more radical agrarian reform has been carried out than in Mexico. More than thirty million hectares of land have been distributed to the benefit of about two million peasant families. Nevertheless at this date there are thousands of landless peasants, and the problem is far from having been completely solved. Some people favour the "public land" (*ejido*) system as the predominant system, while others favour the small holding. Both systems exist, and in my opinion can coexist for some time; but if more and more land is going to be allotted to new public tracts, it will not be possible to increase the total extent of private properties; and if on the contrary the small holding is fostered, soon it will no longer be possible to make new contributions to public lands. In the end one system will be detrimental to the other; both cannot grow together indefinitely along parallel lines, for the simple reason that the quantity of land available is not unlimited.

The present government seems to favour the strengthening and the generalization of the small private holding, protecting it with legal guarantees and assisting its cultivation by means of credit.

As a general rule the Mexican people are not interested in politics; rather, they regard the subject with more or less indifference. Only on occasion do they show signs of activity. At times, on account of the absence of the best citizens at election time, it is the worst who triumph. This is a defect which urgently calls for correction.

It may be said that at the present time there are four political parties: The Institutional Revolutionary Party, the official party; the Party of National Action, of conservative tendencies; that of the synarchists, ultra-reactionary and with many points of resemblance to the Spanish "phalanx"; and the Communist Party, which has about two thousand members in the entire country. None of these parties, as has been frequently said, is abreast of conditions; perhaps their leaders lack imagination, because not infrequently they try to solve new problems with formulas that have been useful in the past, and which are now badly time-worn. None has reached the hearts of the people, because none represents their true aspirations or is capable of interpreting them.

In Mexico much has been said among liberals, socialists, or people with socialistic tendencies, about the necessity of organizing a political party in tune with the historic moment of the splitting of the atom—a party with new ideas, new ethical principles, with the capacity to claim the heritage of what is best in the Mexican Revolution and with an invincible desire to serve the nation disinterestedly.

Unfortunately up to the present nothing practical has been done, and the man, or the group of men, has not been discovered with aptitude and positive qualities capable of carrying out such a vast enterprise. At the present moment and with relation to such an aim, the political scene in Mexico is not encouraging and the prospects for it are still less rosy. It is wrapped in mist and weighted down with interrogation marks.

Mexico's foreign policy has been correct and patriotic. We have always been on the right side, as in the incidents relating to Abyssinia, Austria, and Spain, and also with respect to the last war. We hope that it will be the same in the future, and that foreign influences will never cause us to abandon international decency.

Mexico has just one international problem, one that is permanent, serious, and at times grave. This problem is geographical. We are neighbours to the United States, the most powerful country on earth at the present time; and that country is imperialistic, an economic phenomenon resulting from its formidable industrial and financial development. Imperialism does not stem from the will of a man or of a few men, like the "Good Neighbour Policy." It is like a reservoir constantly supplied by springs of muddy water, which finally overflows and covers the nearby places and sometimes even the distant ones. The "Good Neighbour Policy" and imperialism cannot be united in close bonds. They are incompatible, contradictory; only imperialism is a reality and the other thing, at best, a kindly wish.

The defence of countries which do not have war machines by the thousand and soldiers by the thousand lies in Right. Whether this be a strong or weak defence, and perhaps it is very weak, it is the only one. It is necessary to know how to practise Right; it must be practised with prudence, intelligence, courage, and with clear and far-seeing vision. Before the powerful it is useful to make oneself respected; and we can do this only by the force of our virtues, by being honest, sincere, responsible, and truly patriotic.

The concept of independence is being replaced by that of interdependence, due among other causes to the progress of transportation and international commerce. In our day it is not possible to think of completely autonomous national economies; and if this is not possible, it is likewise impossible in the political domain. One is the inevitable consequence of the other. From this grave problems arise for which it is not easy to see solutions.

Obviously interdependence must not be confused with dependence. The latter means subordination and is intolerable; the former can be founded upon principles of equity, justice, right, and can be a new formula by which peoples live with one another.

There are large clouds covering the horizon. Nevertheless, one feels in one's heart and head, in one's flesh, bones, and blood, that there is a new light slowly approaching, with exasperating slowness, but it is approaching.

Mexico, Country of Paradox

Mexico is an exceptionally contradictory and paradoxical country. The shape of its territory, as we have said, resembles a horn of plenty, and yet most of its inhabitants have lived and are living in poverty. There are terribly lonely deserts in which anaemic shrubs barely grow, here and there; rich pasture lands where cattle graze; fertile valleys and primaeval rain-drenched jungles. There are all the climates, all the fruits, and all the plagues which threaten plant, beast, and man.

There are regions in the Republic where the climate is pleasant and the land a wilderness; and there are others, in the tropical zone, as fertile as the best in the world but treacherous and deadly: malaria and other diseases are always lurking for those who dare to violate the solitude of the forests, mountains, and promising fertile plains.

In Mexico, and this point we stress, there are very few navigable rivers, and none that is navigable for its entire length. Many Mexican rivers are not always rivers, because for a large part of the year they remain dry and idle. At the end of spring or the beginning of summer the streams which come down from the mountains rapidly fill their channels, and roaring waterfalls and fierce rapids are formed. The waters swell hour by hour and sometimes overflow, flooding the neighbouring districts, destroying property and snuffing out lives.

The grey, blue, purple, and reddish mountains which adorn the Mexican landscape, which are a delight to the eyes of the traveller, which conceal in their wombs abundant treasures, are at the same time obstacles to communications and difficult to conquer. They have been and still are barriers to the formation of a genuine nationality; and at times even the metals they contain have remained there, and are still there without yet being wealth, because of the excessive cost of transportation to internal markets, to ports, or to border custom-houses.

The few harbours we have on the Gulf of Mexico that are more or less suited to modern commerce have required very considerable expenditures. We refer to Tampico and especially to Veracruz. Campeche and Progreso have harbours which even vessels of medium draught cannot enter, and something similar can be said, in general, about the harbours on the Pacific. Mexico is a nation with one of the longest coastlines, but without natural harbours to facilitate commercial development.

Everything is paradox and contradiction.

Our history too is constant contradiction and paradox. The Aztecs practised human sacrifice and on occasion even acts of cannibalism; but they had a morality with some principles and precepts which seem to be inspired by Christianity. During the conquest and the colonial period, along with the cruel and bloodthirsty soldier, along with the inhuman and exploiting landlord, along with the Spanish adventurer filled with greed for material benefits, with "gold lust" as Father Las Casas would say, were Las Casas himself, Vasco de Quiroga, Motolinía, and a whole host of austere civilizing friars, full of love for the Indian and impregnated with the highest virtues. And in our evolution as an independent people there are abundant examples of treachery, disloyalty, banditry, rapine, and assassination; while at the same time there are abundant acts which bespeak probity, honesty, patriotism, heroism, and spirit of sacrifice. There crowd into our memories the names Morelos, Gómez Farías, Juárez, Ponciano Arriaga, Altamirano, Justo Sierra,[10] and many others. These are exemplary lives, because in one field of activity or another they were always in the service of their country. These are exemplary lives which youth should emulate.

It appears too that the setting and the historical background have an influence upon the psychology and the attitudes of individuals. The Eskimo has something in him of the frozen regions he inhabits; the gaucho and the bedouin exteriorize in their conduct and customs the influence of the pampa and the desert; the mountaineer preserves in his inner physiognomy the roughness of the mountains; the sailor reflects in his eyes, accustomed to vast distances, the fierceness and the immensity of the sea; and the Mexican, from analogous causes, strange, complex, and almost unexplored, is paradoxical and contradictory like the land in which he dwells, like the drama he lives and which was lived by his ancestors.

The Mexican is paradoxical and contradictory. He is brave, almost always, because he scorns life; but on occasions too he knows something of fear and cowardice. He is at times disloyal and crafty, but in the vast majority of cases he will be inclined to frankness, and to loyalty to the point of allowing himself to be killed for a friend or a noble cause. He is lazy and industrious, selfish and unselfish; capable

[10]Morelos belongs to the Independence movement, the next four listed to the Reform movement of the middle of the nineteenth century, and Justo Sierra to the twentieth-century Revolution.

of the most repulsive vices and the highest virtues; capable too of the most horrible crimes and of acts of the highest nobility. The Mexican people may fall into discouragement and dejection, or they may rise to the loftiest heights in deed and thought, in the achievement of a constructive and creative purpose. Which side will gain control will depend on the people themselves and also, in large part, on their technicians, scholars, artists, writers, and poets, on their apostles and their statesmen.

Final Words

These meditations are inspired by my love for Mexico and by my natural frankness. It is true that I have let fall words of censure, and that at certain times, perhaps involuntarily, passion crept in; but I have always tried to tell the truth, because I know that only with the truth does one truly serve man, and that only with the truth does man truly serve peoples.

Patriotism is not a dithyramb but constructive criticism. Errors are revealed so that they will not be repeated, and vices are pointed out in order to correct them, and sores in order to cure them. Patriotism is in essence admiring love and a passionate yearning for betterment. It is desired that the Fatherland should become better and better, and for that reason it is criticized; it is criticized in order to serve it and because one loves it.

There is no need to flatter rulers. "Incense," says Luis Cabrera, "smells nice, but in the end it smudges the idol." Flattery, we add, is a lackey's weapon.

The history of Mexico is a paradox, just as the Mexican people is paradoxical. True, it has great defects, but its virtues are still greater. For that reason, those of us who know this people well are aware of the human depth of its collective acts and have faith in the brilliance of its destiny.

July 1947

Meditations on Mexico, Essays and Notes (*Meditaciones sobre México, ensayos y notas*), Cuadernos Americanos, Mexico, 1948, pp. 9–46.

Ermilo Abreu Gómez

(b. Mérida, Yucatán, 1894)

In his youth, Abreu Gómez was a dramatic author and an archaizing novelist. As a consequence of this latter tendency may be explained his interest in Colonial literature, to the most distinguished personalities of which—Alarcón, Sigüenza y Góngora, and Sor Juana[1]—he has devoted a number of studies. To Abreu Gómez we are indebted, especially, for having attracted the attention of critics to the work of the great poetess. A large part of the prominence which has been given to studies on Sor Juana in Mexico and abroad was promoted by the numerous essays, editions, commentaries, iconographies, and bibliographies collected in long years of toil by one of the most devoted connoisseurs of the Tenth Muse. To Abreu Gómez we also owe some useful lessons in Spanish literature and critical notes on questions concerning ancient and modern literature.

The autochthonous themes were a happy find for the work of Abreu Gómez. Of the three works on *Mayan Heroes* (*Héroes mayas*), 1942, that on Canek is the most successful. In a lucid, lyrical style, barely shaken by the mute, pathetic rebelliousness which flavours the story, Abreu Gómez brought to life the years of the hero's childhood. In *Quetzalcóatl: Sleep and Vigil* (*Quetzalcóatl: Sueño y vigilia*), 1947, he used similar stylistic devices to organize the legendary traces of the mythological personage. Later Abreu Gómez related, in *Indian Shipwreck* (*Naufragio de indios*), 1951, a tragic episode in the history of the Yucatán people, and began the publication of his memoirs with a volume entitled *It was about the Hour of Dawn . . .* (*La del alba sería . . .*), 1954.

For many years his principal work was teaching and journalism, both in the field of literature. Since 1947 he has lived in Washington and at Middlebury College, occupied in cultural and paedagogical activities.

CRITICISM AND STUDIES: *Classics, Romantics, and Moderns* (*Clásicos, románticos y modernos*), 1934; *Sor Juana Inés de la Cruz. Bibliography and Library* (*Sor Juana Inés de la Cruz. Bibliografía y biblioteca*), 1934; *Iconography of Sor Juana* (*Iconografía de Sor Juana*), 1934; *Spanish Literature. Historical Tables* (*Literatura española. Tablas históricas*), 1937; *Biographical Sketches of Sor Juana Inés de la Cruz* (*Semblanzas de Sor Juana Inés de la Cruz*), 1938; *The Course of Sor Juana*

[1]These are all Mexican writers of the seventeenth century.

(*La ruta de Sor Juana*), 1938; *Juan Ruiz de Alarcón. Critical Biography* (*Juan Ruiz de Alarcón. Bibliografía crítica*), 1939; *Lessons in Spanish Literature* (*Lecciones de literatura española*), 1944.

ESSAYS: *Guide to Lovers* (*Guía de amantes*), 1933, 1943; *Portrait Gallery* (*Sala de retratos*), 1946; *Saint Francis* (*San Francisco*), 1954.

MEMOIRS: *It was about the Hour of Dawn . . .* (*La del alba sería . . .*), 1954.

LITERARY REFLECTIONS

I

VIVES SAID: "Anger is like a boiling of the blood around the heart."[2] This boiling disturbs the powers of the spirit and beclouds the pathways of the body, through which they must express themselves. This accounts for the state of perturbation into which a man falls when he becomes its victim. From this perturbation arise acts which lead to crime or heroism, according to whether the cause of the anger is noble or ignoble.

In like manner the poetic state in men is like the boiling of blood around the imagination. It stirs or it stills spirits; it sweeps them along noisily or it leads them in silence. Upon this boiling depends whether the song will be epic or lyric, whether it rises high or droops. The entire capacity of voices is contained in the miracle of that union of the blood with what is imagined.

II

Only literature can cause words to say more than they contain. To do this it uses a technique unknown in the spoken language. The technique of literature lies in the *combination* it makes with words. This *combination*—as well as the words themselves—produces a new quality. This new quality is ineffable.

III

In literature, part of the original and creative spirit depends on the *relationship* that is established between the writer and the world surrounding him. For example: in oriental literature we can note this fact: the relationship between life and the writer is so intimate that it almost forms a coherent whole, without assembled parts and materials. The personality of the writer is absorbed by the cosmos, by the abso-

[2]Vives was a Spanish humanist of the sixteenth century, who became a professor at Oxford.

lute forces, within which people move. Then there is neither man, nation, nor god: all is fused in a pantheistic nature.

A professor of philosophy would call this: phenomenology of ***relationship*** in literature.

IV

Frequently reference is made to literary schools, giving to them a transcendent sense they do not always have. It must be remembered that in most cases literary schools merely reflect a shift in the occasional postures man assumes. They reflect, for example, an eagerness to be different, a desire to attract attention, to break—artificially—a rhythm. This accounts for the fact that not a few writers, with more skin than marrow, can easily pass through all the schools of their time.

V

The spoken language satisfies one need; the writer satisfies another.

Literary language, spoken or written, provides a pleasure: it satisfies the instinct for selection, taste, enjoyment, rhythm, balance, and organization, which man possesses deep down within him. If literary language does not measure up to all these requirements, it is not literary language. Only an artist can create that literary language, with the intention that it should be of that quality and that it should satisfy such desires.

VI

It was once said that literature begins where life ends, at a moment of spiritual crisis. Here we must declare, as the classicists say, this truth. In fact literature, which is the art closest to man, to such a degree that it can scarcely be separated from him (because it is united to his speech, the very marrow of his being), comes into being at those moments when the expression of the spirit, through excess of pain, through abundance of joy, or through superfluity of vision, breaks and suspends its activity. But this muteness is only apparent because it soon finds its expression, perhaps the most intimate expression, through the medium of the written word. In this situation the spirit rushes forth to capture beauty in speech. In this situation literature coagulates in the voice which is, at the same time, resonance, dialogue, with an emotion that reasons and with a reason that feels emotion. If the proper equilibrium in this exercise is achieved, then literature is born. If the equilibrium is not achieved, other values are born which gravitate to morality, deficiency, or nothing at all.

VII

It may be said that language satisfies two purposes. The spoken language completes its function when it satisfies the need of *men.* The literary language completes its function when it satisfies the need of *man.* To speak more clearly, the spoken language can exist only when men use it with a definite and immediate object in view. The literary language exists already in the very act alone of its invention by man. The first fulfils an extrinsic necessity; the second, an intrinsic necessity. If the literary language is at times put into circulation immoderately, it is due to the appetite of man who is not capable of inventing it, but who is capable, because of his spiritual nature, of enjoying it.

VIII

Ortega y Gasset[3] defines technique in these words: "It is the reform which man imposed upon nature, for the satisfaction of his needs." This definition helps us to understand what literature is. Literature too is technique; it means "the reform which the artist imposes upon the nature of the spoken language, in search of the satisfaction of his spiritual needs. Literature supposes two precise terms: what it is and who creates it. To understand this more clearly, the process may be inverted: who creates it and what it is. It is created by an artist, a person who possesses a value composed of good taste, selectivity, creative instinct, and sense of beauty. What this artist composes must satisfy the requirements noted: creation, selection, beauty. Literature, then, comes to be a beautiful artifice which has a point of departure (the spoken language) and a palpable reality in the genres which contain it.

IX

The writer must remember what Luis Vives said with respect to friendship. "Friendship," said this thinker, "consists of love, equality, simplicity, and confidence."

These terms fit in well with the art of writing, as will be seen immediately. If the theme is not loved with the whole mind, it will be difficult to approach it. If the writer does not feel himself equal to the theme, that is, if its magnitude is beyond his powers, it will be useless for him to touch it. It will always seem to him a theme removed from him. If the writer does not succeed in developing it with simplicity, it is not worth studying. And finally, if the writer lacks confidence in

[3]Modern Spanish philosopher who died in 1955.

himself and in what he is doing, his work will reflect the ineffectiveness of his spirit.

X

A drop of water is a drop of water; but a drop of water and another drop of water, added up, in the end make up an Ocean. Then any one of the drops of water which form the Ocean is also to some extent the Ocean itself. It is already, in a measure, Ocean. It is, in miniature, the Ocean itself. Now we shall be able to say the following: The same thing is true of men and society. A man is a man. But one man and another man and another man come to constitute a society. Then any of the men who form the society is also part of the society. He is already, to some extent, *society*. He is, in miniature, society itself.

XI

A man of letters who is not conscious of the literature to which he belongs is hardly a man of letters. He is an isolated being, a stranger in his own country, a creator of myths—of fruitless myths, without miracle and without life. Only the man of letters who moves within literature, inside the species, can succeed in entering into the universal consciousness of literature.

XII

To the Persians only those suffered from leprosy who had sinned against the sun. And to sin against the sun was to be untrue to truth.

XIII

Striving for literary effect is an evil so great that it even goes as far as to take on disguises, as if to deceive the person suffering from it and practising it. The most dangerous disguise that is commonly used, to validate the deception, is that of simplicity. For this reason the best method for not finding simplicity is to seek it. Simplicity is found in a negative way: by avoiding everything that is not simple.

XIV

By seeing what is not simple, one discovers what is simple. So, from this burlesque passage about Liñán y Verdugo,[4] written in his *Guide and Advice to Strangers* (*Guía y aviso de forasteros*), one may draw

[4]A minor Spanish novelist of the seventeenth century.

profitable lessons. The passage runs: "The twenty he asked me for reals I do not have, though my desire with you great to serve you, the possible for limits to satisfy you, the most that evident you have shown willingness to on all occasions honour me, and favour me with your wonderful in everything visits, subtle, which is ingenious conversation, in which may he who is able, that is God, and who did bless you with it, improve and increase you."[5] To put into good style paragraphs like this, which are more abundant in the country than one might think, is a fruitful exercise. It is an exercise which should be practised not only by novices but also by some who consider themselves masters of the art of writing. And possibly the latter would benefit more than the former.

XV

Hegel said that historical events are sometimes repeated. Marx added that the first time it is as tragedy, and the second time as farce. Still more could be said: the first time it is as reality, and the second time as imitation. Examples abound in literature. To the Classicism of the sixteenth century corresponds the pseudo-Classicism of the eighteenth. In Classicism man takes the form of an attitude, but in pseudo-Classicism he is merely a posture. Classicism produces Lope,[6] and pseudo-Classicism produces Moratín.[7]

Mexican Letters (*Letras de México*), Mexico, February 15, 1942, Year VI, Vol. III, No. 14, p. 4.

[5]One vice of the *culto* or Gongoristic school was hyperbaton. My translation does not exaggerate its manner. Euphuism in English literature bears some resemblance to it.

[6]Lope de Vega, most famous of Spain's dramatists of the Golden Age.

[7]Dramatist of the late eighteenth and early nineteenth centuries, who was strongly influenced by Molière.

Julio Jiménez Rueda

(b. Mexico, D.F., 1896)

Like the majority of the fellow-members of his generation, Jiménez Rueda made his first attempts in the theatre and in the colonialist novel, but when that fashion passed, he devoted himself entirely to criticism, literary history, and research, activities in which he distinguishes himself by the clarity of his syntheses and the sprightliness of his evocations. He has a constant love for the great Spanish figures of the Golden Age and for our national letters. After his manual of Mexican literature, his most important project has been the history of our culture, concerning which he has published the volumes which treat the pre-Hispanic period and the viceroyalty.

Jiménez Rueda has taught literature to many generations, in the National Preparatory School and in the Faculty of Philosophy and Letters, of which he has been dean. As delegate of the National University and of the City Council of Mexico, he visited Buenos Aires and Montevideo, and has delivered many lectures and given short courses in universities and colleges of the United States. He has directed the General Archives of the Nation, and is now director of the *Ibero-American Review* (*Revista Iberoamericana*). He is also a lawyer, a Doctor of Letters, and a member of the Linguistic Academy.

STUDIES: *Outlines of Mexican Literature* (*Resúmenes de literatura mexicana*), 1918; *History of Mexican Literature* (*Historia de la literatura mexicana*), 1928, 1934, 1942, 1946; *Anthology of Mexican Prose* (*Antología de la prosa en México*), 1931, 1938; *Juan Ruiz de Alarcón in His Time. A Lecture* (*Juan Ruiz de Alarcón en su tiempo. Conferencia*), 1934; *Lope de Vega. Interpretive Essay* (*Lope de Vega. Ensayo de interpretación*), 1939; *Saint Teresa and Sor Juana, an Impossible Parallel* (*Santa Teresa y Sor Juana, un paralelo imposible*), 1943; *Mexican Letters in the Nineteenth Century* (*Letras mexicanas en el siglo XIX*), 1944; *Don Pedro Moya de Contreras, First Inquisitor of Mexico* (*Don Pedro Moya de Contreras, primer inquisidor de México*), 1944; *Heresies and Superstitions in New Spain* (*Herejías y supersticiones en la Nueva España*), 1946; *History of Culture in Mexico. The Vice-royalty* (*Historia de la cultura en México. El virreinato*), 1951; *Sor Juana Inés de la Cruz in Her Time* (*Sor Juana Inés de la Cruz en su época*), 1951; *The Constitutions of the Ancient University* (*Las constituciones de la antigua*

Universidad), 1951; *Juridical History of the University of Mexico* (*Historia jurídica de la Universidad de México*), 1956; *Pictures of the Golden Centuries* (*Estampas de los siglos de oro*), 1957.

MEXICO IN SEARCH OF HER EXPRESSION

WITH REGARD TO EACH OF OUR COUNTRIES, trying to find its expression means that it has sought the precise ways of expressing itself that differ from the ways the Spaniards express themselves in their literature and the ways in which the different citizens of the American continent express themselves in their own literatures; that is, it is a theory of collective psychology directly related to our theory of art and our literary history.

The history of Mexico, to confine the theme exclusively to my country, is divided into two main sectors: pre-Hispanic history and Hispanic history, which at a given moment meet to create a new form of expression. It would be necessary to study first what had been and what is still the form of expression of the indigenous peoples; how these cultures have manifested themselves and to what extent they have exerted an influence within our Hispanic civilization. It is known that the principal creation of the native mind has been in the plastic field. Whatever it had of literature has come to us in a few samples preserved by the missionaries or handed down later through the generations. The most important fact of the native world, whether Maya or Aztec, has been that of its great plastic creations: the arts of architecture and sculpture. Thanks to that architectural and sculptural plastic art, pre-Hispanic America plays a very important rôle in the history of universal art. The Pyramid of the Castle at Chichén Itzá, the ruins of Uxmal, the Stone of the Sun, the Aztec Calendar, the Stone of Sacrifices, the Great Head of the Eagle Knight, that of the Dead Warrior, are masterpieces of universal plastic art, and represent the originality of a people, the supreme creation of the soul of a race.

What was this expression? The expression of a religious feeling and a passion for war. Religion and war were intimately linked together in the minds of this pre-Hispanic people.

Huitzilopochtli was the god that presided over the actions of the Aztec people, and in speaking of religion and war, there naturally arises the profound sense of death. It was a people that was constantly facing death and that knew that death was one of its fundamental gods, that the might of the warrior was closely linked to death. Hence, therefore, it is natural that there should appear in the indigenous race that fatalistic sense which moves it to undertake any kind of action which has an end in death. But at the same time they were a sensitive people; alongside warlike action, there was always a deep sense of poetry intimately related to the flowers and the birds. The remnants of lyric poetry which have come to us revolve around the Indian gardens and the birds. At a certain moment, the myth of war and poetic creation intermingle. Huitzilopochtli will become the representation of a bird that represents the god of war; the tiniest and most delicate creature becomes intimately related to the most fearful and implacable war-god. The eagle is linked with the serpent. Quetzalcóatl is a mixture of serpent and bird.

At bottom, too, there is the feeling of the sadness and melancholy of a subjugated people, of a people always living in the presence of death, and that characteristic fatalism of the race is accentuated still further when the conquerors come and conquer them, precisely because of this fatalistic sense. They could fight and die with men, but they could not fight against gods, and the gods were the Spaniards who fell upon the Valley of Anáhuac and subjugated the Indians and replaced their culture with a new one.

Naturally the forms of expression, from that moment, are different. The two races begin to fuse together, and that energetic, vigorous Spanish spirit gradually comes to feel the enchantment of contact with indigenous forms, with the calm, the tranquil, the melancholy. The conquered becomes the conqueror. Hernán Cortés (Cortez) and Bernal Díaz already feel that enchantment, that strange bewitchment through contact with the atmosphere and with the men, and the spirit of the conqueror is so changed, that the conqueror himself has to use indigenous methods to dominate the Indians, and though Cortez was a great warrior, when he goes to Spain and is called to the Emperor's Council in the campaign against Tunis, his opinion is worthless to Emperor Charles V, because his understanding of war conformed to the Indian manner and not the European.

The two races begin to fuse together; a new art is created; poets arise who are sons of our own soil, who begin to express Mexican reality, the spirit of Mexico; grandeur of the city that resembles Venice, luxury of retinue, of horses, new plays that are acted every day. Again Mexican art expresses itself in plastic form. The best of colonial creation is architectural art, created in Mexico with Spanish forms, but done by natives.

The Spaniard directed the building of palaces and churches; but the native was the one in charge of the workmanship, and when he entered into it he recalled his own forms of plastic expression. There are carved crosses which reflect indigenous monuments, and in the doors of churches and cathedrals, the work of native carpenters, there remains the memory of the native plastic art which elaborated a baroque art different from the Spanish. A new element arises, the Oriental. The Chinese ship came to Acapulco every year and brought things from the legendary Orient; it brought silks, clay vessels, ivories, and those objects which gradually were left inside our Mexico and also influenced the baroque art of the eighteenth century. It is not remarkable that in this baroque art the saints in the churches, the work of our image-makers, should appear to be dressed in Chinese kimonos. It is not unusual to find, on the altars of the Cathedral of Mexico City, Spanish saints that are not clothed like the martyr saints of Spain, but in admirable tunics of Chinese cut. The angels that support the candelabra in the passage leading to the altar in the Cathedral of Mexico City show more of the Oriental style of sculpture than of the Spanish. The predominance of blue also recalls Chinese art. Baroque art creates a new form of expression; it also has an influence on literature, in a form perhaps more interesting. Mexican literature of the seventeenth century was aristocratic; it came out of universities and colleges; it was of a learned style, not intended to be appreciated by Indians and mestizos, but only by cultured men; it regarded the mestizos and the mulattos as something decorative and baroque, because the composition of Mexico at that time was baroque too. . . .

The spirit of that baroque period in Mexico is expressed through Sor Juana Inés de la Cruz, Carlos de Sigüenza y Góngora, and other authors. But towards the end of the seventeenth century it begins to have consciousness of nationality. What is Mexico? The poets had already described the landscapes, the nature, and the climate of Mexico. The answer to the question will not be given by poets, but by scholars. Sigüenza y Góngora explores the Gulf of Mexico, to discover the character of this region; he is an astronomer, a geographer, a historian, and he tries to interpret the old manuscripts, and to investigate the past of the native Indians. At bottom, there is the belief that the real nature of Mexico cannot be grasped without a knowledge of past ages; to understand the present, it is necessary to immerse oneself in the past. The historians are going to study that past. Sigüenza y Góngora first, then Clavigero, devote themselves to the study of the ancient history of the natives and exalt the past, in part as a protest against the present. The Indians are exalted just to deprecate colonial organization. Of course, no definition of nationality appears as yet; but the word "fatherland" (*patria*) does come forth: the fatherland is already felt, and the difference between the Spaniard of Spain and the Spaniard of America is already felt too. In the dedication to the University which Clavigero prefixes to his *Ancient History of Mexico* (*Historia antigua de México*), one reads: "To the Mexican fatherland." Now, if in speaking of the Mexican fatherland and in saying "I dedicate my work to the Mexican fatherland," one has no consciousness of nationality, I do not know what having a consciousness of nationality is. In the works of the Jesuits appear these phrases: "Fatherland of Mexico" . . . "Mexican fatherland" . . . "we sigh for our fatherland" . . . "we live in exile because of the injustice of the Spanish government". . . . All the work of the Jesuits expelled from Mexico in the eighteenth century has a character that is not only literary and historical, but political. No study has yet been made of this aspect of the work of the Spanish Jesuits expelled by the government of Charles III.

Another interesting element begins to be mingled with the political life of Mexico. It is no longer the Spain of the Austrian dynasty, of the seventeenth century, but that of the Bourbons, that represents the foreign spirit. The distrust that is shown in the eighteenth century towards the rulers is due to the fact that foreign national elements are beginning to interfere in the history of America. I hold that the colonial period in Mexico ends about the middle of the eighteenth century, with the baroque style. The appearance of the Bourbons coincides with Neoclassicism, which is no longer Mexican. It is an architectural and plastic rationalism, and artificial.

About the middle of the eighteenth century one also sees the intrusion of French rationalism, which appears in the seventeenth century with the philosophy of Descartes. Sor Juana Inés de la Cruz knew Descartes. It is the beginning of the rationalism which will incorporate the ideas of the French philosophers by creating a new ideology and a new sense of the way to express things.

Now we come to the beginning of the nineteenth century. It is true that almost all, or perhaps all, of the leaders in Spanish America show a profound confusion and in their proclamations independence is not mentioned. The cry of independence is a paradoxical cry. "Down with bad government, death to the Spaniards!" The Napoleonic invasion comes to fill up the cup, with its torrent of blood. But the revolution will not be accomplished by the ideologists; it must be accomplished by the people, to whom one does not speak with philosophies but with sentiments. Against whom are we going to fight? Against the Antichrist! And who is the Antichrist? Napoleon! How are we going to fight? With whatever we can fight with, but not against the King, because after three centuries of colonial domination the concept of obedience to the King is thoroughly ingrained in the minds of the people. The Austrian house had exalted, above everything, the majesty of the King: "Only the King Supreme."[1] It was not possible to say to the people: "We are going to fight against the King", when Ferdinand VII at that moment represented the protest of the Spanish people against Napoleonic domination. One could fight against the Antichrist, not against the one who was fighting the Antichrist, the one who was then the confused image of the Fatherland, Ferdinand VII, the Well-beloved. For that reason, the cry of Independence took that form. For that reason, Hidalgo and the first leaders of the Independence movement carried it out in accordance with a paradoxical proclamation. In Morelos there already appears the desire to become independent of the government of Spain. The Constitution of Apatzingán, in 1814, already contains the principle of absolute independence. Morelos represents the political and military genius of the first period of the revolution. There you have expressed the idea of nationality, in a political document written on the battlefield. It was the Constitution of the United States transferred to New Spain, and so democratic, that with Morelos as general, the Commander-in-chief of the army resigned his command in Congress and died defending the Congressists. He could have saved himself by flight, but he preferred to die. He is one of the martyrs not only of the Independence movement, but of the representative and democratic spirit of America in general.

All the proclamations of the leaders of Independence are in the name of America: "Americans of all America"; there is already in mind a clear and precise division between Spain which is the past and America which is the future. In reality, our leaders of 1810 rose up under the influence of French ideas and those of the Constitution of the United States, which was the realization of a desire of the intellectuals. When Bolívar felt the American spirit, he was creating this spirit which has brought us together on this occasion to discuss these problems in this city. Barja has said that America is the future, that it is reaching its majority. That is true: at this moment America is creating a new world which perhaps we shall not see.

[1]*Del Rey abajo ninguno*, the title of a play by Rojas Zorrilla of the Golden Age period, is used in that play in the sense "below the King, none (may insult me)." Here the sense appears to be "below the King, none (has authority)."

Every legist, every poet, every artist, every mind that thinks and speaks for culture, has been creating this new world which will be the world of our grandchildren, or that of our grandchildren's grandchildren. A new world, a world created by the mind through a culture elaborated throughout the centuries, which comes from the East and which in its trajectory towards the West, at this moment, finds America full of vigour and wealth, facing the catastrophe which seems to be annihilating what is best in the world; but we hope it will not die, and we hope it will rise up again from the ashes of our volcanoes.

Report of the Third International Congress of Professors of Latin-American Literature (*Memoria del Tercer Congreso Internacional de Catedráticos de Literatura Iberoamericana*), December, 1942, Tulane University Press, New Orleans, La., 1944, pp. 151–56.

Alfonso Caso

(b. Mexico, D.F., 1896)

Alfonso Caso obtained his law degree and the degree of Master of Philosophy at the National University. He has been Director of the National Preparatory School (1928–29), General Director of Higher Education and Scientific Investigation in the Department of Education (1944), President of the National University (1944–45), a Member of the Board of Governors of the same university, and Secretary for National Property and Administrative Inspection (1946–48). Besides, with relation to his specialty, he has been Head of the Department of Archaeology in the National Museum, Director of the same museum, Director of the National Institute of Anthropology and History, and of explorations at Monte Albán, Oaxaca. He also directs the *Mexican Review of Anthropological Studies* (*Revista Mexicana de Estudios Antropológicos*) and has been director of the *Bibliographical Bulletin of American Anthropology* (*Boletín Bibliográfico de Antropología Americana*). From its foundation, in 1949, he has been directing the National Institute for the Study of Indigenes.

In 1944 he formulated the Organic Law and the Statutes which govern the National University, and in 1951 he presided over the Mexican Scientific Congress, which the University organized on the occasion of its quadricentennial anniversary.

Besides numerous honorary degrees and academic distinctions from European and American universities, Caso received the Viking Fund medal and prize for 1952, awarded by the Wenner Gren Foundation, on the nomination of the Society for American Archaeology, and in 1954 he was awarded the Manuel Ávila Camacho Science Prize, by the Mexican Book Institute.

Alfonso Caso has one of the keenest and most penetrating minds in Mexico. The intellectual impulse, which in the philosopher Antonio Caso, his elder brother, was mainly an urge of the heart and a passion of a romantic character, is rigorous and lucid, of marked scientific sobriety in Alfonso Caso, though on occasion his passion may be aroused in defence of his ideals.

In his youth, in a student group called "The Seven Wise Men," he inclined towards juridical and philosophical studies, but soon his vocation was to be decisively turned towards archaeology and in general towards the study of primitive Mexican cultures. In this field, his discovery in 1931–32 of the jewels deposited in the tombs of Monte Albán, Oaxaca, and his valuable monographs, were soon to make him the most outstanding authority, the organizer and guide of anthropological organizations in Mexico and, through the Institute for the Study of Indigenes, a worker for the betterment of the Indian elements in the country.

STUDIES AND ESSAYS: *What is Law?* (*¿Qué es el derecho?*), 1919; *The Temple of the Sacred War* (*El Teocalli de la Guerra Sagrada*), 1927; *Zapotecan Traces* (*Las estelas zapotecas*), 1928; *The explorations of Monte Albán* (*Las exploraciones de Monte Albán*), *1931–32 Season*, 1932–*1934–35 Season*, 1935; *Explorations in Mitla, 1934–35* (*Exploraciones en Mitla, 1934–35*), 1936; *The Religion of the Aztecs* (*La religión de los aztecas*), 1936; *Mixteca and Zapoteca Culture* (*Cultura mixteca y zapoteca*), 1936; *Thirteen Masterpieces of Mexican Archaeology* (*Trece obras maestras de arqueología mexicana*), 1938; *Explorations in Oaxaca. Fifth and Sixth Seasons. 1936–37* (*Exploraciones en Oaxaca. Quinta y sexta temporadas. 1936–37*), 1938; "Pre-Hispanic Arts," "El arte prehispánico," in *Twenty Centuries of Mexican Art* (*Veinte siglos de arte mexicano*), 1940; *Message to the People of the Universities* (*Mensaje a los universitarios*), 1944; *Preliminary Sketch of the Organic Law of the University* (*Anteproyecto de Ley Orgánica de la UNAM*), 1944; *Outline of the Statutes of the University* (*Proyecto de Estatutos de la UNAM*), 1944; "Contribution of the Indigenous Cultures of Mexico to World Culture" ("Contribución de las culturas indígenas de México a la cultura mundial"), in *Mexico and Culture* (*México y la Cultura*), 1946; *Bibliography of the Popular Plastic Arts in Mexico* (*Bibliografía de las artes populares plásticas de México*), 1950; *Urns of Oaxaca* (*Urnas de Oaxaca*), 1952 (In collaboration with Ignacio Bernal); *The People of the Sun* (*El pueblo del Sol*), 1954; *Pre-Cortezian Indigenous Institutions* (*Instituciones indígenas precortesianas*), 1954; *Studies of Indigenes* (*Indigenismo*), 1957.

IS THE MEXICAN INDIAN A MEXICAN?

WHEN WE ARE CONFRONTED with a problem, we can always take two attitudes. The first—the more comfortable and the less compromising—is to ignore its existence and lull ourselves to sleep with a soothing optimism. The second—the more virile and energetic—consists of facing reality, however bitter it may appear, in order to know the elements of the problem and try to solve them.

Both attitudes have been and are still at the present time shown with regard to the Mexican indigenes.

There are still many people who, when they hear about the problem of the indigene, do not believe it exists; they simply ignore it, or at most, they ask themselves in a rather sceptical way what the problem is.

Fortunately the majority of Mexicans have the other attitude, that is, we know the problem exists in the country and we want to know about it in order to solve it.

But for those who ask what it is we can say, in a general way, what the elements are in this situation with which we are trying to acquaint ourselves, not only with an academic purpose, but fundamentally with a practical purpose in mind.

What Is the Problem of the Indigene?

In the first place, are there any indigenes in Mexico?

If, according to the censuses and the studies that have been made, we know that there are three million people who speak only indigenous languages, or who speak in addition a few words of Spanish, but in a manner as defective as if it were a foreign language, we shall already have one reason to answer that, at least in a fundamental aspect—the expression of thought—there are three million Mexicans who express themselves in languages which are not the national language.

What consequences does this have? Imagine for a moment any one of us, living in a country whose language we do not speak, obliged to live isolated within a small community, from which one not only cannot escape but has no desire to escape, for fear of a strange and hostile world, which one does not understand or feel oneself capable of understanding.

But language is only one of the spiritual expressions of any man who lives in a society. Language, beliefs, customs, habits, costume, techniques, etc., form—when they are all added together—what we anthropologists call by the name of "culture."

The difference in language between the indigene and the rest of the population of the country is an index of a much more important fact: the difference in culture between the indigenous groups and the rest of the Mexican population. And by culture we mean, and we repeat it again, not only the highest expressions of culture, but the sum of technical knowledge; practices, habits, beliefs, etc., which make up the social life of a community.

The problem of the indigene, consequently, does exist in this sense, in that there are at least three million Mexicans who in their "culture" differ from the rest of the Mexican population.

The Problem of the Indigene Is Not Racial

We are not concerned, and this must be emphasized, with a racial problem, but with a social or cultural problem. No one would dream in Mexico, where racial discrimination does not exist, of trying to find out if the indigenous race is or is not capable of being civilized. Race is a purely biological concept and has nothing to do with the intellectual or cultural capacities of an individual; the difference which exists between communities in the country is not a racial difference. From the racial point of view, it may be that these communities do not differ from the others, or differ very slightly. But it is their culture, that is, the total of ideas, practices, habits, utensils, and techniques that distinguishes indigenous communities.

And what consequence has this had for the lives of the Indians? For one thing, the indigene lives in the most remote and isolated regions of the country. He has been driven from the valleys to the mountains, from the meadows to the deserts; for five centuries, those who were better armed than he, from the cultural point of view, have succeeded in despoiling him of his lands, his bodies of water, his woods, and in casting him out to the confines of the territory. There are soils too poor for agriculture, situated on the slopes of mountains, where population cannot concentrate because there is not sufficient land to sustain life except for isolated plots which can support just a few families; lands incapable of supporting a settlement, in the sense in which we understand this word, which accounts for the great dispersion of the indigenes in the areas they inhabit; and that dispersion makes it difficult to reach those people by means of roads, to establish schools and clinics, and to exploit other natural resources and organize industries. The poorness of the land makes it adequate only for the bare support of the family; the productivity is so small that there is hardly any excess to exchange for other products, and so the indigenous family lives exclusively, or almost exclusively, on what it produces. It neither produces for the country, nor does it consume what Mexico produces.

There is backwardness in the technical, sanitary, economic, and educational facilities. Isolated families in the mountains and deserts, with a production barely adequate for daily sustenance, without any possibility, because of their isolation and the roughness and poorness of the localities in which they live, of receiving benefits which the Federal Government or the State Legislatures offer to the rest of the population, by providing highways, irrigation works, hospitals, clinics, schools, etc.

Still more: the indigene who lives in his isolated community cannot feel himself to be a Mexican. He does know that there is a kind of natural power called "Government," whose orders must be respected because it uses force to impose obedience. He knows that "Government" appears at times in the form of alcohol inspectors, who ransack their poor hovels looking for clandestine stills, and he knows that at times "Government" demands that a list of requirements be fulfilled which carry with them as a penalty fines and levies. And there ends his concept of government. He does not feel himself to be Mexican, and he has no sense of being part of an entity which extends beyond his little community. Outside of it everything is hostile to him. Only within does he find sympathy, warmth, and understanding.

What is there strange about the indigene having a strong sense of a bond uniting him to his own people, and of there being nothing for him outside his own community? Mexico is only a word.

Those three million indigenes lack the essential sentiment of the citizen, political solidarity, which is the very foundation on which the principle of nationality rests.

The problem of the indigene is this: there are three million Mexicans, at least, who do not receive the benefits of the country's progress, who form isolated pockets, incapable of following the rhythm of the development of Mexico, and who do not feel that they are Mexicans. Can we now ask if there is a problem of the indigene in Mexico?

But in this matter, as in all those that concern social questions, there are a great many mistaken ideas and mistaken measures, which it is necessary to discuss and reject.

Mistaken Ideas About the Problem of the Indigene

The first mistaken idea, which we have already analysed summarily, is that the problem of the indigene is a racial problem, that is, that there exists an indigenous race, distinct from the Mexican. This is clearly a colonial attitude. Peoples that have conquered other peoples may have the idea they can distinguish two races in absolute terms: the conquerors and the conquered, the masters and the slaves; but in Mexico, right from the time of the beginning of the conquest, races have intermingled. Soon the mestizo appears, and through the centuries when Mexico was a colony and those of our independence, the racial intermingling has gone on in such a way that it is very unlikely that any Mexicans exist who do not have Indian blood in their veins, and it is also possible that many of the indigenes have mestizo and white ancestors.

But what does it matter to us, and to what purpose should we concern ourselves, that an individual should have more or less Indian or European blood? What concerns us is not the race, but the cultural and social condition of the population. For this reason the theories which hold that the Indian problem can be solved by importing Europeans are ridiculous. Or is it really believed that the problem of the indigene in Mexico, of three million Mexicans, is to be solved by the importation of a few breeders from the Old Continent?

The second mistaken attitude holds, with a false romanticism regarding the indigene, that the Indians should be left alone and isolated. Instead of taking to them the benefits of a higher culture, of scientific medicine, of a language that can serve as a vehicle of universal thought and feeling, of more modern agricultural methods, we should leave them, according to this policy, just as they are in their own communities. This view prescribes a system of segregation, and is horrified by the idea of taking to an Indian population the *nixtamal* grinder and ending the use of the autochthonous and picturesque *metate*, to which the Indian woman is attached, on her knees, for hours and hours of toil.

The third mistaken attitude is what we might call the formalistic attitude. It is the attitude which holds that, according to our Constitution, there are no Indians; we are all Mexicans and have the same rights and the same obligations. It is indeed a very noble concept, if considered as an ideal to be attained; but it holds danger of disastrous consequences if it is regarded not only as the expression of an ideal contemplated in our laws, but as the actual condition in which we are living. The propounders of this theory ask themselves: "Is the indigene not a Mexican? Why, then, call him an indigene? Why make a 'discrimination' not recognized in our laws? Why, in brief, consider him apart from the Mexican population as a whole?" The answer is obvious and simple: The indigene is a Mexican, but also an indigene; that is, theoretically he is protected by the law, but in reality he lives in his communities, in the mountains and deserts, isolated from the cultural, social, economic, and political influences of Mexico.

The indigene is a Mexican, since he pays the tax when he goes to sell his products in the cities or to buy the things he does not produce; he is a Mexican when he is hired to work on the pineapple or coffee plantations and receives, as an advance on his wages, a good dose of alcohol which brutalizes and drugs him; he is a Mexican when he falls into the hands of the police who take him to prison to collect fines from him and force him, the following morning, to sweep the streets of the town; and he is also a Mexican when he pays taxes indirectly, when he buys the products sold to him at inflated prices by the town merchants.

But if an epidemic of typhus or smallpox afflicts his community there is then no Mexican doctor or medicines. If he wishes to utilize his lands or his woods, there are no Mexican technicians or credits in Mexican banks to assist him. If he wishes to educate his children, there are no Mexican schools to teach them, and if he wishes to leave his community and make contact with the rest of the country, there are no Mexican roads that pass through his village.

Yes, the indigene is a Mexican according to our laws. He has none of the advantages we have mentioned, but in compensation he can console himself in the knowledge that the Constitution and the laws of the country, written in a language he does not understand, declare him to be a Mexican citizen, "in full use of his rights and privileges."

Can it be possible that anyone does not understand that laws that speak of equality are just only when applied to equals? And that it is the greatest of injustices to declare equal before the law those who are not equal?

Our legislation has made this interpretation, as has also the legislation of all the civilized countries on earth. The minor is not, before the law, the equal of one who has attained his majority; women are not the legal equals of men, they need the protection of law. The workman cannot be considered the equal of the employer, he requires protection; and the agrarian laws are protective laws and not simply restrictive laws.

Equality is just only among equals. Our equalizing laws, to solve the problem of social inequality, do not suffice, for the problem is the result of an exploitation which has gone on for five centuries.

There is still another mistaken attitude, perhaps the worst of all, but so stupid and unjust, that we mention it only to complete our inventory of errors. It is the attitude which holds that the problem of the indigene requires using force against him, forcing him to obey, or as we say in military parlance, "as circumstances may require."

If the Otomis do not want to leave the valley of the Mezquital, they must be forcibly expelled from the land in which they and their ancestors have lived for centuries; that is, it is proposed to treat them as delinquents, forcing them to do what they do not wish to do, as if it were a crime to be an indigene, and it is now completely forgotten that we are living under the rule of law and that the Constitution allows every Mexican the right to live where he pleases.

Fortunately this theory is absolutely repudiated by Mexican public opinion, and is held only by a few reactionaries.

The Right Way

Consequently there is only one way to solve the problem of the indigene, only one that is scientifically correct and also just and generous. To solve the problem of the indigene, Mexico cannot follow any other course. The communities of indigenes must be incorporated into the great Mexican community. Their communities must be transformed by taking to them what already exists in other settlements in the country: roads, hospitals, and schools. They must be given land, water, and woods; their herds must be improved; they must be taught new methods of cultivation, supplied with improved seed, given protection for their crafts and new ones established, taught the national language and offered the benefits of the basic education to which every man and woman in the world has a right.

Since it is not a racial problem but one of cultural backwardness, what is needed is to transform the negative aspects of the indigenous culture into positive aspects, and preserve what is positive and useful in the communities of the indigenes—their sense of solidarity and of obligation to mutual assistance, their popular arts, their folklore. We do not have the right to destroy these forms of their culture, if we are men with sensibilities, if we believe that the world ought not to be populated by individuals governed by a standard system, but that within world culture, as within national culture, variety is necessary in order to enrich the highest forms of culture.

We must transform the communities of the indigene by the only method possible if we are to make the social transformations durable and if they are to be made without the tensions and conflicts that are brought about by the use of force, that is, by education and example. This is not to force, but to invite; not to command, but to demonstrate; not to destroy, but to transform. This is the way. It is a slow way, as all education is a slow process. It is a way which requires not only the acceptance, but the enthusiastic co-operation of the community of indigenes, but in the end it is the only sure way, the way that will enable us to incorporate the three million indigenes, and really make them into three million Mexicans, not only because our laws so declare them, but because they are so as a social reality. If we use education and example, we are sure to win trust and co-operation, and we are sure also to avoid the conflicts which might be caused by too impatient a policy, attempting to solve in a few years a problem that is centuries old.

It frequently happens, in the social sciences, that those who do not know the problems and the techniques for solving them have a belief in the power of magic. Such is the untutored legislator who, on formulating a law, thinks that the next day it will be converted into a social accomplishment; or the economist who, without knowing about the intricate working of economic forces, tries to solve the problem by means of theoretical recipes; or the sociological novice who, without knowing about the inner forces which govern transformations in society and culture, tries to achieve those transformations by hasty measures.

But in the social sciences, as in any other science, the aphorism of Comte is applicable: "We must know in order to foresee, and we must foresee in order to know." Without previous knowledge it is impossible to know what will happen, and without knowing what will happen any action that is taken is blind and condemned to failure.

Mexico has a serious problem before her, one of the most serious of the present day for our country—the problem of the indigene. We already know that we can solve it; the experiments which we have made in Chiapas, Chihuahua, Veracruz, and Oaxaca, in establishing the Co-ordinating Centres (of the National Institute for the Indigenes), show that our methods are the right ones. We have the confidence and support of the indigenous population. We do not need speeches or sentimental attitudes; what we need is that the country should realize the magnitude of the problem, and that the necessary resources be furnished, in money, equipment, and men, to solve it. And in this way, perhaps slowly, but in a scientific, just, and generous manner, Mexico will be able to have those three million Mexicans incorporated into the economic, social, political, and cultural life of the nation.

Mexico in Culture (*México en la Cultura*). Supplement to *Novelties* (*Novedades*), Mexico, Feb. 19, 1956, pp. 1–2.

Samuel Ramos

(b. Zitácuaro, Michoacán, 1897; d. 1959)

Samuel Ramos began his studies at the University of San Nicolás de Hidalgo, in Morelia, and continued them later in the Faculty of Philosophy and Letters of the University of Mexico, where he obtained the degrees of Master and Doctor of Philosophy. In Europe he extended his studies at the Sorbonne and the Collège de France, as well as at the University of Rome. Back in Mexico, along with the constant exercise of his discipline, he worked in varied academic and educational activities. Ramos was Director of University Extension, Head of the Department of Intellectual Co-operation, Dean of the Faculty of Philosophy and Letters, and Co-ordinator for the Humanities. From 1952 until his death, he was a member of the National College. As representative of Mexican institutions he attended international cultural meetings and gave lectures in cultural centres of the United States and South America.

The philosophical investigations of Samuel Ramos have shown a preference for problems of modern aesthetics and the study of the idiosyncrasies of the Mexican. Departing from the lines indicated by his master Antonio Caso—with whom he had a famous controversy—Samuel Ramos was the initiator of the study of the character of the Mexican man which, in later years, a new group of philosophers would be able to convert into a constant preoccupation with Mexican thought.

ESSAYS: *Hypothesis* (*Hipótesis*), 1928; *The Profile of Man and Culture in Mexico* (*El perfil del hombre y la cultura en México*), 1934, 1937, 1951; *Diego Rivera*, 1935; *Beyond the Morality of Kant* (*Más allá de la moral de Kant*), 1938; *The Stravinsky Case* (*El caso Stravinsky*), 1939; *Towards a New Humanism* (*Hacia un nuevo humanismo*), 1940; *Twenty Years of Education in Mexico* (*Veinte años de educación en México*), 1941; *History of Philosophy in Mexico* (*Historia de la filosofía en México*), 1942; *Philosophy* [*in Mexico*] (*La filosofía* [*en México*], 1946; *Philosophy of the Artistic Life* (*Filosofía de la vida artística*), Buenos Aires, 1950.

PSYCHO-ANALYSIS OF THE MEXICAN

"WHAT DOSAGE OF TRUTH can man take?" This question of Nietzsche's comes to our mind and prompts us to warn the reader concerning the contents of the present chapter, which is a harsh, but dispassionate, exposition of what in our opinion makes up the Mexican psychology. It would be an abuse of our thesis to deduce from it a judgement that would be depressing to the Mexican, since we do not make him responsible for his present character, which is the result of an historical destiny beyond his control. It is not very flattering to feel one has a character like the one we are about to portray, but it is a relief to know that it can be changed as one changes clothes, since that character is borrowed, and we are wearing it as a disguise to conceal our authentic nature, concerning which, in our opinion, we have nothing to be ashamed of. It is not a question, then, of just one more self-defamation, but neither is there any squeamish avoidance of unpleasant things for the sole purpose of "pleasing the *bourgeoisie.*"

We are the first to believe that certain traits of the human soul should remain unpublished when nothing is gained by bringing them to the light of day. But in the case of the Mexican we think it would be harmful to him not to know his character when it runs contrary to his destiny, and the only way to change it is to become precisely aware of it. In such cases, the truth is more salutary than self-deception. Take note that in our essay we do not confine ourselves to describing the most salient characteristics of the Mexican character, but we delve down to the point of discovering their hidden causes, in order that we may know how to change our nature.

The object of this work is not to criticize the Mexican with malicious intentions; we think that any Mexican has the right to analyse his nature and take the liberty to publish his observations, if he is convinced that these observations, pleasant or unpleasant, will be advantageous to the others, revealing to them that they bear within themselves mysterious forces which, if not perceived in time, are capable of thwarting their lives. Men not accustomed to criticism think that anything that is not praise is something against them, when often praising them is the surest way to be against them and do them harm.

Others before us have spoken of the inferiority complex of our race, but nobody, as far as we know, has made systematic use of this idea to explain our character. What is attempted for the first time in this essay is the methodical application of the psychological theories of Adler to the Mexican. An inferiority complex must be inferred in all individuals who show an exaggerated concern to assert their personalities, those who are keenly interested in every matter or situation having to do with power, and who have an immoderate eagerness to be predominant, and first in everything. Adler states that the sense of inferiority appears in the child when he realizes how insignificant his strength is compared to that of his parents. When Mexico was born, she found herself in the same position with respect to the civilized world as the child with respect to his elders. She appeared in history when a mature civilization, which a child-like mind can only half understantd, was already dominant. From this disadvantageous situation arises the sense of inferiority which was aggravated by the conquest, the mixture of blood, and even the disproportionate magnitude of Nature. But this feeling does not assert itself in a perceptible manner in Mexican character until the coming of independence, in the first third of the past century.*

It has been held unnecessary to support this interpretation by an accumulation of documents. If the reader is honestly interested in the question and takes these ideas in good part, he will find the data to prove them in his own observations. Before giving a detailed description of Mexican life, we have tried to establish how the soul of the individual functions in general, what his habitual reactions are, and to what impulses he responds.

There is no reason for the reader to take offence on reading these pages, in which it is not stated that the Mexican is inferior, but that he *feels inferior*, which is something very different. If in some individual cases the sense of inferiority reflects real organic or psychic defects, in the majority of Mexicans it is a collective illusion resulting from measuring man according to very high scales of value, corresponding to countries advanced in age. We invite him, therefore, to look into our ideas with complete equanimity. If, in spite of these explanations, the reader feels hurt, we sincerely regret it, but we shall be confirming that in our American countries there exists, as Keyserling

*"Young peoples, for their part"—says Keyserling—"do not have an intense, critical spirit. They are spiritually passive, like all young persons; they are extremely susceptible to suggestion and resent criticism, out of weakness that is both physiological and moral. They are constantly perturbed by a sense of inferiority." *The Future of the European Spirit* (*L'Avenir de l'Esprit Européen*). Edición del Instituto de Cooperación Intelectual, Paris, 1934, p. 28.

says, "a primacy of susceptibility"; and so his reaction of resentment would be the most cogent proof of our thesis.

The Peon ("Pelado")

To discover the mainspring of the Mexican soul it has been necessary to examine some of the great collective movements. Plato maintained that the State was a magnified image of the individual. Below we shall demonstrate that, in fact, the Mexican conducts himself in his private world in the same manner as in public life.

The psychology of the Mexican is the result of reactions manifested for the purpose of concealing a sense of inferiority. Such a purpose is achieved by falsifying the appearance of the outer world, in order to exalt the Mexican's consciousness of his own worth. In his country he imitates the forms of European civilization, in order to feel that he is as good as the European and in order to form in his cities a privileged group which considers itself superior to all those Mexicans who live outside civilization. But the fictional process cannot be confined to external matters, nor is this sufficient to re-establish the psychic balance which the sense of inferiority has broken. That process is applied likewise to the individual, falsifying the opinion he has of himself. The psycho-analysis of the Mexican, in its individual aspect, is the theme we shall now consider.

To understand the working of the Mexican mind, we shall examine it in a social type in which all its movements are accentuated, so that one can clearly perceive the direction of its trajectory. The best specimen for study is the Mexican peon, since he constitutes the most elemental and well drawn expression of the national character. We shall not speak of his picturesque side, which has been reproduced to the point of boredom in the popular theatre, the novel, and in painting. Here we are concerned only with seeing him inside, to find out what elemental forces determine his character. His name *pelado* (stripped) defines him very precisely. He is a man who carries his soul uncovered, without hiding anything in its innermost recesses. He cynically displays certain elemental impulses which other men try to conceal. The "peon" belongs to a social species of the lowest category and represents the human outcast of the large city. In the economic hierarchy he is less than a proletarian and in the intellectual he is a primitive. Life has been hostile to him on all sides, and his attitude towards it is one of bitter resentment. He is a person of an explosive nature with whom communication is dangerous, because he explodes on the slightest friction. His explosions are verbal, and his theme is self-assertion in coarse, aggressive language. He has created a dialect of his own whose lexicon abounds in words in current use to which he gives a new meaning. He is an animal that resorts to pantomimes of ferocity to frighten others, by making them believe that he is stronger and more resolute. Such reactions are an illusory revenge for his real situation in life, which is like that of a zero on the left side of a number. This unpleasant truth tries to come out to the surface of his consciousness, but it is held back by another force which maintains within the unconscious all that could lower his sense of personal worth. Every external circumstance which could bring out the sense of inferiority will provoke a violent reaction on the part of the individual in order to subdue depression. This accounts for a constant irritability which makes him quarrel with others on the slightest pretext. The bellicose spirit is not explained, in this case, by a feeling of hostility towards the human race. The peon seeks a quarrel as a stimulant to elevate the tone of his depressed ego. He needs a prop to recover faith in himself, but since he has no real worth, he tries to substitute a fictitious worth. It is like a ship-wrecked person who plunges about in the deep and unexpectedly discovers a saving plank: virility. The terminology of the peon abounds in sexual allusions which reveal a phallic obsession, which has the effect of making him consider the sexual organ a symbol of masculine energy. In his verbal battles he attributes to the adversary an imaginary femininity, reserving to himself the masculine role. By this ruse he tries to assert his superiority over the rival.

We should like to demonstrate these ideas by examples. Unfortunately, the language of the peon is of such a crude realism, that it is impossible to transcribe many of his most characteristic phrases. We cannot omit, however, certain typical expressions. The reader must not be offended at our citing words here which are not used in Mexico except in intimate conversations, since the psychologist sees, through their vulgarirty and coarseness, another more noble sense. And it would be unpardonable to expunge valuable material for study for the sake of adhering to an ill-understood decency of language. It would be like a chemist refusing to analyse substances that have a foul smell.

Even if the peon of Mexico is completely wretched, he consoles himself by shouting to everyone that he has "many eggs" (the name given to the testicles). The important thing to note is that in these organs for him there lies not only one kind of potency, the sexual, but every kind of human potency. For the peon a man who triumphs in any activity, anywhere, triumphs because he has "many eggs." We shall mention another of his favourite expressions: "I am your father," the intention of which is to assert superiority. It is certain that in our patriarchal societies the father is for any man the symbol of power. It must be observed too that the phallic obsession of the peon is not comparable to the phallic cults, beneath which lies the idea of fecundity and eternal life. The phallus suggests to the peon the idea of power. From this he has derived a very impoverished concept of man. Since he is, in fact, a being without substantial content, he tries to fill his vacuum with the only value within his reach: that of being male. This popular concept of man has been turned into a prejudice that is most regrettable in every Mexican. When the latter compares himself with the foreign civilized man and perceives his own small worth, he consoles himself in the following manner: "A European"—he says—"has science, art, technology, etc., etc.; here we have none of that, but . . . we are he-men." They are men in the biological sense of the word, that is, males that enjoy full animal potency. The Mexican, fond of bullying, thinks that that potency is demonstrated by braggadocio. If he only knew it was all just a smoke screen!

We must not, then, allow ourselves to be deceived by appearances. The peon is neither a strong man nor a valiant man. The appearance he presents to us is false. It is a camouflage to mislead himself and all those that have dealings with him. It may be inferred that the greater the show of strength and valour, the greater the weakness that he wants to conceal. However much the peon may deceive himself with this illusion, so long as his weakness is present, threatening to betray him, he cannot be sure of his strength. He lives in continual fear of being discovered, distrusting himself, and for that reason his perception becomes abnormal; he imagines that the first newcomer is his enemy, and distrusts any man who approaches him.

Having given this brief description of the Mexican peon, it is fitting to outline his mental composition and functioning in order then to understand the psychology of the Mexican.

(1) The peon has two faces: one real, the other imaginary.

(2) The real personality is concealed by the latter of these, which is the one that is apparent to the person himself and to others.

(3) The imaginary personality is diametrically opposed to the real, because the object of the first is to raise the psychic tone which is depressed by the second.

(4) Since the person lacks any human value and is powerless to

acquire any in fact, he employs a ruse to conceal his feelings of inferiority.

(5) The lack of real support for his imaginary personality gives rise to a lack of confidence in himself.

(6) The lack of confidence in himself causes an abnormality in his psychic functioning, especially in his perception of reality.

(7) This abnormal perception consists of an unjustified distrust of others, and an excessive touchiness in his relations with other men.

(8) As our type is living under false colours, his position is always unstable and forces him constantly to stand guard over his ego, without regard for the real facts.

This disregard of reality and the consequent absorption in himself justify our classifying the peon among the "introverts."

It might be thought that the presence of a sense of inferiority in the peon is not due to the fact that he is Mexican, but because he is a member of the proletariat. Indeed, this last situation may in itself give rise to that feeling, but there are reasons for believing that it is not the only factor that causes it in the peon. We point out here that this person associates his concept of virility with that of nationality, creating the erroneous idea that valour is the peculiar mark of the Mexican. To support the opinion that nationality, too, in itself creates a sense of inferiority, one may mention the touchiness of his patriotic feelings and his inflated use of words and slogans. The frequency of individual and collective demonstrations of patriotism symbolizes the Mexican's uncertainty with regard to the worth of his nationality. The decisive proof of our statement lies in the fact that that feeling exists among cultured and intelligent Mexicans who belong to the middle class.

The Mexican of the City

The type we are about to present is the city-dweller. Naturally, his psychology differs from that of the peon, not only because of the kind of life the latter leads, but because in Mexico he almost always belongs to the indigenous race. Even though the Indian forms a considerable part of the Mexican population, in present-day life he plays a passive role in the country. The other group is the active one, the group of mestizos and whites who live in the city. It is to be expected, of course, that the Indian has influenced the spirit of the other Mexican group, since their bloods have intermingled. But the Indian's social and spiritual influence is reduced today to the mere fact of his presence. He is like a chorus silently witnessing the drama of Mexican life. But though it is limited, his influence is still important. The Indian is like those substances called "catalytic," which cause chemical reactions by their mere presence. Nothing Mexican can escape this influence, because the indigenous population creates a dense atmosphere which envelops everything in the country. We regard the Indian, therefore, as the hinterland of the Mexican. But for the present he will not be the object of our investigation.

The trait of the Mexican character which first strikes us is his mistrust. This attitude precedes any contact with men or things. It appears with or without foundation for it. It is not a mistrust on principle, because the Mexican usually lacks principles. It is an irrational mistrust which emanates from the depth of his being. It is almost his primordial sense of life. Even if the facts do not justify it, there is nothing in the universe that the Mexican does not see through the eyes of his mistrust. It is like an *a priori* form of his sensibility. The Mexican does not mistrust such and such a man or such and such a woman; he mistrusts all men and all women. His mistrust is not confined to the human race; it extends to all that exists or occurs. If he is a merchant, he does not believe in business; if he is a professional man, he does not believe in his profession; if he is a politician, he does not believe in politics. The Mexican believes that ideas have no sense and scornfully calls them "theories"; he regards the knowledge of scientific principles as useless. He seems to be very sure of his practical sense. But as a man of action he is sluggish, and in the end does not have much faith in the outcome of his actions. He has no religion and no social or political creed. He is as little of an "idealist" as anyone can be. He denies everything without any reason, because he himself is negation personified.

But then, why does the Mexican live? Perhaps he would answer that it is not necessary to have ideas and beliefs in order to live—provided one does not think. And this is indeed the case. Mexican life gives the impression, on the whole, of unreflecting activity, completely planless. Every man, in Mexico, is interested only in immediate goals. He works for today and tomorrow, but never for a later time. Concern for the future he has expelled from his consciousness. No one is capable of venturing on enterprises that offer only long-term results. Therefore, he has removed from life one of its most important dimensions: the future. Such has been the effect of Mexican mistrust.

In a life circumscribed by the present, only instinct can function. Intelligent reflection can only come in when we make a pause in our activity. It is impossible to think and act at the same time. Thought presupposes that we are capable of hope, and one who hopes is giving a place to the future. Obviously life without a future can have no pattern. So, Mexican life is at the mercy of every wind that blows, following a random course. Men live in haphazard fashion. Naturally, without discipline or organization, Mexican society is a chaos in which individuals move about aimlessly like scattered atoms.

This chaotic world, the direct result of mistrust, reacts upon the mistrust and gives it a kind of objective justification. When the individual feels he is drifting in an unstable world, in which he is not even sure of the soil on which he treads, his mistrust increases and causes him to hasten to snatch from the present moment some immediate profit. So, the horizon of his life is narrowed further, and his morality sinks to such a degree that society, in spite of its appearance of civilization, resembles a primitive horde in which men quarrelled and scrambled for things like starving wild beasts.

A trait intimately bound up with mistrust is touchiness. The mistrusting man is always afraid of everything, and lives on the alert, ready to defend himself. He is suspicious of any gesture, any movement, any word. He interprets everything as an offence. In this matter the Mexican goes to incredible extremes. His perception of things becomes overtly abnormal. On account of his hypersensitive touchiness, the Mexican is constantly quarrelling. He no longer waits to be attacked, but he takes the initiative in offending. Sometimes these pathological reactions carry him too far, to the point of committing unnecessary transgressions.

The psychic anomalies we have just described doubtless spring from an unsureness of himself which the Mexican projects outwards without realizing it, converting it into a mistrust of the world and of men. These psychic transpositions are instinctive devices to protect the ego from itself. The initial phase of the development is an inferiority complex experienced as mistrust of himself, which he then, to rid himself of the unpleasantness that goes with it, objectivizes as mistrust of others.

When the human psyche wishes to rid itself of an unpleasant feeling, it always resorts to processes of self-delusion like the one just described. But in the special case which concerns us, that resort does not bring satisfactory results, because the veil that is drawn over the annoyance one wishes to avoid does not suppress it, but only causes it to change its motivation. The Mexican is habitually in a state of mind that betrays an inner uneasiness, a lack of harmony with himself. He is touchy and nervous; he is almost always ill-tempered, and frequently irascible and violent.

The strength which the Mexican attributes to himself by virtue of his impulsiveness seems to us to be false. Of course, true energy lies in intelligent control of impulses and sometimes in repressing them. The Mexican is impassioned, aggressive, and warlike out of weakness, that is, because he lacks a will to control his actions. Moreover, the energy he displays in these acts is not in proportion to his vitality, which usually is low. How then can we explain the violence of his acts? Only by regarding it as a result of over-excitement which is caused within him by the same psychic disorder.

Our knowledge of the psychology of the Mexican would be incomplete if we did not compare the opinion he has of himself with what he really is. A moment ago we were discussing the strength the Mexican attributes to himself, which leads us to suppose that he has a high opinion of his own person. We also suspect that some readers of this essay will react against our assertions, seeking arguments to reject them. That is because here we have dared to reveal certain truths that every Mexican strives to keep hidden, since he superimposes on them an image of himself which does not represent what he is, but what he would like to be. And what is the strongest and innermost desire of the Mexican? He would like to be a man who stands out prominently among others on account of his valour and his power. The suggestiveness of this image artificially exalts him, obliging him to act in accordance with it, until he comes to believe in the reality of the phantom of himself which he has created.

The Mexican Bourgeois

In this last part of our essay we shall consider the most intelligent and cultivated group of Mexicans, who for the most part belong to the *bourgeoisie* of the country. Most of the traits which mark his character are reactions against a sense of inferiority, which, not having their source in economic, intellectual, or social inferiority, doubtless arise from the fact that he is a Mexican. Basically the Mexican *bourgeois* does not differ from the Mexican proletarian, except for the fact that in the latter the sense of inferiority is aggravated by the concurrence of two factors: nationality and social position. There appears to be a contrast between the coarse and violent tone which is habitual in the urban proletarian, and a certain polish in the *bourgeois*, who expresses himself with a frequently exaggerated courtesy. But every Mexican of the cultivated class is capable of taking on, when a moment of anger causes him to lose control of himself, the tone and language of the lower classes. "You're acting like a peon!" is the reproach hurled at this wrathful man. The Mexican *bourgeois* has the same patriotic touchiness as the common man, and the same prejudices with regard to the national character.

The psychic distinction between the higher and lower classes of Mexicans is that the former completely conceal their sense of inferiority, because the relation between their external attitudes and their unconscious motivations is so indirect and subtle that it is difficult to discover it, while the peon displays, with frank cynicism, the operations of his mind, and the relationship between the conscious and the unconscious in him is very simple. It has already been seen that it is one of opposition.

It is fitting to make clear at this point the nature of these feelings of fundamental deficiency that irritate the psyche of the individual and provoke the reactions described. They are feelings that the individual will not consciously tolerate, on account of the discontent and the depression they cause; and precisely because of the need to keep them hidden in the unconscious, they manifest themselves as vague sensations of discomfort, the cause of which the individual cannot trace or specify. When they succeed in invading the conscious they assume various hues. Let us mention a few of them: weakness of will, self-depreciation (inferiority complex), sense of incapacity and of lack of vitality. The individual's recognition of his inferiority is converted into lack of faith in himself.

The Mexican *bourgeois* possesses more capacity and intellectual resources than the proletarian for achieving perfectly the work of dissimulation required to hide his sense of inferiority. This is equivalent to saying that the imaginary ego built up by each individual is such a finished piece of work, and has such an appearance of genuineness, that it is almost impossible to distinguish it from an authentic ego.

Let us now establish what elements the Mexican utilizes in order to compose his work of fiction, or, in other words, what reactions arise from his sense of inferiority. In its simplest form, the operation consists in superimposing on what one is what one would like to be, and representing this desire as a fact. Sometimes the desire is confined to avoiding scorn or humiliation, and then, on an ascending scale, we come to the desire to be as good as others, to be superior to others, and finally, the will to power.

The work of building up an image conforming to a desire for superiority requires attention and constant care of the self. This turns every Mexican into an introvert, and as such he correspondingly loses his external interests. He considers men and things as mirrors, but he takes into account only those that show the image he wishes them to reflect. It is indispensable that other men should believe in this image, so that he can solidify his own faith in it. So his work of fiction is achieved with the complicity of society. We are not trying to claim that this is a characteristic exclusively Mexican. No normal man, whatever his nationality, could live without the aid of such fictions. But it is one thing to accept pragmatically the effect of a fiction, knowing that it is one, and another thing to live it without realizing that it is false. The first is a matter of possessing ideals or archetypes as stimuli to overcome the obstacles and difficulties in life, while the second means not to live really, but to cheat life. It would be wrong to attach to this attitude a moral appellation, since it is not born of any conscious or deliberate purpose. Recent discoveries in psychology show us that, in spite of its blindness, the unconscious does not lack logic, though it may be a logic that differs from the rational. The Mexican does not know that he is living a lie, because there are unconscious forces that have driven him to it, and perhaps, if he realized the deception he would cease to live in this way.

Since the self-deception consists in believing one already is what one would like to be, as soon as the Mexican is satisfied with his image, he gives up making an effort really to improve himself. He is therefore a man who passes through the years without experiencing any change. The civilized man changes, and new forms of life, art, and thought arise, which the Mexican tries to imitate in order to feel he is of the same stature as the European; but at heart the Mexican today is the same as he was a hundred years ago, and his life slips along, in the city apparently modernized, like that of the country Indian: in an Egyptian immutability.

We may picture the Mexican as a man who flees from himself to take refuge in an imaginary world. But this does not conclude his psychological drama. In the deep recesses of his spirit, inaccessible to his own perception, throbs the inconsistency of his personality, which may vanish at the slightest breath of air, and like the hedgehog, he protects himself with a coat of spines. No one can touch him without getting hurt. He is abnormally resentful of criticism, and holds it at bay by being the first to hurl slander upon his neighbour. For the same reason, self-criticism is paralyzed. He has to convince himself that others are inferior to him. He therefore acknowledges no superiority to himself, and knows no veneration, respect, or discipline. He is ingenious in disparaging his neighbour to the point of annihilation. He indulges in slander with a cannibal cruelty. The worship of the ego is as bloody as that practised by the ancient Aztecs; it feeds on victims. Each individual lives locked up within himself, like an oyster in its shell, with an attitude of mistrust towards others, oozing malice, so that no one will come near. He is indifferent to the interests of society and his acts always have an individualistic character.

We conclude these notes on Mexican psychology by inquiring whether it is an impossible task to drive out the phantom that dwells in the Mexican. For such a purpose it is essential for each one to practise honestly and courageously the Socratic counsel "Know thyself." We know now that the natural faculties of a man are not adequate for the acquisition of self-knowledge, but he must be equipped beforehand with the intellectual tools forged by psycho-analysis. When man thus prepared discovers what he is, the rest of the task is self-operative. Phantoms are nocturnal creations that vanish by mere exposure to the light of day.

The Profile of Man and Culture in Mexico (*El perfil del hombre y la cultura en México*), Mexico, 1934, pp. 65–92.

CREOLE CULTURE

IT IS A CHARACTERISTIC TRAIT of Mexican psychology to think up artificial destinies for each of the forms of national life. It is true that our Europeanism has been largely artificial, but the plan to create a pure Mexicanism is none the less false. The Mexican never takes into account the realities of life, that is, the limitations which history, race, and biological factors impose upon his future. The Mexican plans his life as if he were free to choose any of the possibilities which to his mind appear most interesting and desirable. He does not know that the horizon of life's possibilities is very narrow for any people and for any individual. The historical heritage, the ethnic mental conformation, and the peculiarities of environment predetermine the line along which life will develop with a rigidity that the will of the individual cannot alter. This fatalism we call destiny. The Mexican is a man who for years has systematically striven to thwart his destiny. This attitude has moved him to sow in his land seed that can be cultivated only in a European climate and which here has had a feeble, almost lifeless growth, like plants in a hothouse. Finally he has been convinced of his failure, but, without understanding its causes, he attributes it to the thing itself, that is, to a dubious break in European culture, and not to what it really is: an inner defect of his psyche.

Therefore, in changing his plans he has replaced the external thing, but the psychological approach continues to be the same: artifice. Now he proposes to create a Mexican culture and a Mexican way of life—a Utopia more fantastic than the other, because this presupposes that one can get something out of nothing, unless one intends to work through all over again the whole process of culture, beginning with the neolithic age. The latest exaltation of nationalism arouses in us the fear that the Mexican is already fundamentally in his innermost nature a mixed-up individual, who has superimposed on his real nature, which he does not know, a false image of himself. The virtue which must be most urgently recommended to the present-day Mexican is sincerity, so that he will tear off the mask with which he hides from himself his authentic character.

Europeanism has been in Mexico a hothouse culture, not because its essence is foreign to us, but because of the false relationship in which we have placed ourselves with respect to what is taking place beyond the seas. We must accept the fact that our cultural perspectives are contained within the European framework. A culture is not selected like a certain style of hat. We have European blood, our speech is European, as are also our customs, morals, and all our vices and virtues that were bequeathed to us by the Spaniards. All these things form our destiny and inexorably set our course. What has been lacking is wisdom to develop this European spirit in harmony with the new situation in which it is placed. We have the European sense of life, but we are in America, and this fact makes it necessary that the same vital sense, in a new atmosphere, should be expressed in a different manner.

If we remove the façade of artificial Europeanism, which indeed covers only a small group—just as its influence in architecture affects but a limited cluster of wards in our cities—we come to the true nucleus of Mexican life, made up especially of the middle class, whose whole existence is patterned after European life. Even if the majority of the population is Indian, the mental outlook of this class does not yet permit it to separate itself from its European origin, while at the same time it takes on the atmosphere of primitivism which covers the rest of the population. On account of its quality, the middle class has been the axis of national history and continues to be the backbone of the country, in spite of its being quantitatively a minority. In this class, the concepts of family, religion, morals, love, etc., preserve the European stamp, modified—even impoverished, if you like—but operating as vital realities, so that there is what may correctly be considered a middle culture, assimilated to our geographical background, which we shall call *Creole culture*.[1] This Creole character is pronounced, especially in the provincial centres, less inclined to become denatured through the adoption of foreign fashions. These centres preserve in their spirit, as also in the faces of their women and the architecture of their cities, the European profile already integrated into the Mexican landscape. What a marvellous spiritual influence this would be for arresting the depersonalizing effect of the materialistic metropolis, were it not for its conservatism, basically an inertia and a passivity which neutralize the provincial virtues!

On this humus of generic culture has grown a form of selection, also Creole, that has been effected in a minority of individuals. However modest they might be with relation to a world-wide scale of values, we must recognize that they represent our only tradition of higher culture. The worth of some of these men lies in the person rather than in the work accomplished.

As men they have reached the highest level that can be reached by a Spanish American. Their spiritual grandeur would not have been possible without the nutriment of European culture, which in giving them a deeper consciousness of life has bound their interests more closely to the native soil. Almost all of them have had a social significance of greater or lesser range as educators, guides, and even exemplary personalities. Their enlightened minds have on occasion been flashes of brightness in the dark destiny of Spanish America. It has been thought hitherto that the appearance of these men is inexplicable in the rarefied atmosphere of the New World, and they are regarded as distant products of European influence. It has never occurred to anyone that this influence would be nil, if a predisposition acquired on the native soil did not go out to receive it. Of those figures only one side has been seen, their anarchical bent, their solitary individualism, which appears to make them reducible to one cycle of culture. Nevertheless, from the point of view of Creolism, all these

[1]As used in Ramos' essays, "Creole" means an American-born person of pure white ancestry.

heterogeneous figures can be accommodated within a distinguishable unity. No one has defined Creole culture up to the present, because it has an atmospheric existence that is present everywhere, but invisible because of its transparency.

The vital element which, by co-ordinating our psychic activity from the time of the conquest, puts it into the category of culture, is religiosity. Let it be borne in mind that the idea of a unified whole does not exclude a struggle between opposing principles; what is required is that the conflicts should be polarized towards a single point. In other words, it may be said that the history of Mexico, especially on the spiritual plane, is the affirmation or negation of religiosity. On whichever side our ancestry may have been, that of the Indian or that of the Spanish conqueror, we discover we are of a race of exalted religiosity. The pioneers of culture in Mexico were the missionary monks. The religious nature of the Spaniards was firmly moulded into the architecture they gave to our cities. Almost always the church was erected in the centre of the city, or on the vertex when a hill is its site, so that from any point, inside or outside the limits, the towers point to heaven. From a distance, the first thing one sees in any small Mexican city is the bell-tower and dome of the church, whose silhouette literally stretches out its lines, as if to give a sense of architectural totality to the scattered dwellings. Not only is the church the geometric centre of the city, but before its doors there opens into a large open space the "parade ground," the true heart of civic life, because since here are found "the market," "government house," and the gardens, in and out of this place flow the political and religious activities, commerce, and even all forms of amusement. On account of its size alone it seems that the church holds authority to preside over that human anthill, and often it is the most beautiful building as well. Materially and metaphorically, the church is always on a vertex.

Every culture is built upon a religious sense of life. This feeling is the fountain of energy which inspires creative effort. Perhaps European culture would not have taken hold in America if among the soldiers who came to conquer it there were not some men of the Church possessed by an evangelizing zeal. Chronologically, the cultural works that first appear are intimately related to the religious life or they even form part of it. So in Mexico ecclesiastical art arises as the initial expression of Creole culture. The general outlines of that art were traced by Europe, but it is almost symbolic that they should have been worked out in stones from Mexican soil which the hand of the Indian carved and assembled, on occasions interpreting the ornamental motifs in his manner. First it was the Franciscan style, of an ascetic simplicity, constructed in angles and straight lines which impress upon the silhouette of the church a military stamp of strength. Its geometric masses, with cutting edges, are the expression of an almost aggressive overpowering masculinity, which erected these towers in solitary spots to dominate the forest. In time this primitive hardness becomes softened when the church is surrounded by a city district, and a lively imagination breaks the ascetic discipline to create a national baroque architecture, in which is reflected a life more peaceful and more worldly. As an expression of religious feeling, Creole architecture was a living art which immediately became incorporated into the New World. On a purely aesthetic plane, we feel today that, beside colonial structures, other styles later imported from abroad are out of place.

The seminaries are the purveyors of Mexican education from colonial times to the end of the past century. The priests are, for good or for ill, the directors of the popular conscience. Through the seminary, with Greek and Latin, the humanities are cultivated in Mexico, guiding the intellectual formation of several generations in the standards of Mediterranean culture.* Naturally the type of education then imparted lagged considerably behind European education of the same period. Nevertheless, neither the Pontifical University nor the colleges which formed part of the Church's paedagogical monopoly were proof against modern ideas, which filtered in mysteriously through official and ecclesiastical censorships. The rumble of the French Revolution had been too resounding to be unheard inside academic cloisters. The first leaders in our War of Independence were priests.

The negative phase of religiosity in Mexico begins with the second half of the past century. It is the dramatic beginning of liberalism with the Reform revolution, the result of which was the laic Constitution and laic education. The politicians who agitated and legislated for the movement, with heated Jacobin passion, were intellectuals with a scholastic mentality. What is not rhetorical in their anticlerical polemics is dialectical in the style of the seminary.

From this time the power of the Church was legally destroyed, although only much later was the effective influence of that power really lessened. Can the same thing be said about religiosity as a psychologi-

*Read the *Discourse through Virgil* (*Discurso por Virgilio*) by Alfonso Reyes (ed. *Contemporáneos*), from which we quote the following lines: "The Mexican spirit is of the colour that Latin water, just as it reached us, acquired here in our land as it flowed for three centuries, licking the red clays of our soil."

cal factor in Mexican conduct? Even in the freethinkers who brought about the revolution, the tone of their denials has the fire of religious sentiment, but turned in a contrary direction. We mean that the psychology of the Jacobin is not that of a man emancipated from religion in his mind, but he is an example of that paradoxical phenomenon which the school of psycho-analysts has today explained by the term "ambivalent sentiments." While the weapons with which the freethinkers of 1857 fought were those of rhetoric rather than philosophy—they acted as politicians, not as intellectuals—they did not abandon a method of reasoning in which could be seen, as in the ground glass of a photographic camera, the inverted projection of religious sentiment. Their "equality," a certain vague "humanitarianism," even their rationalistic attitude—a delayed American echo of French "enlightenment"—are not sufficient to reconstruct the image those men had of the world. If some conscientious historian of Mexican ideas someday could bring together their fragmentary thoughts, seeing through to the data lacking for the giving of form to the Jacobin concept of life, it would not be surprising if he discovered how its formation is that of an abstract Catholicism without God, or churches, or dogmas.

Religions have, like any living organism, a natural death due to a slow dissolution of beliefs through the work of intellectual criticism, which finds them incompatible with a new sense of life. When religious sentiment has grown cold, the external practices and ceremonies continue through social inertia, as mechanical gestures without expressive value. Apparently religious passion is gradually withdrawing from the Mexican historical scene and is ceasing to be the central stimulus of our spiritual activity. The Positivism imported after the Reform, as a doctrinal support of laic education, was the philosophy adjudged most satisfactory for the extirpation of religious ideas. Barreda founds the Preparatory School, whose curriculum is organized in accordance with Comte's classification of the sciences, hoping that from its halls youth would come out with a new soul. As a matter of fact, the reform in education did succeed in effecting a very perceptible change of orientation in the mentality of our country.

While it was an immediate historical necessity to nullify the secular power of the Church, perhaps it was not necessary to destroy religious feeling, but external events re-echoed within consciences as an argument against religion. Since the points at issue did not have the spiritual quality necessary for transforming feelings radically, these feelings were simply stifled under materialistic influences. Religiosity, then, was not destroyed, though everybody thought it was, but merely repressed in the unconscious, on account of the external inhibitions operating as anti-religious prejudices. Up to the present no one has undertaken to study the complicated mechanisms which the Mexican mind has engendered, in spite of the fact that this is the only way we can know ourselves. The explanation we now give of irreligiousness seems to us especially useful for the understanding of many psychological abnormalities in the Mexican of the present day. The religious life is not a transitory phenomenon of the spirit, but a permanent and consubstantial function of its nature. So, when its impulse is not transferred consciously to other objects in the same spiritual sphere, and when even its presence is not acknowledged, it is converted into an obscure force which inverts the view of values and causes the individual to live in an illusory world, because he attributes false magnitudes to his ego and to things.* Positivism was included in the curricula of Mexican education with an anti-religious purpose, and soon after its introduction, Positivism and liberalism meant the same thing. The doctrine in question certainly has numerous points of view favourable to the purposes of the liberals; they found there material that was as if made to order for supporting their negations, giving them a scientific appearance and the prestige of modernity. If in this paedagogical enterprise philosophic judgement had prevailed over sectarian passion, it would soon have been discerned that Positivism, as a criticism of religion, is not very satisfactory, and greatly inferior to it as a successor, because of its lack of a metaphysical sense. These congenital weaknesses prevented it from acting as an intellectual corrosive of religious feeling in Mexico, but it did have a mechanical influence as a prejudice for repressing it. With that feeling locked up in the deep recesses of the soul, its tension rises, and seeking an escape, it finds one in scientific superstitution. For lack of a religion, the intellectual classes deify science.

On the other hand, this same religious feeling turned upward has given a stimulus towards idealism in Spanish-American thinkers of the end of the nineteenth century. The most noteworthy of these was José Enrique Rodó, the most complete and representative personality of Creole culture. The great Uruguayan writer was also a product of the French Positivism of Comte and Guyau, and of Taine and Renan, but his Positivism had a Renaissance breadth and nobility. No one has equalled the genius of Rodó in absorbing the most refined European

*See Jung, *The Unconscious.*

culture into the sensibility of our race.* For the first time our race is acquiring consciousness of a spirituality which Rodó symbolizes in the name *Ariel.*

If the youth of America thrilled to the magic of his voice, it was because in the music of his words they discovered themselves, and found principles which gave hope to their noblest desires.

The piquancy and brilliance of his literary form, along with the Hellenism, Christianity, and trust in reason contained in his work, are the particles which have integrated the Mediterranean spirit. How could this spirit be disseminated in America? Note that the elements enumerated above are not things that can be learned at school, but rather predispositions of the sensibilities and the understanding, which will bring order into all that the individual is learning, in accordance with certain invariable forms of representation. These habits which give the soul its character can be formed only by a spiritual power like the Catholic Church, operating continuously from generation to generation, like an atmosphere which individuals see themselves obliged to breathe from birth to death. Catholicism is certainly the vehicle which the classical Mediterranean mind implanted in America, unless one resorts to explaining as a miracle personalities like Rodó, who in the silvan atmosphere of America reproduces a cultural type of very different climates. An individual who becomes emancipated from his religion does not always give up all its ingredients, but in withdrawing his faith from the supernatural and the mythological, he clings to its quintessence, that is, the spiritual sense of life. The spirituality of Rodó still preserves, on the side of sentiment, the Christian form, and on the side of reason, the idea of universality transformed into Pan-Americanism. Rodó takes up the idea of Bolívar, the political unification of America, and in a broader and less concrete sense imagines a "super-country," as the Spanish-American ideal. This would be something like a reincarnation of the Ghibelline spirit.

We could cite many examples of similar religious transpositions in our greatest writers, were it not that our purpose is to define impersonally the common elements in America's culture, and for this purpose we believe the example cited will suffice. Even though our exposition

*Rodó, though so European, and precisely for that reason, is the man of letters who incarnates in the purest manner the civilization we are acquiring, and the death which we are assimilating. For this reason, in the sense of his being an upholder of a modified purism, he is the writer who best represents us." *José Enrique Rodó*, by Gonzalo Zaldumbide, *Revue Hispanique*, New York–Paris, 1921, p. 13.

refers principally to Mexico, we have not hesitated to select a South American writer, because the historical development of Spanish-American countries is such that conclusions arrived at in the analysis of a development in one of them will be valid for all the others. Only an anti-religious prejudice will prevent anyone from seeing that the only bond uniting the capricious individualism of the Spanish-American intelligentsia into a cultural unity is the influence of religion.

As soon as a high consciousness of America expresses itself sincerely, religious uneasiness appears. Thus on one occasion Rubén Darío cried out that his soul was in conflict "between the Cathedral and the pagan ruins." Is this not perchance an image of the American drama? Grave problems are still unsolved on account of the separation of the culture that built our cathedrals from the other culture, that of *our* ruins, which when they met were incapable of forming a new synthesis.

So far as Mexico is concerned, however harmful to culture the consequences of Positivism later became, at a certain moment this doctrine was a factor in the liberation and progress of a minority group of leaders. It drew them out of the scholastic stagnation of the seminaries and made it possible to renew the vitiated air of the schools, opening their doors to scientific study. The success of Positivism is explicable in that it satisfied a spiritual and social need in Mexico. It was an exotic plant, but it found in the atmosphere here oxygen to feed on, and therefore it lived. It lived almost always as a negative passion, contradicting its name "Positivism." Even so, the fact that it burned as a passion meant that it was a living doctrine. It is therefore worthy of being considered as a moment in Creole culture.

An alien element, and one even opposed to Positivism, explains the fact that among some of its partisans it has assumed a high moral tone. But its naturalistic content predestined it to descend in ethical quality in the popular mind, until it became reduced to a philosophy of common sense and a justification of instinctive egotism. Such was the origin of the "scientific" morality of the dominant and exploiting *bourgeoisie* that enriches itself under the régime of Porfirio Díaz.

The cultural task of the Youth Athenaeum (Ateneo de la Juventud), begun about 1908, must be understood as a struggle against the corruption of the Porfirio period. This revolutionary intellectual movement preceded by two years the political Revolution which broke out in 1910.

A forerunner of these events was Justo Sierra, a humanist, and a promoter of Mexican culture as teacher of history and as Minister of Education, an outstanding man who, on account of his impressive personality, merits a place of honour among our most prominent men of culture. Because of the quality of its members and the unity of its activities, the Youth Athenaeum is an important event in our country's history. Each of the members was heterogeneous in vocation. There were humanists, like Pedro Henríquez Ureña; philosophers, like Antonio Caso and José Vasconcelos, the former oriented towards university teaching, and the latter towards political action; essayists, like Alfonso Reyes, Julio Torri, and Jesús Acevedo; critics, like Eduardo Colín; poets, like González Martínez. The Athenaeum was not a cenacle isolated from the world; its programme was to renovate and extend culture. All its members were writers, and most of them later became professors in the University. Within the variety of interests to which each individual was devoted, in the activities of all there was one common purpose: moralization. This means that they strove to enhance in every respect the spiritual calibre of the Mexican. Against Positivism the Athenaeum launches a campaign to replace the philosophical bases of official education. The spiritual nature of the race breaks through the prejudices which were inhibiting it and comes out into the light unashamed of its name. The philosophers of the Athenaeum, Caso and Vasconcelos, informed of the resurgence of spiritualism in Europe, draw support from its most authoritative representatives—for example, Bergson—in order to reproduce here the same current of ideas. Convinced that higher education must be built on a philosophic base, Caso inaugurates the teaching of that discipline in the University. In the activities of the human spirit, in knowledge, art, and philosophy, he brings into relief their moral sense;* Vasconcelos, in his writings, goes further, supporting a mystical conception of life in which the aesthetic element fulfils the decisive function. In the domain of letters it was also necessary to moralize the writers, to teach them that without the discipline of culture, inspiration and even genius are sterile. There was a great difference between the Youth Athenaeum's severe aesthetics and the Bohemian character of a previous generation of literary men, grouped together in the *Modern Review* (*Revista Moderna*) of Jesús Valenzuela, whose view of art was the ivory tower and artificial paradises. Moral too was the voice of the most outstanding poet of the moment, Enrique González Martínez, who opposes to the pure aestheticism of Rubén Darío his own lyrical work, the intent of which is declared in this line: "Wring the neck of the swan of deceptive plumage." Morality appeared likewise in

*There is a study of the work and personality of Antonio Caso in my book *Hypotheses*, Mexico, 1928.

a place where it is just as indispensable as is the artistic sense: in literary criticism. These two qualities were found united in Eduardo Colín.

The work of the Athenaeum in its totality was a shock which came to interrupt the somnolent calm of the intellectual world in Mexico. It propagated new ideas, aroused curiosity and uneasiness, and extended the vision with which problems of culture were here regarded. Through its philosophy it tended to arrest the growing influence of Utilitarianism, inculcating in youth the sense of spiritual values. The result of that agitation in the decade beginning in 1910 was an elevation of tone and a broadening of scope in our intellectual life. Hitherto no stress has been laid upon the circumstance that this intellectual resurgence was effected in an atmosphere of tragedy. The Revolution had broken out precisely in the year 1910. It is true that the Civil War did not become generalized at that time throughout the whole country; it was something like a revolving mill which overturned everything it found in its path, but immediately afterwards life returned to normal. Nevertheless, soon the effects of the war made themselves felt in the entire country. No one could escape the increasingly serious economic crises.

One can read through the work of philosophers, men of letters, and poets who wrote in the midst of the national drama, without finding a word of discouragement, or a shadow of fundamental pessimism or absolute negation. Our thinkers adhered enthusiastically to any philosophy which energetically affirms life in the name of its spiritual values and came near to accepting its religious sense. Their voice is the voice of the Spanish-American race, whose intellectual tradition is a variation on the theme of spiritualism. When Vasconcelos gives to the University of Mexico as its motto: "Through my race the spirit will speak," his thought appears to be obeying a supra-personal will; he expresses himself as one inspired whose intuition suddenly illuminates the mysteries of the collective unconscious.

The high quality of this intellectual work arises from the fact that it developed freely, drawn from the immediate Mexican scene, and its authors for that reason have always a certain heroic magnitude. Vulgar criticism has denied that this work has a national significance, because it does not find in it allusions to the contemporary history of Mexico. But then every intellectual on looking about him saw that the surrounding reality was death, and in defending his faith and his cultural heritage he was defending an expression of life. He was not therefore outside his world, because saving himself meant contributing something to the salvation of his country.

It is not scorn for his country, or a lack of understanding of its problems, that causes the Mexican intellectual to make no references to events about him; it is because when the spirit wishes to express itself it has to do so in a language of its own which the American soil has not yet created, and which only European culture can give him. Our "Europeanism" is not always a frivolous keeping up with the fashion, or a servile imitation; it is also esteem for the effective values in human life and a desire to enter into the world which contains them. Indifference to this would perhaps indicate an inferiority which would condemn us never to pass beyond the boundaries of the homeland, and an inability to mingle with a broader community of men, which is what Europe had in mind to achieve, creating the only type of universal culture in the modern age. Fortunately, the Spanish American is able to rise to spiritual universality and has the will to achieve it in its possible forms. We have already noted that this will is expressed in our best thinkers and is one of the *leitmotifs* of Creole culture. Even if Vasconcelos' doctrine of a "cosmic race" is not a credible prophecy, since it is an ideal disproportionate to the present state of *our* life and its feasible possibilities, we see in this idea, as an abstraction from its content, the will to universality of *our race* mythologically expressed.

A select group of Mexicans feeling the need of a superior culture, and not finding it outside in the world in which they lived, realized it within themselves. They were the soul of Mexico, but a soul . . . without a body. A superior culture, to sustain itself, requires a certain social form of partial culture, which is its vital atmosphere. This element would be the body that is missing for the completion of the organic totality of our culture and which would make it effective. Only when the partial enlightenment is accessible to the community will the spirit of the select minority flow in all directions, and set this culture in motion as the nervous system moves the members of an organism.

The Profile of Man and Culture in Mexico (*El perfil del hombre y la cultura en México*), Mexico, 1934, pp. 95–121.

Daniel Cosío Villegas

(b. Colima, Col., 1900)

Daniel Cosío Villegas, after completing his law studies at the University of Mexico, continued them at various universities in the United States—Harvard, Wisconsin, and Cornell—and then specialized in economics in the schools of London and Paris. Returning to Mexico City, he became a teacher in the National Preparatory School, the Faculty of Law, and the National School of Economics, and in 1933 and 1934 he was the director of the last named. He represented Mexico as Technical Adviser and Delegate Plenipotentiary at the Second Pan-American Commercial Conference, the Seventh American International Conference, the Fifth International Conference on Statistics, the Fifth Inter-American Commercial Conference, and the International Monetary Conference. Cosío Villegas has been the director of the journal *The Economic Quarterly* (*El Trimestre Económico*); he organized and directed, from its beginning in 1934 until 1948, the Foundation for Economic Culture (Fondo de Cultura Económica); he is on the Board of Governors of the College of Mexico and of the review *American Memoranda* (*Cuadernos Americanos*); and he is a member of the National College.

His first works, *Mexican Miniatures* (1921) and a few short novels, were on literary themes and reflected a certain influence of Azorín. During these years Cosío Villegas was one of the disciples of Pedro Henríquez Ureña and a contributor to the review *Modern Mexico* (*México Moderno*). Later, from 1924 to 1934, he devoted himself exclusively to economic themes. In *American Extremes* (*Extremos de América*), he presented a collection of studies as impassioned as *The Mexican Crisis* (*La crisis de México*), which made him one of the most outstanding and lucid Mexican essayists and one of the most penetrating minds in the diagnosis of the problems of Mexico and America.

The last intellectual stage in the life of Cosío Villegas is strongly oriented towards history. After long years of study and investigation, he embarked upon an ambitious and extraordinary cultural undertaking, the *Modern History of Mexico* (*Historia moderna de México*), carried out under his direction by a team of researchers, and of which up to the present four large volumes have appeared, the first from his own pen. In addition, as collateral investigations, he has published interesting books and booklets, also on historical questions.

The essays in the collection published in *American Extremes* show an ironic and sententious keenness of judgement and a phlegmatic detachment which make them peculiarly attractive. In his first historical studies, on the other hand, he seems to have curbed this pungent and satirical inclination in order to produce an objective exposition, at times encumbered with detail. However, in his latest writings, he shows himself again the great essayist, with firm mastery of his material.

ESSAYS: *Mexican Miniatures. Travels, Impressions, Theories* (*Miniaturas mexicanas. Viajes, estampas, teorías*), 1922; *American Extremes* (*Extremos de América*), 1949.

STUDIES: *Course in Mexican Sociology* (*Curso de sociología mexicana*), 1924–25; *The Tariff Question in Mexico* (*La cuestión arancelaria en México*), 1930–32; *The Monetary Problem in Mexico* (*El problema monetario en México*), 1933; *An International Technical Association* (*Un organismo técnico internacional*), 1934; *Porfirio Díaz in the Revolt of La Noria* (*Porfirio Díaz en la revuelta de la Noria*), 1953; *Modern History of Mexico. The Republic Restored. Political Life* (*Historia moderna de México. La Republica restaurada. Vida política*), 1955; *Economic Life* (*Vida económica*), 1955; *Social Life* (*Vida social*), 1956; *The United States versus Porfirio Díaz* (*Estados Unidos contra Porfirio Díaz*), 1956; *The Constitution of 1857 and Its Critics* (*La Constitución de 1857 y sus criticos*), 1957.

AMERICAN PROBLEMS

I PREFACE MY ARTICLE with a little foreword: I am not dealing with all America, but our America, this America which we at times call Latin America, and at other times Ibero-America or Spanish America. The non-restrictive term is used here for mere convenience, and to be frank, for the pleasure of committing a verbal theft, since material thefts are forbidden.

Another point, of major importance, but which also must be presented as a foreword, is this: speaking of someone's problems presupposes the existence of that someone. Are there among the various countries of America a sufficient number of resemblances for them to have problems in common? I do not deny that the question is one of little interest, and that in the present case it ought to be in the nature of a previous question; but although they are the theme of not a few essays and even books,* I shall take those resemblances for granted:

*See, for example, Luis Alberto Sánchez, *Does Latin America Exist?* (*¿ Existe América Latina?*), Mexico, 1945.

the observations on American problems I shall endeavour to make applicable to all America, though with qualifications as often as it may appear necessary.

One useful approach to the theme would be to assert that Latin America has not progressed as much as it should and could. Progress means going forward, which presupposes the existence of a goal, one which will indicate at any time whether there has been an advance, a halt, or a retrogression.

With relation to what goal would we judge our America? The Yankees, victims of a mania for figures as well as for meddling, have tried several times to "measure" the progress of Latin America,* and naturally have concluded that it is slow and scant. They have counted the population, for example, or they have estimated the volume and value of production, of exports and imports, etc., to measure economic improvement; and the social factor they have estimated by counting the school population, or more brazenly, the number of inhabitants per hospital, per washing machine, per telephone, or per automobile.

In spite of that most tender feeling that I have been developing in my long and daily efforts to understand everything about the Americans to the north, I believe that such measurements are misleading, for two reasons among many: first, because if they have been used only from a comparatively recent date, the correct conclusion would be that Latin America has progressed to an incredible degree: for example, beginning from 1922 Mexico established 25,000 rural schools in twenty-five years and in the last seven years she has built an average of ten hospitals per year. Therefore it could be stated that our countries have advanced in the last thirty years at the same feverish pace as the middle western states of the United States a century ago. Secondly, though the day may be near when we shall have to accept the American of the North as the measure of all things, as yet just plain man is that measure, which means that the progress of a community must be measured by a standard proper to itself, and not by a foreign standard.

For me progress is not so measured, or at least, the progress I have in mind: not simply material or economic progress, or even what is called social progress, but general human progress. I do not believe there is any measure for this type of progress but the extent to which men learn to live together. This living in a society depends in part—in large part if you like—on the material well-being enjoyed by the people;

*See, for example, Fitzgibbon and Wooton, *Latin America, Past and Present*, New York, 1946.

but not all life in a society depends upon material well-being, as could be proved, if proof were necessary, by the Argentina of today.

One thing has always attracted my attention in Latin America: the coolness, the aloofness between a man and his neighbours. "Love thy neighbour as thyself," says the Christian law; well, among us this neighbour is neither neighbourly nor near: the distance is wide and the comparison slight.

Indeed, for the American the American land has always been vast: the land is broad and alien, the Peruvian novelist[1] has been able to say; ours is an "empty continent," says a Mexican writer; and in Argentina, the expression "peopled solitude" seems now to have lost its authorship by dint of repetition.

As a matter of fact the geographers* tell us that the common demographic pattern in Latin America is the very primitive one of "closed cloister": one patch of human habitation here, another there, and between the two a vacuum, a lifeless area in which man does not live, let alone live in a society. It is not only that between one patch of humanity and another there is nothing, but each of these patches—whatever its location or size—is dense at its centre and vanishes progressively on approaching the periphery. This means that, both now and for many long years ahead, there is no hope of one patch growing out until it touches the nearest one, by the two of them fusing into one and thus extending the area of human society. For this reason the geographers state that in the whole territory of Spanish America there are barely three regions which have a "healthy" population growth, that is, areas in which the centre is strengthened without detriment to the density of population at the periphery: the highlands of Costa Rica and Colombia, and the southern states of Brazil.

From this cloistered demographic pattern arise numerous and very curious consequences. The first has already been pointed out: the total or almost total lack of any contact between men living in the different populated areas. The second is that the country or nation is in large measure a fictitious entity, or, if you like, a very imperfect creation, for in addition to that territorial continuity which the writers on public law mention as a characteristic of the State, concerning the nation it should be asserted that it has that of being peopled without any prospects of continuity, to express it in extreme terms. The third is that

*See, for example, the excellent geography of Preston E. James, *Latin America*, New York, 1942.

[1]Ciro Alegría, whose novel *Broad and Alien is the World* (*El mundo es ancho y ajeno*), 1941, won him international fame.

in each populated area are created, with obvious waste of time and effort, institutions and services of all kinds, since, by definition, a cloister is a self-governing unit in the economic, political, and social spheres, and even in the spiritual. In brief, the largest populated area tries to govern the smaller ones; but since each one is a cloister, the men in one cloister do not know why those in the other should try to dictate general laws or customs. And they do dictate them, and by violence, extreme or moderate, temporary or permanent. And this ignorance is explicable: if the human body acknowledges the primacy of the heart, it is because the heart serves the whole body; it sends to each part of the body the pure, red blood, and brings back the poisoned, blue blood. The heart governs because in the body it fulfils two functions, not only general, but one might even say sacred: it feeds and it purifies. But why should a distant and isolated cloister wish to govern other distant and isolated cloisters? Why, when their inhabitants have no contact with one another? Simply because one is larger or stronger, or because it is situated in a dominant position on the plateau or the coast? The truth is that communications, power, and strength are concentrated in the largest cloister, and this cloister tries to use that power and strength for its own benefit, and not for the benefit of all the cloisters.

It is almost unnecessary to say that if our demographic pattern is the primitive pattern of the cloister, there are reasons, and very strong reasons, for it. Almost all the American soil is inhospitable, so that there is no country, with the possible exception of Uruguay, in which the progressive occupation and utilization of the land is an easy task, and feasible, so to speak, with the simple passing of time.

In Mexico, for example, the north-central part is a desert, with little or no hope of improvement, even without considering the cost of possible artificial solutions; the great central plateau is dependent upon an insufficient and irregular rainfall; the coastal region along the Gulf and the southern part, near Guatemala, is completely tropical: hot, humid, aggressively fertile, and unhealthful. In reality, the country possesses only isolated little valleys in the great central plateau, with rich extensions into the north-western zone. And let us make no mention of the network of mountain ranges which cut through the country, reducing it literally to fragments. This geographical description of Mexico is essentially valid for Central America and the Caribbean. Colombia, Ecuador, and Peru are victims of the colossal Andean barrier, a theme—not without importance—of a continuous literary exaltation. And though the Colombian has excellent highlands and slopes which he occupies and cultivates with gratifying success, he also must contend with his mountains, and this consumes time and effort in enabling man and his wealth to circulate, and on his soil, in the north-western part, the Colombian has a jungle so dense that we are assailed by the frightening thought that at some time a human being may be caught in it. Brazil has this too, with no lack of desert, and in addition, covering its centre, is the Amazon basin, so aptly called the "graveyard." Ecuador and Peru likewise have the untamed tropical jungle and the lonely desert. Half the Chilean territory is a desert. Argentina is not all pampa, and even less, watered pampa: there is also a desert and a Patagonia which allows itself to be inhabited only if the human wolf clothes himself in sheep-wool.

And the tragic thing is that in those inhospitable lands is found a large part of the wealth which the man of America needs in order to live: the Bolivian Indian and the Peruvian have to climb up to a height of four thousand metres to wrest from the earth the tin or the copper which they sell so that they may feed on corn and wheat. Hence the inhospitable geographical zones force the population to concentrate in those that are least inhospitable, thus isolating one populated area from another.

As always happens, this demographic growth of the cloister type is not altogether disadvantageous: pleasant at times and always useful as human contacts are, they should not become as close as they are in Europe, where a man feels that they are imposed upon him, forcing him to live elbow to elbow with his neighbours, as if he were attached to a rope and being led off to prison or the desert. One of the reasons for the decidedly more healthful human climate in America is that between man and man there has been up to the present enough land to work and pure air to breathe; unfortunately, the separation now is so great that, like the desert, it leads to sterility, and like the desert too, it engenders loneliness and insecurity.

There has indeed been an enormous advance in the occupation and mastery of the land: for example, one is strongly impressed if one reconstructs on a map today the zones populated by the natives of America at the time of the Discovery and the Conquest: three quarters lived in the very small areas in which flourished the great civilizations of the Mayas, Aztecs, and Incas, and the less advanced civilization of the Chibchas; the rest of our enormous territory was either not populated at all, or populated by small, unorganized tribes. Today the population is much greater, its grouping denser, and the distances and obstacles which separate the different demographic nuclei have been diminished. Nevertheless, neither Latin America as a whole, nor any of its countries considered individually, has been able to match the feat of the Americans of the North in populating and mastering territory of such magnitude in barely a century and a half. Not only that, but all the Latin American countries are still a long way from accomplishing it, and in some of them one cannot see when or how they could accomplish it.

The inhospitality of the land* in large measure explains its partial occupation and exploitation; the partial occupation and exploitation of the land explains the primitive demographic pattern of the cloister; and this pattern, in turn, explains in part the point of greatest concern: the limited degree of social unity that the man of our America has achieved. But we cannot explain in this way the fact that this social unity continues to be limited and defective within any unit, whether it be called nation, province, or settlement. Here enter reasons equally obvious and fundamental, but of a very different character: it is no longer nature that separates man from man, but man himself. The Spanish Americans must be very stupid if they have not managed to live in harmony with their neighbours in spite of being condemned to live with them in enclosed cloisters: it is well known that the monk who is actually and physically confined to a cloister does his very best to come to an understanding with those with whom he will have to share his entire life. And yet, apparently the Spanish American has not made to that end as determined an effort as he should, or if he has done so, he has failed in very large measure.

To be convinced of this it would suffice to cast a glance at the social structure of any of our countries, and unfortunately, in this there appear to be no exceptions, even in degree. None has a middle class (or, at least, none has one sufficiently large and concentrated),

*Even today, in the middle of the twentieth century, and not in the fifteenth or sixteenth, there are many people who see the wealth of the American continent as unlimited, especially in comparison with the European continent. As long as both this opinion and its opposite are held, the latter being the one that I uphold in this and other works, within the purely arbitrary area of extreme affirmation and denial, both these opinions can be supported with equal vigour and brilliance. Perhaps there is a sensible compromise between the two extremes, such as the following. There is not the slightest doubt that the natural economic possibilities of Europe have been already explored and exhausted. The natural economic possibilities of Latin America, on the other hand, appear to be very great—unlimited, if you like; but only on condition that the technical skills and the capital used for the exploitation of natural resources is also unlimited. In any case, up to the present, it is indisputable that the man of America has only with difficulty achieved a frugal standard of living.

the existence of which mitigates the sharp and distressing contrast between a lower class of excessive poverty and an upper class with wealth likewise excessive. Perhaps the only thing these two classes have in common is their gross ignorance; in all else, they could neither be more different nor more widely separated. And I insist that we must not gloss over the abominable coldness which separates our lower and upper classes. The superficial observer tends to see the mote in the other's eye, but not the beam in his own, so that very frequently those who come from a country in which European dress is general believe that the social gap is smaller in their country and greater in those with an indigenous population, simply because in the latter there is added to the social gap the "colour note" of a picturesque costume.

Of course there is no modern society in which these social differences do not exist and are not even clearly visible; but ours seem to me to be greater and, as it were, more striking, more poisonous to the entire social body, at times causing it to have violent convulsions, among other reasons because in our America it appears that there ought to be plenty of space, plenty of air and light, and sufficient food and shelter, for everyone. And in speaking of social classes let us not forget that phenomenon to which sociologists attach such importance: social capillary attraction, or the degree of facility or difficulty involved in a man of a lower class breaking away from his class to climb to a higher one.

As for our clear and firm division into classes, I do not think it necessary to speculate a great deal in order to acknowledge it and to appreciate its magnitude: it would suffice to think of a Bolivian or Peruvian Indian, at one extreme, and a gentleman of La Paz or Lima, at the other; of a negro of the Caribbean coast of Colombia, and of the rich industrialist of Antioquia; of a Chilean labourer and the dandy who frequents the Union Club in Santiago; of a Mexican businessman with holiday houses in Cuernavaca, Taxco, and Acapulco, and a nomadic Lacandón Indian. Some ingenuous Spanish American may think that though social differences are great in our America, they are not as great as in Western Europe and the United States, because among us there is no real aristocracy or genuine industrial proletariat: the first being a class really haughty, and the second a class one would call not simply low, but subterranean.

Perhaps our upper classes are indeed less exalted than the traditional European aristocracy or the incredibly wealthy man of the United States, but there is no doubt that there is nothing in the world as low as an Indian of the Bolivian highlands; and even if the first statement is true, it is not a fact favourable to us. For one thing, the European aristocracy is less aristocratic than is commonly supposed, and consequently less exalted than it appears; and for another, it has very little or no part in civic life, so that it is constantly an object of social comparison or a source of envy or rancour; in fact, it is a closed social group. In any case, in so far as it is a true aristocracy, it has had time to become refined and polished. Ours, on the contrary, is so new, and has to such an extent been formed before our eyes, is put together so crudely with money as the sole ingredient, and its wealth has been so directly obtained by despoliation, through governmental connections, or by chance, that it cannot be an object of admiration, and at times it could be one to be shunned to the point of ignoring it; to this must be added its general lack of good taste and refinement. Many of the heroes of our Independence movement were wealthy gentlemen; in all the countries of America the upper middle class which gradually grew up in the second half of the nineteenth century became on occasions enlightened, generous, and progressive; but the rich man of this century has no redeeming feature in whatever way you may look at him. So, it must be borne in mind that our aristocracy, directly or indirectly, is governing or has governed our countries, and even in those in which it has been beaten, it does not accept a merely ornamental social role, but is on the lookout for an opportunity to return to power. This explains why at best it is regarded with suspicion, and at worst as an enemy.

Our economic structure is, of course, another formidable obstacle to a closer social unity in our America. If we have acknowledged the fact that the social structure is characterized by marked class distinctions, we must suspect that these distinctions originate largely in an inequality of economic means and opportunities: at one end, great wealth invested in lands, estates, and now in industries—which makes possible an easy, idle, and carefree life; at the other, a low and insecure wage; on the one hand the palace with a private race-course, as they say in Buenos Aires; on the other, the notorious "low tenement." And let it not be forgotten that the faults of this system have effects which are becoming more and more general and more and more noticeable: in no way does it have the same significance to be poor in the twentieth century as it had to be poor in the twelfth century, since modern industry has awakened the desires of man by displaying before his eyes, in shop after shop, an endless variety of merchandise, services, attractions, and pleasures—in short, things that in other times he could not even imagine, and consequently could not seek either. Man himself has changed, on his own initiative or as a result of external influences; but at all events the human being of this century will not meekly continue to be poor, or tolerate having at his side men who are in all things his equals, save in wealth. For many years, in fact centuries, the Christian religion has been able to restrain man's appetite for material things, or offer him compensation for his poverty. Today Christianity has forever lost that power, retaining the more modest function of lending an innocent air of simple good luck to wealth acquired, perhaps by shady means.

But there is one fact which is often forgotten in analysing the peculiarities of the economic structure of our countries, a fact which also prevents greater social contact between the men of America: the co-existence of primitive economic forms and institutions and of those that are ultra-advanced. We all know the brilliant sign of the Panagra: a monster of the air crosses the sky of Peru and Bolivia at a speed of 500 kilometres per hour and at a height of 6000 metres, while below, in the calcined desert, some Indians with their flock of llamas gaze at it in astonishment.

In reality, the Panagra, an old procuress of imperialism after all, has been kind to us Spanish Americans, since without violating the truth it has been able to replace by the llama another more primitive but not less general means of transportation: the back of the Indian himself, on which have been carried for centuries, and are still being carried, goods and persons.

Not only in transportation, but in the whole economic life of our America, one sees the co-existence of primitive forms and advanced, exceedingly modern forms. Alongside the famous factory of Carretonas, in which glass is blown only by lung-power to produce that special kind of Mexican glass-work, are the modern plain-glass factories of Monterrey; alongside the serape and poncho woven by hand or by foot-loom are the great textile factories of Antioquia,[2] São Paulo, Santiago, or Orizaba;[3] and in Buenos Aires, alongside the great department store in which one can buy, according to the old saying, "anything from a pin to a locomotive," one sees the animal-drawn cart going daily to supply vegetables to the housekeepers and servants of the entire city.

Social living is not easy for men whose economic worlds are radically different: could you expect understanding between the man who

[2]In Colombia.

[3]In Mexico.

carries his wheat or corn on his back to take it to the market—and the man who receives by airplane some new part for the machinery in his factory? In fact, one very frequently finds in American countries groups of people who live in an economy of simple barter, while others operate in an economy based on the most advanced capitalism. *The Pearl*, by Steinbeck, presents precisely this problem in its dramatic plot.

The social and economic differences among our peoples are so great and so firmly established that they cannot be lessened or corrected in a normal, quiet, routine fashion, so to speak; moreover, social "capillary attraction" is either lacking or weak, since the means and opportunities to change one's class or group are either lacking or weak.

The means and opportunities to acquire, for example, an education which would to some extent compensate for a humble social origin or economic poverty, are tragically limited in our countries. Schools are scarce, and those that exist are concentrated in the large urban centres, and are totally lacking or quickly diminish in frequency as one comes into the small towns or the rural communities. The effectiveness of their teaching is very limited, on account of their shifting philosophy, their routine methods, the lack of resources, because they do not serve the vocational needs and the widely varied interests of the modern man, and because they are lacking in a higher, evangelical inspiration up to the level of the work of salvation which they ought to be undertaking. The economic means are perhaps still more limited, since to its concentration in the hands of a few individuals must be added the poverty of the countries as countries: the supply of capital is quite small, and consequently credit is even more restricted; it does not serve the whole country, but only the larger cities, and in these it is given to the one who already possesses wealth and not to the one making his start.

Not only are the means scant, the opportunities are too: societies as rigid, almost static, as ours are, hardly give any opportunity to the person who wishes to change his status. Let us compare, for example, the normal opportunities offered by countries like the United States and Canada with those that exist in the South American countries which most resemble them, Argentina and Brazil. The daily history of the United States is full of bootblacks and newsboys who become magnates; in our countries the closest parallel would be the demagogue or bandit who gets control of the government over night.

Let us summarize what has been said thus far, since there is no harm in occasionally bringing order out of chaos: the inhospitality of the land of America concentrates the population in the least inhospitable zones, isolating it from the population living in other zones; thus there arises the demographic development of the closed cloister type, which prevents or renders difficult the bringing into contact of men of one cloister with those of others. Within each cloister, social living is little developed because the economic and social structure strictly divides men into classes or groups; the division persists because of the lack of sufficient means and opportunities to permit men of a lower class to rise easily to the higher classes or groups.

Let us look at this last conclusion: in a society strictly divided into classes or groups, and in which, in addition, there is a lack of normal means and opportunities to change one's social position, those in the lower groups find and feel strong resistance to their promotion to higher groups. Does this mean that the man of the lower class gives up in the face of this resistance and resigns himself to not ascending in the social scale? That might have happened in some measure in societies far removed from modern times, but not in those of today, even in societies as insignificant as ours.

What happens in reality is very different and very regrettable. Since the social changes are not made with ease, in a normal fashion, day by day as a matter of routine, they therefore take place at certain intervals. But then the change is radical, in the sense of being profound and complete; it is violent, sweeps away laws, institutions, habits and customs, and usually leads to actual civil war. In short, the social change becomes a revolution and on occasions attains the proportions of a genuine geological cataclysm. For example, in the case of the Mexican Revolution which began in 1910, the country ceased to gain in population for the first time in all its long history, so that the census of 1920 registered a net loss in population of 826,000; the land-holding class disappeared completely, and in it had been concentrated from 60 to 70 per cent of the wealth of the whole country; large professional groups, the members of the government and the politicians, the army, the university professorate, were all completely reconstituted, or little short of it; new social classes emerged with decisive political power: the brand-new collectivist landlord, the workers' class, a popular army, and a new upper middle class, so new, tender, and delicate that none of the thousand millionaires in Mexico today has been one for more than fifteen or twenty years.

Anyone having personal experience of changes of this kind which occur from time to time in our countries will not see any exaggeration in the expression "geological cataclysm" which I used a moment ago.

There is still to mention, even though it be in a hasty and sketchy manner, the other great problem in America: the continuous dis-adjustments and adjustments imposed upon our countries through the operation of external factors.

As a matter of fact, though few would be inclined to dispute the assertion that American societies have maladjustments as serious as other peoples, in many doubt would arise immediately if it were asserted, first, that those maladjustments are more serious, and secondly, that most or all of them of any importance are due to forces arising outside of our America. The statement, in any case, has absolutely no ethical implication or suggestion of imputing responsiblity; it does not for a moment imply that outsiders are the cause of our ills; on the contrary, they are caused by a fact as irremediable as the following: once "discovered" by Europe, our America became an appendage of occidental civilization, but not entirely a part of it. Since then our chief concern has been to make a sustained effort to ascertain first what Europe, and today the United States, invents, in order to adapt it to our own situation.*

It may be said that it took us three centuries to assimilate the forms of the political, economic, and social organization of Spain, along with her art, religion, and language. The task was a tremendous one, because Spain was America's first point of contact, and besides being the first, it was comprehensive, bringing each and every one of the phases of a civilization which at that time was already the most complex and dynamic in the world. But Spain, at the very time of the Conquest, or shortly afterwards, which amounts to the same thing, lost the initiative in Europe, that is, ceased to be the mainspring of occidental civilization. The Dutch from the middle of the seventeenth century, the French in the first part of the eighteenth, and the English from that time and right through the nineteenth century, left her farther and farther behind, until Spain became that type of country which has a golden age behind it, and for which any time in the past

*It is a different problem to explain why part of the American continent, the United States, not only remained right in the centre of that occidental civilization, but has finally become its mainspring, at least in the material and political aspects. Perhaps the chief factors—none of which was fully operative in Spanish America—are: the existence of territory without population but containing great riches; but on top of this, and this is very important, the happy historical coincidence that the United States was founded and led by England, the country which gave the tone to contemporary occidental life. To this must be added unusually good luck, which has made the history of the United States an exceptionally happy one.

was a better time. Therefore, instead of originating changes and reforms, Spain received them from Western Europe, to transplant them later to America, but only belatedly and partially, and at times in a rather peculiar form.

Partly for this reason it may be said that the process of disadjustment and adjustment to which America has been subject since its first contact with Europe was more endurable in the period of our dependence upon Spain; other reasons also contributed to this fact. For one thing, the Europe of the twelfth and thirteenth centuries was doubtless a society subject to continuous and occasionally profound changes, but not to rapid or revolutionary changes. In political organization, for example, the English revolution of 1265, mother of the modern Parliament, does not spread to the rest of Europe, as happens to the point of reaching almost world-wide proportions in the other three great revolutions: that of the Independence of the United States of America, the French Revolution of 1789, and the industrial revolution; but these three, in spite of the dates of their beginning, really open the nineteenth century, and are actually a part of contemporary history. Also, difficulty of communication slowed the spread of changes, large or small. Thought was transmitted only in printed form, and in America to a very limited extent: it is estimated that in Mexico, where Spanish colonial culture was more flourishing than anywhere else, there were printed in three centuries of Spanish rule about thirty thousand publications, or barely a hundred per year. Furthermore, transportation facilities by land were exceedingly limited, and by sea not much better: the time it took Columbus' caravels for his voyage to America is shortened appreciably only when, well on in the past century, the famous North American swift-sailing *Clipper* crossed the North Atlantic.

The two circumstances which made our adjustment to new conditions less imperative lose their validity in the course of the nineteenth century, the first century of our independence. On the one hand, the already known means of communication come to countries previously beyond their reach; other means perfecting or completing those already in existence are introduced, and all tend towards the immediate and incessant transmission of ideas and news. On the other hand, European society is decidedly geared to technological and scientific progress, with material well-being the goal of personal and collective life. In this domain changes begin to be continual and of an increasingly obscure and revolutionary significance. In addition, two new circumstances are not long in making themselves felt: if in any field the legacy from Spain was nil, it was in that of science and technology, that is, precisely in that field in which the most dynamic and most gifted nations were working with greatest zeal and success; and then Europe itself, and most peculiarly the Catholic Church, only very belatedly perceived that a world as advanced as the one created by the new science and the new technology could not be contained within the moulds of the same political, social, and moral order. So Europe, and especially the United States, began to be with relation to our America, on the one hand, the source of the most astonishing technical progress, and on the other, the cause of the most lamentable moral and political backwardness.

It is therefore not surprising that though the necessity of adjusting to the changes in European society in the nineteenth century becomes more urgent, our capacity to achieve it without great delay and without serious and irreparable harm was not increased.

Thus we have spent the entire nineteenth century ruminating on economic and political liberalism, not with the languishing, but basically calm, attitude of the ruminant, but with turmoil, pain, terror, and violence. In none of our American countries was the triumph of liberalism ever complete, and in none did it achieve partial control without war and bloodshed. Someday someone of understanding will study the history of liberalism in our America; then will be seen how difficult its progress has been, the incredible contortions it has had to make in order to form its channel, the most curious modifications that it has undergone in being transplanted in our society, so different from the Western Europe in which it was born.

And I have a feeling that such an investigator will not be able to escape this conclusion: we inherited from Spain a central political organization more or less authoritarian, in which the initiative and the ultimate authority rested in the State; we gave up the inherited ideology, institutions, and experience, to embrace the liberal philosophy in which the State is passive, and the individual the only motive and regulative force, only to discover just slightly less than a century ago signs of a return to a political organization similar to the one we had received from Spain, and which was rejected by America's best men in order to put us in tune with modern Europe. I do not suppose it can be said that we have lost a century of our existence; but it certainly can be said that we were victims of the illusion that a politico-economic philosophy has universal validity by the sole fact that model countries originate it and that in them it flourishes. We were indeed victims of an illusion, first because we associated the liberal philosophy with our desire to rid ourselves of the domination of Spain and the Church, and secondly, in a more general sphere, because the human inclination to give universal application to what each man invents or experiences seems to be incurable.

The lack of discernment on the part of the American countries in evaluating the great transformations originating in the creative countries of the Western world in respect of their true significance, their final outcome, their transitoriness or relative permanence, is revealed in a situation which could be observed in Mexico as early as 1920, and which we see at this very moment in other American countries, such as Argentina, Brazil, Chile, and Venezuela.

None of these countries noticed in time that the industrial revolution was coming to them (even though in a carnival disguise), a social-economic revolution which brought loss of power to the land-holding obligarchy and, in consequence, the desperate efforts of this class to hold on to it. With it came the birth of a financial and industrial oligarchy, destined to replace the first one and to prosper at its expense; still more important, there came the transformation of a rural proletariat, disorganized and submissive, into an industrial and urban proletariat, aggressive and organized. These profound transformations are the essence of the whole contemporary history of Western Europe; they have been studied step by step, in all their details and vicissitudes, and also with accuracy. And yet not one statesman of Spanish America, nor any of its thinkers, so far as I know, made a move or uttered an appropriate word.

Our poor America is always lagging behind, and it does not even profit by the advantage of being able to avoid the pitfalls into which others have fallen so tragically and spectacularly. To my mind the most interesting political phenomenon in Latin America in recent times is the phenomenon which years ago, following the First World War, appeared first in Italy, then in Germany and Portugal, next in Spain, France, and Poland, though in the two last-mentioned countries it did not come to its ultimate consequences because the Second World War broke in upon them. The resemblance in this case cannot be considered identity, and therefore it is pointed out simply as a resemblance.

The truth is that in our America this phenomenon presents itself in the following form: the most capable administrative leaders have proved in the end to have the feeblest political vision, since they were unable to see in time—and even yet some of them have no inkling of them—the changes that have taken place in their countries in recent years. The principal changes are two in number, and one is older than the other. The first is a gradual disillusionment concerning the liberal and democratic formulae and methods; the second is the appearance and spread of an industrial proletariat, and in some countries, of a new youth movement. This has brought about the existence of large popular groups in deep discontent and in the most total political disorientation, and consequently easy prey to the first squint-eyed person who gives them a wink. There is a saying that is illustrative in spite of its grotesqueness: the liberal leaders have ceased to have any sex-appeal for the masses.

This phenomenon has shown itself with very great clarity in Argentina, but to my way of thinking with no less clarity in Colombia. The radicals of Argentina—who have represented the liberal side for many years—have ceased to have all the sex-appeal which they had in the highest degree with the first government of Irigoyen, so that it became useless to look for a name or a man who could pull radicalism out of the shadow of grey indifference which covered it: any Tamborini (drum) sounded like any Mosca (fly), and any Mosca seemed to fly like any Tamborini. And in Colombia, what could the name of Mr. Turbay offer that was new? At best, he was the black horse of liberalism, and at worst, not just the black horse, but the black omen: through a long career of political attrition, he had passed from the extreme liberals to the traditional liberals, that is, to those who express clear opinions only on the problems of the rich, but who become dumb, or at least cautious, when the problems of the poor are brought up.

But it must be agreed that the masses who followed Perón until they carried him to his triumph, and Gaitán until they brought about the defeat of the liberal party, did not move, nor do they move, towards the right. A hundred times no! They fell into the tragic trap because they sought and eagerly desired betterment, change, progress, in short, the "leftist" symbol in life, a symbol they did not find in the other camp, the traditional and the outworn. And, as in the romantic novels, they also fell into the trap through . . . a man, through a physical, tangible man, who wins more confidence among the masses when the institutions become dehumanized and depersonalized.

And since nobody noticed it in time, the oversight cost Mexico a long, bloody Revolution, which fortunately, "brought her up to date," at least for the time being. It is costing Brazil a fall into a deadness and confusion which her own jungle could hardly suggest. Argentina is caught in the trap of a demagogy both bungling and deceitful, perhaps costing her her future for the next fifty years; it is costing Peru a relapse into the darkness in which she has lived for a continuous half century; Venezuela, a loss of opportunity to accelerate her progress, not being able to resume the course of peace in which she was beginning to travel so courageously; Colombia, the necessity of resorting to the assassination of her modern demagogue to obtain a breathing-spell, one of which we do not yet know whether it will lead to genuine and modern democratic progress, or will only be one more blood-stain in the history of our oligarchical governments.

To me, in short, America appears to be faced with many problems, but there are two important ones upon whose solution depends in large measure the tempo of its progress: one is the small measure of social contact that one sees there, and the other is to discern and to profit by the course of occidental civilization and history in order to shorten our journey.

It would in no way surprise me if the readers of these notes objected to all or part of what is said in them; but I feel certain that all, weary of the sombre tone (usually insincere, rarely honest) which life these days is taking on, will ask indignantly: "And what is the remedy for all this?"

After first overcoming my natural timidity, I must confess that it has always appeared to me that the division of labour causes men to feel more sure of themselves in the analysis of ills than in the counselling of remedies; but if this time I am to venture into the field of the herb-vendor or the enchanter, I will hazard two conclusions and two remedies.

The government is the chief power in all modern societies; our lives (personal and collective) depend upon it in surprising measure, but this will increase still further. Consequently, the quality of a government is today a major problem in any country, and to obtain the best government possible, no citizen can scorn participation in public affairs.

The American countries belong to the sphere of Western civilization, but more in the material and political areas than in the cultural, this being a situation which will be underscored by the present preponderance of the United States. Since our part in that civilization is more passive than active, we have a very strong tendency both to imitate without reflection and to scorn "the lessons of history." A real need in Spanish America is to believe in its own creative genius and to screen very severely foreign innovations.

March, 1949

***American Extremes,* (*Extremos de América*) Tezontle, Mexico, 1949, pp. 249–72.**

Jaime Torres Bodet

(b. Mexico, D. F., 1902)

The intellectual career of Jaime Torres Bodet has been one of the most remarkable in contemporary Mexico. After studying at the Normal School, the National Preparatory School, the Law School, and the Faculty of Advanced Studies of the National University, he taught literature in the Preparatory School, and while still very young, became registrar of this same school and later private secretary to José Vasconcelos, at that time Minister of Education and Head of the Libraries Department. In addition, along with Bernardo Ortiz de Montellano, he directed the literary review *The Phalanx* (*La Falange*), 1922–23, and some years later he became co-director of *Contemporaries* (*Contemporáneos*), 1928–31, a review which was to give its name to his literary group. The next stage in his life, from 1929, was devoted to diplomatic service in Madrid, The Hague, Paris, Buenos Aires, and Brussels, and upon his return to Mexico, from 1940 to 1943, he was Under-Secretary for External Affairs.

From 1943 to 1946 he was Secretary for Public Education, a post which he filled with the greatest distinction. He initiated a broad programme of school construction, reorganized and gave fresh impetus to the campaign against illiteracy, created the Institute for Teacher Training, organized the commission for the revision of plans and programmes, initiated the Popular Encyclopaedic Library, directed the excellent compendium *Mexico and Culture* (*México y la Cultura*), 1946, built numerous schools (of which outstanding examples are the Teachers' Normal School, the Higher Normal School, and the National Conservatory in Mexico City), and in short established consistent objectives in Mexican education. On completing his educational service, he became Secretary for External Affairs, and in 1948 he received the honour of being named Director General of UNESCO, a post which he occupied until 1952.

Torres Bodet is a member of the Linguistic Academy and of the National College, and has received the highest honours from Mexican and foreign institutions. Since 1955 he has been Mexican Ambassador to France.

In his essays and studies in literary criticism—for the most part published originally in the review *Contemporaries*, with some of them later being collected in a volume bearing the same name (1928)—Torres Bodet combined a complete and constantly recultivated knowledge of ancient and modern letters with an alert mind and a pliant and luminously rich style. His criticism in its time corrected the evaluation of many false lights and made very important contributions to the literary education of the younger generations.

His writings in connection with his public offices, addresses, and messages —among which are found admirable pages, such as his address to motherhood or his Academy discourse on the responsibility of the writer—are devoted to elucidating educational problems and problems of international concord between Mexico and the rest of the world.

Recently Torres Bodet returned to the literary field with two excellent books. In *Time of Sand* (*Tiempo de arena*), the first part of his memoirs, the balance is tilted in the direction of spiritual biography, while the incidents in his life barely constitute a framework or a reference. Perhaps for that reason the best pages, of a consummate and elegant quality, are those which tell of the revelations of literary or artistic figures like Racine, Beethoven, Proust, Antonio Caso, or José Vasconcelos. *Three Discoverers of Reality* (*Tres inventores de realidad*), which gathers together the lectures he gave at the National College on Stendhal, Dostoievski, and Pérez Galdós, is a work of intellectual depth and maturity. His analyses of the profound problems of literary creation and of the fundamental dilemmas which life and art presented to these great novelists are a model of literary criticism.

MEMOIRS: *Time of Sand* (*Tiempo de arena*), 1955.

ESSAYS AND CRITICISM: *Contemporaries* (*Contemporáneos*), 1928; *View of Present-day Literature* (*Perspectiva de la literatura mexican actual*), 1928; *Landscape of Garcilaso* (*Paisaje de Garcilaso*), 1936; *Three Discoverers of Reality* (*Tres inventores de realidad*), 1955.

STUDIES: *Mexican Education. Addresses, Interviews, Messages* (*Educación mexicana. Discursos, entrevistas, mensajes*), 1944; *Work in Education from 1940 to 1946* (*La obra educativa en el sexenio 1940–46*), 1946; *Education and International Concord. Addresses and Messages, 1941–47* (*Educación y concordia internacional. Discursos y mensajes, 1941–47*), 1948.

REFLECTIONS ON THE NOVEL

Themes

"CAN IT BE THAT, since the novel is the freest of all literary genres, it is from fear of the very liberty it enjoys that the novel has clung to reality in such a cowardly fashion?" exclaims Edward, the most intellectualized character in André Gide's *The Counterfeiters* (*Les faux monnayeurs*) in referring to the works he has undertaken and which are confused, not unintentionally, with those of the author.

The problem of the novel is defined along the above lines with the most extraordinary acumen. It is not a problem of decadence, nor of logical vertebration, as Eugenio d'Ors is on the point of informing us in his commentaries on contemporary novelists: Morand, Romains, and René Benjamin. It is, more simply, a problem of pure art.

The nineteenth century appears to have taken pleasure in leaving us the greatest number of traditions to oppose. It would be the same as admitting defeat to try to continue in the current of ideas accepted by the men of the eighteen hundreds. The works produced under the domination of orthodox Positivism may have been beautiful. We do not refuse them our admiration, but let us refuse them our obedience. Like every period which succeeds in attaining an individuality, a characteristic tone, the nineteenth century did not disappear without denigrating the intellectual movement that was to follow it. In order to denigrate it, it hit upon a pretext and a formula: decadence.

Verlaine calls himself decadent in 1875, and in America Darío is accused of decadence in 1905. This idea must have been animated by a peculiar form of vitality when, like an over-used coin, it still keeps circulating among us, and when even today people try to buy with it the world's gift of art. The Naturalist critics continue to call the imaginative poetry of the United States decadent, and find no better word to attach to the methods of contemporary painting in Europe. Spengler takes advantage of an hour of national disaster, in Germany, to speak in his book *The Decline of the West* (*Der Untergang des Abendlandes*), and José Ortega y Gasset founds a *Western Review* (*Revista de Occidente*), publishing a series of observations on the "decadence" of the novel.

There is always this need to erase the work of today by appeal to the memory of the work of yesterday, coloured too strongly by the exaggerated reality of Romanticism! But contemporaries cannot content themselves with memories of a youth they have not lived, and for this reason it will be necessary to seek another explanation that can go beyond explaining everything by decadence—an explanation more concerned with investigation than with denial, the only one really adequate for discerning the element of aesthetic truth which the essays of today contain.

As we approach the novel, immediately an objection to Ortega's theories occurs to us. "We should imagine the novel," he says, "as a quarry with an enormous but finite maw. Those who worked there first easily found new materials, new figures, and new themes. The workers today, on the other hand, find that only small and deep veins of stone are left."

There remains one positive affirmation: the novel is outside of man; it is a genre to which it will be necessary to go as women go to the well for water. So long as the spring is active, the work of the artist will be limited to sinking his jug into the fountain. For Ortega y Gasset, the decadence of the novel is a matter of the number of themes. We are not going to make common cause with him in this retrogression to Naturalism.

No work of art derives its life from the theme treated. To state that the merit of a novel is in direct ratio to the novelty of its subject matter, is to assume that the words "merit" and "success" have a significance in common. According to this pre-eminence given to plot (which is the episodic element) over art (which is the essential element), *The Lady with the Camelias* (*La dame aux camélias*) would be superior to *The Red and the Black* (*Le rouge et le noir*), and *L'Atlantide* by Pierre Benoît, in which there is an out-and-out riot of action, would overshadow the qualities of Constant's *Adolphe*, in which nothing happens.

The novel is not a genre in decadence. Joyce's *Ulysses* and, more recently, Gide's *The Counterfeiters* are not works of decadence. The only thing that has entered a period, not indeed of decadence, but of sheer abandonment, is the naturalistic novel, the novel for the shop-boy's and shop-girl's market, the novel of the type of Zola's *Germinal* and Blasco Ibáñez's *The Four Horsemen of the Apocalypse* (*Los cuatro jinetes del Apocalipsis*). And it has fallen into desuetude because it was not a pure literary form and because, for that reason, it could not compete with the cinema, which has a firmer grasp of industrial resources, the solid food for that hunger after effortless imagination which characterizes people when they constitute a public.

The same character in André Gide's novel that I mentioned at the beginning of this essay refers to the genre in these terms: "A slice of life! said the naturalist. But its defect was always that it was cut in just one direction: in the direction of time, in length. Why not in breadth or depth?" This is what the contemporary novel has set out to do, the novel of Proust or Joyce: free itself from the notion of time, to which I attribute the demise of the theatre as a traditional art form, and penetrate into the most intricate depths of the consciousness, through the medium of a series of besetting scenes—of experiences in the memory—in which the artist brings into focus the field of lower modes of expression, the world of little acts, and there finds, with the same shrewdness which in Freud is a defect, the flower of hidden intention into which action and thought are resolved.

However deeply it becomes involved in this investigation, the novel will not run the risk of becoming pure psychology, since as a work of art it will cause to coincide with these resources of "surrealism" a synthesis and harmony of emotion nowhere discovered in science, and which are exclusively the product of beauty.

Will the novel alter its purposes? We hope so. Why should every sort of change be decadence? Had it nothing left to do, then, but die?

What is true for apples, in the picturesque succession of seasons, ought not to be applied to a work of art. Maturity, the last period of botanical life, is nothing but a pause in the history of literature. This may mean that the reader is weary of novels that amuse him, and now wants them to interest him. What the new authors must aim at is to succeed in this.

Reality and Memory

The novel already knows its masters, has learned to love them, and is beginning to feel the need of selecting them. First of all it must not be forgotten that the novel, with its present characteristics, is a genre of yesterday—when "novel" was mentioned, Balzac was implicity associated with it. More than the Napoleon of French literature he dreamed of being some day, Balzac was the Christopher Columbus of a genre which, before him, had found its formula only in the production of a few masterpieces, isolated or in series, as in the Spanish picaresque novel of the reign of Philip II, for which nationalism was both a basis and a limitation.

Balzac took possession of the novel with that robust zest which enabled him to compete in fecundity with the offices of vital statistics, and he modelled it in his own manner—a manner which, unfortunately, was not always a style. The Romantics admired this development of the novel in the direction of psychological reality and mistook the terms. When they said of Balzac that he was moulding the profile of the French novel, would it not have been more exact to say he was deforming it?

The favourite device of this madman was precisely to reduce intelligence, goodness, art, and passion itself to the category of manias. This was an anticipation of the Realistic school in modern psychology, which our contemporaries have managed to brush aside in the nick of time. The shifting canvas of the spirit which Montaigne already described as fluctuating and diverse was for Balzac a specimen for a sectional cross-cut in the direction of greatest immobility, of sedimentation of habit, of the automatism which the consciousness attains by dint of repetition. A good fairy nevertheless watched over the birth of each of Balzac's novels: the creatress of exact types. Père Goriot, Baltazar Claes, and old Grandet are hardly men as Naturalism was to understand the term. They are types. Goriot is not really the perfect father. He is paternity itself in what lies concealed in it of vice, self-abnegation, and maternity. If Molière had not traced with the same porcelain the statue of Harpagon, in the seventeenth century, in that same French language, would it not have been more appropriate to give to *Eugénie Grandet* the title of *The Miser* (*L'avare*)? And what about *The Lily in the Valley* (*Le lis dans la vallée*) and *Cousin Bette* (*La cousine Bette*)? What work by Balzac does not define that general type of mania which constitutes a human type? In this Balzac is simply a Classicist, and this he is in spite of himself, even though his sole ambition was to escape from Classicism. Being ambitious—and does not "ambitious" already say "Romantic"?—what he dreamed of doing was "to fashion men."

The modern novel begins at the moment when it becomes too easy to make them, and when it is understood that to study them is more interesting and perhaps more amusing. The aptitudes of the novelist which in Walter Scott, Balzac, and Dickens were gifts for creation, for imagination, are rapidly being converted into gifts for definition, for subtlety in exegesis, for true analytical magic. The third person in the narrative loses his transcendence as spectator. It becomes a more profound pleasure to intervene in the spectacle, and therefore, day by day, autobiographical novels are more frequent, those in which the memory pours its treasures into the vessel of pure forms, and illuminates them within by the warmth of its later experience which has now completely matured in the form of spirit, and which barely at intervals is vitiated by tangible existence.

The best quality of the modern novel will therefore be its scrupulous fidelity to memory. In a tale by Kipling a young Englishman who is most profoundly conscious of having lived in Greece six centuries before Christ, and of having rowed as a galley slave in its galleys, gives this precious detail to the writer: "The sea, in enveloping the ship at the moment of the wreck, seemed to be the string of an immense stretched bow." And this single sentence animates the tale and vivifies it. Proust—whom one cannot accuse of having made excessive concessions to the spirit of his time—put all his self-abnegation into cultivating this faculty of the novelist: the memory. Always ill, death found him correcting the chapters in which he described the sensations of a dying man.

There is nothing simpler than to close the circle in a formula, but nothing is solved if the field circumscribed by the formula is not that of a truth repeatedly tested. We are assured that the novel is a descriptive genre. There is nothing richer in contradiction than a description. What kind, then, must the description be that is worthy of constituting a novel?

Stendhal, Dostoievski, the most perfect masters, have been content to describe a few profound cases, and have succeeded in interesting us by placing themselves at every moment both inside and outside of their theme. Their works are never the history of an event as in Galdós or Zola. They do not take hold of their theme except at the point where passion, in every way human and natural, takes an unknown course. The novel, then, in its most perfect realization is a genre too big for Classicism, which separates from it in a natural manner, because of its essence; because in it the interesting element evoked by the subject dominates too completely the interest which the simple form would be able to suggest. Just as in lyric poetry, in the essay, and even in tragedy, it is difficult to mark the precise limit, the needle on which the scale-pans of the balance oscillate, so in the novel the problem of style, if it does not cease to exist—a thing which can never happen in art—changes its centre. From being a form of expression, it becomes a form of exploration. In poetry, style is a frontier; in the novel, it is a highway.

To write a novel is as captivating as to start on a journey. A novel that does not compel us to read it right to the end is like a city which sends us back quickly to our point of departure: its way of life, or its melody, was not in tune with our sensibilities.

A poem is listened to; a drama is suffered; a treatise is thought. A novel is different. Either one lives in it or it does not exist for us. A perfect novel would be one that would make us die of the asphyxia of reality, by the substitution of its atmosphere for ours, while mediocre novels are known by the atmosphere of reality that filters in through the cracks. The slightest breath of life spells failure to the intention, and we fall heavily, slaves of reconquered gravity, to the level of the known.

Some Pathways

Back of the journey along the pathway of the novel, from the turbulent romantic city of Balzac—a city of northern France during the Napoleonic Wars—to the Siberia of Dostoievski, or the Chartreuse of Stendhal, lies this undiscovered territory: the contemporary novel.

All the modern tendencies in poetry, painting, and ideas have found an echo in the novel and have tried to destroy its essential unity, by imposing upon it a foreign stamp.

While drama was becoming lyrical in d'Annunzio, Maeterlinck, and Lord Dunsany, poetry—so confined within the tight tunic which the schools succeeding Symbolism prescribed for it—was being poured in its entirety into the novels of Régnier, Jammes, and later those of Giraudoux and Larbaud. In these authors the value of the image is exaggerated into a vicious voluptuosity. The refinement of the style thins the profile of the characters and barely clothes them in that lucid lace with which the sea-foam, without erasing it, covers the name we write with our finger in the sand of the shore.

From the psychology of the characters of Balzac, so given to blurred generalizations, made up entirely of plans superposed, confused and gigantic like the form in the sculptures of Rodin, to the mastery of psychology in Flaubert and the Goncourt brothers, the road travelled was already disquieting. We know Emma Bovary, Mr. Homais, and Bouvard through and through. Our memory holds them tight—just as the poet holds his sweetheart in Gerardo Diego's madrigal—in the way that the water, inside, holds tight to the glass that contains it.

We shall be able to discover, at a happy moment, the colour of Madame Bovary's eyes, but from the very first, in an almost painful manner, we feel her within us, her tragedy grips us, and there is not a single obscure corner in her tormented consciousness with which Gustave Flaubert's finger has not brought us into contact. Flaubert was not a doctor's son in vain. In the tenacity with which he describes the defects of his characters there is something of piqued curiosity, of morbid pleasure. He touches the sore spot. He withdraws from it. But his hands, the cruel hands of the surgeon, do not rest till he touches it again.

Thus interpreted, psychology would be an insoluble problem for novelists of the type of Giraudoux or Régnier. The first, if he had been born in 1800, would have written Lamartine's *Grazielle*. The second has an ideal, and this ideal hardly separates him from Marivaux's

Mariane . . . when he is not infected by the eroticism of *The New Héloïse* (*La nouvelle Héloïse*).

Balzac, Flaubert, and Dostoievski were not in the habit of penetrating into the spirit of their heroes in a single flash of insight. They besieged it like an enemy fortress and took it in slow stages. The modern novelist tires of this tedious toil and prefers to work on material previously defined. Comparing their work with that of the sculptor, we might say that Balzac, Flaubert, and Dostoievski drew from the innermost parts of the stone the original figure, while the novelists of today content themselves with cutting down to the point of transparency the figure they receive from real life or literature.

It will be understood why to this type of author the subject matter would be the part of least concern. On the contrary, the subject matter hems them in. Neither Giraudoux, nor in Spain, Salinas[1] or Jarnés,[2] has the gift of invention. Any story-writer of the Naturalistic school, even the most colourless, would be able to think up a theme more readily. But this is because their art does not derive its life from invention, and the kind of imagination they cultivate is not the kind used to adorn a baroque plot, but the other more subtle kind, which finds connections between opposites, which disassociates ideas which the commonplace has associated, and brings together images which the traditional way of seeing things would never venture to bring next to one another.

While this kind of novel emanates from poetry—the work of Jules Romains contains other human concerns—we shall have to go to Proust in France and to Joyce in Ireland to find, in living literature, examples of the pure psychological novel. Joyce's *Ulysses* is the history of one day. Readers accustomed to being born with their characters, to accompanying them all through a book for twenty or even fifty years of adventures, will feel dissatisfied with the short period of time in which this novel of more than seven hundred rich pages develops. A curious phenomenon has occurred. The subject which the novelist of yesterday saw looking the wrong way through his opera glasses, moving it far away and reducing its size, the novelist of today contemplates through a magnifying glass. From such an exaggeration of reality, the resulting reaction is that surprise with which we recognize the presence of any new, healthy art, incapable of resigning itself to following the models of tradition—the master of the mediocre.

The contemporary novel has not been satisfied with receiving into its

[1]Professor at Johns Hopkins University, who died in 1951.

[2]A contemporary Spanish novelist and critic.

treasury the contribution of poetry: Giraudoux, Souppault, Valery Larbaud. Neither has it been content with the psychological frenzy of Proust. Moreover, it has endeavoured to continue along the pathways opened by the best writers of the past. André Gide and François Carco are, from two different points of view and with unequal merits, disciples of Dostoievski. Romain Rolland would be worthy of comparison with Tolstoy in the dramatic intensity with which *Jean Christophe* is conceived, if the polemicist, and at times the impatient journalist, did not too frequently overpower the thinker. There is no present-day concern which has not tortured this strange writer, to whom may apply at the same time the attributes "lucid" and "disordered."

In Spain, Ramón Pérez de Ayala also follows a tradition, but he inherits the genuine Spanish tradition and therefore even the titles of his books have the smell of the living Spanish soil, for example, *Trotters and Dancers* (*Troteras y Danzaderas*), *The Fox's Paw* (*La pata de la raposa*).

Azorín,[3] whom I intentionally place among the poet-novelists, has made out of criticism the best of his novels. He has the defect, along with the opportune talent, of placing the writers he judges in the literary atmosphere which applies to them. Like Zuloaga, he is an excellent portrayer of backgrounds. At times what is lacking in these canvases is the portrait itself.

Baroja[4] defies classification. He would not accept a judgement excluding him from tradition nor would he tolerate being limited to it. His strength lies in a kind of crude originality which makes him appear as an intruder into literature. He loves life with the coarse love of some Italian women novelists of the end of the past century, but his works, even those which treat matters of style and language with the greatest indifference, never achieve the ease and freedom of the novels of Blasco Ibáñez, which are the crowning triumph of a good digestion.

A dissection of the modern novel which neglected sense of humour would be lacking in comprehensiveness and pitifully incomplete. Paul Morand[5] and Gómez de la Serna[6] know how to find the comic elements

[3]The pen name of José Martínez Ruiz, born in 1873 in Manóvar, Alicante and now living in Madrid.

[4]Pío Baroja, born in San Sebastián in 1872, was a famous Spanish novelist. He died in Madrid in 1956, and was visited shortly before his death by Ernest Hemingway.

[5]Contemporary French writer.

[6]Spanish writer who died in Buenos Aires in 1963.

in the characters they describe. Gómez de la Serna discovers them quickly and utilizes them to excess. His smile runs the risk of becoming merely a gape. Morand, on the other hand, seems to have evolved in the direction of a greater purity. His latest books show less of a desire to surprise the reader. Perhaps the advice of Proust to *Tendres Stocks* is now bearing fruit: one must not seek a metaphor, but find it.

Contemporaries. Critical notes (*Contemporáneos. Notas de crítica*), Herrera, Mexico, 1928, pp. 7–21.

DUTY AND HONOUR OF THE WRITER

Inaugural Address in the Mexican Academy, affiliated with the Spanish Academy, Mexico, delivered on April 11, 1945

THE ENTRANCE OF A WRITER into membership in a body like this is certainly not free from a severe, autumnal solemnity. The reason is that it is not usual for anyone to find his way into precincts of this kind without having suffered that noble devastation with which age keeps pulling out the profusion of leaves on the burning trees and denuding the souls of that vesture of changing attitudes and unnecessary words which, in earlier years, one wishes to have taken for authentic youth.

Such a high distinction is not a trophy in recognition of the past of the one who obtains it, but a stimulus to greater severity in his work and conduct, a command to impose silence on many sterile fancies and set limits to the caprice with which the artist who takes delight in eluding regular methods seeks to compensate, in unrestrained self-indulgence and free-ranging idleness, for his position as a soldier without a regiment and a musical note without a staff, elusive and alone.

Nevertheless, from such meditations—which do not deny the vague melancholy with which reflection is coloured in maturity—there arises finally the certainty that the line of the staff for that note we imagine to be excluded from it, basically represents the firm scaffolding of its logical and natural order. Without its lines and spaces—limited, but precise—the most ambitious note would lose significance, because where there does not exist a school, that is, a definite relating of values, how could the sign, isolated and individual, however lofty we might wish it in its conception, attain any exact sense?

This lesson in modesty is the first instruction which your Academy gives to its new members. If I praise it, upon my entrance here, it is because I have never dissimulated my liking for all that awakens a healthy confidence in a unity, capable of making those who compose it more loyal to themselves in proportion to the degree to which they perceive and recognize that, among independent men, absolute unity means monotony, since true unity emanates from an equilibrium of harmonized liberties and of mutual tolerance and respect.

Even if I had not spontaneous belief in what I have said, it is my opinion that I should be induced to suggest it by the circumstance, taken along with different other reasons, that I find myself taking the place of a writer so different from what I have been, Mr. Teodoro Torres, a person of great prestige for whom I express my most cordial esteem, and whose death leaves in the letters of our nation a place which posthumous adjectives do not mark as the pathetic vacuum of an absence, but on the contrary, as the actual presence of a smiling, lucent, and faithful man of letters.

After rendering homage to his illustrious name, and after thanking you most cordially for the honour you have done me in inviting me to add my efforts to the brilliant traditions of this Academy, allow me, gentlemen, to utilize the attention you are according the recipient to reason with you, for a moment, concerning the problems with which the crisis afflicting the world confronts us, as writers and as men. This crisis is so deep and so disturbing that there is no group able to escape its grave influences, and no conscience which does not feel obligated to seek a solution for it.

We are passing through a dark forest, out of which we shall emerge at the cost of every sacrifice, except one: that of faith in human virtue.

In this descent into the darkness, all peoples, all human beings—it must be acknowledged sincerely—were in some measure guilty, even though in infinitesimal measure, through action or inaction. The culprits which history will inscribe in its registers are the tyrants: leaders of automata, who seized to their own profit all the mechanisms of technology and science, all the capabilities of discipline and economy, and at times including all the external forms of culture.

But if in political matters it is a consolation to perceive the unanimity with which the free nations have pronounced against the mad passions of those culprits, in personal matters we cannot confine ourselves to condemning them. It would really be too comfortable to incarnate evil in a few bloodthirsty despots, because to an impartial thinker it is obvious that those despots would long ago have been in prison or in a mental hospital if, at the time they made their bid for power, there had been throughout the entire world an active hierarchy of spiritual values that would render useless their conspiracy of cruelty.

This, gentlemen, is the burning problem of our time. The crisis in which we live is today a crisis of war. Yesterday it was, and perhaps it will also be tomorrow, an economic crisis. It has always been marked by an insufficiency in the rule of law, but for many years now it has indicated something more alarming: an ethical crisis. Concerning this last crisis, who would have a right to say he was not responsible? And the responsibility for this crisis is shared by the writers, the intellectuals, and the philosophers, in accordance with the quality of their vocation.

I am sorry if I am here disturbing the habitual serenity of these meetings by referring to a deep anguish, instead of offering you, for example, the clean autopsy of a question of literary criticism. I also regret, however, that in a period like the present it is no longer possible for the writer to forget the man, and that when all is in danger of perishing (since a badly organized peace would bring with it as many ills as a series of convulsions and conflicts), coming to speak to you about the decline of the elegy, about the twilight of the eclogue, or about the enfeeblement of the sonnet, would suggest a lamentable deformity on my part, and would be as if I imagined you to be detached from the army of the only profession for which any institution of this importance is an academy opening upon the earth: the profession of men who love righteousness.

Precisely because there have existed, for many years, many generations who thought they could serve intelligence without serving humanity; precisely because there have existed, for many years, many specialists in culture who built their utopias in the air, and many practitioners of art who declared unhealthful for their work anything outside the narrow space they called their "ivory tower," there came to be established, in many nations, a painful divorce between life and intelligence, and between politics and culture.

Well now, this divorce has caused so many disasters that we could not venture to make accusations exclusively against the majorities that permitted it. Where the intellectual has given up his function as an orientator, future peace would require an end to the divorce to which I refer, because although a Spanish thinker[7] spoke of the rebellion of the masses before the conflict, the intelligence has experienced other

[7]José Ortega y Gasset.

subtle forms of rebellion: pride of isolation, denial of public service, and the belief that civics is only a profession, a mere specialty.

If you disagree, reconstruct the scene of the years which followed the first terrible war of our century. With a few most honourable exceptions, what did the statesmen do? They distrusted intelligence. And what did numerous intellectuals do in their turn? They withdrew from the meeting places of the citizenry, and repudiated their obligation to give direction.

Removing themselves thus from the common effort, how could they expect that to supplant them there would not offer themselves those simulators—pseudo-philosophers and pseudo-artists—who quickly converted pure science into cunning tactics of aggression, talent into smartness, and art and thought into monstrous systems of propaganda?

In Mexico, fortunately, the phenomenon I mention appeared with less acuity than in other countries. Many found ways to participate—from the pages of their books, the columns of newspapers, the public platform, the university chair—in the combined work of affirmation and, at the same time, of constructive criticism which the evolution of society requires from the possessors of culture. But it is no longer a matter of limiting to one country the rectitude of that vigilance over the things of the spirit. For the world that is being born, amid ruins, sobs and bombardments, machine-gun fire and death, wretchedness and bloodshed, all of us, all writers, all artists, all thinkers, are under obligation to think up a better way of life.

After the hour of the strategists will come that of the politicians. Diplomacy will strive to settle many differences, and to bind and fuse together many wills. Nevertheless, our appointment with destiny is inescapable. To the noblest political and economic charters, peoples are demanding the addition of another fundamental charter: one in whose clauses is established the order of moral postulates for conduct; one in which, to live together, all races and all continents finally agree upon plans for a union which would be, at most, a precarious alliance of regional political interests, if we were not able to support it upon a supreme alliance of the spirit.

No nation, no group, no individual will be capable of serving the peace of the world, so long as that peace is not linked to a philosophy of life which gives to life its full significance: the fulfilment of a mission.

Undoubtedly it is quite right that we should be concerned about defending ourselves against the adversaries which liberty always finds; but it is equally important never to forget that not a few of those adversaries will perish by their own actions, as a punishment for their violence, as happened in the case of the hypocritical rival of Theagenes when he went to tear from its pedestal the statue which the Thapsians had consecrated to him. The image of the conqueror fell; but in becoming detached it rolled over on the body of the envious attacker, and buried him under its weight.

On the other hand, though we are frequently saved from external enemies by circumstances, who would be able to save us, but ourselves, from that enemy we carry inside of us wherever we go; that enemy who listens to our secret before it strikes our own ears, however mysterious the message it contains and however quiet the voice that carries it to us alone; that enemy who sometimes defeats us in our victory and whom we conquer only when we succeed in stifling within our consciousness the cry of egotism, the bloodthirstiness of hatred and the sordid lust for pleasure?

No one will succeed in living in peace with his fellow-men who is unworthy to live in peace with his own self. Therefore in these times, when we wish to construct an education serving peace, democracy, and justice, let us appreciate how urgent it is to stress in our teaching not only the aspect of a holy struggle animating man in the determination of his political and social faculties, but also, concomitantly, the discipline of his inner equilibrium as a person, and his capacity to subdue, in himself, the dark urge of passions. Or, to express it differently: man is not liberated only by guaranteeing him the use of his rights. He is liberated, and possibly more truly so, by raising him above shameful slavery to his instincts and making him understand his obligations to himself, to his fellows, to his country, and to all humanity.

Much has been said about the rights of the citizen, the rights of women, the rights of the writer, the rights of youth, of the technician, and of the artist. We have been creating, in all ranks of society, a mentality of unsatisfied collectors. Consequently he who makes demands does less than he makes claim for, and gives in service less than he asks as the price of his service. There is thus accumulated in peace-time, over the short or long term, a collective deficit, which the nations know no way of paying except with their contribution towards some war; and this, after all, is the same as trying to settle a debt indirectly, by way of the general liquidation of a bankruptcy.

What I have just said makes clear to us that one of the values that it behooves us to instil, within the human sense of culture, is the spontaneous and intrinsic value of duty—but not any longer the military duty of killing or dying, which peoples accept when offensives are launched, but the civil duty to live and make live in accordance with standards above suspicion; the duty to sacrifice a little of our pleasure, every day, in order not to sacrifice it in its entirety on the tragic altars of war; the duty to be strong, in time, in order not to have to learn to be strong in conflict, when strength is measured by what is denied us and not by what is assured us, by what it destroys and not by what it builds.

We have before us the complete and laboriously contrived sketch of a new world, a world which was not formed by a chance of geography, but by an insistent, solid, and stern will—the will of human history. That sketch will be at most an insensitive, uncultivated, and mute form so long as we do not give to it a soul of its own. And that soul can be given to it only by those who possess the capacity to give to their work their entire being.

For many years we have heard some intellectuals express in an abstract manner their opinions concerning themes relating to the causes of peace and war among nations. Even immediately following the armistice in 1918, there was a leading European writer who would define peace as merely an equilibrium of symbols. With frightful irreverence his literary gift had taken pride in playing with metaphors in this manner. But it happens that metaphors are just a moment of reality—the rapid, photographic moment in which matter turns to sign, allusion, or emblem. And we are seeing, by the experience of our sufferings, that our immediate role is going to consist in resuscitating the figures which lie beneath the symbols.

If the artists of old took pleasure in seeing how Daphne became transformed into a laurel and Lot's wife into a statue of salt, duty demands that our time should be marked by precisely the contrary phenomenon, and that at the touch of our poetic or philosophic rod, Lot's wife should live again, escaping from her salty, frigid prison, that the laurel should become again the living Daphne, and that we should find, under the oppressive symbols, the tremulous and vulnerable flesh through whose arteries will run a blood no longer fictitious, but red and afire like our own, amid nerves and muscles of truth.

This means, without allegory, that on the new generations is imposed a task whose purest marks of glory will be derived from bringing culture to life, from humanizing it, and from combating the arid abstractions which were threatening to stifle art, science, and thought.

The soul awaiting this new world would tomorrow rise up in wrath against us if we did not all strive to create it out of the purest elements in our faith. What has been most lacking in the builders of our present-day civilization is faith in man, devotion to his ideals, and the critical examination necessary in order to distinguish clearly between hope and mirage.

Upon the technique of haste it is indispensable to superpose the technique of solidity. Let everyone acquire the psychology of the architect, "the architect of his destiny." In this the writers and artists of Mexico are under the same obligations as those of any nationality. It is indeed essential that the world we help to organize should be a world of order, and that the order regulating it should be derived from the only discipline which can be united with our love of liberty: order by the power of spirit.

In a debate presided over by Professor Osorio de Almeida there was discussed, some time ago, the matter of the transposition of cultural values. Among others, Werner Thormann, a political exile from Germany, spoke on that occasion. From him I quote the following sentences, the repetition of which I do not consider out of place here: "In all domains of public life," exclaimed the speaker, "our task is to prevent man from being made into a simple instrument." And he added: "We have witnessed the liberation of the masses, but we still have to reconcile that emancipation with the concept of personality." To this Raymond de Saussure immediately made the objection: "A lessening of individual responsibility towards the whole of society, a desire to ask everything of it and to offer it nothing in return, was the principal characteristic of the pre-war period."

We note that in this supposed antinomy between the responsibility of society and the responsibility of the individual, or between the emancipation of the masses and the disinvolvement of the person, the positive solution unquestionably will have to be a moral one. As early as the end of the eighteenth century, Kant advised: "Act in such a way as always to treat the free and reasonable will, that is, humanity, in yourself and in your neighbour, as an end and not a means."

There is no juridical postulate which this reflector does not illuminate: liberty of being in the democracy of the nation, as well as the sovereignty of peoples in the democracy of nations. For what economic imperialism or totalitarianism, technical or practical, has tried to accomplish, both in the internal society of countries and through the tortuous combination of powers, is the use of the neighbour as a means, of one's fellow-man as an inferior, and the subjection of the will (which in itself is a noble end) to transitory aims which disturb social life and upset the universal order.

In all latitudes, in all climates, under all skies, the men who write, think, and teach must try to make of peace and liberty something dynamic and of real substance, and not situations of timid stability and simple absence of death and servitude. Interest in peace and zeal for liberty were on the decline among nations and in the minds of men before the outbreak of the actual hostilities from which we are suffering, in part because under the shadow of ideas of peace and liberty, many injustices had taken form and many false ideas had thrived; but in part, too, because the leaders in culture did not succeed in inculcating among the masses a living image of those ideas, and contented themselves with defining them in their negative aspects: peace, as a repudiation of war, and liberty, as a repudiation of tyranny.

It happens, however, that the minds of individuals and popular conviction are difficult to stir up with something that is offered them in restrictive terms, and that liberty and peace are conditions which must be esteemed, first of all, for their positive aspects. After Versailles there were a good many books which propagated the hatred and fear of armed conflict. Barbusse and Duhamel, Arnold Zweig and Dorgelès, Remarque and Romain Rolland—to mention only novelists whose success is beyond question—made of their works vehement outcries against war.

As a counterpart to those outcries, how many writers dared to sing the positive praises of peace? However dark the novelizing of war may have been, the novelizing of peace, as well, bred bitterness and discouragement, pessimism and desolation.

What samples of humanity did the most famous writers offer to their readers? In France, there were the immoral "counterfeiters" described with such persuasive talent by André Gide, and the decadent society which provided material for the admirable analyses of Marcel Proust. In Germany, we had Thomas Mann's cult of death and the cruel investigations of Jakob Wassermann. In Italy, there were the nocturnal characters of Svevo and Pirandello. In Prague, we find the agonizing disquietude of a Kafka, and in England, either the ironical excursions of Aldous Huxley or the exacerbated unwholesome sensuality of *Lady Chatterley's Lover.*

Between prospects of an armistice without nobility and the portrayals of a war without magnanimity, what naturally germinated among the public was indifference. Was it worth while to renounce struggle only to fall into the marasmus we were given as the epitome and anaesthetic of peace? In order to counteract the tearful sentimentality of certain periods in nineteenth-century literature, exaggerated claims were made on behalf of a geometrical and sensational intellectualism. Poets, possessed of an angular talent, went so far as to declare that the heart had forever gone out of fashion. Before being removed from real characters, virtue, creative passion, integrity, and manly elegance in conduct were removed from the pages of books. And, making allowance for some exceptions, most of the literary production scattered about the world between 1918 and 1940 may be classified under two long series: that of works tending towards idealism, through evasion of reality, and that of works proclaiming, as the only realism possible, the elimination of ideals.

What did such a serious antithesis signify, but a fundamental abandonment of intelligence? But we must not resign ourselves to having the role of intelligence reduced to the copying of vulgar portraits and ignominious profiles, but on the contrary it must take the scattered elements in nature and organize them with determination, in order that we may be offered a gallery of models, fortunate or unfortunate, noble or base, but contrasting them, as has always occurred in periods of greatness, against the background of a coherent, inspired, and firm concept of life.

In these days we all find ourselves somewhat in the position of Renan,[8] when he wrote his *Prayer on the Acropolis* (*Prière sur l'Acropole*). All of us indeed, some more truly than others, could say with him: "We arrived late at the threshold of the mysteries of true and simple beauty." Because we have been ill with scepticism, and because, to say it in his words, "a philosophy indubitably perverse induced us to believe that the good and the evil, the ugly and the beautiful, pain and pleasure, could be transformed into their opposites, through indiscernible shadings, like those on the neck of a dove," we now feel ourselves confronted with the duty to choose the good boldly and to reject the evil decisively, to serve right with the entire force of our convictions and to oppose wrong indefatigably and constantly.

Our worthiness, and perhaps not ours alone, will depend upon how well we choose between the road over the plain, which leads with mild undulations to comfort and to relaxation, and the road through the mountains, which leads through rocks to the heroism of beauty and truth.

The highest duty of the artists and writers of our time is to restore hope to men. But it must not be the soft, effeminate hope that makes peace the equivalent of an insurance policy against all the risks of life,

[8]Ernest Renan is best known for his *Life of Jesus* (*Vie de Jésus*), 1863, in which he explains away any supernaturalism he find in his Scriptural sources.

but the manly hope which holds that living means to accept dangers, to overcome them and to find a way to control them valiantly, as the function and operation of an ideal.

May the aim of Mexico be that all her writers, present and absent, will be worthy to assume this obligation. Such, gentlemen, is the prayer I fervently offer as I join your Assembly.

Education and International Concord. Addresses and Messages (Educación y concordia internacional. Discursos y mensajes), 1941–47, El Colegio de México, Mexico, 1948, pp. 38–47.

Xavier Villaurrutia

(b. Mexico, D.F., 1903; d. Mexico, D.F., 1950)

Even though Xavier Villaurrutia was essentially a poet, he was also a poet-critic. With implacable severity, the cold, nocturnal light of his mind reduced and organized the great themes of his poetry—love, night, death—until he gave to them the maximum of expressive intensity. This same lucidity, bequeathed to us in his brief and concentrated work as a poet, shines through his criticism and essays as well. His sober, keen, pointed style shows his contact with French prose, especially that of André Gide, who taught him his clarity, elegance, and conciseness. The essays and critical notes which he collected in *Texts and Pretexts* (*Textos y pretextos*), and those not yet collected, for the most part contain sagacious and penetrating analyses. As examples we have the masterly essay on López Velarde and the brilliant pages on theatre and painting.

Villaurrutia studied at the French College and the National Preparatory School of the City of Mexico, and at a very young age began to devote himself exclusively to literature, which therefore constitutes his only biography. His first poems date from 1919, and in 1923 his work was represented in the anthology *Eight Poets* (*Ocho poetas*). Along with Salvador Novo he directed *Ulysses* (*Ulises*), 1927–28, the first Mexican review frankly of the "Vanguardist" school, and later he was one of the principal promoters of the review and the group called "Contemporaries" (1928–31). In 1935 and 1936 he studied dramatics at Yale University, on a Rockefeller Foundation scholarship, continuing an interest which had begun with the experimental groups "Ulysses" and "Orientation," which offered performances of modern dramas in 1928 and 1932. Later Villaurrutia, a distinguished dramatic author, became a master of the histrionic art, and on rare occasions he gave lectures or literary courses. In his last years he frequently wrote for the reviews *Mexican Letters* (*Letras de México*), 1937–47, and *The Prodigal Son* (*El Hijo Pródigo*), 1943–46. His poem *Song to Spring* (*Canto a la primavera*) received first prize at the Spring Festival of Mexico City in 1948, perhaps his only contact with official and academic ceremonies, which he always shunned.

ESSAYS AND CRITICISM: *The Poetry of Youth in Mexico* (*La poesía de los jóvenes en México*), 1924; *Texts and Pretexts* (*Textos y pretextos*), 1940.

PAINTING UNMARKED

I

THE ARTISTS REPRESENTED in this exhibition, with those who are also represented by virtue of that poetic reality we might call the presence of an absence, are free, independent painters who aim to be personal. And is not that aim the most living form, perhaps the only desirable form, of personality? Their work does not spring from any school, nor does it deliberately set out to form a new school. Having been developed in the warmth, or in the coldness (which also burns and matures and preserves), of intimacy and of solitude, it is nourished by their aspirations and desires. No political creed and no educational system imposes upon it the brand of bondage.

Like the latest Mexican poets, the latest painters, living in an atmosphere hostile because indifferent, without a definite public to appeal to, nevertheless produce work which tends to spiritual unity with the rest of the world, and if it appears to be aesthetically and morally isolated, it is due to the fact that it opposes the work of the artists who preceded them in time, without surpassing them in merit.

Of lyrical poetry and painting which bear on their face the marks of their isolation, some say this is their weakness, but I believe it to be their strength.

It is the work of lyrical poets and painters, Mexican poets and painters, who have been able to find in their own poems and pictures the precious fruit of moral liberty.

We have poetry and painting; we know that in the eyes of all there are visible relations, and of an order we might call reasonable, between the world of poetic forms and the world of plastic forms. I speak of certain aesthetic affinities which render it possible to bring together for a moment, into the same plan, through the fine rhetoric of drawing, through the savouring of certain delicacies of a language of precise forms, an excellent poem and an excellent picture, a poem by José Gorostiza and a picture by Julio Castellanos, for example. Though the affinities are so interesting, I do not wish to pause to speak of them.

I prefer to point out the existence of other more subtle relations between the world of poetry and the world of painting. Having them under the protection of deep solitude and silence, in the horizontal fall of insomnia, in the uplift of the night; catching them with our customary opening and closing of the eyes in our slumbers; interpreting these subtle relations which at times have left in my hands the keys to open communicating doors between rooms, or wings, of painting and poetry—all this has been one of the purest and freest pleasures of my mind.

The fruits of this stationary and silent search, of this aerial or under-sea navigation of the spirit, are my poems which have wished to be not merely unreal creatures, mathematical entities or musical existences, but also, and especially, plastic objects.

I well know that the relations of which I speak to you exist between the other arts, but I know too that if it is true that contact beween them is possible, it is certain that everything in them would have an immediate break-up. We cannot imagine, without an ironic smile, a picture that sings; and even less can we imagine a picture that dances. On the other hand, no one would be surprised, except in a pleasant way, to find himself suddenly before a picture that dreams. And is the dream not the exceedingly fine network of conducting wires stretched between the worlds of painting and poetry? But it must not be forgotten that a true artist must always be, even in his dreams, completely awake.

Why should you be surprised, then, that in a spasm of what we might call unselfish egotism, I should wish our new painters to intercept those mysterious relations, and that, operating in the opposite direction to the one I have followed, they should make their painting more poetic, as I have tried to make my poetry more plastic!

There is no doubt that the first man to compare poetry with painting was a man of very delicate taste. To revive in our day the *ut pictura poesis* of Horace would not reveal the same good taste or the same shrewdness. What could be done then cannot be done now. Neither the art nor the times which it has fallen to our lot to live in or experience are the same as those Horace lived in or experienced, because art and time are not immutable things, but, on the contrary, they are subject to incessant change, and to a constant becoming. The time that *was* Horace's is now past. And since the friend of Maecenas has not died completely, no one will prevent us from saying that his art *is* of this kind or the other. It is not that art and present time simply are, because they *are being.*

I have not attempted, therefore, to compare the two fine arts, and still less to advise fusing them, but I have merely tried to tell you that they are interrelated and to make you see that some of their relations are invisible. It would be stupid for me to try to make you see the invisible through the use of logical discourse. That is for the artist to do. The reading of a poem or the contemplation of a picture, if they are alive, will give you better than anything else that consciousness of the imponderable which the reason cannot produce, and much less convey.

One generation of artists was able to consider art as an escape from reality. Fleeing from the reality which surrounded them, they attempted the impossible: to escape from themselves. The vehicle of fancy transported them to times and worlds which were alien and temporary: the Middle Ages, the Orient, the Tropics. Theirs was a life of emigrants, and their work, even in their own land, a work of exiles. Some thought they could find in suicide, that journey without a return ticket, the solution to their drama. But interrupting the drama is not solving it. The drama continues to stand right there.

Tired of not finding satisfaction in their constant flight, other artists decided to face the reality which had been revealed to them by a man who ran out into the street shouting: "The external world exists." But this man was a workman, an artist only in the sense that he was a technician, not an inventor or a poet. His work and the work of those who listened to him reflected a very narrow conception of the imitation of external reality. As if the means could justify the end, they thought that the secret of art was to manipulate the material with dexterity. They put in everything, without any place for poetry, mystery, or chance.

The first, the Romantics, fled from reality. In the case of the second, the Naturalists, reality fled from them.

But the artist is always living in unstable equilibrium on a dangerous point between two abysses, that of the reality that surrounds him and that of his inner reality. Sometimes he has been content to look outwards; at other times he has merely glimpsed at his inner abyss; and at others, for fear of not being able to endure the vertigo, he has closed his eyes.

Reality contains man, and the whole content of man is reality. The artist of today appears not to be satisfied with only one of these realities. Neither the external nor the internal reality is sufficient to him separately. And to express only one of them implies the renunciation of the other. "How can he," I ask myself, "express the two realities when standing in between them are the walls of the vessels which contain them?" This he can do by destroying these walls, or better, by making them invisible and porous in order to achieve a filtration, a circulation, or a transfusion of realities.

With a few outstanding exceptions, the new painters of the entire world, and quite a few Mexicans among them, have abused what we might call the external model, as opposed to the purely internal model in which André Breton finds the only justification for plastic art.

If you transfer my hypotheses to the field of painting, you will think with me of a third model, whose realities are no longer external or internal, because the frontiers which kept them isolated have now disappeared.

Do not expect of me a commentary on each of the pictures you will presently see. Some of their creators I should have to praise timidly, and others with moderation, and Vauvenargues has told us that to praise moderately is a sign of mediocrity. And how could I appear timid and mediocre before a group of persons whose mere presence at this exhibition would suffice to gain for them the title, if they did not already possess it, of connoisseurs?

If it is true that the trees prevent us from seeing the woods, it is at times no less true that the woods prevent us from seeing the trees. Now that the woods you are forming before me are breaking up, I invite you to see, one by one, the trees which show themselves at the windows which open about you. And for this purpose you have come, because a picture is something as simple and as complete, as deeply rooted and as aerial as a tree, an external tree and also that other tree which each of us carries in his body, through whose arteries and veins the blood mysteriously circulates.

II

Surrounded as I am by a considerable number of works by mature artists and by new artists, the first thing I feel is a kind of excitement. Works of plastic art have always had an *appeal* for me, a peculiar magnetic effect. It is impossible for me to remain cold and indifferent in their presence! They attract me like a passing adventure; they speak to me, when they are capable of it, in a voice to which I cannot help listening eagerly. Like an imprudent Ulysses, I confess to you that I have never tied myself to any mast so as not to hear the clamour of these sirens which come forth from a sea of canvas, stone, or paper. To try to explain the pleasant excitement that comes over me; to try to discover precisely what I feel in the presence of the work of art and why I feel it, is to throw away the free enjoyment of my sensations, my sensibilities, and my instincts, to surrender to pride in the exercise of my reason. It is avoiding the correspondences of my senses, the impact of my memories and feelings, and the mysterious impulses of my blood, my breathing, and my nerves. And if, with the same gesture with which a shipwrecked man prefers the narrow plank of an improbable rescue to the magnificent spectacle of certain shipwreck in which he is at the same time the victim and the fortunate spectator, I abandon, avoid, and erase this thing that is nothing but mystery, I must say to you that if we wish the mystery to continue as mystery, it is necessary that we should not try to explain it, but we must preserve it carefully in its own atmosphere, moving round it, feeling it, and at most striking it momentarily, in just vengeance, since it strikes and blinds us.

There are those who consider plastic art a systematic game of values, colours, and lines. Others see in it nothing but the triumph of matter, and just as in oil painting they prefer to consider the quality of the paste used and the brightness or opaqueness of the colours, in a drawing they take delight in the endless musical, tactile, and visual gamut of the greys which a hard or soft pencil has left on the sheet of paper. The former believe that plastic art should appeal only to the mind. The latter believe that it is all for the senses. But truth is a goddess, and we must not seek her just in one place, but everywhere. Therefore we are not satisfied with the pure painting of the first group, for whom the work of art sallies forth armed from the artist's head to go directly to the head of the spectator, nor with the feast of oil and lead of the second group, for whom the work of art is hard or soft, rough or smooth, dry or greasy, just like the human skin.

Neither in its origin nor in its purpose is the work of art a pure act of the mind. Neither is it a mere projection of the feelings. Still less is it the simple presence of matter. It is none of these things, and yet it is all these things and more. Let us not wish to have it singular, because perhaps its only permanence is to be found in its constant change of content. It is better for it to be plural, and though finite, still unlimited. The play of mind and matter is only the brain and skin of the work of plastic art. And it seems to me that nothing is more simple or more accurate than to compare a work of plastic art to a living human being. Like man, it has in its inner world zones that are known and zones that are unexplored, aerial terraces, dark tunnels, where our intentions and hidden desires, our feelings, our formed and unformed ideas, rise up, move about, and struggle to express or repress themselves.

A simple Euclidean knowledge of man calls these zones instinct, soul, and mind. But where does one zone end and another begin? Where do our instincts start, and where is the beginning of our ideas? Being accustomed to this simplified knowledge of the inner man, which in more than one way parallels the concept of geometry before Einstein, our reason has placed our instincts in our skin and muscles, and our feelings, our soul, in the heart, and our intelligence in the brain. But nature demands a solution less simple and more correct. Would it not be better to say that these zones pile on top of one another and mingle together, and that the roots of their flora, subterranean or aerial, invade and cross the zones inside our body, rendering impossible an unnecessary delimitation of frontiers?

As a human work, a work of art must be the external expression of this living and varied world, with its invisible fusions of the innumerable and complex elements which dwell within our bodies.

The work of plastic art will make use of matter (canvases, colours, oils, and papers) as a simple means of rendering them visible.

The object of painting, Valéry has said, is vague. But the same may be said of all the arts. Prompted by an imperative necessity, which according to period and fashion sometimes takes the name of faith, luxury, pleasure, or pastime, man produces works of art to satisfy the no less imperative necessity of other men to gratify their appetites with them. This would be the only object of the arts, if each art did not have, besides this mechanical one, another or other objects more peculiar to itself and more subtle.

With full understanding of the dangers involved in my statements, I think that the object of music is to make heard the unheard, expressing all that is significant in sound and also in the sound made by silence, and I think that if the end of poetry is to make one think of the unthinkable, perhaps the object of painting is none other than to make seen the invisible.

To make seen the invisible! That is the work of magic, religion, and poetry. It is the common denominator of all the arts of poetry: "The substance of things unexpected, the evidence of things not seen."

If painting has been till now the art most submissive to the external models which nature and reality have suggested to it, it must be added that for that reason, of all the arts, painting has been the one offering the fewest means of becoming acquainted with the inner world of man. Only a few painters have done something more than transpose or reconstruct, sometimes magnificently, the world of stimuli which strikes their eyes outside of themselves, but these few have enriched the world with new, unexpected visions, born of dream, hallucination, or unconfessed desire, adding to common reality fragments of an inner reality no less intense, and more profound. I do not dare mention them because the name of each one is already, and clamorously, on every tongue. Only a few painters have been truly creators and inventors.

To invent, and not transcribe; to create, and not repeat—these are the duties, and also the only joys, of the poet. Those of the painter must be no different. Though the painter is not like the poet, painting *is* like poetry. In essence, the letters of one are in no way different from the lines and colours of the other, and we already know, since Rimbaud, that letters have colour, and since Nietzsche, that poems must be written (I was about to say, painted) with blood.

A somnambulist, a mystic, a man possessed, a poem, a drawing—all resemble one another in that all speak in solitude.

It has not been my purpose to speak of the drawings of this exhibition. For fear of marking them up, I have not traced these lines over them, but around the mystery which is exuded from some of them. They await only my silence to tell you their particular secrets, and to make heard to you their inner voices. I can imagine their impatience, and to them I yield the floor.

Exhibition of Modern Art, 1932

Texts and Pretexts. Literature, Drama, Painting (*Textos y pretextos. Literatura, drama, pintura*), La Casa de España en México, 1940, pp. 193–206.

THE FACE AND THE PORTRAIT

MEDITATION CONCERNING THE PORTRAIT leads us inevitably to the consideration of the eternal and the ephemeral, of what is permanent and what passes away.

Just as there exists in man an instinct to preserve, we might say that, whether it be obscure or clear, conscious or unconscious, there exists in him an instinct towards immortality. Man knows he is ephemeral, but he does not resign himself to it. Man wants to endure, and as soon as he establishes relations between the eternal and the transient, in the midst of an agonizing shipwreck he seeks safety-planks to grasp, and not only to survive, but to survive his own self.

Man knows that he changes every moment and that that moment is irreversible. Tormented by a thirst for continuity, by a longing for immortality, he seeks the way to see himself outside of himself, immobilized in time, and stabilized in space. Has not man attained a view of his gods or his god in pictures and images? Has not man converted divine principles into images? Has he not humanized, to come right out with it bluntly, his gods? God created man in his image and likeness, but has not man represented his gods in effigies that are anthropomorphous and even zoomorphous? Has he not for this purpose utilized matter, seeking first the hardest, the most durable, and the propitious for continuing to be? Has he not turned to the three dimensions of sculpture which allow him not only to see, but to walk around and even touch these representations of principles, of gods, which man comes to confuse with the principles and gods themselves? And has he not consented to the representation of his gods in the two dimensions of drawing and painting?

In a trajectory in the opposite direction to the one he followed in the case of the gods, pursuing his own immortality in the same way as he pursued the humanization of the divine, man seeks a way not only to see himself outside of himself in an ephemeral way, but in a durable and permanent form which will defy time.

And who can succeed in attenuating, calming, or sating this thirst for a continued life, this longing for survival, except the artist? To achieve this gratification of his pride, man resigns himself, momentarily, to a form of servitude; he offers himself, for the time being, as a model to the artist who will immortalize him.

To halt the fleeting, in time; to stabilize the mutable, in space—these are the magical objectives which the artist sets for himself before his model. From this to saying that the artist aspires to immortalize the mortals is only a step. And this step, which in turn implies an undeniable act of pride, a Satanic act, a Promethean challenge to the gods, who are in their essence immortal, is the step which the artist dares to take.

When André Gide, in a statement which seems like a new proverb from William Blake's Hell, wrote that "there is no work of art without the collaboration of the Devil," he must have been thinking of the subtle intrusions of self-aggrandizement, vanity, and pride in the work of art. And this infernal proverb helps me to uphold the opinion that art diabolically serves to gratify or appease this instinct for immortality, patent not only in the man who wishes to immortalize himself, but also in the artist who, if he really is one, not only aspires to self-immortalization, but achieves it, using the model offered him as a medium. And let us note how (and a mental excursion through a gallery of portraits of all times will help us to prove it) it is not the model that has attained his desire, but the artist who has achieved his own identical desire, since with rare exceptions what survives is not the person or spirit of the subject of the portrait, but the person and spirit of the artist.

Let us suppose, then, that the devil has intruded once more, subtly, in these human and artistic aspirations, to exchange the ephemeral for the eternal.

There is a myth which lies over this anguished racing of man in pursuit of his own image. The myth is none other than that of Narcissus.

Narcissus knows his own soul, but not its form; he knows his own body, but not its form. He knows his face is handsome, through the effect it has on others, through the personal satisfaction which this effect gives him. But Narcissus does not know his own face or image. An eagerness to know himself consumes him. Narcissus starts off in pursuit of his image. He goes along a road. The road is a motionless river. He sees a river, and the river is a moving road. Narcissus does not wish to lose time, which he knows is flowing along like the river before his eyes. And as he longs to see his image, exactly as it is, outside of time and outside of the ceaselessly flowing river, he seeks till he finds that part of the current which, by virtue of a special conformation, forms a quiet pool. This is a place within the river and yet, miraculously, outside of the river; it is in time, and yet, miraculously, outside of time. He bends over, and the miracle happens. Narcissus discovers the mirror. Narcissus discovers the self-portrait. Henceforth, Narcissus will spend the entire day leaning over the mirror of the pool, contemplating his image.

But the dangers involved in finding something are never sufficiently terrifying to prevent man from rushing madly in search of it. When once man had discovered in the mirror a way to contemplate his image; when once he had found in "the congealed waters" a space capable of reflecting his image, so that he could know it and love or hate it, he conceived the mirror which retains it without requiring that the model should remain, like poor Narcissus, motionless in front of himself. There was then born the idea of the mirror that would hold, without need of the model, a static, eternal image, in the form which we now know, use, and see.

Our instinct for immortality is nourished, supported, or simply consoled in what one of our poets, Sor Juana Inés de la Cruz, has called in a moralizing reflection

> . . . coloured deceit,
> which displaying the splendours of art,
> with false syllogisms of colours,
> is a subtle delusion of the senses;
> the senses by which flattery has sought
> to rescue us from the horrors of the years,
> and, conquering the harshness of time,
> to triumph o'er old age and oblivion.

On a less general plane, on the plane of painting itself, what is a portrait? It is simply a kind of painting, "a kind modest in appearance but requiring a great intelligence," Baudelaire said of the portrait. And he added: "When I see a good portrait, I imagine all the efforts of the artist who has had to see, of course, all that allowed itself to be seen, but in addition he has had to imagine all that was concealed."

The artist has two duties to perform, then, with respect to his model. The first is the one which insensibly, coldly, and precisely is performed by the mirror (the impartial mirror, be it understood), in reproducing what the model shows to the eye. The second and more subtle duty is that of bringing out what is submerged, raising to the surface what is hidden, and showing what is concealed inside the model. This second duty Baudelaire calls, attributing to it a magical value, "divination." A less poetic mind, what we call a scientific mind, might use another word to designate the same thing, and call this second duty an "investigation."

A portrait is not, therefore, a copy, but it is a divination, or, expressed in different terms, it is an investigation of a human model.

Mexican Letters (*Letras de México*), Mexico, Mar. 15, 1942, Year VI, Vol. III, No. 15, pp. 1–2.

THE POETRY OF RAMÓN LÓPEZ VELARDE

THE MATURITY OF A LIFE, like the maturity of the day, is not revealed in the vague hour of nightfall, but in the full, vibrant moment when the noon-day sun is at its zenith, at the moment when the sun, having completed its ascending trajectory, appears to stop to contemplate, stealing the shadow from persons and things, the results of its journey before commencing a descent which is, at the same time, a return. Disappearing in the noon-day of his life, death did not come to shatter hopes or to cut down promises in flower, because Ramón López Velarde had realized the former and fulfilled the latter. His journey was the perfect journey without a return.

Three books of verses, of which the third, published posthumously, contains along with a number of finished, well-turned poems, others that are incomplete and blurry sketches, with no value except to serve for the study of the peculiar manner he had of perfecting his verses to the point of reaching, through a sought-after and calculated accommodation, unforeseen expressions, together with a book in prose which contains poetic pages of unquestionable merit, constitute the work of Ramón López Velarde. But the rare quality of that work, the interest it arouses, and the irresistible magnetism which it effects on minds that do something more than read it superficially, make of it a remarkable event in Mexican letters. Though we have poets of broader scope and more richly and more compellingly endowed, none is more intimate, more mysterious, and more covert than Ramón López Velarde. The intimacy of his voice, his mysterious chiaroscuro, and his profound reserve have retarded the diffusion of his work, let us not say beyond our frontiers, where he is not admired because he is not known, but even within our own country, where even minorities have rapidly granted him, before they understood him, nothing but a blind and gratuitous admiration.

Blind admiration is almost always a kind of injustice. At least such is my opinion when I consider that Ramón López Velarde is more admired than read and more read than studied. An admiration without reservations, a superficial reading, and an immediate reaction stirred by the less profound themes of his work, sufficed to carry him directly to glory without making him pass through purgatory and still less through the hell in which, according to his own confession, Ramón López Velarde believed.

After the appearance of a number of the review *Modern Mexico* (1921), devoted entirely to honouring the memory of the poet, and in which, among many studies more moving than accurate and more sentimental than true, a study by Genaro Fernández MacGrégor was distinguished by real critical acumen, I but vaguely remember the lecture in which José Gorostiza traced the precise portrait of the "peasant" which Ramón López Velarde never concealed, and a study by Eduardo Colín, confused like all of his. Nevertheless, the glory of the poet has been growing like a snowball as time rolls on, taking a form that is alien to him, too spherical and precise, too simple when we remember that we are dealing with poetry that is polyhedric, irregular, and complex. The proselytes of Ramón López Velarde have contributed not a little to detracting from the personality of the poet and to simplifying in a conclusive form, unjustly, the features of a physiognomy full of character, changing, and mobile. I have said his "proselytes" and not his "disciples," because I believe that Ramón López Velarde, a poet without any discernible descent, has not yet had a worthy disciple. Of his work there have been imitated the provincial softness of the skin that clothes him, the local colour of his familiar themes, and even the tone of voice, opaque and slow, with which he delighted in confessing, along with the venial sins, the most intimate and obsure agonies which his admirers and his proselytes have hastened to forgive him without examining them, without considering that the complexity of the poet's mind is expressed precisely in them.

Serpents of typography and thought, interrogation marks surround and bite us. Is the spiritual complexity of López Velarde's poetry real and profound? Was his obscurity of expression necessary? Was his unusual style the price of his concern for precision, or was it only the outcome of his desire to be different? Were the metaphors of his poetry sought after or were they inevitable? . . .

It is impossible to deal with all the suggestions which, almost simultaneously, are forming in my mind. But how can I avoid lifting for at least some of them, even though it be only in order not to fall into the vice of unconscious admiration, the corner of the veil which keeps them concealed?

The truth is that the poetry of Ramón López Velarde attracts and repels, pleases and displeases, alternately and at times simultaneously. But when once displeasure and repugnance are overcome, the seduction is effected, and sometimes in admiration, at other times confused, always interested, it is not possible to fail to enter into it as into an intricate labyrinth in which perhaps the poet himself had not found the guide-wire, but in which, in some way or other, the anguish of his mind was in itself the prize of the adventure.

In the eyes of everyone, the poetry of Ramón López Velarde is set in a provincial, Catholic, orthodox atmosphere. The Bible and the catechism are indisputably the ever-handy books of the poet; his love is romantic love; his only loved one, Fuensanta.

But these are the general characteristics, the visible limits of his poetry, not the more special lines or the more secret frontiers. In his very first book, *Devout Blood* (*La sangre devota*), Ramón López Velarde belies, once and for all, the apparent simplicity of his mind, and indicates two periods of his inner life, saying:

> Then was I a seminarist
> without Baudelaire, rhyme, or sense of smell.

And yet his imitators have tried to continue to see in him the seminarist who has not discovered the secrets of rhyme, the pleasures of the senses, and the new thrill of Baudelaire. In reality, from that time onwards and forevermore will be definitely established the conflict which makes of his work a complex drama, situated in

> the chiaroscuro atmospheres
> in which Heaven and Earth convene.

In a perfect epigram of light and synthesis, an outstanding Mexican writer has concentrated the drama of certain minds by saying of one of them that "he never could understand that his life was two lives." In fact, how many minds come to their death without having paid attention to the contradictory ideas which stir up irreconcilable dialogues within them! How many others strive to stifle one of these two voices and even succeed, or at least succeed in refusing it audience, in order to gain a coherence which is nothing but a mutilation of their minds!

Ramón López Velarde does not belong to this unhappy family. His drama was not one of ignorance or spiritual deafness, but of clarity. Very soon he realized that in his inner world two lives, in mutual enmity, were locked together in an incessant struggle, in an open conflict, and with them two irreconcilable aspirations which, attracting him with equal force, drew him outside of himself.

With magnificent clarity he understood that his life was two lives. And this acute consciousness, before the very force of the opposing lives that stirred within him, was sufficiently clear to allow them to coexist, and fortunately did not lead him to the mutilation of one of them in order to achieve, as did Amado Nervo, a simplified coherence and, in the end, an empty serenity.

I wonder whether the significance, and the very manner of title and content of his most important book, are other than the painful anguish of his spirit before the reality of two different lives which, coexisting within him, were struggling to express themselves and finally were actually expressing themselves, in the most fruitful moments of his poetry, not only alternately, but simultaneously.

Heaven and earth, virtue and sin, angel and demon contend with each other, and it matters not that at moments heaven, virtue, and the angel are victorious, if what upholds the drama is the continuance of the conflict, the locked hold of the adversaries, in the mind of Ramón López Velarde, whose life was escorted by a guardian angel, but also by a "wild demon."

Ecstasies and pleasures attract him with identical force. His mind and body will live under the sign of two opposing groups of stars:

> You reveal to me the synthesis of my own zodiac:
> the Lion and the Virgin.

What memories of childhood readings about the paradises which the fancy of the Mussulmans created for the blessed, and what vision of coloured prints of those memories left in López Velarde the trauma which endures like an obsession throughout his entire work?

If in his constant thirst for the love of women he finds no way to reconcile his Christian religiosity and his eroticism; if, at first, in *Devout Blood* he asks himself:

> Can this constant longing be Franciscan or polygamous?

he soon finds in the Mohammedan paradises a way to extend his religiosity, but also his eroticism. Then, in a first statement, he becomes bold and says:

> meanwhile I act like an Arab without a houri,

and seeking obscure genealogical antecedents in his soul's family tree, he does not know whether his devotion is caught in the madness of the first theologian who dreamed of the first woman

> or whether, atavistically, I am an Arab without qualms
> always just returned from the cruel continence
> of the desert, and in the midst of the merriment of houris
> finds all of them beautiful, and all his favourites.

Instead of blotting out one of the two contradictory elements in his nature, he learns to let them coexist within him, carrying on an incessant dialogue, a conflict which feeds on itself. In this way he reconciles monotheism and polygamy, Christ and Mohammed:

> I, a whole man,
> nourished by the honeycomb
> of Mohammed
> and by the one over which Rome watches
> on the Central Plateau

he says in *Anguish* (*Zozobra*), and then, years later, in Poem 33 of *The Sound of the Heart* (*El son del corazón*), there is heard again the voice called forth by the insoluble problem of the man who, instead of dissimulating his torments, his preoccupations, his inner conflicts, has learned to live with them open in the agony of his sufferings:

> The age of the blue Christ afflicts me
> because Mohammed follows me
> tinging the mind with green and the flesh with red
> and chisels them, the Bedouin and the houri,
> like an emerald on a ruby.

And in the same poem:

> The parable courses in and flares,
> and I waste my talents in the struggle
> of Happy Arabia with Galilee.

What matters it that at one moment he should venture to call unhappy the duality which we know has also brought him ecstasies of joy,

> I am smothered, in unhappy duality,
> by Ligia, the martyr with stiffened eyelash,
> and the bissextile croup of Zoraida,

when the Christian Ligia and the infidel Zoraida will henceforth be embracing him forever!

Pleasure and pain, opulence and wretchedness of the flesh, delight of a present paradise and sadness because of a forced earthly exile for the sake of the promise of a paradise without pleasures—these are the weights which oscillate in his balance.

When Ramón López Velarde wishes to give a formula for himself, when he tries to objectivize his inner drama, he finds only the image of something, suspended between these two worlds, which oscillates incessantly like a pendulum over them:

> I am hanging in the infinite
> stir of the ether, like
> a wretched thread of silk

or:

> I am a harem and a hospital
> Hanging together from a dream.

And making it still more concrete, objectivizing more precisely, he discovers his symbol in comparing himself, in a beautiful poem, to the lamp on which he hangs his sores like prisms.

In the Baudelairian minute of religiosity which is no longer distinguishable from amorous frenzy, when we see him come out with hands and mind empty, returned from an immersion in the sea of his own anguish, I imagine him, as in two of his verses of incomparable desolation, swaying over the abysses which open within and without, "with the widower—oscillating on the trapeze."

The blood which circulates in the most recondite vessels of Ramón López Velarde is not, therefore, constantly devout blood. This blood is disturbed, tempered, and even yields through the impulse of a current of erotic blood, to such an extent that at moments the two are confused, becoming one single blood, red, dark, composite, and mysterious.

Never is this poet nearer to religiosity than when he has touched the ultimate extreme of eroticism, and never is he nearer to eroticism than when he has touched the ultimate extreme of religiosity:

When the last odalisque,
my garden now loveless,
flits off in search of fresh honey,
what psalmody of my heart
will be worthy to sigh
through the empty harem?

He who functioned at intervals as a lone Arab now feels himself definitively forsaken. And at the mere thought that the pleasures of the senses may no longer exist for him, at a given moment, the moment when "the effective, live rose" of his virility becomes superfluous and impeding, in the final spasm of fear he will confess himself dead in life, an Arab without a houri:

Divine fire on whose tongues
each morning I wake:
one day, eyes half-opening,
I'll be dead before I die.

Can it be necessary to say that this duality of Ramón López Velarde is very far from being an external and purely verbal game and that, on the contrary, it is very close to the profound antithesis which one sees in the mind of Baudelaire? In Ramón López Velarde too "the antithesis bursts forth spontaneously in a heart that is also Catholic, which knows no emotion whatever of which the outlines do not fly off at once and immediately meet their opposite, like a shadow, or rather, like a reflection."

And yet his work continues to be seen with eyes that remain at the surface without venturing to plunge into the depths of the body in which man has been concealing man. So Ramón López Velarde continues to be for everyone a simple Catholic poet who expresses simple feelings. I wonder if it can be possible now to keep on speaking of simple feelings in the poetry of Ramón López Velarde. I recall the revealing words of André Gide: "The only thing that permits a belief in simple feelings is a simple way of looking at feelings."

It is not by chance that the name of the great French poet has arisen on more than one occasion in considering one of the most personal aspects of Ramón López Velarde. He himself has confessed to having been changed after becoming acquainted with Baudelaire. Was his knowledge of him precise and clear? Did Ramón López Velarde read Baudelaire in French? Or did he know him only through Spanish translations, that of Marquina, for example? What Ramón López Velarde takes from Baudelaire is not the form; it is the spirit of the poet of *The Flowers of Evil* (*Les Fleurs du mal*) that helps him discover the complexity of his own.

I have already said that, according to an uttered confession, López Velarde owed to Baudelaire the discovery not only of rhyme, but also, and especially, that of odours, coming to a knowledge of the most characteristic, the most refined, the most precious and the most sensuous of the senses which no poet has ever brought into play like Baudelaire.

It would be unjust and artificial to establish a parallel between the two poets, and it would be impossible even to detect a direct imitation or point out a precise, external influence. Between the forms used by the two poets lies a veritable abyss. But though an abyss lies between the forms of the art of these two men, another abyss, the one that opens within their minds, makes of Baudelaire and Ramón López Velarde two members of the same family, two protagonists of a drama that is repeated through time with a rending and magnificent anguish. Agony, emptiness, fear, and sterility, themes of Baudelaire, are also themes of our poet. And if the religiosity of López Velarde is resolved in eroticism, by following an opposite course, but one no less dramatic, the eroticism of Baudelaire is converted, in the ultimate analysis, into a prayer:

> O Lord, give me the strength and courage to contemplate
> my body and heart without disgust.

Certain verses of our poet, verses of truest ring, communicate an indefinable Baudelairian quiver when they are the expression of a tortured mind:

> with the arid agony of an exhausted heart

or, when he tells us:

> I am drinking a cup of terror

or when, in *Worshipping Spirit* (*Ánima adoratriz*), he wishes life to end at precisely the same time as pleasure,

> and when of the wine of gladness not a dreg of a dreg remains
> on the table, may the mocking legacy of a sterile coal slip
> into the grave.

In an identical obsession with death, Ramón López Velarde confesses in anguish that the prodigal life

> . . . flows over into the false
> feast, and the torture of my growing hunger,
> as a cornucopia overturns on a scaffold.

And this shows still more when he superposes the images of full life and of inevitable death, as at the end of the poem in which he has sung with sensual rapture of the teeth of a woman, perfectly accommodated in the infinitesimal aqueduct of the gum. He stops, and suddenly, passing without transition from the erotic madrigal to the macabre vision, he says:

> Because the earth swallows every bright amulet
> and your idol's teeth will be left quite lone
> in the bristly grimace of the hostile skeleton.

Of all the poems of Ramón López Velarde, three from *Anguish* (*Zozobra*): "The Tear" ("La Lágrima"), "Ants" ("Hormigas"), "I Honour Thee in Terror" ("Te honro en el espanto"), illustrate, better than the detached verses I have quoted, this affinity of atmosphere, of obsession, and even of expression which López Velarde did not go to Baudelaire to seek, but to recognize as his own.

Precise influences have been pointed out in the work of Ramón López Velarde. Mention has been made of Luis Carlos López. With equal propriety we may mention Julio Herrera Reissig, and with greater exactness Leopoldo Lugones. I think that rather than speak of the influence of the poetry of Luis Carlos López on that of López Velarde, it would be more correct to note certain superficial affinities, of a purely thematic character. These affinities appear only in *Devout Blood*, and it is appropriate to point out that the very slight family resemblance is due to the provinces which are similar, if not everywhere identical, in Colombia and Mexico. But the ironic and bitter tone, the caricaturish or satirical relief, not always neatly achieved in the poetry of Luis Carlos López, is absent in that of López Velarde. Certain expressions used by Julio Herrera Reissig, and the use of an affected vocabulary, might cause some verses of the Uruguayan to be confused, when first read, with verses by Ramón López Velarde. But literary taste, that gift which keeps the poet in balance, is always more sensitive in the Mexican than in Herrera Reissig, who placed horrible phrases alongside unquestionable felicities of expression, apparently without distinguishing them, in his ambition to discover startling images. Besides, the love of the decorative for its own sake, which is a vice of Modernist poetry, fortunately does not appear in the poetry of the Mexican López Velarde.

Achievement of the Lugones mode of expression appears to Antonio Castro Leal to be the aim in certain poems by Ramón López Velarde. There is a good deal of discernment and truth in this observation, which he illustrates by quoting a few lines from López Velarde:

> My power to feel follows the scale
> of the slipp'ry barometer, which in violet garb
> holds the voluble shadings of climates
> with an instant and precise honesty,

to which it is easy to add these, in which he speaks of

> the stars and the jovial perimeter of women,
> the sparkling of your slippers,
> the crackling of your dismal skirt,
> the incisive whip of your eyebrows,

and even others in which the Lugones of the *Sentimental Calendar* (*Lunario sentimental*) shows itself:

> Obesity of those moons that went
> rolling along, sleepy and coquettish,
> through a softened blue
> over the trees of the sidewalks.

Indeed, for Ramón López Velarde the poetry of Lugones is both a model and a patent influence in certain effects learned in the magnificent school of the *Sentimental Calendar*, and in the aim to hit the mark by employing the most unusual means. Lugones was for our poet, "the most sublime and most profound poet of the Spanish tongue." "The reduction of sentimental life to psychological equations, a feat attempted by Góngora, has been consummated by Lugones," wrote López Velarde in an article in which he also speaks very lucidly of the role of the critical faculty in poetic creation. "The poetic system has been converted into a critical system," he said. A better judge of himself than of others, the predilection of López Velarde for Lugones is intelligent, and also reveals and establishes his temperament with relation to that of the Argentinian poet. The words concerning the commonplace which Lugones wrote in the prologue to *Sentimental Calendar* seem never to have been forgotten by Ramón López Velarde.

But perhaps it is not justifiable to go seeking the psychological key to poetical composition in Ramón López Velarde beyond the concentrated passion with which he strove to find startling images, and both subtle and precise relationships among people and things. He put the same passion into hating, as the worst enemy, the commonplace, the blurred and worn expression, like a coin passing from hand to hand without leaving or permitting a trace, smooth and conventional, with no value except that ascribed to it by custom.

He would willingly have created a whole language for his personal use, which they say seems to have been the aim of Góngora, whom he loved passionately. But giving new names to things would have confined him to the circle of perfect reason, that is, to the circle of madness. As with any good poet, there was still open to him the resource of submitting nouns to the test of adjectival fire; from it they came out remade, with a different, unaccustomed form, which he sought, and with very frequent success, to give to them. Recovering a paradisical faculty, he started, like Adam or Linneus, to name things, adding adjectives to them in such a way that, in his hands, the eyelids are the "narcotic eyelids," the waist, "the musical waist," and the road "the ruby road." Thus he became the creator and inventor of expressions of "unheard flowers."

Throughout all the work of Ramón López Velarde, from the pages of *Devout Blood* to the poems which formed *The Sound of the Heart*, the presence of the Bible makes itself felt; but not as a source of decorative images, to which the so-called Modernist poets were so inclined, but as indispensable food for the nourishment of the mind and for the expression of his personality.

Like a body clasped tightly to him, he carried it all through his poetic life, not like war booty or a romantic cargo, but like a body which, by loving it, he came to find undistinguishable from his own.

Christian mythology does not serve him, as Greek and Latin mythology served Góngora, to make his poetry more learned and ornamented, but to make it more sincere, as if it formed part of a life lived, or at least desired, by Ramón López Velarde.

When in a poem in *Devout Blood* he wishes to remain and sleep on the pillow of the silken arms of a woman, our poet ingenuously confesses that it is

> to see, in the night of bliss,
> Jacob's ladder filled with fantasies.

The women who pass through his poems have biblical names: Ruth, Rebekah, Sarah. The last-mentioned he finds no longer faithless like the wave, but flexible "like David's sling."

In a curious refrain, the name of Zion appears in several poems. At times he asks a woman to lead him to Zion by the hand, and at other times he is desolate as he sees that women on their way to Zion forsake him. Also he peeps into the breast of a woman and finds it "free of Purgatory and Zion."

He would have liked to be one of the kings of Israel, when the fear, in López Velarde a fear with marks of an obsession, of reaching the "bone-dry and impotent hour of old age" assails him. He then calls upon the coolness of the company of the provident woman not to fail him

> along with the decrepit kings who bound the sickles
> of Israel, and sang
> in psalms, and slept on wild beasts' skins.

He finds, especially in the Old Testament, the concentrated juice of lives which are simultaneously health, religiosity, gaiety, and fleshly pleasure, and which will give him not the ignoble intoxication of Noah, but the perfect intoxication of lucidity.

So, from the paradisical allusions when he confesses himself:

> Attentive to the violin
> of the cherub
> and susceptible
> to the earthly apple-tree,

or when with a tear of gratitude he would like to "salt Paradise," to the curious picture which reminds us of an adorable composition of El Bosco, in which he imagines himself in Thebaid beneath a flight of ravens:

> The legendary raven which feeds the Cenobite
> flies through my desert and leaves me no bread;
> another transports a flower most strange,
> another bears in its beak the spouse of Adam,
> and not even seeing me, all three pass on.

The forty nights of the Deluge made on López Velarde an impression which, in his poems, appears in the form of allusions or images with reference to a personal state of mind:

> My rain is now a deluge, and I shall not see the ray
> of the sun o'er my bow, because on the fortieth night
> my heart will be broken;

or:

> Amber, cinnamon, flour, and cloud
> which, weaving their caresses into my flesh,
> link themselves with the effluvium
> which binds the shipwrecked clusters
> over the crests of the Deluge.

Another time it is not Genesis, but Exodus. The plasticity and mystery of the curtain of smoke and fire, which served as a guide to Moses and the Israelites in leaving Egypt, reappear with equal mystery and singular intimacy when he says to a woman:

> Your shadow
> guided my heart-beats, as the column
> of fire guided the Israelite.

And then, the Book of Numbers, with the beautiful myth of the twelve tribes, serves him for a comparison of a woman's teeth with manna

> with which the twelve tribes fascinated
> by your voice sate their hunger and their retinas.

Less than the Old Testament, the New Testament serves him for the attainment of a full expression of his private voices of anguish. Nevertheless, when he thinks of a return, a maleficent return to his home town, his thoughts go back to the Prodigal Son of the parable related by Saint Matthew, returning this time to a Mexican town, riddled by the grapeshot of the Civil War.

> The rifle shots engraved in the lime
> of all the walls
> of the spectral village,
> black and doleful maps,
> so that in them the prodigal son
> might read on returning to his threshold
> in a nightfall of witchcraft,
> by the light of a petroleum wick,
> his hope destroyed.

And when he sings of the women who were martyrs in the provinces, he recalls, in an anecdote about his native town, the cruelty of Herod, saying:

> This epic also groans, written
> in blows upon innocence, when Herod
> beheads a child of my town.

His first vocation as a seminarist is not absent from this love for the Bible, a love which, when transferred from a feminine to a masculine object, not even the most profane adventures of the senses would be able to wrest from him thenceforth.

The Catholic religion with its mysteries, and the Catholic Church with its offices, symbols, and vessels, serve Ramón López Velarde to achieve the expression of his intimate and innermost intuitions. As in the case of the Bible, his vocation as a seminarist is shown in this precise knowledge of the form which the Church has approved for the celebration of the divine offices. Soon there is observed in his poetry a familiarity with objects and symbols which is far from being sought after. Moreover, there is an intense obsession with certain atmospheres in which are intermingled richness of ornament and its opposite: the wretchedness of the loathsome flock which does not go to the magnificent cathedrals, but to the gloomy and repulsive common churches.

A strophe of a poem in *Anguish* (*Zozobra*) gives us the key to his preferences:

> My spirit is a tapestry of souls, a tapestry
> of souls in a church ever needy;
> it is a tapestry of souls spotted with wax,
> trodden upon and torn by the loathsome flock,

revealing the correspondence between the drama of his spirit and the drama which appears to move and breathe, and in fact does move and breathe, in the precincts within which the religion of Christ, as in a mysterious theatre, performs its offices, and receives its faithful both as spectators and actors.

And still further: Ramón López Velarde appears not to be agreeable to comparing his spirit with a tapestry of souls; to be precise, it is necessary that the tapestry of souls should be spotted, trodden upon, and torn; he must add these epithets to make his wretchedness palpable. In the same way, when he compares himself to the nave of a parish church, he hastens to add "of a parish church in penury."

The Passion of Christ is also his passion. His soul is the vinegar; his pain, an offering; and Christ is not the Christ of everyone, but his Christ:

> But today my soul is vinegar,
> and my ecumenical pain a holocaust
> which smokes in the desert.
> My Christ, before the gall-soaked sponge, pants
> with the arid agony of an exhausted heart.

The vinegar, the sponge, the gall, and also the nails and thorns of the Passion of Christ are also instruments of his eternal passion, which is the passion of love.

Holy oils, monks' girdles, monstrances, and candles appear in his poems with a special, intimate significance. And even in the accidents of the external landscape and in its transformations, he finds a poetical relationship to liturgical objects. Thus he finds:

> the stole of violets on the shoulders of the Dawn,
> the purple monastic girdle of the sunset.

The flames of the purgatory and hell of Christian mythology show their fiery tongues in the poetry of López Velarde as in the pictures of souls of the dead in the churches. And even in the mouth of a woman they reappear:

> your mouth, in which the tongue vibrates protruding into the world
> like a reprobate flame, springing forth from a furnace.

And of his heart he tells us:

> One day I would hurt it like a tongue of fire
> which is brought out to the light from the depths of purgatory.

At other times, the poetry of the *Salve*, which to Ramón López Velarde is a holy oil and a fountain, makes him shudder with a childish shudder.

And so, in an endless procession, sacraments and mysteries of the Christian religion serve him to render more expressive the moods of a soul in which, with erotic bent, woman and religion are indiscriminately embraced. "A virgin was my catechism," he confesses in *The Sound of the Heart*. And in the same book:

> God, who sees in me that without a woman I fail
> in the small and in the great, gave me
> as guardian angel an angel that was feminine.

And just as he impregnates religion itself with an erotic feeling, everything he sees and touches, even the things most inert, becomes humanized and throbs at the slightest contact with the poet:

> In my happy breast was nothing
> of crystal, terra-cotta, or wood,
> which, embraced by me, had not
> human movements as of a spouse.

Expressed with extreme lucidity, concealed in one of the pages of *The Minute-hand* (*El minutero*), we find the consciousness of this peculiar attitude: "I can understand or feel nothing except through woman. This explains why even abstract questions come to me with an erotic temper." Right to his death he retained his erotic temperament which, like his poetry, knew no decadence or decline, because, consistent with his own prophecy, his thirst for love was like a ring set in the flagstone of his tomb.

In Mexican poetry, the work of Ramón López Velarde is up to the present moment the most intense and the most daring effort to reveal the inner soul of a man; to bring to the surface the most submerged and intangible affections; to express the most painful torments and the most recondite distresses of the mind called forth by eroticism, religiosity, and death.

Prologue to *Selected Poems* (*Poemas escogidos*), by Ramón López Velarde, Cultura, Mexico, 1935, pp. 9–32. I follow the text, corrected by its author, published at the beginning of *The Lion and the Virgin* (*El león y la virgen*), an Anthology of Ramón López Velarde, Publications (*Ediciones*) of the Autonomous National University of Mexico, 1942, pp. vii–xxxiii, Library of the University Student (Biblioteca del Estudiante Universitario), Vol. XI.

Jorge Cuesta

(b. Córdoba, Veracruz, 1903; d. Mexico, D.F., 1942)

In Jorge Cuesta the intellectual and moral doctrines of the literary group "Contemporaries" had their most dramatic intensity. He was not the most outstanding of those writers, but yet in some way he was their keenest and most uncompromising mind. He spent his youth in Córdoba and about 1922 he came to Mexico City to study chemical sciences. "This inclination to chemistry," he wrote Xavier Villaurrutia, "was to enable him to establish between literature and science subtle and perilous capillary communications." "Later," adds Villaurrutia, "his friends would call him 'The Alchemist.' And Jorge liked to repeat the famous verse: 'The Saddest of the Alchemists.'"

His first essays, which already showed the complexity and keenness of his mind, appeared in the review *Ulysses*, 1927–28, and then, in the latter of these years, he signed as sponsor the *Anthology of Modern Mexican Poetry* (*Antología de la poesía mexicana moderna*), an expression of the poetic doctrine of his group. In the reviews of the time, *Contemporaries* (1928–31), *Examination* (*Examen*, 1932), *The Book and the People* (*El Libro y el Pueblo*, about 1934), *Mexican Letters* (1937–47), *Workshop* (*Taller*, 1938–41), and *Romance* (1940–41), his poems and essays were dispersed. Of the former, Alí Chumacero made the first attempt to make a collection in a special number of the review *New Land* (*Tierra Nueva: Poesía*, 1942), to which must be added the sonnets found by Rubén Salazar Mallén and published in the review *America* (No. 62, January, 1950). On the other hand, the essays which Xavier Villaurrutia proposed to call *Transmutations* (*Transmutaciones*), in spite of their importance, have not been collected. Paradoxically, the only publications bearing the name of Cuesta are some political articles of the long series published in the dailies of Mexico City.

The constant theme of the essays of Jorge Cuesta was Mexican poetry, concerning which he put forward some of the most sagacious and subtle observations. The complexity of his analyses, which frequently are "clearly obscure," reflect an intellectual strictness which, amid the swarm of perspectives in philosophy, aesthetics, science, criticism, and poetry, appear unable to hit upon the dominant note. Thus his essays are a repertory of problems and suggestions rather than orderly expositions of concepts. Like Richard Gómez Robelo, that strange writer of the time of the "Athenaeum," Jorge

Cuesta, according to his friends, put the best of his mind into his conversations, polemics, and verbal lucubrations. His inner drama was that of an implacable intelligence which annihilated everything, and which, as Alí Chamacero pointed out, could only bring to him "after playing with shadows —the clearest consciousness of nothingness." Finally, confused in this struggle, Jorge Cuesta succeeded in annihilating himself.

ESSAYS: *The Plan Against Calles* (*El plan contra Calles*), 1934. *Criticism of the Amendment to the Third Article* (*Crítica de la reforma al Artículo Tercero*), 1934.

MODERN ART

Irrationalism and Mysticism

MODERN ART is bound up in two significant facts: the reappraisal of primitive art and the reappraisal of El Greco. They are significant because in both one witnesses a deformation of objects, which the academic criterion always regarded, scornfully, as a defect in reasoning: in the first case attributing it to a lack of maturity, and in the second, to an individual organic aberration. Modern art came to show that the deformation was not involuntary, but deliberate and artistic, sought for the purpose of satisfying a certain poetic conception of things. If in primitive art it is ingenuous and in El Greco artificial, this does not make any radical difference in the artistic character of the two. By different routes one arrives in both cases at the same artistic sacrifice of reason. And this sacrifice of reason, this irrationalism, is what modern art, recognizing itself in it, has made prevail over traditional scruples.

This shows us why, with so much appearance of plausibility, it has been possible for all works of modern art to be regarded as mystical where there is seen a deformation of objects, similar to what one sees in the work of El Greco and in primitive painting. But this conclusion is equivalent to attributing a mystic sense to any irrationalistic attitude, and this is wrong. Primitive painting and the painting of El Greco are both characterized by the scorn of reason; both possess a profound religious sense; in both a Catholic sentiment operates; in both "the reasons of the heart which reason does not know" hold sway, as also the pious "Make yourselves as fools" of Pascal. Nevertheless, only the painting of El Greco, strictly speaking, merits the name of mystical. Primitive painting is naturalistic; its religiosity is not in conflict with the happy cult of appearances; it is descriptive and even ornamental;

it does not retreat into any inner world. The baroque character of El Greco, on the other hand, is impregnated with metaphysics; its irrationalism is not ingenuous and sensuous, but tortured and ascetic. El Greco learned from classical idealism to disdain the immediate appearances, the superficial meanings; but he does not stay with it in its impassioned intellectual investigation of nature through appearances.

If, therefore, the inclination of modern aesthetics towards the painting of El Greco were a mark of mysticism it would be necessary to consider contradictory its affinity to primitive painting. But there is no such mysticism. The fact is that the mystical attitude is also a form of total irrationalism, and that mysticism too is a kind of irrational conception of the world. Therefore, we must say that if the mystical expressions of art find a correspondence in modern art, it is because the mystical sentiment is one of the irrational forms of consciousness, which modern art does not hesitate to utilize, attributing to it a natural artistic value.

The question is clarified if one considers that in modern art appreciation has also been accorded to works of popular art, the spontaneous artistic expressions of children, the material of dreams, and even the lucubrations of the insane, none of which can be correctly connected with mysticism. But all are alike in their irrational character.

Modern art is therefore properly defined when one says it is irrationalism in its broadest sense. Nevertheless it may be pointed out that irrationalism is a necessary condition of art, that it is present in all the artistic expressions of humanity, and for that reason cannot be considered as something that is a peculiar characteristic of modern art. But if we remember that it is said of modern art that it is the most artistic, the purest as art, "art for art's sake," we see in what sense the aforesaid definition is true, because in modern art must be seen the purest, the most absolute aesthetic irrationalism that humanity has known.

Strictly speaking, none of the previous irrationalisms, of a mystical, popular, traditional, or other character, was completely irrational; they were always bound to some kind of significance, that is, to the understanding. Primitive painting shocks reason; likewise the painting of El Greco; likewise the art of the negroes and the creations of children. But the fact that this circumstance has always been attributed to an involuntary defect, or to a utilitarian limiting of the understanding, shows that in those cases we are not confronted, as in the case of modern art, with an irrationalism to which is attributed an aesthetic value in its character of pure irrationalism. In the irrationalism of modern art there is no place given to any kind of meaning; reason is not renounced in order to maintain the coherence of the world in which our senses are satisfied; the natural order of the outer world is not renounced for the benefit of the feelings of the subject: *It is an objectivist irrationalism.*

What does this mean? Well, it means nothing less than that irrationality is considered as an essential property of the object, and not as an inner defect of the consciousness, and that, therefore, the very consciousness of the external world is considered to be of an irrational character. According to this conception, the creations of both mystics and madmen acquire objective validity, and relate to the same reality as the creations of laymen and men that are sane; in other words, lack of meaning, or irrationality, is considered to be an essential and natural quality of the reality which confronts our understanding.

To this view modern art owes its profoundly revolutionary character and its profoundly non-popular character, for the ordinary viewer, as happens when he contemplates popular works and even primitive painting, would find pleasure in the non-pleasure of his heart before the works of modern art, if in them he recognized that the sacrifice of reason is due to the usefulness of the sentiment, and to the will of the subject—that is, he would gladly accept irrationalism, if it were subjectivist. But he will not tolerate a sacrifice of reason without a sentimental advantage, *for the benefit of reality itself.*

Form and Meaning

Under the title "Expressionism in Art," the American critic Mr. Sheldon Cheney has published an interesting study on contemporary art. In this manner he explains the title, as well as the object of the work: "I believe that history will give the name 'expressionism' to the development of art which began with Cézanne in painting, Sullivan in architecture, Duncan in the dance, and Craig and Appia in the theatre. It appears to me to be the only exact term to cover the works of Cézanne as well as those of Picasso, Orozco, Wigman, Wright, and Lehmbruck; the only term sufficiently broad to include that varied production of the so-called post-impressionists, *Fauves*, cubists, functionalists, purists, etc." This statement also shows us immediately the method which Mr. Cheney follows in his explanation: that of establishing the *a priori* or possible content of the term "expressionism," according to a certain conception of art that is also *a priori*, and then describing the different ways in which this potential content is realized in experience.

This method obviously is ingenuous; for it is just as ingenuous to try to adapt philosophically, to an historical experience of any kind, a name that will explain it, as to try to gain knowledge of a place from its geographical name. Nevertheless, perhaps to this ingenuousness we owe the fact that Mr. Cheney's book is more useful than other critical studies for the understanding and appreciation of the artistic production of recent years.

Mr. Cheney obviously fails in his attempt to formulate a clear and congruent "expressionist" theory of art; like other critics who previously attempted the same thing, he cannot avoid, in the end, coming up with such ideas as "expressive form," "plastic architecture," "dynamic rhythm," "abstract painting," "mystical significance," in the vagueness of which he smothers his purpose of clarifying modern aesthetic ideas. These expressions, as the author himself also observes, have a purely descriptive and a purely empirical content, which refuses to be fixed by the reason, or to offer a clear concept to the mind. In this way the reader, in the end, finds that his own artistic experience, vague and confused, comes to be the final support of his critical thought for which that experience is hoping to find a base that it lacks.

But this very deficiency in Mr. Cheney's criticism is what enables it to be so valuable and so instructive, because it obliges him to appeal so much to experience that I believe few commentators on modern art have succeeded in setting before our eyes as incisively as he does the aesthetic problems which challenge us in works of contemporary art.

Starting from the idea that, according to the "expressionist" conception, art is a form that is expressive, imagined, and an original creation, Mr. Cheney devotes the major portion of his study to analysis of form. Form is all that enters into painting in a purely plastic fashion: the bidimensional nature of the surface painted, the physical character of the canvas, the inner movement of the painting, the movement with relation to the viewer, the dynamic relations between the different planes, the distribution of space, the volumes, the tensions, the tonality of the colouring, the texture, the decorative order, etc. None of these elements have a "natural" significance; they mean nothing "in nature." But within the artistic concept they constitute form, in which lies the whole emotional value, the whole significance of art.

This analysis of the "formal" elements of painting, by its ingenuous character and by its rigorous empiricism, is valuable as a description of the "expressionist" attitude of the painter and the spectator before the work of art, and for that reason it is extraordinarily interesting. But it is valuable also, and especially so, on account of the aesthetic problem to which it inevitably leads. What does form express? How does form express anything?

As another critic chose to speak of "significant form" to characterize the modern artistic concept, Mr. Cheney takes a special interest in pointing out the impropriety of this term. In "expressionist" art, form *expresses*, but it does not *signify*; in other words, its whole significance lies in its being pure form. But this idea of art evades the problem, and Mr. Cheney does not fail to face up to it, in the following terms: What does form signify in itself? What significance has form without content, form without signification?

This is where the reader must turn to his own experience, and recognize what form signifies, by a "mystical revelation." And this is what is surprising and disconcerting. It is difficult to accept modern art as mysticism. It does not seem consistent that an art which aspires to having a purely formal character, to depriving itself of every external significance, "in nature," should have a significance in the end. Why not take, with a greater ingenuousness, the evident purpose of modern art with precise literalness? Why not deprive it of all meaning? Why not see form as pure form, without meaning in itself and completely empty?

Because when in an "expressionist" picture one recognizes no object adapted to our judgements and feelings, its purpose is evidently that it should not be the object either of our feelings or our judgments, and that it should be a presentation to which no logic and no moral can be applied. This picture means absolutely nothing; its object is to deny meaning, and this negation is what its form *expresses*. Every "natural" presentation is immediately an object of judgements and feelings; in this lies its meaning, and its "nature." If, therefore, the "expressionist" presentation is not a "natural" presentation, it must be concluded that it really signifies nothing. And in the inconsistent aim to seek in it a mystic meaning, a meaning beyond its natural one, one must see simply the repugnance of the mind towards presenting to itself things that are not natural; that is, there must be seen an attitude which no longer harmonizes with the "expressionist" intention, with which it is incongruous and in conflict.

If, then, we carry Mr. Cheney's explanation to its logical conclusion, instead of to its mystical conclusion, what we recognize in modern art is, clearly and simply, a purpose of having no meaning; and if we name this purpose expressionism, we must define the expressionist concept of art as form without meaning. Of course this aim, thus limited, is no longer recognizable in all modern works of art, nor is it identical in the different schools which Mr. Cheney has included in expressionism, but though in this way we deny ourselves a general theory to explain all contemporary artistic production, we gain in the precise definition of the sense of part of this production.

Making of art an imagining of forms without meanings is, in fact, an aesthetic view which has a meaning, without any need to resort to the mystical and supernatural in order to interpret it. It is sufficient to observe it as the product of a logical and moral scepticism, in order to understand in how natural a way it communicates with our minds. In the same way, also, to understand how it can have a purely "plastic" content, devoid of meaning, but without this depriving us of our liking for it, it is sufficient to present a world in which we abstain from evaluating and judging, but not from living.

Is this world possible? This is the question which modern art has asked itself and which it has tried to answer through "expressionism."

Naturalism and Antinaturalism

Mr. Cheney's criticism again sets before us the problem created by what Ortega y Gasset called "the dehumanization of art," that is, by the situation in which the viewer was placed before some artistic works which did not represent the world that was intelligible to him. From the time when the first works of this character appeared, right up to the present moment, the number of those interested in modern art has everywhere increased, but the great gulf separating them from the average viewer has not disappeared. Mr. Cheney's book is a new attempt to translate the language of the former into the language of the latter.

Nevertheless, we see how we inevitably come to a mystical conclusion as soon as we attempt to give a meaning to an artistic creation which has defined itself as "form without meaning." For resorting to an "aesthetic meaning," which can be found in creations which have lost all logical and moral meaning, does not get us away from the mystic explanation. What a thing means is the result of a judgement concerning the thing; if there is no judgement there is no meaning or, what amounts to the same thing, there is meaning only in a supernatural way. And the meaning of any reference to an object which is not a logical or a moral reference, must therefore be, as meaning, nothing but supernatural.

In other words, in Mr. Cheney's criticism there continues to present itself the same abyss which opens up between "the meaning" of the "expressionist" works of modern art and the intelligence of the viewer. He obviously fails in his intention to make of "expressionism" an intelligible art. But this failure is, in the end, the key to the question, for he makes us understand that the meaning of modern art in its "expressionist" aspect really consists in its lack of meaning, in its not being intelligible, in its giving us the vision of the world that makes no sense to the intelligence, in its being the product of a conscious anti-intellectual attitude. From this we conclude that the people who "understand" the works of "expressionism," "understand" them through having avoided any intellectual attitude in viewing them, through having accepted the fact that they are not logical and moral references to the objects offered to the consciousness. We further conclude that if the common viewer does not succeed in understanding them and continues to feel repugnance towards them, it is because he does not set aside an intellectual attitude and insists upon really understanding them, in this way preventing what these works represent from appearing in his consciousness as something proper to it, in an entirely natural manner.

Mr. Cheney, following other theorists in this view, comes to consider modern art to have an anti-naturalistic spirit. Actually, the truth is quite the contrary: modern art, from the time of symbolistic poetry and impressionistic painting, has been the artistic expression of naturalism. Never has there been a more natural art, more removed from all metaphysics. Those strange forms it paints, those unreal bodies, those formless objects, are as natural as those we see in dreams, and it paints them precisely because they are natural. And in this lies its difference from traditional art. What critics like Mr. Cheney, who consider traditional art to be naturalistic, really mean, is that while traditional art imposes upon our representation of things a logical order, in accordance with the nature of the things represented, modern art makes manifest that the *natural* order of our representations does not *logically* coincide with the nature of things; they therefore consider that the representations of traditional art are really less natural than those of modern art, even though the latter do not present to us the nature of the objects represented. But in this view, obviously it is traditional art that, in all justice, is not regarded as naturalistic. Naturalism consists not in the represented thing's being natural, but in the representation being natural.

The idea is false too that modern art was a reaction against impressionism, for in fact, it was nothing but its logical and necessary extension. It was impressionism that liberated the senses, so to speak, from the logical function of constituting natural objects. In impressionism the outlines and the character of objects disappeared; colours became individual in the background of the illumination; meanings began to become confused and unnecessary; the plastic order of the painting ceased to be identical with the special order of the object; contradiction arose as an aesthetic value; the shadows became luminous, the vacuums became filled, the background came to the foreground. Over this new spiritual mood of painting, the post-impressionists were able to discover the "nature" of our representations, the figuration of unforeseen and surprising objects, following a purely pictorial order, as an expression of "pure painting." This could not be the discovery of a mystical or supernatural order; it was merely the discovery that, naturally, in the significance of things there are gaps, real abysses which are ignored by the contours and perspectives in which the significance is presented.

When modern art has been associated with the psychological theories of Freud, whose naturalism is undeniable, more has been done than to establish a purely fortuitous and accidental correspondence, but not because it must be admitted that works of "expressionistic" art are psychological documents that must be interpreted by psycho-analysis; according to this criterion, all works of art of all ages are psychological documents to attract the attention of the psychiatrist. Both error and correctness in a mathematical operation have a psychological content; but pure psychological data do not allow us to pronounce upon the mathematical value of the operation. The same applies to works of art: they may be originated by the repression of a desire or by a sexual frustration, but this has nothing to do with their artistic significance. No, the relationship between modern art and the new psychological theories is due to the irrationalism, to the anti-intellectualism they have in common. Both concede a value, in one case artistic, in the other exclusively psychological, to the irrational and non-moral creations of the consciousness, to the presentation of our sense of things, that is to say, to our expressions, even if they lack any logical or moral sense, even if they lack meaning. The difference between the two cases, that of art and that of psychology, lies in the fact that for the "expressionist" artist, the absurd, the senseless expression, has a value which does not need to be referred to the world of meaning, while for the psychiatrist it has the value of signifying a certain psychological condition in the subject.

This, of course, does not mean that all senseless expressions must have a value for "expressionistic" art. Among the innumerable images which dwell in the consciousness of the artist, some have value and others do not. What must not be lost from view, in judging "expressionistic" works, is that the artistic value of these works is not made to lie in the significance of their representations, even though it may happen that they do signify something.

ca. 1932

The Prodigal Son (*El Hijo Pródigo*), Mexico, August, 1943, Year I, No. 4, pp. 281–85.

SALVADOR DÍAZ MIRÓN

MY ADMIRATION FOR SALVADOR DÍAZ MIRÓN is the culmination of a reservation which extended over many years. So, with the greatest assiduity I have dealt with everything said against the obfuscations in his work, his weaknesses, both aesthetic and moral, and the dark spots that are pointed out in his life. I had an opportunity to meet him and speak with him shortly before he died; but my admiration was already feeling its chains, and I did not make the attempt, though I might also point out in my hesitancy the social shyness from which I have always suffered. But in this case my social shyness was also that same shyness which in solitude has kept awake my distrust of a poetry which never explained its strange capacity to contain, alongside negligences and weaknesses which must be regarded as lamentable, the brightest and most dazzling mental sparks. *Stone Sparks* (*Lascas*) is a more apt title for a book of verse than any other I know. In fact, its bright spots are intermittent and flashing, just like the stone sparks which continually return to their mineral darkness, cold and incombustible. When they were kindled, what was kindled in me was distress because their light was not constant, and the resistance which this distress offered to an admiration which suffered from being restricted. The essay which don Genaro Fernández MacGrégor wrote on Díaz Mirón, in which he deals with him as a pathological case, greatly perturbed me, and this I sought to explain to myself. The same moves me to write today: I find that my admiration remains, and even increases. I now suspect that the humiliations to which I have subjected my admiration have given it a vengeful spirit, and I should not be surprised to see it express itself with rancour.

Even one with no knowledge of the life of Díaz Mirón finds reasons for regarding his work with very little sympathy. From the first, one is struck by the originality of his style as by something sought after, something arbitrary. His small production, furthermore—because Díaz Mirón is practically a one-book poet—causes to appear presumptuous the insistence with which is presented, as a subject and as a moral, the formulation of an "artistic criterion," which in the prologue to the book is called "definitive." Following this declaration, which he makes in 1901, Díaz Mirón is still more definitively silent, as though he were abandoning an instrument that he had proposed only to possess, but not to use. So his poetic activity appears to express nothing but an imagining of what it should be like, given an opportunity which is always reserved for the future: thus, at one time it is idle theory, at another an image of the silence in which he shuts himself up and which probably was not interrupted by any further definitive creation. There is mention, indeed, of the existence of unpublished originals, but apart from the fact that there is need of an explanation for the indolence which has been the cause of his silence, everything points to the conclusion that, if they really existed, if they belonged either to the period of *Stone Sparks*, in which the poet stated that he was publishing only a small part of his original work, or to a later period, they continue to belong to the perceptive spirit for which *Stone Sparks* appears to be the simple, sufficient, and swollen vehicle, and that they were then felt by Díaz himself to be a kind of redundance. The abstinence can be explained in no other way, since right to the end of his life he never ceased to give free rein in his conversations to his love for displaying his talent.

The indifference with which the themes of the poems of *Stone Sparks* appear to be selected and treated is also offensive to the reader, especially when he sees it formulated into the most conscious aesthetic principle of the poet. For that the nature of the subject should be indifferent to beauty is a principle, indeed, which very soon comes into conflict with the morality of our senses, which cannot conceive of pleasure being a sufficient end in sentiment. An indifference of this kind seems to us to lack soul, or to be the product of a sentimental aberration. And even from a merely aesthetic point of view, the lack of necessary connection between the form and the matter of poetry appears to us an organic defect of the imagination. A pure form seems to us to be a hollow form. And we see this borne out in the poems in which the anecdotal element ceases to be the image which guides and contains the poetic sense, and shows itself naked as an idle and empty accessory. And when we perceive this, we find satisfaction in seeing aesthetic pride thus humiliated, that is, in realizing that the splendour of beauty is not a pure profit or pure recreation of art, but that in so far as it is a necessity of its object, it is an essential element in its power.

This same cruel indifference with which, through themes and sentiments most distant and foreign with respect to one another, Díaz Mirón seeks the acquisition of a mere aesthetic pleasure—a selfish pleasure, as he himself calls it—leads us to the distaste for his biography, to the consideration of the accidents of his life (the deaths of which he was the author) which give to don Genaro Fernández MacGrégor his pathological foundation for defining him as an antisocial character. In fact, the resemblance in his case is a good illustration of the disputed unity of temperament which may occur between the life and the work of a writer. The satisfactions which Díaz Mirón gave in his lifetime to his "honour" do not appear to obey any "aesthetics" that are different from those ruling the satisfactions which he gave to his pleasure in poetry. The insensibility, or if we say it with the required emphasis, the scorn he had for what his satisfaction was sacrificing, in both cases prompted him to judge in the same manner that the *subject* in itself[1] lacks importance: so he did not hesitate to victimize it (him)[1] in reality, as in his imagination, whenever his satisfaction became stern and implacable. And, turning this comparison around, the life projects on the work, to increase the repugnance of the reader, the "vast and fierce abyss" which the poet advises us to seek in the "hollowness" of form, in "lyricism" (and the quotation marks for this last word are his), through a sounding, which indeed spontaneously verifies the transparency of the water, since everybody sees it, though preferring not to look.

Leaving for later on a discussion of the morality of Díaz Mirón, it is pertinent that we should observe here that when an alienist defines the characteristics of an antisocial temperament, the society he takes as a reference is an entity free from abnormality by virtue of the same definition. I do not know whether originally there may have been in this medical procedure a begging of principle. But when society is identified with the law in this way, what I see clearly is that in the deduction of the consequences the health of society is confused with the health of the individual as if they were one and the same thing. I imagine the homicide which I might commit, and I am not astonished that the law should punish it mercilessly; but I am immediately astonished at the possibility that it should be considered an antisocial

[1]For "itself" and "it" in this sentence, the meanings "himself" and "him" are also applicable.

act according to the criterion of psychiatry. Society does not appear to me to be in any way a pathological absolute. On the contrary, it appears to me as an organism, whose state of health no one is able to define. But, just the same, as a practical convenience, if society thinks it is suffering as a consequence of my crime, it seems to me natural that it should impose a penalty. All organisms, healthy and unhealthy, react with hostility against what causes them a suffering which society realizes I do not share. The chances are that the crime has in me the healthiest physiological consequences. In consideration of these, I do not think that I could admit my crime to be my illness rather than my healthiness, merely because it was demonstrated that it caused social suffering.

The aesthetics of Díaz Mirón are not, really, any abnormality in taste. If in the view of his sentimental victims the aesthetic crime he commits presents itself as a hurt suffered by the inner society of the soul, the health of beauty is benefited by it. This is also a clear fact, the lustre of which never suffers through all the vicissitudes that an admiration for Díaz Mirón may experience. I have followed the course of this fact like a drama, and I see it as the same thing as the drama to which the poetry of Díaz Mirón owes its character and its immortality. The ups and downs of my admiration are identical to the ups and downs of his taste, which is the only appetite and the only instinct of his genius, since he "definitively" establishes himself in it. Well then, to know the ups and downs of a taste is more than to share in the entertainment of a "lyricism," in the idleness of pure form; it is to know it as true suffering. The weaknesses of the poetry of Díaz Mirón acquire another colour as soon as they are viewed with eyes that have entered into the intimacy of aesthetics which appear as insensibility, only on account of the gratuitous character of their torment. And then there is the distance that lies between the vanity of his themes and the strangeness of the glory that pervades them, together with the strange anguish that could not be contained in anything but a great serenity, which must be very far removed from insensibility or an absence of sentiment, and signifies the silence which Díaz Mirón kept for the many long years following the publication of his *Stone Sparks*. One cannot quite understand why in this most strange book there are brought forward such insoluble lyrical problems, such inescapable aesthetic contradictions, so unfamiliar to poetic culture, so barbarous, in short, and so lacking in transcendency. But it is the fact that he has brought them forward and has withstood them that explains why an admiration for his work, through him, is able both to withstand the most obstinate reservations and the most uncompromising disagreements that admiration for any poetry can have.

ca. 1932

The Prodigal Son (*El Hijo Pródigo*), Mexico, August, 1943, Year I, No. 5, pp. 285–87.

FRENCH CULTURE IN MEXICO

THERE ARE STILL FREQUENT EXPRESSIONS of censure in our letters concerning the influence of French literature upon ours; it is even said that the work of a certain Mexican writer lacks all value for us because it could have been written in France and in French. It is a nationalistic sentiment that expresses itself in this way, but I think that its passion, instead of enriching the country with a knowledge of its originality, comes forth in such a light and superficial way that its end result is a greater ignorance of our history and of the original character of our will as a nation. For I observe that the influence of French culture has been so constant and profound in Mexico that anyone feeling a repugnance towards it runs the risk of repudiating the most personal part of his own life. Mexico is already a country that is French in all orders of its culture, and has been so from its birth as an independent nation, from the first evidence of a will that was free and conscious of itself. And certainly this has not been by chance or because of a passing obfuscation, for then necessarily the time to emerge from it would have come. A century in the life of a people is a sufficient period of time to bring about the separation, evident to anyone considering the question, of the perishable incidentals the people experience and the positive determinants which mark their destiny. Well then, the influence of France has not been an accidental or capricious factor in our national development, but a determining or inseparable part of it, and still more is this so with regard to her personal character, distinction, and quality. Take away this factor and hardly any sense is left to our national existence, and nothing remains of our literature or politics, our society, or our moral concepts. For more than a century now all our cultural life has found its sustenance in France, and it is in acts that spring most directly from our own originality that especially must be noted the effect of such a decisive influence and its justification found, for indeed it exerts a greater influence upon the roots of our liberty than upon its conscious or superficial details.

Our culture is French without any artificial resolution; it is French in a natural manner.

Of course there will be those who will appeal to history and ethnological data to refute the foregoing observation, showing that even though certain French thoughts have had important Mexican repercussions in the past century, one century is much thinner than four in the incrustation of traditions, and that therefore those thoughts do not lose their external character with relation to our true tradition, the sources of which are and must be only aboriginal and Spanish. It will certainly be said that with the same superficiality it may justifiably be claimed that our culture has an American (United States) origin. It will be noted that during the life of our independence the influence of France has affected such a small number of people, that the correct view is to consider them as a group apart, and not as representative of the nation. Even with regard to the nature of the influence, it will be pointed out that it is the modern and superficial manifestations of French thought that have had repercussions in Mexico, while we have been indifferent to its truly traditional and authentic forms. And finally it will be noted that twice we fought against France, thus expressing our determination to expel her from our life.

In view of these justifiiable arguments, I must make plain the purport of my observation. I say, precisely, that French thought has been the most important influence that our national culture has experienced; that this influence is patent in our literary, artistic, scholastic, political, and juridical works—that is, in our strictly cultural expressions; that certainly our internal national life has been more than insensible to this bent of our minds, in which is recognized a minority, small indeed, which may properly be considered as foreign and uprooted with respect to the vast majority of the population. But it must be noted that apart from this small minority the Mexican nation has not had a true existence of its own, and has never grasped its historical responsibility as a nation; that our national society has been a creation and the exclusive responsibility of this minority, and that—outside of its outcast culture, outside of its uprooted works—no national will or consciousness worthy of the name has existed. Regarding the internal sources of our tradition, that is, the aboriginal and Spanish, I point out that they have been profoundly indifferent to our recent national spirit and even constantly hostile to it, and that it has been in a perpetual struggle against these internal reactions that this spirit has succeeded in asserting its characteristic independence and personality. I find already formulated, in an admirable and shrewd historical theory conceived by Vicente Riva Palacio, the thesis that our existence as a nation has been the product of an act fundamentally *external* to our history, that it does not have its roots either in our indigenous life or in our Spanish life.

This *external* act has its roots in France. Certainly more than one mind will find it repugnant to hear it said that Mexico is the result of an "importation of culture," and that the victory of the "imported" culture over our historical data is what lends significance to the latter. The war of the "Reform," even fought for a long period against France itself, was a triumph for republican ideas and the laic state, the most representative French political creations. It may be said that it was a triumph of France over France, and its nature as an intestine war is quite evident. Our existence subsequent to the Reform War, up to our most recent revolution, is characterized as a social movement for the purpose of establishing in a definitive manner the authority of a revolutionary political system, which has no historical or revolutionary significance that differs from that of French radicalism. The history of the French nation has been marked by these two essential principles in their political system: laicism and radicalism, which represent merely the same attitude of mind, manifested now with respect to religious sentiments, and now with respect to economic sentiments. Its result is a free political system, external to the habitual religious and economic interests of the individual. Well now, the national history of Mexico is the history of a free political system, uprooted from the economic and religious life of the country, and interested only in consolidating its liberty; for no other reason has it been forced to contend with our traditional Spanish way of life, symbolized in the Church, and with our traditional indigenous way of life, symbolized in our economy. Our independence meant the radical foundation of an original and free State; our Reform, the radical liberation of our political society with respect to its religious independence; our last revolution is nothing but a radical liberation of this same political society of ours with respect to its economic independence. The three movements are pure radicalism, French radicalism.

The ignoring of this *external* tradition (which on its part does not replace or deny, but on the contrary affirms our Spanish tradition, the original slant of which is that of Renaissance culture, the same that is followed by the cultural development of France) makes even our most immediate and correct political thought appear inexplicable and arbitrary, and renders the language in which it is expressed hollow and senseless. And it must be noted that this ignoring of it is the characteristic attitude of the "Reaction," that this is the essence of that reaction: ignoring and misunderstanding the deep and disinterested life of the mind, whether it be manifested in politics, literature, religion, or art. An alert mind does not fail to perceive the danger involved, even for our political life, in the general intransigence which prompts opposition to manifestations of our culture, feeling that they are alien to it, and that they do not hold to the requirement which is expressed in these terms: "Let us be original as Mexicans." For there is only one way to be original, and that is to be radically so, which already is almost the equivalent of saying: with a French culture. Indeed, this is the most significant existing culture, the truest culture of originality, the most representative revolutionary culture. Repugnance towards it, on account of its character as "imported culture" does not prove our authenticity, but our lack of culture and the dependent nature of our spirit. On the other hand, we are faithful to our spirit if we desire that there should return to our school, for example, the sense of direction and the strictness of its original French culture. I have already stated that justification could be found for claiming that the French influence we have undergone is superficial; but this superficiality is only an indication of how little we ourselves penetrate into the substance of our significance. Indeed, unless we are to end by being unoriented in our most proximate and most necessary spiritual life, we are obliged to penetrate into its "external" and "superfluous" sources, until we find its true and fundamental elements. In the lack of understanding of our "Gallicized" literature there is manifesting itself only a public that is vacuous, uncultured, and divorced from the roots of its own spirit. And the early consequences of its obfuscation are not obscure: it will be left without nutriment or will become a parasite.

In previous times the Romanticism in our literature was no mere chance, nor were its later Parnassianism and Symbolism. Today it is not because our literature lacks a significance of its own that the most recent French literature finds in Mexico a living extension of its aspirations. In the philosophic order it was no arbitrary and meaningless act on the part of Gabino Barreda when he founded the Mexican school of Positivism; nor was it so later in the case of the French thought of Justo Sierra or the impassioned Bergsonism of Antonio Caso. On the contrary, this is where is manifested the most profound and genuine will to achieve a Mexican cultural destiny. And if its manifestations have been timid and of "little significance," it has not been due to the falsity, but to the poverty of its intellectual decision; it has been because an isolated production of French thought does not suffice to give satisfaction to the spirit which recognizes itself therein, but does so in a much more profound manner than the way in which it conforms its accidental and incidental connivance with it. Our lack of significance in this respect is caused in a way contrary to what is generally supposed: by our resistance to a penetration into the sources which, though justly considered external to ourselves, are nevertheless the most fundamental sources of our culture. To ignore them, to despise them as extraneous, to consider them alien to our significance, is what prevents us from penetrating into our own spirit, because of not penetrating into those sources of it. So long as works like those of Alfonso Reyes are censured for their alien spirit and their lack of native roots, we are merely insisting upon divorcing ourselves from our genuine and authentic spirit, making a knowledge of it and its gratification inaccessible to us. It is precisely in that "lack of native roots," in that "alien spirit" that no Mexican can fail to find the true reality of his significance. So long as this is overlooked there will be only confusion in our minds. This will result from our neglecting the duty which our own culture actually imposes upon us, and which is none other than to find, in a will that is external, what is in fact the essence of our own inner will, the origin of our own significance; but within this it is necessary that our responsibility and our profound consciousness of it should be made manifest, and not only a vague, repentant, hypocritical, and obscure spiritual dependence.

ca. 1932

The Prodigal Son (*El Hijo Pródigo*), Mexico, August, 1943, Year I, No. 5, pp. 287–90.

MEXICAN CLASSICISM

THE HISTORY OF MEXICAN POETRY is a universal history of poetry; it could have happened in any other country; it has a significance for any cultivated mind that pays attention to it and aspires to an understanding of the ideals it has served and which have characterized it. These ideals which, in a limited geographical area, Mexico, within a particular society, the Mexican, and in a definite historical period, fascinated different minds, have also been, on account of the variety of their appearances and the variability of their forms, the same ideals that have been followed by the poetry of any other modern nation. Even when, following multiple Romantic tendencies, its products have been most individual or most exotic, Mexican poetry has not been able to avoid showing in this way a universal destiny in poetry. When it has become "Mexicanized," or "Americanized," when for example it has been sought through the use of indigenous words and expressions, inevitably even then it has been just one of a number of exoticisms which have accidentally distracted and captivated the consciousness of a single culture: the Occidental. For this reason, Mexican poetry is a "European" poetry, just as is, strictly speaking, any American poetry.

In a narrow sense, Mexican poetry is a Spanish poetry; but this too is not the base which gives it its individuality, or creates for it a necessary organic dependence; on the contrary, it is one of the bases for making of Spanish poetry a universal poetry. If one were asked to state the particular contribution of Mexican poetry to Spanish poetry, one would be obliged to say, ambitiously but truthfully, that it is universality. This is the goal attained when, within Spanish literature, Mexican literature is capable of possessing independence, a spirit of its own. I am not saying that in Mexico thought has attained its universality, but that necessarily it had been obliged to attain it in order to become Mexican. Thanks to its universality, Spanish poetry was able to provide an origin, and constantly faithful to that origin, the function of Mexican poetry, "within" the Spanish, has been to maintain and recall that universality.

The origins of Mexican poetry are closely linked to one of the most brilliant periods of poetic creation. Its first lisps were classical, perfect works, which do not see their worth diminished by the most admirable universal poetic competition that has ever taken place. At birth it entered into maturity; from its infancy it assumed a higher responsibility which fascinated the greatest minds of a great period, in the greatest nations. Immediately it entered fully into the most honourable tradition and had to satisfy the most exacting standards. It is impossible even to imagine the probability that Mexican thought, at birth, would not have felt the domination of a mode of thought which universally dominated, as it is impossible to imagine either that it could have been born and could have developed in an original manner without the effect of that fascination.

In the history of Mexican literature that identity of its origins with Spanish literature has been a source of embarrassment. Do the works of Juan Ruiz de Alarcón and of Sor Juana Inés de la Cruz belong to Spanish literature, or can they be considered already to belong to Mexican literature? But this problem is absolutely idle, if it is remembered that one is dealing with a *classical* Spanish literature, that is, with a universal language and significance. The odes of Fray Luis de León or of Francisco de Rioja do not belong exclusively to Spain either. The life of a Spanish culture in America is not explicable without a detachment from Spain, that is, those poems were inexplicable without a Spanish classicism and universalism. The domination of Spain in America—in poetry too—was the domination of a universal idea, an idea which also belonged to Italy, France, and England, and one which drank from the "classical" fountains of Greece and Rome. There would not have been a Spanish literature in America if the Spanish language had not been a universal cultivated language, capable of being used to express any temperament, and capable of giving form to a new and original literature in any latitude. In a similar manner in the United States, Latin, for example, would have been adopted as the literary language if English had not possessed, thanks to its culture, and thanks to its adaptability to the most varied ways of thinking and feeling, the capacity to receive within its forms any new and unforeseen concepts. Along with the cultivated forms of Spanish, the popular forms also passed over to Mexico. But if only the latter had passed over, now would be the time when perhaps one could not speak of an original Mexican literature, though on the other hand there would be a "pure" literature in Mexico, which the Spanish writers would always regard with benevolence and which would have figured in their anthologies as their own. But this is not what has happened: from the beginning there flourished in Mexico the critical and reflective forms of Castilian literature.

As a consequence, Spanish writers have traditionally regarded with scorn even the works of Ruiz de Alarcón and Sor Juana Inés de la Cruz, which no mixture of Indian blood excludes from Hispanicism. But they are excluded, apparently, by their critical and reflective character, by their universal nature. The Spanish literature of Mexico has had the good fortune to be considered in Spain as a literature out of caste. This view was quite correct, for it brings it back to the best Spanish tradition, which is not the pure-Spanish tradition, but the classical tradition, the tradition of heresy, the only possible American tradition.

In Mexico there is no indigenous poetry, and no possible autochthonous popular poetry. The popular forms of Mexican poetry are merely the popular forms of Spanish poetry after undergoing the same operation that the academic Mexicanists performed upon the cultivated forms of bucolic poetry, in applying it to the landscape of Mexico. Therefore, there is no pure-caste Mexican poetry, authentically. Mexican purity has not been a *pastiche* of Spanish purity, the "purity" of which, moreover, is very difficult to prove, whereas its adulteries are otherwise. The originality of Mexican poetry is not attributable to anything but its radicalism, its universality. This is what Spanish poetry gave to it in giving it its origin, classically and radically: not some habiliments hereditarily accumulated, but the capacity to carry its roots in its universality, and to find its inspiration therein. Even the indigenous poetry picked up by the Spanish colonizers, like the songs attributed to Netzahualcóyotl, was in its Spanish translation cultivated poetry, related to the themes and figures of Horace; that is, they were "uprooted" and added to a universal and transmigrant tradition.

Any classicism is a universal and transmigrant tradition. In the Spanish thought which came to America from Spain, what emigrated was not Spain but a universalism, a universalism which Spain was unable to retain, since she ceased to emigrate—intellectually. Not only Mexico, but all America was born under the influence of the universal passion which stirred the European mind in the sixteenth and seventeenth centuries, opening their eyes to nature, awakening scientific curiosity, inspiring in it the eagerness to explore its passions profoundly. The influence of America was profound in Europe "viewed from the future" and viewed from a distance. The idea of America became the most live revolutionary ferment, destroying the habitual frontiers of the world, by the sheer power of imagination. This ferment did not lose its force in the present and in actual reality. America, in the thought and action of the Europeans populating it, became representative of heresy. This original situation has rendered impossible a Mexican purity or an American orthodoxy in terms of blood. This situation very soon rendered suspect to orthodox Europeans what was produced in America and naturally aspired to universality.

The American originality of Mexican poetry must be sought nowhere except in its classical tendency, that is, in its preference for universal norms as opposed to individualistic norms. In this way, its fidelity to its origin has been expressed, and in this lies originality. That tendency could not disappear even in Mexican Romanticism, which was a leaning towards individualization, and for this reason our Romanticism was derived directly, and not by inversion, from our academic poetry. Just as the works of Sor Juana Inés de la Cruz and Juan Ruiz de Alarcón are distinguished within Spanish Classicism by their greater radicalism, our later academic poetry is distinguished from its counterpart in Spanish poetry by a greater liberty, by a less rigid adherence to the artificial forms of a "Spanish" Classical school, by a natural desire to keep alive a universal classical school. In other words, Mexican academicism was much less an academicism than the Spanish model; no purism forbade it to find directly in Greek and Latin classical sources authorization for its heresy, and a precedent for its independence and its revolutionary tendencies. One of these was, and this in Spain was blasphemy, that of having no qualms about seeing its models and norms, "in addition," in "French" Classicism.

The relationship which is established in Mexican poetry between academicism and Romanticism remains obscure and appears arbitrary and senseless if judged according to the narrowest scholastic conceptions, which do not generally distinguish perfectly between Classicism and academicism and cast Romanticism against them both. Against Classicism, academicism was the attacking foe. Academicism was a Classicism "without universality," a "private" Classicism. If it is borne in mind that Romanticism was love for the particular in art, reasons will be found for bringing it into line with academicism and not seeing it as its opposite. Nevertheless, Romanticism does differ in its worship of modernity, which made of it, rather than a special point in space, a special point in time, though it has also been both things at once. Well then, Mexican academicism, without a tradition that was classically, historically, and geographically its own, was philosophically made incapable of being a pure and particular Classicism: in it universalism was "necessarily" present. When Romanticism came, since it was a particularism "in time," since it was a cult of "universal modernity," it immediately satisfied the need of Mexican academic poetry, allying itself with it rather than combating its tendencies. The most important outcome of this strange but fortunate and explicable concord was the appearance of Manuel José Othón and Salvador Díaz Mirón, Classicists, Latinists, and Gallicists, modern and American.

The constancy of a classical attitude, even in Mexican "nature" poetry, was what enabled it to resist seeing the landscape romantically, that is, animating it with the sentimental reactions of the spectator. It was necessary to await the appearance of "Modernism" for attempts along these lines to prosper fully, that is, for them to encounter no resistance. In Mexican landscape poetry it may be said that Parnassian forms took precedence over forms strictly Romantic, and this is accounted for by the fact that they were brought in by academic poetry. Doubtless this is not strictly true, and a poet as academic as Pagaza was not free from Romanticism. Moreover, this is already a poetry "of nature" that belongs to Romanticism, however Parnassian, descriptive, and impersonal it may be, for there are no strictly impassive descriptions. For the same reason it might be said that even a poet like Pesado did not keep clear of the Romantic virus, since he found satisfaction in descriptive poetry. But what merits special attention is the reciprocal movement, that is, the influence exerted upon the Romantic attitude by academic poetry, or in other words, the humanism which academic poetry cultivated with admirable rigour.

This influence is what is to be observed in Manuel José Othón. What gives to his poetry such special value is his strict adherence to it. Superficially, Manuel José Othón was only a Romantic poet, slow to abandon academic habits. But if the question is considered from the opposite angle, one discovers how profoundly interesting it is. It might be said that in Manuel José Othón is shown the absurdity of a humanism of the landscape. There is something more than a geographical reference in his two sonnets to Clearco Meonio, in which he shows how different are the respective landscapes which surround Clearco Meonio and himself. He himself is surrounded by an arid, desert landscape, a landscape which does not reflect human sentiments, and remains insensitive to them. This contrast is brought out with a profound meaning, that is, with a literary meaning. If Clearco Meonio is the academician who is slipping towards Romantic beaches, Manuel José Othón is the man who, on the contrary, is rising towards a more demanding ideal than that of the complicity of nature. Manuel José Othón is the man who is poetically disillusioned about landscape, and naturally, therefore, about the American landscape.

When the first "Modernistic" poems were published, Manuel José Othón could not restrain his disgust. That Romanticism could go as far as that, to him made no sense. The thought is disconcerting that Othón should have conceived a "strict" Romanticism and that he should have been shocked on finding in poetry that the emerald of the trees was more than a rhetorical metaphor, and that the lakes were actually confused in the minds of poets with silver, sapphire, and lapis lazuli. For in poetry are already verses like these:

> evening's pale elegy
> and the blue ballad. . .

But it is beyond question, with all his constant lapses into Romantic sentimentalism, that Othón did not notice that his Romanticism was opposed to Classical ideals which were living in academic forms. It is certain that he did not feel different in his Romanticism, not only from his contemporary Joaquín Arcadio Pagaza, but even from his predecessor José Joaquín Pesado. And certainly in the poetry devoid of academic scruples which caused his alarm, he did not condemn acts, the sin itself, but the theory, the conscience that took pleasure in sin and divinized it. Years later, Enrique González Martínez resuscitated and justified the shock of Othón, within "Moderism" itself, making a philosophy of it, as it were, and recalling significantly, though perhaps not deliberately, the apprehensions of Othón with regard to inanimate things, to which "Modernism," following the Romantic tendencies, fearlessly and disrespectfully attributed the most intemperate and the most superficial animation. These verses, which González Martínez might claim, are by Othón:

> Climb the harsh rock, and with me you will hear
> What things are saying in the night

and these others, much more significant:

> But who can hear the mysterious voices
> raised in mystic murmur
> by the deepest hidden womb of things?

The lack of comprehension with which Manuel José Othón received "Modernism" is a judgement which will never cease to weigh heavily upon "Modernistic" works, and which explains the isolation and remoteness that Salvador Díaz Mirón maintained to his death, while "Modernism" prospered and succeeded in momentarily muffling voices more durable than its own. The voice of Díaz Mirón was silenced not only metaphorically. From the publication of *Stone Sparks*, his poetic activity stopped, because he was undoubtedly incapable of overcoming the unhappiness caused in his mind not only by the nature of the new literary lights, but also by his own conflicts, out of which he proposed to create in his poetry an impassive and diaphanous consciousness. The fullness of the soul was greater than the strength of the mind, but not greater than its pride. The fate of this poet was the same tragic fate which maintained the dignity of Othón's poetry; not with Othón's ingenuousness, but with a demoniacal penetration; not with traditional limits deliberately accepted, but with a critical passion that devours all limits; not with academic temperance, but with an implacable dogmatism.

In order to understand the greatness of Díaz Mirón, he must be read with acumen; one must avoid hearing his voice directly; one must cast doubt upon what he states in a direct manner in order to catch hold of what he is responding to. In Díaz Mirón there is a demoniacal interlocutor whose voice is one we like to get at by penetrating through the poet's direct words. His thought and his reasoning are interrupted in every utterance. Between the reading and the reader there is interposed an external sound which removes the text to a distance, so that it must be gone over again. A "no" is thrust in, which renders necessary an insistence, on the part of the poet, in order to answer it and to prevail over it. The poetry of Díaz Mirón is a tortured poetry, but it is tortured deliberately; it is a poetry without kindliness, a poetry with an enemy, incapable of expressing itself except in conflict, as the product of hostility. The attention he wins for himself by this effort allows one "also to hear his silence."

If one regards Salvador Díaz Mirón as "Mexican Romanticism," it is made clear what was meant by the observation that Mexican poetry, paradoxically, came to Romanticism in its search for universality, in its search for a deeper discipline; one then has the truest explanation for Mexican poetry's abandonment of the Spanish school and for its turning its eyes towards France, where it could discover that "Romanticism was Baudelaire," a modern Classicist, fascinated by the "American" temperament of Edgar Allan Poe, the philosopher of poetic radicalism. Salvador Díaz Mirón is a Romanticist, but one must go to French Classical poetry to find an idiom logically as rigorous as his. He is a Romanticist, a poet of nature, but it is difficult to find universal examples of the implacable reasonableness of his nature. In Othón's desert one still sees that

> . . . the carnation bud
> in the straw-hued plantation of cotton
> lifts up from its "snowy" crest the white note;

but Díaz Mirón's desert is a desert in which no whiteness remains and in which there is no mist or shadow to protect fancy:

> The spot is unpleasant, with stench and gloom.
> The teasel, nopal, and nettle
> Thrive; and the air smells of dung,
> shellfish, and mire; and the gnat
> swarms and plagues.

Díaz Mirón's Romanticism certainly did not aim at releasing the concept from its promises and obligations, or at liberating the fancy and giving free range to dreams. The consequence of this sternness is also one of those which cannot be attributed to Romanticism; the poet became unfruitful, sterile, and arid, like the landscape he portrayed. My admiration finds the tragic heroism which inspires it in this proud fate: Díaz Mirón preferred to kill his fancy rather than sacrifice his reason. I am not one of those who lament it. For me, his fruitfulness is in his silence. His silence is what one listens to especially: other poets were unworthy of silence.

In reality, Mexican Romanticism did not limit itself to a tortured life in company with the academic poetry which kept alive the Classical ideals, but the Romanticism which remained faithful to the strict Romantic manner did nothing at first but repeat Quintana, Martínez de la Rosa, Espronceda, Bécquer, and Campoamor. It cannot be called Mexican, except for the accident that placed it in Mexico; it has no personal significance. Until the advent of "Modernism," it did not feel it possessed complete liberty, and it lacked authority, for academic poetry took authority from it, confining it, and limiting it to the satisfying of uncultivated and popular tastes. In the "Modernist" poets Romanticism finally found its fullness and its triumph; no longer was it restrained by any discipline. It was the "Modernist" poets who made intoxicating cadences and glows of the Arabian Nights freely swarm over the landscape; there was no object, however lifeless, which in falling within the radius of their attention, did not lend itself to indulging their sentiments and obscuring its own reality. It was they who definitely made poetry sensitive, tender, and plaintive; it was they who made nature historical and history phantasmagorically novelesque, and elaborated a moving bourgeois civic poetry. It is impossible to deny that some of the works possess merit; but these are the works that get away from their true inclination, the inclination that is noticeable in the two most noted poets of the movement: Manuel Gutiérrez Nájera and Amado Nervo, who are two sad, melancholy, grief-stricken, neuralgic, and exceedingly bad poets.

In the midst of the romantic expansion of "Moderism," Enrique González Martínez becomes alarmed in the same way as Manuel José Othón, and provides him with a new and vigorous reinforcement for his scruples:

> He seeks in all things a soul and a hidden
> sense. . . .

Just as significant as that Díaz Mirón has been our greatest Romanticist is the fact that González Martínez has been our greatest Symbolist. Most certainly it was no accident or tolerated aberration that there should have been placed at the head of an "aestheticist" school in Mexico a man with the temperament of a moralist, who does not brook in poetic thought any kind of intoxication and who takes no pleasure in it. The well-known verse:

Wring the neck of the swan of deceitful plumage,

is a heresy within Symbolism. Nevertheless, González Martínez "is Mexican Symbolism," not in spite of, but because of that heresy. The morality in his poetry is a reserve formed by a reflective penance, a kind of repentance; its aim is to keep satisfaction at a distance, and to keep pain alive and awake; on account of this morality he approaches beauty with distrust, preferring that it should be falsely imagined rather than falsely present. This distrust is named with exactitude if it is said that it is precisely a "Mexican distrust," that it is the fear of being individual, of not being within a universal harmony. Beauty, González Martínez appears to be saying, is not familiar to me, it is not near to me; and in this consciousness he restores to it its true extraordinary and furtive character, and does not yield to the Romantic fatuity of thinking that one brings it clinging to one's lips. Martínez's ambition is certainty, clear evidence, and his virtue is strengthened in a proud indifference similar to that of Díaz Mirón. The effect of his reserve is that his spirit must be sought in the profundity in which he keeps his conflict, and that one must admire an attitude which leads Mexican poetry to reflection, and which restores it, if not to universality, at least to universalism.

Mexican "Modernism" has for literary history the interest of having been a "Gallicizing" movement which detaches itself completely from Spanish traditions. Therefore, relatively, in its totality it also represents an heretical decision, but only in González Martínez does it remember its goal of universality. In this movement the possibility that a Spanish spirit might come to thrive in Mexico was completely ruled out; but not only was it unable to avoid a Mexican spirit, but its own particularist tendency has created and fomented it. Mexicanism in our contemporary poetry is merely a "Modernism" applied to the Mexican landscape. All the Mexicanisms in our literature have been merely terms applied to the landscape, that is, they have had nothing but a purely ornamental character. Moreover, they have been able to exist only when a foreign poetry, through its tendency towards the particular, has turned its attention to "things Mexican" as its object. In other words, Mexicanist literature has not been Mexican literature, but the exotic element in a foreign literature. Historic Romanticism made a Mexican poetry out of Mexican history; the Spanish literature of customs made a Mexican literature of customs; the exoticism of the French Symbolist and post-Symbolist poetry made possible a new Mexicanism, just as in Spain, from as early as the time of Juan Ramón Jiménez,[1] it has made possible a new Spanish spirit. Consequently it is not surprising that in no Mexicanism of Mexican literature is it possible to find the slightest originality.

Ramón López Velarde, a poet who died in 1921 at the age of thirty-three, has been made the representative of a Mexicanist school; he has been made its representative, but wrongly so, since Ramón López Velarde is one of the most original of Mexico's poets. It seems as though in him the silence of Díaz Mirón and the reserve of González Martínez became manifestly fruitful and revealed their direction. It is true that, apparently, López Velarde is the poet of the social landscape of Mexico; his most lauded poem, *The Gentle Homeland* (*La suave Patria*) is a song to the picturesque element of Mexico; his first book of verses is the song of the provinces. Nevertheless, in this aspect of López Velarde one must see a tolerance on his part rather than his true character. Within his own treatment of landscapes he does not succeed in concealing a classical sentiment, similar to that of Othón, but a much more significant one. López Velarde is also a man disappointed with landscapes. His treatment of landscape reflects a sense of pleasure in the feeling of his disappointment, a feeling which becomes all the more tragic because it is not physical nature that reveals to him its aridity and implacability, but the human landscape; it is man that becomes diaphanous as a desert, and who exposes himself to the most ardent and arid rays of light, and loses his innocence.

In Ramón López Velarde Mexican poetry is reflected upon passionately, repudiates its artifices and acquires a consciousness of its aims which is comparable, in its penetration, to the immortal poetic consciousness of Baudelaire. The poems in which this poet left the best of himself are not numerous—there are only a few—but they are sufficient to have him acknowledged as the most personal poet that Mexico has ever had. The flame kindled in his poetry is not only enough to give to his verse its brightness, but it illuminates the entire destiny of Mexican poetry. In Ramón López Velarde a sense is found

[1]Won the Nobel prize for literature in 1956; he died in Puerto Rico in 1958.

in all the Mexican poetic endeavours whose originality it is difficult to perceive on account of their indecision, their reserve, or their proximity to the different schools. Even the most forgotten academic poetry recovers a value, certainly unknown to itself, when it is considered from the position of López Velarde. In this great poet, prematurely deceased, the poetic experience of Mexico is isolated, summed up, and purged; it grasps in a profound way "the American character" of its destiny, and makes that destiny universality.

The Book and the People (*El libro y el Pueblo*), Mexico, August, 1934, Vol. XII, No. 8, pp. 367–78.

Agustín Yáñez

(b. Guadalajara, Jalisco, 1904)

Agustín Yáñez continued his studies to the point of obtaining, in 1929, admission to the bar. About that time he was one of the leading spirits in the literary group which published the excellent review *Provincial Banner* (*Bandera de Provincias*, 1929–30), which Yáñez directed in co-operation with the poet Alfonso Gutiérrez Hermosillo. He came to Mexico City to study philosophy, and received his Master's degree in 1951. For years he taught literature and history in different schools in Guadalajara, Tepic, and in the capital of the country, and also in the National University and the College of Mexico. He has been President of the Publication Committee, Co-ordinator for the Humanities, and President of the Technical Council for Research in the Humanities, at the National University, and Vice-President of the International Institute of Ibero-American Literature. In addition, he has directed the Section of Libraries and Economic Archives of the Department of Finance, and has represented the University and the Government of Mexico at international cultural gatherings. He was also Secretary-General of the Organizing Committee for the celebration of the Fourth Centenary of the University of Mexico, and was in charge of the publication of the *Complete Works* (*Obras completas*) of Justo Sierra, which the National University published in commemoration of the centenary of the birth of its founder.

Besides the *Provincial Banner*, Yáñez directed the review *Occident* (*Occidente*, 1944–45), and contributed to literary and cultural reviews and to daily newspapers of Mexico City. He has been a member of the Seminary of Mexican Culture, and has served as its President. He is a member of the Linguistic Academy and of the National College, and in the period 1953–59 he was Governor of the State of Jalisco.

Agustín Yáñez is one of the most outstanding contemporary prose-writers. In addition to his historical and philosophical essays, Yáñez, who made himself known in the world of letters as a narrator, has written beautiful recollections of his childhood and youth in Jalisco; also a fine work of description, *Mirage of Juchitán* (*Espejismo de Juchitán*, 1940), and a few novels, among which are distinguished for their originality and richness of imagination those of the volume *Archipelago of Women* (*Archipiélago de mujeres*, 1943) and *At the Water's Edge* (*Al filo del agua*, 1947), a powerful analysis of the dramas of conscience in the provincial medium, and one of the most important Mexican novels. Yáñez's essays and studies in literary criticism are mainly devoted to Mexican themes, with a predilection for those following the course of writers who have contributed to the constitution and definition of our nationality. His biography of Father Las Casas, his essay on the capacities of the indigenous soul, his study of the life, thought, and work of Justo Sierra, and his essay on Fernández de Lizardi[1] are fundamental contributions to the study of these themes.

BIOGRAPHY: *Fray Bartolomé de las Casas, the Conqueror Conquered* (*Fray Bartolomé de las Casas, el conquistador conquistado*), 1942; *Don Justo Sierra. His Life, Thought, and Work* (*Don Justo Sierra. Su vida, sus ideas y su obra*), 1950.

ESSAYS: *The Social Content of Ibero-American Literature* (*El contenido social de la literatura iberoamericana*), 1944; *Mexican Notes* (*Fichas mexicanas*), 1945; *Alfonso Gutiérrez Hermosillo and Some Friends* (*Alfonso Gutiérrez Hermosillo y algunos amigos*), 1945; *The Spiritual Climate of Jalisco* (*El clima espiritual de Jalisco*), 1945; *Yahualica*, 1946.

MEDITATIONS ON THE INDIGENOUS SOUL

AUTHENTIC TESTIMONIES PERSIST with regard to what our pre-Hispanic ancestors possessed and bequeathed to us by way of culture.

In the first place, the plastic arts, from ceramics to architecture, passing through the stages of sculpture and codices; whatever the place and time of their making, those forms leave no room for doubt concerning the magnificence and subtlety of the spirit which inspired their creations. The work of time, neglect, errors, and sectarianism, far from destroying their majesty, accentuate the powerful mystery with which today, as in the early days of the conquest, monuments, masks, and codices astonish the mind that contemplates them.

In the second place, the genius of the indigenous languages bears no less powerful witness to the native capacity of those who used them and cultivated them. The effectiveness and the beauty of a language must be measured by its ability to express abstract ideas and spiritual concepts. Of the Náhuatl language Clavijero[2] states that the friars had no need to introduce foreign words to explain the truths of Christian theology and philosophy; a language of surprising elasticity,

[1]Satirical novelist at the time of the Mexican independence movement, most famous for his *The Mangy Parakeet* (*El Periquillo sarniento*), 1816.

[2]Mexican historian of the eighteenth century.

it possesses a great treasure of transformations, inflectional endings, and shadings. Within the same sound, as in that of the vowel *u*, according to whether it is open or closed, are contained different meanings. Thanks to the variety of tonic accents, Náhuatl possesses short, long, and half-long syllables, with full and partial pauses. The tendency to the use of metaplasms and the conglutinating prosody bring difficulties and fresh splendours to this language, pronounced exquisite and most elegant by the missionaries who delved into its secrets with evangelical purposes. The Tarasco language is elegant, harmonious, and rich in onomatopoeia. The Zapatecan language is one of precision and beauty, adapted to the ready creation of images, amenable to a conglomeration of meanings, delicate and musical through the play of interposed vowels and accents which modify the sense of the words. No less effective, powerful, beautiful, and perfect is the Mayan language, "which appears to have been the language closest to the one which through the lips of our first father gave to each thing its essential and natural name," according to Father Gabriel de San Buenaventura. Otonomí has thirteen vowels. Mixteco changes the meaning of many of its verbs through modification of the tense, and is a language full of gravity and majesty. Totonaco, Matlacinga, Huaxteco, etc., are other fecund languages, rich in synonyms and in combinations of letters and rhythms, adapted to the expression of delicate thoughts and feelings. Looked upon as a whole, the indigenous languages surprise us by the differences which mark them off one from another and which are produced by different racial units and different ways of living; but they also show ultimate analogies which reflect characteristics common to the native peoples, and may be compared to the resemblances between the different forms of pre-Cortezian plastic art. Even if the most recent critical efforts had not demonstrated the existence of genuine literary forms, and in spite of the transcriptions and deliberate reworkings of those who later collected them, passing them through the sieve of an alien sensibility and of the apostolic concern for converting the people to Christianity, it would be impossible to accept the contrary conclusion, and even more so to fail to recognize the cultural maturity reflected by the linguistic maturity. Languages never attain a maximum splendour and the highest degree of expressive possibilities through natural and spontaneous developments; rather, they are the sure index of the cultural history of social groups, and of the growth, plenitude, and decline of peoples. Expressive amplification and refinement result from compelling anxieties and collective successes; they reflect needs which have enriched the storehouse of life, either as projects proposed or as attained realities. As a neat sociological and linguistic theorem, the one just enunciated recalls to mind that principle concurrent with our thesis, according to which, as José Vasconcelos states, "wherever there has been architecture there has also been philosophy; one cannot construct with grace and lightness, with majesty and harmony, unless one conquers, in the realm of the spirit, the harmonious and firm order of a coherent and comprehensive philosophic doctrine." With greater cogency arises the connection between language and culture, the former being an integral mark of culture the development of which requires not only the full vigour of the intelligence, but also the maximum development of the sensibilities. Thinking and feeling, or stated more precisely, styles of living, are made manifest in the genius of languages.

The wealth of religious beliefs, the ritual, and the customs derived from these are the third great witness to the indigenous soul, which is not invalidated by the obscurities that go with it, or by the errors in interpretation which it has suffered from the very beginning of the conquest, or by the mingling of ideas, rites, and customs which commonly disfigure it when viewed through the centuries elapsed. The fear or ignorance of some of the aborigines who were consulted about such matters by the missionaries, the insufficient understanding of some of the latter, and their concern to explain the old ways from the Christian point of view, and to use the old feeling as magic to make an opening for the new religion, the distortions of the subject by the various chroniclers who gathered the information, and the policy of persecution and relegation to oblivion are other sieves which, by allowing certain living, invariable, and unanimous notes to escape, only prove their authenticity. This is well stated by one of the early and outstanding recorders, Fray Bernardino de Sahagún, when he says: "What is written in this volume it is impossible for the human understanding to feign." That was so suggestive that the completion and the publication of the work of Sahagún were prevented because it was considered a dangerous encouragement of indigenous sentiments never completely subdued.

The authentic traits of the primitive religions which we preserve, whether regarded as objective realities or as an aggregate of subjective attitudes, coincide with the essential notes that we discovered in the plastic arts and the linguistic forms, fusing together to give categorical testimony to autochthonous faculties, later doubtless greatly transfused, as action and as power or multiple disposition, over what today constitutes Mexicanism.

In all areas of pre-Cortezian cultures, a power of abstraction, systematically and very energetically exercised, appears as an outstanding endowment. It is not difficult to discover it in the testimonies of the plastic arts which have come down to us. Abstraction marks one of the invariable characteristics observed by Alfonso Caso in pre-Hispanic art, and in Mexican art in general, even in its most recent manifestations: "The naturalistic representation of the details, while the work as a whole is purely imaginative and conceptual. Minute observation is expressed in the artistic production with almost photographic exactitude, but the work itself does not represent an objective reality, but an idea, a product of the fancy, an entity which lives only in the unreal world of myth." The abundance of abstract names and facility in the use of other words to represent ideal objects, the metaphorical and imaginative tendency, the inflections employed as semantic modifiers, and the variety of meaning introduced by the use of accents all show in the languages the mark of abstraction. But the religious sphere is the one from which it is projected with greatest clarity and over broad areas, characterizing the theogony, cosmogony, and cosmology, in general the philosophy of the indigenes (primarily, metaphysics and sociological foundations), because the entire life of those peoples is immersed in religion, and everywhere (in war and peace, in the home and in public commerce, private conscience and collective enterprise) is directed towards supernatural ends.

The idea and the representation of the gods are mere abstractions; even today, anyone contemplating the ancient idols requires a great capacity for abstraction in order to understand the sculptural and hieroglyphic forms, and still more so in order to capture their elemental symbolism. There were ethnic groups on our soil that made no use whatever of material means to represent the ideas of their form of worship: they lacked idols, temples, ministers, and organized public rites, but the religious bent of their lives is beyond question. "The religion of the first inhabitants of Mexico consisted in the adoration of a being which originally was not represented by any visible image." . . . "The Zuinametin lacked priests and rites." (Cf. Francisco Plancarte y Navarrete, *Prehistoric Mexico* [*Prehistoria de México*], Chap. 2). Not even at the peak of the theocratic hegemony in peoples like the Aztecs, when religion came to be a strict formula for the outer and the inner life, and when the esoteric character of the religious principles reserved for a caste was accentuated, did idols and ceremonies become ends in themselves. Popular consciousness merely saw in them symbols of "invisible and impalpable" realities, the working of the epithet constantly applied to the gods in the prayers collected by Father Sahagún. Sun, stars, forces of nature, etc., are also separate manifestations of the supreme principle which rules the universe. Even Father Las Casas explained this metaphysical concept on which is based the very broad idea of aboriginal monotheism. Of course, archeological investigations have proved beyond question the absolute identity of many divinities, for example, Zuetzalcóatl and Xólotl, morning and evening symbols of the crepuscular stars. The great and fearful god Tezcatlipoca is Telpochtli the eternally young; he is Yáoth, the lord of warriors, who because he is a representation of the nocturnal heavens is in a way identified and contrasted with Huitzilopochtli, the blue, diurnal sky. Huitzilopochtli is bound up with Xiuhtecuhtli, lord of fire, who also receives the names of Huehuetéotl, the archaic god, and Frocozauhqui, the god with the yellow face. Possibly in esoteric religious circles could be seen clearly the relationships and the identification of the long line of gods and goddesses, which archeological investigation may at a later time bring to light. The major myths explain celestial phenomena connected with the other forces of nature: winds, water, origin of the earth, etc., which were also objects of particular myths. The marvellous Mayan and Aztec chronologies demonstrated the unification of all these mythical ideas into a single idea, regulating both time and life. This most certainly shows a great power of abstraction. In the different types of heroic deaths, in the urge to warfare, in the exceedingly severe penances, in the pedagogical ideas, in every form and in every act, the metaphysical is present, abstracted from life in systematic fashion.

Alongside the power of abstraction, and in constant interplay with it, realism appears as a supreme category in the indigenous soul. The observations of Alfonso Caso regarding the plastic arts are confirmed in every area of pre-Hispanic cultures: realism in linguistic forms, realism in religious concepts and representations, an awful and absolute realism in the human sacrifices, in the palpitating hearts as supreme offerings worthy of the supernatural: a sustained, detailed, naturalistic realism in which some see only the gross aspects insufferable to Christian sensibility. Springing from the regions of realism is a succession of metaphysical objects, through abstraction from phenomena: the sun, as a heavenly body, is Tonatiuh; as a giver of life, lord of our flesh, the creator being his own first creature (according to Fábrega), he is Tonocatecuhtli; finally, as supreme creator, at the summit of this series of abstractions from the reality of the heavenly body, the sun is Ometecuhtli, the representation of which is the first and most prominent figure at the beginning of the *"Vatican" Codex*. The artist portrays him in the highest region of the heavens, richly attired, with the sign of light on his brow, engaged in the act of creating both the higher or divine heavens, six in number, and the seven lower heavens which are within the view of man. All thirteen are at the feet of Ometecuhtli, on the first lamina of the codex. Then he continues with the creation of the earth and of the first creature, which is Ometecuhtli himself made into Tonocatecuhtli, now abstracted as an operative force, detached from the divine essence, through which, by union with the earth, are created Zuetzalcóatl, the evening star, and Tezcatlipoca, the moon, which also came to be a symbol of the nocturnal heavens and of the occult powers. This is followed by prolonged acts of creation whose attributes correspond to those of the real things of the universe, and express the cosmic order in the mind of the Nahoas, the dominant, wise, and able race.

In the interplay of realism and abstraction appears another faculty which might be called the flair for paradox, conciliating opposing terms, and by means which must have been ready and habitual, even though they may never be thus understood, or the congruence of their forms grasped by the Western mind, for which the terrible grandeur of Coatlicue, or the nexus of mutual support between life and death, will always be insoluble enigmas. The beauty of the astronomical myths and the mingling with blood of the materials which could serve for the making of idols; the reverential ceremonies offered to captives who, representing the figures of certain gods, would then be sacrificed; the marriage of Cipactly, the first created, ethereal light, and Oxomoco, meaning literally "the place that serves as a way for the feet," or the earth, the place of toil and misery; the materialism of the offerings and funeral rites along with the belief in the supernatural destiny of certain dead men; rigid asceticism along with sensuality and licence, mainly in certain religious festivals of the highest order; the supreme exaltation of life by the shedding of blood and by the death of thousands of human beings; the glorification of enemies sacrificed in acts of worship, etc.—all these are customs in the lives of the aborigines practised with the greatest naturalness and in which they found a rigorous logic, through their mental, emotional, and volitional agility, which brought into a close relationship very different places of reality, adjusting symbols and styles with an astounding eloquence, with profound meaning and a disconcerting originality.

This sets in relief another of the constituent elements of the indigenous soul, namely, its poetic capacity, in the strict sense. The pre-Hispanic man moves within an intricate network of fictions made out of heterogeneous realities, and there is no situation which lacks a cabalistic sense. At the moment of birth, and even before, he is enveloped by the intricate systems: nuptial ceremonies with their sorcery, techniques in magic during pregnancy and childbirth, astrological fatalism with regard to the newly born, the inseparable connection between the calendar and religious ideas, conventions which controlled the educative process and social destiny. In the heavenly bodies, in the skies, mountains, fountains, rivers, lakes, and seas, in trees and plants, in every animal species, there lies a hidden sense which is breathed into them by invisible spirits. There is scarcely a place which is not dedicated to some divinity. Homes, streets, roads, markets, schools, have their tutelary god; however humble they may be, all things possess magic virtues, for good or for evil, qualities more important for man than the immediate utilitarian properties they can offer him, and which he will not use if the anterior mythical prejudice stands in the way of his need. The indigenous soul is a persistent sentimental projection in all directions and the power of its fancy creates around it a world of double dimension, and a double perspective.

In this situation is developed the faculty which has been best observed and which we shall call that of detachment. It engenders many characteristic attitudes of the Indian: his states of mind that range from melancholy to deep and heavy sadness; from expectancy to inertia, scorn for life and its vanities, joyous familiarity with death, imperturbality of countenance in the face of sufferings and calamities. The newborn babe was greeted by the midwife with these words: "You have come into this world in which your parents live in toil and hardship, where there are fierce heat, cold, and winds, where there is no pleasure or happiness. . . . This is not your house into which you have been born, because you are a soldier and a servant, you are the bird they call *quecholli*, a bird they call *zaquan*, a bird and soldier of one who is everywhere; but this house into which you have been born is but a nest, an inn at which you have arrived, it is your entrance into this world. . . . Your own land is another land. . . . It is for you to give drink to the sun of the blood of your enemies, and to give food to the earth, whose name is Tlaltecuhtli, with the bodies of your enemies. Your own land, and your heritage, and your father, is the house of the sun, in the heavens. . . . Perchance you will have merit and be worthy of dying in this place and will there receive a flowery death. . . ." The phrases and tones of the discourse were repeated on the most important occasions in life. When the Aztecs elected an emperor, he was counselled in this manner: "Perchance for some length of time you will bear the burden entrusted to you, or perchance you will be cut off by death, and your election to reign over this kingdom will be as a dream; take heed that you be not ungrateful, despising in your heart the bounty of our lord god, for he sees all secret things and will send upon you some punishment, as he deems fitting, for it may be in his wish and will to obscure you and cause you to disappear, or he will send you to the mountains, and to the grassy plains, or he will cast you into the dung heap, amid its filth, or he will cause some ugly or vile thing to befall you. . . . You are the image of our lord god and represent his person; in you he is resting and you he is using, as a flute. In you he speaks, and with your ears he hears. . . . Take heed that it shall never cross your mind to say: 'I am lord; I will do as I will' . . . but rather it behooves you often to remember what you previously were, and the low place from which you were taken to be placed in the high station where you now are, without merit of yours . . . for this seems more like a dream than like reality. . . . Our lord god holds us in the hollow of his hand, and is moving us about there, and we are as round balls of clay in his palm, who go rolling here and there and make him laugh, and he uses us. . . . Perhaps he wants to test you and find out the stuff of which you are made, and if you fail in your duty, he will put another in this high place. There are many that are generous, most prudent, and of great ability. Humble yourself and bow down and weep in sadness . . . consider, lord, the place in which you are, which is very high, and a fall from there has great danger. . . ." (Cf. Fray Bernardino de Sahagún, *General History of New Spain* [*Historia general de las cosas de Nueva España*], Book VI.) When the foreigner destroyed the double dimension of the indigenous world, the detachment and static disorientation of the natives constituted the gravest problem for the new nationhood.

In the course of previous considerations one might have observed another essential faculty which, with a scope similar to that of religion, embraces and limits intuitions of a different order and the emotional proclivities of the indigenous soul; this faculty is plastic expression. The Indian is capable of representing by means of lines, colours, and volume both immediate realities, discernible to the senses, and the most abstruse intellectual concepts, poetic creations, religious mysteries, and volitive decisions. In the hieroglyphics we find impressive and exact proof of plastic power; even with complete ignorance of the actual meaning, the honest contemplation of the hieroglyphics makes deep impressions, which from visual and aesthetic astonishment lead us to a sense of the scope of those images and the richness of spirit of their authors. For example, will anyone reading the indigenous literary version of the myth called the Myth of the Four Suns fail to appreciate the fact that the expressive elements in the corresponding paintings of the *"Vatican" Codex* are more eloquent and complete? What we now call the epic attitude of the creative imagination, or the outlook on the external world (the world as a spectacle), from which are gathered materials which later the imagination will transmute into peculiar forms of the said attitude (the epic forms), appears with magnificent proportions in the autochthonous hieroglyphics, demonstrating what we would call the egregious and constant capacity for epic of the ancient races; but this would not be the sole characteristic, strictly speaking, either of their plastic art, or of their varied forms of expression, or of the spirit of those cultures. The hieroglyphics capture the external world with a compository power which lends exceptional mobility to its representations, whether considered in isolation or, better still, considered as a whole. The plethora of realistic elements and details, especially in the Aztec codices, covers the plastic panorama; but there is also evidence of the totalizing, conceptual, and symbolic aspiration. The codices are not mere photographic successions, even within the Hispanic period, and even in the treatment of facts. Back of these realistic, historical circumstances, which we would properly call epic, arise the metaphysical ideas, the sense of the deepest inner life, which we would call lyrical attitudes and forms. The double basis, real and ideal, of the indigenous world is represented in such paintings in an integrated manner. Consider the hieroglyphic transcription of the Christian *Lord's Prayer.* Consider some scenes of the so-called *Canvas of Tlaxcala,* which are true elegiac forms. We thus come to the conclusion that our old cultures did not know or realize as distinctive forms what from the time of the Greeks has been designated epic, lyric, and dramatic genres, but when these terms are used with direct reference to literary creations they are nevertheless valid for all types of creative imagination, since they correspond to different attitudes of the mind. The indigenous attitude includes all possible planes, internal and external, real and ideal, and expresses them all together. Plastic art, in spite of its obvious power to express the external with its multiple complications, differs from Western canons; it conceives and realizes its aims by most peculiar means, with complete originality in relation to the forms which here, for greater clarity, we shall call European. And the same may be said of literary samples which oral tradition brought to the knowledge of the Spaniards, who preserve them written in phonetic characters, and these samples positively do not fit into the classifications of Western rhetoric.

The aptitude for plastic expression is manifested in the structure of languages by the symbolic power of words, whose morphology brings out different meanings; and just as in the visual arts colours have a metaphoric value, so in languages the change of accent and the introduction of particles develop the content of words, the etymological decomposition of which is equivalent to an accurate analysis of plastic expressions: consider, for example, the wealth of meanings in the etymology of names given to the Aztec divinities, true linguistic hieroglyphics which reveal the plastic sentiment projected in them.

All religion, with its absolute power of absorption into life, is an uninterrupted series of concepts, emotions, and forms of a plastic order. Perhaps if those peoples had achieved a phonetic script, abandoning the pictorial angle from which they did their thinking, feeling, and willing, the physiognomy of their life and culture would have been different.

Expression in the plastic implies a series of admirable aptitudes: sense of proportion, which presupposes, in turn, mathematical mastery; aesthetic taste, which governs a very marked rhythm, patent in all the works of old cultures that have come down to us; physical and chemical knowledge on which are founded the most varied techniques in all the crafts; popular competition animated by a single spirit; hierarchical ordering of the elements, which doubtless reflects a very deep-rooted idea which, moreover, is confirmed by the testimony of social life. One of these aspects has been pointed out by Alfonso Caso as a constant characteristic of Mexican art, a characteristic which consists in "transforming each motif into a decorative motif; Mexican art is a decorative art whose fundamental mode of expression is rhythmic repetition. Hence there is the necessity of symmetry, and also the desire to cover with decoration every possible space, without leaving large plain surfaces"; the sum of the attributes of the gods, the identity of many of them, the repetition of ceremonies and prayers, the complicated ritual—all these are manifestations of the decorative in religion. And as for languages, we can still see the importance in them of the ornamental elements: adjectives, epithets, images, metaphors, and the free prosodic rhythm in a pleasing symmetry. Outstanding in this aspect of rhythmic, decorative repetition is that literary fragment which has come into the hands of Sahagún, in which is related the birth of Huitzilopochtli. As for the rhetorical knowledge implied in this plastic art, we are immediately astonished by the aptitude for mathematical calculation, especially when before the great architectural structures we recover from the first emotional shock and analyse the technical process of the construction. Sometimes the site of the work is a marvel of orientation, of understanding of geography and landscape, of surveying (we have in mind the sites of Xochicalco, Monte Albán, Tepozteco, Uxmal, Chichén Itzá, Teotihuacán, and Tenayuca). At other times, in the general lines and in the distribution of the decorative elements, the sense of number, which is the basis of the rhythmic sense, flourishes without solutions in series: an unconscious amplification, upwards, of the high platforms or ornamented motifs in order to give a harmonious total impression. There are also the splitting up of surfaces in accordance with esoteric ideas and the grouping of solid masses and ritual edifices. Nothing is left to chance. In everything there enters a calculation, with a rigorous foresight which keeps in mind the solemnity of the place. Even the acoustic conditions were taken into account. As a ready example, take the citadel of Teotihuacán, which makes one of the most powerful impressions that can be had anywhere on earth. And if we consider the durability of the materials, the secrets in the colouring of statues, buildings and codices; or if we think of the knowledge of astronomy which produced chronological systems like the Aztec and Mayan, of the devices for carving rock crystal and precious stones, for digging quarries, smelting metals, preserving feathers and making mosaics of them, etc., we shall agree upon the spiritual greatness demonstrated by the plastic art of those races.

Under the influences of four centuries, which have been an alluvium of different bloods, devastations, building, beliefs, ideas, doubts, new needs, problems, anxieties, and contradictory forms, the Mexican of today still feels some kind of mysterious atmosphere, subterranean and familiar, which is given off from the domestic vessels and other forms of ceramics, from the toys and other forms of popular handicraft, from the melodies, rhythms, colours, dances, linguistic forms, dress, politics, and household furniture, the accumulation of images in the homes, the religious hybridism, the lotteries with astronomical and zoological insignia, the superstitions, the burdens, the hopes, the cunning, the indifference, the habitual activities, the common gestures and attitudes of the people, all marks that become more pronounced as one penetrates more deeply into the social strata whence they come. These are all living realities which make up the atmosphere of the national life and through whose more or less occult power efforts to annihilate them have been scotched. There the indigenous soul lives on with its heritage, and it has been a vain error to try to ignore it and to deny its force. By such action its vices have become more dangerous, and its virtues are neglected as lost forces, lying stagnant in the history of the nation. A certain kind of absurd shame has come to be felt for the indigene, a mark of one of our greatest shortcomings and of ignorance with regard to what the indigenous was and is, so far as it subsists within the national soul.

Preface to *Indigenous Myths* (*Mitos indígenas*), Publications of the Autonomous National University, Mexico, 1942, pp. vii–xxxv, Library of the University Student, Vol. XXXI.

Justino Fernández

(b. Mexico, D.F., 1904)

Justino Fernández' first published works were on historical themes, but he was later to devote himself completely to art criticism and aesthetic investigations. In spite of having contributed some fine studies on colonial architecture and popular art, his most important studies are on aesthetics and the modern and contemporary art of Mexico, on which he has published an excellent treatise. With regard to the painter José Clemente Orozco, Justino Fernández wrote a book debatable in its enthusiasm and methods, but fundamental for an understanding of the great mural painter. In addition, he is the author of a work on the general interpretation of the spirit of present-day painting, and of a mature study of the aesthetics of indigenous art.

The peculiar tone of Fernández' essays and studies is the investigation of a philosophical character which he applies to his view of art. The memorable philosophical lessons of Dr. José Gaos left a profound impression upon his mind, and this impression has been enriched and refined in his latest writings.

Justino Fernández studied at the National University. Along with Edmundo O'Gorman he published the Alcancía collection. He is a Doctor of Philosophy and master of his specialty in the Faculty of Philosophy and in the School of Plastic Arts. At the present moment he is director of the Institute for Aesthetic Investigations at the National Universiy.

ESSAYS AND MONOGRAPHS: *Biographical Sketch of don Vasco de Quiroga* (*Semblanza de don Vasco de Quiroga*), 1937; *Modern Art in Mexico* (*El arte moderno en México*), 1937; *Tomás de Suria and His Journey with Malaspina in 1871* (*Tomás de Suria y su viaje con Malaspina en 1871*), 1939; *The Dance of the Shell Gatherers of San Miguel Allende* (*La danza de los concheros de San Miguel Allende*), 1941 (In collaboration with Vicente T. Mendoza); *Catalogue of Religious Constructions in the State of Hidalgo* (*Catálogo de construcciones religiosas del Estado de Hidalgo*), compiled by J.F., I: 1940, II: 1942; *José Clemente Orozco. Forma e idea* (*José Clemente Orozco. Form and Idea*), 1942; *Prometheus. Essay on Contemporary Painting* (*Prometeo. Ensayo sobre pintura contemporanea*), 1945; *Catalogue of Religious Constructions in the State of Yucatán* (*Catálogo de construcciones religiosas del Estado de Yucatán*), compiled by J.F., 1945, 1946, 1952; *Rufino Tamayo*, 1948; *The Mining Palace* (*El palacio de Minería*), 1951; *Coatlicue*,

Aesthetics of Ancient Indigenous Art (*Coatlicue, Estética del arte indígena antiguo*), 1954; Claudio Linati, *Civil, Military, and Religious Costumes of Mexico* [1828] (*Trajes civiles, militares y religiosos de México*), Introduction, study, and translation by J.F., 1956.

OROZCO, GENIUS OF AMERICA

OROZCO IS DEAD and Mexico is in mourning. In all America there will be hearts seized with pain and sadness because his prodigious hand will never again paint the truth as he could paint it; because the drama of the man will never again climb the steps to illuminate enclosures with stirring forms; because the nails have been drawn from the last scaffoldings and a wreath has been placed upon his tomb.

But at the death of the genius, weeping is out of place. We shall hold our tears in the silence of our own hearts for the great friend, the man, who really leaves a void. The greatness of his work does not permit the spirit to be cowed, since it infuses fresh stimulation to keep in motion, untiringly, in harmony with his life, art, and example.

Real genius is rare, because those men are rare who achieve the unstable equilibrium of their being. For some, genius is an explosion out of orbit, a divine intoxication; for others, genius is calm and serenity, absolute equilibrium; for me, it is dominated passion, a lyrical sense of limitations, being there, but in movement, a paradox, a sustained equilibrium which gets lost in one's hands, to return continually to a state of suspension. There is no better example than that dome of Guadalajara, where all the possibilities of being become present in its essential and limited repertory, like all that is human, with the greatest possibility of man's greatness remaining at the centre: being through burning up.

And so Orozco lived, burning up until he consumed his material substance and was converted for others into a living essence; for how could he fail to live in the walls and vaults he painted, at least till this or other worlds live with some sense of humanity? As some are converted into books or into good or bad memories, Orozco became converted into painting of the best kind, that kind that is not made by painting, but with the red-hot and entire being, always working at the limits of its own possibilities.

Orozco is the first great creative genius of American art, the first since America has been America; with full consciousness of his action he burned his ships to "see if he could" have being without them. He wrote: "Why should we be always on our knees before the Kants and the Hugos? All glory to the masters! But we also could produce a Kant or a Hugo. We also could extract the iron from the bowels of the earth to make machines and boats. We knew how to build marvellous cities and create nations and explore the universe. Were not the two races from which we sprang of the breed of titans?"

"Glory to the masters!" he says. They are the others, or the past, that he respects. It was not a matter of unconscious rejection, but of the programme for a new and magnificent adventure: being his own self, by his own efforts, feeling himself heir to glorious traditions and aspiring to their renewal in America.

On another occasion, at Dartmouth College, he expressed himself in these terms: "It is useless to talk of Tradition. Certainly we have to place ourselves in line and learn our lesson from the masters. If another way exists, it has not yet been discovered. It appears that the cultural line is continuous, without breaks, from the unknown Beginning to the unknown End. But now we feel pride in saying: This is not a limitation; it is our own effort within the limits of our own strength and experience, with full sincerity and spontaneity."

His life was a continuous effort to be himself in his American surroundings, and therefore out of himself, from this starting point, he faced the spiritual problems of our times with such profundity and with expressions of such a high order, that the line of titans to which he belongs is evident, and among them he takes his place.

In his painting he meditated upon and expressed (for in Orozco the thinker and the artist are one) this America in its origin, as a new and human world, not as a new *thing*, and the significance of the Conquest in terms of human understanding, not of "philias and phobias," of Hispanicisms or indigenisms equally discredited; he could see how from the clash of cultures of different types, as from a painful childbirth, there arose a world with a new significance of its own. He never played politics with the theme, because he was trying to clarify the real nature of our being, not to erect statues to anyone, though his work turns out to be a monument to America.

With a keen sense of contemporary reality he portrayed the Mexico of today with its historic world, and from this he interpreted the historic significance of the world; therefore his work has universality, since he never considered America, Mexico, or himself as an isolated fact, but always in relation *with* everything and *with* all humanity.

At the outset in his mural painting he painted *Christ Destroying His Own Cross*, as if he despaired of all salvation, as if he definitively rejected such a possibility, and while he re-introduced into art a transcendant sense, he decided simply to *burn himself.* It is the road he travels from the walls of the Preparatory School to the vaults of Guadalajara; when he comes to those of Jesus, the incandescent man can no longer show his face because it would inspire terror.

His authentically liberal sense of human existence is reflected in his politics; always truthful, he hated falsehood and sham, never offered aspirins, and therefore could strike right and left. For this reason some have considered him a destructive anarchist or a contradictory and negative spirit. It might be said that his ideal was "Liberty for truth," and though difficult, nothing could be loftier or more expressive of his absolute good faith. Liberty and creative action in art were something more than lures for him. He never allowed himself to be brutalized by politics, and few have understood what he meant when he said: "Artists do not have, and never have had, political convictions of any kind, and those who think they have them are not artists." Orozco is an exemplary sample of liberty, the liberty that man makes for himself, that he takes for himself, that Orozco has made for himself; therefore in contemplating his works the spirit moves freely and passes through the horrors and anguish of this world *burning itself*, leaving its body in it.

I said earlier that genius too is a paradox, for nobody has expressed the present and the concrete as Orozco did, and nobody has been able to equal him in giving to it its exact value and in remaining suspended in his own fire. His work is related to the immediate in a very direct relation, but he converts everything into the mediate, and what is here of interest is his creative activity and his ultimate sense of existence. Thus his immediate and specific themes have their own substance, like chapters of a work that must be read between the lines, and every printed letter forgotten. Precisely because his work is all shot through with history it is in the ultimate analysis exceedingly human, and great art viewed from any angle.

His only true and explicit theme is man here and now, in his individual concreteness, because he knew that to be a man is to be an individual, to accept one's own personal responsibility and to live burning oneself. Needless to say, his concern was not for the isolated individual but for the necessary relationship *with* others and *with* all that constitutes his historical world. Those who abominate this individualism do so because they hope that others will save them or burn them, or burn or serve "humanity." Orozco condemned himself to action.

The "beyond" this world appears in his work as a limit to man, as an unknown, as a dark hole always open to any kind of possibility, but dark. He knew about existence here, between the *unknown Beginning* and the *unknown End*; he had experience of only the fire.

According to the above notes, Orozco is a modern man more than any other that has lived in the world of art, and he is American. The first of these he is in his decision to *burn himself*; the second in his intention and his work. The significance he comes to have in the history of twentieth-century culture is a thing to be pondered.

Among the great artists of the Modern Age, Orozco has his standing and his place. Raphael is an idealist anchored to tradition and with his face turned towards Antiquity; he is a new beatitude, there is no drama in him. Michelangelo is another type of idealist, tormented and unsatisfied, who found in Neo-Platonism, according to Panofsky,[1] the metaphysical justification of his own being; in him coincide the nonacceptance of the reality of existence and its cure at the same time, and therefore it is dramatic. Goya is a believer in immanence, in the modern sense, and his cures are related only to those that belong to this world. Orozco is the one who achieves modernity with his full consciousness, and fully, because he is neither the pious man with his eyes turned towards the past, nor is he an unsatisfied man, nor does he swear by a possible or impossible "beyond," but decides to *burn himself* here, in the reality of what is here, and in the very fire of his creative activity. Of course, though all I have said would require greater development, Orozco is more closely related to Goya than to any other, but he differs from him in that he carries everything to its extreme and to a heroic magnitude, which, however one may account for it, Goya did not achieve.

After Ingres and Delacroix, painting was thrown into that ingenuous trifling with "art for art's sake" or "pure art," actually an absurd invention of the bourgeois world, a formalism in which painting continues to be sunk right to our own day, and more than ever turned into a plaything, into little abstractions or childish decorative impulses, save for Mexican mural painting and a few exceptions in Europe: Rouault and Dalí, in a certain measure, and the great Picasso. This last artist, of doubtless genius and admirable, holds a position with respect to modernity which consists in saying something old in a new way, because Picasso appears to me as an *essentialist*, since apart from the *joie de vivre*, so dear to "art for art's sake," his constant falling back on the symbol of the "woman sitting," besides others, leads the viewer to

[1]A contemporary German-American art historian.

one essence that is permanent, immutable, eternal, one that is reflected in the mirrors of the past and future in a repetition which changes only in form, but is actually always the same. Picasso really gives little importance to historical forms, to time, which becomes an accident; what interests him is that permanent and unique essence, and therefore he plays with forms, but not with the content. Picasso is a modern classicist, whose classicism consists in being an essentialist and whose modernity is expressed in taking life as best one can, and at times, of course, one must overlook certain lapses, like *Guernica*; but in his work there are few of them.

In relation to the other two creators of Mexican mural painting, Rivera and Siqueiros, Orozco is different, as was to be expected, because Rivera is a classicist in his forms and a modern who is indifferent to everything except the triumph of man in this world—in the historico-mechanistic way—and back of the turbulence of history, as a good classicist, he aspires to a final rest; in him the drama is historico-remediable, because the important thing is to reach the calm and serene goal. Siqueiros appears to be a modern classicist in a certain portion of his forms, but in another portion he is not, for he is also indifferent to anything that is not action. If the oppressed did not exist, he would invent them, provided he had a reason to be in motion. It is the motion itself that interests him; rather than *burn himself*, like Orozco, he wears himself out in it.

Of course, in making a sketch in this way, I lose sight of other directions taken by the painters I am here considering, including Orozco, but I wanted to reduce the picture to its essentials. Well then, in relation to the attitudes taken in the past and present of modernity, I said that Orozco is the one who has the fullest grasp of the modern man, but without being unconcerned about his transcendency, having solved it with matchless courage, deciding not for the *joie de vivre*, but for the pain of living, seeing clearly the pain of man, grieving for him, and taking him on his own back.

It is interesting to see how, in spite of the sufferings and imminent danger of further sufferings, the consciousness revealed by contemporary painting, in a general way, is of the type *joie de vivre* (read "art for art's sake"), or a refusal to face historico-spiritual problems and an abandoning oneself to the *jouissance* of forgetting them, a sin which perhaps Baudelaire himself would have condemned. Before this panorama the mural painting of Mexico has a place apart as an exception, because in one form (with Rivera or Siqueiros, in the historico-social), or in another (with Orozco, in the historico-philosophic), it has made special themes of concern out of the problems of man in our time. That America should express a consciousness of this kind, and that in thinking of itself it should think and feel itself to be in a relationship of solidarity with others, and that it should express itself in great forms of art, seems to be in tune not only with the times, but with an ultimate sense of human dignity that is laudable in every respect. While the world is arguing and rending itself in the present for a supposedly better "tomorrow," European painting, in a general way, expresses a clinging to the only absolute that it seems to have left: the *joie de vivre*, as opportunity presents itself, and there is no doubt that this also has a profound meaning, perhaps an ultimate instinct for self-preservation, with or without dignity.

Orozco is the greatest exponent in contemporary art of the most modern and most up-to-date American consciousness, and of course not only because of his spiritual attitude, but because of the moving, grandiose, and original forms in which he expressed himself, I name him: *Genius of America.* I call him so, besides, because his mode of expression has an authentic boldness which is inconceivable anywhere else, without detriment to universality.

Picasso is the greatest exponent in contemporary art of the European consciousness; as a classicist, he is a traditionalist in his forms in some original way. Nevertheless, these do not match, and only occasionally do they approach, the monumental forms of Orozco.

If Orozco is a fully modern man, as I see him, with an ideal of fire, Picasso is a half-modern man, with an ideal of *joie de vivre.* Is it possible that the Mexican resolved, and was bold enough, to take a step into modernity which the Spaniard, more cautious, has not made up his mind to take? A question of tastes, some will say, or of circumstances, according to others. Certainly it is a question of ways of life elevated into artistic categories. In any case, they are two ways of feeling, thinking, imagining, and painting what human life is.

With this question of the American and the European consciousness it is not my intention to show a radical dualism, which from any point of view is untenable, or to deny the values of European painting. It is a matter of the spiritual circumstance of Western culture in which two great artists operate in different ways. Orozco operates by drawing near to the danger, Picasso by keeping a certain distance away from it. Both do their work with supreme mastery.

Many will still have to become informed, for their benefit, that Mexico, or America, has produced the great painting of our time, and that this painting, so penetrating in historical consciousness, has been carried to its limits by the new and fertile genius of Orozco, whose dramatic expression has a compass still unsuspected in the culture of the century which, moving along other currents, has achieved the atomic bomb. Orozco abominated everything mechanical; he was vital movement converted into art, with a keen critical sense, which for him meant being an artist. He felt and expressed as no one else did the pain of being man and the joy of creating, and he accepted his condition completely. Through his infinite joy as an artist, he elevated that transcendent pain to the category of a strong and beautiful art. He had faith in life, and by converting it into fire he made of himself a torch. This is the meaning his capricious biography holds for me.

American Notebooks (*Cuadernos Americanos*), Mexico, Nov.-Dec., 1949, Year VIII, Vol. XLVIII, No. 6, pp. 247–53.

César Garizurieta

(b. Tuxpan, Veracruz, 1904)

The stories and tales with which Garizurieta made his beginning as a writer were praised for the naturalness of their humour and their imagination, for a certain easy charm, of a popular flavour, which expressed one of the main features of the personality of this native of Veracruz. In maturity, César Garizurieta successfully attempted the essay, and following his interest of those years in investigating the "essence of the being of the Mexican," he wrote some pages which—once they escape from academic style and structure and freely adopt a very Mexican tone of "relaxation"—in their treatment of the same questions that are analysed seriously by others, hit upon, if not the right answer, at least a new and fresh perspective.

Garizurieta graduated in law from the National University. He was deputy to the National Congress, and later had a prominent post in the Department of Agriculture. At the present time he is our diplomatic representative in the Republic of Haiti.

ESSAYS: *Agrarian Policy* (*Política agraria*), 1931; *Reality of the Communal Land* (*Realidad del ejido*), 1938; *Catharsis of the Mexican* (*Catarsis del mexicano*), 1946; *New Theory of Colours* (*Nueva teoría de los colores*), 1947; *Mexican Realities* (*Realidades mexicanas*), 1949; *Introduction to Things Mexican* (*Isagoge sobre lo mexicano*), 1952.

CATHARSIS OF THE MEXICAN

THE ARTIST ACCOMPLISHES HIS WORK by objectivating his sensibility through the medium of "lyric intuition"; out of his feelings, which are intangible, he creates something material or immaterial, but capable of being captured through the senses. The contemplation of sentiment constitutes art. The artist projects his feelings through images, whether in the plastic arts, music, or poetry. These ideas are not his own; they are a precipitate extracted from "Aesthetics in a Nutshell" by Benedetto Croce, which he wrote for the *Encyclopaedia Britannica.*

We can explain the above by the example of Alexandre Dumas Senior, who in writing his novels represented his heroes objectively by means of puppets which he himself made, for since the characters were numerous, he did this in order not to make a mistake with them, such as by killing one that he had already buried in the previous chapter. In one drawer of his writing desk he would hide the personage who was travelling, and in another drawer the one who was in love or dying. A good way to understand art is to do this staging that Dumas did with his novels: his personages were materialized sentiments.

Man creates his work of art in accordance with his sensibility and the nature which surrounds him, but principally in accordance with the social world which men themselves integrate. The maxim of Seneca may be repeated: "Man cannot jump on his own shadow." The artist, like the madman, is a realist; he exacerbates his sentiments with deep roots of reality. The madman of Mexico City may feel himself to be a general, a millionaire, or President of the Republic, but never an Eskimo, because this lies outside his sphere of experience. The artist accomplishes his work through the medium of his feelings and with images drawn from the medium to which he belongs.

Literature, as social content, is the image of the reality in which the artist lives; it is the representation of the world in which he lives with respect to time, customs, habits, or language. Lope de Vega and Calderón de la Barca, in their theatrical works, concern themselves with the problems of their time: the struggle of the feudal lords against the king, at that time the protector of the people. The monarch, in the advent of the monarchy, is a revolutionary who constitutes himself a defender of the poor against the greed of the feudal lords. Miguel de Cervantes Saavedra, in *Don Quijote*, expresses his personal thought in relation to the period in which he lives, criticizes a false literature of shepherds and knights which do not exist, and spares the rogue, who is an authentic part of Spanish reality. Voltaire, speaking through *Candide*, destroys with his satire the philosophy of Leibnitz, the so-called philosophy of optimism. In any tragic or comic circumstance, the character is in the habit of repeating: "I am in the best of all possible worlds," the basic premise of the author of *Fundamental Treatises*. Jonathan Swift, through his character Gulliver, whether in the country of the pygmies or in that of the giants, criticizes the philosophy of the senses of George Berkeley, which makes of the senses the only form of knowledge. Literature is not a simple spontaneous creation of the human mind; it corresponds to a reality which the artist feels with his reason and brings out in a poetic form.

Mexican literature has not yet created a character who represents the Mexican type, to characterize it from a psychological point of view, because it does not penetrate down to popular roots, even though there do exist toddling profiles which may serve to create it in the future. The literary characters are pure costuming; they lack soul. In their psychology they lack depth. They act in the face of life like puppets. They are false cinematographic cowboys dressed like private individuals or puppets with the head of a chick-pea and wrapped up in *crêpe* paper. We see them in the personages of don Carlos González Peña or don Federico Gamboa. *Santa,* despite the archaic 606 and the turbid permanganate and its best successors, neosalvarsan and penicillin, is actually Emile Zola's *Nana,* depicted by the photographer Napoleon as dressed like a Puebla doll, away off in the stony land of San Ángel.[1]

The spiritual metabolism of the writer must live in harmony with its time; but writers, particularly those of the past century and part of the present century, have imported, like commodities from overseas, form and content originating in other countries. This is why the character in a novel or tale is not incubated. Up to the present, writers are just beginning to take note of the local and popular. In psychological types we have not yet created anything like Quijote or Candide. In the national atmosphere there is a mixture of dissimilar social strata, some still unliquidated and others yet to be born: feudalism, liberalism, capitalism, and socialistic dreams. Out of these social groups has come nothing definitive for the creation of the Mexican type; but, I repeat, there is a nascent national literature with brilliant psychological outlines of what the Mexican type may be in the future.

To understand art, which is a product of society, we must possess an idea of the man who constitutes it, and know his essence. We must therefore discover a man who is the archetype of the Mexican, who is the measure, pattern, or highest common factor of the society in which we live. It is not necessary to invent him, because he can be extracted from reality; he could not, of course, be Diego Rivera, José Vasconcelos, or Lázaro Cárdenas.[2] It is necessary to select a type of man who in his vices and virtues appears as if seen in perspective. He could be

[1]A suburb of Mexico City.

[2]Cárdenas was a soldier and statesman, President of Mexico from 1934 to 1940.

studied in the Castañeda asylum for the insane, because in madmen there does appear, as if seen through a magnifying glass, the character of the Mexican. That is where, in the sum of them all, one finds what constitutes the personality of the Mexican, seen in comic or tragic form as if it were a map in high relief. There, magnified and outside the reality of reason, one can analyse the character and the temperament of the Mexican; their sum is what Mexican society can be in its psychic aspect, this being understood as a caricature. In the schizophrenics, the deranged in reason, and the manic depressives, who are deranged in the senses, the zealous investigators can determine characteristics of what is Mexican.

We have already seen that the elements in our national literature for the study of the Mexican are scant; to find him we must seek him in other sources. Professionals in the subject have done something by turning to some systems implied in the biotypes of Viola, in the psychological types of Jung, in the psychosomatic classification of Ernest Kretschmer; but without satisfactory results, since in the relating of knowledge which must exist between subject and object, the latter was lacking. The investigator carried out his introspection and thought he was himself the Mexican, like the one who said that because he was ugly and swarthy he had an inferiority complex. The systems of psychological investigation already mentioned are good, provided that many individuals are studied to establish rules. The Mexican of these gentlemen is in their memory, which repeats what they have read; but in reality he does not exist, because there has been no object of knowledge.

Lexically, *to know* means: "To have ascertained by the exercise of the intellectual faculties the nature, qualities, and relationships of things." With this elemental primary definition of knowledge, we shall investigate what constitutes the Mexican type, for the investigators have lacked material, sources of information, and equipment, and we are well aware that science is perfected to the extent that its deficiencies, attributable to human error or to the instruments of investigation, are corrected. It was sufficient that calculus and the telescope should be perfected to learn that some stars of the heavens had taken off their age as many as five million years—not as many as some ladies take off theirs—in the age they had confessed to previous astronomers.

Aided by my own understanding, I wish to determine in an approximate way the Mexican type, setting aside completely the traditional methods for attaining philosophical knowledge. Making use of the comic, which is a faculty of the intelligence and an attribute of culture,

I shall try to approximate the truth. The comic ought to be a source and means of investigation. Philosophy, too academic and confined, has forgotten the comic because it is not very serious; it ought to give it its citizenship credentials in spite of everything. It does not do so because the comic, at the same time, both is and is not the subject, but possesses all its qualities, and all the essences which connect and define it. The "comic" is a word so alive that it has no need of definition. It is sufficient to pronounce it and everyone will laugh; it always brings its card of introduction with it.

I am using the comic as a new method of philosophical investigation because from a comic subject, extracted from reality, I am going to study the psychological type of the Mexican.

The study has to be made, then, if you like, in metaphor, which is poetry, and this is the forerunner of science because it is an instinct of the human species. The comic, like the poetic, is a vehicle for the expression of feelings. The comic is the horizon which divides the real and the unreal. In the comic, in the grotesque (which is the caricature of man), we must convey the deepest root of what is Mexican. We shall therefore select that man who, in becoming individualized, in the Mexican social setting, represents it in its best expression. The Mexican, undoubtedly, is represented by "Cantinflas." We have all suffered the anguish of the gendarme; we have been "authority," or we have been struck dumb in the presence of the woman loved. He represents in a powerful manner the varied moods of the Mexican.

Richard Bell was an English clown suited to the dictatorship of Porfirio; his jokes contained no social venom; Leopoldo Beristáin was an unreal rancher suited to tourists. Roberto Soto is a product of the bourgeois who enables them to laugh at their own defects; "Tin-Tan" was a momentary creation of social discontent, with its living expression: the day labourers.

The comic, like art, must be popular; this explains the success of "Cantinflas." The comedian, who is an artist, must be local and popular; in this can be found the universal. There is nothing that is more of an expression of our capital city than "Cantinflas"; but what a universal effect he has had as well!

"Cantinflas" is a man who came out of a little hut near the Guitarro ward; he dressed in the rags discarded by other rag-wearers who were less ragged than he. His clothes, if one admits that he is clothed at all, do not match: his hat is an iceman's hat, the shirt stuck on his body is a bartender's, his trousers are an old clothes dealer's, his belt a porter's of the Merced, and oh! his jacket—a dream, an attempt to be "Fifi," "Rags," or "Tarzan." The costume of "Cantinflas" is a mosaic, a plumage in which each of the city wards presented him with a feather. His dress makes him appear the poorest and most wretched man in Mexico, so low in his social status that his existence does not represent any economic phenomenon. He rarely lives by stealing; he feeds himself, when he can, on cheap food, usually left-overs from restaurants, or failing that, out of garbage cans, in stubborn competition with the stray dogs. His work is ill paid; he prefers to be an idler. He has no fixed domicile or legal status; his affections go to vagabonds or transients, and the Civil Code gives him no name—that is, legally he is not a man. He does not comb his hair, and so he does not take off his hat; his moustache he uses as "sweetener," not as a luxury, but because he lacks money to tidy himself up. He is physically weak, on account of his scant and bad diet. He is sad, not because he is a Mexican, but because any man, of any country whatever, is sad when he has not eaten. For the same reason the hidalgo and the picaroon of the Spanish novel were sad. "Cantinflas" lives and operates in a city like Mexico City, close to a well-developed bourgeoisie: the social distinctions are brutal. To realize this, it suffices to compare the Bankers' Club of Mexico City with one of those wards that have been thrown into the dung-heaps of the city. "Cantinflas" moves between the dung-heap and the handle of his "pan," in front of the Hotel Reforma.

He does not aspire to a better way of life; he is resigned to being as he is, since he has a realistic appreciation of his social status. Although he is almost without relationships, love, or profession, he has not developed an inferiority complex, because unconsciously he does not aspire to improving himself. He does not want a better world even in his dreams; he wants to live just as he is living; with regard to the elegance, food, and women that others enjoy, which he knows he can never have, since he is sufficiently intelligent to believe them impossible for him, he feels no envy. On account of this he does develop a sense of inferiority, consciously, with respect to others. The complex is a phenomenon of the subconscious which tends to overcome itself; the feeling is conscious and rather inhibits the subject. This is why "Cantinflas" is timid socially and prefers to be lost in the anonymity of the ward.

According to Freud, two vital constructive and destructive forces operate unconsciously in the human species: Eros and Thanatos, love and death. These symbols, in the real and the dream world of "Cantinflas," are represented by a gendarme and a woman. Before them he is always timid, because a word might get him involved. He may either get married or go to jail, the worst things that can happen to our hero because of his precarious economic situation.

The person "Cantinflas" ("mask" in Latin) represents cunning, the crafty one, the Latin, the one who has learned Latin, the ecumenical language of the conquistador–he who knew it defended himself better. "Cantinflas," in defence of his person, expresses himself in an ingenious style, not bombastic, as a result of certain features of his incapacity. With his great sense of inferiority, he knows that he compromises himself by either denying or affirming; so he neither denies nor affirms–he oscillates between affirmation and denial. Unintentionally, when he speaks he provokes laughter or tears indiscriminately, because there are no frontiers delimiting for him the tragic and comic. His picturesque language shows intelligence; he speaks with naturalness, without wishing to appear either stupid or clever. He is not affected in his manner; he is simple. He has wit, sociability, or, as Gracián[3] said, "social grace." In his speech he does not concern himself about style, he acts with reserve, defending himself in his speech, saving or concealing his person in an attitude suggested by "throw the stone and hide the hand." A yes or a no, before a woman or a gendarme, would be fatal to his life as a city nomad. "Cantinflas" has to defend himself boldly against an environment that is hostile to him; but as he cannot do it physically or legally, he substitutes cunning, using his most highly developed faculty, intelligence, with a language of his creation which is not thieves' slang or "gang cant," because he does not belong to the underworld; he uses a language which does not compromise him. He does not affirm, doubt, or deny, but conveys the sense of "yes, but no." He denies an affirmation or affirms a denial; so when he sells snacks in the street, he cries: "Cigars, sir"; or when he sells cigars he calls out: "Snacks, sir, snacks."

Mario Moreno has created his own character out of his own flesh, as the snail makes its shell: he has achieved it by an objective operation upon himself, expressing his feelings, his "pure intuition," in his language, which is comic language.

The success of "Cantinflas" must be attributed to its popular foundation: he is the people, part of oneself, looking at oneself in a mirror.

[3]Seventeenth-century Spanish writer, most famous for his *The Critic* (*El Criticón*), published in parts from 1651 to 1657.

In a semi-colonial country like ours, with its illiterates (in which we ought to teach to read those who can already read), the way to knowledge must be rooted in the objective and penetrate through two senses: sight and hearing. "Cantinflas" is seen and heard, and this is part of his popularity. The criticism he makes of the social set-up, the struggle of the strata forming it, everybody understands. "Cantinflas" is basically a romantic character, unconsciously struggling against social injustice. Mario Moreno has saturated himself with his character; he has the "Cantinflas" complex. That is why he tried to become a leader.

"Cantinflas," a thorough realist, is not a representative of the proletariat, bourgeois, or socialist, he is simply an idler without any economic relationship; as a comic personage he is real and unreal, but he is a critic of the society in which he lives. As he never has permanent employment he cannot become a bourgeois or a proletarian, and he laughs at these; he represents the smile, mockery, the concept of the liberty of the idler, who is under no social obligations of any kind; he does not sink into poverty because that is no longer possible, and he does not rise in the world because he has not the inclination. Charles Chaplin, on the contrary, with bowler, cane, bow tie, and dress suit, does represent the pauper who aspires to becoming an aristocrat. If he does not achieve it, it is because of his constant failures.

"Cantinflas," in the depths of his subconscious, is a frustrated romantic. His humour is merely the sublimation of his lack of love: the humorist is a romantic who failed. His economic want in a world socially unjust causes him to struggle against what is higher, which is represented in the gendarme. He struggles for himself, defending himself and those like him, using mockery as an offensive and defensive weapon. He carries with him a kind of militant rebelliousness as an emblem on behalf of the underdogs, those who suffer like him and pay debts unwillingly incurred. He knows, for example, that the "bite" is a constitutional precept.

When our hero mocks at everything, he does so without envy because he is not resentful; he criticizes the falsity, the insolent elegance, the extravagant character of the society in which he lives. Consciously or unconsciously, "Catinflas" and Vicente Lombardo[4] represent the same disquietude which comes in very different ways. When Lombardo ordered Luis N. Morones to debate with "Cantinflas," in order to get rid of him, he made a jest at which everyone laughed; the mechanics of the comic is self-explanatory. It is as if

[4]Prominent contemporary leader of labouring classes.

Lombardo had said: "I am 'Cantinflas,' debate with me," or as if "Cantinflas" himself had said: "I am the dialectal Lombardo; come to the tent and we'll argue it out." Unconsciously, in the mind, there is a confusion of persons; hence the laughter of those who heard Lombardo.

"Cantinflas" is a Lombardo who criticizes the social environment in which he lives, not dialectically, but with the most terrible form of human expression: irony. Lombardo, for his enemies, is a "Cantinflas" as they would like to see him: ignorant, poor, and timorous, without the two thousand suits of the same colour his enemies have invented for him. Just as much "Cantinflas" is a serious Lombardo too, a Lombardo transformed into a leader, not in the wretched attire which he wears for farce, but in the legendary cashmere in which he really carries on his work. If we put on Lombardo the costume of the actor, in spite of his brilliant oratory he would no longer be Lombardo, and if we dress up "Cantinflas" in an ordinary suit, he becomes Mario Moreno the leader. Both, then, are confused in principles and in aims. Mario Moreno is the author of "Cantinflas," and his actor. His personality bifurcates: the serious and the comic, reality and farce; as opposed to harsh social criticism, he criticizes alimony. The bourgeoisie does not find the enemy, as in the story of the squint-eyed man of Yucatán and the Palomeque bull. Lombardo is not a farcical character, he is a dialectician. In him they do indeed personalize the enemy, and that is why they hate him. He incites to the social struggle in order that the "Cantinflases" of real life in Mexico may cease to exist. "Cantinflas," on the contrary, provokes merriment with his jokes. The aims of Lombardo equate him to "Cantinflas" in his social rebellion. The jests of the daily papers do not strike or destroy Vicente Lombardo Toledano, because he is immunized against them; he has formed his antibodies, a kind of antidote against the comic, and they do not finish him off in the domain of the serious because in his intelligence he has his most highly developed defence. His enemies necessarily wish him to cut a comic figure. The protean nature of his personality, which sways him between the comic the enemy desires and the dialectic interest of his follower, saves him and exalts him.

In the field of psychology, it is exceedingly rash to generalize from the particular case of a single man and make him a kind of attribute of the social mass, and this not only with respect to Mexico, but even in countries having a uniform and balanced population, in which each man, like a cell, is representative of the entire social structure. Nevertheless, I can declare that "Cantinflas" is what is most representative of the Mexican manner. By his way of thinking and feeling, and his attitude towards life, he is undoubtedly a "wretched," "depraved", and "unsteady" loafer.

If we select "Cantinflas," a comic character, as representative of what is Mexican, we can look at him in caricature, stereotyped in his vices and virtues. Seen in this way, outside the bounds of reality, one can pretty nearly deduce permanent characteristics which define the Mexican type, with due reservations, of course, as I have reiterated.

In speaking of the Mexican manner we must be exceedingly careful, because a permanent architecture of its spirit has not yet been devised, owing to the fact that there has been no smooth evolution of its economic structure, and also on account of the diversity of racial origins which make up the Mexican family: indigenes, Creoles, mestizos, and foreigners, who have not definitively settled in their places so that one can define the nuclear substance and the spiritual protoplasm which form what Mexicanism will be in the future. Mexican society is in constant ebullition owing to its social and economic struggles; the bases which could explain its spiritual content have not been allowed to form.

The Mexican, individually, has a sense of inferiority, which becomes a collective whole, made up of many souls, formed like the sea, in the Leibnitz manner, in which each of them is as a drop of its waters and has been formed by its old-style poverty, its never-ending slavery, and its insecurity, not only individual, but social. The Mexican, therefore, lives his life in fear, as if he did not wish to do anything in order not to compromise himself. When he makes mock of the man involved in politics, it is always under the cover of anonymity in order not to suffer want or imprisonment. Unconsciously, he does not wish to be individualized, but to be perpetually in community with others; he does not aspire to being authentically himself, but to depersonalizing himself in a "we," dissolving or mingling himself in the social mass.

Since the time when literature, on the basis of synthetic knowledge gleaned from the newspapers, has given out scientific knowledge to the layman, many of these, under the influence of barbers and druggists, have become denatured, and among the public there have arisen certain scientific concepts that lead to outworn commonplaces which, on account of their easily falsified coinage, circulate in the black market of ideas. One of the many that can be mentioned are the so-called complexes of Sigmund Freud or the modest self-depreciation of Alfred Adler, concepts of modern psychology which, as idle chatter, pass from mouth to mouth. These things are talked about with equal glibness by a minister of state, a prostitute, or a snake-charmer. As a result there has been persistently asserted the following false statement which everyone repeats: The people of the United States have a superiority complex, and those of Mexico an inferiority complex.

There is nothing more false than these two beliefs. The Mexican does not have an inferiority complex; the one who suffers from this is the American of the United States. Since he has created a great civilization which stifles him and a monstrous world of gigantic machines that hem him in, undoubtedly these cause his spirit to shrink. His individual inferiority complex is fired off collectively to rise up towards the grandiose; that is, according to Adler's thesis, the self-depreciation is transformed into the superiority complex. For this reason they seek after everything that is big: they boast of having the biggest bridge, river, boat, and even the biggest giant in the world. The smallest dwarf in the world they would have sent to the electric chair. There was once even a Yankee painter of miniatures who painted a picture a hundred metres square, in order to appear in the eyes of his fellow countrymen as the biggest miniature artist in the universe.

The Mexican does not have an inferiority complex, as is said (even though many individuals may have it), because this concept belongs to the world of the subconscious. Intelligent and vivacious by nature, he knows his destiny and his poverty. He is conscious of his spiritual world and the natural conditions surrounding him, in which he has to struggle and defend himself; and so, consciously analysing his situation, he acquires a feeling of insecurity and inferiority. He knows his world and lives in it—his real world that he sees with his eyes, with a panorama of dreams and mirages. He does not unsettle his fancy with an unreal world. He placidly extends his culture to the place in which he lives, and in the real there is a permanent equilibrium in his economic expectations and his psychological world of sentiment.

The Mexican cares nothing for the big because he does not have to overcome any inferiority. As a realist *par excellence*, he sees his world shrunken and accommodates himself to dressing fleas or placing a married couple or a corpse in a nutshell. If he had an inferiority complex, to overcome it he would take it into his head to conquer Guatemala and liberate the ethnical minorities in British Honduras. The Mexican who sees things big is put into the insane asylum. No Mexican writer has ever thought of writing the universal epic or the universal great novel. He is content to be a modest novelist, short story writer, or writer of spicy anecdotes, in each case simply Mexican.

Not wishing to be himself, not individualizing himself, hiding his true personality—these are characteristics of the Mexican. We see that the dress that gives uniformity, like "overalls," is becoming popular. Aristocracy, which is an ambition to be superior to others, has not infected Mexico because the common Mexican type does not seek it on account of his fear of authority, whether it be the gendarme or the academician.

To become aristocratic means to become individualized in dress, manners, and diet, which are things at variance with the Mexican mode of living, since our conventions require clothing of a certain cut, a special diet: ham, sausages, salad, hors-d'œuvres; and an unconscious urbanity of manner. To us nothing is funnier than a gentleman in a dress suit going by himself with a barbecued tamale, or one hitting his neighbour with a turkey foot covered with chili sauce, or spattering his starched shirt-front with the blush of the violet-coloured sauce.

The uniforms of the aristocrat or gendarme are not allowed because they represent the authority of money or the club. Formerly the motormen and conductors of electric trains wore a blue uniform and caps like the gendarmes. They had an air of authority and were rude and insolent to the passengers. An agreement of the union took away their uniforms and they again became somewhat pleasant. Heaven deliver us from taxi drivers with uniforms! An army without uniforms, instead of defending governments, would defend peoples.

Even in the comic, which is medullary to him, and his deepest dimension in the matter of natural phenomena, the Mexican is inhibited: he laughs furtively and with his back turned to others. The smile and the outburst of laughter do not come out in virginal fashion like water, but are beclouded with sobs and tears. Pain and smile come across each other as though in a partial eclipse.

In Mexico, the social setting has been transformed as a result of the shock of three successive revolutions. As if it had been subjected to a pruning, it bore fruit very early, like a leafy tropical tree. One is surprised by the fact that in the course of a very few years, less than a century, in different aspects of its economy and its cultural life, undreamed-of goals have been reached. This is seen mainly in the arts, which are of such a quality that they may be compared with the very old countries of ancient cultures without being put to shame. We can note this, dispassionately, in music, painting, and literature, in spite of the newness of our culture.

Through the comic attitude of an imaginary personage like "Cantinflas," but with a real existence in farce, I have tried to establish psychological norms which characterize and define the Mexican. I shall now try to prove my statements, not in the field of the hypothetical or inductive, but by the example of persons who live in a social setting which we see and know because it is near us. I shall refer to the artist not as an individual, but as a social group suitably differentiated on account of being something that is most clearly characterized in Mexican society. It has a very well delimited cultural and social level, and its field of action is marked off, and professionally it has frontiers of its own. It is not the same with other occupations. The artist breathes only his own atmosphere; on account of a typically bourgeois culture which has nurtured him, his reflexes respond to the stimuli of the superstructure that has formed him. There are also some other professions which, like the batrachians, live indiscriminately in the water or on land, that is, they breathe in a world both feudal and capitalistic, and they therefore have no uniform characteristics. Therefore, since the work of art corresponding to the type with which I am concerned is uniform in its expression, the personal origin of the artist with respect to his economic status or his connection with an ethnic group is of no importance.

The artist has a real existence. We see him, talk with him, listen to his works or come to know them, and therefore we can study him perfectly and refer to his habits and customs. We can establish his psychological climate, treading on firm ground, and not, as we did with respect to the comic, by reduction to the absurd. Besides, the artist, in thinking and feeling, creates his works, which are his fruits, and as the Bible says, through them we can know him.

Art individualizes man, and makes him singular. He ceases to belong to the common herd because he thinks and feels differently from the masses. Authentic artistic worth takes account of personal worth in relation to others and closely examines sensibility and creative faculties, but does not become vain by overestimating the ego; on the contrary it conceals it, as certain animals do with their eggs, so that they may be hatched by the rays of the sun. The artist does his work with a certain aloofness, as if he did not wish it to be known that he was doing it, without over-compromising himself, in the phenomenological attitude of "throwing the stone and hiding the hand," trying to hide his work as if it were of shameful paternity. In hiding from others he is trying not to stand out as an individual, showing in his consciousness his sense of inferiority as an artist and as a Mexican, because up to the present to be an artist means voluntarily to condemn oneself to perpetual poverty or to work in spare time while tied to the bureaucratic desk of some office. The artist rarely lives by his artistic work; few in Mexico live by their pens or by their work as artists. What their works bring in is insufficient for them to live even modestly. Anyone who works as an artist sees himself obliged, in order to live comfortably, to take on some employment to provide a complement to his small income from artistic production, thus wasting part of the basic metabolism of his sensibility in tedious, impermanent, and unnecessary work; for example, a mural painter earning his living as a steeplejack, or an etcher, composer of "strong waters," working in the deleterious waters of the drain.

The artist aspires to not individualizing himself; he does not wish to be an artist. But at the same time, he carries in his subconscious an imperative which obliges him to be one, that is, he desires to express his artistic sentiments in order to communicate them to others. He has in constant conflict a wish and an unwillingness to be an artist; therefore he tries to dissolve in his problem what he has that is exceptional, thus becoming a common man. In accordance with the nature of the Mexican, he creates his work with a certain insecurity, as though making fun of himself, almost hiding what he has done.

I do not remember where I have read that George Brummel, the most elegant man in England in his time, said on a certain occasion that his elegance consisted in that when he went to some party, the next day nobody remembered the cut of his suit, and not even that of the flower he wore in his buttonhole; that is, true elegance, which is the external style of the elegant man, ought not to be noticed. If it is noticed it is no longer elegance; it is affectation or freakishness. Real Mexican art is not noticed because its creator has dissimulated his work, hiding his true personality with scandal, or with a certain indifference despising his own creation.

There is a close similarity between "Cantinflas'" method and that of the artist. In their meagre intercourse with society, with the same external stimuli, they react in the same way. Both are idlers; usually neither has definite employment which would enable him to live decently in society. They are both social pariahs. The artist, on account of a marked sense of inferiority, when among others assumes an attitude of indifference towards his work and his person. Once I learned that a certain publishing house asked many outstanding men, some in the sciences and others in the arts, for their biographical data for publication in an encyclopaedic dictionary. They were sent a questionnaire to make up the files. Very few of them answered. I think that it certainly was not a matter of an almost incomprehensible demonstration of modesty; I rather believe that it was due either to shyness or to indifference.

The artist, with deliberate premeditation, deforms his physical or mental personality until he achieves freakishness, or hides behind the anonymity of a pseudonym, or resorts to the smoke-screens of scandal, in the political or ideological domain or in the boldness of his aesthetic conception, always in an endeavour to hide his work. As if it were all a mere trifle, he gives it an insignificant title.

We have already seen, in a summary fashion, what constitutes the essense of things Mexican, their temperament and their attitudes toward themselves and others. The artist, with his temperament and sensibility exacerbated, in his work and actions shows the characteristics which I have previously mentioned as belonging to the Mexican type.

I do not deny that many artistic values do not fit in with the characteristics I have indicated, but they are not the most representative. What is best, what has most value in Mexican art, can be found among that unexhibited work, done as in play, to put in time, or for entertainment, "muddling" or indifferent. For example, it must be sought in literature in out-of-the-way places, hidden among the pages of great humour which were written with serious intent.

When I speak of idleness I do not do so deprecatingly, but in the Greek manner. I refer to what was called Hellenic idleness, for which Plato wished protection by the Republic, because he considered it a necessary condition for the cultivation of the fine arts and political ideas. Business, a purely economic social activity, is the opposite of idleness, that is, its negation, non-idleness, which is what it means etymologically. Art is idleness because it has no economic phenomenon as its basis. It is simply a passion, like hatred or love; it has no price-tag. Idleness has to do chiefly with the spirit. Vagrancy is a material question, and extra-vagrancy (freakishness) is a vagrancy externalized.

We must not seek the best artistic values in the works of those who owe their prestige to propaganda, but in those who present their work with a certain timidity, as though they did not wish to excel, and play what we call in Mexico "the vacillating game." For that reason there is value in the constant "vacillator," careless and indifferent, whether we are considering José Vasconcelos, "The Little Black Poet," or José Vasconcelos "The Philosopher." Vasconcelos is of greatest value not for his *Aesthetics* (*Estética*), but for those pages written without effort of will, like those appearing in *Ulysses the Creole* (*Ulises criollo*), which are of such human penetration and literary value that they can be compared to *The Confessions* of Jean-Jacques Rousseau, the *Autobiographical Pages* of Maxim Gorki, *From the Last Turn of the Road* (*Desde la última vuelta del camino*) by Pío Baroja, and *Persons and Places* (*Personas y lugares*) by George Santayana.

This negligent manner, as though not taking oneself seriously, which is observed in the arts, is found even in scientific activities. People do not take seriously the predictions of the eminent astronomer don Joaquín Gallo, whose scientific excellence no one can deny, and he is better known through jokes at his expense than through his learning. He has taken science very seriously, but has not done the same with respect to his person, for the public makes fun of him. Of course I do not refer to the society of the few learned men there have been in the world, in which Gallo is a figure of great intellectual prominence. On the other hand, Dr. Leopoldo Salazar Viniegra, a master of the difficult art of psychiatry, who works at science in fun-making fashion, with scandalously original theories, does not take science very seriously, but he still has, both in the scientific and the popular worlds, a place of distinction.

To prove my statements, I will mention a few concrete examples which will help to demonstrate my theory, using as specimens works and artists in different fields. I shall begin with music.

Silvestre Revueltas, a genius prematurely lost, represents the highest art in music. There is nothing more Mexican than he in his musical expressions. In the personal sphere he never made any effort to get away from his environment, in spite of his prodigious talent. He was modesty itself. As an artist he always hid from others. He was as simple as his works of art, to which he never gave high-sounding names. He called them: *The Strolling Tadpole* (*El renacuajo paseador*), *The Colonel's Wife* (*La coronela*), *Corner* (*Esquina*), *Window* (*Ventana*), *Bright Colours* (*Colorines*). His tone was a purely popular one, with the language of the people coming out in each note.

Another great "vacillator" is Carlos Chávez with his *H.P. 32*, or his *Concerto for Piano and Orchestra* (*Concerto para piano y orquesta*), the music of which seems more like a landslide than mere music-making. He tries to hide his personality in the way he makes up his elegant hair, which seems like a wig but is not.

In the plastic arts, the painting by young painters, which we can already call Mexican, is my best argument. The works and their authors support my thesis. The creators have expressed popular values, the essence of what is Mexican with all its characteristics: mockery, hatreds, laughter, rancours, and its struggles for liberty. The plastic nature of the colouring is turned forcefully to didactic purposes. Painting will be the future leader that will point the way for other arts, so that they may balance form and content, and so that there may be no cleavage between the sentiments of the artist and social reality. A national painting has been created that has a universal resonance because it has taken popular foundations for its architectural structure. In painting, nucleus and protoplasm are found in a balanced harmony.

There is nothing more Mexican than our painting, beginning with the engravings of José Guadalupe Posada. His mockery continues right to the grave: skulls dressed up as dandies or ladies of the time of Porfirio, with broad hats and frocks in the style of the period. His creative genius he employed to laugh at the most serious things in the experience of man, like death. His works have the full flavour of the popular at the festival of All Souls' Day. His drawings served to illustrate the popular verses (*corridos*) of Vanegas Arroyo, the best popular form for poetic composition. At the present time the other vigorous and gifted engraver, Leopoldo Méndez, is indicating by his art the evils of a present-day world which he regards as unjust. His works are characterized by their strength, vigour, and human depth, also by the deeply-rooted popular character of his concepts. His art has a function to fulfil: his works disseminate his ideas, which point to the liberation of the people from old and relentless enemies. In spite of its being art with a purpose, this does not detract from it; on the contrary, it enhances its vigour and passion.

The three greatest painters, Diego Rivera, José Clemente Orozco, and David Alfaro Siqueiros, are the creators of the Mexican style in painting. Their works are concerned with the same aim: to cut the umbilical cord connecting us to the traditional art of old Europe. They nationalized art, just as oil was nationalized. As for their respective personalities, they are as well matched in their activities as if they had rehearsed their steps together. Diego changes ideas right and left. Constantly creating scandal, even when he passed himself off as a gluttonous eater of prepared human flesh he was trying, in spite of his corpulence, to conceal his genius. José Clemente Orozco, by the absence of his hand, seems to be saying that he has never painted any mural. David tries to soften his artistic genius by taking part in street meetings and sensational conspiracies.

Among Mexican writers too there is the characteristic I have indicated. I shall not mention them in alphabetical order because I am not trying to make up a directory. I wish to show the phenomenon and not the writer as a person, and so many will please pardon my leaving them out in my deliberate amnesia.

Joaquín Fernández de Lizardi, with *The Mangy Parakeet* (*El Periquillo sarniento*), in spite of its being the old Spanish picaresque novel adapted to our environment, certainly sets and fixes Mexican literature in the course it is following today. The author of *The Quixote Girl and Her Cousin* (*La Quijotita y su prima*) was called, and liked to be called, "The Mexican Thinker." Just as we laugh at the *Parakeet*, our ancestors praised its cleverness and wit.

Juan Bautista Morales, the hemiplegic strummer of the guitar and Minister of the Supreme Court of Justice, struggled during the most tragic period of Mexican history, which was the dictatorship of don Antonio López de Santa Anna; therefore he composes his famous work without compromising himself greatly. His characters express their political ideas in true allegorical fashion, but one always recognizes the dictator at whom the poisoned darts are aimed. His work *The Pythagorean Cock* (*El Gallo pitagórico*) is written in the manner of the *Moral Dialogues* (*Diálogos morales*) of Luciano Samosata, with humanistic and high-flown language. A cock and José María Luján carry on a dialogue, and in their daily chat they criticize the social and political life of their time.

Manuel Gutiérrez Nájera, who gave himself the name "Duke Job," as a good Mexican never ceased to be a joker, in spite of his artificial elegance with clothes in the style of Braniff or Mr. De la Cantoya y Rico, the enormous flower in his buttonhole, his big Havana cigar made with tobaccos of San Andrés Tuxtla and his aggressive moustache in a cup-like cover with bright red roses and gilded ridges. He represents the sly mockery of a baroque and Frenchified society like that of the period of the Porfirian[5] dictatorship. His verses about false princesses, duchesses, and young ladies sound like the music and songs of blind vendors of one-cent "twist-candy and trifles." "Duke Job" always made mock with his constant smile which he covered with his enormous cigar and its white ash. His ambulating mockery strolled from "The Surprise" (La Sorpresa) to the Jockey Club.

Another very characteristic leading writer is our Ángel de Campo. He always hid his physical smallness behind a bureaucratic desk, and his creative talent by two words continually oscillating between "Micrós" and "Tic-tac." In spite of the subconscious modesty shown by

[5]The reference is to Porfirio Díaz, Mexican dictator from 1884 to 1910.

his pseudonyms, he is beyond doubt the master designer of the contemporary Mexican short story.

In present-day literature the examples are numerous; as I have said, they are characterized by scorn of their work, using as titles insignificant names, and hiding their personalities in different activities, in most cases far removed from their artistic refinements. For example, we have Octavio N. Bustamente, at present deeply involved in priestly ministrations, with a very serious literary work: *Invitation to the Dance* (*Invitación al dancing*), *General Theory of Cagancho* (*Teoría general de Cagancho*), and *Six Novels All Alike* (*Seis novelas iguales entre sí*). Another case is Renato Leduc, a great poet of exceptional talent, at present occupied in journalism, and who has already many works published: *The Lecture Hall* (*El aula*), *etc., The Beige Corsair* (*El Corsario Beige*), *The Banquets* (*Los banquetes*), and *Poems Deliberately Romantic* (*Poemas deliberadamente románticos*). His concealed work, like his secret verses, mostly pornographic, does not detract from his talent and proved value as a poet. These poems, which circulate in secret like the pirate editions, are known even to the most respectable ladies in society.

The list would be interminable. There are Efrén Hernández, with his *Blemishes* (*Tachas*), *A Little Nail in the Air* (*Un clavito en el aire*), *A Very Grateful Writer* (*Un escritor muy agradecido*), and *A Few Tomatoes on a Little Shelf* (*Unos cuantos tomates en una repisa*); Juan de la Cabada with his *Promenade of Lies* (*Paseo de mentiras*) and *Melodic Incidents of the Irrational World* (*Incidentes melódicos del mundo irracional*); José Rubén Romero, with his *Pito Pérez*, and José Vasconcelos, the best humorist who writes with seriousness.

Giovanni Pascoli,[6] in his *Theory of Art*, once said: "There exists within us a child that not only has vibrations, as Cebes of Thebes[7] thought, who was the first to discover it in himself, but also tears and joys of his own."

The Mexican artist carries within himself a "Cantinflas," who speaks and acts in easy indifference, without ever compromising himself, where tears and laughter are interfused like the horizon with drops of sea or pieces of sky.

1946

Mexican realities (*Realidades mexicanas*), Secretaría de Educación Pública, Mexico, 1949, 53–74, Popular Encyclopaedic Library (*Biblioteca Enciclopédica Popular*), Vol. CCXIII.

[6]Italian lyric poet of the late nineteenth and the early twentieth centuries.

[7]Greek philosopher of the fifth century B.C.

Andrés Iduarte

(b. Villahermosa, Tabasco, 1907)

Iduarte began his studies at the National University, continued them in Spain, and finally obtained the degree of Doctor of Philosophy at Columbia University, New York. He travelled in Europe and America, and since 1940 he has lived in the United States as a professor of Spanish-American literature at Columbia University, except for the period 1952–54, when he was director of the National Institute of Fine Arts.

The great figures in the literature and culture of Spanish America are the special field of André Iduarte's essays. He has a profound understanding of the sensibility, the spiritual creations, and the deep conflicts in Spanish America. His study of Martí as a writer is, among many, the best on this aspect of the Cuban revolutionary leader, and the pages he has devoted to Gabriela Mistral, Rómulo Gallegos,[1] and Alfonso Reyes show a spirit in which fervour is allied with intelligence.

ESSAYS AND STUDIES: *The Moral Problem of Mexican Youth* (*El problema moral de la juventud mexicana*), 1932; *Martí, Writer* (*Martí, escritor*), 1944–Havana, 1951; *Spanish American Chats* (*Pláticas hispanoamericanas*), 1951; *Eulogy of Mexico* (*Elogio de México*), New York, 1956; *Alfonso Reyes: The Man and His World* (*Alfonso Reyes: el hombre y su mundo*), New York, 1956.

CORTEZ AND CUAUHTÉMOC: HISPANICISM, INDIGENISM

THE RECENT EXHUMATION of the remains of Cortez and his subsequent re-interment are simply characteristic episodes of polemic history concerning the conquest of America, and consequently new milestones in the integration of the Spanish-American spirit. The very form in which the two events occurred underlines its traditional significance, and at the same time a new and novel transcendency. The continual

[1]Venezuelan novelist, most famous for his *Doña Bárbara* (1929). He was president of his country in 1947–48.

fluctuation with the same violence as in the past, the flux and reflux, is still in full swing. But at the same time the outlines are becoming firm, the lines are being clarified on all sides, and they are moving towards a complete and harmonious conclusion. The oarsman advances steadily, with strong and rhythmic strokes, and with full consciousness of the distance that has been covered. His *appoggiatura*[2] is the point on the horizon that has been, by hard and persistent effort, left behind.

I cannot assert, since I lack sufficient data, that the discovery of the bones of the conquistador has been a simple hoax; but it is unquestionable that the way in which it was communicated to the public reveals a plan, an elaboration, and a thesis. If it was not a hoax, it can be assured that the remains of Cortez will necessarily be followed immediately by manipulation and fixing-up. This means that the remains in themselves are a thesis against which the antithesis is clashing, both of them still rough and violent, but visibly nearer to a completing synthesis.

The details which preceded and followed the re-interment are revealing: the key to the urn that contained the remains was in the possession of the descendants of don Lucas Alamán, whose very name is a banner and a call to action. The discovery of the place in which they lay was made, according to the press, behind the back of the Embassy of the Spanish Republic in Mexico, whose secret documents were ingenuously or cunningly violated, that is, without the approval of liberal Spain. The historians and others who initiated the plan to exhume the body, with some exceptions, were definitely of clerical or conservative stamp.

And no less eloquent are the facts which form the response: the street, the pulpit, and the newspaper article came to a victorious and worthy culmination through the decision made by the government to rebury the remains. This ceremony was performed in proper form: with the law represented by a notary of high standing in the Mexican legal profession; with the proper official representation, headed by the Secretary for Public Education; with intellectual representation (historians, writers) of the first rank; with the proper solemnity and respect, aside from debated merits, for a figure of first importance in the history of Mexico and the Hispanic world. Also, and this must be underlined because it is a new and significant ingredient, there was represented the Embassy of the Spanish Republic, in the person of General José Miaja, leader of the popular army which defended Madrid from 1936 to 1939, exiled in Mexico. Symbolically, by lifting up and

[2]Accessory or embellishing note in music.

burying the ashes of Cortez, there was present the Spanish spirit which defended Madrid on May 2, 1808, which organized the junta for defence and gave birth to the first popular representative bodies (*Cortes*) in which there were delegates from the American colonies (those of Cádiz), which produced the Navarrese hero who fought and died for Mexican independence, Francisco Xavier Mina, and which fought in Spain in 1936 against the same feudal, clerical, and military privileges which were fought against in 1810 by the founders of the Spanish-American republics. It is obvious that in the last skirmish between the two Americas and the two Spains, part of two antagonistic and universal political outlooks, the liberal answer not only surpassed in cogency the conservative thesis, but also in skilfulness and tact. As regards reason and truth, we are among those who believe they have always won out.

In the Paseo de la Reforma, the great avenue of the Mexican capital, rises the statue of Cuauhtémoc,[3] and Cortez' statue is not there. The last hard-fought battle to erect a monument to the latter, in the same Paseo de la Reforma or in some other place in the city, has failed completely, in spite of the fact that the moment selected was a fitting one, and that the weapons engaged were powerful, and in skilled hands. And this is because the avenue that bears the name of the political struggle headed by Juárez is still, despite a long series of confusions, a living symbol of Mexican consciousness, also confused in many respects, but not in the essentials of its existence.

Polemics over the conquest touch incidentally, though not strictly or mainly, upon the problem of culture in America. The major problem concerns life and justice. This was settled in favour of the political liberty of America, that is, in favour of the organization as free peoples of the groups of humanity that formed the Spanish Empire. The Spaniards and the Spanish Americans who, out of passion or deceitfully, involve one problem with another, resemble the ostrich that buries its head in the sand and leaves the body and heart exposed to the perpetuation of the right of the strongest. When Mexico denies a monument to the conquistador it does not deny it to the Spanish culture of which it is part, and at first approach it does not deny it either to the complex personality of the man from Estremadura, so full of merit and spirit, but it does deny it to the right of conquest.

The argument advanced in favour of honour to Cortez, which on occasion goes so far as to ask for or suggest the destruction of the honour paid to Cuauhtémoc, is as follows: we do not speak Náhuatl,

[3]Aztec leader of the resistance against the Spaniards. He was executed in 1525.

but Spanish; what gives us Spanish-American unity, and with it a common personality, is the language of Cervantes and Iberianized Mediterranean culture, which reached our lands in the heyday of Spain. At times the argument becomes aggressive: that is the only claim to dignity which we can present to the world. Without Spanish culture, this only claim to dignity, we should still be sacrificing our brothers before the altar of Huitzilopochtli; the obsidian knife would be in the place of the cross of Golgotha; the carriers would not have been liberated by the beast of burden; we should be dressing in coarse cloth or simple loin-cloths; we should be wearing feathers on our heads; we should be drinking beverages like *pulque* instead of cow's milk and wine from Mediterranean grapes; we should have our hair straighter or more bristling, our skins darker, our lips thicker and more protruding. . . . Along this line the original argument, debatable but not censurable, follows a sectarian course until it reaches disgusting extremes of confessional fanaticism and even barbarous Nazi racism, so crude or so odious that they are unworthy of the slightest comment. The only asseveration that is unchallengeable is the one which concerns the high quality of occidental culture, introduced by fire and sword through the Spanish conquest.

Alfonso Reyes has written a sentence in his *Vision of Anáhuac* (*Visión de Anáhuac*) which, like many of his, is a fine representation of the complicated event: "The vessel of clay was broken when it collided with the vessel of iron." . . . Only a fanatical upholder of the opposite view can say that the indigenous cultures were coming to the point of surpassing Spanish culture at the moment of the Conquest. Beautiful theogonies, astronomical discoveries, architectural marvels, and artistic beauties place our indigenous cultures alongside those of Egypt and Babylon, but these things do not bring them to the level of the Greco-Latin world or the Christian world of the sixteenth century. And no normal, unbiassed mind can fail to see that our brotherhood with millions of men rests upon the common denominator of Hispanicism, or that this fact is really what gives us international importance and may presently enhance this status. Also, it is simply a naïve or mad illusion to hold that, if Spaniards had not come, the thousand American groups would today be speaking and writing one indigenous language.

Moreover, the lamentation is not only absurd, but useless in every respect. The fact is that European culture triumphed over the indigenous, the cross over the sacrificial stone, the brigantines over canoes of Xochimilco, Seville over Uxmal, the Latin alphabet over hieroglyphics, the book over the codex, gunpowder over the arrow, the horse over the footsoldier, without succeeding in effecting total destruction, and at times without attempting it. Out of the battle in which Spain was victorious, but in which the Indian did not disappear, came the mingling and grafting which produced our Spanish-American nationalities, unhappy and restless, colourful and strange, with a personality not achieved by other colonized lands like those of Africa, and with more savour than other nationalities in which the Indian disappeared from the scene.

But between recognition of these facts—the triumph of the Spanish conquistadors, the greater power and cultural development back of them, our present Hispanic character—and singing of Conquest and Colony, attributing to the former the right to subjugate and to the latter the right to enslave the population of America, there is a tremendous difference. In such songs the only ones who can find entertainment are the ingenuous or propagandists inspired by self-interest or hatred, who of course also have their stupid, ill-natured, or mean counterpart in those who devote themselves to creating the Spanish black legend and the idyllic legend with respect to the indigenous empires. Spanish culture of the sixteenth century as a point of departure for our present cultural formation is one thing, and the violence of the Conquest with the social injustice built up during the colonial period is another. Our present blemishes can in large measure be traced to those brought by the Spaniard of the sixteenth century, those possessed by the Indian of 1492, and the clash of arms between the two in the act of conquest, apart from later complications. Anyone who affirms the Spanish black legend is just as untruthful as one who invents the rose-coloured legend of the Indian, and *vice versa*. The Spanish Conquest is not to be attacked because it is Spanish, but simply because it is a conquest, as one should also condemn the Protestant or Mohammedan or Jewish conquest which had overtrodden the earth and the rights of others. It is possible that the Spaniards' division of the land and their *encomienda* system have been more tolerable than the sacred wars of the Aztecs, followed by horrifying sacrifices, but this does not justify singing hymns of praise to the land-distribution and the *encomienda*. We will not praise the bad in order to point out the worse, and still less can we pray for its survival. The fact that our fathers the conquistadors have brought better weapons and have established institutions slightly less unjust than the bloody sacrifices of those vanquished in war does not move us to applaud the enslavement of the Indian as a thing in their favour. And in brief, the fact that the conquistadors were our ancestors, or that they were so daring and valiant, does not move us to celebrate the tragic victory which gave us birth. If we became filled with this racial passion and religious fervour, by what right could we condemn the passion and fervour of those who remember in the same way the indigenous ancestor, overpowered and debased in his own home, and who daily express both violent and useless invectives against Spanish culture? By that dark route no progress is made towards the spiritual edification we need; instead, we advance by it towards the breaking-up and undoing of all that has been accomplished and organized in the century and a half of independence.

We are bound in every way to Spanish culture; to it we belong. We are in no way bound to the Conquest, even though of it have been born all of us who speak Spanish: whites, mestizos, and Indians. Culture binds us also to the Indian of yesterday. Our Spanish-American numerators (I speak of Mexico, Peru, Guatemala, and the other countries where the Indians were strong and numerous) are filled with their presence. In every case the indigenous numerator is in vassalage to the solid base of the Spanish common denominator. But we are bound to the Indian by possession of the same land, by admiration for his arts, of which we are heirs, and by the heroism with which they defended our land against foreign interference. If we are pleased at having inherited a universal language, the Spanish language, why should we not be equally pleased at having before our eyes, as an example and lesson given over this very valley of ours, the epic resistance to the attack of a stronger enemy? The Mexican of today, admittedly, has the Spanish language as a weapon of defence; but there is still more inspiration to defence in the memory of the Aztec emperor. In the same way our hearts are touched, though from a greater distance, by the name of Viriato[4] and by the defence of Numancia[5] and of Sagunto,[6] because Iberian Spain, Latinized by the Roman conquest, for the integration of its personality, did not forget the names of its defenders, even while speaking a Latin language. Should we deny the sentimental tie and the moral example of the indigenous ancestors who resisted the Spanish conquistadors, merely because we speak the latter's language?

[4]Guerrilla leader against the invading Romans who came to conquer Spain in the second century B.C.

[5]Famous for its heroic resistance to the Roman conquest, to the point of its own utter annihilation, in the second century B.C.

[6]Renowned for its resistance to the Carthaginians under Hannibal, in the third century B.C. Sagunto, too, was annihilated without surrender.

But that is not all. The Indian is not only history and archaeology, but presently a living being. The Spanish-speaking Indian is here, and takes part in government and contributes to literature, under the name of Benito Juárez, Ignacio Ramírez, and Ignacio Manuel Altamirano. There is no Mexican art, or Mexican historical event, in which there is lacking the figure of an Indian, or at least of a mestizo with a high percentage of indigenous blood. It is not just, or reasonable, or right, to take from our tradition the part that we see every day in songs, dances, books, in the streets, in our veins, and in our hearts as men and as friends. If these Indians speak Spanish and belong to Hispanic culture, the whites of Mexico, as a transfusion in their sensibility, also bear traces of the indigenous. And beside the whites and the mestizos, the Indian Juárez—of pure Zapoteca blood, and of Spanish speech in his cultural and political life—was the symbol of national defence. Party feeling has cast many shadows over Juárez, but the place he holds in the history of Mexico and of human liberties stands firm, and will always stand firm, against malevolent investigators and wrathful denigrators. Paraphrasing a well-known saying, we may state that "Cortez (better, Cervantes) does not remove Altamirano." In the development of our Mexican culture it is suicidal to pull out the Spanish root, but it is suicidal also to cut off the branches of the tree watered and grown with blood and soul taken from the race of its first inhabitants.

Besides, the Mexican Indian is not only the heroic ancestor, nor only the Mexican who defended his nationality and created his culture, but the most unfortunate sub-stratum of the national population. Vanquished in the war of defence, incorporated into the Catholic faith and then disciplined and subdued by religious superstition, exploited by the victors and by the victors' descendants during the colonial period and the subsequent period of independence, and also by their half-brothers the mestizos and some of their brothers of indigenous blood who have climbed to power and wealth, the Indian today forms part of the great unfortunate majority. Being of indigenous blood does not make him a farm labourer or a badly paid workman, since mestizos and whites are also in the same situation in the defective economic organization of our day, but the man of indigenous origin has still fewer opportunities to become emancipated than one of more fortunate birth. And in the remote areas there are still indigenous tribes which do not enjoy the benefits of civilization. Championing of the indigene, or idolatry of a racist character, cannot be justified; but there is a social and cultural interest in the indigene—justice for the exploited, incorporation into society of the forgotten elements, vindication of the qualities possessed by those suffering under racial discrimination—which must necessarily be found in every noble heart. In the domain of social action this concern for the indigene is, will be, and will continue to be an indisputable duty and necessity, an inescapable categorical imperative. Anyone in Mexico who rejects the Indian on the basis of racial prejudice, and points out inaptitudes and blemishes as inherent in the indigenous race, is unconsciously or artfully speaking against the disinherited and the oppressed, and is advocating the continuation of wrong and privilege.

Historical scholars (or rather, scholars in petty, superficial pseudo-history) are asking for a statue of Cortez. They are joined by the extollers of our Hispanic culture. Sometimes within their own hearts, without daring to acknowledge it to themselves, and on occasion in a clear and wicked manner, there beats the desire to lift up higher the one who is up, and to push down farther the one who is down. Doubtless in the course of time a day will come, with the reshuffling of the Mexican population, new immigrants, new wars, new besetting problems of the modern world, the evolution of the concept of the native land, and a general new organization, when the statue of Cortez will not mean a song to the Conquest, but merely the recognition and cultivation of our deepest root: Hispanic culture. But today we cannot yet make of Cortez the symbol of Spanish culture, and so long as this is true only an ingenuous Hispanicism, or a military and clerical Hispanomania, enveloped in the smoke of war and eager for a new battle for the authority enjoyed yesterday, can call for his monument. Any glorification which can appear to applaud force and social injustice, even though done in the name of culture, will tomorrow give rise to movements of a more sinister character. In strong countries it fosters the lust for expansion and domination; in weak countries it brings something worse: the loss of the necessary dynamic, in a world full of dangers, for self-defence and survival.

Those concerned about the honour due to Spanish culture can be satisfied: in Mexico City and in the outlying parts of the country monuments are being erected to the missionaries. Have we indeed not enough with the statues of Columbus and of Vasco de Quiroga, and the streets of Isabella the Catholic and of Peter of Ghent and of Motolinía? It is significant too that it is the liberal groups that are the most insistent concerning the commemoration of the missionaries. This is because in them, rebels against the Church itself by their saintliness, in a wrathful manner in the case of Las Casas and in gentle fashion in Motolinía, one cannot see the slightest trace of benediction of the

Conquest, but merely of culture which is allied, as culture should be, to the defence of the vanquished.

In this essay have come out a few references to Cortez the man, the soldier, and the ruler, but we have had no intention of going into this delicate matter. It would require a great deal of investigation and long reflection. Cortez was an extraordinary man, an exceptional soldier, and an expert ruler. His energy and ability are surprising, amazing, tremendous, repulsive, and irritating. From admiration one passes to indignation. His gifts as a ruler were great, and also his virtues. His conduct towards the vanquished race was much better than the conduct of other conquistadors, especially if judged according to the ideas of the time. If we place ourselves within the compass of those ideas, the conquistador of Estremadura merits the statue. But within this compass one must not put, or attempt to do so, a free people born of a Conquest and in whose sky there has always been the storm-cloud of that day. Moreover, one cannot overlook one unpardonable act, fraught with an unfortunate and inevitable symbolism: the hanging of Cuauhtémoc. We do not know what went on in the mind of the conquistador at the time of the blackest deed in his life. We cannot judge precisely the military or political circumstances that might explain the terrible misstep. The misstep is there, and it had unpleasant consequences in his lifetime, as Bernal Díaz pointed out, and it has been and will continue to be an oppressive burden upon his life's story. It is to be hoped that someday the man will be freed from such a frightful curse. The human heart, fearful of what is decreed by fate, knowing the crossroads encountered on the way, refuses to pass judgement upon an event which forever darkened a man's lustre and definitively detracted from the qualities of an historic figure. Before such a drama the human heart does not pass sentence, but neither can it fail to convict, without regard for the extenuating circumstances and the practical considerations which lay behind the execution. But today the least important thing is that man, Cortez, and his terrible chain. What is important is that in him everything becomes symbolic, and also in Cuauhtémoc, and there remains the terrifying impression that the strangulation of Cuauhtémoc is the cruelest symbol: the victory of the stronger required the disappearance of the vanquished, now handed over and disarmed, now subdued and prostrate. It is impossible to speak of the monument to Cortez, beside that of Cuauhtémoc, without thinking that a statue is being erected to the killer in the symbol of the vanquished.

Only those who carry the justification of the Conquest to its ultimate and absurd extreme, only those who believe that the triumph of the Spaniards should have been absolute, and that no stone should have been left whole and no man left alive, only those who believe that the indigenous world should have been left dead and buried, can forget the fateful hour of Cortez. Perhaps this act of war, if one could delve more deeply into the story, might be considered an accident, an incident, a mere detail. But this is impossible. And the door to the glorification of Cortez is almost hermetically sealed.

1948

Spanish-American Chats (*Pláticas hispanoamericanas*), Tezontle, Mexico, 1951, pp. 9–18.

Antonio Gómez Robledo

(b. Guadalajara, Jalisco, 1908)

Gómez Robledo began his higher education at the University of Guadalajara, from which he graduated in law, and in that city he belonged to the generation of the *Provincial Banner* (*Bandera de Provincias*) and directed the periodicals *Proa* and *Forma*. At the National University he graduated with the degrees of Master and Doctor of Philosophy. Diplomatic posts took him to Brazil, on whose philosophy he wrote an authoritative study, and also to the United States. At the present time he is teaching philosophy at the University of Mexico, and he belongs to the Centre for Philosophical Studies. He has been a member of the Linguistic Academy since 1955.

The philosophical career of Gómez Robledo has followed an uninterrupted line in rigour and classification. After his juridical studies, and especially those in international law, his first task in the study of philosophy was the learning of the essential languages, his knowledge of which is attested in his translation of Aristotle's *Nicomachean Ethics*, his studies of Augustine, and the Latin discourse which he gave at the celebration of the Quadricentenary of the National University. His philosophical creed might be defined as a Christian humanism. An essayist of pure and forceful style, among our thinkers he is one who has the strictest and most orderly of minds.

ESSAYS: *Two Essays* (*2 ensayos*), Guadalajara, 1931 (In collaboration with Alfonso Gutiérrez Hermosillo. That of A.G.R. is entitled *Catholicism and the League of Nations* [*Catolicismo y Sociedad de Naciones*]); *Policy of Vitoria* (*Política de Vitoria*), 1940; *Christianity and Philosophy in Augustinian Experience* (*Cristianismo y filosofía en la experiencia augustiniana*), 1942; *Philosophy in Brazil* (*La filosofía en el Brasil*), 1946; *Philosophy and Language* (*Filosofía y lenguaje*), 1956; *Essay on the Intellectual Virtues* (*Ensayo sobre las virtudes intelectuales*), 1957.

PHILOSOPHY AND LANGUAGE*

Philosophy of Language and Language of Philosophy

PHILOSOPHICAL EXPRESSION can of course be studied in many aspects and in strata of more or less profundity, though I venture to hold that partial criteria in each of them will always depend in the final analysis upon the criteria adhered to in what pertains to the ultimate stratum, or to the deepest element in the problem. As a simple enumeration, which in no way seeks to be exhaustive, I might mention the following problems: the literary genres in which philosophy can or should be expressed; the relative capacity of languages, classical of modern, for serving as vehicles of expression in this sphere; the general conditions of philosophical style, with the debated question regarding the two forms of language, the esoteric and the exoteric, which have such an interesting historical alternation, and finally the particular conditions, of a preponderantly logico-grammatical order, which would be the more or less normal standards of that style. Beneath all this contexture of problems, however, lies the ultimate problem as to whether human language as such is or is not capable, and in what measure, of transposing philosophic thought, and this underlying problem is the one which I propose to elucidate in these reflections. To them I shall add just a few considerations concerning philosophic style, in special contrast to poetic style.

It is immediately obvious that the solution of the problem depends in large part upon the idea one holds of language in general, of its capabilities as well as its limitations, so that this question of the language of philosophy postulates in its turn the other correlative, the philosophy of language. Since it is impossible here to go deeply into such a vast theme, a theme that till now has been under constant revision, I shall limit myself to a bare, succinct enunciation of the fundamental convictions I have concerning the matter.

By the two main roads known and travelled by any philosopher, *a priori* and *a posteriori*, before or after the concrete expression, it is possible to arrive at a philosophy of language and to regard it, as it was regarded by ancient wisdom and confirmed by modern science, as a typically human phenomenon for the communication of thought.

By the first road, starting from a metaphysical concept and from

*Main part of A.G.R.'s address on the occasion of being received into the Mexican Academy, December 14, 1955.

a philosophical anthropology which for the moment I am unable to base upon a more ample foundation, it is obvious that if man is among the finite entities and, according to Aristotle, the only rational living being, the animal endowed with the "word," and that if from this mere fact there lies between him and the rest of creation a gap which evolution cannot close, then human language will have to be an incommunicable attribute of the species, the most excellent function of which consists in its being a vehicle for the transmission of what the understanding is capable of apprehending in the use of ideas. This is expressed in the famous definition of Wilhelm von Humboldt, who says that language is "the constantly repeated act of the mind in the utilization of sounds articulated so as to express thoughts."

But also *a posteriori*, with data contributed by sciences as rigorously empirical as ethnology, anthropology, comparative linguistics, and other auxiliary disciplines, the same conclusions can be reached. The Darwinian epoch, in which our language appeared to be merely, in the words of Anatole France, "cries of the forest corrupted and complicated by anthropoid apes" (*The Garden of Epicurus, Aristus and Polyphilus or the Metaphysical Language* [*Le jardin d'Epicure, Ariste et Polyphile ou le langage métaphysique*]), or with greater euphemism, but with the same denigrating intention, a mere method of adapting to the medium, and therefore totally incapable of apprehending or expressing anything but physical entities—this epoch, I say, I believe in all sincerity to have been definitively superseded. To mention only the names of highest authority in this field, suffice it to say that such a distinguished anthropologist as Köhler summarized his long observations over many years in the thesis that the phonetic expression of the non-rational animals, even the higher apes, has only an emotive function, and totally lacks, and not by reason of secondary glotto-labial limitations, the indicative and representative functions. In human expression, on the contrary, the majority of linguists recognize today, after the salutary anti-naturalistic reaction led by Charles Bally, this triad of significative functions: emotive, indicative, and representative; and the last of these, as Cassirer has pointed out, extends from mere literal and imitative representation to analogy and symbol.

In this way, the conclusions at which Köhler arrived through the methods of the natural sciences have been in every way substantiated in the other great branch of the sciences of the mind. In the calm, documented judgement of Cassirer, observations in the most recent studies of animal psychology "seem to widen rather than narrow the gap between natural communication and human language" (*The Philosophy of Symbolic Forms* [*Philosophie der symbolischen Formen*], I, III). And reflecting the present position of investigations in this matter, a linguist and philosopher as outstanding as Urban has been able to conclude that human language "is not a part of nature, but rather an expression or incarnation of the mind; not a product of mechanical evolution, but of creative activity" (*Language and Reality* [*Lenguaje y realidad*], Fondo de Cultura Económica, 1952, p. 73).

And so we have happily returned, after the vain attempt to make of man merely the final form of the higher vertebrates, to the ancient confidence in the word as taught to us by the Greeks, at least by their greatest philosophers. Speech is the messenger of the understanding, all the Middle Ages say with Aristotle: *Sermo intellectus est nuntius.* And Plato on his part, in that dialogue in the *Sophistes* between the stranger and Teetetes, makes the correspondence between the two terms so intimate that it practically amounts to identity, to the point where speech is already in the mind before it passes to the lips, and, as will be said in the Middle Ages, mental speech and concept are in reality one and the same thing. "But is it not true," asks the stranger, "that thought and speech (*dianoia* and *logos*) are the same, except that thought is the inner, silent dialogue of the soul with itself, while the flux that goes out from the soul and passes through the mouth in sound we call speech?" "It is true" (*Sophistes*, 263*e*), answers Teetetes, "and for my part I believe it too with an unshakable conviction."

The Problem of Philosophic Language

However, here we are barely in the prodromes of our reflections, and the most arduous part still lies before us. Indeed, a general equation of thought and language is one thing, but it is a very different thing to know: firstly, if the understanding is capable of grasping what traditionally philosophy has endeavoured to grasp; and secondly, the aforesaid being deemed possible, if the articulated phoneme can express, and to what extent, that final thought experience. To make a decision about the two questions, it is no longer sufficient that we know scientific or philosophical anthropology, *a priori* or *a posteriori*, or however we may care to imagine it, but it is necessary to inquire into the deepest roots of being and thinking. I am really very sorry, gentlemen, to force you into making this effort, but here and now you will have to think hard with me.

If philosophy were, as for many it is (and on occasion I certainly envy such a comfortable attitude), nothing but the methodical articulation of individual sciences, or the formulation of categorical hypotheses which *a priori* render science itself possible, the problem under these conditions would be much less difficult to solve, since then there would enter into the question only the validity of the scientific knowledge and its consequent vocabulary. This philosophizing, indeed, which converts the former handmaid of theology into a slave of science, actually depends upon declaring metaphysics impossible. For me, nevertheless, and of course I claim no originality for an assertion backed by twenty-five centuries of philosophizing, philosophy is nothing, or very little, without what Aristotle called "first philosophy," philosophy *par excellence*, philosophy as a general term, philosophy which, in the course of the years, and by a fortuitous bibliographical inventory that in such a marvellous way involuntarily gave to it its irreplaceable name, was called metaphysics. It, in fact, has as a correlative the entity and entities which are beyond the *physis* (physical), beyond this visible and palpable nature, that is, the supreme principles and causes of entities in general, and entities most positively immaterial (positively, I say, and not only negatively like the quiddities captured through ideational abstraction) like God and spirit.

There has not been a single great philosopher who was anti-metaphysical. Heidegger calls metaphysics the fundamental event in human existence.* Kant himself, who because of limitations of historical comprehension in his time could not, greatly against his inner desires, lay a basis for speculative metaphysics, had the greatest reverence for it, and so at times calls it "the crown and consummation," and at other times "the full and complete development of the human reason."

Is the human intelligence capable of going that far, of in some way penetrating into the *omnitudo realitatis* (totality of reality), an intelligence whose own object is doubtless unlimited being, but whose sufficient object in this life, as incarnated intelligence, is the entity implied in sentient substance: *ens concretum quidditati sensibili*? And supposing it to be capable of it, can intuitions of such a character be expressed by a language whose vocabulary has been forged primarily to master the environment, to make things manageable, as Heidegger sees it, or to satisfy, says Bergson for his part, the practical requirements of life? In this, in the purely genetic aspect of language, I am in complete agreement with these philosophic currents, and even if

*"Die Metaphysik ist das Grundgeschehen im Dasein" (*Was ist Metaphysik*? [*What is Metaphysics*?], 5th ed., p. 38).

you like with so-called behaviourism, though I do not agree, of course, when its exponents, looking upon that single aspect, deny the possibility of metaphysical language, or at most allow, as for poetry, the possibility of a metaphysical predication. Metaphysics would then not be, as they say themselves, anything but an "adulterated poetry" (Montaigne), or a "justifiable poetry" (Lange), or a "dismal form of poetry" (France).*

Analogy of Word and Entity

But let us leave these facile ironies in which is demonstrated, as Kant said, what little minds can do with great problems, and let us treat seriously what is serious and great. Gentlemen, I believe that the problem will never have a satisfactory solution as long as we do not return sincerely (and not by halves or with a sense of shame, as the philosophers of symbolism usually do) to the fruitful idea which, dimly conceived by Plato and formulated with full precision by Aristotle, received all its marvellous development in the Church fathers and mediaeval scholasticism, so as to render possible, as its greatest expression, the constitution of speculative theology—the idea, in a word, of the analogy of being. There can be no doubt that it is one of the greatest discoveries of the human mind; one of its intuitions, which at the same time keeps in mind the vast space between the different steps of the ontological scale, and still is capable of throwing across all of them the bridge that supports the two correlative operations of concept and predication.

On the first page of the *Corpus Aristotelicum*, at the beginning of the treatment of Situations or Categories, and also at the end of the Metaphysics, analogy is found in the highest intuition of God which classical antiquity had; a Pure Act upon which, as Dante will say later in translating Aristotle literally, *dipende il cielo e tutta la natura* ("heaven and all nature depends," *Paradiso*, XXVIII, 42). Without analogy Aristotle could not have taken a single step, and for his exposition he begins by saying that just as there are terms whose significance (*ratio per nomen significata*) is rendered fully in all the subjects and predicates to which it is applied, and that just as on the contrary there are others whose significance is totally different though with identical phoneme, so also there are still others in which the meaning of the name is in part the same and in part different in the different entities included under the said terms or concepts. To these

*"Dismal poets . . . they indulge in empty mythology" ("Tristes poètes . . . ils font de la mythologie blanche," *Le jardin d'Epicure*).

last terms called analogues, and not to terms univocal or equivocal, belongs being; and for this reason we can predicate the being both of Being for itself and of being for another (God and his creatures), and both of being in itself and of being in another (substance and accident), without being obliged either to confine being inside the set Parmenidean sphere, or on the contrary to be silent, like the representatives of negative theology, before the other thing which is absolutely inconceivable and incommunicable.

It is not appropriate here to go more deeply into the technical terminology of the School to determine, for example, to what kind of analogy the analogy of being belongs, a question which, besides, is keenly debated even today in the scholastic school, which has a philosophy much less dogmatic than people believe. Suffice it for me to say here that whatever name it is given or whatever the differences are in its way of thinking, the fundamental thing is that in any comparison the significant reasoning must be given truly and intrinsically, whether by attribution, or only by proportional equality, in both items in the analogy (*vere et intrinsece in utroque analogato*), since otherwise it would be impossible to predicate by analogy in metaphysical discourse.*

It is not so much that we must be cured of technical terminologies as of the active intuition which animated Aristotle and the great patristic and mediaeval doctors of analogy, which is nothing but the metaphysical and religious intuition of the Entity which is Being itself, the subsistent Being (*ipsum Esse subsistens*), and the imitations of

*As I see it, this is the only point of agreement between the two schools, the Thomist and the school of Suárez [Spanish Jesuit theologian of the late sixteenth and early seventeenth centuries], who even today dispute heatedly, and with a good supply of arguments on both sides, concerning the interpretation of the analogy of being. In everything else, however, the difference is great, since while for St. Thomas (at least in Cayetano's exegesis) that analogy would be barely of intrinsic proportionality (God is to his being as the creature is to his), for Suárez, on the other hand, it would be of intrinsic attribution, and then there would be a concept or reason common to every entity, depending of course on the first term of the analogy (God). Both solutions have obviously advantages and disadvantages. The Thomistic solution more perfectly preserves divine transcendence, but the analogy is reduced to a proportional ratio. The solution of Suárez, on his side, postulates a common form, but is dangerously close to the concept of the univocal. I refrain from going more deeply into the problem, both because it is out of place here, and because of my conviction that this is one of those problems with respect to which the human intelligence will always come up against a residue of unintelligibility (*to us*, of course) which in this life at least appears to be irreducible.

which, always deficient, are all the other things, all that in any way falls into the category of entity. For them the universe was like a mirror in which is refracted into an infinity of images the most simple Light, in which, in turn, all things are, as Dante said too, *nella profonda e chiara sussistenza dell'alto lume* ("in the deep and clear subsistence of the high light," *Paradiso*, XXXIII, 115). Analogy, this intrinsic analogy of which I am speaking (the extrinsic is hardly a subject for rhetoric and literature), would be nothing but a manner of speaking, a metaphorical predication, without the theological foundation which sustains it.* Analogy is, in the final analysis, participation; and the philosophies of analogy are therefore philosophies of participation. If analogy is to be something more than a "discrete dosage of the univocal and the equivocal,"† in the final analysis a verbal dosage; or if a ratiocination which, evading the anathema of Kant, does not move in a vacuum, is to have true entitative force and render possible metaphysical ratiocination, it will not be able to ignore its original source. "A primary illumination of its origin" is the only sense in which the entire creation can be understood. As is explained by Przywara[1] (*Antología entis*, Munich, 1933, pp. 68–9), one of the great modern theorists of analogy, analogy is not something fundamental, as is suggested by the adverbial prefix of the word (*análogos*), but an ascent of the mind along the entire current of being, and in an ordered succession (since *aná* means both "upwards" and "in series") to its prime origin and source, just as Herodotus, expressing himself in the same terms, spoke of ascending the current of the river: *aná potamón plein*. In this way metaphysical ratiocination is the bold and arduous movement of the mind with the current and against the current and over the current of being and thinking, until it captures and lives, as far as it is possible for us, the life of the fountain-head. This is the nature of philosophy in those who have truly lived it on a great scale, because this is likewise the nature of being in general, in the heart of which lies, in embryo or in full consciousness, the impulse to rise above its ontological finiteness, at least in the sphere of intention. Aristotle gave finished form to this thought in conceiving the whole cosmic process as a movement of love towards Pure Union, and Fray Luis de León said the same thing, in one of the loftiest

*"Ipsa analogia entis recte declarata supponit emanationem et dependentiam omnium entium a Deo" (Suárez, *Disp. Met.*, 29, III, 7).

†José Hellín, S.L., *Analogy of Being and the Knowledge of God in Suárez* (*La analogía del ser y el conocimiento de Dios en Suárez*) Madrid, 1947, p. 64.

[1]A leading contemporary Catholic philosopher.

passages written in our language, when he told of how that unremitting endeavour of the being to return to its first cause is "the general longing of all things, and the end and, as it were, the mark towards which all creatures direct their desires" (*Of the Names of Christ* [*De los nombres de Cristo*], *Of Names in General* [*De los nombres en general*]).

So for precisely this reason, that of being analogous, that of there being in all entities a common ratio or at least a proportionality, being without limitations, the *plenitudo entis* is conceivable and expressible by man. If "in the beginning was the Word," this means as well (as the Greeks saw previously, though without this resplendent clairvoyance) that also in the end, and at the bottom of all things, the word likewise is: an intelligible structure, a *logos* which the intelligence —a *logos* also on its part—is to make known in ideational abstraction, in this way intuiting the truth and proclaiming it. It was Heidegger who restored to us this pristine sense of truth by merely calling our attention to the beautiful word by which in Greek one says "truth": *aléthia*, which denotes an operation which consists in saving from oblivion or in discovering what was hidden (*a-lethos*, *lanthano*), or from still another angle, to keep removing veils, those veils which interpose the inevitable deformations of practical life between our perception and intelligible reality. So reality, reality human and extra-human, abundant off-pouring of the first Word, is, all of it, at least by right, fundamentally intelligible. It is all discoverable, all rational, as an image or vestige of prime Reason. We must row hard, once more, in the current and against the current; but this current is not a Heraclitan or Bergsonian flux of essential irrationality, but in the mirror of its waters, however turbulent they may at times appear to us, is the spark and projection of the eternal mind.

Nobody as much as Saint Augustine lived through the agitated and vertiginous course of becoming; a torrent—said he also—which as soon as it is stemmed runs over, and then rushes wildly and runs precipitously along its course (*torrens . . . colligitur, redundat, perstrepit, currit et currendo decurrit* [*In Ps.* 109, 20]); a torrent in which things no sooner come into being than they cease to be (*antequam sint, non sunt* [*de lib. arb.*, III, 7,21]), but in which, nevertheless, there is perceptible the beauty and harmony of the whole, just as in a poem in which verses and syllables must end successively in order thus to make comprehensible the beauty of the entire poem (*de vera rel.*, XXII, 42–3). And it is so—concludes this great philosopher who is a philosopher both of becoming and of analogy—because all things have their most authentic being and their incommutable life in the eternal repository of uncreated Ideas.*

Whenever we can be permitted to contemplate its refraction, whenever in the wild current we can discern a sound without a shadow of obscurity, or, expressed in philosophical terms, a perfection of absolute postivity, we can then without any fear transfer it and predicate it out of the most pure simplicity of the source, but raising to the power of infinity the finite splendour which has once struck our eyes. It is not possible for me to clarify it further, but in these images the initiated will certainly have seen what Saint Thomas, and along with him Catholic theology, has called the *via eminentiae, per modum excellentiae et remotionis* ("way of eminence, through excellence and sacrifice"), and which constitutes the natural way of access to the divine.† Removing veils, separating impurities, clearing away perceptible rubbish, with dexterous hand and clear eye (with the latter especially), the theologian and the metaphysician open up to us the kingdom of Forms and introduce us into the mystery of being. I say the theologian and the metaphysician because both consummate, so far as conceptual form is concerned, an operation which might be called identical, since metaphysics and theology differ only slightly in that one has as its object God *sub ratione entis* ("under argument for being"), and the other, with the added habiliment of faith, *sub ratione Deitatis* ("under the reason of the Deity"). Theology, says Przywara in a beautiful phrase, is the entelechy of metaphysics (*Antología entis*, p. 48).

It is one of the greatest feats of the human intelligence to have made of this poor earthly speech of ours an instrument capable of expressing

*The immutable essence of things is therefore not the "identity of reaction," or "habit, going back from the field of action to that of thought," or arbitrary "cuts" in real duration, or other Bergsonian fancies (*Thought and Change* [*La pensée et le mouvant*], pp. 67, 68, and *passim*), but the expression of the Logos immanent in the world; that is, Aristotelian "form," and not any geometrical *découpage* (carving) taken from universal mobility.

†Of course, to connote its perfections, but never the divine nature in itself, which is completely ineffable. Saint Thomas was as conscious as anyone of the limits of analogical predication, as can be seen in a thousand places like the following: "Deus est super illud quod de ipso intellectui repraesentatur" ("God is above what is represented to the intellect about Himself," *de Ver.*, *q.* 8, *a.* 1 to 8); "Hoc est ultimum cognitionis humanae de Deo quod sciat se Deum nescire" ("This is the ultimate in the human knowledge of God, that he should know that he does not know God," *de pot.*, *q.* 7, *a.* 5 to 14); "Ita quod intellectus noster secundum nullam formam intelligibilem Deo assimiletur" ("So because our intellect will conceive of God in no intelligible form," *de pot.*, *q.* 7, *a.* 5 to 13), etc. etc.

meaningfully those supreme and mysterious realities.* To say, like Bergson, that because language has been shaped primarily for everyday uses, it cannot transcend this sphere, is an invalid objection. The meaningful transposition does not need to be chained to its original meaning, since as Saint Thomas teaches (*Sum. Theol.*, I, *q.* 13, *a.* 2), the *a quo* of the invention of the name is one thing, and quite another the *ad quod* of the further signification, an operation which has its foundation in the analogical function of language, and the latter in its turn is founded on the analogy of being. With words of everyday use, of the most trivial and practical use (one need only recall the stale example of the *ousía* [being]) Plato and Aristotle forged the marvellous world of the non-temporal and the eternally valid, as Windelband[2] would say, or rather, they did not forge it (they were not, really, philosophers of the transcendental subject or the consciousness in general), but with this marvellous verbal instrument they gave us the key just barely to allow us access to that world in whose contemplation lies (this is also the case with Aristotle) the happiness most proper to man. They did this because for Plato the world of fact was a replica of the world of idea, the phenomenon of the spirit; or, as is said still more clearly in the *Timaeus*, this world is an image of the divine pattern, a thought which, integrated and expanded by Saint Augustine in the theology of the Word, is the unexhausted and inexhaustible source of analogy and symbol. In those great philosophers there was *avant la lettre* the feeling, both humble and bold, of confidence in the word, in the finite word and the infinite Word "by whom all things were made," and through which, consequently, they have voice and meaning, this feeling which, under the dazzling light of the Johannine gospel, finds incomparable expression in the sonorous voice of Victor Hugo: "Car le mot c'est le verbe, et le Verbe c'est Dieu" ("For speech is the word, and the Word is God").

Greatness and Deficiency of Philosophic Language

And yet, gentlemen, I still find it necessary, at this stage of my discourse, to beg your indulgence again, and most earnestly, because

*On the other hand, there are philosophers blind to metaphysics, like William James, for example, who believes that the attributes which the human reason can predicate concerning God constitute nothing but a "metaphysical monster . . . an absolutely worthless invention of the scholarly mind" (*The Varieties of Religious Experience*, Longmans, 1923, p. 447). These evaluations are, of course, enthusiastically adhered to by Ogden and Richards, "drug-store" philosophers, whose popularity in environments like ours, of a genuine metaphysical tradition, is simply inexplicable.

[2]German philosopher of the Neo-Kantian school, who died in 1915.

after having praised at length its great qualities, I have to do the same with regard to the deficiencies in philosophic language, I mean its essential inadequacy (however adequate it may be in other respects) to give us by its power alone this knowledge, the highest in the natural order, which we call philosophy.

Philosophy is the perfect work of reason (*opus perfectum rationis*), of this there is no doubt. But just because of this, because it is an operation so eminently vital and demands so unreservedly, by virtue of the indestructible unity of man, the aid not of the reason only, but of all his powers, and finally because its object, in spite of the analogical scale, is so far beyond the customary business of this human intellect immersed in matter—on account of all this, I say, it is pertinent to inquire how far and under what conditions philosophical language will be able to make patent to us (as even Husserl demanded, voicing the aspiration of all the great philosophers), the things themselves. Words alone, says Paul Valéry, cannot consummate the act of spiritual possession (*Leonardo and the philosophers* [*Léonard et les philosophes*]). Philosophy is not a logomachy, but, as Plato says literally, a "gigantomachy," a "struggle of giants to have being."

It was not exactly the philosophers of becoming and irrationality, but the great champions of the power of the intellect and word themselves, who first of all valiantly posed the problem of the communicative value of philosophic language. Those unfortunate voyages of Plato to Sicily, where he went with the fallacious illusion that in that island he would make a trial of his great dream, the philosopher-king, have left us among other things, as a complete compensation for the failure of the immediate objective, the most conclusive demonstration of the inanity of philosophy when it is nothing more than logomachy, a texture of *philosophemata* (philosophic items"), a mass of verbal statements, however true it may literally be. For then this Dionysius the Young, tyrant of Syracuse, in whom Plato had such high hopes, knew the sayings of the philosophers very correctly, and had even written a little treatise, something like what today we would call an "Introduction to Philosophy," but of the thing itself (*peri tou prágmatos*), says Plato (*Ep.* VII, 340*e*), he knew absolutely nothing. He knew nothing, according to the philosopher, because unlike what happens in other sciences (note well the contrast), philosophical intuition "cannot be reduced to a formula, but only after an assiduous cultivation and after living for a long time with these problems, just as when the spark leaps, the truth is suddenly kindled in the depths of the soul, and then grows by itself" (*Ep.* VII, 341*c*). And continuing this happy digression of his Seventh Letter, Plato enumerates the five elements which, like so many veils or barriers, the philosopher must apprehend and transpose until he really arrives at the conquest of the truth, namely: the name, the definition, the image, the concept, and finally the object itself, that is, the truly intelligible and real entity.

There was therefore no need for Hegel and Bergson to come and rend their clothes and talk with such indignation, moreover very just indignation, against the novices, scribes, and Pharisees of philosophy who content themselves, according to Bergson, with "collecting ready-made thoughts and phrases" (*Thought and Change*, p. 42). Plato had shared an identical *pathos*, though without despairing, as Bergson did, of the power of the intelligence, since even right there, in that Sicilian epistle in which he goes so far as to say, in a moment of discouragement, that philosophy is incapable of any graphic expression, he asserts once more that metaphysical objects are in themselves accessible to the understanding by virtue of "the relationship and resemblance" which the latter bears to them, the capital argument, as I see it, which Plato uses in the dialogue about the death of Socrates, to demonstrate the immortality of the soul.

But here it is not merely a question, as might appear at first sight, of a purely natural relationship and resemblance, revealed once for all for everyone, but of a proportion or analogy (here we are again with the key term) which comes to show itself between the soul and its highest and most fitting object, only after a continuous and daily exercise of reflection and purification, an exercise in which virtue plays a part as great as dialectics, or perhaps a greater part. In short, it is a question of a second analogy, an existential analogy between subject and object which Saint Thomas will call adaptation (*connaturalidad*), and which the saint himself considers a surer road to knowledge than rational argument itself; according to him, a gift of the Holy Spirit (*Sum. Theol.*, II *a*, II *ae*, *q*. 45, *a*. 2). Well, the minds of these philosophers of whom I am speaking are also saturated with this mystic sense, and for this reason they considered wisdom a divine and not a human possession, as Aristotle says (*Met.* I, 2, 982 *b*), and philosophy, this love of wisdom, as we still say today, but without any longer knowing what we are saying, was for them a way of life, the highest of all, followed in the bosom of an erotic and mystic community which aspires to share in what is properly divine, and in what, thanks to an incessant dialogue (it is seen that in no way is the power of the word disregarded) between souls of the same high temper, there occasionally comes, Plato says further, "the shining of wisdom and intelligence with all the intensity that human strength can endure" (*Ep.* VII, 344*b*). Socrates has reason (it matters little whether it is the real or the fictitious Socrates) for comparing philosophy to the Orphean mysteries and initiations, and of himself he says that for his whole life he has been a priest of Apollo, god of light and intelligence, in whose honour, like the swans, at the moment of death he sings the song of immortality (*Phaedo*, 85*b*).

This corporative and organic sense of wisdom, these beautiful communitarian forms of life, these laic cenobies or homes of wisdom, the latest example of which I think was Port Royal, seem to have passed away forever, and there hardly remains a vestige of them in the universities. This dismal civilization in which we live inexorably demands a selection among other types of community, which while they differ in many respects, all agree in being institutionally coercive and incompatible up to a certain point with free and absorbing dialogue, which is the atmosphere and instrument suitable for philosophizing. The philosopher today, no longer able to be a cenobite, must be more or less an anchorite, in which appears, in this new fashion, the heroic requisite which is and always has been consubstantial with his calling. Philosophy, as Heidegger says, is an oblation, "the farewell to entities" to deliver themselves over to being (*What is Metaphysics?*, 5th ed., Epilogue [*Nachwort*], p. 45). Though those social forms are irremediably outworn, what really matters is that there should be preserved intact the impulse that animated them, that is, the resolution to conquer at all costs that existential analogy between the spirit and the supreme spiritual realities, so that, through that medium, the inner sight may be opened to the infinite maze of the analogy of being.*

Concerning Philosophic Style

After we have arrived at this point, the question of manner, style, or form of expression in general to be employed by the philosophic writer is to a certain degree secondary. This term "philosophic writer" is far from being an analytical category. Apart from the fact that here, as in everything else, the apothegm of our poet holds its full value: "The form enslaves; the reason governs," reflecting the dominant indifference of the mind to its means of expression, what is really

*No great philosopher is untouched by this participation in the divine which philosophy carries with it. Thus Bergson has been able to write: "There is already something almost divine in the effort, however humble, of a mind that reinserts itself in the vital impulse (*élan vital*)." (*Thought and Change*, p. 76.)

important and decisive is the fertilizing of the soul, of the listener or reader, so that he may transcend, as Plato desires, the name, definition, and concept, and can by himself kindle and utter his inner word, without which there is no spiritual fruitfulness either in heaven or on earth.

This operation can be aided equally by the dialogue, the essay, or the treatise, or any of the varieties comprised in these three general terms, provided (and this would be the only requirement common to them all) the philosophic style is always direct and dramatic, of a kind of dramatism, of course, that is intrinsic and basic, that is, with live ideas set up against one another, in a tension both antagonistic and complementary. Philosophy, in fact (authentic philosophy, that is), has always been, as Plato said, dialectical, because in turn the analogy of being is dialectical and dramatic, a mystery of resemblances and differences (*tanta similitudo et maior dissimilitudo*, as the Fourth Lateran Council said) and understanding can therefore not progress except by cancelling, conserving, and replacing, in an *Aufhebung* ("ascent") which is in the same way applicable to every profound philosophy, with whose contrasts and oppositions the participation of being is permeated. In this sense, a Platonic dialogue is dramatic, as are also the antinomies of Pure Reason and any article of the *Summa Theologica*, a live counterpoint of opposing voices, the objections and answers of which integrate into the body of the article a unity, increasingly simple and rich, of dialectical conquest. The only difference between the so-called dialectical philosophies, by antonomasia, and the others, is that for the latter we arrive at a point where, as Aristotle said, we have to stop, the point where every *Werden* ("becoming") rebounds and comes to an end, as when the waves strike the escarpment, in the subsistent *Esse* ("being") of Pure Action.

Without this, not even philosophy itself will escape an unauthentic existence which Heidegger calls "empty talk" or "empty writing," since the characteristic of empty talk or gossip is not exactly slander, but loss of contact with things; repeating the talk of others without verifying it personally; making out of words things in themselves or enigmas; repeating philosophizings of others, now emptied of the original intuition. What marks a philosopher, according to Alloys Müller (*Introduction to Philosophy* [*Einleitung in die Philosophie*], p. 29), is the gift of vision (*die Gabe des Schauens*), and anyone who does not feel it in the depths of his soul had better think of something else.

By the same criterion, both liberal and inflexible, we can settle the other allied question, which is so greatly discussed these days, as to whether philosophy should be expressed in concepts or in metaphors.

Concerning this I shall say no more than that metaphor, whose philosophical foundation is simply the analogy of extrinsic proportionality, cannot be scorned on the ground that, according to very respectable opinion, the analogy of being would hardly be of intrinsic proportionality. Moreover, a large number of philosophic concepts, among those which today appear most certainly to be such concepts, were originally metaphorical concepts. Think again of *ousía* (being), of *persona* (person), and of many more. If we believe Leibniz, the "influence" (*in-fluere*) of cause on effect seemed a daring metaphor to the contemporaries of Suárez. Nobody today would call the scholastic vocabulary metaphoric, and yet to Leibniz himself it appeared to be a style abounding in metaphors: *eorum oratio tropis scatet* (*De stilo philosophico Nizolii*, XVIII).

Let us look then, without any animosity—indeed quite the contrary—at the progressive enrichment of philosophic language thanks to the introduction of new terms and concepts which at first, in their native state, will appear bold metaphors, on account of the inevitable necessity to express unpublished intuitions in words originally intended for other uses. Nevertheless, except by looking at being, in its ultimate foundations, as something irrational, it is not possible to maintain, as Bergson did, and apparently Heidegger ultimately, that metaphor (it seems to me that we must understand metaphor as in its virgin state) is the only means, or at least the most adequate means, of philosophical expression. Such a claim, then, must be rejected when one considers that the concept, in spite of all its imperfections, is nevertheless the normal way of access to the intellectual intuition of the entity which is fundamentally true and intelligible.* Philosophy is, or ought to be, learning universally valid, and "only the concept," says Hegel, "can produce universality of learning" (*Phenomenology of the Mind* [*Phenomenologie de l'esprit*], translated by Hyppolite, Vol. I, p. 60). The fierce invectives of *Phenomenology of the Mind* against the invasion of *Sturm und Drang* (storm and stress) in philosophy, "phantasmagorias that are neither fish nor flesh, neither poetry nor philosophy" (*Phenomenology*, Vol. I, p. 58) are still alive and pertinent.

If philosophy is not to end by becoming poetry (which I think would ordinarily be bad poetry), it absolutely must restore the concept as its most suitable instrument. No one made more abundant use of

*Bergson himself acknowledges this when he says: "Intuition will moreover be communicated only by intelligence. It is more than idea; nevertheless, to be transmitted, it will have to be mounted on ideas." (*Thought and Change*, p. 52).

metaphor, allegory, and myth than Plato, and yet he takes good care to warn us that the poet and the philosopher differ precisely in that one uses *mythoi* ("myths") and the other *logoi* ("statements") (*Phaedo*, 61*b*). The philosopher, after all, is not a mystagogue, even less a hater of reasoning, but on the contrary his mission consists in propagating rational clarity as far as possible, and by the use of adequate concepts.

Will it be necessary to say that in these considerations there is not the slightest disparagement of poetry, but rather a desire to assure proper status and autonomy to what, along with philosophy, is worthy of our greatest reverence? Poetry also lives by analogy, by *l'universelle analogie*, as Baudelaire says (*Art romantique, Victor Hugo*), who elsewhere adds that "nature is a word, an allegory" (*Baudelaire à Alphonse Toussenel*),[3] and that "the earth is a correspondence of heaven" (*Art romantique, Théophile Gautier*), words with which he gives us, in plain, undebatable prose, the antological foundation of those marvellous poetic "correspondences" in which "man passes through beautiful gardens of symbols." Drinking from the same spring, poetry thus gives us the profound sense of life, the affective impletion, the direct contact with that thing which the concept does not succeed in representing except abstractly and schematically. We might say that it is the Eros informing the Logos, or perchance another Logos which for lack of words, and because it itself alludes to something not directly namable, we should have to designate simply as Spirit. For that very reason, nevertheless, the finite mind would be unable to unite in one operation what, being still above it, without ceasing to be one thing, is distinct. If I am permitted to express what I think concerning this matter by means of one of those Trinitarian analogies to which one is irresistibly led by the reading of St. Augustine, I shall say that the human mind, productive of many things: science, technology, politics, law, etc., also produces two fruits, philosophy and poetry, in which alone it fully reveals its nature, and which for that reason are, so to speak, its two processes, on an equal footing, one through intelligence, and the other through love, both having the same perfection and the same substance, but really distinct and opposite to each other.* The poet

*"We may conclude, then, with Paul Valéry that metaphysics is a special literary genre, characterized by certain themes, and by the recurrence of certain terms and forms, which distinguish it clearly from the types known as poetry and science. To subsume its language, which has terms like "ideas," "essences," "noumena," etc., under poetry, is to have a mistaken conception of both poetry and metaphysics" (Urban, *Language and Reality*, p. 534).

[3]Nineteenth-century French journalist and writer.

and the philosopher "live near each other on mountains separated by abysses."*

With poetry philosophy shares the highest aristocracy of the mind, and it is the final fruit, historically later than poetry, of a culture in its perfect maturity. That we should come to have it in Mexico, and as soon as possible, is my most sincere and heart-felt wish. And as our philosophy bursts into flower on the edges of the light, our Academy will have to be there, vigilant and understanding, to sanction the beneficent renovation of the philosophical lexicon in harmony with the nature and modules proper to the Spanish language, for if the language is the collective soul, philosophy is the perfect generation of the soul fertilized by being. In my opinion, this is a beautiful aspect of the general duty incumbent upon the Academy, this community of men bound together by love of the word.

Philosophy and Language (*Filosofía y lenguaje*), Imprenta Universitaria, Mexico, 1956, pp. 20–83.

*From the *Patmos*, by Hölderlin, applied by Heidegger to the relationship between the thinker and the poet (*What is Metaphysics?*, *Epilogue*, at conclusion).

Leopoldo Zea

(b. Mexico, D.F., 1912)

Leopoldo Zea began to study philosophy about 1939 as a student of Dr. José Gaos, who was the definitive guide to his philosophical vocation, since his earliest writings were literary in intention. His first studies were in the field of Greek philosophy: his later examination of positivism in Mexico and Spanish America induced him to cultivate the same themes; in recent years, faithful to this decision, he has devoted himself to the investigation of the philosophy "of the Mexican" and to the advancement of the study of the history of ideas in America. Historicism, existentialism, and the historical concept of Toynbee have been his principal philosophic affinities.

The quality of Zea's studies does not lie in the brilliance of the style or exposition, but in his mental precision and concentration, the extraordinary discipline and passion with which the author devotes himself to his philosophic work, even in its less academic aspects. This accounts for the force he puts into his polemics and the inner persuasiveness which gives life to his writings.

At the National University, where he teaches his specialty, Leopoldo Zea studied and obtained the Master's degree and that of Doctor of Philosophy. He has travelled and given lectures in America and Europe on projects related to philosophy, and his name is known and respected in the philosophical centres of the world. He formed and actuated the Hyperion group, dedicated to existentialism and engaged in the philosophical investigation of "Mexico and things Mexican" ("México y lo mexicano"), the theme and name of an interesting collection of publications directed by Zea.

ESSAYS: *Proud Philosopher* (*Superbus philosphus*), 1942; *Positivism in Mexico* (*El positivismo en México*), 1943; *Apogee and Decline of Positivism* (*Apogeo y decadencia del positivismo*), 1944; *Essays on Philosophy in History* (*Ensayos sobre filosofía en la historia*), 1948; *Two Stages of Thought in Spanish America* (*Dos etapas del pensamiento en Hispanoamérica*), 1949; *Consciousness and Possibility of the Mexican* (*Conciencia y posibilidad del mexicano*), 1952; *Philosophy As Commitment, and Other Essays* (*La filosofía como compromiso y otros ensayos*), 1952; *The Consciousness of Man in Philosophy* (*La conciencia del hombre en la filosofía*), 1953; *The West and the Consciousness of Mexico* (*El Occidente y la conciencia de México*), 1953; *Philosophy in Mexico* (*La filosofía en México*),

1955; *Scheme for a History of Ideas in Spanish America* (*Esquema para una historia de las ideas en Iberoamérica*), 1956; *From Liberalism to the Revolution in Mexican Education* (*Del liberalismo a la Revolución en la educacion mexicana*), 1956; *America in History* (*América en la historia*), 1957.

CONCERNING AN AMERICAN PHILOSOPHY

I

A FEW YEARS AGO a young Mexican writer, Samuel Ramos,[1] published a book which aroused expectations. In this book, called *The Profile of Man and Culture in Mexico* (*El perfil del hombre y la cultura en México*), a first attempt was made to interpret the culture of Mexico, taking it as a theme for a philosophical interpretation. Philosophy descended from the world of ideal entities to a world of concrete entities like Mexico, a symbol of men who live and die in its cities and fields. This rashness was scornfully called "literature." Philosophy could be nothing but an ingenious game of words taken from a foreign culture, words which of course lacked a meaning, the meaning they had for that original culture.

Years later another writer, this time an Argentinian, Francisco Romero, emphasized that Spanish America had to begin to concern itself about themes proper to itself, about the need to turn to the history of its culture and draw from it themes for a new philosophic interest. But this time the exhortation was supported by a series of cultural phenomena indicated in an article entitled "On Philosophy in Spanish America" ("Sobre la filosofía en Iberoamérica"). In this article he shows us how interest in philosophic themes has been growing in Spanish America day by day. The outside world follows and eagerly asks for works of a philosophic type or character, out of which numerous publications have arisen: books, reviews, newspaper articles, etc., as well as the formation of institutes and centres of philosophic studies in which this activity is carried on. This interest in philosophy appears in contrast to other periods when this activity was the work of a few misunderstood men, something that did not pass beyond the esoteric circle or the university chair. Now a point has been reached which Romero calls "a stage of philosophical normality," that is, a stage where philosophical exercise is regarded as an ordinary function of culture, the same as other activities of a cultural nature. The philosopher ceases to be a queer fellow whom no one is

[1] See p. 238.

interested in understanding, and becomes a member of the cultural élite of his country. There is established a kind of "philosophical climate," that is, a public opinion which pronounces judgement upon philosophical creation, obliging it to concern itself with themes that agitate those who form so-called "public opinion."

Well then, there is a question that concerns not merely a few men on our continent, but the man of America in general. This question is that of the possibility or impossibility of an American culture, and as a partial aspect of this question, that of the possibility or impossibility of an American philosophy. But to pose and attempt to resolve such a question, independently of whether the answer is in the affirmative or the negative, is already engaging in American philosophy, since it means trying to answer an American question affirmatively or negatively. Therefore works like those of Ramos, Romero, and others on such a theme, whatever their conclusions, are already American philosophy.

The question of the possibility of an American culture is one imposed by our times, by the historical circumstances in which we find ourselves. In the past the name of America had not become the topic of such a debate because no one cared about it. An American culture, a culture proper to the man of America, was a theme without interest; America was living comfortably in the shadow of European culture. Nevertheless, this culture is astir in our times, and seems to have disappeared from the entire European continent. The man of America who had lived so trustingly finds the culture upon which he relied failing him, facing an empty future, and the ideas in which he had placed his faith turning into useless, senseless contrivances, without value to their originators. He who had lived so confidently in the shade of a tree he had not planted finds himself unprotected when the planter cuts it down and casts it into the fire as worthless. He now has to plant his own cultural tree, and make his own ideas. But a culture does not rise up miraculously. The seed of such a culture must be procured somewhere, and must belong to someone. Well (and this is the matter that preoccupies the man of America), where can he procure this seed? That is, what ideas is he going to develop? In what ideas is he going to put his faith? Will be continue to trust and develop ideas inherited from Europe? Or are there ideas and topics to be developed that belong to the American setting? Or will it be necessary to invent those ideas? In a word, there is posed the problem of whether there are or are not ideas proper to America, as well as that of whether or not to accept the ideas of European culture now in crisis. More concretely, it is the problem of relations between America and European culture, and that of the possibility of an exclusively American ideology.

II

By the preceding we see that one of the first themes for an American philosophy is that of relations between America and European culture. Well, the first thing to ask is what kind of relationship exists between America and that culture. Some have compared this relationship to that which exists between Asia and the same European culture. It is assumed that America, like Asia, has assimilated only European technology. But if this were so, what would American culture have of its own? For the Asiatic, what has been adopted of European culture is considered to be something superposed, which it has had to adopt due to change of circumstance when the European intervened. But what he has adopted of European culture is not precisely the culture itself—that is, a way of life, a concept of the world—but only its instruments, its techniques. The Asiatic knows himself to be heir to a very old culture which has been passed down from father to son, and thus he knows himself to be in possession of a culture of his own. His concept of the world is practically the opposite to that of the European. From the European he has taken only his techniques, and this has been forced upon him by the European himself, by intervening with his techniques in what was a purely Asiatic circumstance. Our day is showing what an Asiatic can do with a concept of the world that is his own by utilizing European techniques. Such a man is totally indifferent to the future of European culture, and will certainly try to destroy it if it interposes itself or continues to intervene in what he considers as his own culture.

Well then, can we of America take the same view with respect to European culture? Such a view means to regard ourselves as possessors of a culture which is our own and which perhaps has not attained expression because Europe has stood in our way. Then it would indeed be fitting to take this as the opportune moment to liberate ourselves culturally. In that case the crisis in European culture would be a matter of indifference to us. Instead of such a crisis presenting itself as a problem, it would present itself as a solution. But this is not the case: the crisis in European culture concerns us deeply, and we feel it as a crisis of our own.

And this is because the kind of relationship which as people of America we have with European culture is different from that possessed by the Asiatic. We do not feel ourselves, as the Asiatic does, heirs to a culture of our own continent, that is, autochthonous. An indigenous culture did indeed exist—Aztec, Mayan, Incan, etc.—but to us it does not represent, to us who live in America today, what the ancient Oriental culture represents to present-day Asiatics. While the Asiatic continues to view the world as it was viewed by his forefathers, we of America do not view the world as it was viewed by an Aztec or a Mayan. If we did, we should feel for the divinities and temples of pre-Columbian culture the same devotion that the Oriental feels for his very ancient gods and temples. A Mayan temple is just as alien and meaningless to us as a Hindu temple.

What is our own, proper to America, is not found in pre-Columbian culture. Is it something European? Well, with respect to European culture we are in a strange position—we use it but we do not consider it ours; we feel ourselves to be "imitators" of it. Our way of thinking, our concept of the world, is similar to that of the European. European culture has for us meaning that pre-Columbian culture lacks. And yet, we do not feel it is ours. We feel like bastards using property to which they have no right. We feel like one putting on a suit that is not his, and we feel it is too big for us. We adapt their ideas but we cannot adapt ourselves to them. We feel we should realize the ideals of European culture, but feel ourselves incapable of achieving them; we content ourselves with admiring them, thinking they are not made for us. In this lies the core of our problem: we do not feel ourselves heirs of an autochthonous culture, since this culture lacks meaning for us; and the culture which, like the European, has a meaning for us, we do not feel is ours. There is something inclining us towards European culture, but at the same time fighting against being part of that culture. Our concept of the world is European, but the achievements of this culture we feel are alien to us, and when we try to emulate them in America, we feel we are imitators.

What inclines us towards Europe and at the same time resists being European is something peculiarly ours, the spirit of America. America feels inclined towards Europe like a son towards his father, but at the same time he resists being his own father. This resistance can be seen in the fact that despite its inclination towards European culture, when it achieves what that culture achieves, America feels itself to be an imitator, and does not feel that it is achieving something of its own, but something that only Europe can achieve. This explains our feeling of being inhibited, inferior to the European. The trouble is that we feel American things, our own possessions, to be something inferior. The resistance of the American against being European is felt as incapacity. We think like Europeans, but this is not sufficient for us; we also want to have the same achievements as Europe. The trouble is that we want to adapt American circumstance to a concept of the world which we inherited from Europe, and not adapt this concept of the world to American circumstance. This accounts for ideas and reality remaining unadapted. We need the ideas of European culture, but when we bring them into our setting we feel they are too big and do not dare to cut them down; we prefer to be ridiculous, like one who puts on a suit which does not fit him. This is explained by the fact that until a very short time ago the man of America wanted to forget he was of America in order to feel himself just another European. This is the same thing as a son forgetting he is a son and trying to be his own father; the result would have to be a poor imitation. And this is what the man of America feels who has tried to imitate instead of to realize his personal potential.

Alfonso Reyes very wittily portrays for us this resistance of the man of America to being American. The American felt, "on top of the misfortunes of being human and being modern, the very specific misfortune of being American; that is, born and rooted in a soil that was not the present focus of civilization, but a branch office of the world."* Until yesterday to be of America had been a great misfortune, because it did not allow us to be European. Now it is completely the reverse: not having been able to be European, in spite of our great determination, allows us now to have a personality. It allows us in this moment of crisis in European culture to discover that there is something peculiar to ourselves, and which therefore can serve to sustain us. What this something is, is one of the questions which American philosophy must consider.

III

America is a daughter of European culture, and is rising up in one of the latter's great crises. The discovery is not simply a matter of chance, but the result of a need. Europe needed America; in the mind of every European was the Idea of America, the idea of a Promised Land, a land to which the European could direct his aspirations, when once he could not keep on directing them to the air above him. He could no longer look to heaven. Thanks to the new physics, the heavens ceased to be the abode of ideals, to become transformed into something

*Alfonso Reyes, "Notes on the American Intelligence" ("Notes sobre la inteligencia americana"), *Sur* review, Buenos Aires, Sept., 1936, No. 24.

unlimited, into a mechanical infinity which was for that reason dead. The idea of an ideal world came down from the heavens and was set in America. For that reason the European went out in search of the ideal land and found it.

The European needed to rid himself of a concept of life with which he felt himself sated; he needed to free himself from his past and begin a new life. He needed to make a new history, well planned and calculated, in which there would be neither scarcity nor surfeit. What the European did not dare to propose openly in his own land, this new land called America took for granted. America was the pretext for criticism of Europe. What they wished Europe to be was in their imagination realized in America. In these lands were imagined fantastic cities and governments which corresponded to the ideal of the modern man. America was presented as the idea of what Europe should be. America was the European Utopia, the ideal world in conformity with which the old Occidental world was to be remade. In a word: America was the ideal creation of Europe.

America comes into history as a land of projects, a land of the future, but projects which are not its own, and a future not its own either. These projects and this future belong to Europe. The European who set foot in America—becoming involved in the American scene, bringing into being the man of America—was not able to see the genuine America, for he had eyes only for what Europe wanted it to be. Not finding what European fancy had put on the American continent, he felt disappointed, which gives rise to the uprooting of the man of America with respect to his environment. The man of America feels himself to be European in origin, but inferior to the European on account of his dwelling-place. He becomes an unadapted person, considers himself superior to his environment and inferior to the culture which formed him. He feels scorn for anything American and resentment towards anything European.

The man of America, instead of trying to realize possibilities that were America's own, strove to realize a European Utopia, naturally coming into conflict with American reality which resists becoming anything but what it is, namely, America. This is the cause of the sense of inferiority of which we have already spoken. The surrounding reality is considered by the man of America to be inferior to what he believes to be his destiny. This feeling has shown itself in Anglo-Saxon America as an eagerness to achieve on a large scale the same thing that Europe achieved to satisfy needs peculiar to itself. North America has striven to be a second Europe, a copy magnified. Creation of one's own is of no importance; the important thing is to copy the European models on a large scale and with maximum perfection. Everything is reduced to numbers: so many dollars or so many metres. At heart all they are trying to do in this is to conceal a sense of inferiority. The American of the United States tries to show that he is just as capable as the European, and his way of showing it is to do on a large scale, and with the greatest technical perfection, the same thing that the European has done. But in this he has not demonstrated cultural capability, but simply technical ability; for cultural capability is shown in the solution given to problems which pose themselves to man as he lives, and not in the mechanical imitation of solutions which other men have arrived at in solving their own problems.

As for the Spanish American, he has resigned himself to feeling inferior not only to the European, but also to the American of the United States. Not only does he not try to conceal his sense of inferiority, but he displays it by depreciating himself. The only thing he has tried to do up to the present has been to live as comfortably as possible in the shadow of ideas he knows are not his own. The important thing is not ideas, but the way one lives by them. Therefore our political organization has been turned into a bureaucracy. Politics ceases to be an end and is turned into an instrument for obtaining a certain bureaucratic post. Banners and ideals are of no importance; what matters is that these banners or ideals should open the way to a certain position. This explains those miraculous and rapid changes of banner and ideals; it also explains those everlasting projects and that constant planning, without ever achieving definitive results. Projects and plans are continually inspired by ever shifting ideologies. There is no plan to be carried through by the nation as a whole, because there is no sense of nationhood. And there is no sense of nationhood for the same reason that there is no feeling for things American. Anyone feeling inferior as a man of America also feels inferior as a national, as a member of one of the nations of the American continent. And do not think that the rabid nationalist has a sense of nationhood, the one who talks about making a culture that is Mexican, Argentinian, Chilean, or of any other country of America, excluding everything with a foreign smell. No, basically he will try only to eliminate everything before which he feels inferior. Such is the case with all those who think this the opportune moment to eliminate everything European from our culture.

This would be a false position; whether we like it or not, we are children of European culture. From Europe we have our cultural body, what we may call the framework: language, religion, customs; in a word, our view of the world and of life is European. To break away from it would be to break away from the kernel of our personality. We cannot renounce that culture, just as we cannot renounce our parents. But as without renouncing our parents we have a personality which prevents anyone from confusing us with them, so also we shall have a cultural personality without renouncing the culture from which we sprang. Consciousness of our true relationship to European culture eliminates every sense of inferiority, giving rise to a "sense of responsibility." This sense is what animates the man of America in our day. He regards himself as having attained his "majority," and like any man who has reached that age, he recognizes that he has a past and does not renounce it, in the same way that none of us is ashamed of having had a childhood. The man of America knows himself to be heir to Western culture and claims his place in it. The place he claims for himself is that of contributor. A son of such culture does not wish to continue to live by it, but he wants to work for it. In the name of this America with a sense of responsibility, a man of America, Alfonso Reyes, claimed from Europe "the right to the universal citizenship which we have won," considering that now "we have attained our majority".* America stands at the historic point where it must carry out its cultural mission. What this mission is to be is another theme, to be developed by what we have called American philosophy.

IV

Having recognized our cultural relations with Europe, another of the tasks of this possible American philosophy would be to continue the development of philosophic themes which belong to that culture, but especially the themes which European philosophy considers as universal themes; that is, themes whose abstractness makes them valid for any time or place. Such themes are those of being, knowledge, space, time, God, life, death, etc. An American philosophy would contribute to Occidental culture by trying to solve the problems which such themes would pose and which had not been solved by European philosophy, or whose solution was not satisfactory. Well then, those interested in formulating a philosophy with an American stamp might think that this is of no concern in a philosophy preoccupied with the strictly American. Nevertheless this would be untrue, because both the questions we have called universal and the questions peculiar to American circumstance are intimately bound together. When we deal

*A. Reyes, "Notes on the American Intelligence."

with certain questions we must also deal with others. Abstract questions will have to be viewed from circumstances applicable to the man of America. Every man will see in these questions what has the closest connection with his circumstance, and will focus them from the point of view of his interest, which is determined both by his mode of life and by his capacity or incapacity—in a word, by his circumstance. In the case of America, its contribution to the philosophy of these themes will be coloured by the American circumstance. Hence, when we approach abstract questions we shall focus them as questions of our own. Being, God, etc., while questions valid for any man, will be questions to which solutions would be given from an American point of view. Concerning these questions we should not be able to say what they are for every man, but what they are for us as men of America. Being, God, death, etc., would be what such abstractions represent for us. Do not forget that all European philosophy has worked on the same questions in an endeavour to offer solutions of a universal character. Nevertheless, the result has been a number of philosophies differing from one another. In spite of all their striving for universality, there have come out a Greek philosophy, a Christian philosophy, a French philosophy, an English philosophy, and a German philosophy. In the same way, independently of our trying to create a philosophy of America, and in spite of our endeavour to give solutions of a universal character, our solutions would bear the stamp of our circumstance.

Another kind of question that could be treated by our philosophy would be any that is related to our own circumstance; that is, this future philosophy of ours must try to solve problems which our circumstance poses. This point of view is as legitimate as the preceding, and valid as a philosophic theme. As men of America we have a number of problems that arise only in our circumstance, and which therefore only we can solve. The posing of these problems does not diminish the philosophic character of our philosophy, because this philosophy attempts to solve problems which are set before man in his existence. Hence the problems set before the man of America will have to be peculiar to the circumstance in which he exists.

Among these themes is that of our history. History is part of man's circumstance: it gives him his figure and profile, making him capable of performing certain tasks and incapable of performing others. This is why we must consider our history, for in it we shall find the basis of our capacities and incapacities. We cannot continue to be ignorant of our past, refusing to consider our experience, for without this knowledge we cannot consider ourselves mature. Maturity, attaining our majority, means experience. Anyone ignorant of his national history lacks experience, and anyone who lacks experience cannot be a mature, responsible man.

Concerning the history of our philosophy, it will be thought that we cannot find in it anything but bad copies of the European philosophic systems. In fact, this will be what is found by anyone seeking in it philosophic systems, peculiar to our America, that are as important as the European systems. But this would be a wrong point of view; we must go to the history of our philosophy with a different perspective. This must be that of our negations, of our incapacity to do anything but make bad copies of our European models. We must ask ourselves why we do not have a philosophy of our own, and the answer may just be that philosophy itself, since we should be discovering in ourselves a way of thinking that is our own, which perhaps has not acquired expression in the forms used by European philosophy.

We must further ask ourselves why our philosophy is a "bad copy" of European philosophy, because possibly in this fact of being a bad copy there may also be the thing that is essential to an American philosophy; for being a bad copy does not imply that it must be bad, but that it is simply different. Perhaps our sense of inferiority has caused us to think of anything of our own as bad, merely because it does not match or come up to its model. To acknowledge that we cannot produce the same systems that European philosophy has produced does not mean that we confess our inferiority to the makers of that philosophy; it is simply to acknowledge that we are different. Starting from this angle, we shall not see in what our philosophers have done a mass of bad copies of European philosophy, but interpretations of this philosophy made by men of America. The American element will be present in spite of our philosophers' endeavour to be objective. The American element will be present regardless of attempts to depersonalize.

V

Philosophy in its universal character has been preoccupied by one of the problems which have most agitated man in all times, that of man's relations with society. This theme has been posed as a political matter, the organization of our living together. These relations are the responsibility of the State, and for this reason philosophy has inquired by whom it ought to be formed, and who ought to govern. The State must see that the balance is not disturbed between the individual and society; it must see that it does not fall into either anarchy or totalitarianism.

Well, to achieve this balance a moral justification is required. Philosophy tries to offer this justification, whereby any metaphysical abstraction culminates in an ethic and a political scheme. Any metaphysical idea serves as a basis for a concrete fact, as a justification for a type of political organization that is almost always proposed.

We have a great many philosophical examples in which metaphysical abstraction serves as a basis for a political construction. One example we have in Platonic philosophy, of which the theory of Ideas serves as a basis and justification for the *Republic.* In St. Augustine's *City of God* we have another example; the Christian community, the Church, is supported by a metaphysical entity which in this case is God. The Utopias of the Renaissance are other examples in which rationalism justifies forms of government out of which has arisen our present-day democracy. Some thinker has said that the French Revolution finds its justification in Descarte's *Discourse on Method* (*Discours de la méthode*). Hegel's dialectics inverted by Marxism have given rise to forms of government like Communism. The same totalitarianism has tried to justify itself metaphysically by seeking that justification in the ideas of Nietzsche, Sorel, or Pareto. Many further examples may be found in the history of philosophy, in which metaphysical abstraction serves as a base for social or political practice.

By this we see how theory and practice must go together. Man's material acts must be justified by ideas, because this is what differentiates him from the animals. Now, our age has been marked by the rupture between ideas and reality. European culture finds itself in a crisis on account of this rupture. Man finds himself lacking a moral theory to justify his acts, and so he has not been able to solve the problem of his living in society, and the only thing he has achieved is going to extremes, to anarchy or totalitarianism.

The different crises in Western culture have been crises caused by lack of ideas to justify human acts, and the existence of man. When certain ideas have ceased to justify that existence, it has been necessary for man to seek another set of ideas. The history of Western culture is the history of the crisis which man has suffered by the rupture of the co-ordination which existed between ideas and reality. Western culture has gone from crisis to crisis, sometimes saving itself with ideas, sometimes with God, at other times with reason, until our own day, when it has been left without ideas, God, or reason. Culture is crying out for new bases on which to support itself. Well, the answer to this cry, from our point of view, appears practically impossible to obtain. And yet, this point of view is that of men in crisis, and it could not be otherwise, because if it seemed to us that such a problem was easy to solve, we should not be men in a crisis. But the fact that we are in a crisis, and that we do not possess the solution longed for, does not mean that no solution exists. Men in other ages who have found themselves, like us, in a crisis, have suffered from the same pessimism; nevertheless, the solution has been found. We do not know what values can replace those we see lost, but one thing certain is that they will appear, and it is up to us as men of America to make our contribution to this work.

By the above we can be led to another kind of task for a possible philosophy of America. The Western culture of which we are sons and heirs requires new values for its support. Well, these values will have to be extracted from new human experiences, from experiences which come when man finds himself in new circumstances like those which are now arising. America, given its particular position, can bring to culture the novelty of its still unexploited experiences. Hence it is necessary that it proclaim to the world its truth, but a truth without pretensions, a truth that is sincere. The fewer pretensions it has, the more sincere and authentic that truth will be. America must not have aspirations to set itself up as a director of Western culture; its aspiration must be, purely and simply, to produce culture. And this can be done by trying to solve the problems that come up from its own, the American, point of view.

After this crisis America and Europe will find themselves in similar situations. Both will have to solve the same problem: that which concerns the form of life they will adopt in the new circumstances that confront them. Both will have to continue the work of universal culture which has been interrupted, but with the difference that this time America will not be able to continue to linger in the shadow of what Europe is achieving, because now there is no shadow, and no place to find support. On the contrary, it is America that finds itself in a privileged situation which may be of short duration, but which must be utilized to take on the appointed task of one that has become an adult member of Western culture.

An American philosophy will have to initiate this work, which consists in seeking the values that will serve as a basis for a future type of culture. And this work will have as its aim the safeguarding of the human essence, that by which man is man. Now, man in his essence is both an individual and a social being, and thus it is necessary to preserve the balance between these two components of his essence. This balance is what has been disturbed by carrying man towards his extremes: individualism to the point of anarchy and a sociability so complete that he has become one with the mass. It is therefore necessary to find values which make sociability possible without detriment to individuality.

This universal type of work, and not one that is simply American, will have to be the supreme goal of this possible philosophy of ours, which must not be limited to problems strictly American, to those of American circumstance, but must include those of that broader circumstance, in which we also have our place as the men we are, the circumstance called humanity.

It is not enough to try to discover an American truth, we must also try to discover a truth valid for all men, even though we may not in fact succeed. We must not consider things American as ends in themselves, but as frontiers of a more extensive purpose. That is why any attempt to form an American philosophy, with the sole aim that it be American, will be doomed to failure. One must endeavour to form a philosophy, purely and simply, and the American part will be added unto it. For the philosophy to be American, it will suffice that those who philosophize are American people, in spite of the attempt to depersonalize them. If the opposite way is taken, what will suffer will be philosophy.

In attempting to solve man's problems, whatever his situation in space or time, we shall have to start from ourselves as the men we are; we shall have to start from our circumstances, our limitations, from the fact of being of America, just as the Greek started from a circumstance called Greece. But like him, we cannot limit ourselves to remaining inside that circumstance. If we do remain there, it will be in spite of ourselves. Thus we shall form American philosophy just as the Greek developed Greek philosophy in spite of himself.

Only by starting from these bases can we fulfil our mission in the context of universal culture, contributing to it in the consciousness of our capabilities and our incapabilities, conscious of our reach as members of that cultural community called humanity, and of our limitations as the product of a circumstance, which is peculiar to us and to which we owe our personality, a circumstance called America.

1942

Essays on Philosophy in History (*Ensayos sobre filosofía en la historia*), Editorial Stylo, Mexico, 1948, pp. 165–77.

Octavio Paz

(b. Mixcoac, D.F., 1914)

Of the generation of *Poetic Workshop* (*Taller Poético*, 1936–38), Octavio Paz is the most prominent poet, and today he is one of the most important of those writing in the Spanish language. In his first book, *Root of Man* (*Raíz del hombre*, 1937), eroticism as a lyric force was brought back to Mexican poetry, inflamed by juvenile ardour. *On the Bank of the World* (*A la orilla del mundo*, 1942) reveals a poetry that abandons intimacy to turn to the world and ask of it the meaning of existence. In *Liberty Pledged* (*Libertad bajo palabra*, 1949), *Seeds for a Hymn* (*Semillas para un himno*, 1954), and in the prose poems of *Eagle or Sunshine?* (*¿Águila o sol?*, 1951), Paz returns to his constant themes: sensuality, beauty, the secret realm of poetry. He explores the circumstantial and the anecdotal. He struggles with words. He enriches himself in the oneiric realm of Surrealism, but he is still the same poet who sang that song in his earlier books, and now he is in complete control of his vigour in expression.

Like many major poets who, along with their lyric poems, have expounded their personal *ars poetica*, Octavio Paz has extended his poetry in brilliant essays, of which some of the best are uncollected. In *The Labyrinth of Solitude* (*El laberinto de la soledad*), he began by trying to explain the secret of the Mexican man, and with regard to some of his aspects—solitude, feast days, injustice, impermeability, the Revolution—he advanced bold theories. *The Bow and the Lyre* (*El arco y la lira*), a book whose intellectual value may be compared with Alfonso Reyes' studies of literary theory, is a poetic anthology which in principle has the rare merit of being excellent both as aesthetics and as poetics, that is, it offers a philosophic concept and also, from within, an intimate concept of poetry. In his doctrine one arrives at a happy synthesis of various currents in contemporary thought; but, at bottom, he expresses a single coherent poetic concept: that of the poet which the author is.

Octavio Paz studied at the National University. In 1936 he went to Spain during the Civil War. He directed the review *Workshop* (*Taller*, 1938–41) and was editor of *The Prodigal Son* (*El Hijo Pródigo*, 1943–46). From 1943 to 1953 he held diplomatic posts in the United States, France, India, and Japan.

ESSAYS: *The Labyrinth of Solitude* (*El laberinto de la soledad*), 1950; *The Bow and the Lyre* (*El arco y la lira*), 1956; *The Pears of the Elm Tree* (*Las peras del olmo*), 1957.

•

INTRODUCTION TO THE HISTORY OF MEXICAN POETRY

SPAIN, A WORD THAT IS RED AND YELLOW, black and purple, is a romantic word. Devoured by extremes, with Carthaginian against Roman, Visigoth against Mussulman, the Middle Ages against the Renaissance, hardly any of the ideas which mark the stages of European history are completely applicable to her development. Actually, it is impossible to speak of a Spanish "evolution," because the history of Spain is a succession of abrupt leaps and falls, sometimes in a dance, sometimes in lethargy. Thus it is not strange that the existence of the Spanish Renaissance has been denied. Indeed, just when the Renaissance revolution emigrates from Italy and inaugurates the modern world, Spain shuts herself off from the outside world and withdraws within herself. But she does not do this without first giving herself freely to this very spirit which later she was to deny with the same passionate fervour with which she had given herself to it. That moment of seduction, in which Spain receives the literature, art, and philosophy of the Renaissance, is also that of the discovery of America. As soon as the Spaniard treads American soil, he transplants the art and poetry of the Renaissance. These constitute our oldest and most genuine tradition. Spanish-speaking inhabitants of America came into being at a moment of Spain's universality. That is why Jorge Cuesta maintains that the most noteworthy characteristic of our tradition is "uprootedness" (*desarraigo*). And that is the truth; the Spain that discovered us is not mediaeval Spain, but the Spain of the Renaissance. And the poetry that the first Mexican poets recognize as their own is the same that in Spain was regarded as outcast and foreign: the poetry of Italy. Heterodoxy with regard to the pure Spanish tradition is our only tradition.

Immediately after the Conquest, the Creoles imitate the Spanish poets most detached from the Spanish soil, sons not only of Spain but of their time. If Menéndez y Pelayo asserts that "the primitive poetry of America may be considered as a branch or continuation of the Sevillian school," could his assertion not be expanded to say that the latter, in turn, is but a branch off the Italian trunk? Situated on the periphery of the Hispanic world, facing a world of nameless ruins and also a landscape still unnamed, the first poets of New Spain wish to overcome their marginal position and their isolation by using a universal form which makes them contemporaries, if not fellow-countrymen, of their masters in old Spain and of their Italian models. What we have left of their works is far removed from the vacillations and violent outbursts of a language in formation and which, in being formed, creates a literature and moulds a spirit. Possessors of a clear form, they move effortlessly in a universe of ready-made images. Francisco de Terrazas, the first poet of merit in the sixteenth century, does not represent a dawn, but a noonday.

If anything distinguishes the poetry of New Spain from that of Old Spain, it is the lack or scarcity of mediaeval elements. The roots of our poetry are universal, like its ideals. Born in the time of the language's maturity, its sources are the same as those of the Spanish Renaissance. As daughter of Garcilaso, Herrera, and Góngora, it has not known heroic stammerings, popular innocence, realism, and myth. Unlike all modern literatures, the development was not from the regional to the national, and from this to the universal, but the reverse. The infancy of our poetry coincides with the noonday of Spanish poetry, to which it belongs in language and on account of the fact that for centuries it does not deviate except in its constant inclination to prefer the universal to the purely national, and the intellectual to the racial.*

The abstract and clear form of the first poets of New Spain did not tolerate the intrusion of American reality. But the baroque opens doors to landscape, to flora and fauna, and even to the Indian himself. In nearly all the baroque poets one observes a conscious utilization of the native world. But those elements only tend to accentuate, by their very exoticism, the sense of strangeness demanded by the art of the period. The baroque could not scorn the aesthetic effects offered by all these materials in almost raw form. "The Mexican feather costume" of Góngora was utilized by many. The poets of the seventeenth century, like the Romantics, discover American nature through European models. Allusions to the native world are the fruit of an aesthetic doctrine and not the result of a personal intuition.

In the work of Bernardo de Balbuena has been seen the birth of nature poetry in America. But this learned and prolific poet does not so much express the splendour of the new landscape as indulge in the play of his fancy. Between the world and his eyes is interposed the

*This is not entirely applicable to popular Mexican poetry, which does develop and modify traditional Spanish forms like the ballad.

aesthetics of his time. His long poems have no framework, because they are not supported by true poetic imagination, which is always the creator of myths; but his inexhaustible fantasy, his love of the full and resonant word, and his most rich and excessive verbosity have something about them that is very American, and which justifies the opinion of Pedro Henríquez Ureña,[1] who writes: "Balbuena represents the American portion at the central moment of the great baroque poetry. . . . His baroque style is not a complication of concepts, as with the Andalusians, but a profusion of adornment, with a clear structure of concept and image, as on the baroque altars of the Mexican churches." The originality of Balbuena must be sought in the history of styles and not in unhistorical nature. He himself has left us an excellent definition of his art:

> If the carving and the brush console
> the curious eyes with their splendours
> and are intent upon remaking the world. . .

Baroque art is an imitation of nature, but that imitation is also a recreation which underlines and exaggerates its image. For Balbuena poetry is a sumptuous and exciting game, both rich and eloquent. Being an imitative art, colonial poetry tends to exaggerate its models, and in going to extremes in this way it is not difficult to discern a desire for singularity.

Exaggeration of the Spanish element was only one of the ways in which our distrust of Spanish art was expressed, excessive and inflated as that art already was. The other way was the way of reserve, incarnated in Juan Ruiz de Alarcón. This great dramatist—and fair lyric poet—sets up against the theatre of Lope and his dazzling facility a work in which it is not far-fetched to perceive an echo of Plautus and Terence. In contrast with Lope and Tirso, the Mexican poet creates a theatre of characters rather than of situations, a world of reason and equilibrium; and above all, a world of reasonable probability, as opposed to that of impossible combinations as presented by his rivals. Alarcón's reserve thus stresses the true explanation of the exaggerations of poets like Bernardo de Balbuena. The nascent Mexican literature asserts itself at one time as a restraint upon the Spanish spirit, at another time as an excessive indulgence in it. And in both cases it shows a distrust of a spirit which does not yet dare to be itself, oscillating between two extremes.

[1]Contemporary Dominican critic and scholar, who has been a professor at the University of Mexico and the University of Minnesota.

Religion was the centre of society and the true spiritual nourishment of its components. It is a religion on the defensive sitting on its dogmas, because the splendour of Catholicism in America coincides with its decadence in Europe. The religious life of the colony lacks a mystic impulse and theological audacity. But if it is difficult to find figures comparable to San Juan de la Cruz or Fray Luis de León, there are many religious writers of merit. Among them there stands out Fray Miguel de Guevara, the author of some sacred sonnets among which appears the famous "What moves me to love Thee, my God, is not. . . ." As happens with a number of masterpieces in the Spanish language, it is impossible to say with certainty whether this sonnet is really by Guevara. For Alfonso Méndez Plancarte the attribution is more than probable. Moreover, other sonnets by Guevara, adds this discerning critic, "can bear comparison with this composition, especially the one beginning: 'Putting the Son on the cross, his bosom open. . . . ,' which brings to mind the most profound of the sacred sonnets of Góngora, surpassing him in emotion and even in imaginative fire."

The curiosity aroused by the Indian past must not always be seen as a simple thirst for exoticism. In the seventeenth century many wondered how the colonial order could assimilate the indigenous world. The old history, the myths, the dances, the material objects, and even the very religiosity of the Indians formed a closed world, impenetrably sealed; and yet, ancient beliefs were mingled with the modern, and the remnants of indigenous cultures posed questions to which there was no answer. The Virgin of Guadalupe was also Tonantzin, the arrival of the Spaniards was confused with the return of Quetzalcóatl, and the ancient ritual of the indigenes showed disturbing coincidences with the Catholic. If in Mediterranean paganism there had been signs foretelling the coming of Christ, why should they not be found in the old history of Mexico? The Conquest ceases to be a unilateral act of will on the part of the Spaniards, and is transformed into an event looked forward to by the Indians, and prophesied by their kings and priests. Thanks to these interpretations, the ancient religions are linked supernaturally with the Catholic. Baroque art takes advantage of this situation, mingles the Indian and the Spanish, and for the first time tries to assimilate the indigenous cultures. The Virgin of Guadalupe, in whom it is not difficult to see traces of an old goddess of fertility, a constellation of many beliefs and psychic forces, is the meeting-point between the two worlds, the centre of Mexican religiosity. Her image, at the same time as it embodies the reconciliation of the two opposing halves, expresses the originality of the merging nationality. Mexico, through the work of the Virgin, claims a heritage from two traditions. Almost all the poets write poems in her praise. A strange variety of the baroque—which may quite legitimately be called "Guadalupan"—becomes the prevailing style of New Spain.

Among the poems dedicated to the Virgin the one written by Luis de Sandoval y Zapata is outstanding. Each of the fourteen lines of this sonnet—"winged eternity of the wind"—contains a memorable image. Zapata best represents the apogee of baroque art, and is an excellent incarnation of the *creativity* of the age, of a type which is to some extent analogous to the *wit* of the English metaphysical poets. We barely know his work, buried for centuries and rejected by a criticism which did not understand the baroque and was too lazy to try to understand it. The remnants which have come to us show him as an artist both subtle and grave, both brilliant and intriguing, a personal heir to the double lesson of Góngora and Quevedo. From each of his poems can be selected perfect lines, not in the soulless sense of mere correctness, but terse or scintillating, weighty or winged, and always effective. His liking for the unusual image, as well as his love for the geometry of concepts, lead him to construct delicate musical cages for intellectual birds. Therefore, not only is it possible to extract from the few poems still accessible to us some strange, resplendent fragments, but two or three sonnets complete and still living, isolated towers amid the ruins of his work.

Sor Juana Inés de la Cruz is not only the loftiest figure in Spanish-American colonial poetry, she is also one of the richest and most profound minds in our literature. Beset by critics, biographers, and apologists, nothing of what has been said about her person since the seventeenth century is more penetrating and true than what she herself tells us in her *Reply to Sor Filotea de la Cruz* (*Respuesta a sor Filotea de la Cruz*). This letter is the history of her intellectual vocation, the defence—and the mockery—of her love of learning, the story of her toils and triumphs, the criticism of her poetry and of her critics. In these pages Sor Juana reveals herself as an intellectual, that is, as a person to whom life is an exercise of the understanding. She wishes to understand everything. Where a religious spirit would find proofs of the presence of God, she finds occasion for hypotheses and questions. The world appears to her more as an enigma than as a place of salvation. While a figure of plenitude, the Mexican nun is also an image of a society about to be cleft asunder. A religious by intellectual vocation —and also, perhaps, to escape from a society which condemned her as an illegitimate child—she prefers the tyranny of the cloister to the tyranny of the world. In her convent she maintains for years a delicate balance and a daily struggle between her religious duties and her intellectual curiosity. When overcome, she keeps silence. Her silence is that of the intellectual, not that of the mystic.

The poetic work of Sor Juana is abundant, varied, and uneven. Her innumerable poems written by request bear testimony to her charming facility, and also to her careless attitude. But a goodly portion of her work is free of these defects, not only because of the admirable rhetoric of the structure that supports it, but because of the truth of what it expresses. Though she says she found pleasure only in the writing of "a little trifle they call the *Dream* (*Sueño*)," her sonnets, *liras*, and *endechas* are works of a great poet of terrestrial love. The sonnet is transformed into a form natural to this keen-minded, passionate, and ironical woman. In her luminous dialectic of images, antitheses, and correspondences, she consumes herself and saves herself, plays coy and yields herself. Less ardent than Louise Labé,[2] also less direct, the Mexican poetess is more profound and relaxed, bolder in her reserve, more self-controlled in her aberration. Her intelligence does not enable her to restrain her passion, but deepens it and so renders its inevitability more free and cherished. In her best moments the poetry of Sor Juana is something more than a sentimental confession or a felicitous exercise in baroque rhetoric. And even when it is a deliberate game—as in the disturbing portrait of the Countess of Paredes—sensuality and love of the body inspire the erudite allusions and the plays on words, which are converted into a labyrinth of crystal and fire.

First Dream (*Primero sueño*) is the most ambitious composition of Sor Juana. Though it was written confessedly as an imitation of the *Solitudes* (*Soledades*), its profound differences are greater than its external similarities: Sor Juana wishes to penetrate reality, not to transmute it into a resplendent surface, as Góngora does. The vision presented to us by *First Dream* is that of the dream of universal night, in which man and the cosmos dream and are dreamed of: dream of knowledge, dream of being. There is nothing further removed from the night of love of the mystics than this intellectual night, with wakeful eyes and precise time. The Góngora of the *Solitudes*, says Alfonso Reyes, sees man as "an inert form in the midst of the nocturnal landscapes"; Sor Juana approaches "the sleeper like a vampire, enters into him and his nightmare, seeks a synthesis of vigil, half-sleep, and dream." The substance of the poem has no antecedents in the poetry

[2]French poetess of the sixteenth century.

of the language, and only recently has it found an heir in José Gorostiza. *First Dream* is the poem of the intelligence, of its ambitions and its defeat. It is intellectual poetry, poetry of disillusionment. Sor Juana closes the golden dream of the rule of the viceroys.

Though the baroque continues to the middle of the eighteenth century, this century is an age of prose. Journalism is born; criticism and erudition prosper; science, history, and philosophy grow at the expense of the creative arts. Neither the golden style of the preceding century nor the new Neoclassical tendencies produce any figures of importance. The most outstanding poets of the period write in Latin. Meanwhile the ideas of the Enlightenment awaken a somnolent world. The revolution of the Independence movement is foreshadowed. The artistic sterility of Neoclassicism contrasts with the intellectual fervour of the best minds. At the end of the century there appears a poet of merit, Manuel de Navarrete, a scrupulous disciple of Meléndez Valdés. In his poems Neoclassicism and its shepherds are tinged with a vague sentimental mistiness, harbinger of Romanticism.

The nineteenth century is a period of internal conflict and external wars. The nation suffers two foreign invasions and a long civil war, which ends with the victory of the liberal party. The Mexican intelligentsia shares in the politics and the struggle. To defend the country, and in a certain sense to bring it into being; to invent it, so to speak, is the task that concerns Ignacio Ramírez, Guillermo Prieto, Ignacio Manuel Altamirano, and many others. In this exalted atmosphere the Romantic influence begins. The poets write. They write incessantly, but above all they fight, also incessantly. The admiration aroused in us by their ardent and dramatic lives—Acuña commits suicide at twenty-four, and Flores dies blind and poor—does not prevent us from realizing their weaknesses and inadequacies. None of them, perhaps with the exception of Flores (who did have poetic vision though he lacked originality in expression), had any conception of what Romanticism really meant. Therefore they extended it into an eloquent and sentimental literature, false in its superficial sincerity and impoverished in its very emphasis. The irrationality of the world, the dialogue between the world and man, the full powers conferred upon dreams and love, nostalgia for a lost unity, the prophetic value of speech, and finally the use of poetry as a loving apprehension of reality, a universe of hidden correspondences which Romanticism discovers, are preoccupations and evidences foreign to almost all these poets. They move in the sphere of sentiment and take pleasure in telling us their loves and enthusiasms, but they barely touch the region of the sacred, which is part of any genuine Romantic art. The greatness of these writers lies in their lives and in their defence of liberty.

The persistence of Neoclassical poetry in this atmosphere of change and revolt is remarkable. Correct versifiers almost invariably, the academicians preserve the language from Romantic collapse. None of them is a true poet, but José Joaquín Pesado and Joaquín Arcadio Pagaza achieve a modest recreation of the Mexican landscape. Their influence and teaching will later benefit Manuel José Othón. The beautiful paganism of Ignacio Ramírez, perhaps the most representative mind of the period, is expressed with dignity in a few disdainful tercets. Altamirano, teacher of a younger generation, tries to conciliate the opposing tendencies and initiates a timid literary nationalism, which produces no immediate results of merit.

Manuel José Othón appears as heir to the academic current. His work is not inspired by any seeking after novelty. If he avoids Romanticism, he is also averse to "Modernistic" rhetoric, which he sees triumph towards the end of his life. The academic poets, and he himself, thought that this attitude made him a member of their school. And it is true that a large part of the work of Othón is undistinguishable in purpose and intention from that of Pagaza, a poet to whom he was bound not only by common tastes, but by a common aesthetic attitude. But the sonnets *Wild Idyll* (*Idilio salvaje*), *To a Steppe of Nazas* (*A una estepa del Nazas*), and a few others represent something more than that "poetry of nature" in which the academic school delighted, becoming thereby turned to stone. The solitary regions of the North, "dry basin of a dead ocean," and its high, cruel sky cease to be a spectacle or a symbol. As a mirror of his exhausted self, the aridity of love and the ultimate sterility of passions are reflected in the bareness of the savannah. Beneath traditional form and language, there shines the fixed eye of a nature which sates itself only by annihilating what it loves, and has no other aim than to be consumed in consuming. A sun of the paramo burns the rocks of the desert, which are merely the ruins of its being. Human solitude is one of the rhymes of the plural solitude of nature. The sonnet deepens and its correspondences and echoes allude to another inexorable geometry and to other rhymes more deadly and empty.

If Othón is an academician who discovers Romanticism and so escapes the Parnassianism of his school, Salvador Díaz Mirón sets off in the opposite direction: he is a Romanticist aspiring to Classicism. The poetry of his first period shows marks of the eloquence of Hugo and the emphasis of Byron. After years of silence, he publishes *Stone*

Sparks (*Lascas*), the only book he acknowledged to be entirely his. This title describes his poetry; or more precisely, the moments of poetry wrung out, by anger and impatience, from a form that is always applying the brake. *Stone Sparks*: sparks, brief flashes illuminating for a brief second a dark and proud soul. The Parnassian Díaz Mirón does not reject the Romanticist: he holds him in check without ever taming him completely. And from this struggle, at times merely a sterile command and a torturing of the language, come forth pure, tense verses "like the silence of the star o'er the tumult of the wave."

As opposed to the dull language of the poets preceding him, and also in contrast to the false jewels of almost all the Modernists, the poetry of Díaz Mirón has the hardness and splendour of a diamond; and a diamond with an excess, rather than a deficiency, of lustre. Being a poet who strives only for mastery, he finds no form which expresses him without oppressing him. After this strenuous effort, his work settles back into silence. Spirit is his form, and the definitive form of his spirit. Or, as Jorge Cuesta has said: "his fecundity is in his silence. Other poets were unworthy to keep silence." As precursor and leader of Modernism, the adventure of Díaz Mirón is above all a verbal adventure. But that adventure is also a drama: that of pride. For this artificer is also the first Mexican poet who is conscious of the ailment and of its atrocious creative possibilities.

Modernism is not merely an assimilation of Parnassian and Symbolistic poetry avidly seized upon by a few Spanish-American poets. In discovering French poetry, Modernism also discovered the Spanish classical poets, forgotten in Spain. And above all it created a new language, which was to serve in a moment of extraordinary fecundity as a vehicle of expression for a few great poets: Rubén Darío, Leopoldo Lugones,[3] and Julio Herrera y Reissig.[4] In Mexico Modernism would perhaps have been poetically more fruitful if the Mexicans had discerned the true significance of the new movement. Modernism presented itself as having an indifferent attitude towards Spanish traditionalism, but at the same time it revived the true Spanish tradition. How could we fail to see in it an heir of the tradition which had been our foundation? For the rest of Spanish America, it opened the doors of the universal poetic tradition; to Mexicans, on the other hand, it gave an opportunity to resume their own tradition. Every revolution possesses a tradition or creates one: Darío and Lugones create theirs; Gutiérrez Nájera and Amado Nervo were not fully con-

[3]Argentinian poet who died in 1938.

[4]Uruguayan poet who died in 1910 at the age of thirty-five.

scious of the tradition which belonged to them, and therefore they were also not fully conscious of the profound significance of the Modernist renovation. Their Modernism is almost always a form of exoticism, that is, a revelling in the more decorative and external elements of the new style.

In spite of his limitations, in some poems by Manuel Gutiérrez Nájera one glimpses that other world, that other reality which is the patrimony of every real poet. Sensitive and elegant, when he does not indulge himself in his tears or his discoveries, he attacks with a melancholy charm the theme of the shortness of life. His poetry, as he himself says in one of his most quoted poems, "will not entirely die." In his Modernistic period, Amado Nervo manipulates without good taste, but in a novel and authentic fashion, the repertory of Symbolism. Later, he decides to strip himself bare. In reality, it is a matter of a simple change of costume. The Symbolist costume, which was becoming to him, is replaced by the topcoat of the religious thinker. Poetry lost by the change, without gain to religion or morality.

Other poets, less applauded in their day, draw nearer to the electrically charged zone of poetry. Francisco A. de Icaza, bitter and sober, achieves in his short poems a conciseness that is both sententious and opaque. Luis G. Urbina, in a large part of his work, continues the sentimental line of Nájera, but he is saved by having the temperament of an impressionist painter. The best part of his poetry, made up of twilights and seascapes, show him as an excellent heir of the landscape tradition. With less intensity than Othón, though with more fantasy and richness of shadings, Urbina accomplishes a delicate expressive equilibrium. A curious thing to observe is how the Mexican poets escape Modernist affectation by turning to a universal tradition. Mexican poetry does not find its native form, and every time it ventures to express the best and the most intimate in its being, it can do nothing but use an abstract language which it possesses only by intellectual conquest.

To the Modernist poets, who glean from Symbolism the least enduring elements, Enrique González Martínez opposes a deeper and more reflective sensibility and an intelligence which dares to interrogate the dark face of the world. The severity of González Martínez, the absence of any unforeseeable element, which is the salt of poetry, and the didacticism which tinges part of his work, have caused him to be considered the first Spanish-American poet to break with Modernism: the swan is confronted with the owl. In reality, González Martínez does not oppose Modernism: he undresses it and strips it of its trappings. In despoiling it of its sentimental and Parnassian adherences, he redeems it, makes it conscious of itself and of its inner significance. González Martínez adopts Mexican originality and links it to a tradition. Thus he does not repudiate Modernism, but is the only truly Modernist poet Mexico has had, in the sense in which Darío and Lugones in America, and Machado and Jiménez in Spain, were Modernists. The attention he gives to landscape, especially to nocturnal landscape, is impregnated with meaning—the dialogue between man and the world is resumed. Poetry ceases to be a description or a plaint and again becomes a spiritual adventure. After González Martínez, Parnassian eloquence and Romantic outpourings of the heart will be impossible. In making of Modernism a consciousness, he changes the attitude of the poet to poetry, even though he may leave intact the language and the symbols. The value of his example does not lie in his opposition to the language of Modernism—which he never rejected except in its aberrations, and he remained faithful to it till death—but in his being the first to restore to poetry the sense of the *gravity* of words.

One of Alfonso Reyes' first books of poems is called *Pause* (*Pausa*). This title not only defines his poetry; it also shows his place in relation to his immediate predecessors. Reyes does not break with Modernism; he simply withdraws, and after a pause, consisting precisely of the poems in the book so entitled, he turns his back upon it for ever. A spirit both ethereal and substantial, made up of both air and earth, Reyes has approached many fountains, has passed through a variety of temptations, and has never said "of this water I will not drink." Popular language, colloquial turns of phrase, Greek classics, and French Symbolists are all interallied in his voice; and with these, he is not forgetful either of the Spaniards of the Golden Age. A man who moves about in different languages on this continent and others, a writer with affinity to Valéry Larbaud by virtue of the universality of his curiosity and experience, at times true expeditions of conquest in lands till recently unknown, he mingles his readings with his life, the real with the dreamed, the dance with the march, and erudition with the freshest invention. In his work, prose and verse, and criticism and creation, are interwoven and mutually influence each other. For that reason it is impossible to reduce his poetry to his verses; one of his poems is a vast fresco in prose, *Vision of Anáhuac* (*Visión de Anáhuac*), a recreation of the landscape and pre-Columbian life in the Valley of Mexico. Over against this text must be mentioned *Cruel Iphigenia* (*Ifigenia cruel*), which is something like a reply to the *Vision*, in which the drama of mind and world, heaven and earth, blood and speech, is incarnated in language at once subtle and barbarous, giving us a double surprise in its archaism and its refinement. It would also be unfair to forget among his poetical works several translations which are genuine recreations, and among which one cannot fail to mention two names which are like opposite poles: Homer and Mallarmé. It is said that Alfonso Reyes is one of the best prose-writers in the language; it must be added that that prose would not be what it is, were it not the prose of a poet.

José Juan Tablada and Ramón López Velarde broke openly and definitely with Modernism. The first was a deserter from that movement. The poetry of his youth appears to be a typical example of the brilliant and vacuous vices of that school. Tablada, curious, eager, without ever looking behind him, with wings in his shoes, hearing the grass grow, was the first to get the smell of the new beast: the fierce, magnificent beast that was about to devour so many dozers—namely, the image. Infatuated with Japanese poetry, he introduced the *haiku* into our language, a little before the fashion caught on in France, according to his own story. His bestiary shows a profound understanding of the animal world, and his monkeys, parrots, and armadillos gaze at us with fixed, sparkling eyes. Like a diminutive sun, Tablada's *haiku* is very rarely an isolated image detached from a longer poem, but a fixed, pulsating star, only apparently motionless, since it is constantly revolving about itself. The *haiku* has a very natural connection with the popular *copla*, which explains its tremendous vogue. On our continent many adopt it, and in Spain Juan Ramón Liménez and Machado have written some of the best "maxims and witticisms" in poems of three or four lines, which, while they echo Andalusian poetry, at the same time call to mind this oriental form.

As soon as the *haiku* becomes a commonplace, Tablada abandons it and starts to write his "ideographic" poems. His attempt, less inspired of course, is an echo of that of Apollinaire, who just then is publishing *Calligrammes*. The poetic typography attracts him only for a moment. Always smiling and hurrying, in a few years he traverses many poetic lands. In the end, he returns to his country and publishes a series of "Mexican" poems, which it would be unjust to regard as a simple imitation of those which López Velarde brought out a little while before, though they show his marks and follow his pattern. Less profound than López Velarde, and less personal, his vision is brighter and has more colour. His language, almost entirely free of Modernistic tinsel, is elastic, ironical, and sprightly—reflecting the Mexico of ballet and fair, of firecracker and tumult. In his poems appear, alive for the first time, the sacred and common animals, idols, the old regions, and the ancient art. López Velarde was always outside of that world. Fascinated by the deadly struggle between the provinces and the capital, his eyes light upon the Mexico of the creole and the mestizo: Mexico popular and refined, and Catholic even when revolutionary. Tablada's vision is more external; as an occultist and a traveller, he sees his country with other eyes, and appropriates the exoticism of the gods and the colours. He is one of the first to be conscious of the richness of our indigenous heritage and the importance of its plastic arts. Tablada has a nature less profound than that of López Velarde, and his style is more invented than created, more premeditated than inevitably imposed. But at the same time he is more susceptible and agile; he plays more, and knows how to smile and laugh; he flies, and falls, more frequently. In a word, he is more daring.

In spite of the differences between them, something brought these two poets together: the love for the novel image, and their common belief in the value of surprise. This explains why Tablada was one of the first to discover López Velarde, and why, years later, he had no difficulty in recognizing what he owed to the poet from Zacatecas. Ramón López Velarde was a provincial, silent and intense. While Tablada was the visual poet, capable of apprehending an instantaneous flash of reality in three verses, the other was a man of slow tempo and in dialogue with himself. His imagination did not enable him to burn in fireworks, but to penetrate into his own heart and express more faithfully what he had to say: "I long to expel from within me any syllable not born of the combustion of my bones." López Velarde was a poet with a destiny.

Like any true poet, he is preoccupied with language. He wishes to make it his own. But he wishes to create for himself a personal language because he has something personal to say. He has something to say to us and something to say to himself and until it is said it will not cease to torment him. His feeling for words is very acute because he has a profound consciousness of himself and his own personal conflict. And it should be added that if his consciousness of himself leads him to invent for himself a language, that language also brings him closer to himself and reveals to him a part of his being which otherwise would have remained unformulated and invisible.

Two facts, apparently external, favour the discovery which López Velarde will make of his country and himself. The first is the Mexican

Revolution, which breaks with a social and cultural order which was a mere historical superposition, a straightjacket which stifled and deformed the nation. In destroying the feudal order—which had been disguised beneath the European fashion of progressive Positivism—the Revolution tears off the successive masks which covered the face of Mexico. The Revolution reveals to López Velarde a "country Castilian and Moorish, striped with Aztec." And while the other poets turn their eyes outward, he peers inside it, and for the first time in our history dares to give it expression without disguises or without reducing it to an abstraction. The Mexico of López Velarde is a living Mexico, that is, a Mexico lived day by day by the poet.

The other decisive fact in the poetry of López Velarde is his discovery of the capital. The revolutionary tide, along with his own literary ambitions, brings him to Mexico City when his mind was already formed, but with his taste and his poetry still unformed. His surprise, shock, joy, and bitterness must have been tremendous. In the city he discovers women, solitude, doubt, and the devil. And while he is undergoing these dazzling revelations, he comes to know the poetry of some South-American poets who dare to break with Modernism by carrying its conquests to the extreme limit: Julio Herrera y Reissig and Leopoldo Lugones. Contact with these writers change his manner and his vision. The critics of his time found him contorted, incomprehensible, and affected. The truth is the very opposite: thanks to his search for the image, to his almost perfidious use of adjectives that till yesterday were rare, and to his disdain of forms already established, his poetry ceases to be a sentimental confidence in order to become converted into the expression of a mind and a tortured anguish.

The discovery of the poetry of Lugones would have made of López Velarde a distinguished rhetorician, if at the same time he had not remembered the idiom of his native town. His originality consists in the fortunate fusion of the opaque and ardent language of the centre of Mexico with the artifices of Lugones. In contrast with Laforgue, who comes down from the "poetic idiom" to the colloquial and from that shock attains a strange splendour, López Velarde constructs with everyday elements, apparently realistic, a sinuous and labyrinthine phrase which, in its greatest moments, comes forth in a surprising image. That language, so personal and inimitable, permits him to discover his own intimate nature and that of his country. Without that language, López Velarde would have been a sentimental poet; and only with it, could he be an accomplished rhetorician. His drama, and the drama of his language, turn him into a genuine poet; nay more, into the first really Mexican poet. For with López Velarde we have a beginning of Mexican poetry, which till then had not found its language and had poured itself into forms which were Mexico's only because they also belonged to everyone.

Beyond the intrinsic value of López Velarde's poetry, his influence—as to a lesser extent that of Tablada—stems from the fact that these two poets do not hold to forms already proven and sanctioned by a universal tradition, but they dare to invent others, which are their own and not transferable. In the case of López Velarde the invention of new forms is allied to fidelity to the language of his time and of his people, as with all true innovators. If part of his poetry seems to us ingenuous or limited, nothing prevents us from seeing in it something that even his successors have not achieved completely: the seeking, and the finding, of the universal through the genuine and through what is possessed by the self. The heritage of López Velarde is arduous invention and loyalty to his time and his people, that is, a universality that does not betray us and a fidelity that neither isolates us nor smothers us. And even if it is true that it is not possible to go back to the poetry of López Velarde, it is also true that such a return is impossible precisely because it constitutes our only point of departure.

Contemporary Mexican poetry starts from the experiment of López Velarde. His brief development proves clearly that all poetic activity feeds on history; I mean on the language, the instincts, the myths, and the images of the time. And likewise, it proves that the poet tends to dissolve or transcend the mere historical train of events. Each poem is an attempt to resolve the opposition between history and poetry, to the benefit of the latter. The poet is always aspiring to extract himself from the tyranny of history, even though he may identify himself with his society and participate in what they call "the trend of the times," an ideal that is becoming less and less imaginable in the modern world. All the great poetic efforts, from the magic formula and the epic poem to automatic writing, aim to make of the poem a place of reconciliation between history and poetry, between fact and myth, between the colloquial phrase and the image, between the unrepeatable date and the commemorative festival, a living date, endowed with a secret fertility, which continually returns to usher in a new day. The nature of the poem is analogous to that of the festival which, while a mere calendar date, is also a breaking of the sequence, and the irruption of a present which periodically returns, and which has no yesterday nor tomorrow. Every poem is a festival: a precipitate of pure time.

The relationship between men and history is one of slavery and dependence. For while we are the only protagonists of history, we are also its objects and its victims: it is fulfilled only at our expense. The poem radically transforms this relationship: it is fulfilled only at the expense of history. All its products—the hero, the murderer, the lover, the myth, the legend in rags, the proverb, the coarse word; the exclamation uttered by the playing child almost involuntarily, the man condemned to ascend the scaffold, the girl who has fallen in love; and the phrase born away by the wind, the shred of an outcry, along with the archaism and the neologism and the slogan—suddenly these do not resign themselves to death, or at least, they do not resign themselves to being smashed against the wall. They wish to arrive at their end, they wish to *be* fully. They detach themselves from cause and effect and hope to be incarnated in the poem which redeems them. There is no poetry without history, but poetry has no other mission but to transmute history.

Since poetry is made of the very substance of history and society, namely, language, it tends to re-create language through laws differing from those which govern conversation and discourse. Poetic transmutation operates in the very heart of language. The sentence, not the isolated word, constitutes the cell, the simplest element of speech. Well, the word cannot live without words, or the sentence without sentences. Any phrase or sentence always contains, implicitly or explicitly, a reference to some other phrase or sentence, and is open to being explained by a new sentence. Every sentence has a meaning that can be conveyed by another sentence. Language is an *attempt to express a meaning*, and accordingly it makes up a combination of signs and sounds that are movable and interchangeable. But poetry transforms language radically; words suddenly lose their mobility and become irreplaceable. There are several ways of saying the same thing in prose, but there is only one way in poetry. Poetic language is not an attempt to express a meaning; it is an irrevocable utterance. The poet does not talk about horror, love, or the landscape; he presents them, he re-creates them. Irrevocable and irreplaceable, the words become inexplicable—except by themselves. Their sense does not lie beyond them, in other words, but in just those words. Every poetic image is inexplicable; it simply *is*. And in the same way, every poem is an organism of inner meanings, irreducible to any other form of expression. Once more, the poem is not something to be explained, it *says* its message in final form. It is not a sentence or a series of sentences, but an indivisible constellation of images, a verbal world peopled with heterogeneous or opposing visions, which resolve their discord in a solar system of correspondences. It is a universe of corruptible and opaque words, but they are capable of taking fire and burning every time a pair of lips brushes against them. At certain times, and coming forth from certain lips, the mill of phrases is converted into a gushing spring of evidences without recourse to demonstration. Then one lives in the fullness of time. In affirming history, the poet dissolves it, denudes it, and shows it what it is: time, image, and rhythm.

When history seems to tell us that perhaps it has no meaning beyond a phantasmal march without direction or end, language accentuates its equivocal character and impedes true dialogue. Words lose their sense, and therefore their communicative function. Degradation of history to a mere succession of events involves the degradation of language to a mass of lifeless signs. All use the same words, but there is no understanding; and it is useless for men to try to agree about linguistic meanings—the meaning is uncertain because man himself has become an incarnation of uncertainty. Language is not a convention, but an inseparable dimension of man. Therefore every verbal venture bears the mark of a totality—the whole man stakes his life on a word. If the poet is the man of words that man is a poet whose very being is interfused with speech. For this reason, too, only the poet can establish the possibility of intercommunication. His mission, and particularly in times like ours, consists in "giving a purer sense to the words of the tribe." But words are inseparable from the man. Therefore, poetic activity is not consummated outside the poet, in the magic thing which is the poem, but in his very being. Poem and poet are fused together because the two terms are inseparable: the poet is his uttered word. Such has been, for the last hundred years, the aim of the leading poets of our culture. And the same course is followed in the last great poetic movement of the century: Surrealism. The greatness of this endeavour, with respect to which no poet worthy of the name can remain indifferent, consists in its having sought to solve in one stroke, forever, and with a desperate sense of urgency, the duality that divides us. Poetry is a leap of derring-do, or it is nothing.

In present circumstances it may seem absurd to speak of these extravagant pretensions of poetry. Never has the domination of history been so strong or the pressure of "facts" so stifling. As the despotic call to the immediate task becomes intolerable, for it is a task concerning which no one has asked our assent, and one which is almost always directed towards the destruction of man, poetic activity becomes more and more secret, isolated, and strange.

Quite recently, writing a poem, falling in love, expressing astonishment, and dreaming out loud were subversive acts which endangered the social order, showing it up in its duplicity. Today the very idea of order has disappeared, and has been replaced by a combination of forces, masses, and resistances. Historical reality has discarded its masks and contemporary society shows itself for what is it: a combination of factors "homogenized" by the whip or by propaganda, directed by groups distinguished from the rest only by their brutality. Under these conditions, poetic creation again becomes a clandestine activity. If the poem is a feast, it is a feast at strange hours and in places little frequented, an underground banquet. Poetic activity rediscovers all its former effectiveness by the very fact of its secret character, impregnated with eroticism and with occult rites, a challenge to an interdict no less condemnatory because of being unformulated. The poem, previously called out into the open air of universal communion, continues to be an exorcism capable of preserving us from the sorcery of force, numbers, and ambiguousness. Poetry is one of the means which modern man utilizes to say *no* to all those powers which, not content with controlling our lives, also want our minds.

Paris, 1950

Introduction to *Anthologie de la poésie mexicaine*, Les Editions Nagel, UNESCO Collection, Paris, 1952. In Spanish in O.P., *Pears of the Elm Tree* (*Las peras del olmo*), Imprenta Universitaria, Mexico, 1959, pp. 3–31.

THE DISEMBODIED WORD

THE NOVEL AND THE THEATRE are forms which permit a compromise between the critical and the poetic spirit. The former, morever, requires it; its very essence consists in its being a compromise. On the other hand, lyric poetry sings of passions and experiences irreducible to analysis or which constitute an expenditure and a waste. The exaltation of love, for example, involves a provocation, a challenge to the modern world, since it is something that eludes analysis and constitutes an unclassifiable exception—hence the strange prestige of adultery throughout all our modern age. Whereas for the ancients it was a crime or an act without importance, in the nineteenth century it became an act of defiance to society, a rebellion and a deed consecrated by the ambiguous light of being under a curse.* Like love, death is absurd and responds with a "nothing makes sense" to the foresights of reason. Dreams, wandering thoughts, the play of rhythms, idle fancy—these also are experiences which disturb the economy of the mind and becloud the judgement, without any possible compensation. For the bourgeois, poetry is a distraction. But whom does it distract, except a few eccentrics? Or else it is a dangerous activity, and the poet is an inoffensive but costly crackpot, a madman or potential criminal. Inspiration is a fraud or a disease, and one can classify poetic images (a strange confusion which still persists) as products of mental illnesses.

The "accursed poets" are not a creation of Romanticism: they are the fruit of a society which casts out what it cannot assimilate. Poetry neither enlightens nor diverts the bourgeois. Therefore he exiles the poet and turns him into a parasite or a vagabond. This also accounts for the fact that for the first time in history poets do not live by their work. Their product has no value, and this *having no value* is translated precisely into *earning nothing*. The poet must seek another occupation, from diplomacy to swindling, or else starve to death. This situation is related to the birth of modern society: the first poet who was a "madman" was Tasso; the first "criminal" was Villon. The golden centuries of Spain are peopled by beggar poets and the Elizabethan period by lyric ruffians. Góngora begged all his life, cheated in gambling, and ended his life besieged by creditors. Lope made use of arbitrators. In Cervantes' old age there is a painful incident in which women of his family appear in an equivocal light. Mira de Mescua, a canon in Granada and a dramatist in Madrid, collected remuneration for an office without fulfilling its functions. Quevedo, with varying fortunes, devoted himself to politics.† Alarcón took refuge in the higher bureaucracy. Marlowe was assassinated in a mysterious intrigue, after having been accused of atheism and libertinism. Ben Jonson was a poet laureate, and received, besides a sum of money, a cask of wine annually—the two together inadequate. Donne changed coats

*The metamorphosis of love, from "courtly love" to bourgeois adultery, may be seen in the different images of Tristan and Isolde that were formed in each period. The naturalness and lightness with which such love is treated in *The Book of the Valiant Knight Tristan of Leonis*, a novel of chivalry, is most striking.

†On Quevedo as a realistic politician, see the essay by Raimundo Lida, "Quevedo's letters" ("Cartas de Quevedo"), in *Hispanic letters* (*Letras hispánicas*), pp. 103–23, Fondo de Cultura Económica, 1958.

and so succeeded in rising to become Dean of Saint Paul's. In the nineteenth century the poets' social status worsens. The Maecenases disappear and their incomes diminish, with exceptions, as in the case of Hugo. Poetry carries no price-tag; it is not something that can be turned into money, like painting. The "de luxe editions" have not been so much a manifestation of the sectarian spirit of the new poetry as they are a device to sell at a higher price, because of the small number of copies, books which in any case the general public will not buy. The *Communist Manifesto* states that "the bourgeoisie has turned the doctor, the lawyer, the priest, the poet, and the scientist into a paid servant." This is true, with one exception: the bourgeoisie closed their cash-boxes to the poets. They are neither servants nor buffoons; they are pariahs, phantoms, and idlers.

This description would be incomplete if I failed to point out that the conflict between the modern spirit and poetry began as an accord. Based on the same decision as in the case of philosophic thought, poetry tried to found poetic speech upon man himself. The poet did not see in his images the revelation of an external power. Unlike the Holy Scriptures, poetic writing was the revelation which man gives to himself about himself. From this circumstance arises the fact that modern poetry is also a theory of poetry. Moved by the necessity of basing its activity upon principles denied it by philosophy and conceded to it only in part by theology, the poet develops into a critic. And here it is appropriate to repeat that these lines propose to clarify the situation of modern poetry, not so much from the point of view of the poems themselves, as from the perspective of the poets' writings on theory. Therefore they deal with poets who, besides being poets, have endeavoured to justify poetic activity by a philosophy of poetry. This philosophy is also, as will be seen, a theory of history, a religion, and even a political doctrine.

Coleridge is one of the first to scrutinize poetic creation, to ask it what the poem really means or says. For Coleridge, imagination is man's greatest endowment, and in its primordial form "the faculty which originates all human perception." This view is not very different from that of Kant, at least according to Heidegger's interpretation of the *Critique of Pure Reason*: "Transcendental imagination" is the root of sensibility and understanding, and is what makes judgement possible. . . . Imagination reveals or projects objects, and without it there would be neither perception nor judgement; or rather, as a manifestation of the temporary thing that it is, it reveals and presents objects to the sensibilities and the understanding. Without this operation, out of which what we call "imagination" is really formed, perception would be impossible. (Heidegger: *Kant and the Metaphysical Problem*, F.C.E., 1954). Reason and imagination ("transcendental" or "primordial") are not opposite faculties; the second is the foundation of the first, and is what enables man to perceive and to judge. But Coleridge, in addition, as a second sense of the word, conceives of imagination not so much as an organ for acquiring knowledge as the faculty of expressing it in symbols and myths. In this second sense, the learning which our imagination yields us is not really knowledge: "It's a form of Being, or indeed it is the only Knowledge that truly is, and all other Science is real only as far as it is symbolical of this" (*On Method*, Essay XI). Imagination and reason, originally the same thing, finally fuse together in a concept which is incommunicable except by a symbolical representation, the myth. In short, imagination is fundamentally an organ of knowledge, since it is the necessary condition for all perception; and besides, it is a faculty which expresses, through myths and symbols, the higher knowledge.

Poetry and philosophy culminate in myth. Poetic and philosophical experience are confused with religious experience. But religion is not a revelation, but a state of the soul, a sort of ultimate accord between man's being and the being of the universe. God is a pure substance, concerning which reason can say nothing, except that it is inexpressible: "the divine truths of religion should have been revealed to us in the form of poetry; and that at all times poets, not the slaves of any particular sectarian opinion, should have joined to support all those delicate sentiments of the heart . . ." (*Literary Biography*). Religion is poetry, and its truths, beyond all sectarian opinion, are poetic truths: symbols or myths. Coleridge strips religion of its essential quality, that of being the revelation of a divine power, and reduces it to intuition of an absolute truth, which man expresses through mythical and poetic forms. Moreover, religion "is the poetry of Mankind." Thus, he founds poetic-religious truth upon man, and converts it into an historical form. For the sentence "religion is the poetry of Mankind" means in fact: "The manner in which poetry is incarnated in man, and becomes rite and history, is religion." In this idea, common to all the great poets of the modern age, is to be found the root of the opposition between poetry and modernity. Poetry is proclaimed as a principle at variance with the critical spirit, and as the only one that can replace the old and sacred principles. Poetry is conceived of as the original principle upon which, as secondary and historical manifestations, if not as tyrannical superpositions and concealing masks, rest the truths of religion. For this reason the poet cannot but view favourably the criticism of religion made by the national mind. But as soon as that same critical spirit proclaims itself the successor to religion, it condemns the poet.

Doubtless the reflections just expressed oversimplify the problem. It is well known that reality is richer than our intellectual systems. Nevertheless, reduced to its essentials, this is precisely the position of German Romanticism, since Hölderlin,[5] and from that time on, of all European poets, whether they are named Hugo or Baudelaire, Shelley or Wordsworth. It is not pointless to repeat, furthermore, that all these poets at some time fall in with the revolution in the critical spirit. It could not be otherwise, for we have already seen that poetic endeavour has a lateral coincidence with the revolutionary movement. The mission of the poet consists in being the voice of that movement which says "no" to God and his hierarchies and "yes" to men. The Scriptures of the new world will be the words of the poet revealing a man free from gods and overlords, left without any intermediaries before death and life. Revolutionary society is inseparable from society founded on the poetic word. It is therefore not strange that the French Revolution should arouse great expectations in all minds and that it should command the sympathy of German and English poets. True, hope is followed by hostility; but later, with the mitigation or justification of the double scandal of revolutionary terror and Napoleonic Caesarism, the heirs of the first Romantics again identify poetry with revolution. For Shelley the modern poet will occupy his former place, usurped by the priest, and will again be the voice of a society without monarchs. Heine asks for the warrior's sword for his tomb. All see in the great rebellion of the critical spirit the prologue to an event still more decisive: the advent of a society founded upon the poetic word. Novalis informs us that "religion is only practical poetry," that is, poetry embodied and lived. Through rites and mysteries the sacred images assume bodily reality and become action and living presence. Bolder than Coleridge, the German poet asserts: "Poetry is the original religion of humanity." To re-establish the original word, the poet's mission, is the same as to re-establish the original religion, still free from the dogmas of Churches and States.

The attitude of William Blake illustrates perfectly the true direction of poetry and the place it occupies at the beginning of our period. Blake does not spare his attacks and sarcastic comments on the

[5]One of the greatest German poets of the late eighteenth and early nineteenth century; he died in 1843.

prophets of the Age of Enlightenment and especially on the Voltairian spirit. But with the same vehemence he continually mocks official Christianity. The word of the poet is the original word, which precedes Bibles and Gospels. For him "the poetic genius is the true man. . . . The religions of all nations are derived from different receptions of the poetic genius. . . . The Hebrew and Christian Testaments are originally derived from the poetic genius . . ." (*All Religions Are One*, 1778). Blake's man and Blake's Christ are the opposite of what the official religions offer us. Original man is innocent, and each one of us carries within him an Adam. Christ himself is Adam. The ten commandments are an invention of the Devil:

Was Jesus chaste? or did he
Give any lessons of chastity?
The morning blush'd a fiery red:
Mary was found in adulterous bed.
. . . .
Good and Evil are no more,
Sinai's trumpets, cease to roar!

The mission of the poet is to re-establish the original word, thrown off course by priests and philosophers. "Prisons are made with the stones of the Law; brothels, with the bricks of religion." Blake sings to the American and French Revolutions, which break open the prisons and bring God out of the churches. But the society prophesied by the poet's word cannot be confused with a political Utopia. Reason creates darker prisons than theology. The enemy of man is called Urizel (Reason), the "god of systems," the prisoner of itself. Truth does not come from reason, but from poetic perception, that is, from imagination. The natural organ for acquiring knowledge is not the senses or the power of reason; both are limited and indeed stand in opposition to our ultimate essence, which is infinite desire: "Nothing less than everything can satisfy man." Man is imagination and desire:

Abstinence sows sand all over
The suddy lambs and flaming hair,
But desire gratified
Plants fruits of life and beauty there.

By his imagination man sates his infinite desire and he himself is converted into an infinite being. Man is an image, but an image in which he himself is incarnated. Amorous or mystical ecstasy is that incarnation of man in his image: being one with the object of his desire, he is one with himself. Therefore, the true history of man is that of his images: mythology. Blake relates to us in his "prophetic books" the history of man in mythical images. It is a history on the march, occurring right now, at this very moment, and culminating in the erection of a new Jerusalem. Blake's great poems are nothing but the history of the imagination, that is, of the avatars of the primordial Adam. It is a mythical history, a sacred scripture, a basic scripture. It is a revelation of past origins, one that unveils archetypal time, which precedes all times. A fundamental and prophetic scripture, it tells what was, is, and will be through all eternity. And what do these poetic sacred scriptures prophesy to us? They prophesy the coming of a man who has recovered his original nature and has thus found sin's law of gravity. Relieved of the weight of guilt, Blake's man flies, has a thousand eyes, and fire in his hair. He kisses what he touches, and sets aflame what he thinks. He is now image, action. Desire and its realization are the same thing. Christ and Adam are reconciled; Urizel is redeemed. Christ is no longer Rimbaud's "perpetual robber of energies," but energy itself, tense, and with action its target. Imagination that has become desire, desire that has become action: "Energy, eternal delight." The poet cleanses the sacred books of its errors and writes "innocence" where previously it read "sin," "liberty" where "authority" was written, "moment" where "eternity" had been engraved. Man is free; desire and imagination are his wings; heaven is within reach of his hands and is called "fruit," "flower," "cloud," "woman," "action." "Eternity is enamoured of the works of time." The kingdom prophesied by Blake is that of poetry. The poet again becomes a Seer and his vision proclaims the founding of a city the cornerstone of which is the poetic word. The poetic society, the new Jerusalem, is outlined for the first time, freed from the dogmas of religion and the Utopia of philosophers. Poetry goes into action.

It is not difficult to discover in German Romanticism similar preoccupations and ambitions. In the review *Athenaeum*, which served as the organ of the first Romanticists, Friedrich Schlegel thus defines his programme: "Romantic poetry is not only a universal progressivist philosophy. Its aim is nothing less than to bring together all the different forms of poetry and to re-establish communication between poetry, philosophy, and rhetoric. Also it must mingle and fuse together poetry and prose, inspiration and criticism, natural poetry and artificial poetry; it must vivify and socialize poetry, make life and society poetic, poeticize the mind, fill and saturate artistic forms with a substance appropriate and varied, and animate the whole with humour." This programme may be reduced to the formula: "Poeticize life;

socialize poetry." The tendencies of the Jena group find in Novalis[6] the clearest voice and the most trenchant and audacious thought, in conjunction with the authenticity of the great poet. The religion of night and death in the *Hymns* (*Hymnen an die Nacht*), the impressive *Fragments* (*Fragmente*)—each like a piece of stellar stone on which were engraved the signs of the universal analogy and the erotic correspondences which bind man to the cosmos—the search for the lost Middle Ages, the resurrection of the myth of the poet seen as a triple figure in which are united the knight errant, the lover, and the seer, make up a star of many facets. One of them is a plan for social reform, the creation of a new Europe, made up of the alliance of Catholicism and the Germanic spirit. In the famous essay *Christendom or Europe* (*Die Christenheit oder Europa*), written in 1799, the year of the fall of the Directory, Novalis proposes a return to mediaeval Catholicism. But it is not a question of a return to Rome, but of something new, though inspired by Roman universality. (Let us point out, in passing, that unity and universality are ideas which never cease to fascinate the Romanticists.) The universality of Novalis is not an empty form; the Germanic spirit will be its substance, since the Middle Ages are alive and intact in the depths of the popular Germanic soul. And what are the Middle Ages but the prophecy, the dream, of the new Romantic spirit? The Romantic spirit is poetry. History and poetry are fused together. A great Peace Council will reconcile liberty with the Papacy, and philosophic reason with the imagination. Again, and by unexpected routes, poetry enters into history.

Novalis' dream is a disquieting portent of other and more ferocious ideologies, and so it has been recently denounced by Albert Beguin, to whom we owe studies of inestimable value on German Romanticism. But the same disquietude, to be just, should be aroused in us by certain discourses of Saint-Just, another pure young man, which are also a prophecy of the future feats of the geometric mind. The attitude of Novalis, moreover, reflects a double crisis, personal and historical, impossible to analyse here. Suffice it to say that the French Revolution put between the sword and the wall the best German minds, as it did with the English and the Spaniards.* The Jena group, after being

*Nobody, among us, has better portrayed the dual character of that moment than Pérez Galdos, in the first two series of the *National Episodes* (*Episodios Nacionales*). Gabriel Araceli and Salvador Monsalud are still contending in every Spaniard and Spanish American.

[6]Pseudonym of Georg Friedrich Philipp, Freiherr von Hardenberg, German poet and novelist who died in 1801.

seduced for a moment, and not without torment of spirit, rejects many of its initial views. Some throw themselves into the arms of the Holy Alliance; others choose a less militant Catholicism; and the remainder penetrate into the great Romantic night of death. These oscillations are the counterpart of the revolutionary crises and convulsions, from the Reign of Terror to Thermidor, and its final culmination in the coup of Bonaparte. It is impossible to understand the Romantic reaction if historical circumstances are forgotten. To defend Germany against the Napoleonic invasions was to fight against foreign oppression, but also to strengthen internal absolutism. This was an insoluble dilemma for most of the Romantics. As Marx has said: "The struggle against Napoleon was a regeneration accompanied by a reaction." We, contemporaries of the Revolution of 1917 and the Moscow Trials, can understand better than anyone the alternatives presented by this Romantic drama.

Stripped of its accessory elements and purged of certain Germanic obsessions, Novalis' concept appears as an attempt to set poetry in the centre of history. Society will be made into a poetic community and, more precisely, a living poem. The relationship between men will cease to be that of master and servant, employer and employee, in order to usher in a poetic community. Novalis even foresees communities engaged in producing poetry collectively. This communion is, first of all, a penetration into death, the great mother, because only death (which is night, illness, and Christianity, but also the erotic embrace, the feast in which the "rock becomes flesh") will give us access to health, life, and sunshine. Novalis' communion is a reconciliation of the two halves of the sphere. In the night of death, which is likewise that of love, Christ and Dionysius are one. There is a magnetic point where the great poetic currents cross: in a poem like *Bread and Wine* (*Brot und Wein*), the vision of Hölderlin, a solar poet, for a moment touches that of *Hymn V* by Novalis, a poet of the night. In the *Hymns* there burns a secret sun, the sun of poetry, the black grape of resurrection, a heavenly body covered with black armour. It is no chance occurrence that that image of the sun should break in like a knight bearing crape-covered arms and plume, because Novalis' communion is a mystic and heroic supper in which the guests are knights who are also poets. And the bread that is shared in this banquet is the solar bread of poetry. "We will drink that wine of light, we shall be heavenly bodies," says the *Hymn*. As communion in poetry, the supper of German Romanticism is a rhyme or response to Blake's Jerusalem. In both visions we go back to the origin of time, in search of the original man, the Adam who is Christ. In both, woman, who is the "highest corporal nutriment," is a mediation, a gateway to the other shore, where the two halves make their covenant and man is one with his images.

From its birth modern poetry presents itself as an autonomous enterprise struggling against the current. Even though it is a spiritual endeavour that is incompatible with the "march of time," it finds no place to get hold of in the churches either. It is revealing to note that for Novalis the triumph of Christianity does not involve the negation, but the absorption, of the pre-Christian religions. In the Romantic night "all is delight, all is an eternal poem, and the sun that sheds its light on us is the august face of God." Night is sunlight. And the most surprising thing is that this solar victory of Christ should be achieved not before, but after the scientific era, that is, in the Romantic age, in the present. The historical Christ who preached in Galilee is obviously not the same as the night-sun deity invoked by the *Hymns*. The same occurs with the Virgin, who in like manner is Persephone and Sophia, the poet's beloved, the death that is life. The new Catholicism of Novalis is, taken literally, something new and different from historical Catholicism; and at the same time it is older, because it summons the divinities that were worshipped by the pagans. From this perspective the essay *Europe or Christendom* is illuminated with another sense. Poetry, once more, shows a double face: it is the most revolutionary of revolutions, and simultaneously the most conservative of revelations, because it consists merely in re-establishing the original word. The attitude of the other great precursors (Hölderlin, Blake, Nerval) is still more clear: their Christ is Dionysius, Lucifer, or Orpheus.

The root of the rupture between modern poetry and religion is of a different character from that which opposes the poetic spirit to the rational spirit, but its consequences are similar: the churches, too, like the bourgeoisie, expel the poets. The opposition of poetic and sacred writings is of such a nature that all alliances between modern poetry and established religions always end in scandal. There is nothing less orthodox than the Christianity of a Blake or a Novalis; there is nothing more suspect than that of a Baudelaire; there is nothing further removed from official religion than the visions of a Shelley, a Rimbaud, or a Mallarmé, not to mention the man who made of rupture and negation the most powerful funeral song of the century: Isidore Ducasse.

It is not necessary to follow the episodes of the sinuous and subterranean course of the poetic movement of the past century, ever oscillating between the two poles of Revolution and Religion. Each adherence ends in a rupture; each conversion, in a scandal. Monnerot has compared the history of modern poetry with that of the gnostic sects and that of those belonging to the occult tradition. This is true in two senses. The influence of gnosticism and hermetic philosophies on poets like Nerval, Hugo, and Mallarmé is undeniable, not to mention poets of our own century: Yeats, George, Rilke, and Breton. Moreover, every poet creates around himself little circles of the initiate, so that without exaggeration we may speak of a poetic secret society. The influence of these groups has been enormous and has succeeded in transforming the sensibility of our age. From this point of view it is not an exaggeration to assert that modern poetry has been embodied in history, not in full light, but as a nocturnal mystery and a clandestine rite. An atmosphere of conspiracy and of an underground ceremony surrounds the poetic cult.

Condemned to live in the subsoil of history, solitude is the distinguishing mark of the modern poet. Even if no decree forces him to leave his homeland, he is an exile. Dante never abandoned Florence, because in past times society always kept a place for the poet. The ties with his city were not broken; they underwent transformation, but the relationship continued to be live and dynamic. To be an enemy of the State, to lose certain civil rights, to be exposed to the vengeance or justice of one's native city, is a very different thing from lacking any personal identity. In the latter case the person disappears, and becomes a phantom. The modern poet has no place in society because, as a matter of fact, he is a "nobody." This is not a metaphor: poetry does not exist for the bourgeoisie or for the masses in contemporary society. The writing of poetry may be an amusement or a disease, never a profession: the poet does not work or produce. That is why poems have no value; they are not products that can be traded commercially. The effort expended in their creation cannot be reduced to a labour value. Commercial circulation is the most active and most total form of interchange known to our society, and the only form that produces anything of value. Since poetry is not subject to interchange like commercial commodities, it is not really of value. Since it has no value, it has no real existence in our world. The volatilization works in two ways: what the poet talks about is not real (and it is not real, primarily, because it cannot be reduced to a commodity), and poetic creation is not a definite occupation, job, or activity, since it is not possible to pay its price. From this it follows that the poet has no social status. The controversy about "realism" would be seen in another light if those who inveigh against modern poetry on account of its disdain for "social reality" realized that they are merely copying the attitude of the bourgeoisie.

Modern poetry does not deal with "real things" because previously the decision has been made to do away with a good part of reality: precisely that part which, since the beginning of time, has been the source of poetry. "The marvellous thing about the fantastic," says Breton, "is that it is not fantastic, but real." No one recognizes himself in modern poetry because we have been mutilated and we have now forgotten what we were like before this surgical operation. In a world of one-legged people, anyone who speaks of there being people with two legs is a visionary, a man who flees from reality. With the world reduced to those things that are evident to the consciousness, and all activities to their labour-market value, automatically the poet and his works were expelled from the sphere of reality.

While the poet vanishes as a social element, and while the circulation of his works in the open become less common, his contact increases with something which we shall call, for want of a better expression, the lost half of mankind. All the ambitions of modern art are directed towards re-establishing communication with that half. The supremacy of popular poetry, the turning to dreams and delirium, the use of analogy as a key to the universe, the attempts to recover the original language, the return to myths, the descent into darkness, the love of the arts of primitive peoples—all this is a search for the lost man. A phantom in a city of stone and wealth, dispossessed of his concrete and historical existence, the poet crosses his arms and dimly perceives that we have all been torn away from something and hurled into the void: into history, or time. His situation as an exile, from himself and from his fellows, causes the poet to surmise that only by touching the farthest point of the solitary state will the condemnation be terminated. For just when it seems there is no longer anything or anyone, on the last frontier appears the *other one*, and *all of us* appear. Man alone, hurled into this darkness of which we know not whether it is of life or of death, helpless, with all his moorings lost, endlessly descending, is the original man, the real man, the lost half. The original man is all men; or, as the Upanishads say: "You and I are one." Born of solitude, modern poetry is a poetry of communion.

The most desperate and total attempt to break out of limitations and make of poetry a common good was made in those places where objective conditions had become critical—in Europe after the First World War. Among all the adventures of that time, the most clear-sighted and ambitious was Surrealism. To examine it will be to realize, in its most extreme and radical form, the pretensions of contemporary poetry.

The Surrealist programme, that of transforming life into poetry and thus effecting a decisive revolution in the thinking, the customs, and the life of society, is the same as the project of Friedrich Schlegel and his friends: to make life and society poetic. To achieve this, both appeal to subjectivity. The disintegration of objective reality, as a first step towards its poeticization, will be a matter of inserting the subject into the object: Romantic "irony" and Surrealistic "humour" clasp hands. So, love and woman occupy a central place in both movements—complete liberty in love is allied to belief in the unique love. Woman opens the doors of darkness and truth; physical and psychic union is one of the most exalting experiences of man, and in it man comes into contact with the two sides of being: death and life, night and day. The Romantic heroines, beautiful and terrible like that marvellous Caroline of Gunderode, are reincarnated in women like Eleanor Carrington. The political vicissitudes are also similar: between the Bonapartist reaction and the Holy Alliance, Schlegel goes over to Metternich and others take refuge in Catholicism; in the opposite direction, but no less in renunciation of their past, before the world of the bourgeoisie and the Stalinist reaction, poets like Aragon and Eluard embrace the latter. The others disperse (until the concentration camp or the insane asylum swallows them up, as in the cases of Desnos and Artaud). They isolate themselves like Char or try to regroup, seeking a third way which will reconcile poetry and revolution, as exemplified by Breton and Peret.

The differences are no less noteworthy. Among the Surrealists the metaphysical outlook is less acute and comprehensive; even in Breton and Artaud, the only ones with a truly philosophical vocation, the vision is partial and broken. The atmosphere surrounding the Romantics is German philosophy; surrounding Surrealism are the poetry of Apollinaire, contemporary art, and Freud. On the other hand, its historical consciousness is clearer and deeper, and its relation to the world more direct and aggressive. The Romantics end by denying history and taking refuge in dreams; the Surrealists do not give up the game, even if this means, as in the case of Aragon, submitting the word to the necessities of action. Differences and resemblances are fused in a common circumstance: both movements are a protest against the spiritual sterility of the geometric spirit; both coincide with revolutions that are transformed into Caesarean or bureaucratic dictatorships; and finally, both are attempts to transcend reason and religion and thus found a new haven of refuge. Before such historical crises twilight and dawn fall simultaneously. The first reveals the common insufficiency of feudalism and the Jacobin spirit; the second exposes the ultimate nihilism of the rationalistic concept and the perils of bureaucratic Bolshevism. They do not achieve a synthesis, but in the midst of the historical tempest they lift up the banner of poetry and love.

Like the Romantics, the Surrealists attack the idea of subject and object. It is futile to stop and describe their attitude. It is fruitful, on the other hand, to stress the fact that the affirmation of inspiration as a manifestation of the unconscious, and the attempt to create poems collectively, imply a socialization of poetic creation.

Inspiration is a common possession—it is enough to close the eyes, and the images flow. We are all poets, and we must in fact ask for pears from the elm tree. Blake had said: "All men are alike in the poetic genius." Surrealism tries to demonstrate it by its recourse to the dream, to dictation from the unconscious, and to the collectivization of speech. The hermetic poetry of Mallarmé and Valéry, and the conception of the poet as an elect person and a being set apart, are violently assailed—we can all be poets. "We give back the talent with which we are entrusted. Speak to me of the talent of that metre of platinum, of that mirror, or that door. . . . We in ourselves have no talent," says Breton in his first manifesto. The destruction of the subject implies that of the object. Surrealism places works under an interdict. Any work is an approximation, an attempt to get hold of something. But at the point where poetry is within the grasp of everyone, poems and pictures are superfluous. We can all produce them. Nay more, we can all be poems. To live in poetry is to be poems, and images. The socialization of inspiration leads to the disappearance of poetical works, dissolved in life. Surrealism does not so much aim at the creation of poems as at the transformation of men into living poems.

Among the means that will consummate the abolition of the antinomy poet and poetry, poem and reader, you and I, the most efficacious and radical is automatic writing. Having destroyed the shell of the ego, with the partitions of the consciousness broken down, possessed by that other voice that rises from the depths like a swelling tide, man returns to the thing from which he was separated when consciousness was born. Automatic writing is the first step towards restoring the golden age in which thought and word, fruit and lips, desire and action are synonyms. The "higher logic" to which Novalis called us is automatic writing: I am you, this is that. The unity of contraries is a state in which knowledge ceases, because the knower has been fused with the known; and man is a source of evidences.

The practice of automatic writing is confronted with several difficulties. In the first place, it is an activity engaged in by following a direction contrary to the ideas that prevail in our world. In no uncertain manner, it attacks one of the foundations of present-day morality: the value of effort. To abandon oneself to automatic writing involves a very grave decision, since it contradicts commonly accepted principles. Furthermore, the passivity it demands implies another decision of an opposite kind: the will not to intervene. The tension engendered is unbearable, and only a few succeed in achieving, for a short time, that state of passive activity. The experience is not very different from the ecstasy of the Christians or the vacuum which is the plenitude of the Buddhists, although the Surrealistic experience may not have given us texts comparable to those of the great mystics. Thus, contrary to Breton's notion, automatic writing is not within reach of all.

It is not enough to hold out one's hand and close one's eyes and let the fruit of poetry fall. This accounts for the paucity of texts really produced by the automatic method. And I might even venture to say that the practice of automatic writing is impossible in present circumstances. If inspiration consists in that forward self-projection of man, continually reaching out for the image and continually detaching himself from his own self, automatic writing will be possible only when a radical transformation takes place in man's being, that is, when man ceases to be man.

The difficulties just mentioned are not the only ones. There is another objection that is more decisive and immediate. Automatic writing is a means for achieving a certain state of perfect facility in creation. But it is a means that is an end; what one tries to achieve with automatic writing is automatic writing, that point where the space separating man and his utterance ends. Automatic writing is a method within the reach of everyone for composing poems. The poems, on their part, have no other object than to create in the reader a state similar to that of the poet engaged in writing by the automatic method; therefore, the products of automatic writing are superfluous.

Our view of the possibilities of automatic writing changes as soon as we set it in focus within its own historical perspective. The *First Manifesto* announced a poetic revolution. The *Second* makes a single slogan out of the phrase of Rimbaud: "Change man," and that of Marx: "Change the world." As soon as class struggle ends, as soon as the State is liquidated and the infernal dialectic of slave and master is resolved into a real community, distances will be shortened between man and men, between man and things, and between man and his consciousness. The human being will be restored and consciousness and existence will be one and the same reality. In a Communistic society poetic automatism, far from being a paradox, would be the normal state of men. Work would be transformed, according to Lenin's well-known phrase, into art. And according as the human consciousness subjected existence to its will, all of us would be poets because all our actions would be poems, that is, creations. The night that is "an eternal poem" would be a daily reality, right out in the open sunshine. In the light of the *Second Manifesto*, excessive confidence in automatism shows itself for what it really is: a noble historic error.

In 1954, after the Second World War and the tense years which followed it, one can see more clearly the nature of the revolutionary fiasco of Surrealism. None of the revolutionary movements of the past had adopted the closed form of the Communist Party; none of the preceding poetic schools had appeared as a group so compact and militant. Surrealism not only proclaimed itself as the poetic voice of the Revolution, but it identified the latter with poetry. The new Communistic society would be a Surrealist society, in which poetry would circulate in social life as a perpetually creative force. But in historical reality that new society had already engendered its myths, its images, and a new form of refuge. Before the cult of the Leader arose, there had already appeared the keepers of the sacred books and a caste of theologians and inquisitors. Finally, the new society began to resemble too closely the older societies, and many of its acts recalled not so much the Reign of Terror of the Tribunal of Public Safety as the deeds of the Pharaohs. Nevertheless, the transformation of Lenin's Workers' State into a huge and efficient bureaucracy merely hastened the rupture; it did not cause it. With Trotsky in power the difficulties would not have been in any way different. The reading of *Literature and Revolution* is enough to make us realize that the liberty of art also had certain limits for Trotsky; if the artist passes beyond them, it is the duty of the revolutionary State to take him by the shoulders and shake him.* The compromise was impossible, for the same reasons which had prevented the poets of the preceding century from forming any permanent union with the Church, the liberal State, or the bourgeoisie.

After this rupture, Surrealism again becomes like the old poetic

*Years later, when he was already in exile, Trotsky modified his point of view and asserted that the only régime possible for the artist was that of anarchism, absolute liberty, independent of the circumstances prevailing in the revolutionary State. But these statements came from a man in opposition.

clubs, a semi-secret society. It is true that Breton has not ceased to proclaim the eventual identity of the revolutionary and the poetic movements, but his actions in the sphere of daily reality have been sporadic, and he has not gained any decisive influence upon political life. At the same time, it would be unjust to overlook the fact that, beyond this historic failure, the sensibility of our times and their images, particularly that incandescent triangle formed by liberty, love, and poetry, is in large measure a creation of Surrealism and its influence upon the majority of contemporary poets. Moreover, Surrealism is not a survival of the first post-war period, nor is it an archaeological specimen. In reality, it is the only movement that has remained alive to the middle of the century, after passing through a war and an unparalleled spiritual crisis. What distinguishes Romanticism and Surrealism from the other modern literary movements is their power of self-transformation and their ability to cut a subterranean passage under the historical surface and come up again. One cannot bury Surrealism, because it is not an idea but an inclination of the human mind. The undeniable decline of the Surrealistic poetic style, turned into a recipe, is that of a set form of art, and does not essentially affect its ultimate powers. Surrealism can create new styles, fertilize old ones, or even avoid all form and make itself into a method of inward searching, like Zen Buddhism. Well then, apart from what the future has in store for this group and its ideas, it is evident that solitude continues to be the dominant note of present-day poetry. Automatic writing, the golden age, night that is an unending feast, the world of Shelley and Novalis, of Blake and Hölderlin, are not within the reach of men. Poetry has not been incarnated in history; poetic experience is an exceptional condition; and the only way left to the poet is the old way of creating poems, pictures, and novels. But then this return to the poem is not a simple going back, or a restoration. Cervantes does not repudiate Don Quijote: he takes on his madness, and does not sell it for a few crumbs of common sense. The future poem, to be a true poem, will have to spring from the great Romantic experience. Do the questions that the greatest poets have been asking themselves for a century and half have any answer?

The Bow and the Lyre: The Poem, The Poetic Revolution, Poetry and History (*El arco y la lira: El poema, La revolución poética, Poésia e historia*), Fondo de Cultura Económica, Mexico, 1956, pp. 229–48.

José E. Iturriaga

(b. Mexico, D.F., 1914)

José E. Iturriaga is one of those Mexicans for whose mind national and human problems are its most compelling concern. His is a serious and reflective mind, and he appears to write not for intellectual reasons but with civic motives, directed solely towards the launching and the defence of great causes: education, social and political integration, lessons from our past history.

Iturriaga studied law and philosophy. In his youth he was a fervent admirer of Ortega y Gasset, on whose thought he wrote an extensive book which, because of moral scruples, he never carried through to publication. He belongs to the Board for the Economic Investigation of National Finance. Most of his essays and studies have appeared in cultural journals and in the daily press of Mexico City.

ESSAYS: *The Tyrant in Latin America* (*El tirano en la América latina*), 1944; *The Social and Cultural Structure of Mexico* (*La estructura social y cultural de México*), 1951.

THE CHARACTER OF THE MEXICAN

General Considerations

A MUCH MEDITATED THEME has been that of the existence of a national character for any given people, by virtue of which individuals that come into being and grow up in its bosom possess an unmistakable stamp which distinguishes them from other peoples. Along with this thesis, or more precisely, in opposition to it, there is another theory which holds that a man, quite apart from his place of birth, in the final analysis is exactly the same as any other.

But setting aside the polemic spirit common to both theses, and likewise keeping away from all the strictly philosophical implications which these theses suggest, it may be stated that every people has, as a matter of fact, a distinctive national character, a specific system of reactions brought about by the circumstances of life in which it is placed, namely: its geographical, economic, historical, social, political, and juridicial setting.

Throughout the different essays describing the national character of certain peoples, one may discern a series of *a priori* generalizations and arbitrary judgements easily refuted (e.g., in Salvador de Madariaga's[1] *Englishmen, Frenchmen, Spaniards* [*Ingleses, franceses y españoles*]), so that to describe the Mexican character is a difficult task to embark upon, apart from the concomitant presence of other reasons still more obstructive. Among these difficulties the following may be mentioned: (*a*) the complexity of our past history; (*b*) the multiplicity of aboriginal groups that occupied our territory before the arrival of the Spaniards; (*c*) the fact that the conqueror was not completely European, but a mixture of Celtiberian and Arab*; (*d*) the fact that Spain had not yet left behind her the mediaeval mode of life when she conquered and colonized these lands by virtue of her vigorous Counter-Reformation movement; (*e*) Mexico's situation next to a country like the United States of America, whose cultural structure has its origin in the Reformation and in "free examination," a direct and decisive antecedent of her scientific, technological, and economic leadership which stands in such total contrast to us in political and economic power;† and (*f*) as if all this were not enough, a piece of territory for the most part poor, broken up into a large number of regions closely delimited and isolated by their orography.

*From the anthropological point of view, Spaniards are the end product of a most complicated process of cross-breeding among different races: Iberians, Phoenician Semites, Romans, Goths of Germanic origin, Moors (Arabs and negroes), etc., so that the intermingling of such disparate racial elements within the nation (internal cross-breeding), had not yet reached a point which would justify considering Spaniards as a homogeneous ethnic group." Siegfried Askinasy, *Indigenous Mexico* (*México indígena*), Imprenta Cosmos, 1939, p. 147.

†See Waldo Frank's book *You and We* (*Ustedes y nosotros*), which points out the differences in cultural origin between Spanish America and Anglo-Saxon America. Editorial Losada, Buenos Aires, 1942, pp. 66–68. Daniel Cosío Villegas in his essay entitled *Mexico and the United States* (*México y Estados Unidos*) points out an interesting contrast: "Mexico was born of an important power. Not only were the vital energies of that power diminished to the point of virtual extinction, but Spain, incapable of creating any longer, necessarily fell into the position of hiding, for the sake of holding on to it, all that she had given to the world and derived from it. Mexico, like all the Spanish colonies of America, thus lived under an order of conservation and reaction, and was not moved, as was the country which later was to become the United States, by the great creative forces of modern society." (*Cuadernos Americanos*, No. 6, 1947, p. 16.)

---

[1]Spanish diplomat and scholar, who has been a professor at Oxford University since Franco overthrew the Spanish Republic in the Civil War of 1936–39.

But to all these historical, racial, cultural, international, and geographical factors, which have produced a type having a psychological make-up so full of shadings and so rich in its ingredients, many of these contradictory, there must be added still another, deriving from our uncompleted mingling of bloods: the two bloods we carry in our veins have not yet made peace; they are in a state of perpetual conflict.

Here it behooves us to pause a moment to clarify this point somewhat. A proof that the cultural cross-breeding is in the process of formation and that the reconciliation of our two bloods has not yet been achieved may be found, for example, in the fact that the name of Cortez continues to be polemical even among the most level-headed indigenists, apart from the fact that in a certain way the Conquistador continues to be taken as a symbol of reactionary political credos. And it is curious to note how the average Mexican feels more closely bound to the figure of Cuauhtémoc than to that of Cortez, which stands out in contrast to the situation in Peru, where the average Peruvian feels more closely bound to the figure of Pizarro than to that of his indigenous ancestors. In Mexico, Cortez has no statue, and Cuauhtémoc on the other hand has one. In Peru, Pizarro has a large number of statues, and Atahualpa on the other hand has none. The Peruvian history texts, in relating the battles of the Conquest, read as if those describing them were Spaniards. On the other hand, in our official texts one frequently finds: "Here we defeated the Spaniards." What is revealed by this contrasting historiographical outlook in two countries with a high percentage of indigenous population is indeed of great cultural significance, as has been shown by Leopoldo Zea (*Mexico in Spanish America* [*México en Iberoamérica*], *Cuadernos Americanos*, No. 6, 1946).

In like manner the change that has taken place in the popular consciousness during the nineteenth century with respect to the symbols represented in the two antitheses, Cortez–Las Casas and Cortez–Cuauhtémoc, is most impressive. Indeed, in the great liberating era of our Independence movement it was customary to compare two figures, both Spanish: Cortez and Las Casas. One was the symbol of the oppressor of Indians, the other the symbol of their defender (Cf. Silvio Zavala, *The Philosophy of the Conquest* [*La filosofía de la Conquista*], Fondo de Cultura Económica, 1947, pp. 117–50). But as early as the great days of the Reform and the French intervention the figure of Cortez was commonly contrasted with the heart-stirring personality of Cuauhtémoc.

This replacement of the Spaniard Las Casas by the Indian Cuauhtémoc as "defender of the Indians" by antonomasia, with the latter as a representation of the image of Juárez,* clearly indicates a collective evolution to a preference for the indigenous, a phenomenon which is observed even more clearly in the concept of the Mexican Revolution, for the Indian is placed in the foreground in the minds of the precursors of our social movement of 1910.† This means that as the country matures, the preference for the indigenous side of our blood mixture becomes stronger, and simultaneously, the figure of Cortez continues to have the polemical character to which we have already referred. It appears therefore that our two bloods will know no rest until the two and a half million bilingual and monolingual indigenes are completely brought up to the average cultural level and the average economic level of the country. Perhaps then we shall be able to view Cortez objectively and without animosity, and shall recognize him as one of our ancestors, as in fact he is.‡

An example of this collective inclination towards the indigenous is found in the popular enthusiasm aroused by the finding of the remains of the last Aztec emperor, an enthusiasm which did not cool down after the official declaration that those remains were spurious. And the notion of the average man in Mexico that his most illustrious ancestor is Cuauhtémoc, was recognized and consecrated in the decree of October 10, 1949, drawn up by the Congress of the Federation, which in Article 1 says precisely: "Of course, be it here declared categorically that *the heroic figure of Cuauhtémoc is the symbol of our nationality* and therefore merits the sincere devotion of the Mexican people."

Mexican Traits of Character

Before making an inventory of the character traits of the Mexican, an initial statement may be made—that the soul of the Mexican, like his corporeal aspect, is undergoing active gestation, in the same way as

*"Juárez is called 'the Indian' as a derogatory term by his political enemies, but this name was also given him by his followers to glorify him." Emilio Rabasa, *The Historical Evolution of Mexico* (*La evolución histórica de México*), Librería de la Vda. de Ch. Bouret, Mexico, 1920, pp. 31–2.

†In the programme of the Liberal Party of 1906, contained in the San Luis Potasí Plan, Point 48 mentions expressly the redemption of the indigenes. Cf. Jesús Romero Flores, *Historical Annals of the Mexican Revolution* (*Anales históricos de la Revolución Mexicana*) edition of El Nacional, Mexico, 1939, p. 207.

‡The urgency of this reconciliation is strongly proclaimed by Héctor Pérez Martínez in his *Cuauhtémoc*, Editorial Leyenda, Mexico, 1945.

this is happening, for example, in the mingling of bloods in Indo-China. That is to say, his is a soul charged with a dynamism directed towards being fixed and set in an unmistakable type. This is so true that many thinkers eager to grasp Mexican reality—sociologists, philosophers of culture, psychologists—believe it is impossible to define the peculiar Mexican character precisely because its peculiarity has not yet shown itself in outlines sufficiently plain to individualize it. Nevertheless, setting aside this objection, it may be stated that the degree of Indo-Spanish cultural intermingling that has taken place in three centuries makes it permissible to speak of a spiritual profile peculiar to the Mexican, which is nothing less than the collective national subconscious. But it must be understood that, when we speak of the Mexican, we shall be referring to the man who lives in the central states of the Republic, since it is here that the intermingling has gone furthest, and above all, it is here that the population is densest, for in 1946 the northern states had 4.9 million inhabitants, the central states 11.0 million, those along the Gulf of Mexico 2.8 million, those of the Northern Pacific area 1.5 million, and those of the Southern Pacific 3.1 million. Thus the Mexican of the central area constituted the greatest section of the population of the country.

The differences in character observed in the Mexican of other regions that bear a mark of individuality, for example, in the Mexican of Jalisco or of the North or of the state of Veracruz, or in that of Oaxaca or the Yucatán Peninsula, must be systematized by some scholar who is capable of offering a kind of spiritual geography of Mexico. In this way, then, within inevitable limitations of arbitrary judgements, there will be indicated the psychological traits which appear to be most distinctive in him, placing the typical *Mexican* in the central states and in the popular and semi-poor classes, for, as Dr. Mora said, "the character and the virtues of the Mexican are not to be looked for, as many foreigners have done, among the privileged classes, but in the great mass of the citizenry" (*Mexico and Its Revolutions* (*México y sus revoluciones*), Ed. Porrúa, Mexico, 1900, Vol. I, p. 121).

First of all, the Mexican suffers from a deep sense of inferiority which stems from his colonial past, from his position as a member of a conquered race, from the technical inferiority of his civilization compared to that of the conqueror* and from the fact that the inter-

*Naturally this inferiority does not apply to each and every element constituting a civilization or a culture, as is shown by the Aztec calendar and aboriginal medicine. On this topic the reader may consult the work of Alfonso

mingling took place not as a result of love, but through violence.* From this sense of inferiority arise all his virtues and all his shortcomings, for, as Adler has pointed out in *Knowledge of Man*, the prerequisite for the acquirement of any human impulse towards higher things is having that type of springboard that is provided by a previous consciousness of one's own inferiority and owing to which man is propelled onwards. Sometimes the acquirement is frustrated and he develops the so-called false superiority complex, grotesque and antisocial. But at other times the sense of inferiority gives rise to impressive cases of super-compensation. Towards this last phenomenon the Mexican has shown a strong inclination.

A frequent characteristic found in him is timidity. On the other hand, he can be extremely daring and courageous when circumstances require it, perhaps on account of a profound and atavistic contempt for life, which is another way of rendering homage to death.† Indeed, this tacit necrolatry is apparent in several facts, for example in the tie which binds the Mexican to the idea of death, and he is so familiar with its figure, that a strange phenomenon takes place in him: he ends by making it concrete in tidbits to be eaten, or else he utilizes its image to make playthings for his children or masks for his dances. His unconscious death cult does not merely lead the Mexican to observe the day dedicated to the dead, but he cleans up and arranges the pantheons with a care which shows a marked contrast to the carelessness in the cities.‡

He is usually reserved and has a great capacity to conceal his feelings. "The Mexican," observed Alexander von Humboldt 150 years ago, "likes to make a mystery of his most ordinary acts"; but this mystery, this timid attitude of his, is doubtless explicable by his

---

Caso, "Contribution of the Indigenous Cultures of Mexico to World Culture" ("Contribución de las culturas indígenas de México a la cultura mundial"), *Mexico and culture* (*México y la Cultura*), Secretaría de Educación, 1946.

*Almost all Spaniards left their wives, sisters, and daughters back home, and this inevitably brought about the propagation of the mestizo among the population, without the latter being the offspring of a healthy and moral union, but of the urge to gratification of the procreative instinct in the conquistador, producing an offspring that very frequently lacked affection and a sense of responsibility in its progenitor.

†On this theme there has been a profusion of writing, but perhaps the best work we owe to Gabriel Fernández Ledesma, of which an advance instalment appears in *Mexico in Art* (*México en el Arte*), No. 5, 1948. Organ of the National Institute of Fine Arts.

‡This characteristic is pointed out by Andrés Henestrosa, *Excélsior*, July 23, 1950.

consciousness, frequently mistaken, of his own frailty, as well as by the impact upon his ancestors of centuries of exploitation, for the Indian never knew whether the white man approaching him would treat him well or ill. Therefore he dissembled. Octavio Paz is right in saying:

> Perhaps dissimulation arose during the colonial period. Indians and mestizos, as in the poem of the Magi, had to sing softly, since words of rebellion muttered between the teeth are not well heard. The colonial world has disappeared, but not the fear, the distrust, or the suspicion. And now we dissemble not only our anger, but our tender sentiments. . . . The Mexican appears to me as a person who locks himself up and preserves himself, with both face and smile a mask. Set in his sullen solitude, simultaneously gruff and courteous, he uses all the means of self-defence: silence and speech, courtesy and contempt, irony and resignation. (*The Labyrinth of Solitude* [*El laberinto de la soledad*], Ed. Cuadernos Americanos, Mexico, 1950, p. 42.)

His sparing of gesture bears some resemblance to English phlegm or Oriental imperturbality. This is particularly true in such proportion as the Mexican is submerged and saturated in autochthonous cultural elements. Humboldt likewise had noticed this reserve when he said of the Mexican: "We do not find in him even that changeability in sensations, features, and gestures which characterizes many peoples of the equatorial regions in Africa. There is no contrast more striking than that observed in comparing the impetuous vivacity of the negroes of the Congo with the inner phlegm of the copper-coloured Indian."

To classify him with respect to the two basic types of temperament, the sentimental and the rational, the Mexican is sentimental, in spite of his external appearance of coldness or indifference. His tendency to self-isolation and immobility, which causes him to pass over and over through the few events which occur in the world about him, are the result of his distrust of social and natural surroundings that have been hostile to him. And perhaps his lack of vivacity is also due to the century-old malnutrition from which he has suffered and still suffers lamentably, for the nutrition of the Mexican is indeed distressingly deficient, since the quantity of strength-giving food he consumes is less than in 32 countries of so-called Western culture. So, for example, while the Mexican consumed an average of 9.8 kilogrammes of meat per year, the Argentinian ate 136.6 kilogrammes. As for the average consumption of milk per inhabitant, in our country it was 30 litres a year, while in Sweden or Norway it was 300, or ten times more. (See *Study of Fundamental Education in Mexico* [*Estudio* *acerca de la educación fundamental en México*], SEP, Mexico, 1947, pp. 104–5.) This malnutrition from which the Mexican has suffered, and is still suffering, causes him to be underweight, for in relation to his average height the male should weigh 59.8 kilogrammes, but his actual average weight is only 53.3, which means, in brief, that the average Mexican is 6.5 kilogrammes underweight.*

The Mexican is sad by nature. Nevertheless, he possesses a keen sense of humour which he can use as an offensive and a defensive weapon, on the terrain of his gruff social manner, in the form of poisoned darts within a precarious patriotism frequently cast in the direction of electoral politics.

Since he uses a language not his own, for it was not evolved by his autochthonous ancestors, and therefore is not incrusted upon the collective subconscious, he speaks little, in a low voice, with difficulty or obliquely, and generally uses a lot of diminutives (See Jorge Carrión: "Mexican science and magic" ["Ciencia y magia del mexicano"], *Cuadernos Americanos*, No. 2, 1948). But when the phenomenon of supercompensation takes place in him, he can be rhetorical and a good orator, though his skill is shown more in letters than in oratory. His liking for blasphemous language, not always frequent in its manifestation, is not really an indigenous trait; it is rather a tribute he pays to his Spanish forebears.† When he quarrels, he prefers innuendo to open insult; for this reason he says "the understanding mind needs few words."

The Mexican, "desiring both his own privacy and that of others, does not even venture to cast a glance at his neighbour: a look might unleash the wrath of those souls charged with electricity" (Octavio Paz, *The Labyrinth*, p. 29). In fact, the Mexican is very touchy and irritable and frequently gets into quarrels, as is shown by these figures: out of every 100,000 inhabitants 8.4 commit homicides.

If we compare such figures with those for other countries, we find corroboration of the statement just made. For example, in Scotland, out of every 100,000 inhabitants, 0.66 committed homicide; in Ireland, 1.08; in France, 1.41; in Belgium, 2.01; in Austria, 2.28; and in Spain (the other blood in our cross-breeding), 5.54. Only in Italy were

**Image of the Contemporary Mexican* (*Imagen del mexicano contemporánes*). Lecture given in October 1947 by Dr. José Gómez Robleda, under the auspices of the Sociedad Mexicana de Estudios y Lecturas (Mexican Society for Studies and Readings), in the Bolívar Amphitheatre.

†In Alvarada and Veracruz, towns in which the Spanish character predominates, the inhabitants customarily misuse blasphemous language.

higher figures recorded than in our country; while out of every 100,000 Italians 9.86 commit homicide, out of every 100,000 Mexicans 8.4 commit that crime.*

But in spite of his long-standing poverty, and contrary to what has been commonly believed, the Mexican commits more crimes against persons than against property, for in 1940 the crime of causing bodily harm was 400 per cent more frequent than the crime of robbery. In fact, the quarrelsomeness of the Mexican comes from an excessive concern for his personal importance, indicative of his sense of inferiority; but, as over-compensation for this, he manages to be haughty and proud.

The Mexican, so rich in contrasts, shows one that is most remarkable: that which one notes between his acrimony and violence on the one hand, and his fine delicacy and capacity for tenderness on the other (See Emilio Uranga: "Towards an ontology of the Mexican" ["Ensayo de una ontología del mexicano"] *Cuadernos Americanos*, No. 2, 1949, pp. 135–48); and this contrast is shown with greatest plasticity in popular art and the love of flowers, which attests to his profound vocation as a creator of beauty. Humboldt was puzzled by "how strange it was to find a love for flowers in a nation whose bloody religion ought to have obliterated all sensibility of spirit." And he also added: "In the great market of Mexico City the native of the country does not sell his fruits and vegetables, and even pulque, without adorning his stand with flowers, which he daily renews."

The Mexican has an acute sense of the ridiculous, which arises from his strong habit of self-criticism, and this is because his inhibition and underdeveloped character also derive from his fear of debasing his ego in the eyes of others (Adolfo Menéndez Samará: "The complex of the ridiculous in the Mexican" ["El complejo del ridículo en el mexicano"], *Letras de México*, Sept., 1940). Fortunately he is losing this feeling slowly but steadily as he realizes he can do things he previously had considered impossible because they were ordinarily done in countries more highly developed than ours.

Contrary to general belief, the Mexican is not gregarious but an individualist, and consequently he frequently lacks a spirit of col-

*"The Mexican of the common class," says Abad y Queipo, "is excessively prone to crime, but it is marvellous that he does not fall into crime oftener, and that among this class we should find the regular customs recognized in many of its individuals." Gregorio Torres Quintero, *Mexico towards the End of the Spanish Viceroyalty* (*México hacia el fin del virreinato español*), Librería Bouret, Mexico, 1921, p. 35.

laboration. His unsociability and gruffness incapacitate him for associating with others without friction or for working creatively as a member of a team. Probably this accounts for his limitations in the political sphere, his apathy as a citizen, and his inclination to break the laws in force; and for his unconsciously or unconcernedly making a mere abstraction out of the lives of other people. It is true that the individualistic spirit of the Mexican does not derive so much from his indigenous stock as from his Spanish ancestry,* as may be seen from a series of essays on Spanish individualism written by brilliant representatives of the "generation of '98" in Spain. But, be that as it may, one thing certain is that the Mexican has not developed his "social ego," as for example it has been developed by the American of the United States, whose social sense and vigorous patriotism contrast so strongly with our attitudes.

This difference between the Mexican-American and the United-States-American is somewhat tilted in our favour by the fine observation of a sociologist: "In few matters are the American of the North and the Mexican so widely separated as in the impression made by them when they are outside their own country: the Mexican makes a better impression, and the American appears in a worse light. . . . The strong point of the United States is its collective character and not the individual; the best of Mexico is the individual, and not the social person. (Daniel Cosío Villegas, *American Extremes* [*Extremos de América*], F.C.E., 1949, p. 75.)

Now, the unsociability and the individualism of the Mexican would cause him to be unbalanced in his emotional life if these two deficiencies were not counterbalanced by an aptitude for making loyal and lasting friendships, which he customarily elevates to the rank of a spiritual relationship by a solemn and religious oath: the "sworn companionship," an institution with origin not only Hispano-Catholic, but having strong precolonial antecedents, as is shown by one investigator.† This aptitude for friendship is also stressed by Dr. Mora when he says: "Fidelity and constancy in their friendships, affections, and pledges surpass anything one can imagine. Being suspicious by nature, and also on account of the oppression under which they have lived,

*See in this connection Ganivet's *Spanish Ideas* (*Ideario español*), José Ortego y Gasset's *Invertebrate Spain* (*España invertebrada*), and Miguel de Unamuno's *The Life of Don Quixote and Sancho* (*La vida de Don Quijote y Sancho*).

†Francisco Rojas González, "The institution of sworn companionship among the Indians of Mexico" ("La institución del compadrazgo entre los indios de México"), *Revista Mexicana de Sociología*, Vol. V, No. 2, 1943, pp. 201–2.

they do not easily enter into relations with others, but once committed, only very rarely do they break them" (*Mexico and Its Revolutions*, Vol. I, p. 69). The tracing back of this sociological syndrome, that of the Mexican's great capacity for friendship, to a point where the category of friendship means more to him than fidelity to ideas, especially in the domain of public life, is a theme that is truly fascinating. Bulnes used to call that tendency of ours "friendliosity" (*amistosidad*), while Quevedo y Zubieta called it "amification" (*amificación*).*

As a balance left in his consciousness by the pressure of the viceregal authorities, the Mexican feels a basic antagonism towards governmental machinery. Abad y Queipo has already expressed it: "What affection, what kindly feelings, can they [the Mexicans] have towards the ministers of the law who exercise their authority only to send them to prison, to the pillory, to the penitentiary, or to the gallows?" (Brown Castillo, *Studies of Abad y Queipo* [*Estudios de Abad y Queipo*], p. 14.)

The effect of such tyranny was to leave in his consciousness an inability to express his contrary opinions and his aspirations by means of civil political action, so that he does so only by armed conflict when the pressure exerted by the governmental authorities accumulates around him.

This lack of training in political life leads to a marginal type of civic life. So, instead of joining political parties, he prefers to oppose the government under the protection of the anonymity afforded by the walls of rooms, on which he imprints, as an expression simultaneous with another form of catharsis, his political opinions. This strange rostrum serves him likewise for the expression of his resentments and complaints against the hated enemy or the oppressive leader, and his bashfulness with regard to the woman he likes and whom he does not dare to woo he relieves in those private places by means of compensatory symbols.

We have made up an "anthology" and an "iconography" of inscriptions and drawings found in such places—workshops, barracks, schools, public offices, moving picture theatres—and they are documents of inestimable value for the knowledge of certain psychological areas

*See F. Bulnes, *The True Díaz and the Revolution* (*El verdadero Díaz y la Revolución*). Ed. Eusebio Gómez de la Puente, Mexico, 1920, pp. 171–9, and Salvador Quevedo y Zubieta, *The Leader* (*El Caudillo*), cited by Molina Enríquez, p. 14.

which the scholars have not yet touched. The constant notes of this material are lack of civic courage, an unsatisfied sexual urge, and diluted forms of sexual relations.

The sense of being magnificently masculine—the so-called "he-man-ism" (*machismo*)—and also a fondness for the pun,* for the flirtatious remark, and for pornographic suggestions and gestures, are other characteristics of the Mexican. One would say that he always has a balance owing to himself, a sexual deficit that he has not yet satisfied, and this in spite of his long history of malnutrition which logically should bring him to a more ascetic mode of life, at least mentally.

That the Mexican is persistently preoccupied with eroticism was proved by an investigator† by means of a close inquiry conducted by radio broadcast. The results were as follows: 34.34 per cent of the people questioned stated that the predominating interest which motivated their lives was sexuality and eroticism; 17.17 per cent said they preferred the mystic-religious life; 11.48 per cent said they liked the imaginative life; 8.63 per cent confessed that their interests inclined towards good food and health; 6.92 per cent expressed their desire to rise higher in the economic scale; 5.69 per cent showed a strong love for family; 4.88 per cent said they were chiefly preoccupied by a concern for their own importance; 4.27 per cent declared they had a vocation for the arts; 3.80 per cent sought power; and the remaining 2.82 per cent showed an interest in political and social problems.

The Mexican has exalted patriotic feelings, although he lacks a clear sense of nationhood; that is to say, his patriotism does not lie in the sphere of the rational, but in the sphere of the emotional; or if you like, he has a deep feeling for his country but has no clear concept concerning it. The reason for this may perhaps lie partly in the lack of geographic cohesion, a condition which is disappearing owing to the highways that have been constructed during the last twenty years, and partly in the large number of aboriginal groups that there are in the country (more than fifty), as well as in a firm and sure conservative

*See Samuel Ramos' book *The Profile of Man and Culture in Mexico* (*El perfil del hombre y la cultura en México*), the chapter entitled "The peasant" ("*El pelado*"), where the customary terminology of this human type is studied; the pun frequently carries the obvious message suggesting sexual relations. Pedro Robredo, 2nd edition, amplified. Mexico, 1938, pp. 75–84.

†José Gómez Robleda, "Image of the contemporary Mexican" (Imagen del mexicano contempráneo"), a lecture arranged by the Sociedad Mexicana de Estudios y Lecturas in the Bolivar Amphitheatre of the UNAM, October 1947, mimeographed edition, p. 38.

instinct with relation to any outside influences which might destroy or alter our national identity.*

The Mexican, when he governs, or when he accidentally is set in a position higher than his fellows, is ordinarily harsh, doubtless due to the reaction of resentment, studied at great length by modern psychology, which holds that any sense of vassalage is coupled with a strong inclination towards despotism. This fact is best illustrated by the men in authority in the numerous rural communities, a condition which produces the plague of cacique rule, and the extirpation of which will be beneficial to the democratic development of the country.

The Mexican is not much given to reflection and analysis; he is the product of two cultures which did not find the truth by the use of reason. One of these cultures, the aboriginal, was pre-logical, and to it the supernatural was natural (Lévy-Bruhl, *Primitive Mentality* [*La Mentalité primitive*]). The other was non-positivistic, dogmatic, and based on faith. Nevertheless, the Mexican is intelligent and quick in comprehension,† although superficial through his lack of the reasoning habit. But when he can combine his innate intelligence with persistence, there is then produced a man who can utilize the highest scientific disciplines, as has been happening recently.

The Mexican has a quickness and a richness of imagination which explain both a fundamental virtue and a fundamental defect: his prodigious creative capacity in the domain of art, and his tendency to a mania for myth. That is, the Mexican does not content himself with reality, or submit to it, just as it is offered to his eyes; therefore he distorts it with the supplementing fancy of his own desires or through a work of art. His hostile surroundings (other things and other people), the ungenerous reality in which the Mexican lives, he does not respect; he attacks it either ethically or aesthetically. In this sense, the painter Diego Rivera is the archetype of the Mexican.

Among the great cultural values—truth, goodness, justice, beauty, sanctity—the Mexican does not hesitate in his preference: beauty is a gravitational force which attracts him, so that the other values are subordinated to it.

*Jorge Carrión, in his work entitled "Psychic Trauma of the Mexican in the War of 1847" ("Trauma psíquico del mexicano en la Guerra de 1847"), studies the hypersensitive patriotism of the Mexican as an effect of those painful times. *Cuadernos Americanos*, No. 6, 1947.

†President Valentín Canalizo, in his message to Congress on January 1, 1844, at that early date was already speaking of "the precocious cleverness of Mexicans." *Public Education in Mexico as Seen through the Presidential Messages* (*La educación pública en México a través de los mensajes presidenciales*), p. 9.

The Mexican in his daily life is temperate, perhaps on account of so many centuries of poverty; but he can be lavish in his dress, his parties, and his meals, and is fond of excessive noise and skyrockets, when he enjoys any transitory prosperity. "The native of these lands is grave and silent so long as he is not set off by strong drink," observed Humboldt even a century and a half ago.

The Mexican is weak-willed, and is moved to action only by the impulse of desire; that is, he lacks a will that is applied towards changing surrounding reality. Of course this defect in his character, like many others, is not constitutional but provisional; it is not a definitively established attribute, but a mere consequence of a myriad of adverse œcological factors. Indeed, the poorness and the hostility of the geographical surroundings, the low productivity of his work, centuries of malnutrition, and the great prevalence of ill health, can explain this collapse of will-power. According to the 1940 census, 12.41 per cent of the population was suffering from illness, exclusive of a large mass of the same population that was potentially so, owing (among other things) to the lack of good drinking water supplied by water works; for in 1940, of the 3,800,000 houses showing in the records of the aforesaid census, more than 2,500,000 were huts and hovels, and barely 6.7 per cent of the total had drinking water with sewers and drainage. (See Gómez Robleda, "Image of the contemporary Mexican," p. 15.)

The most wide-spread illnesses, according to the census, were the infectious and parasitic. Of 857,000 cases of diseases of all kinds, 287,000 were diseases of the digestive tract and 202,000 were of the respiratory organs. The diseases showing the smallest number of victims are the neo-plasmic diseases and cancer.

With respect to the total mortality, of 458,000 people who died in 1940, the diseases which because of their severity caused the greatest number of deaths were those of the digestive tract, at 20.77 per cent, and those of the respiratory organs, at 18.78 per cent. Among these diseases the most prevalent are: diarrhoea and enteritis, which caused 96,000 deaths; pneumonia, which caused 70,000; and malaria, which caused 23,000. Canada differs from us in this respect, for there the greatest number of deaths caused by disease are due to heart ailments and cancer.

The premature death of the average Mexican likewise shows how illness is always with him in a potential state. Of all the Mexicans that are born, only 54 per cent reach the age of thirty, the remaining 46 per cent dying before attaining that age. If we compare these figures with those for Australia, for example, we see the extent to which the centuries of malnutrition suffered by our people, the lack of health services, and overwork, reduce the span of human life in Mexico. In Australia 82 per cent of the population passes the age of thirty, only 18 per cent dying before reaching that age. In Sweden 77 per cent attains the age of thirty, in the United States 74 per cent, in England 73 per cent, in Germany 67 per cent, and in Italy 65 per cent.*

In 1930 the Mexican lived to an average age of thirty-five years, the Swede to an average of sixty-six, the Australian sixty-four, the Englishman and American fifty-nine, and the German and Italian fifty-five. The differences from the figure for Mexico are striking, since the Mexican lives to little more than half the age attained by the Swede.

The Mexican has another defect related to the lack of will previously mentioned: a divided will, indecision, since the form which will-power takes in him, when he applies it, is that of being applied not in a single direction, but in two or several directions. Well, this multiple will and indecision is possibly due to this fact: in the underlying regions of his mind there is a strong desire to avoid all responsibility with regard to other people which may result from any decision he makes. Therefore the Mexican does not say "yes" or "no" emphatically and straightforwardly, but eludes any categorical statement that may put him under obligations. This instability of will has its repercussions in the emotive sphere, a phenomenon that has been seized upon by popular jargon in an expression full of semantic intuition: "an uneven character," which indicates that the Mexican is, using the customary language of psychology, a *schizotimic*, whose unsteady and oscillating character causes him alternately to assume one attitude or another; to be both quickly elated and quickly depressed; to feel himself readily both master of things and mastered by them,† and therefore he moves easily from the most unrestrained optimism to the blindest form of pessimism. This division of will also explains his frequent lack of convictions and his forsaking of the political ideas he holds.

The Mexican is improvident, perhaps owing to his lack of any sense

*The figures for foreign countries apply to 1930.

†Emilio Uranga ("Towards an ontology of the Mexican") states that the Mexican is always "up or down" (*en zozobra*), giving back to the word *zozobra* its etymological sense; "sub-supra," or, being in *zozobra* [usual sense: "anxiety"], means being alternately below and above things, or our circumstance.

of the passing of time. This comes from a culture, the aboriginal, which, like the oriental, perceived time as something static, something immobile in which little or nothing happened. His tendency to unpunctuality is likewise explained by the low value he attaches to time. His notion of space is usually vague too, perhaps because of the custom (especially in rural areas) of moving without mechanical aids over vast areas broken up by geography.

The Mexican is irresolute. His inability to make a continued effort leading to results is daily apparent in his mode of living; therefore, no sooner does he start projects than he abandons them, a defect which accompanies the trait of the divided will that we have mentioned. He is unenterprising, that is, he lacks the pragmatic spirit. His incapacity for sustained action in the world of business prevents him from having it. Perhaps for this reason, when he decides to make a change in his fortunes he usually prefers the quickest way and not always the most licit. His inclination towards the lottery and games of chance has the same source: a desire to solve his painful economic problem without the least effort.*

The Mexican is a spendthrift. His prodigality and recklessness are shown by the fact that he spends more than he earns and is continually in debt. In short, he lacks the habit of saving. Of course such a habit, like many others, has arisen from strictly economic causes, for the fact is well known that the average Mexican has always suffered and is still suffering from under-consumption,† as is shown in the 1940 census: 13,000,000 Mexicans slept on the floor or ground; 7,000,000 wore white breeches; 6,000,000 went barefoot; 4,000,000 wore sandals, and 9,000,000 wore shoes. These figures show their poverty, and so prove that the vast majority of Mexicans have been, and still are, unable to save, although those who are able to do so either squander

*Dr. Mora mentioned in his time the "abominable vice of gambling, so common and widespread in all classes of society, and which reflects so little credit on the character of the Mexican." *Mexico and Its Revolutions*, Vol. I, p. 129.

†But this poverty does not move the Mexican to use his earnings in hand for the satisfaction of his most elementary needs; rather, he does the opposite: he postpones this in order to treat himself to a moment of gay life. A minute study of the distribution of the expenditures of the heads of families belonging to the labouring class, the peasantry, the middle class, and the poor would show that the category of amusements is high on the list, as can be seen immediately from the habit of going to the bull-fights (a very costly spectacle), the indispensable celebration of saints' days, the festival in honour of the patron saint of the town, the alcoholic Saturdays (always a heavy burden on family life), etc.

their resources in an absurd manner or go to the opposite extreme and practise the most unproductive hoarding, either in their houses, or in the savings banks.*

The Mexican has a great capacity for absorption and adaptation; he is mimetic, and possesses a strong imitative faculty. And when a thing is imitated, according to Samuel Ramos (*The Profile of Man*, p. 12), it is because it is considered worthy of imitation, for there lies in the consciousness a previous evaluation which places one's own culture in a lower category than the culture one tries to imitate. This was probably the way the so-called *malinchismo* (mania for the foreign) worked, consisting, as is well known, of considering everything foreign to be superior merely because it is foreign. In this connection, an observation of Humboldt's concerning a custom of the sacristans of the Capuchins is most illustrative. These sacristans "wanting to look like their absolute masters, the friars," daily shaved off their scant beards to make them grow and thus resemble the Spaniards in appearance; this same phenomenon is seen in the Castilian *ceceo* [use of the *th* sound] used by Indian clerks in bakeries and grocery stores owned by Spaniards.†

The Mexican is an improviser; more precisely, he is marked by having a surprising facility for doing what was previously unknown to him (remember the *Periquillo Sarniento* (*Mangy Parakeet*), a personage created by Fernández de Lizardi), a virtue the roots of which one would have to seek both in his remarkable adaptability and in his recognized manual dexterity and richness of imagination. All of this enables him to have relative success in the most contradictory forms of activity. This aptitude for improvisation is obviously the result of the lack of a differentiated specialization applying to official positions and professions, as one finds in countries more highly developed economically and technologically, since the absence of that

*As the standard of living has gradually risen in recent years in certain strata of society, the habit of depositing money in savings banks (abandoning the classic mattress) is becoming established, for while in 1942 there were 99,300,000 pesos in the banks in savings accounts, in 1949 the figure had risen to 356,300,000 pesos, which means that the habit of saving in the social classes capable of doing so rose 358.75 per cent, or more than three and a half times.

†The fondness for everything foreign just because it is foreign, as one of the traits of the Mexican, is noted by José Joaquín Fernández de Lizardi in his "Dialogue between a Frenchman and an Italian on North America ("Diálogo entre un francés y un italiano sobre la América Septentrional"), written December 16, 23, and 30 of 1813 in *The Mexican Thinker* (*El Pensador Mexicano*), Vol. II, Nos. 16, 17, and 18.

division of work obliges the Mexican to engage in all kinds of activities. Any attempt at improvisation made by a people endowed with less imagination than ours would have catastrophic consequences, but because of this imagination no great harm results. The proverb "He's just as good for sweeping as for scouring" describes this remarkable aptitude; nevertheless, many administrative disasters can be charged to the account of improvisation. Fortunately, however, the increasing technical organization of the Public Administration, the economic development recorded in recent years, and the creation of new courses in the new technological institutes and universities that have been established in the country, will gradually expel from our land the utilization of such a picturesque and suppletory aptitude.

The Mexican is fatalistic and superstitious, precisely because the two cultures which have formed him made life and plans depend upon transcendent forces and divine purposes. Much of what happens to him he attributes to good or bad luck, which also explains his fondness for the lottery and games of chance. The reputation still enjoyed by charmers, practitioners of cartomancy, and herbists, whose forgetting of the great empirical tradition of our aboriginal medicine is frequently fatal, can be verified in the "bargain offer" pages of the press, where daily there appear new and weird names of persons engaging in such an anachronistic and lucrative profession.

Of the three parts into which religion is commonly divided,* the Mexican is more inclined towards dogma and the scrupulous observance of ritual than he is towards morality (Carrión, "Psychic Trauma"). This fact is clearly explicable if we remember that the two cultural worlds of which he was born were characterized by the preponderant role of a spectacular liturgy and an unshakable and hermetic dogma, on the Spanish side, and on the indigenous side, by the savage observance of rite. In this he differs notably from the Anglo-Saxon, for the latter prefers morality or social service to rite or worship, which is almost always unimpressive in Protestantism.

The Mexican is "micromanic," as was first perspicaciously pointed out by Jorge Carrión, that is, he has a predilection for the small, in which he is the opposite of the United-States-Americans, who, in contrast, are "macromanic." In no other country, in fact, has that "macromania" been produced to the degree in which it is observed in

*Every religion is divided into three parts: dogma, morals, and worship. See in this connection R. de la Grasserie, *Psychology of Religions* (*Psicología de las religiones*), Ediciones Pavlov, Mexico, 1948.

the United States. That "megalolatry," as Röpke* calls it, is really a religion which comes into being in the nineteenth century and which had become most perceptible in North America, possibly as a result of mass production in industry and as a consequence of the hypertrophy produced by its technological machinery. This contrast between the Mexican and the United-States-American is thus noted by a prominent investigator:

> The United-States-American, a fabulously rich man, is in the habit of counting what he has, earns, and loses; he therefore tends to base many judgements of value upon magnitude, or quantity. The Mexican, usually wretchedly poor, has literally nothing, or very little, to count, and consequently the idea of magnitude, or quantity, seems to him somewhat strange. This explains why his judgements are based or seek to be based on the idea of quality. (Cosío Villegas, *American Extremes*, F.C.E., p. 50.)

This "micromania" of the Mexican is implicit in the abuse of diminutive forms used in daily speech and in street cries, but above all in his peculiar fondness for miniatures, as can be observed by contemplating in village markets the rich variety of toys and popular dainties, or the work in bone and ivory done by convicts, or the dressed fleas, etc. Few peoples, indeed, possess this peculiar characteristic, and a more thorough and systematic investigation would lead to most interesting conclusions. For the time being we might hazard this one: the abuse of the diminutive in speech must be attributed to a delicacy that is expressed in the form of courtesy, although at times the excess of courtesy reflects a sense of inferiority; and the fondness for miniatures can be explained as a relic of aboriginal fetichism, or the mere pleasure it gives the Mexican to show to himself and others the cleverness and dexterity of his hands.

In all these generalizations and judgements, not free from the arbitrariness which is inevitable in describing the character of the Mexican, it must be remembered that the virtues and defects apply, as was clearly indicated at the beginning of this chapter, more particularly to the popular and lower middle classes living in the centre of the Republic, though frequently the Pueblan is mentioned as the type most representative of this zone.

*Wilhelm Röpke, *The Moral Crisis of our Time* (*La crisis social de nuestro tiempo*), Revista de Occidente, Madrid, 1947, chapter entitled "The Cult of the Colossal," pp. 78–90. The cult of the colossal means, for this economist and cultural sociologist, "prostrating oneself before what is merely big, accepting this as sufficient evidence of greater quality and value," this along with "the scorn for the externally small, but intrinsically great."

The contrasts observed between Mexicans of the central region and those of other parts of the country are indeed striking. For example, the inhabitant of Veracruz, on the coast, is not timid or introverted, and unlike the man who lives on the central plateau, he talks loudly. His frankness and hospitality, in which he resembles the Cuban or the Venezuelan, are proverbial, but the latter of these qualities he is slowly losing on account of the influence of the highways and tourism upon the population of this province. In brief, in the people of Veracruz, as in the case of the inhabitants of Tabasco, the Spanish character prevails over the indigenous.

The inhabitant of the northern states, likewise, is frank and energetic; and his relative lack of religiosity is doubtless explicable by the fact that the influence of the Catholic Church in that part of our territory was less highly developed, as is indicated by the paucity of religious monuments to be found there, for while the State of Puebla alone, in 1939, had 1898 Catholic churches, Sonora, Chihuahua, Coahuila, Nuevo León, and Tamaulipas together had only a third of that number, or 682 churches.*

But, as we have stated, the tracing of a "characterological map" of the country, the establishment of a "spiritual geography" of the Republic, is a task which requires a careful systematization on the part of scholars.

It is unnecessary to emphasize that many of the traits of character which today appear to be peculiar to the Mexican may disappear as soon as there is a change in the economic, political, and social conditions which favoured their appearance. And in spite of the balance-sheet presented, apparently unfavourable, one thing must be emphatically declared: the Mexican possesses a great underlying spiritual strength. At times we scorn it or fail to see it, but it will enable us to continue to be ourselves, and it is something which will save our vigorous national personality and lift us upwards towards a position of greater historical importance. This strength is something in which many Latin American peoples place their trust, and in which we must trust with greater reason than they.

*José Vasconcelos, in a passage of his autobiography, observes the scant Spanish influence in the northern part of the country, not only in the small number and lack of impressiveness of the churches, but in the poorness of the cuisine.

Arturo Arnáiz y Freg

(b. Mexico, D.F., 1915)

Lucas Alamán, Dr. José María Luis Mora, Justo Sierra, and some scientists of the nineteenth century (Elhúyar, Del Río), have been studied by Arturo Arnáiz y Freg, who enjoys high prestige as an historical essayist. His published works can be collected in a single volume, but his contribution to the historical disciplines is constant in his university chair, in research, and in his very active participation in national and international meetings and congresses. His essays are marked by a precise and lively style, a thorough understanding of the themes studied, and a penetration that lays bare the essential vital forces of an historical personality.

Arnáiz y Freg studied history and economics at the National University, where he is now a professor.

STUDIES: *Andrés Manuel del Río. Biographical Study* (*Andrés Manuel del Río. Estudio biográfico*), 1936; *Personalities and Ideas* (*Semblanzas e ideario*) by Lucas Alamán, Prologue and selection by A.A.F., 1939; *Essays, Ideas, and Portraits* (*Ensayos, ideas y retratos*) by José María Luis Mora, Prologue and selection by A.A.F., 1941; *Juárez, His Work and His Times* (*Juárez, su obra y su tiempo*), by Justo Sierra, edition and notes by A.A.F., 1948.

PANORAMA OF MEXICO*

CONCERNING MEXICO, most outsiders know only that it is a country of beautiful landscapes, some volcanoes, a good climate, and many revolutions, and very few have the intellectual patience necessary to obtain some information about what Mexico is, what it has been, and what it aspires to become.

We were born into Occidental life in the sixteenth century as a product of the fusion of the most powerful European empire and the most powerful American empire. Cortez arrived on our shores in 1519,

*Lecture read before the General Assembly of UNESCO, in Mexico City, November 7, 1947.

the year of the death of Leonardo da Vinci. The child Saint Theresa was just four years old.

Received as gods, the Spaniards here lived "the way of the book of Amadis." As victors, they demonstrated by their colonizing enterprises that they had the same capacity for agglutination as Rome in its best days.

Since those days, the process of learning to comprehend things Indian on the part of peoples of Occidental culture has been long and arduous. The conquistadors had no interest in ethnology. Occupied with saving the people of these regions for living together as Christians, they were not too particular about preserving the sculpture, jewels, and codices which the natives had produced.

Incapable of understanding the symbolical language of sanguinary rites, the conquistador reacted to them as one convinced that they had a diabolical origin. In systematically destroying the symbols of the old pagan practices, the Iberian believed he was contributing to the salvation of the heathen.

With a clear-cut universalistic mania, and opposing anything that might weaken the unity of the Empire, Spain finally prohibited the study of things pertaining to the Indians. The Royal Decree of April 1577 which proclaimed the seizure of the manuscripts and papers of Fray Bernardino de Sahagún read as follows: ". . . and be warned not to permit in any circumstances that any person write anything touching upon the Indians' superstitions and way of life, in any language, for so it becomes the service of God our Lord and Master."

Not until the eighteenth century, with Clavigero, does the pre-Hispanic begin to be freed from this idea that it was diabolical. In the nineteenth century begins in earnest the systematic salvaging of vestiges hidden underground.

The investigations of modern archaeologists have recently succeeded in unearthing, in the Valley of Mexico, the oldest human skeleton hitherto found on the American continent. It is a male, and according to the most conservative calculations, he lived fifteen or sixteen thousand years ago. The "Man of Tepexpan," a hunter of elephants and a descendant of the first discoverers of the continent, was found in mesolithic terrain, which suggests that his ancestors came from Asia to America after the glacial period.

The American Indian was the first to face the American enigma and the first to find solutions to it. They did the first developing of the continent's resources, without which the European occupation would have been exceedingly difficult.

Passing from the stage of being gatherers of the earth's offerings to that of agricultural life, men with ancient modes of cultivation succeeded in producing maize. And this was only the beginning. Agriculture came to be regarded by them as something sacred. And having hit upon the right course, they cultivated and domesticated plants and animals which later spread over the world.

Maize, cacao, vanilla, the tomato, chicle, Mexican cotton, the turkey, and India rubber figure in the list which the illustrious Alfonso Caso has given us as an impressive compilation of inventions and discoveries that pre-Hispanic Mexico gave to Western culture.

In freeing him from the anxieties of the nomadic life, agriculture gave to the Indian an opportunity to turn his eyes towards the celestial vault. And on observing the first regularities, he fell down in adoration before the forces which he recognized as not being subject to his will. Then rose the astronomical religions, and all those elaborate theogonies were rocked and lulled by the rhythm of dances, hymns, and prayers.

All that could be burned, all that could be consumed by putrefaction, has disappeared, and yet, such is the richness of the archaeological treasures Mexico still offers, that we have entire peoples for whom no place whatever has been found in any general chronological scheme.

With their complicated religious systems destroyed, their cosmogonies forgotten, their liturgy brought to nought, their priests forever silenced, there remain standing the statues of the terrible gods in which the men living here, like those of other climes, symbolized the processes of nature which, because inscrutable, could then be assimilated into human motivations.

Many religious secrets still remain hidden in frets and friezes; the pomp and colour that accompanied their liturgy have disappeared; the smoke of their incense will never rise again, and the eyes of the stone idols have become opaque. But it is evident that in those hieratic relics, in those statues which are, as it were, their subconscious brought into the open, the Mexican of today finds elements that lead him to a better understanding of his tortured inner life.

Shortly after the eye becomes trained, it discovers the dynamic details which a highly intellectualized study has left hidden inside the inert mass. Symmetry, proportion, personal imprint are found in every sculptural detail. The deformations introduced into the hard modelling of each stone or into the delicate outlines of the clay and the obsidian were carefully calculated.

For good reason our contemporary painters have been able to discover many of the shadings which give an individual essence to their message in those monuments of religious art which place the creative capacity of the Mexican Indian at the same high level as that of the artificers who erected the imperishable structures of Egypt and Mesopotamia.

In the last three decades we have seen a fresh evaluation of Spanish American art. European art is now only a part of universal art, and the new sensibility (less confined within narrow Greco-Latin moulds) has given us a better understanding of the vigorous Indian accent that is present in the most important periods of our artistic history. The Indian element is still a mystery that has not been completely unveiled. Every day we have at our disposal better data for establishing its historical position. For us the task brooks no delay, because when one lives in these parts, one may have nothing Indian in the flesh, but yet always carry something of the Indian in the deep recesses of the spirit.

We are appreciating more and more the delicate intimacy of his poetic creations, the dignified attitude of the Indian in the face of the enigmas with which life confronts him, the impressive sense of urban elegance shown in his cities, and the dazzling magnificence of his gold and silver work.

And on studying the hieroglyphics that we still find on his stones and on the yellowed leaves of the codices, and on noting that there have not yet occurred all the eclipses which they predicted, we are astonished by the accuracy of their calendars and chronologies.

When the Spanish-Arab culture was flourishing in Granada, and when the author of the *Divine Comedy* had been dead barely four years, the Aztecs, in 1325, reached the Central Valley of Mexico. After almost three centuries of incessant warfare they succeeded in integrating the most powerful organized society in North America. Their old habit of exacting tribute enabled them to draw up a true economic map of the regions they occupied.

In the central zone of their great political and military structure lived and prospered the *calpulli*, a system of holding land that was based upon a thousand-year-old tradition of mutual service which let its advantages be felt by all members of the community.

And it is also not until our times that, provided with the data furnished by the archaeologists and specialists in the history of religions, we have learned to understand the symbolic significance of their sanguinary rites. These peoples of the central part of Mexico fought periodically in knightly wars. To solicit divine favour they shed their own blood. The desire to keep the sun burning by the abundant offering of the most precious of liquids, human blood, led them into the tragic error which for the sixteenth-century Spaniard could only have been inspired by the infinite wickedness of the devil, but which now, without any lessening of our repugnance towards the terrible error that made it possible, rises up before us as one of the highest forms of generosity. In keeping with this generosity, the whole collective life of these peoples was oriented towards one purpose: "One must know how to die."

And they knew how to die heroically when the conquistador came in 1519. The arrows, darts, and heated rods could not compete with fire-arms. The wooden clubs with stone knives turned out to be useless against swords of Toledo steel.

The Spaniard of the sixteenth century, seasoned by the struggle with the Arabs, gave to the conquest of these lands the character of a crusade. The astonishment of the conquistadors at the beauty of the native's cities is apparent in all their descriptions.

While the presence of the whites, within the magic world of the Indians, was merely the fulfilment of prophecies which in recent years they had seen reinforced by the appearance of several portents outside the natural order, the Spaniard, on the other hand, advanced with the conviction that anyone had the right to destroy myths if he replaced them with something better. In Mexico, he always felt that he was fighting the infidel, and under the influence of the long war in the Iberian peninsula, he called the Indian temples mosques and claimed that the Aztecs wore burnouses. And the soldiers of this armed retinue, an extension of the mediaeval world on American soil, when it was their fate to fall before the Indians, used their own blood to form a cross on the ground, in order to die kissing it.

The passions which beclouded the judgement with regard to the conquest of Mexico by the Spaniards have cooled off a great deal among us. We are learning more and more about the lives of other peoples, and so every day we discover a more just historical orientation of the exploit of Cortez and his companions.

As a Mexican mestizo, I become calmer and calmer about the history of the conquest. It is like a family quarrel, like the indispensable requisite that half of me should join the other half.

Cortez doubtless had great faults, but I cannot help admiring one of the qualities which he imprinted on the Spanish conquest. While for other peoples "the best Indian is a dead Indian," Cortez showed by his conduct that for him the best Indian was an Indian girl in love. Cortez was the great collector of loving Indian girls!

Impressed by his heroic defence of Tenochtitlán, the Mexican clings to the admirable figure of Cuauhtémoc. He is one of the objects of our most profound patriotic devotion on account of the epic note which lends character to the life of the young prince, and because of the dramatic end to his life as a ruler faithful to the destiny of his people.

With the conquest ended and the chivalric novel once concluded, the exploit of a more extended range began: draught animals arrived, and many unfamiliar European plants were brought over. The wheel was applied to transportation, and with the presence of horses and asses, there slowly disappeared the inhuman institution of the *tameme*, or human carrier. Burdens ceased to be carried on the backs of men.

The Spaniard in Mexico came to be a new and vigorous synthesizing factor. In a certain way, Cortez and his men continued the work that the Aztecs had taken upon themselves. A few decades after the fall of Tenochtitlán, the unification of the warlike tribes had already been achieved under the banner of Castile.

To this end the missionaries had made an enormous contribution. It was they who enabled the Spaniard, for undeniable merits, to win a guerdon which no one would take from him. The best opportunity in history to lead the indigenous nuclei of America into an active partnership within Western civilization was created by him. Moreover, as the Bishop of Michoacán, don Vasco de Quiroga, has written, the Indians were "people so gentle, so unsophisticated, so simple, and so like soft wax that one could do with them whatever one would."

In the sixteenth century we received our heavy dose of the Middle Ages. The Spanish soldiers spread over the plains of America and, when the time came to build, churches, palaces, and fortress-castles filled out the Mexican landscape with the monumental grandeur of ecclesiastical and military Spain. In this way an Empire based on spiritual solidarity laid the foundations of its rule.

A few years ago an eminent European professor said to me with regard to the different shadings which may now be observed in the former Spanish colonies: "No, don't speak to me of the captaincies-general! I believe in the viceroyalties."

And I had to answer him: "My friend, I believe in the viceroyalties, but I also believe in the Indian empires, because there was no great viceroyalty where there did not previously exist a powerful pre-Columbian people."

The greatest wealth of Middle America was the cheap and skilful work of the indigenes. Since before the consummation of the conquest,

Indians have done the hardest work that is done in the country. The four centuries during which this situation has continued have not been sufficient to stop in them the springs of artistic creation.

Throughout the whole colonial period we were, along with Peru, one of the two great pillars that supported Spanish power in America. With funds from the coffers of Mexico the deficits of Spain's colonies in the northern hemisphere were covered. From our coasts sailed the expeditions which brought Western civilization to the Philippine Islands.

In the seventeenth century the Renaissance touched our shores. The grandchildren of the conquistadors are now living as colonists. This extensive portion of the empire shares in the splendour of the Spanish Golden Age through the fine sensibility of don Juan Ruiz de Alarcón.

Along with the Spaniards and Indians, there arises the group of humanity in which is effected the synthesis of these two elements. The mestizos make their appearance, "capable of all good and all evil," according to don Lucas Alamán,[1] but to them entrance into the schools of higher learning was expressly forbidden.

On the throne of Spain, the Bourbons replace the house of Austria. French influence is accentuated, and in the eighteenth century the colonial world, built on economic inequality, and in its hierarchies and refinement distributed according to categories, sees the fine atmosphere of its baroque peace disturbed by the first pressures of modernity. Eighteenth century Spain, its energy now exhausted, tried to shut itself in behind its walls. But ideas infiltrated past all obstacles, as always happens, and in Mexico there arose various indications of the influence of the encyclopaedists.

The Saint Charles Academy and the Royal School of Surgery opened their doors. The Royal School of Mining was established. When Baron von Humboldt visited us early in the nineteenth century, he had to acknowledge that no city of the new continent showed institutions as solid and durable as did the capital of New Spain.

In 1810 the peace of centuries was finally broken by the insurrection of the insurgents in the town of Dolores; a man who had been principal of one of the leading centres of higher learning in the colony launched the first important challenge to Spanish power in our territory.

In almost all provinces of the country the civil war for independence was kindled. Guanajuato, Morelia, Guadalajara, and Toluca fell, and Mexico City itself was within reach of insurgent troops.

When after the defeats of Aculco and Puente de Calderón it

[1]Mexican statesman and historian of the early nineteenth century.

appeared that the tide was ebbing, don José María Morelos y Pavón rose up in the south.

A shepherd of souls, he was able to break the bonds subjecting him to the ecclesiastical hierarchy in order to serve the urgent needs of his people.

His unmartial form began to increase in stature with the engagements. A nimble horseman on his tall horse, he organized his troops with rigorous discipline. Without officers or soldiers, he was able to create armies led by a group of admirable leaders. He accustomed his men to standing firm on the battle field against the onslaughts of the powerful viceregal enemy. In him were united cunning, personal valour, physical vigour, and aptitude for command. Over the fields of central Mexico, which always smell of ripened harvests, he came to acquire the habit of beating the royalists.

The privileged classes of viceregal Mexico placed themselves at the side of the Spanish government. After several years of fighting, with the principal leaders captured and afterwards shot, the movement was left without any headquarters capable of co-ordinating the efforts of the guerrilla fighters scattered throughout the different parts of the country. The viceregal government, now victorious, could afford a policy of amnesties. Many secondary leaders agreed to lay down arms and began to live peaceful lives in regions remote from the areas in which they had operated. Francisco Javier Mina went to Soto la Marina, and after six months of military operations carried out with dazzling rapidity, he was finally overcome by superior forces. His execution marks the end of the last appreciable threat to the firm authority of the viceregal régime in this country.

Our separation from Spain was brought about in a paradoxical manner. We became independent of our mother country when it offered us greater liberties. It was the conservative elements in Mexico, the same that in earlier years had overpowered the efforts of the insurgents, that now regarded as no longer of any value to their interests the link with a peninsular Spain that had accepted the application of the liberal constitution of 1812.

Now independent, we lived two years under the régime of Iturbide, more properly termed a dream or a theatrical performance than an empire. The first Emperor dethroned, the attention of our theoretical politicians turned towards the manner in which we should constitute ourselves a republic. Those were years of vertiginous political and military action, but decisive in the history of our nation on account of the different solutions that were tried, the conflicts that were resolved in that period, and the high moral calibre of the patricians who directed public affairs.

Our Constitutive Congress of 1824 decided on a federalist solution. As a governmental programme, federalism at that time had the merit of having kept the nation intact.

With frontiers embracing territory from Upper California to the boundaries of Great Colombia, and with an area of more than four million square kilometres, our ancestors found themselves confronted with a dilemma which unfortunately they were unable to solve. We were incapable of offering to all the parts which then constituted the country a good programme for the future. In 1823 we lost Central America because we had not been sufficiently conservative. In 1835 the first of our old northern provinces separated from us because we had not known how to be sufficiently liberal.

On our northern frontier we inherited a problem which Spain had been incapable of solving. Before the progressive advance of the Anglo-Saxons, our former mother country had been adroit in postponing any clash by means of diplomatic concessions which always entailed a withdrawal to positions farther and farther south.

In all those early decades of our life as an independent country, our most discerning minds were in constant anxiety with respect to Mexico's internal weakness. They felt that the time for mutilations was approaching. And the conflict did not take long to settle.

The Mexico of a century ago offers an interesting panorama.

We began our independent life as a country of armed injustice. In the top leaders and the petty officers, one sees a touching resolve to ape the Napoleonic model. In our political life, all the important decisions were made by military men. The Mexican civilians who managed to gain any decisive influence in politics always had to seek out a docile tool in order to get anything done. The pain they felt on account of operating in the background often caused them to despise their executive arm.

With the abuses of the Church, which in those times owned two-thirds of the country, and with the crimes and spoliations of the professional soldiers, there was gradually formed a liberal group opposed to the two dominating classes. It was an intellectual group, the first germ of a true middle class which by the end of the century was to be a vigorous free-thinking and anti-militaristic bourgeoisie.

Our history of the past century is almost completely filled by the antinomy between liberals and conservatives. Those rich in material goods, desiring security, thought somewhat ingenuously that the country's ills would disappear if one could manage to bring things back to the conditions prevailing in the pleasant final years of the eighteenth century.

After the noble attempt at reform by Gómez Farías and Dr. Mora, which was suddenly interrupted in 1834, the conflict remained undecided until the revolution in Ayutla. Santa Anna, who filled three decades of Mexican life with his name, was, in the end, decisively defeated. After having served under all banners, he fell defending the interests of the traditionalists. After their victory on the field of battle, the liberals finally succeeded in bringing into Mexico's fundamental code the separation of Church and State, the disentailment of ecclesiastical property, and the abrogation of the clerical monopoly of public education. The new constitution seemed too advanced to President Comonfort, who by a coup d'état tried to prevent its enforcement. After further military conflict he was defeated.

In Mexico, no head of state has been able to gain the support of the party opposing the one that brought him into power. The mere attempt to change colours has with us usually meant quick political suicide.

And after the last great effort of the conservatives, when with the support of the armies of Napoleon III they tried to establish here the imperial régime of Maximilian of Hapsburg, the victors under Juárez put an end to the last vestiges of the old professional army. If since that time Mexico has ever for some years evaded, in a few periods of her history, the painful spectacle shown by the typical Latin-American dictatorships, it has been because the reformers found the way to divide the united strength of the clergy and the professional army. On account of the strict discipline to which they are subjected, both bodies in these countries of ours impress upon their men a kind of fundamental intolerance which in former days profoundly affected national destinies.

Liberalism was able to exist among us as a stable form of government from the day when it was made possible for a non-professional army, improvised and revolutionary, to stand on guard against the ecclesiastical hierarchy.

Later, the dictatorship of General Díaz, established under the slogan of a programme of progress, prevented the country for the time being from having a normal political development. Many of our gravest present-day economic problems are due to the mistakes made at that time. Mining, the most important of the Mexican industries, is still today in foreign hands. The establishment of large estates in land was permitted. Most of the rural population of Mexico was reduced to the condition of serfs. On the large estates sometimes not even a tenth of the land was utilized, which caused many of them to be really nothing but broad tracts of desert.

The Mexican Revolution has in large measure remedied this situation. By its agrarian policy it has made it possible for thousands of serfs to become men. The great movement which was begun in 1910 does not have, in the political thinking of the people who contributed to its preparation, any direct links with ideological stimuli from outside the country. The solutions proposed are not suggested by examples elsewhere, but by the painful situation in which the majority of the inhabitants of the nation lived.

Time has slipped by and these words must necessarily come to an end. In the next few days you will get a view of different facets of Mexican life. When you have passed through our streets, when you have been shown in our museums the jewels that our archaeologists have been able to discover, the day when after having set foot upon the age-old stucco of our pyramids it is possible for you also to get a view of the beauty of our landscapes, I am sure you will agree with me that in order to get an integrated view of Mexico, nothing will be able to take the place of the effect of your own impressions.

The study of History is first of all a great lesson in humility.

When it is necessary for you to return to your countries, I am convinced you will take with you the conviction that among us, as among many other peoples of the earth, there are still grievous inequalities, there are still many goals to reach, and in many ways the distribution of the material wealth is unjust. In the next few days you will hear right in this place what men who are recognized authorities will tell you about our literature, our arts, and our sciences. They will give you your bearings with respect to the serious study of things pertaining to us. And by the tenor of their words you will see, on skimming over even as rapidly as I have done the various stages of the historical life of Mexico, that their voices do not assume the tone of a dead man's testament, but in large part that of a portent filled with hope.

It cannot be denied that the groups that have here been vanquished in history lay special stress upon the sombre aspects of our internal struggles. They have lacked understanding of the Mexican scene. They judge it in both a humorous and a tragic light, but history cannot be reduced to a long lamentation interrupted by a few outbursts of laughter.

On the other hand, the average Mexican looks back on his dramatic past to draw from it arguments to support his strong desire for liberty, for the equitable distribution of material goods, and for peaceful relations with the other peoples of the earth.

When, back once more enjoying the stimulating warmth of your own hearths, you begin to reflect upon Mexican life, it is very probable that you will come to the conclusion that though there are greater or smaller economic resources, though there are greater or smaller numbers of machines, in spite of the different languages and the different types of social organization, the people of our nations are fundamentally the same in their deepest concerns.

This nation, to whose formation men of all origins have contributed, is now convinced that it is an urgent matter to reduce its serious technological deficit. We are poor; the fields of our high plateau lack water. It is also true that both city and country lack machinery. But, without forgetting the magnitude of our past and present economic problems, we are interested in man. We are interested in giving a good internal structure to the man of Mexico.

Since we gained independence, we have opened our land to all influences. Here, as elsewhere in America, we are witnesses to the creation of a true Latin-American cosmopolitanism. We are free ports for the activities of the mind. Our historical antecedents provide us with a good preparation for the understanding of peoples born outside our boundaries. When Spain came to these lands, she did not bring a message from one locality, but she brought the finest things the West could give. To her spirit we remain faithful when we hearken to the voices of the geniuses that breathe beyond our frontiers.

Therefore, in having the honour to be host in its capital city to the Second General Assembly of UNESCO, my country takes pleasure in welcoming this display of intellectual and moral solidarity which humanity offers us. Since we are united in great emergencies, our coming together must not appear to be imposed upon us by external factors, but by mutual understanding. It behooves us all not to allow ourselves to yield to forces which, inside all national boundaries, have only had their rancours lulled to sleep.

May this meeting in Mexico, at the same time as it clarifies our sense of responsibility, permit us to make new friendships. And, with its hues light and dark, may the image of our country that you carry away in your memories be a just one. In your understanding alone we shall find an eloquent token of friendship. With it we shall feel flattered, for as an indigenous poet said more than four centuries ago:

> A necklace of jewels is placed about our necks
> When we know that the hearts of our friends are faithful.

Supplement of "*El Nacional,*" Mexico, Nov. 30, 1947, No. 35, pp. 8–9.

Emilio Uranga

(b. Mexico, D.F., 1921)

Among the young philosophers who in about 1948 gathered around Leopoldo Zea to form the "Hyperion" group, Emilio Uranga was outstanding for his decidedly philosophical bent, for his disciplined intellect, and for his keen curiosity concerning other forms of culture. At the National University he began to study medicine, which he was to abandon in favour of philosophy. In this field, as member of the Faculty of Philosophy and Letters, he is now a professor and lecturer, and throughout the years 1948 to 1953 he began the publication of the initial results of his meditations on the nature of the Mexican. At the same time he is engaged in research in the Institute of Social Sciences of the University and also in the College of Mexico. From 1953 to 1957 Uranga amplified his philosophical studies at the German universities which are still the greatest centres of philosophical activity in the world, Freiburg, Tübingen, and Cologne, and also at Oxford University and at the Sorbonne. As a result of his work during those years we have his books *Goethe and the Philosophers* (*Goethe y los filósofos*), *Marx and Philosophy* (*Marx y la filosofía*), and *Introduction to the Reading of George Luckacs* (*Introducción a la lectura de George Luckacs*).

ESSAYS: *Analysis of the Nature of the Mexican* (*Análisis del ser del mexicano*), 1952.

THE MEXICAN AND HUMANISM

WITHOUT THERE BEING ANY NEED for the formulation of a theory concerning the nature of the Mexican, we may say that he spontaneously regards himself as a very peculiar representative of a human style of living. Pre-ontologically or pre-conceptually, the Mexican makes himself and his world explicit *as* human, which means that he sees in his life an *image* of man. At the first blush, the express statement that the Mexican conceives of himself *as* man appears to be a triviality unworthy of consideration. And yet in this expression, so comprehensible in itself, is concealed an assertion the justification of which in one period of our history required learned theories and conceptual elaborations, of a type predominantly theological, the significance of which we are still very far from grasping with adequate discernment. We are alluding to that famous dispute which arose in the sixteenth century concerning the "humanity" of the Indian, concerning his rather obvious and patent "bestiality" and not "humanity," to use the words of one of our most renowned and profound historians. By still unknown paths the Mexican asserts himself in the course of his unhappy history as "man," even when he caricatures this human dimension of his and degrades it into "he-manism" (*machismo*). Being a Mexican, then, does not mean, if one penetrates right into the marrow of his being, a peculiar nationality, but the quality of being human. In a certain way his libertarian efforts, like the Reform and the Revolution, are copies of a struggle for the human to which the Mexican finds himself committed, a struggle which he takes up with such *originality*, that from this root other qualities sprout as genuine offshoots and not as tumours to be eradicated.

But with equal *originality* the Mexican rejects the human, and cloisters himself, with indelible vows of ferocity, within his *nationality*, and boasts of it with loud protestations which pass the limits of the prudent to overflow into the grotesque, brutal, coarse, and even sanguinary. With equal spontaneity the Mexican asserts himself *as* Mexican and *as* man, but the nationality hardens and calcifies the first interpretation by converting it into something official, by creating a complicated set of exceptions and privileges which, though justified in certain points, in most points are absurd. The Mexican clings to his nationalism by repudiating his fundamental human qualities. The two interpretations are incompatible, and contend in a tragic conflict that has coloured with its iridescent light all our history from the War of Independence to the Revolution. In the Mexican, in the form and manner in which history offers him to us, there is a ready intermingling of humanism and nationalism. We respond with equal naturalness to the human and the Mexican, and an understanding of this bilateral character gets at the root of many of our attitudes. From historical motivations easy to enumerate, the Mexican has sought in nationality a refuge, a shelter that will protect him against the appropriative voracity of foreigners. The idea of a rich *nation* has been joined to that of a collection of its legitimate proprietors. "Mexico for the Mexicans" is the motto of a nationalistic claim for the return of national property. The nation is not regarded as a creation in which Mexicans are expected to participate energetically, but as a *possession* or reality at his immediate disposal and for his immediate use, without effort, without work, by merely stretching out the hand to gather the fruit, with his appropriating action well protected against intervention by foreign hands. *Making* a nation is obscured by the stubborn belief that he *has* a nationality. The nationalists imagine Mexico to be a lot of ready-made good things that they can enjoy without effort, and they are concerned about safeguarding this gratification against intruders who also without effort might put our riches in their wallets. This mercantile concept has not disappeared from popular and official mentality, and it has even been aggravated to a pathological degree by the Revolution. Salvation by possession, by property, is a deceptive salvation, which sooner or later leads to despair. Moreover, it is an immoral and unethical solution to the problems of human conduct, which finds its dignity in doing and not in having, and this is the only way for human morality to be represented.

But the most serious thing about nationalism is not its concept of the nation as a possession, which is serious and dangerous enough, but the separation or secession which takes place in the Mexican, cutting him off from general humanity and making of him a particular reality which rules out any participation in what others are doing, because he believes that their fortunes, remote from his own, have no effect on the nearby and immediate. But it is degrading to be a nationalist when one can be a man. For our purposes it is sufficient to have pointed out, in the Mexican, this interpretation of his own person, as a Mexican, in nationalism, stressing that it is not the only interpretation, and far less the readiest, despite appearances to the contrary.

When the Mexican shows himself in complete forgetfulness of his nationality, his life in itself assumes a form in which one finds an original contact with the source of all humanism. The "sentiments" of self-abandonment, spontaneity, inconstancy, oscillation, sorrow, among others, which are familiar to the Mexican as the fabric or "material" of his own nature, afford the only base upon which to establish humanism. In the innermost recess of his nature, the Mexican conceives of himself as "accidental and precarious," which means that he exposes himself openly to the human condition in the deepest stratum of his being. In general, he tends to evade these "painful" sentiments and to seek, in any way possible, by faith, science, culture, or history, something for a man to cling to, a point where he feels himself secure and "of substance." But the Mexican does not evade, with any ready agility, those "categories" or "existential states" of man's nature, he stands right there and keeps them company; he has them in his presence, not in the innocuous sense of being theoretical representations, but as part of his life, both his daily life and his extraordinary experiences. He has them with him, and feels them each day, each night, at all hours. This peculiar "courage" or "perceptivity" that causes him to open himself up to what is "unhappy" and "forsaken" in the human lot is the originating principle that lays him open to what is human, to the more submerged area in which there has been prepared or brought into being a capacity for communication of feeling, by comparison, sympathy, or affinity with other people, and with all that tries to represent itself as human. The Mexican understands the human apart from himself by means of a transposition of the inner feeling of his own life. The compassion he shows so frequently in all aspects of his behaviour (and the Mexican feels compassion for animals, and even plants, and his calling "poor" every human being he comes across, or coming within the sphere of his experience, is not something that merely falls from his lips) is the outward expression of that continuous operation by means of which he is transferring the sense of his own life to what is other than himself. This complicated operation requires that one have an unobscured sense of the point from which the transmission is effected; that one's own life, which figures as an absolute centre of reference from which the sense emanates, be truly known; that we carry it with us as we carry our own bodies—for the moment communications with the original source are broken, all compassion becomes paralyzed. And the converse too is true. When the Mexican sees that somebody is trying to pass off as human something that to him does not appear human, something that does not tie up with the original meaning of the word "human," he immediately strips it of all claim to humanity and treats it as a thing and not as "human." In the same way that he is compassionate, he is also indifferent and brutal, and inconsiderately passes by with icy indifference what is "evidently" human. As long as the supposedly "human" bears no obvious relationship to what is Mexican, compassion is inoperative, and it is not even recognized as human.

Our lives are based on familiarity with the human, because the characteristics we ascribe to man are also applicable to a description of the Mexican. We do not have to run through the register from the Mexican to the human, but there is an original coupling in a "team" of the Mexican and the human. We have seen the same phenomenon for the Mexican regarding life and death. We have said that death is, for the Mexican, a symbol of his own life, because the conclusions which we applied to life are also those which gave us a definition of death. Life and Death figure as "mates." They are linked together; not only that, they mutually call to each other. By turns, each invokes the other. Edmund Husserl[1] was the first of our philosophers to call attention to the peculiarities of an association by "pairs," or of a "pairing" (*Verkoppeln*). The curious way in which the two things go together gives rise to strange phenomena. When two entities, like life and death, or the Mexican and the human, appear as paired, this means that they are at the same time "similar" and "different." There is a kind of family air, a touch of resemblance, between life and death, but at the same time we are struck by differences between them. The resemblance is not so great as to permit us to speak of equality, but the difference is not so sharp that we can say they are really different. The coupling is upheld within the limits of resemblance and difference. This being the case, it permits the effectuation of a "transmission" or "transference" of characteristics of both things represented in the "pairing." There is a reciprocal lending of sense. One term is explained by the other, and this, in turn, is reversible. There is a continuous circulation of sense, a to-and-fro movement, a receiving and returning, and interminable going and coming of meanings from one term of the pair to the other, out of which rises its unitary sense, which belongs to the pair and not exclusively to one of it members. We apprehend one of the terms in a relationship, a conformity, with the sense of the other, in the measure that no differences are created that would prevent the transposition, and likewise no equality that renders impossible the transference of the sense.

In our case the Mexican and the human function as a pair. The human is understood by starting from the Mexican. It derives its primary sense from its resemblance to the Mexican. If this resemblance does not exist at the base of relations between us and others, no humanism can be produced. But also the resemblance is given double force by the consciousness of a difference. Though the Mexican is compassionate, thereby showing that he senses the universal similarity of all men, he also has an uneasy feeing that his lot is not one that can be altogether shared, that there is a nucleus in which communication is impossible.

Extremely sensitive foreigners have pointed out to us that a curious

[1]Czechoslovakian-born Jewish philosopher, the "father of phenomenology," who died in Freiburg, Germany, in 1938.

feeling prevails with regard to the Mexican. The openness to everything human, the intermingling and close association without fear or scruple seem to create between the Mexican and other men unlimited communication, in which equality shines out as a supreme ideal. But in spite of this undeniable communicability, there is an impassable limit. While the Mexican comes to resemble the foreigner, the latter, on his part, cannot become fully Mexican. There remains a territory that cannot be entered, that will not open. Hospitality does not remove a kind of redoubt closed to outsiders. The creation of this difference destroys the coupling of the Mexican and the human. If the separation is made on the part of the Mexican himself, it leads almost immediately to nationalism. If no separation is made, and if the cleavage is not seen by the Mexican himself, it is none the less apparent to others. Just what is this barrier? The Mexican will never be able to say what it is. In his humanism he refuses to recognize it and this he does legitimately, because in conceiving of it as based upon a "coupling" he has to ignore it *a priori*. So, rather than a sense of equality with respect to others, there is in a sense of "coupling"; and in the nationalist, one of "difference." Not all humanism is built upon this peculiar structure that we have revealed. It is generally believed that humanism presupposes the affirmation of equality, and that without it there is no humanism possible. But this is a mere supposition. The same notion prevails with regard to life and death, that the "difference" between the two phenomena is the indispensable premise for any theory about life and death. But we have seen that this is not so. The Mexican "couples" them by exaggerating their resemblance to the point of forming an "equality." The same thing occurs with humanism. The human is familiar to the Mexican because he keeps company with it in his life as if it were the opposite pole with which he establishes a sense communication, a reciprocal loan of services and favours, a transference of meaning which enables him to explain his own life as human, and at the same time, the human as Mexican. The results of this operation cannot be considered here.

Analysis of the Nature of the Mexican (*Análisis del ser del mexicano*), Collection *Mexico and things Mexican* (*México y lo Mexicano*), No. 4, Porrúa y Obregón, Mexico, 1952, pp. 38–44.

Pablo González Casanova

(b. Toluca, Mex., 1922)

Pablo González Casanova became known through two excellent historico-philosophical investigations, which arose out of the seminars of the College of Mexico: *Misoneism and Christian Modernity in the Eighteenth Century* (*El misoneísmo y la modernidad cristiana en el siglo XVIII*), a treatment of the first inroads of modern philosophy in New Spain, and *An American Utopia* (*Una utopía de América*), which studies the strange predictions of Juan Nepomuceno Adorno in the middle of the nineteenth century.

But when González Casanova completed his academic investigations, he turned whole-heartedly to live social questions, on which he has written essays that show his best qualities to be scrupulousness and a controlled passion. He is a sociologist who, rather than being impassive and governed by a strict scientific discipline, is especially interested in achieving a diagnosis of our modern society that will be of some service to its development.

Pablo González Casanova began his studies at the National University. At the College of Mexico he took part in philosophical and sociological seminars, and finally he studied at the Sorbonne, where he obtained the doctorate in history. At the present time he is Director of the School of Political and Social Sciences of the National University.

ESSAYS: *Misoneism and Christian Modernity in the Eighteenth Century* (*El misoneísmo y la modernidad cristiana en el siglo XVIII*), 1948; *An American Utopia* (*Una utopía de América*), 1953; *Anonymous Satire of the Eighteenth Century* (*Sátira anónima del siglo XVIII*), 1953 (In collaboration with José Miranda; *Study of Social Technique* (*Estudio de la técnica social*), 1958.

PROPAGANDA OR THE NEW RHETORIC*

IN A CURIOUS NOVEL, *Story of the Greatness and Decline of César Birotteau* (*Histoire de la grandeur et de la décadence de César*

*Lecture delivered October 21, 1954, in the series on "The Great Topics of Our Time," organized by the National University of Mexico.

Birotteau), Balzac tells us of a novelty store that presented to Paris for the first time all "those commercial seductions," all those illusions and optical effects which, brought to a supreme degree of perfection, made of the shop windows "true poems in matter." At this very point he speaks to us of what he calls an "immense revolution," an assault upon public opinion: paid advertisements in the newspapers, the success of which was extraordinary. At that time, more than a century ago, publicity was called, perhaps unjustly, charlatanism. Things have changed greatly. Today the world is flooded with poems in matter; newspapers are for the most part "commercial enterprises directed towards making money by the sale of advertising," and a professor at New York University, George Burton Hotchkiss, as early as 1924 wrote that publicity is an art that can be classed with poetry, the novel, and drama. It would occur to no one to call the publicists charlatans. It would occur to no one to say that the daily spice of life (showcases, billboards, illuminated signs, displays of merchandise, advertisements by radio, cinema, and television) is an act of violence against public opinion. And yet today, with greater reason than in the time of Balzac, one could be in agreement with him, since with the added technical development, the continual production of machines and apparatuses which at that time did not exist, and the growing number of advertising firms and schools of advertising, a stupendous metamorphosis has taken place in this social phenomenon, a metamorphosis which you may regard with a certain air of amused superiority and with shrewd mistrust, but which is a fact becoming more and more evident as one looks upon it and studies it.

A century ago the object of advertising was to inform the prospective customer of the qualities of the merchandise. The information that was given him, deceptive or honest, was intended chiefly to enable him to select merchandise that was most suited to his tastes, or that he would consider most satisfactory with relation to his needs. Today advertising has as aim and predominating method the deformation of the customer's reflexes, that of creating in him, according to Hayakawa, the eminent expert in semantics, automatic reactions: "Nothing would be more useful to an advertising expert," he states, "than to make us order a Coca-Cola automatically every time we approach a soda fountain, or automatically to ask for an Alka-Seltzer every time we do not feel well. . . . " And what does this mean, if not that whereas a century ago the customer chose the merchandise, today the merchandise strives, even successfully, to choose the customer? Yes, today merchandise is made known to us and offered to us through advertising, and our subconscious mind is influenced when we least expect it—when we are stopped by the traffic policeman, when we neglect the girl friend in the movies, when we listen to the radio while the children play. They smell us out, waylay us, follow us, point out to us their preferences on the market, and select us with no thought for anything but our money. A whole art that has utilized the advances in social psychology, that calls for a concise, vivid, striking style, and the constant use of exciting phraseology and figures of speech, has been built up into a complete system of rhetoric, into the rhetoric of "salesmen who can write," as advertising specialists are called in the United States.

And this point, one of the highest importance, would take up our whole evening, as one of the great problems of our day, if the national and international tragedy involving trade for the last fifteen years or more had not led to another phenomenon which has a still greater effect on the entire consciousness of contemporary man. It is a commonplace among students of the economic cycle to say that when it reaches its apogee, wars arise among the great producing countries with the object of extending the necessary markets, and that with a recession or depression comes an increase in the intervention of the state, discontent, and even revolutions. Keynesians and Marxists recognize these facts after long and careful study. When the demand for merchandise declines, advertising increases in intensity and importance, and when advertising does not suffice for finding customers for the merchandise, that merchandise becomes more and more aggressive, demanding, and truly tyrannical. It becomes definitely integrated into the political life of nations, their parliamentary discussions, and their plans and purposes in State intervention. Advertising passes from its golden age, or its natural state, to an age in which it forms part of a *Weltanschauung* of advertisers, of a whole publicity programme of political, moral, religious, and philosophical ideas. This integral publicity is commonly called propaganda. Kymball Young defines it as "the more or less planned and systematic use of symbols, through suggestion and psychological techniques, with a view to altering and controlling opinions, ideas, and values, and finally to change ways of acting, in accordance with predetermined patterns." In propaganda an attempt is made not only to induce automatic reflexes and reactions with respect to merchandise, but to induce automatic reflexes and reactions with respect to opinions, values, and ideas as desired by the propagandist. For this reason this phenomenon prevailing in the life of contemporary man passes the bounds of advertising and merchandise, although from these it may have taken a large portion of their techniques and discoveries, and recognizes broader limits and more distant origins: it is the new rhetoric, in the sense Aristotle gave to the word, as "the art of employing, in a given case, the necessary means of persuasion." And it is as a new rhetoric, the rhetoric of our time, that we propose to undertake its analysis.

"That art of discursive prose, literary in form and with a useful, and especially a political purpose, intermediate between learned and popular, and for that very reason oratorical or glibly persuasive, intermediate between theory (which it resembles in its preceptive character) and practice (which it resembles in being immediately translated into action and even in being in demand for that purpose)—this is rhetoric," according to the analytical explanation of Alfonso Reyes.

His definition of the classic exercise includes several elements worthy of consideration: (1) Rhetoric is an art, that is, it has an aesthetic and formal aspect; (2) Rhetoric has a political purpose, meaning, in general terms, that it is a persuasive art, which aims to convince by the use of a logical and psychological technique directed to that end; (3) Rhetoric is used by scholars turned politicians, or by politicians turned scholars, or by religious men turned preachers; in short, it is used by leaders to guide the flock, the citizens, or the people; (4) The proper terrain of rhetoric is one where at the same time both theory and practice prevail, that is, a religious, philosophical, political, and juridical system, and on the other hand, a situation which presupposes the existence of an enemy (deceived or deceiving), of a potential ally, of a public or a judge (deceived or indifferent, but convincible), and of a means of communication; (5) All these elements combine around a problem that is the nucleus of the discourse and in reality the cause of the dispute.

From the above it may be seen that rhetoric has not ceased to exist since the state of nature came to an end, or since the more direct weapons, like the lance, the harpoon, or the bludgeon, which were used to kill, were replaced by more intellectual weapons, like the suggestion, the apothegm, or the innuendo. In civilization these give an ideological turn to lawsuits, conquests, and revolutions, in some cases delaying the killing, and in others even succeeding in finding an alternative, as among juridical and administrative personnel, where everything is settled by sentence or judgement. But in spite of its prevalence everywhere in social life, rhetoric has certain limits and shows enormous discrepancies.

The limits of rhetoric stem from their two primordial functions, the literary or aesthetic, and that of method or persuasion. Though rhetoric is the art of discursive prose and therefore poetry falls outside its pale, by extension it is said that poetry is rhetoric when it attempts to convince and persuade, and when the forms it employs have no correspondence to the sentiments it expresses, and are not the product of creation but of precept. In such circumstances one can censure any art of rhetoric. From the point of view of persuasive method, rhetoric has an essential limit which, from the time of Aristotle, has been sentiment. Persuasion proper to rhetoric has been and still is a sentimental persuasion, in which logic and science, when used, are in the service of sentiments. Philosophy and science are rhetorical only when they adopt a technique of emotional conviction, that is, when they cease to serve their own ends and follow their own methods, and so cease to be philosophy and science.

Moreover, rhetoric presents radical variations in the course of history. These variations depend upon the advance in the means of communication, upon psychological knowledge, upon the technique of persuasion, upon the State, the enemy, and the reason for the struggle. The present situation with regard to these factors causes propaganda to stand at the opposite pole to the old rhetoric, and to have as the only feature in common the preservation of its characteristic of being a technique of persuasion, of suggestion, and of arousing emotion and sentiment, with a view to political action. To this great difference we may perhaps attribute the fact that propaganda has not been regarded as the new rhetoric, the rhetoric of our times, and essentially the same thing; but historically it is much more vast, more complex, more refined, and possessed of greater knowledge, as we shall see in this attempt to give a brief account of its possibilities and present position, as well as the significance it has for contemporary man.

According to the latest census of the United Nations in 1952, in the United States there were being published 55,370,000 copies of daily newspapers, in Mexico 1,300,000, in Japan 30,218,000, in Belgium 3,343,000, in Sweden 3,490,000, in France 10,193,000, in Germany 12,732,000, in England 31,000,000, in Afghanistan 153,000, etc. Thus there were countries like England that published 615 copies of daily newspapers for every thousand inhabitants, with Sweden publishing 490 per thousand, Belgium 383, the United States and Japan 353, less developed countries like Mexico 48, and in such countries as Afghanistan, Laos, and Liberia, 1. According to the same census there were in the United States 3,761 radio broadcasting stations, in Mexico 212, in Japan 89, in Sweden 53, in France 74, in Germany 120, and in England 42. In Equatorial Africa, the Bahamas, the Gold Coast, and in many other regions, there was only one broadcasting station. The figures for radio receiving sets are perhaps more revealing. In 1952 there were in the United States 110 million radio sets; in 1951 there were in Mexico 1,200,000 sets; in 1953 there were in Japan 10,364,000; in 1952 there were in France 7,926,000, and in Germany 10,507,000; in 1953 there were in England 12,946,000. This means that in countries like the United States there were at that time 705 radio sets for every thousand inhabitants. Last year, in the different regions of the world, there were in Africa 10 sets for every 1000 inhabitants, in North America 520, in South America 40, in Asia (exclusive of the USSR) 12, in Europe (exclusive of the USSR) 175, in Oceania 220, in the USSR 75, and—to sum it all up—in the whole world there was an average of 95 radio sets for every thousand inhabitants. In 1950 the United States produced 395 full length films, Mexico 125, Japan 215, France 106, Germany 78, and England 125. The census does not give a figure that would be still more impressive: the number of moving picture theatres and of tickets sold at the ticket windows. But we know that as early as 1940 there were 70,000 moving picture theatres in the world, 29 per cent of which were in the United States. In that country from 60 to 80 million tickets were sold per week. To these figures we should add those for television—an every-day moving picture show, a home movie—the success of which is evident and sweeping; we should add the number of people who lend newspapers to one another, and the number of newspapers and radios that are used by a whole family, the number of people who listen to the radio all morning or all day, the number of movie fans that go to the movies two or three times a week, and the number of television fans who watch programmes hour upon hour. From the preceding data we can get an idea of communications in our time, terraqueous communications that cover every region of the earth; communications in which, quantitatively, the countries most highly developed have the greatest number of means of communications and reception, and, qualitatively, these countries exert over the others evident control and influence, through associations and large organizations that gather information for the press, through records, films, the most powerful radio stations and other indirect means by which they extend their zone of influence right into the heart of underdeveloped countries. These means of communication are excellent for the spreading of culture, advertising, and propaganda. The relative proportion of these three activities varies in different countries and in the different media within a country, but we may be sure that propaganda does not leave uninfluenced a single country or a single means of communication. It is omnipresent, and rhetoric is no longer merely the art of discursive prose, but the art of violent statements, the art of seasoning and firing what the famous journalist George Creel called from the time of the First World War "paper bullets," to which have been progressively added "sound bullets" and "image bullets."

Psychology, which in the time of Aristotle was the science of the soul, in our time has passed through great crises, but has also made notable discoveries; the knowledge of the unconscious, through psychoanalysis, and social psychology, remain as a very favourable balance which has proved itself efficacious and true in experiment and practice. From propaganda's point of view, studies of the dynamics of behaviour, the view of the world and the reorganization of perceptions, studies of the beliefs and attitudes of men, the means whereby they may be measured and altered, and finally investigations of public opinion, groups, leaders, and their psycho-social functions are all of inestimable usefulness. In the United States, England, and Germany, the universities, individuals, and the government have spent huge sums to advance knowledge of social psychology. Apart from the investigations in laboratory and study, experimental and theoretic, large-scale research has been carried out. From the decade of the thirties there have been famous soundings of public opinion made by George Gallup, the *Literary Digest*, *The Nation*, the American Institute of Public Opinion, the Social Science Research Council, and other institutions more or less scientific. The "gigantic investigations" concerning *An American Dilemma* and *The American Soldier*, *Yankee City* and *Middletown*, are impressive, with their examination of large conglomerations of human beings in their minutest details, covering their reactions, hopes, fears, attitudes, and tendencies. With reason it has been said that psycho-social investigation in the United States is reaching the status of a national industry. The results are formidable: methods are being perfected more and more, and they have even gone so far as to measure and compute the intensity and importance of the attitudes and beliefs of human groups. The margin of error has been greatly reduced in the great surveys, and can be mathematically foreseen to be between 3 and 10 per cent. Moreover, science has reached conclusions of fundamental importance for education and propaganda: it has been discovered that simple and isolated pieces of knowledge are most easily reorganized by direct attack, while differentiated and interdependent combinations can be attacked only indirectly, and offer greater resistance. It has been discovered that isolated and rigid attitudes prevent changing ways of acting; so, according to Krech and Krutchfield, "a man can go on seeking security and justice within the confines of an economic and political system that everlastingly frustrates his endeavours . . . because his thoughts on every aspect of that system are isolated from one another and he cannot see existing interrelations and the scope of the changes he must seek to effect." Likewise it has been discovered that when one wishes to change beliefs and attitudes in a given direction one must proceed in an integral fashion and not piecemeal, encourage certain wants and discourage others, develop certain types of group consciousness and suppress others, support or set up certain leaders and put down others. These scientific techniques which social psychology has acquired, and the strict standards of which no one calls in question, are the fundamental basis of the scientific development of education, but also the basis of education for propaganda, which will tend to develop in an integral form simple and isolated mental concepts, and to train men to be children, helpless, credulous, dependent upon the standard opinion fed them by radio, press, television, and cinema. This aim in education is a conscious or subconscious fact in all countries where they do not teach the great structures of philosophic, scientific, and artistic thought, the categories and facts together, where they teach and require only isolated facts, dates, and numbers, and where to the natural division of labour is added a total and integral division, which isolates and leaves underdeveloped men alone and exposed, in a way in which this never occurred among the Greek citizens, and ready to believe and cherish what the new rhetoric repeats every hour of the day and night, by every kind of medium, apparatus, and machinery.

If Demosthenes had thus prepared his Greek citizens before taking them to the public meeting-place, he would not have needed any of his oratorical gifts to convince them of anything he cared to make them believe.

"Before Pearl Harbor," writes the German-born psychologist Kurt Lewin, "in the United States, perhaps more than in any other country, one could easily discern the tendency to consider psychological factors such as frustration or 'destructive urges' as the basic cause of war. Accordingly it was believed that the avoidance of frustrations was the best way to peace. Since that time there has appeared to prevail a much more realistic point of view with regard to the importance of economic and political factors." The Anglo-American social sciences, in their most recent manifestations, tend to abandon the dominant psychological mania of former times, and to consider the data of psychology as integrating factors of ideologies and of the total social phenomenon. This point of view causes the techniques of American propaganda to align themselves in their formal assumptions with the techniques of Nazis and Communists, and has enabled them to achieve a much higher degree of effectiveness. The present state of investigations into propaganda shows the precision and finesse of the knowledge that is possessed on this subject, and given time, can be discovered by analysing the fundamental principles that govern the technique of propaganda today. These principles have been clearly explained by the American investigators Krech and Krutchfield, and they are as follows:

(1) "A suggestion relating to an existing need will be accepted more easily than if it does not relate to any need." So, in case the need does not exist, the propagandist will have to create it by arousing psychological tensions in the individual and then making his suggestion. The following example is cited: "If the people feel no need of promulgating any anti-labour legislation, the propagandist will try to arrange that in the newspapers, over the radio, and in political discussions there will be emphasized and magnified any 'labour incident,' especially cases of strikes and violence, without paying attention to the fact that it is an insignificant or isolated incident. If the propagandist is successful he will have aroused in the citizen a fear of labour problems and created the need of imposing peace upon labour."

(2) "A suggestion relating to an ambiguous situation will be accepted more easily than one relating to a situation clearly outlined." The good propagandist, accordingly, must adjust his suggestions to the beliefs, attitudes, and ideologies prevailing within the group to which he addresses himself. The following example is cited: "In one situation the propagandist may present Communistic suggestions as congruent with the ideals of Christianity; in another he may present the same suggestions as congruent with a purely rational, scientific, and atheistic philosophy." When that congruence is impossible he may alter the systems of thought, by means of a long-term propaganda, by all the means of communication at his disposal.

(3) "A suggestion that can incite the observation of new attributes in a familiar object will be more easily accepted than one that does not do so." That is, the good propagandist will not try to attack an idea

or a belief, but he will turn his suggestions in the direction of the object, trying to find virtues or defects independent of the idea.

(4) "A suggestion congruent with the people's need to identify themselves or live in concord with other people will be more easily accepted than one that runs counter to popular approval." The good propagandist will try to have his suggestions come from people of prestige, or he will try to give the impression that the majority of people are in accord with his suggestions, or at least that the best people are.

(5) "A suggestion that makes effective use of principles that govern stimulation will be more easily accepted." These principles relate to the timbre of the voice, to the intonation, the pronunciation, the dress, the appearance, and have been the topic of monographical and experimental studies.

(6) "The best way to oppose propaganda is through counter-propaganda. The good propagandist will not waste his time (so it is said) in exposing the techniques of the opposing propagandist, but he will offer counter-suggestions." And, in this regard, here is a final statement of the authors mentioned: "The best kind of counter-propaganda is a social and economic system that satisfies most of the needs of most of the people, most of the time."

Among all these principles there is one that is certainly alarming: the vicious circle of propaganda, the need of states to counter propaganda with more propaganda. But there is another principle complementary to it, which is certainly encouraging: "The best justice is the best counter-propaganda."

Krech and Krutchfield, professors at the University of California and Swarthmore College, respectively, have left in their seven principles of propaganda the *summum* of this social phenomenon, and of their knowledge at the present moment, but in order to know how that knowledge is applied, how it lives and permeates the air, and the images, it is necessary to take a look at contemporary history. That history we are living. From the War of 1914 till today we have been continually hearing about that of "war against war," "arming for peace," "self-determination of peoples," "the defence of democracy," "the struggle for social justice." Since then we have been seeing how the propagandists have tried to accentuate "the technical specialization and the irrational motivations of the masses." The Nazis, masters in the art, have left a precious legacy: set the goals clearly; repeat and repeat the simple themes, constantly and persistently; exploit the divisions in the group towards which the propaganda is directed; and use emotional rather than rational techniques. The words of Hitler still resound regarding the falsification of facts, regarding the advisability of telling big lies and not little ones, "because the masses" (as he says in *Mein Kampf*), "by virtue of the simplicity of their minds are readier to believe a big lie than a little one, since they themselves tell little lies, but would be ashamed to tell big ones." Following these tactics, many people were led to believe that Poland was threatening the stability of the Third Reich and that Guatemala was threatening the security of the Panama Canal. These grotesque campaigns call to mind a comic strip, *Cicero's Cat*, reproduced by Allport in his *Psychology of Rumour*. In the first picture, the cat says: "Oh, a new dog in the neighbourhood . . . !" In the second she tells a spotted cat: "I have just seen a new dog in the neighbourhood." The spotted cat runs to see a friend: "Mind, there's a big black dog in the neighbourhood." The friend thinks it necessary "to warn the girls": "Yes, a black dog, that big." The others have to be told: "He has enormous white teeth and is the size of a lion." Cicero's cat, entering: "Here comes the dog." The others, in their flight, cry out: "Help! The monster will kill us!" In the last picture, all the cats appear up on a post, and down below, walking along slowly, is a dog the size of a mouse. In human life things happen in similar fashion; but the process is far more perfected, and in the last picture the cats will have ended by destroying the mouse, and feeling justified by the belief which for them had turned into a reality, that they were dealing with a real and authentic monster. Propaganda achieves this, consciously, deliberately, with studied techniques and with scientific precision. It spreads rumours, formulates myths, strengthens prejudices, and advances arguments in favour of aggression. It succeeds in giving to all words a new meaning, making black appear white, and white black, causing people to be divided into Germans and human beings, into Communists and human beings, into Jews and human beings. It fosters reasoning like the following, on the part of a Congressman from Mississippi, concerning a weekly paper of his country: "The *Survey-Graphic* contains 129 pages that are outrageous, foul, and sickening, anti-Christian, anti-American, and pro-Communist, ostensibly directed against the custom of racial discrimination in the South." According to this Congressman, Christianity is on the side of racial discrimination and only Communism is on the side of race equality. Propaganda manages to dehumanize everything, to destroy all spirit of tolerance, criticism, and resistance, identifying concrete liberty, real democracy, with the name he utilizes to destroy the evil spirit. Whenever propaganda grows, there grow with it state intervention, censorship, taboos, suppression of free speech, restrictions, and the power of the police. Propaganda is against ideological competition, against decisions arrived at after a process of reasoning. It is the magnificent projection of the existential and material elements in society, the amplification of a real irrationalism, evident in social crises. Propaganda is the antithesis of democracy in its genuine sense, and would destroy traditional and revolutionary liberty. It prevents reasoning, discussion, and a choice of opinions. Nazism assumed this responsibility, and created an ideology of superior races, opposed to the decadent democracies, as it called them. This fostered the establishment of a close congruence between the ideology of violence and propaganda. But democracy and liberty are destroyed in spite of their becoming contradictory to the classic ideologies of democracy and liberty. Propaganda can eliminate them under the pretext of defending them. It is able to bring about the metamorphosis that it desires and that best suits its interests. For this reason, and on account of the advances made by the social sciences in our day, the problem of contemporary man is a problem more of deceit than of error, more of bad faith than of ignorance. It is as if a man of the eighteenth century had lived for two centuries, and after asserting that "religion is the opiate of people" he had encouraged religion, without being religious himself, in order to put the people to sleep. Formerly myths were formed naturally; they were man's philosophy. Today they are fostered, spread abroad, and are created artificially; they are "anti-philosophy."

It might appear from the foregoing that man is in a defenceless position, and yet this is entirely false. The fundamental bases of propaganda are a threat to the propagandists themselves. The latter know that there are two possible ways of changing the world, the first of which is to change the real world, and the second, to change the psychological world and keep the real world just as it is. In other words, they have the choice of dispensing terrestrial or mythological nourishment. In the first case they designate real property as a real benefit, and in the second case as an evil, as deriving from acts artificially stimulated by an execrable energy.

When the propagandist elects psychological change, he tries to create, as in *The Brave New World*, a motion picture in which the spectator will feel the kisses of the heroine on the screen as if she were bestowing them upon his own lips. But he refuses to permit him any contact with a girl of flesh and blood, and if the spectator is unimaginative, and from his desire to satisfy his romantic needs demands to see his sweetheart to kiss her, the propagandist allows the police to take charge of him—that spectator is unorthodox, disloyal, and unpatriotic.

Well, what possibility is there of deceiving our spectator by satisfying his sentimental hunger with motion picture girls, of pure celluloid? Since Leibnitz made the egregious error of replacing heaven by the world, and of saying that the latter is the best of all possible worlds, there is practically no ideology at our disposal that does not propose an imminent solution. Every ideology tries to create a happy world on earth and to justify itself by the terrestrial felicity that it offers. In other times, when the dominant ideologies were transcendental, though the technique and rhetorical devices may have been less scientific, man was promised felicity in Nirvana, Heaven, or Paradise. Felicity was not of this world, and man had to wait for death to see if the promise was to be fulfilled. This was advantageous for the rhetoricians. Now the propagandist is handicapped by the thought that men demand happiness on earth, with the proviso in many cases, of course, that they will continue to be happy in Heaven, Paradise, or Nirvana. Things are more immediate in the political field; the possibility of belief has diminished with the increased possibility of contrasting the ideal perfection that is sung with the reality that is lived. Both are of this world for the majority of men. And the propagandist sees that the dilemma confronting him, whether to transform the psychological world exclusively, or to transform the real world, is tilted in favour of the transformation of the latter. If he cannot or will not transform the real world, we shall see him making desperate efforts which only magnify his failure and drive him to madness. His efforts may consist of promoting the idea anew of a transcendental felicity, by speaking technically of Nirvanas and Heavens; or on the other hand he may gently and gradually turn into a taboo, a forbidden fruit, any talk of one's own happiness, of one's own liberty, and ask the masses not to strive for their own happiness and liberty, but to fight against the iniquity and servitude of someone else. This is what psychology calls inhibition and projection; people are inhibited from acting in their own interests, and they are induced to project their ills towards a stone, a demon, a scapegoat, or a people. In such a case the crisis in relation to reality is accentuated—the distance becomes greater and greater between words and things, and one notes a centrifugal movement of things in their relation to the words of the propagandist. The propagandist progressively dehumanizes words and turns them into cries. He comes to identify everything human with the enemy, and as humanity moves away from him and he is left alone, only he believes in his propaganda and in psychological propaganda. When he loses, he thinks his rivals have won the psychological war. The last thing he would imagine would be that he has at last turned into the propagandist of his own enemy, who in his vocabulary has been identifying everything human with evil; the idea of evil has been turned into an idea of good, and the concept has been divested of the cover word, the cry. As man, for the propagandist, loses every human quality, and as he is given a place among things, his real essence is revealed: he seeks where he can the words for the things he wishes to take and possess. He may possibly pass through an intermediate stage of psychosis, in which the traditional conception of good is obliterated and the traditional conception of evil maintained. It is the time for irrational and desperate philosophies. But that time passes. No man can endure it. And a radical explanation is sought, which completely alters the structures of perception and establishes new correlations. It is as if we were to say that things are looked at with new eyes. And when they are looked at in this way, hope is restored in true human action, which consists in initiating a centrifugal movement from things to words, so that the latter may recover their genuine nature and cease to be mere cries. Words are humanized again, finding their sense and their reality. For this reason, unhappily for any propaganda that goes in for mere psychological changes, the conclusion reached by the scientists quoted above is true: "The best kind of counter-propaganda is a social and economic system that satisfies the needs of most of the people most of the time." That counter-propaganda, more effective and more scientific, is the one that will inevitably win. How can it be found in time? How can it be discovered, when the suspicion has been established that everything is propaganda, and that everything is *appearance*?

"If a playful little imp were to set out to deceive me in everything," Descartes asked himself at the dawn of the Modern Age, "and were capable of achieving his objectives, in what might I believe?" Descartes remained with his Self. Contemporary man does not need to invent playful little imps that try to deceive him; out there, there are being restated, with their machines and techniques, the old problems of philosophy. Neither does contemporary man need to find refuge in solitude, an area in which propaganda causes most havoc. Fortunately, for him, the contemporary little imp is less powerful than Descartes' little imp, since he is not the product of imagination. If he deceives him he loses, and when he tries to deceive him he cannot conceal the rules of his game. The solution to the philosophical problems with which the propagandist confronts us cannot be found in a simple chat. It requires some of the most profound reasoning; it rejects propaganda. And yet it is unquestionable that a study of the methods employed by the new rhetoric to keep us in childhood and adolescence will enable us to preserve and strengthen our intellectual maturity and our human condition.

Novelties. Mexico in Culture (*Novedades. México en la cultura*), Mexico, Nov. 14, 1954, pp. 1 and 6.